Nissan Primera
Service and Repair Manual

Mark Coombs and Steve Rendle

(1851-336-7Y1)

Models covered

Nissan Primera models with petrol engines, including all special/limited editions
4-door Saloon, 5-door Hatchback and Estate models
1597 cc & 1998 cc

Does not cover Diesel engine

GW00481813

© Haynes Publishing 1996

A book in the **Haynes Service and Repair Manual Series**

ABCDE
FGHIJ
KLMNO
P

ISBN **1 85960 194 4**

British Library Cataloguing in Publication Data
A catalogue record for this book is available from the British Library.

Printed by **J H Haynes & Co Ltd, Sparkford, Nr Yeovil, Somerset BA22 7JJ, England**

Haynes Publishing
Sparkford, Nr Yeovil, Somerset BA22 7JJ, England

Haynes North America, Inc
861 Lawrence Drive, Newbury Park, California 91320, USA

Editions Haynes S.A.
Tour Aurore - La Défense 2, 18 Place des Reflets,
92975 PARIS LA DEFENSE Cedex, France

Haynes Publishing Nordiska AB
Box 1504, 751 45 UPPSALA, Sweden

Contents

LIVING WITH YOUR NISSAN PRIMERA

ROUTINE MAINTENANCE

Routine maintenance and servicing

Contents

Introduction to the Nissan Primera

The Nissan Primera was first introduced in the UK in September 1990. The Primera was a new vehicle brought in as a replacement for the Nissan Bluebird, the Primera being much-improved and more refined in all respects. This manual covers models fitted with petrol engines, but other models in the range are available with Diesel engines.

Two sizes of petrol engines are available in the Primera range; 1.6 and 2.0 litre double overhead camshaft (DOHC) units. The 1.6 litre engines were originally fitted with a carburettor, whereas the 2.0 litre models were available in both single-point and multi-point injection forms. A multi-point injection 1.6 litre engine was introduced into the range in 1993. All engines are fitted with a range of emissions control systems. The engines are of a well-proven design and, provided regular maintenance is carried out, are unlikely to give trouble.

The Primera is available in 4-door Saloon, 5-door Hatchback and Estate body styles, with a wide range of fittings and interior trim available depending on the model specification.

Fully-independent front suspension is fitted; on Saloon and Hatchback models, the rear suspension is fully-independent, while on Estate models, semi-independent rear suspension is fitted.

All models are fitted with a five-speed manual transmission. On most 2.0 litre models, a four-speed electronically-controlled transmission was available as an option.

A wide range of standard and optional equipment is available within the Primera range to suit most tastes, including central locking, electric windows, an electric sunroof, an anti-lock braking system and an air bag.

For the home mechanic, the Primera is a straightforward vehicle to maintain, and most of the items requiring frequent attention are easily accessible.

Acknowledgements

Thanks are due to Champion Spark Plug, who supplied the illustrations showing spark plug conditions. Thanks are also due to Sykes-Pickavant Limited, who provided some of the workshop tools, and to all those people at Sparkford who helped in the production of this manual.

We take great pride in the accuracy of information given in this manual, but vehicle manufacturers make alterations and design changes during the production run of a particular vehicle of which they do not inform us. No liability can be accepted by the authors or publishers for loss, damage or injury caused by any errors in, or omissions from, the information given.

Project vehicles

The main project vehicle used in the preparation of this manual, and appearing in many of the photographic sequences, was a 1994 Nissan Primera 2.0 litre SLX Hatchback. Additional work was carried out and photographed on various other 1.6 and 2.0 litre Saloon and Estate models.

Nissan Primera 1.6 LX five-door Hatchback

Nissan Primera 2.0 SLX Estate

Working on your car can be dangerous. This page shows just some of the potential risks and hazards, with the aim of creating a safety-conscious attitude.

General hazards

Scalding

• Don't remove the radiator or expansion tank cap while the engine is hot.
• Engine oil, automatic transmission fluid or power steering fluid may also be dangerously hot if the engine has recently been running.

Burning

• Beware of burns from the exhaust system and from any part of the engine. Brake discs and drums can also be extremely hot immediately after use.

Crushing

• When working under or near a raised vehicle, always supplement the jack with axle stands, or use drive-on ramps. *Never venture under a car which is only supported by a jack.*
• Take care if loosening or tightening high-torque nuts when the vehicle is on stands. Initial loosening and final tightening should be done with the wheels on the ground.

Fire

• Fuel is highly flammable; fuel vapour is explosive.
• Don't let fuel spill onto a hot engine.
• Do not smoke or allow naked lights (including pilot lights) anywhere near a vehicle being worked on. Also beware of creating sparks
(electrically or by use of tools).
• Fuel vapour is heavier than air, so don't work on the fuel system with the vehicle over an inspection pit.
• Another cause of fire is an electrical overload or short-circuit. Take care when repairing or modifying the vehicle wiring.
• Keep a fire extinguisher handy, of a type suitable for use on fuel and electrical fires.

Electric shock

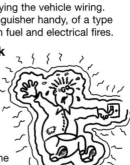

• Ignition HT voltage can be dangerous, especially to people with heart problems or a pacemaker. Don't work on or near the ignition system with the engine running or the ignition switched on.

• Mains voltage is also dangerous. Make sure that any mains-operated equipment is correctly earthed. Mains power points should be protected by a residual current device (RCD) circuit breaker.

Fume or gas intoxication

• Exhaust fumes are poisonous; they often contain carbon monoxide, which is rapidly fatal if inhaled. Never run the engine in a confined space such as a garage with the doors shut.
• Fuel vapour is also poisonous, as are the vapours from some cleaning solvents and paint thinners.

Poisonous or irritant substances

• Avoid skin contact with battery acid and with any fuel, fluid or lubricant, especially antifreeze, brake hydraulic fluid and Diesel fuel. Don't syphon them by mouth. If such a substance is swallowed or gets into the eyes, seek medical advice.
• Prolonged contact with used engine oil can cause skin cancer. Wear gloves or use a barrier cream if necessary. Change out of oil-soaked clothes and do not keep oily rags in your pocket.
• Air conditioning refrigerant forms a poisonous gas if exposed to a naked flame (including a cigarette). It can also cause skin burns on contact.

Asbestos

• Asbestos dust can cause cancer if inhaled or swallowed. Asbestos may be found in gaskets and in brake and clutch linings. When dealing with such components it is safest to assume that they contain asbestos.

Special hazards

Hydrofluoric acid

• This extremely corrosive acid is formed when certain types of synthetic rubber, found in some O-rings, oil seals, fuel hoses etc, are exposed to temperatures above 400°C. The rubber changes into a charred or sticky substance containing the acid. *Once formed, the acid remains dangerous for years. If it gets onto the skin, it may be necessary to amputate the limb concerned.*
• When dealing with a vehicle which has suffered a fire, or with components salvaged from such a vehicle, wear protective gloves and discard them after use.

The battery

• Batteries contain sulphuric acid, which attacks clothing, eyes and skin. Take care when topping-up or carrying the battery.
• The hydrogen gas given off by the battery is highly explosive. Never cause a spark or allow a naked light nearby. Be careful when connecting and disconnecting battery chargers or jump leads.

Air bags

• Air bags can cause injury if they go off accidentally. Take care when removing the steering wheel and/or facia. Special storage instructions may apply.

Diesel injection equipment

• Diesel injection pumps supply fuel at very high pressure. Take care when working on the fuel injectors and fuel pipes.

⚠️ *Warning: Never expose the hands, face or any other part of the body to injector spray; the fuel can penetrate the skin with potentially fatal results.*

Remember...

DO

• Do use eye protection when using power tools, and when working under the vehicle.

• Do wear gloves or use barrier cream to protect your hands when necessary.

• Do get someone to check periodically that all is well when working alone on the vehicle.

• Do keep loose clothing and long hair well out of the way of moving mechanical parts.

• Do remove rings, wristwatch etc, before working on the vehicle – especially the electrical system.

• Do ensure that any lifting or jacking equipment has a safe working load rating adequate for the job.

DON'T

• Don't attempt to lift a heavy component which may be beyond your capability – get assistance.

• Don't rush to finish a job, or take unverified short cuts.

• Don't use ill-fitting tools which may slip and cause injury.

• Don't leave tools or parts lying around where someone can trip over them. Mop up oil and fuel spills at once.

• Don't allow children or pets to play in or near a vehicle being worked on.

Note: *All figures are approximate, and may vary according to model. Refer to manufacturer's data for exact figures.*

Dimensions

Overall length:
Saloon and Hatchback models . . . .   4400 mm
Estate models . . . .   4460 mm

Overall width:
Saloon and Hatchback models . . . .   1700 mm
Estate models . . . .   1695 mm

Overall height (unladen):
Saloon and Hatchback . . . .   1390 mm
Estate models:
   With roof rails . . . .   1500 mm
   Without roof rails . . . .   1470 mm
Wheelbase . . . .   2550 mm

Front track:
Saloon and Hatchback models . . . .   1470 mm
Estate models . . . .   1460 mm
Rear track . . . .   1460 mm

Weights

Kerb weight:
Saloon models:
   1.6 litre models . . . .   1125 to 1140 kg
   2.0 litre manual transmission models . . . .   1185 to 1230 kg
   2.0 litre automatic transmission models . . . .   1210 to 1230 kg
Hatchback models:
   1.6 litre models . . . .   1145 to 1160 kg
   2.0 litre manual transmission models . . . .   1205 to 1250 kg
   2.0 litre automatic transmission models . . . .   1230 to 1250 kg
Estate models:
   1.6 litre models . . . .   1180 to 1200 kg
   2.0 litre manual transmission models . . . .   1215 to 1240 kg
   2.0 litre automatic transmission models . . . .   1235 to 1260 kg
Maximum towing weight (with a braked trailer):
Saloon and Hatchback models:
   1.6 litre models . . . .   1150 kg
   2.0 litre models . . . .   1350 kg
Estate models:
   1.6 litre models . . . .   1100 kg
   2.0 litre models . . . .   1500 kg

Jacking, towing and wheel changing

Jacking

The jack supplied with the vehicle tool kit should only be used for changing the roadwheels - see "Wheel changing" later in this Section. When carrying out any other kind of work, raise the vehicle using a hydraulic jack, and always supplement the jack with axle stands positioned under the vehicle jacking points.

When using a hydraulic jack or axle stands, always position the jack head or axle stand head under one of the relevant jacking points (note that the jacking points for use with the vehicle jack are different from those for a hydraulic trolley jack). Nissan recommend the use of adapters when supporting the vehicle with axle stands - the adapters are grooved, and fit over the sill edge to prevent the vehicle weight damaging the sill **(see illustrations)**. **Do not** jack the vehicle under the sump or any of the steering or suspension components other than those indicated. **Never** *work under, around, or near a raised vehicle, unless it is adequately supported in at least two places.*

Towing

Towing eyes are fitted to the front and rear of the vehicle for attachment of a tow rope. The towing eyes can be accessed through slots, or from underneath the bumpers **(see illustrations)**. Always turn the ignition key to "ON" position when the vehicle is being towed, so that the steering lock is released, and that the direction indicator and brake lights will work.

Before being towed, release the handbrake; select neutral on manual

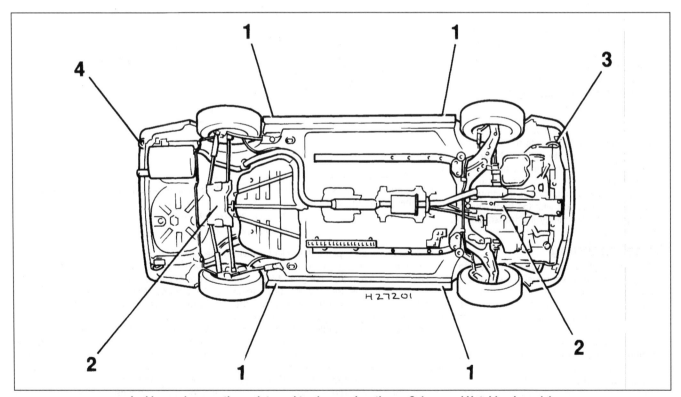

H 27201

Jacking and supporting points and towing eye locations - Saloon and Hatchback models

1 Vehicle jack and axle stand location points   2 Hydraulic jack locating points   3 Front towing eye   4 Rear towing eye

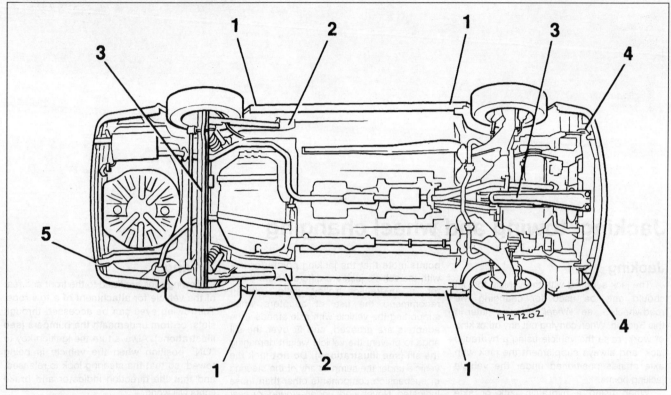

Jacking and supporting points and towing eye locations - Estate models

1   Vehicle jack and axle stand location points (for use with adapters)
2   Axle stand location points (for use without adapters)
3   Hydraulic jack locating points
4   Front towing eye
5   Rear towing eye

transmission models, or "N" on automatic transmission models. Note that greater-than-usual pedal pressure will be required to operate the brakes, since the vacuum servo unit is only operational with the engine running. Similarly, on models with power steering, greater-than-usual steering effort will be required.

Note that a vehicle with automatic transmission should always be towed forwards. To avoid damage to the automatic transmission, do not tow the vehicle any faster than 30 mph (50 km/h), or any further than 45 miles (60 km). Where it can be arranged, models with automatic transmission should ideally be towed with the front wheels off the ground, particularly if a transmission fault is suspected.

Wheel changing

The spare wheel and toolkit are located under the carpet or cover panel in the luggage compartment, and the jack is located behind cover panel on the right-hand side of the luggage compartment. Open up the cover panel and remove the jack, then lift up the carpet/cover and unscrew the spare wheel retaining bolt. Remove the toolkit and spare wheel from the vehicle.

To change a wheel, proceed as follows.

Apply the handbrake, and place chocks at the front and rear of the wheel diagonally opposite the one to be changed. On automatic

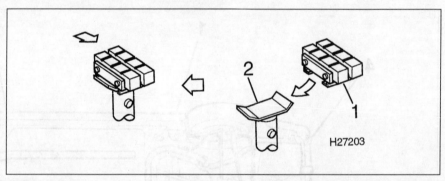

Nissan special adapters for use when supporting vehicle on axle stands. Fit the adapter to the stand, and position it underneath the vehicle so the sill edge is located in the adapter groove (arrowed)

1   Adapter   2   Axle stand

transmission models, place the selector lever in position "P", or with manual transmission models, select first or reverse gear. Make sure that the vehicle is located on firm, level ground, and then prise off, and remove, the wheel trim using the pointed end of the wheel brace (if applicable). Slightly loosen the wheel nuts with the brace provided. Locate the jack head in the jacking point nearest to the wheel to be changed, and raise the jack by turning its handle with the hooked rod (supplied in the toolkit) and wheel brace; engage the hook of the rod with the jack, and use the brace to raise and lower the jack. Note that the lug on

the jack head must engage with the cut-out in the jacking point. On certain models, plastic covers must be unclipped for access to the jacking points. When the wheel is clear of the ground, remove the nuts and lift off the wheel. Fit the spare wheel, and moderately tighten the nuts. Lower the vehicle, and then tighten the nuts fully in a diagonal sequence. Refit the wheel trim, where applicable. If possible, check the tyre pressure on the spare wheel. Remove the chocks and stow the jack, tools, and the damaged wheel. Have the damaged tyre or wheel repaired, or renew it, as soon as possible.

Jump starting

Jump starting will get you out of trouble, but you must correct whatever made the battery go flat in the first place. There are three possibilities:

1 *The battery has been drained by repeated attempts to start, or by leaving the lights on.*

2 *The charging system is not working properly (alternator drivebelt slack or broken, alternator wiring fault or alternator itself faulty).*

3 *The battery itself is at fault (electrolyte low, or battery worn out).*

When jump-starting a car using a booster battery, observe the following precautions:

✔ Before connecting the booster battery, make sure that the ignition is switched off.

✔ Ensure that all electrical equipment (lights, heater, wipers, etc) is switched off.

✔ Make sure that the booster battery is the same voltage as the discharged one in the vehicle.

✔ If the battery is being jump-started from the battery in another vehicle, the two vehcles MUST NOT TOUCH each other.

✔ Make sure that the transmission is in neutral (or PARK, in the case of automatic transmission).

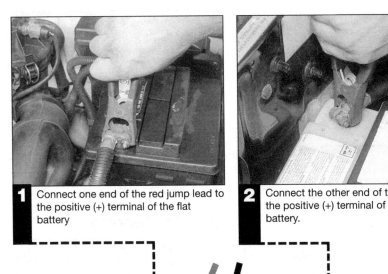

1 Connect one end of the red jump lead to the positive (+) terminal of the flat battery

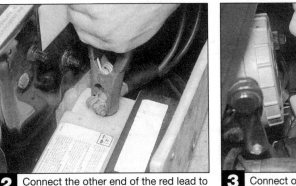

2 Connect the other end of the red lead to the positive (+) terminal of the booster battery.

3 Connect one end of the black jump lead to the negative (-) terminal of the booster battery

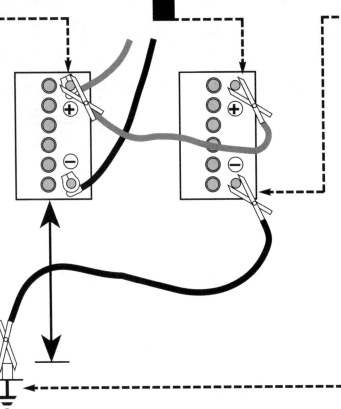

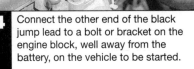

4 Connect the other end of the black jump lead to a bolt or bracket on the engine block, well away from the battery, on the vehicle to be started.

5 Make sure that the jump leads will not come into contact with the fan, drive-belts or other moving parts of the engine.

6 Start the engine using the booster battery, then with the engine running at idle speed, disconnect the jump leads in the reverse order of connection.

Identifying leaks

Puddles on the garage floor or drive, or obvious wetness under the bonnet or underneath the car, suggest a leak that needs investigating. It can sometimes be difficult to decide where the leak is coming from, especially if the engine bay is very dirty already. Leaking oil or fluid can also be blown rearwards by the passage of air under the car, giving a false impression of where the problem lies.

 Warning: Most automotive oils and fluids are poisonous. Wash them off skin, and change out of contaminated clothing, without delay.

 The smell of a fluid leaking from the car may provide a clue to what's leaking. Some fluids are distinctively coloured. It may help to clean the car carefully and to park it over some clean paper overnight as an aid to locating the source of the leak.

Remember that some leaks may only occur while the engine is running.

Sump oil

Engine oil may leak from the drain plug...

Oil from filter

...or from the base of the oil filter.

Gearbox oil

Gearbox oil can leak from the seals at the inboard ends of the driveshafts.

Antifreeze

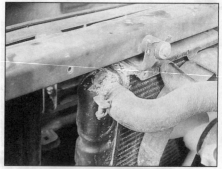

Leaking antifreeze often leaves a crystalline deposit like this.

Brake fluid

A leak occurring at a wheel is almost certainly brake fluid.

Power steering fluid

Power steering fluid may leak from the pipe connectors on the steering rack.

Radio/cassette unit anti-theft system - precaution

The radio/cassette unit fitted as standard equipment by Nissan is equipped with a built-in security code, to deter thieves. If the power source to the unit is cut, the anti-theft system will activate. Even if the power source is immediately reconnected, the radio/cassette unit will not function until the correct security code has been entered. Therefore, if you do not know the correct security code for the radio/cassette unit, **do not** disconnect the battery negative terminal of the battery, or remove the radio/cassette unit from the vehicle.

To enter the correct security code, follow the instructions provided with the radio/cassette player handbook.

If an incorrect code is entered, the unit will become locked, and cannot be operated.

If this happens, or if the security code is lost or forgotten, seek the advice of your Nissan dealer. On presentation of proof of ownership, your dealer will be able to unlock the unit and provide you with a new security code.

Chapter 1
Routine maintenance and servicing

Contents

Degrees of difficulty

Easy, suitable for novice with little experience	**Fairly easy,** suitable for beginner with some experience	**Fairly difficult,** suitable for competent DIY mechanic 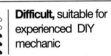	**Difficult,** suitable for experienced DIY mechanic	**Very difficult,** suitable for expert DIY or professional

Specifications

Engine
Oil filter type:
1.6 litre engine	Champion C109
2.0 litre engine	Champion C141

Cooling system

	Antifreeze	Water
Antifreeze mixture (ethylene glycol antifreeze):		
Protection down to -15°C	30%	70%
Protection down to -35°C	50%	50%

Fuel grade
Minimum octane rating:

Models without a catalytic converter ("non-catalyst" models)	95 RON unleaded or 97 RON leaded (eg UK "4-star")
Models with a catalytic converter ("catalyst" models)	95 RON unleaded. Leaded fuel must **not** be used

Fuel system
Air filter element type:

1.6 litre carburettor models	Champion W247
1.6 litre fuel injection models	Champion type not available
2.0 litre single-point injection models	Champion W255
2.0 litre multi-point injection models	Champion U548

Fuel filter type:
1.6 litre carburettor models:	
Saloon and Hatchback models	Champion L206
Estate models	Champion L110
1.6 litre fuel injection models	Champion type not available
2.0 litre single-point injection models:	
Saloon and Hatchback models	Champion L206
Estate models	Champion L215
2.0 litre multi-point injection models	Champion L215

Idle speed and mixture settings

Carburettor models without a catalytic converter:
Idle speed	750 ± 50 rpm
Idle mixture CO content	1.5 ± 0.5 %

Carburettor models with a catalytic converter:
Idle speed	750 ± 50 rpm
Idle mixture CO content	1.0 ± 0.5 % (at exhaust gas sampling pipe)

Single-point fuel injection models:
Idle speed (not adjustable)*	850 ± 50 rpm (controlled by ECU)

Idle mixture CO content:
Models without catalytic converter	Less than 2.0 %
Models with catalytic converter	Less than 1.0 % (not adjustable - controlled by ECU)

Multi-point fuel injection models:

Idle speed (not adjustable)*:
1.6 litre models	700 ± 50 rpm (controlled by ECU)
2.0 litre models	800 ± 50 rpm (controlled by ECU)

Idle mixture CO content:
Models without a catalytic converter	Less than 2.0 %
Models with a catalytic converter	Less than 1.0 % (not adjustable - controlled by ECU)

Note: *Although the idle speed is not adjustable, the base idle speed can be set as described.*

Ignition system

Spark plug type:
1.6 litre models	Champion RC9YCC

2.0 litre models:
Single-point injection models	Champion RC9MCC
Multi-point injection models	Champion RC7YCC
Spark plug electrode gap	0.8 to 0.9 mm
Spark plug HT lead set	Champion LS-34

Spark plug HT lead resistances (genuine Nissan leads only):*
Bougicord HT leads	4.48 to 6.72 k ohms
Sumitumo HT leads	13.6 to 18.4 k ohms

HT lead types can be identified from their markings

Auxiliary drivebelt deflection

1.6 litre engines

	Setting (mm)	Limit (mm)
Alternator:		
With power steering	7 to 9	11
Without power steering	7 to 9	10
Air conditioning compressor	6 to 8	9.5
Power steering pump	4 to 6	7.5

2.0 litre engines

	Setting (mm)	Limit (mm)
Alternator:		
With air conditioning	7 to 8	11.5 to 12.5
Without air conditioning	8 to 9	12 to 13
Power steering pump	4 to 5	6 to 7

Note: *In all cases, the drivebelt deflection is measured by applying a force of 98 N (10 kg) as described in the text. All figures are quoted for a "used" drivebelt - if a new belt has been fitted, the setting deflection should be decreased by 1 mm.*

Braking system

Minimum front brake pad friction material thickness	2.0 mm
Minimum rear brake pad friction material thickness	2.0 mm
Minimum rear brake shoe lining thickness	1.5 mm

Number of clicks required to fully apply handbrake:
Saloon and Hatchback models	6 to 8 clicks

Estate models:
Models with rear disc brakes	7 to 9 clicks
Models with rear drum brakes	8 to 10 clicks

Number of clicks required to operate handbrake "on" warning light:
Saloon and Hatchback models	1 to 2 clicks
Estate models	0 to 1 click

Tyres

Pressures	Refer to manufacturer's tyre specification plate fitted to driver's door rear pillar

Wheel alignment

Front wheel toe setting:
Saloon and Hatchback models . . . . Parallel to 2.0 mm (0°12') toe-in
Estate models . . . . 1.0 to 3.0 mm (0°6' to 0°17') toe-in
Rear wheel toe-setting:
Saloon and Hatchback models:
"Phase I" models . . . . 2.0 mm (0°12') toe-out to 2.0 mm (0°12') toe-in
"Phase II" models . . . . 1.0 mm (0°6') toe-out to 3.0 mm (0°18') toe-in

Note: *All wheel alignment specifications given are for an unladen vehicle - ie, no driver or passengers, fuel tank full, engine coolant and oil levels normal, and spare wheel, jack and tools fitted in normal locations.*

Torque wrench settings	Nm	lbf ft
Air conditioning compressor drivebelt tensioning pulley		
nut - 1.6 litre models	28	21
Automatic transmission drain plug	34	25
Cylinder block coolant drain plug	40	30
Engine sump drain plug	35	26
Manual transmission:		
Filler/level plug:		
1.6 litre models	29	22
2.0 litre models	15	11
Drain plug	29	22
Rear suspension parallel link securing nuts* (Saloon and Hatchback		
models)	120	89
Roadwheel nuts	110	81
Seat belt mounting bolts	50	37
Spark plugs	25	18
Track-rod end-to-steering arm nut:		
Recommended torque	35	26
Maximum permissible torque	49	36

*Use new nuts.

1

Lubricants and fluids

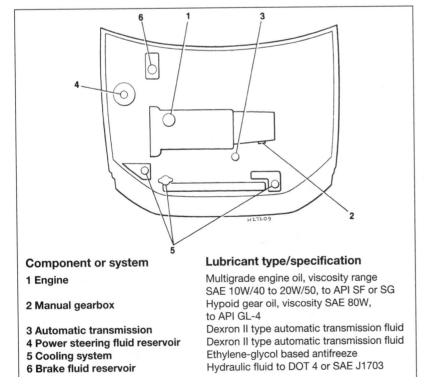

H17209

Component or system	Lubricant type/specification
1 Engine	Multigrade engine oil, viscosity range SAE 10W/40 to 20W/50, to API SF or SG
2 Manual gearbox	Hypoid gear oil, viscosity SAE 80W, to API GL-4
3 Automatic transmission	Dexron II type automatic transmission fluid
4 Power steering fluid reservoir	Dexron II type automatic transmission fluid
5 Cooling system	Ethylene-glycol based antifreeze
6 Brake fluid reservoir	Hydraulic fluid to DOT 4 or SAE J1703

Capacities

Engine oil

At oil change:
    1.6 litre engine . . . . 3.1 litres (5.5 pints)
    2.0 litre engine . . . . 3.7 litres (6.5 pints)
At oil and filter change:
    1.6 litre engine . . . . 3.5 litres (6.2 pints)
    2.0 litre engine . . . . 3.9 litres (6.8 pints)
Difference between "MAX"
and "MIN" dipstick marks
(approximately) . . . . 1.0 litre (1.8 pints)

Cooling system

1.6 litre engine . . . . 6.4 litres (11.2 pints)
2.0 litre engine . . . . 6.5 litres (11.3 pints)

Manual gearbox

1.6 litre models . . . . 2.9 litres (5.1 pints)
2.0 litre models . . . . 3.6 litres (6.3 pints)

Automatic transmission 7.0 litres (12.3 pints)

Fuel tank . . . . 60.0 litres
(13.2 gallons)

Nissan Primera maintenance schedule

1 The maintenance intervals in this manual are provided with the assumption that you, not the dealer, will be carrying out the work. These are the minimum maintenance intervals based on the schedule recommended by the manufacturer for vehicles driven daily. If you wish to keep your vehicle in peak condition at all times, you may wish to perform some of these procedures more often. We encourage frequent maintenance because it enhances the efficiency, performance and resale value of your vehicle. If the vehicle is driven in dusty areas, used to tow a trailer, or driven frequently at slow speeds (idling in traffic) or on short journeys, more frequent maintenance intervals are recommended. Nissan actually recommend that many service intervals are halved for vehicles which are used under these conditions.

2 When the vehicle is new, it should be serviced by a factory-authorised dealer service department in order to preserve the factory warranty.

Every 250 miles (400 km) or weekly

- [ ] Check the engine oil level (Section 3)
- [ ] Check the engine coolant level (Section 3)
- [ ] Check the brake fluid level (Section 3)
- [ ] Check the power steering fluid level (Section 3)
- [ ] Check the screen washer fluid level (Section 3)
- [ ] Visually examine the tyres for tread depth, and wear or damage (Section 4)
- [ ] Check and if necessary adjust the tyre pressures (Section 4)
- [ ] Check the condition of the battery (Section 6)
- [ ] Check the operation of the horn, all lights, and the wipers and washers (Sections 5 and 7)

Every 4500 miles (7500 km) or 6 months - whichever comes first

Note: *Frequent oil and filter changes are good for the engine. We recommend changing the oil at the mileage specified here, or at least twice a year if the mileage covered is less.*

- [ ] Renew the engine oil and filter (Section 8)

Every 9000 miles (15 000 km) or 6 months - whichever comes first

- [ ] Check and adjust the idle speed and mixture settings - carburettor models (Section 9)
- [ ] Renew the spark plugs - models without a catalytic converter (Section 10)
- [ ] Check all underbonnet components and hoses for fluid leaks (Section 11)
- [ ] Check manual transmission oil level (Section 12)
- [ ] Check the brake pads (front and, if fitted, rear) and renew if necessary (Section 13)
- [ ] Check and adjust the handbrake (Section 14)
- [ ] Check and adjust the clutch (Section 15)

Every 18 000 miles (30 000 km) or 12 months - whichever comes first

In addition to all the items listed above, carry out the following:

- [ ] Check the condition of the air conditioning system components (see Section 16)
- [ ] Renew the spark plugs - models with a catalytic converter (Section 17)
- [ ] Renew the fuel filter (Section 18)
- [ ] Check the condition of the emissions control system hoses and components (Section 19)
- [ ] Check the operation of the lambda (oxygen) sensor (Section 20)
- [ ] Check the condition of the auxiliary drivebelt, and renew if necessary (Section 21)
- [ ] Check the rear brake shoes (where fitted) and renew if necessary (Section 22)
- [ ] Change the brake fluid (Section 23)
- [ ] Check the automatic transmission fluid level (Section 24)
- [ ] Check the steering and suspension components for condition and security (Section 25)
- [ ] Check the condition of the driveshaft rubber gaiters (Section 26)
- [ ] Check the wheel alignment (Section 27)
- [ ] Check the balance of each roadwheel (Section 28)
- [ ] Check the operation and security of all seat belts (Section 29)
- [ ] Lubricate all hinges and locks (Section 30)
- [ ] Carry out a road test (Section 31)

Every 36 000 miles (60 000 km) or 2 years - whichever comes first

In addition to all the items listed above, carry out the following:

- [ ] Renew the air filter (Section 32)
- [ ] Check the ignition system components (Section 33)
- [ ] Renew the PCV filter - 1.6 litre models and 2.0 litre single-point injection models (Section 34)
- [ ] Check the operation of the braking system servo unit and check-valve (Section 35)
- [ ] Renew the coolant (Section 36)
- [ ] Renew the manual transmission oil (Section 37)
- [ ] Renew the automatic transmission fluid (Section 38)

Underbonnet view of a 1.6 litre carburettor catalyst model

1 Engine oil filler cap
2 Engine oil dipstick
3 Battery
4 Master cylinder brake fluid reservoir
5 Relay box
6 Auxiliary fusebox
7 Radiator filler cap
8 Alternator
9 Fuel pump
10 Braking system vacuum servo unit
11 Coolant expansion tank
12 Fuel filter
13 Exhaust gas sensor
14 Air cleaner housing
15 Power steering fluid reservoir
16 Air induction valve (AIV)
17 Distributor
18 Windscreen washer reservoir

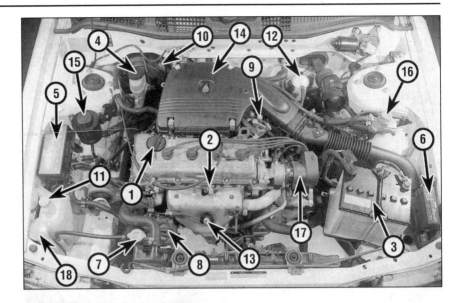

Underbonnet view of a 1.6 litre fuel-injected model

1 Engine oil filler cap
2 Engine oil dipstick
3 Battery
4 Master cylinder brake fluid reservoir
5 Relay box
6 ABS unit
7 Radiator filler cap
8 Alternator
9 Throttle housing
10 Braking system vacuum servo unit
11 Coolant expansion tank
12 Fuel filter
13 Exhaust gas sensor
14 Air cleaner housing
15 Power steering fluid reservoir
16 Windscreen wiper motor
17 Distributor
18 Windscreen washer reservoir

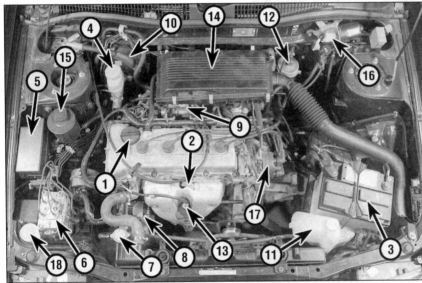

1

Underbonnet view of a 2.0 litre fuel-injected model

1 Engine oil filler cap
2 Engine oil dipstick
3 Battery
4 Master cylinder brake fluid reservoir
5 Relay box
6 ABS unit
7 Radiator filler cap
8 Carbon canister
9 Throttle housing
10 Braking system vacuum servo unit
11 Coolant expansion tank
12 Fuel filter
13 Airflow meter
14 Air cleaner housing
15 Power steering fluid reservoir
16 Windscreen wiper motor
17 Distributor
18 Windscreen washer reservoir

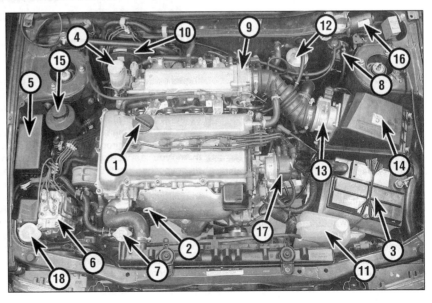

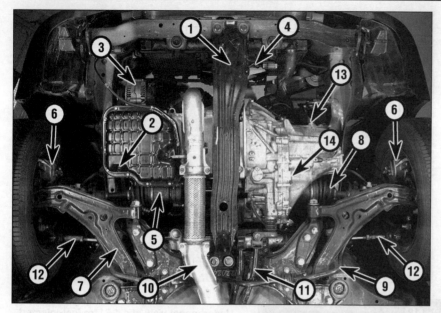

Front underbody view - 2.0 litre model (1.6 model similar)

1 Centre member
2 Sump drain plug
3 Alternator
4 Radiator cooling fan
5 Driveshaft support bearing
6 Brake caliper
7 Lower arm
8 Driveshaft
9 Anti-roll bar
10 Exhaust system front pipe
11 Gearchange linkage selector rod
12 Track rod
13 Transmission filler/level plug
14 Transmission drain plug

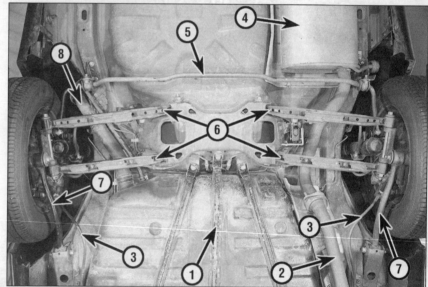

Rear underbody view - Saloon model

1 Fuel tank
2 Exhaust system intermediate pipe
3 Handbrake cable
4 Exhaust system rear box
5 Anti-roll bar
6 Parallel link
7 Radius rod
8 Fuel tank filler neck

Maintenance procedures

1 Introduction

1 This Chapter is designed to help the home mechanic maintain his/her vehicle for safety, economy, long life and peak performance.
2 The Chapter contains a master maintenance schedule, followed by sections dealing specifically with each task on the schedule. Visual checks, adjustments, component renewal and other helpful items are included. Refer to the accompanying illustrations of the engine compartment and the underside of the vehicle for the locations of the various components.
3 Servicing of your vehicle in accordance with

the mileage/time maintenance schedule and the following sections will provide a planned maintenance programme, which should result in a long and reliable service life. This is a comprehensive plan, so maintaining some items but not others at the specified service intervals, will not produce the same results.
4 As you service your vehicle, you will discover that many of the procedures can - and should - be grouped together, because of the particular procedure being performed, or because of the close proximity of two otherwise-unrelated components to one another. For example, if the vehicle is raised for any reason, the exhaust can be inspected at the same time as the suspension and steering components.
5 The first step in this maintenance

programme is to prepare yourself before the actual work begins. Read through all the sections relevant to the work to be carried out, then make a list and gather together all the parts and tools required. If a problem is encountered, seek advice from a parts specialist, or a dealer service department.

2 Intensive maintenance

1 If, from the time the vehicle is new, the routine maintenance schedule is followed closely, and frequent checks are made of fluid levels and high-wear items, as suggested throughout this manual, the engine will be kept in relatively good running condition, and the need for additional work will be minimised.

2 It is possible that there will be times when the engine is running poorly, due to lack of regular maintenance. This is even more likely if a used vehicle, which has not received regular and frequent maintenance checks, is purchased. In such cases, additional work may need to be carried out, outside of the regular maintenance intervals.

3 If engine wear is suspected, a compression test (Chapter 2A or 2B) will provide valuable information regarding the overall performance of the main internal components. Such a test can be used as a basis to decide on the extent of the work to be carried out. If for example a compression test indicates serious internal engine wear, conventional maintenance as described in this Chapter will not greatly improve the performance of the engine, and may prove a waste of time and money, unless extensive overhaul work (Chapter 2C) is carried out first.

4 The following series of operations are those most often required to improve the performance of a generally poor-running engine:

Primary operations

a) *Clean, inspect and test the battery (Section 6).*
b) *Check all the engine-related fluids (Section 3).*
c) *Check the condition and tension of the auxiliary drivebelt(s) (Section 21).*
d) *Renew the spark plugs (Section 10 for non-catalyst models, or 17 for catalyst models).*
e) *Inspect the distributor cap and rotor arm (Section 33).*
f)l *Inspect the ignition HT leads (Section 33).*
g) *Check the condition of the air filter, and renew if necessary (Section 32).*
h) *Check the condition of all hoses, and check for fluid leaks (Section 11).*

5 If the above operations do not prove fully effective, carry out the following secondary operations:

Secondary operations

All items listed under "Primary operations", plus the following:
a) *Check the ignition system (Chapter 5).*
b) *Check the charging system (Chapter 5).*
c) *Check the fuel system (Chapter 4A, 4B or 4C).*
d) *Renew the air filter (Section 32).*
e) *Renew the distributor cap and rotor arm (Section 33).*
f) *Renew the ignition HT leads (Section 33).*

Weekly checks

---

3 Fluid level checks	

Engine oil

1 The engine oil level is checked using a dipstick which extends through a tube and into the sump at the bottom of the engine. The dipstick is located at the front of the engine.

2 The oil level should be checked with the vehicle standing on level ground. The check should be carried out before the vehicle is driven, or at least 5 minutes after the engine has been stopped. If the oil level is checked immediately after driving the vehicle, some of the oil will remain in the upper engine components and oil galleries, resulting in an inaccurate reading on the dipstick.

3 Withdraw the dipstick from the tube, and wipe all the oil from the end with a clean rag or paper towel. Insert the clean dipstick back into the tube as far as it will go, then withdraw it once more. Note the oil level on the end of the dipstick. Add oil as necessary until the level is between the upper (maximum) mark and lower (minimum) mark on the dipstick. Note that approximately 1.0 litre of oil will be required to raise the level from the lower mark to the upper mark.

4 Always maintain the level between the two dipstick marks. If the level is allowed to fall below the lower mark, oil starvation may result, which could lead to severe engine damage. If the engine is overfilled by adding too much oil, this may result in oil-fouled spark plugs, oil leaks, or oil seal failures.

5 Oil is added to the engine after removing the filler cap (twist it anti-clockwise and withdraw it) from the engine cylinder head cover. It is advisable to use an oil can with a spout or a funnel, to avoid spillage. Always use the correct grade and type of oil as shown in *"Lubricants, fluids and capacities"* **(see illustration)**.

Coolant

> ⚠ **Warning: DO NOT attempt to remove the radiator pressure cap when the engine is hot, as there is a very great risk of scalding.**

6 All vehicles covered by this manual are equipped with a pressurised cooling system. An expansion tank is incorporated in the cooling system; on all except 1.6 litre carburettor engine models, the expansion tank is located on the left-hand side of the engine compartment, in front of the battery; on 1.6 litre carburettor engine models, the expansion tank is located in the front right-hand corner of the engine compartment, behind the washer fluid reservoir. As engine temperature increases, the coolant expands, and the level in the expansion tank rises. As the engine cools, the coolant is automatically drawn back into the system, to maintain the correct level.

7 The coolant level in the expansion tank should be checked regularly. The level in the tank varies with the temperature of the engine. When the engine is cold, the coolant level should be between the "MIN" and "MAX" marks on the side of the tank. When the engine is hot, the level may rise slightly above the "MAX" mark.

8 If topping-up is necessary, wait until the engine is cold, then remove the expansion tank cap, and top-up the level as required.

9 Add a mixture of water and antifreeze (see Section 36) through the expansion tank filler neck until the coolant is approximately halfway between the two level marks, then refit the cap.

10 If the expansion tank is empty, check the coolant level in the radiator. Ensure that the engine is cold, then turn the pressure cap on the radiator anti-clockwise until it reaches the first stop. Wait until any pressure remaining in the system is released then push the cap down, turn it anti-clockwise to the second stop and lift off. The coolant level should be up to the filler opening.

11 If necessary, top-up the radiator to the level of the filler opening **(see illustration)**, then refit the pressure cap, turning it clockwise as far as it will go to secure. When the radiator has been topped-up, top-up the expansion tank, as described previously.

12 With a sealed-type cooling system, the addition of coolant should only be necessary at very infrequent intervals. If frequent

3.5 Topping-up the engine oil level

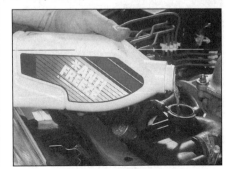
3.11 Topping-up the radiator coolant level

1

3.14 Topping-up the brake fluid level

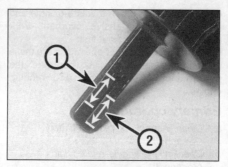

3.20 Power steering fluid level dipstick markings

1 "HOT" level range   2 "COLD" level range

3.21 Topping-up the power steering fluid level

topping-up is required, it is likely there is a leak in the system. Check the radiator, all hoses and joint faces for any sign of staining or actual wetness, and rectify as necessary. Coolant leaks will usually appear as a white stain. If no obvious leaks can be found, it is advisable to have the pressure cap and the entire system pressure-tested by a dealer or suitably-equipped garage, as this will often show up a small leak not previously visible.

Brake fluid

13 The brake master cylinder and fluid reservoir is mounted on the front of the vacuum servo unit in the engine compartment. The maximum and minimum marks are indicated on the side of the reservoir, and the fluid level should be maintained between these marks at all times.
14 If topping-up is necessary, first wipe the area around the filler cap with a clean rag before removing the cap. When adding fluid, pour it carefully into the reservoir to avoid spilling it on surrounding painted surfaces **(see illustration)**. Be sure to use only the specified brake hydraulic fluid, since mixing different types of fluid can cause damage to the system. See *"Lubricants fluids and capacities"* at the beginning of this Chapter.

> ⚠ **Warning: Brake hydraulic fluid can harm your eyes and damage painted surfaces, so use extreme caution when handling and pouring it. Do not use fluid that has been standing open for some time, as it**

absorbs moisture from the air. Excess moisture content can cause a dangerous loss of braking effectiveness.

15 When adding fluid, it is a good idea to inspect the reservoir for contamination. The system should be drained and refilled if deposits, dirt particles or contamination are seen in the fluid.
16 After filling the reservoir to the correct level, make sure that the cap is refitted securely, to avoid leaks and the entry of foreign matter.
17 The fluid level in the master cylinder reservoir will drop slightly as the brake pads and shoes wear down during normal operation. If the reservoir requires repeated replenishing to maintain the proper level, this is an indication of a hydraulic leak somewhere in the system, which should be investigated immediately.

Power steering fluid

18 The power steering fluid reservoir is located on the right-hand side of the engine compartment, in front of the suspension turret.
19 For the check, the car should be parked on level ground, with the front wheels pointing straight-ahead. The engine should be switched off. Note that, for the check to be accurate, the steering **must not** be turned once the engine has stopped.
20 The fluid level should be checked using the dipstick fitted to the underside of the reservoir filler cap. Wipe the area around the

filler cap, then unscrew the cap, and read off the level on the dipstick. If the fluid temperature is between 50 and 80°C (if the vehicle has recently been driven on a reasonable run), the level should be read from the "HOT" range on the dipstick. At fluid temperatures of 0 to 30°C (vehicle has not recently been driven, and engine cold), the level should be read from the "COLD" range on the dipstick **(see illustration)**.
21 If necessary, top-up to the relevant "MAX" mark using the specified type of fluid. Take great care not to allow any dirt or foreign matter to enter the hydraulic system, and do not overfill the reservoir **(see illustration)**. When the level is correct, refit the cap. Note that the need for frequent topping-up of the system indicates a leak, which should be investigated immediately.

Washer fluid

22 The windscreen/tailgate/headlight washer fluid reservoir filler is located at the front right-hand corner of the engine compartment, behind the headlight **(see illustration)**.
23 Certain models are fitted with a facia-mounted warning light, to indicate when topping-up is required.
24 On models without a warning light, a level indicator tube is fitted to the reservoir filler cap. To check the level, use a finger to cover the breather hole in the top of the filler cap, then pull the cap from the reservoir. Fluid will be retained in the tube to indicate the level in the reservoir.
25 When topping-up the reservoir, a screenwash additive should be added in the quantities recommended on the bottle.

3.22 Topping-up the washer fluid level

4.1 Checking a tyre tread depth with a depth gauge

| 4 | Tyre checks | |

1 The original tyres fitted on this car are equipped with tread wear safety bands, which will appear when the tread depth reaches approximately 1.6 mm. Tread wear can be monitored with a simple, inexpensive device known as a tread depth indicator gauge **(see illustration)**.

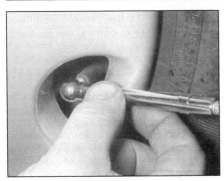

4.3 Checking a tyre pressure with a tyre pressure gauge

2 Wheels and tyres should give no real problems in use, provided that a close eye is kept on them with regard to excessive wear or damage. To this end, the following points should be noted.

3 Ensure that tyre pressures are checked regularly and maintained correctly **(see illustration)**. Checking should be carried out with the tyres cold, and **not** immediately after the vehicle has been in use. If the pressures are checked with the tyres hot, an apparently-high reading will be obtained, owing to heat expansion. **Under no circumstances** should an attempt be made to reduce the pressures to the quoted cold reading in this instance, or effective under-inflation will result.

4 Note any abnormal tread wear **(see illustration)**. Tread pattern irregularities such as feathering, flat spots and more wear on one side than the other are indications of front wheel alignment and/or balance problems. If

any of these conditions are noted, they should be rectified as soon as possible.

5 Under-inflation will cause overheating of the tyre owing to excessive flexing of the casing, and the tread will not sit correctly on the road surface. This will cause a consequent loss of adhesion and excessive wear, not to mention the danger of sudden tyre failure due to heat build-up.

6 Over-inflation will cause rapid wear of the centre part of the tyre tread coupled with reduced adhesion, harsher ride, and the danger of shock damage occurring in the tyre casing.

7 Regularly check the tyres for damage in the form of cuts or bulges, especially in the sidewalls. Remove any nails or stones embedded in the tread before they penetrate the tyre to cause deflation. If removal of a nail does reveal that the tyre has been punctured, refit the nail so that its point of penetration is marked. Immediately change the wheel, and have the tyre repaired by a tyre dealer - **do not** drive on a tyre in such a condition. If in any doubt as to the possible consequences of any damage found, consult your local tyre dealer for advice.

8 Periodically remove the wheels, and clean any dirt or mud from the inside and outside surfaces. Examine the wheel rims for signs of rusting, corrosion or other damage. Light alloy wheels are easily damaged by "kerbing" whilst parking, and similarly, steel wheels may become dented or buckled. Renewal of the wheel is very often the only course of remedial action possible.

9 The balance of each wheel and tyre

assembly should be maintained to avoid excessive wear, not only to the tyres but also to the steering and suspension components. Wheel imbalance is normally signified by vibration through the vehicle's bodyshell, although in many cases it is particularly noticeable through the steering wheel. Conversely, it should be noted that wear or damage in suspension or steering components may cause excessive tyre wear. Out-of-round or out-of-true tyres, damaged wheels, and wheel bearing wear also fall into this category. Balancing will not usually cure vibration caused by such wear.

10 Wheel balancing may be carried out with the wheel either on or off the vehicle. If balanced on the vehicle, ensure that the wheel-to-hub relationship is marked in some way prior to subsequent wheel removal, so that it may be refitted in its original position.

11 General tyre wear is influenced to a large degree by driving style - harsh braking and acceleration or fast cornering will all produce more rapid tyre wear. Interchanging of tyres may result in more even wear; however, if this is completely effective, the added expense is incurred of replacing a complete set of tyres at once, which may prove financially restrictive for many owners.

12 Front tyres may wear unevenly as a result of wheel misalignment. The front wheels should always be correctly aligned according to the settings specified by the vehicle manufacturer.

13 Legal restrictions apply to many aspects of tyre fitting and usage. In the UK, this information is contained in the Motor Vehicle

1

Tyre tread wear patterns

Shoulder Wear

Underinflation (wear on both sides)
Under-inflation will cause overheating of the tyre, because the tyre will flex too much, and the tread will not sit correctly on the road surface. This will cause a loss of grip and excessive wear, not to mention the danger of sudden tyre failure due to heat build-up.
Check and adjust pressures
Incorrect wheel camber (wear on one side)
Repair or renew suspension parts
Hard cornering
Reduce speed!

Centre Wear

Overinflation
Over-inflation will cause rapid wear of the centre part of the tyre tread, coupled with reduced grip, harsher ride, and the danger of shock damage occurring in the tyre casing.
Check and adjust pressures

If you sometimes have to inflate your car's tyres to the higher pressures specified for maximum load or sustained high speed, don't forget to reduce the pressures to normal afterwards.

Uneven Wear

Front tyres may wear unevenly as a result of wheel misalignment. Most tyre dealers and garages can check and adjust the wheel alignment (or "tracking") for a modest charge.
Incorrect camber or castor
Repair or renew suspension parts
Malfunctioning suspension
Repair or renew suspension parts
Unbalanced wheel
Balance tyres
Incorrect toe setting
Adjust front wheel alignment
Note: *The feathered edge of the tread which typifies toe wear is best checked by feel.*

Construction and Use Regulations. It is suggested that a copy of these regulations is obtained from your local police if in doubt as to current legal requirements with regard to tyre type and condition, minimum tread depth, etc.

5 Electrical system check

1 Check the operation of all the electrical equipment, ie lights, direction indicators, horn, etc. Refer to the appropriate Sections of Chapter 12 for details if any of the circuits are found to be inoperative.
2 Note that stop-light switch adjustment is described in Chapter 9.
3 Visually check all accessible wiring connectors, harnesses and retaining clips for security and for signs of chafing or damage. Rectify any faults found.

6 Battery check

Caution: Before carrying out any work on the vehicle battery, read through the precautions given in "Safety first!" at the beginning of this manual.

Maintenance-free battery

1 A "maintenance-free" battery is fitted to some models covered by this manual. Although this type of battery has many advantages over the older refillable type, and never requires the addition of distilled water, it should still be routinely maintained according to the following procedure.
2 The battery is located on the left-hand side of the engine compartment. The exterior of the battery should be inspected periodically for damage such as a cracked case or cover.
3 Check the tightness of the battery cable clamps to ensure good electrical connections,

7.2 Press the locking tab (arrowed) to release the wiper blade

and check the entire length of each cable for cracked insulation and frayed wiring.
4 If corrosion (visible as white, fluffy deposits) is evident, remove the cables from the battery terminals, clean them with a small wire brush, then refit them. Corrosion can be kept to a minimum by applying a layer of petroleum jelly to the clamps and terminals after they are reconnected.
5 Make sure that the battery tray is in good condition, and that the retaining clamp is tight.
6 Corrosion (white deposits) on the tray, retaining clamp and the battery itself can be removed with a solution of water and baking soda. Corrosion of this nature is caustic, so don't get any on your hands, or in your eyes. Thoroughly rinse all cleaned areas with plain water.
7 Any metal parts of the vehicle damaged by corrosion should be covered with a zinc-based primer, then painted.
8 Further information on the battery, charging, and jump-starting, can be found in Chapter 5 and in the preliminary sections of this manual.

Standard and low-maintenance batteries

9 Carry out the checks described above in paragraphs 2 to 8. In addition, the battery electrolyte level should also be checked as follows.

Batteries with a translucent casing

10 On this type of battery, the electrolyte level is visible through the casing. Make sure that the level in each cell is between the UPPER and LOWER level marks on the side of the battery casing.
11 If topping-up is necessary, remove the cell cap(s) and top-up the relevant cell to the UPPER level marking using only distilled water. **Note:** *Do not use ordinary tap water, as this will damage the battery.* Refit the cell cap(s), ensuring each one is securely fitted, and mop up any spilt water.

Batteries with a solid (non-translucent) casing

12 On batteries where it is not possible to see the electrolyte level through the casing, the level is checked via the cell filler cap apertures. Remove the cap from each battery cell and, looking down through cap apertures, check that the electrolyte level is up to the base of the aperture neck.
13 If topping-up is necessary, top-up the relevant cell to the base of the neck using only distilled water. **Note:** *Do not use ordinary tap water, as this will damage the battery.* Refit the cell cap(s), ensuring each one is securely fitted, and mop up any spilt water.

7 Wiper blade check

1 Check the condition of the wiper blades; if they are cracked or show any signs of deterioration, or if the glass swept area is smeared, renew them. For maximum clarity of vision, wiper blades should be renewed annually, as a matter of course.
2 To remove a wiper blade, pull the arm fully away from the glass until it locks. Swivel the blade through 90°, press the locking tab(s) with your fingers, and slide the blade out of the arm's hooked end **(see illustration)**. On refitting, ensure that the blade locks securely into the arm.

Every 4500 miles or 6 months - whichever comes first

8 Engine oil and filter renewal

 Frequent oil and filter changes are the most important preventative maintenance procedures which can be undertaken by the DIY owner. As engine oil ages, it becomes diluted and contaminated, which leads to premature engine wear.

1 Before starting this procedure, gather together all the necessary tools and materials. Also make sure that you have plenty of clean rags and newspapers handy, to mop up any spills. Ideally, the engine oil should be warm, as it will drain more easily, and more built-up sludge will be removed with it. Take care not to touch the exhaust or any other hot parts of the engine when working under the vehicle. To avoid any possibility of scalding, and to protect yourself from possible skin irritants and other harmful contaminants in used engine oils, it is advisable to wear gloves when carrying out this work.
2 Access to the underside of the vehicle will

be greatly improved if it can be raised on a lift, driven onto ramps, or jacked up and supported on axle stands. Whichever method is chosen, make sure that the vehicle remains level, or if it is at an angle, that the drain plug

Note: It is antisocial and illegal to dump oil down the drain. To find the location of your local oil recycling bank, call this number free.

8.9 On 2.0 litre models, access to the oil filter is very poor, and removal may prove difficult without the special Nissan tool

8.11a Apply a coat of oil to the filter sealing ring prior to fitting

8.11b Fitting the oil filter - 2.0 litre engine (viewed from above)

is at the lowest point. The drain plug is located at the rear of the sump.

3 Remove the oil filler cap from the cylinder head cover (twist it anti-clockwise and withdraw it).

4 Using a spanner, or preferably a suitable socket and bar, slacken the drain plug about half a turn. Position the draining container under the drain plug, then remove the plug completely. If possible, try to keep the plug pressed into the sump while unscrewing it by hand the last couple of turns.

> **HAYNES HiNT** *As the plug releases from the threads, move it away sharply, so that the stream of oil from the sump runs into the container, not up your sleeve!*

5 Allow some time for the oil to drain, noting that it may be necessary to reposition the container as the oil flow slows to a trickle.

6 After all the oil has drained, wipe the drain plug and the sealing washer with a clean rag. Examine the condition of the sealing washer - renew it if it shows signs of scoring or other damage which may prevent an oil-tight seal. Clean the area around the drain plug opening, and refit the plug complete with the washer. Tighten the plug securely - preferably to the specified torque, using a torque wrench.

7 The oil filter is located at the rear right-hand side of the cylinder block. Note that on 1.6 litre engine models, access is most easily obtained from underneath the vehicle.

8 Move the container into position under the oil filter.

9 Use an oil filter removal tool (if required) to slacken the filter initially, then unscrew it by hand the rest of the way **(see illustration)**. Empty the oil from the old filter into the container. **Note:** *Oil filter removal is simplified if the special Nissan filter removal tool is used (Part No. KV10105900 on 1.6 litre models or KV10115800 on 2.0 litre models); the tool is in the form of a socket which fits over the end of the filter, and can be turned using a suitable ratchet or extension bar.*

10 Use a clean rag to remove all oil, dirt and sludge from the filter sealing area on the engine. Check the old filter to make sure that the rubber sealing ring has not stuck to the engine. If it has, carefully remove it.

11 Apply a light coating of clean engine oil to the sealing ring on the new filter, then screw the filter into position on the engine. Lightly tighten the filter until its sealing ring contacts the block, then tighten it through a further two-thirds of a turn **(see illustrations)**.

12 Remove the old oil and all tools from under the vehicle then, if applicable, lower the vehicle to the ground.

13 Fill the engine through the filler hole in the cylinder head cover, using the correct grade and type of oil (refer to Section 3 for details of topping-up). Pour in half the specified quantity of oil first, then wait a few minutes for the oil to drain into the sump. Continue to add oil, a small quantity at a time, until the level is up to the lower mark on the dipstick. Adding a

8.11c Fitting the oil filter - 1.6 litre engine (viewed from below)

further 1.0 litre will bring the level up to the upper mark on the dipstick.

14 Start the engine and run it for a few minutes, while checking for leaks around the oil filter seal and the sump drain plug. Note that there may be a delay of a few seconds before the low oil pressure warning light goes out when the engine is first started, as the oil circulates through the new oil filter and the engine oil galleries before the pressure builds up. Do not run the engine above idle speed while the warning light is on.

15 Stop the engine, and wait a few minutes for the oil to settle in the sump once more. With the new oil circulated and the filter now completely full, recheck the level on the dipstick, and add more oil as necessary.

16 Dispose of the used engine oil safely, with reference to *"General repair procedures"* in the Reference sections of this manual.

Every 9000 miles or 6 months - whichever comes first

9 Idle speed and mixture check and adjustment

1 Before checking the idle speed and mixture setting, always check first the following.

a) *Check that the ignition timing is accurate (Chapter 5).*

b) *Check that the spark plugs are in good condition and correctly gapped (Section 10 or 17).*

c) *Check that the accelerator cable is correctly adjusted (see relevant Part of Chapter 4).*

d) *Check that the crankcase breather hoses are secure, with no leaks or kinks (Section 19).*

e) *Check that the air cleaner filter element is clean (Section 32).*

f) *Check that the exhaust system is in good condition (see relevant Part of Chapter 4).*

g) *If the engine is running very roughly,*

check the compression pressures as described in Chapter 2.

h) *On fuel-injected models, check that the fuel injection/ignition system warning light is not illuminated (see relevant Part of Chapter 4).*

2 The idle mixture (exhaust gas CO level) is set at the factory, and should require no further adjustment. If, due to a change in engine characteristics (carbon build-up, bore wear etc) or after a major carburettor overhaul, the mixture becomes incorrect, it

1

9.5 On carburettor models, the idle speed adjusting screw is situated at the rear of the carburettor (shown with air cleaner removed for clarity)

9.12 On catalyst carburettor models, the exhaust gas CO level is checked at the take-off pipe (arrowed) on the exhaust manifold

9.19 On 1.6 litre fuel injection models, the idle speed adjusting screw (arrowed) is on the right-hand side of the throttle housing

can be reset. Note, however, that an exhaust gas analyser (CO meter) will be required to check the mixture and to set it with the necessary standard of accuracy; if this is not available, the car must be taken to a Nissan dealer for the work to be carried out.

3 Take the car on a journey of sufficient length to warm it up to normal operating temperature. **Note:** *Adjustment should be completed within two minutes of return, without stopping the engine. If this cannot be achieved, or if the radiator electric cooling fan operates, wait for the cooling fan to stop. Clear any excess fuel from the inlet manifold by racing the engine two or three times to between 2000 and 3000 rpm, then allow it to idle again.*

4 Ensure that all electrical loads are switched off; if the car is not equipped with a tachometer, connect one following its manufacturer's instructions. Note the idle speed, comparing it with that specified. Proceed as described under the relevant sub-heading.

1.6 litre carburettor non-catalyst models

5 The idle speed adjusting screw is situated at the rear of the carburettor, and is accessible from behind the air cleaner housing. Screw it in or out as necessary to obtain the specified speed **(see illustration)**.

6 If an exhaust gas analyser is available, follow the manufacturer's instructions to check the exhaust gas CO level. If adjustment is required, it is made by altering the mixture adjustment screw which is situated directly below the idle speed adjusting screw.

7 Using a suitable flat-bladed screwdriver, turn the mixture adjustment screw in very small increments until the level is correct; screwing it in (clockwise) weakens the idle mixture and reduces the CO level, screwing it out will richen the mixture and increase the CO level.

8 When adjustments are complete, disconnect any test equipment and recheck the idle speed, adjusting as necessary.

1.6 litre carburettor catalyst models

9 Adjust the idle speed as described above in paragraph 5.

10 Referring to paragraph 2, check and adjust the idle mixture as follows.

11 Stop the engine and turn off the ignition switch. Disconnect the wiring connector from the exhaust gas sensor (which is screwed into the exhaust manifold) and the air induction solenoid control valve (which is mounted onto the left-hand side of the inlet manifold) (see Chapter 4 for further information).

12 Remove the cap from the top of the exhaust gas take-off pipe which is situated on the left-hand side of the exhaust manifold, and connect the CO meter to the take-off pipe **(see illustration)**.

13 Start the engine, clear excess fuel from the inlet manifold by racing the engine two or three times to between 2000 and 3000 rpm, then allow it to idle again. Check the exhaust gas CO level is within the limits given in the Specifications.

14 If adjustment is required, using a sharp instrument, hook out the tamperproof plug from carburettor to gain access to the mixture adjustment screw, which is situated directly below the idle speed adjusting screw.

15 Using a suitable flat-bladed screwdriver, turn the mixture adjustment screw in very small increments until the level is correct; screwing it in (clockwise) weakens the idle mixture and reduces the CO level, screwing it out will richen the mixture and increase the CO level.

16 When adjustments are complete, disconnect any test equipment and fit a new tamperproof plug to the mixture adjustment screw. Refit the cap to the exhaust gas take-off pipe, and reconnect the exhaust gas sensor and solenoid valve wiring connectors.

17 Check the idle speed and, if necessary, readjust.

1.6 litre fuel-injected models

18 Stop the engine and turn off the ignition switch. Disconnect the wiring connector from the throttle potentiometer, which is mounted onto the side of the throttle housing (see Chapter 4 for further information).

19 Start the engine, clear excess fuel from the inlet manifold by racing the engine two or three times to between 2000 and 3000 rpm, then allow it to idle again. Check that the idle speed is within the limits given in the Specifications. If adjustment is necessary, the idle speed adjusting screw is situated on the right-hand side of the throttle housing **(see illustration)**. Screw it in or out as necessary to obtain the specified speed. When the idle speed is correctly set, switch off the engine and reconnect the throttle potentiometer wiring connector.

20 Experienced home mechanics with a considerable amount of skill and equipment (including a good-quality tachometer and a good-quality, carefully-calibrated exhaust gas analyser) may be able to *check* the exhaust CO level. However, if it is found to be in need of *adjustment*, there must be a fault in the ECCS control system; no adjustment of the mixture is possible.

21 If the exhaust gas CO content is incorrect, check the operation of the exhaust gas sensor and fuel injection system components using the ECCS control unit self-diagnostic function (see Chapter 4B). If this fails to show the problem, the vehicle must be taken to a Nissan dealer for testing.

2.0 litre single-point injection non-catalyst models

22 Stop the engine and turn off the ignition switch. Disconnect the wiring connector from the throttle potentiometer, which is mounted onto the side of the throttle body (see Chapter 4 for further information).

23 Start the engine, clear excess fuel from the inlet manifold by racing the engine two or three times to between 2000 and 3000 rpm, then allow it to idle again. Check that the idle speed is within the limits given in the Specifications. If adjustment is necessary, the idle speed adjusting screw is situated on the left-hand side of the throttle housing, and is accessed from the rear. Screw it in or out as necessary to obtain the specified speed.

When the idle speed is correctly set, switch off the engine and reconnect the throttle potentiometer wiring connector.

24 If an exhaust gas analyser is available, follow the equipment manufacturer's instructions to check the exhaust gas CO level. If adjustment is required, it is made via the mixture adjustment potentiometer screw on the right-hand side of the ECCS control unit. To gain access to the control unit, release the retaining screw and fastener, and remove the right-hand trim panel from the front of the centre console; the screw is located behind the stick-on label on the side of the unit.

25 Peel off the label and, using a suitable flat-bladed screwdriver, turn the mixture adjustment screw in very small increments until the level is correct; screwing it in (clockwise) richens the mixture and increases the CO level, screwing it out will weaken the mixture and decrease the CO level.

26 When adjustments are complete, disconnect any test equipment then fit a new label over the mixture adjustment screw and refit the trim panel. Check the idle speed and, if necessary, readjust.

2.0 litre single-point injection catalyst models

27 Adjust the idle speed as described above in paragraphs 22 to 23.

28 Experienced home mechanics with a considerable amount of skill and equipment (including a good-quality tachometer and a good-quality, carefully-calibrated exhaust gas analyser) may be able to *check* the exhaust CO level. However, if it is found to be in need of *adjustment,* there must be a fault in the ECCS control system; no adjustment of the mixture is possible.

29 If the exhaust gas CO content is incorrect, check the operation of the exhaust gas sensor and fuel injection system components using the ECCS control unit self-diagnostic function (see Chapter 4B). If this fails to show the problem, the vehicle must be taken to a Nissan dealer for testing.

2.0 litre multi-point injection non-catalyst models

30 Stop the engine and turn off the ignition switch. Disconnect the wiring connector from the throttle potentiometer (which is mounted onto the side of the throttle housing - see Chapter 4 for further information).

31 Start the engine, clear excess fuel from the inlet manifold by racing the engine two or three times to between 2000 and 3000 rpm, then allow it to idle again. Check the idle speed is within the limits given in the Specifications. If adjustment is necessary, the idle speed adjusting screw is situated on the top of the idle air adjusting unit, which is bolted to the right-hand end of the inlet

manifold. Turn the screw it in or out as necessary to obtain the specified speed. When the idle speed is correctly set, switch off the engine and reconnect the throttle potentiometer wiring connector.

32 If an exhaust gas analyser is available, follow the equipment manufacturer's instructions to check the exhaust gas CO level. If adjustment is required, it is made via the mixture adjustment potentiometer screw on the top of the airflow meter.

33 Using a sharp instrument, hook out the tamperproof plug from top of the airflow meter to gain access to the mixture adjustment screw. Using a suitable flat-bladed screwdriver, turn the mixture adjustment screw in very small increments until the level is correct; screwing it in (clockwise) richens the idle mixture and increases the CO level, screwing it out will weaken the mixture and decrease the CO level.

34 When adjustments are complete, disconnect any test equipment and fit a new tamperproof plug to the airflow meter. Check the idle speed and, if necessary, adjust as described above.

2.0 litre multi-point injection catalyst models

35 Adjust the idle speed as described above in paragraphs 30 and 31.

36 Experienced home mechanics with a considerable amount of skill and equipment (including a good-quality tachometer and a good-quality, carefully-calibrated exhaust gas analyser) may be able to *check* the exhaust CO level. However, if it is found to be in need of *adjustment,* there must be a fault in the ECCS control system; no adjustment of the mixture is possible.

37 If the exhaust gas CO content is incorrect, check the operation of the exhaust gas sensor and fuel injection system components using the ECCS control unit self-diagnostic function (see Chapter 4B). If this fails to show the problem, the vehicle must be taken to a Nissan dealer for testing.

10 Spark plug renewal - models without a catalytic converter

1 The correct functioning of the spark plugs is vital for the correct running and efficiency of the engine. It is essential that the plugs fitted are appropriate for the engine (the suitable type is specified at the beginning of this Chapter). If this type is used and the engine is in good condition, the spark plugs should not need attention between scheduled replacement intervals. Spark plug cleaning is rarely necessary, and should not be attempted unless specialised equipment is

available, as damage can easily be caused to the firing ends.

2 If the marks on the original-equipment spark plug (HT) leads cannot be seen, mark the leads one to four to correspond to the cylinder the lead serves (No 1 cylinder is at the timing chain end of the engine). Pull the leads from the plugs by gripping the plug cap, not the lead, otherwise the lead connection may be fractured.

3 It is advisable to remove the dirt from the spark plug recesses using a clean brush, vacuum cleaner or compressed air before removing the plugs, to prevent dirt dropping into the cylinders.

4 Unscrew the plugs using a spark plug spanner, suitable box spanner or a deep socket and extension bar **(see illustration)**. Keep the socket aligned with the spark plug, otherwise if it is forcibly moved to one side, the ceramic insulator may be broken off. As each plug is removed, examine it as follows.

5 Examination of the spark plugs will give a good indication of the condition of the engine. If the insulator nose of the spark plug is clean and white, with no deposits, this is indicative of a weak mixture or too hot a plug (a hot plug transfers heat away from the electrode slowly, a cold plug transfers heat away quickly).

6 If the tip and insulator nose are covered with hard black-looking deposits, then this is indicative that the mixture is too rich. Should the plug be black and oily, then it is likely that the engine is fairly worn, as well as the mixture being too rich.

7 If the insulator nose is covered with light tan to greyish-brown deposits, then the mixture is correct and it is likely that the engine is in good condition.

8 The spark plug electrode gap is of considerable importance as, if it is too large or too small, the size of the spark and its efficiency will be seriously impaired. The gap should be set to the value given in the Specifications at the beginning of this Chapter.

9 To set it, measure the gap with a feeler blade and then bend open, or closed, the

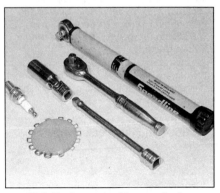

10.4 Tools required for spark plug removal, gap adjustment and refitting

10.9a Measuring the spark plug gap with a feeler blade

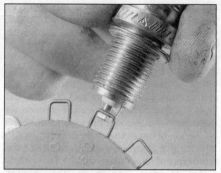

10.9b Measuring the spark plug gap with a wire gauge . . .

10.9c . . . and adjusting the gap using a special adjusting tool

outer plug electrode until the correct gap is achieved **(see illustrations)**. The centre electrode should never be bent, as this may crack the insulator and cause plug failure, if nothing worse.

10 Special spark plug electrode gap adjusting tools are available from most motor accessory shops, or from some spark plug manufacturers.

11 Before fitting the spark plugs, check that the threaded connector sleeves are tight, and that the plug exterior surfaces and threads are clean.

12 Tighten the plug to the specified torque using the spark plug socket and a torque wrench. Refit the remaining spark plugs in the same manner.

HAYNES HINT

It's often difficult to insert spark plugs into their holes without cross-threading them. To avoid this possibility, fit a short piece of rubber hose over the end of the spark plug. The flexible hose acts as a universal joint, to help align the plug with the plug hole. Should the plug begin to cross-thread, the hose will slip on the spark plug, preventing thread damage.

13 Connect the HT leads in their correct order, ensuring that they are correctly clipped into their retaining clips.

11 Hose and fluid leak check

1 Visually inspect the engine joint faces, gaskets and seals for any signs of water or oil leaks. Pay particular attention to the areas

around the camshaft cover, cylinder head, oil filter and sump joint faces. Over a period of time, some very slight seepage from these areas is to be expected - what you are really looking for is any indication of a serious leak. Should a leak be found, renew the offending gasket or oil seal by referring to the appropriate Chapters in this manual.

2 Also check the security and condition of all the engine-related pipes and hoses. Ensure that all cable ties or securing clips are in place and in good condition. Clips which are broken or missing can lead to chafing of the hoses pipes or wiring which could cause more serious problems in the future.

3 Carefully check the radiator hoses and heater hoses along their entire length. Renew any hose which is cracked, swollen or deteriorated. Cracks will show up better if the hose is squeezed. Pay close attention to the hose clips that secure the hoses to the cooling system components. Hose clips can pinch and puncture hoses, resulting in cooling system leaks. If the crimped-type hose clips are used, it may be a good idea to replace them with standard worm-drive clips.

4 Inspect all the cooling system components (hoses, joint faces, etc) for leaks. Where any problems of this nature are found on system components, renew the component or gasket with reference to Chapter 3.

HAYNES HINT

A leak in the cooling system will usually show up as white or rust-coloured deposits on the area adjoining the leak.

5 Where applicable, inspect the automatic transmission fluid cooler hoses for leaks or deterioration.

6 With the vehicle raised, inspect the petrol tank and filler neck for punctures, cracks and other damage. The connection between the filler neck and tank is especially critical. Sometimes a rubber filler neck or connecting hose will leak due to loose retaining clamps or deteriorated rubber.

7 Carefully check all rubber hoses and metal fuel lines leading away from the petrol tank. Check for loose connections, deteriorated

hoses, crimped lines and other damage. Pay particular attention to the vent pipes and hoses, which often loop up around the filler neck and can become blocked or crimped. Follow the lines to the front of the vehicle, carefully inspecting them all the way. Renew damaged sections as necessary.

8 Check the condition of all brake fluid hoses.

9 From within the engine compartment, check the security of all fuel hose attachments and pipe unions, and inspect the fuel hoses and vacuum hoses for kinks, chafing and deterioration.

10 Where applicable, check the condition of the power steering fluid hoses and pipes.

12 Manual transmission oil level check

1 Park the car on a level surface. The oil level must be checked before the car is driven, or at least 5 minutes after the engine has been switched off. If the oil is checked immediately after driving the car, some of the oil will remain distributed around the transmission components, resulting in an inaccurate level reading. To improve access, position the car over an inspection pit, or raise the car off the ground and position it on axle stands, making sure the vehicle remains level to the ground.

2 Wipe clean the area around the filler/level plug, which is on the front face of the transmission. Unscrew the plug and clean it.

3 The oil level should reach the lower edge of the filler/level hole. A certain amount of oil will have gathered behind the filler/level plug and will trickle out when it is removed; this does **not** necessarily indicate that the level is correct. To ensure that a true level is established, wait until the initial trickle has stopped, then add oil as necessary until a trickle of new oil can be seen emerging. The level will be correct when the flow ceases; use only good-quality oil of the specified type **(see illustration)**.

4 Refilling the transmission is an extremely awkward operation; above all, allow plenty of time for the oil level to settle properly before checking it. If a large amount had to be added to

12.3 Topping-up the manual transmission oil

the transmission and a large amount flows out on checking the level, refit the filler/level plug, and take the vehicle on a short journey. This will allow the new oil to be distributed fully around the transmission components. On returning, recheck the level when the oil has settled again.

5 If the transmission has been overfilled so that oil flows out as soon as the filler/level plug is removed, check that the car is completely level (front to rear and side to side). If necessary, allow the surplus to drain off into a suitable container.

6 When the level is correct, refit the filler/level plug, tightening it to the specified torque wrench setting. Wash off any spilt oil.

13 Front and (where fitted) rear brake pad condition check

Front brake pads

1 Chock the rear wheels, apply the handbrake, then jack up the front of the car and support it securely on axle stands (see "Jacking, towing and wheel changing"). Remove the front roadwheels.

 For a quick check, the thickness of friction material remaining on each brake pad can be measured through the aperture in the caliper body. If any pad's friction material is worn to the specified thickness or less, all four pads must be renewed as a set.

2 For a comprehensive check, the brake pads should be removed and cleaned. This will permit the operation of the caliper to be checked, and the condition of the brake disc itself to be fully examined on both sides. Refer to Chapter 9 for further information.

Rear brake pads

3 Chock the front wheels, then jack up the rear of the vehicle and support securely on axle stands. Remove the roadwheels.

4 Proceed as described for the front brake pads in paragraphs 2 and 3.

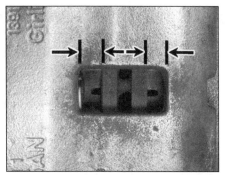

13.2 The front brake pad thickness can be measured through the aperture in the caliper body

14 Handbrake check and adjustment

1 The rear brakes are of the self-adjusting type, and the only adjustments required are to the operating cables.

2 The handbrake should be capable of holding the parked vehicle stationary, even on steep slopes, when applied with moderate force. The mechanism should be firm and positive in feel, with no trace of stiffness or sponginess from the cables, and the mechanism should release immediately the handbrake lever is released. If the mechanism does not operate satisfactorily, it should be checked immediately.

3 To check the operation of the handbrake, chock the front wheels, then jack up the rear of the vehicle and support on axle stands.

4 Fully release the handbrake, and check that the rear roadwheels can be rotated by hand - slight dragging is acceptable, but it should be possible to turn each wheel easily without undue force.

5 On models with rear disc brakes, check that the handbrake levers on the calipers return to rest against the stopper bolts with the handbrake fully released (see illustration).

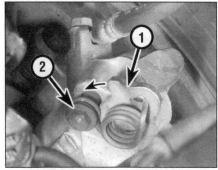

14.5 Ensure that, when released, the handbrake lever rests against the stopper bolt - models with rear disc brakes

1 Handbrake lever (shown here with handbrake applied)
2 Stopper bolt

This will prove easier if the rear roadwheels are removed.

6 Depress the brake pedal several times to establish the correct shoe-to-drum, or pad-to-disc clearance, as applicable.

7 With the pedal released, again, check that the rear roadwheels can be rotated.

8 Apply normal moderate pressure to operate the handbrake lever, and count the number of clicks necessary to bring the lever to the fully-applied position (check that the roadwheels are locked with the lever fully applied). The number of clicks should be as specified (see Specifications).

9 If the number of clicks required to fully apply the handbrake is not as specified, proceed as follows.

10 Working inside the vehicle, remove the centre console as described in Chapter 11.

11 The handbrake adjuster nut is located under the lever on the threaded end of the front cable.

12 Turn the adjuster nut as required (see illustration), and re-check the adjustment as described in paragraph 8, until the handbrake operates correctly over the specified number of clicks.

13 Check that the handbrake "on" warning light illuminates after the specified number of handbrake clicks (see Specifications). If necessary, bend the switch bracket to give the correct adjustment.

14 On completion, where applicable refit the roadwheels, then lower the vehicle to the ground.

15 Clutch adjustment check and control mechanism lubrication

1 Check that the clutch pedal moves smoothly and easily through its full travel. Check also that the clutch itself functions correctly, with no trace of slip or drag, then adjust the clutch cable as described in Chapter 6. If excessive effort is required to operate the clutch, check first that the cable is correctly routed and undamaged, then remove the pedal to ensure that its pivot is properly greased. Refer to Chapter 6 for further information.

14.12 Using a spanner to turn the handbrake adjuster nut

1

Every 18 000 miles or 12 months - whichever comes first

16 Air conditioning system check

Note: *Before proceeding, refer to the precautions given in Chapter 3, Section 10 regarding work on the air conditioning system.*
1 Check the tension and condition of the auxiliary drivebelt which drives the air conditioning compressor, as described in Section 21.
2 Check the condition of the condenser fins, and clean if necessary (remove the front grille panel for access (see Chapter 11). Clean dirt and insects, etc, from the fins using compressed air, or a soft brush. Be careful not to damage the condenser.
3 Operate the air conditioning system for at least 10 minutes each month, even during cold weather, to keep the seals, etc, in good condition.
4 Regularly inspect the refrigerant pipes, hoses and unions for security and condition.
5 The most common cause of poor cooling is simply a low system refrigerant charge. If a noticeable drop in cool air output occurs, one of the following checks will help to determine if the refrigerant level is low.
6 Warm up the engine to normal operating temperature.
7 Move the temperature control knob to the coldest setting, and move the blower motor control knob to the highest setting. Open the doors (to ensure that the air conditioning system does not shut off as soon as it cools the passenger compartment).
8 With the compressor engaged - the compressor clutch will make an audible click, and the centre of the clutch will rotate - inspect the sight glass on the top of the receiver/drier bottle, where applicable. if air bubbles are present in the sight glass, or the refrigerant looks foamy, the charge is low.
9 If no sight glass is fitted, feel the inlet and outlet pipes at the compressor. One side should be cold, and the other hot. If there is no perceptible difference in temperature

between the two pipes, this indicates a fault with the compressor, a low refrigerant charge, or some other system fault - consult a Nissan dealer or air conditioning specialist for advice.
10 The air conditioning system will lose a proportion of its charge through normal seepage - so it is as well to regard periodic recharging as a maintenance operation. Recharging must be done by a Nissan dealer or an air conditioning specialist.
11 Do not under any circumstances attempt to open any of the refrigerant lines, or renew any or the components.

17 Spark plug renewal - models with a catalytic converter

Refer to Section 10.

18 Fuel filter renewal

⚠️ *Warning: Before carrying out the following operation, refer to the precautions given in "Safety first!" at the beginning of this manual, and follow them implicitly. Petrol is a highly-dangerous and volatile liquid, and the precautions necessary when handling it cannot be overstressed*

1 The fuel filter is situated in the engine compartment, mounted on the engine compartment bulkhead.
2 Release the retaining clips and disconnect the fuel hoses from the filter. On fuel injection models, bear in mind the information given in the relevant Part of Chapter 4 on depressurising the fuel system before the hoses are disconnected **(see illustration)**.
3 Slacken the retaining clamp screw **(see illustration)**, then slide the filter out of the clamp, noting the direction of the arrow marked on the filter body. Remove the filter from the engine compartment.

4 Dispose safely of the old filter; it will be highly inflammable, and may explode if thrown on a fire.
5 Slide the filter into position in the clamp, ensuring that the arrow on the filter body is pointing in the direction of the fuel flow, ie. towards the carburettor/throttle body/fuel rail **(see illustration)**. This should be as noted on removal, but can be determined by tracing the fuel hoses back along their length.
6 Connect the fuel hoses to the filter, and secure them in position with their retaining clips.
7 Start the engine, and check the filter hoses connections for leaks.

19 Emissions control systems check

1 Details of the emissions control system components and testing are given in Chapter 4D.
2 Checking consists simply of a visual check for obvious signs of damaged or leaking hoses and joints.

20 Exhaust gas sensor check - models with a catalytic converter

Carburettor models

1 On carburettor models, the exhaust gas sensor is tested as described in Section 2 of Chapter 4D.

Fuel-injected models

2 On fuel-injected models, the exhaust gas sensor can be tested using the ECCS control unit self-diagnosis facility as described in Chapter 4B, Section 12.

18.5 On refitting, ensure that the filter is fitted the correct way round so its arrow (arrowed) is pointing in the direction of fuel flow

18.2 Slacken the retaining clips and disconnect the hose from the filter . . .

18.3 . . . then slacken the clamp bolt and slide the filter out of position

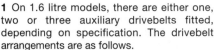

21 Auxiliary drivebelt checking and renewal

1 On 1.6 litre models, there are either one, two or three auxiliary drivebelts fitted, depending on specification. The drivebelt arrangements are as follows.

Models without power steering or air conditioning - one drivebelt (drives alternator and coolant pump).

Models with power steering - two drivebelts (one drives the alternator, and the other the power steering pump and coolant pump).

Models with power steering and air conditioning - three drivebelts (as for models with power steering, with an additional belt for the air conditioning compressor).

2 On 2.0 litre models, there are two auxiliary drivebelts; one drives the power steering pump and coolant pump, and the other the alternator and (where fitted) the air conditioning compressor.

Checking the auxiliary drivebelt condition

3 Apply the handbrake, then jack up the front of the car and support it on axle stands. Remove the right-hand front roadwheel.

4 From underneath the front of the car, undo the retaining screws and remove the plastic cover from underneath the wing to gain access to the crankshaft pulley. If necessary, also undo the retaining screws and remove the engine undershield to improve access.

5 Using a suitable socket and extension bar fitted to the crankshaft pulley bolt, rotate the crankshaft so that the entire length of the drivebelt(s) can be examined. Examine the drivebelt(s) for cracks, splitting, fraying or damage. Check also for signs of glazing (shiny patches) and for separation of the belt plies. Renew the belt if worn or damaged.

6 If the condition of the belt is satisfactory, check the drivebelt tension as described below under the relevant sub-heading.

Air conditioning compressor drivebelt (1.6 litre models) - removal, refitting and tensioning

Removal

7 If not already done, proceed as described in paragraphs 3 and 4.

8 Disconnect the battery negative lead.

9 Slacken the nut securing the tensioning pulley assembly to the engine.

10 Rotate the adjuster bolt to move the tensioner pulley away from the drivebelt until there is sufficient slack for the drivebelt to be removed from the pulleys

Refitting

11 Fit the belt around the pulleys, ensuring that the belt is of the correct type if it is being renewed, and take up the slack in the belt by tightening the adjuster bolt.

12 Tension the drivebelt as described in the following paragraphs.

Tensioning

13 If not already done, proceed as described in paragraphs 3 and 4.

14 Correct tensioning of the drivebelt will ensure that it has a long life. Beware, however, of overtightening, as this can cause wear in the alternator bearings.

15 The belt tension is checked at the mid-point between the pulleys on the top belt run. Referring to the Specifications given at the start of this Chapter, apply the specified force and check that the belt deflection is within the specified range.

16 To adjust the tension, with the tensioner pulley assembly retaining nut slackened, rotate the adjuster bolt until the correct tension is achieved. Once the belt is correctly tensioned, rotate the crankshaft a couple of times and recheck the tension.

17 When the belt is correctly tensioned, tighten the tensioner pulley assembly retaining nut to the specified torque setting, and reconnect the battery negative lead.

18 Refit the cover(s), securely tightening their fasteners, then refit the roadwheel and lower the vehicle to the ground.

Power steering pump drivebelt (1.6 litre models) - removal, refitting and tensioning

Removal

19 If not already done, proceed as described in paragraphs 3 and 4.

20 Disconnect the battery negative lead. On models with air conditioning, remove the air conditioning compressor drivebelt as described in paragraphs 9 and 10.

21 Slacken the power steering pump mounting nuts/bolts (as applicable).

22 Back off the adjuster bolt to relieve the tension in the drivebelt, then slip the drivebelt from the pulleys.

Refitting

23 Fit the belt around the pulleys, ensuring that the belt is of the correct type if it is being renewed, and take up the slack in the belt by tightening the adjuster bolt.

24 Tension the drivebelt as described in the

following paragraphs. Where necessary, refit and tension the air conditioning compressor drivebelt as described in paragraphs 11 to 17.

Tensioning

25 If not already done, proceed as described in paragraphs 3 and 4.

26 Correct tensioning of the drivebelt will ensure that it has a long life. Beware, however, of overtightening, as this can cause wear in the alternator bearings.

27 The belt tension is checked at the mid-point between the pulleys on the upper belt run. Referring to the Specifications given at the start of this Chapter, apply the specified force and check that the belt deflection is within the specified range.

28 To adjust, with the upper mounting nut/bolt just holding the power steering pump firm, and the other mounting nut/bolt loosened, turn the adjuster bolt until the correct tension is achieved. Rotate the crankshaft a couple of times, recheck the tension, then securely tighten both the power steering pump mounting nuts/bolts.

29 Refit the cover(s), securely tightening their fasteners, then refit the roadwheel and lower the vehicle to the ground.

Alternator drivebelt (1.6 litre models) - removal, refitting and tensioning

Removal

30 If not already done, proceed as described in paragraphs 3 and 4.

31 Disconnect the battery negative lead. On models with air conditioning, remove the air conditioning drivebelt as described in paragraphs 9 and 10. On models with power steering, remove the power steering drivebelt as described in paragraphs 21 and 22.

32 Slacken both the alternator upper and lower mounting nuts/bolts (as applicable) **(see illustration)**.

33 Back off the adjuster bolt to relieve the tension in the drivebelt, then slip the drivebelt from the pulleys **(see illustrations)**.

Refitting

34 Fit the belt around the pulleys, ensuring that the belt is of the correct type if it is being

21.32 Slacken the alternator mounting bolts . . .

21.33a . . . then loosen the adjuster bolt . . .

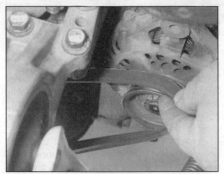

21.33b . . . and slip the drivebelt off the alternator pulley

renewed, and take up the slack in the belt by tightening the adjuster bolt.

35 Tension the drivebelt as described in the following paragraphs. Where necessary, refit the air conditioning compressor drivebelt as described in paragraphs 11 to 17.

Tensioning

36 If not already done, proceed as described in paragraphs 3 and 4.

37 Correct tensioning of the drivebelt will ensure that it has a long life. Beware, however, of overtightening, as this can cause wear in the alternator bearings.

38 The belt should be tensioned is checked at the mid-point between the pulleys on the upper belt run. Referring to the Specifications given at the start of this Chapter, apply the specified force and check that the belt deflection is within the specified range.

39 To adjust, with the upper mounting nut/bolt just holding the alternator firm, and the lower mounting nut/bolt loosened, turn the adjuster bolt until the correct tension is achieved. Rotate the crankshaft a couple of times, recheck the tension, then securely tighten both the alternator mounting nuts/bolts.

40 Refit the cover(s), securely tightening their fasteners, then refit the roadwheel and lower the vehicle to the ground.

Alternator drivebelt (2.0 litre models) - removal, refitting and tensioning

41 Refer to the information given in paragraphs 30 to 40, ignoring the remarks

21.41a Loosen the alternator upper . . .

about removing/refitting the air conditioning compressor and power steering pump drivebelt(s). **Note:** *On models without air conditioning, on refitting ensure that the drivebelt is seated in the same grooves of both the crankshaft and alternator pulleys, so that the belt run is true* **(see illustrations).**

Power steering pump drivebelt (2.0 litre models) - removal, refitting and tensioning

42 Refer to the information given in paragraphs 19 to 29, ignoring the remarks about removing/refitting the air conditioning compressor drivebelt. Note that it is necessary to remove/refit the alternator drivebelt instead (see paragraph 41).

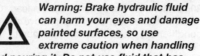

22 Rear brake shoe check

1 Remove the rear brake drums, and check the brake shoes for signs of wear or contamination. At the same time, also inspect the wheel cylinders for signs of leakage, and the brake drum for signs of wear. Refer to the relevant Sections of Chapter 9 for further information.

23 Brake fluid renewal

⚠️ *Warning: Brake hydraulic fluid can harm your eyes and damage painted surfaces, so use extreme caution when handling and pouring it. Do not use fluid that has been standing open for some time, as it absorbs moisture from the air. Excess moisture content can cause a dangerous loss of braking effectiveness.*

1 The procedure is similar to that for the bleeding of the hydraulic system as described in Chapter 9. The brake fluid reservoir should be emptied by siphoning, using a clean poultry baster or similar before starting, then refilled with fresh fluid. Allowance should be

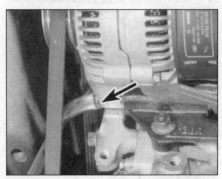

21.41b . . . and lower mounting bolts (arrowed) to allow adjustment of the drivebelt

made for the old fluid to be expelled when bleeding a section of the circuit.

2 Working as described in Chapter 9, open the first bleed screw in the sequence and pump the brake pedal gently until nearly all the fluid has been emptied from the master cylinder reservoir. Top-up to the "MAX" level with more fresh fluid, and continue pumping until new fluid can be seen emerging from the bleed screw. Tighten the screw and top the reservoir level up to the "MAX" level line.

3 Old hydraulic fluid is invariably much darker in colour than the new, making it easy to distinguish the two.

4 Work through all the remaining bleed screws in the sequence until new fluid can be seen at all of them. Be careful to keep the master cylinder reservoir topped-up to above the "MIN" level at all times, or air may enter the system and greatly increase the length of the task.

5 When the operation is complete, check that all bleed screws are securely tightened, and that their dust caps are refitted. Wash off all traces of spilt fluid, and recheck the master cylinder reservoir fluid level.

6 Check the operation of the brakes before taking the car on the road.

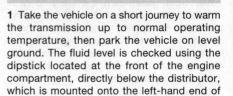

24 Automatic transmission fluid level check

1 Take the vehicle on a short journey to warm the transmission up to normal operating temperature, then park the vehicle on level ground. The fluid level is checked using the dipstick located at the front of the engine compartment, directly below the distributor, which is mounted onto the left-hand end of the cylinder head.

2 With the engine idling and the selector lever in the "P" (Park) position, withdraw the dipstick from the tube, and wipe all the fluid from its end with a clean rag or paper towel. Insert the clean dipstick back into the tube as far as it will go, then withdraw it once more.

21.41c On 2.0 litre models not fitted with air conditioning, ensure that the drivebelt (arrowed) is correctly seated in the same grooves of the alternator pulley as those of crankshaft pulley - ie. so that the spare grooves are at the front

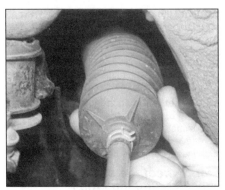

25.2 Checking a steering gear gaiter

25.4 Rocking the roadwheel to check steering/suspension components

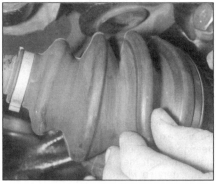

26.1 Checking driveshaft constant velocity joint (CV) joint gaiter

Note the level on the end of the dipstick, noting that there are two sets of level markings. On one side of the dipstick are the "COLD" upper and lower marks (which are in the form of cut-outs on the edge of the dipstick - for use when the fluid temperature is between 30 and 50°C); on the other side are the "HOT" upper and lower marks (which are in the form of lines marked on the dipstick - for use when the fluid temperature is between 50 and 80°C). If the vehicle is fully warmed-up, the "HOT" marks should be used.

3 If topping-up is necessary, add the required quantity of the specified fluid to the transmission via the dipstick tube. Use a funnel with a fine mesh gauze, to avoid spillage and to ensure that no foreign matter enters the transmission. Add fluid as necessary until the level is between the relevant set of upper and lower marks on the dipstick. **Note:** *Never overfill the transmission so that the fluid level is above the upper mark.*
4 After topping-up, take the vehicle on a short run to distribute the fresh fluid, then recheck the level again, topping-up if necessary.
5 Always maintain the level between the two dipstick marks. If the level is allowed to fall below the lower mark, various problems, and even severe transmission damage, could result.

25 Steering and suspension check

Front suspension and steering check

1 Apply the handbrake, then raise the front of the vehicle and securely support it on axle stands.
2 Visually inspect the balljoint dust covers and the steering rack and pinion gaiters for splits, chafing or deterioration **(see illustration)**. Any wear of these components will cause loss of lubricant, together with dirt and water entry, resulting in

rapid deterioration of the balljoints or steering gear.
3 On vehicles with power steering, check the fluid hoses for chafing or deterioration, and the pipe and hose unions for fluid leaks. Also check for signs of fluid leakage under pressure from the steering gear rubber gaiters, which would indicate failed fluid seals within the steering gear.
4 Grasp the roadwheel at the 12 o'clock and 6 o'clock positions, and try to rock it **(see illustration)**. Very slight free play may be felt, but if the movement is appreciable, further investigation is necessary to determine the source. Continue rocking the wheel while an assistant depresses the footbrake. If the movement is now eliminated or significantly reduced, it is likely that the hub bearings are at fault. If the free play is still evident with the footbrake depressed, then there is wear in the suspension joints or mountings.
5 Now grasp the wheel at the 9 o'clock and 3 o'clock positions, and try to rock it as before. Any movement felt now may again be caused by wear in the hub bearings or the steering track-rod balljoints. If the inner or outer balljoint is worn, the visual movement will be obvious.
6 Using a large screwdriver or flat bar, check for wear in the suspension mounting bushes by levering between the relevant suspension component and its attachment point. Some movement is to be expected as the mountings are made of rubber, but excessive wear should be obvious. Also check the condition of any visible rubber bushes, looking for splits, cracks or contamination of the rubber.
7 With the car standing on its wheels, have an assistant turn the steering wheel back and forth about an eighth of a turn each way. There should be very little, if any, lost movement between the steering wheel and roadwheels. If this is not the case, closely observe the joints and mountings previously described, but in addition check the steering column universal joints for wear, and also check the rack-and-pinion steering gear itself.

Suspension strut/shock absorber check

8 Check for any signs of fluid leakage around the suspension strut/shock absorber body, or from the rubber gaiter around the piston rod. Should any fluid be noticed, the suspension strut/shock absorber is defective internally, and should be renewed. **Note:** *Suspension struts/shock absorbers should always be renewed in pairs on the same axle.*
9 The efficiency of the suspension strut/shock absorber may be checked by bouncing the vehicle at each corner. Generally speaking, the body will return to its normal position and stop after being depressed. If it rises and returns on a rebound, the suspension strut/shock absorber is probably suspect. Examine the suspension strut/shock absorber upper and lower mountings for any signs of wear.

26 Driveshaft gaiter check

1 With the vehicle raised and securely supported on stands, turn the steering onto full lock, then slowly rotate the roadwheel. Inspect the condition of the outer constant velocity (CV) joint rubber gaiters, squeezing the gaiters to open out the folds **(see illustration)**. Check for signs of cracking, splits or deterioration of the rubber, which may allow the grease to escape, and lead to water and grit entry into the joint. Also check the security and condition of the retaining clips. Repeat these checks on the inner CV joints. If any damage or deterioration is found, the gaiters should be renewed as described in Chapter 8.
2 At the same time, check the general condition of the CV joints themselves by first holding the driveshaft and attempting to rotate the wheel. Repeat this check by holding the inner joint and attempting to rotate the driveshaft. Any appreciable movement indicates wear in the joints, wear in the driveshaft splines, or a loose driveshaft retaining nut.

1

27 Wheel alignment check

Definitions

1 A vehicle's steering and suspension geometry is defined in four basic settings - all angles are expressed in degrees (toe settings are also expressed as a measurement); the steering axis is defined as an imaginary line drawn through the axis of the suspension strut, extended where necessary to contact the ground **(see illustration)**.

2 Camber is the angle between each roadwheel and a vertical line drawn through its centre and tyre contact patch, when viewed from the front or rear of the car. "Positive" camber is when the roadwheels are tilted outwards from the vertical at the top; "negative" camber is when they are tilted inwards.

3 Camber is not adjustable, and is given for reference only; while it can be checked using a camber checking gauge, if the figure obtained is significantly different from that

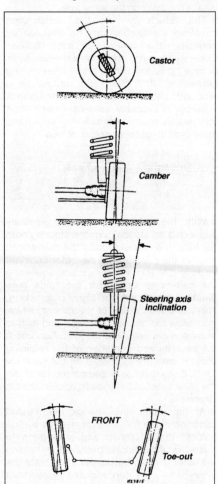

27.1 Wheel alignment and steering angle measurements

specified, the vehicle must be taken for careful checking by a professional, as the fault can only be caused by wear or damage to the body or suspension components.

4 Castor is the angle between the steering axis and a vertical line drawn through each roadwheel centre and tyre contact patch, when viewed from the side of the car. "Positive" castor is when the steering axis is tilted so that it contacts the ground ahead of the vertical; "negative" castor is when it contacts the ground behind the vertical.

5 Castor is not adjustable, and is given for reference only; while it can be checked using a castor checking gauge, if the figure obtained is significantly different from that specified, the vehicle must be taken for careful checking by a professional, as the fault can only be caused by wear or damage to the body or suspension components.

6 Steering axis inclination/SAI - also known as **kingpin inclination/KPI** - is the angle between the steering axis and a vertical line drawn through each roadwheel centre and tyre contact patch, when viewed from the front or rear of the car.

7 SAI/KPI is not adjustable, and is given for reference only.

8 Toe is the difference, viewed from above, between lines drawn through the roadwheel centres and the car's centre-line. "Toe-in" is when the roadwheels point inwards, towards each other at the front, while "toe-out" is when they splay outwards from each other at the front.

9 The front wheel toe setting is adjusted by screwing the track-rod ends in or out of their track-rods, to alter the effective length of the track-rod assemblies.

10 On Estate models, rear wheel toe setting is not adjustable, and is given for reference only. While it can be checked, if the figure obtained is significantly different from that specified, the vehicle must be taken for careful checking by a professional, as the fault can only be caused by wear or damage to the body or suspension components.

11 On Saloon and Hatchback models, the rear wheel toe setting is controlled by the position of the eccentrics on the bolts securing the inboard ends of the rear parallel links (see Section 9 of Chapter 10).

Checking - general

12 Due to the special measuring equipment necessary to check the wheel alignment, and the skill required to use it properly, the checking and adjustment of these settings is best left to a Nissan dealer or similar expert. Note that most tyre-fitting shops now possess sophisticated checking equipment.

13 For **accurate** checking, the vehicle **must** be at the kerb weight, ie unladen and with a full tank of fuel.

14 Before starting work, check first that the tyre sizes and types are as specified, then check the tyre pressures and tread wear, the roadwheel run-out, the condition of the hub

bearings, the steering wheel free play (front wheels only), and the condition of the suspension components (Chapter 1). Correct any faults found.

15 Park the vehicle on level ground, check that the front roadwheels are in the straight-ahead position, then rock the rear and front ends to settle the suspension. Release the handbrake, and roll the vehicle backwards approximately 1 metre, then forwards again, to relieve any stresses in the steering and suspension components.

Front wheel toe setting - checking and adjusting

Note: *If adjustment is required, a balljoint separator tool will be required, and a new track-rod end-to-steering arm nut split-pin should be used on refitting.*

16 The front wheel toe setting is checked by measuring the distance between the front and rear inside edges of the roadwheel rims. Proprietary toe measurement gauges are available from motor accessory shops.

17 Prepare the vehicle as described in paragraphs 13 to 15 above.

18 A tracking gauge must now be obtained. Two types of gauge are available, and can be obtained from motor accessory shops. The first type measures the distance between the front and rear inside edges of the roadwheels, as described previously, with the car stationary. The second type, known as a scuff plate, measures the actual position of the contact surface of the tyre in relation to the road surface, with the vehicle in motion. This is achieved by pushing or driving the front tyre over a plate, which then moves slightly according to the scuff of the tyre, and shows this movement on a scale. Both types have their advantages and disadvantages, but either can give satisfactory results if used correctly and carefully. Alternatively, a tracking gauge can be fabricated from a length of steel tubing, suitably cranked to clear the engine and gearbox assembly, with a setscrew and a locknut at one end.

19 Many tyre specialists will also check toe settings free, or for a small charge.

20 Make sure that the steering is in the straight-ahead position when taking measurements.

21 If adjustment is found to be necessary, clean the threaded ends of the track-rods.

22 Note that the following adjustment operation is easier if the front of the vehicle is raised and supported on axle stands (see *"Jacking, towing and wheel changing"*).

23 Counterhold the track-rod end using the flats provided, then loosen the track-rod end locknut **(see illustration)**.

24 Still counterholding the track-rod end as before, turn the track-rod as required (clockwise to increase toe-in, anti-clockwise to decrease toe-in) **(see illustration)**. Note how far the track-rod is turned, so that the remaining track-rod can be turned an equal amount.

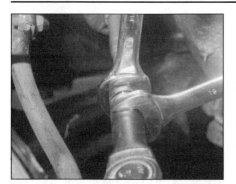

27.23 Loosen the track-rod end locknut

27.24 Counterhold the track-rod end, and turn the track-rod

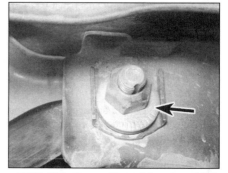

27.35 Note the position of the eccentric (arrowed) on the parallel link inboard securing bolt

25 Tighten the locknut on completion.

26 Repeat the procedure described in paragraphs 23 to 25 on the remaining side of the vehicle, ensuring that the track-rods are turned exactly the same amount.

27 Where applicable, lower the vehicle to the ground, then again check that the front roadwheels are in the straight-ahead position, and rock the rear and front ends to settle the suspension. Release the handbrake, and roll the vehicle backwards approximately 1 metre, then forwards again, to relieve any stresses in the steering and suspension components.

28 Re-check the tracking as described previously.

29 If further adjustment is necessary, repeat the operations described in paragraphs 23 to 28 until the adjustment is correct.

30 On completion, tighten the track-rod end locknuts, whilst counterholding the track-rod ends.

31 Check that the track-rod lengths are equal, and that the steering wheel spokes are in the straight-ahead position.

Rear wheel toe setting (Saloon and Hatchback models) - checking and adjusting

Note: *The rear wheel toe setting on Estate models is set in production at the factory, and no adjustment is possible. If the toe setting is not as specified, this is likely to be due to accident damage or excessive wear in the rear suspension components.*

32 Prepare the vehicle as described previously in paragraphs 13 to 15.

33 The toe setting should be checked using a tracking gauge as described previously for the front wheel toe setting.

34 If adjustment is required, chock the front wheels, then jack up the rear of the vehicle and support securely on axle stands.

35 Working under the rear of the vehicle, on one side, note the position of the eccentric on the rear parallel link inboard securing bolt, then loosen the nut **(see illustration)**.

36 Turn the bolt to move the eccentric by one graduation (if necessary, make an index mark on the body bracket), then tighten the nut to the specified torque.

37 Repeat the procedure described in paragraphs 37 and 38 on the remaining side of the vehicle, ensuring that the eccentric is moved exactly the same amount (ie, one graduation) in the opposite direction to the previous adjustment - if the previous eccentric was moved clockwise, the remaining eccentric should be moved anti-clockwise, and vice-versa. Tighten the nut to the specified torque.

38 Lower the vehicle, then rock the rear and front ends to settle the suspension. Release the handbrake, and roll the vehicle backwards approximately 1 metre, then forwards again, to relieve any stresses in the steering and suspension components.

39 Re-check the toe setting, as described previously.

40 If further adjustment is required, repeat the adjustment procedure until the correct toe setting is obtained.

28 Roadwheel balance check

This task should be entrusted to a Nissan dealer or a suitably-equipped tyre specialist, who should be able to carry out the work for a nominal fee.

Note that the manufacturers recommend that the wheels are balanced off the vehicle.

29 Seat belt check

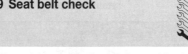

1 All models are fitted with three-point lap and diagonal inertia reel seat belts at both front and at the rear outer seats. The rear centre seat has a two-point lap-type belt of static type (ie, not inertia reel).

2 Inspect the belts for signs of fraying or other damage. Also check the operation of the buckles and retractor mechanisms, and ensure that all mounting bolts are securely tightened. Note that the bolts are shouldered so that the belt anchor points are free to rotate.

3 If there is any sign of damage, or any doubt about the condition of a belt, it must be renewed. If the vehicle has been involved in a collision, any belts in use at the time should be renewed as a matter of course, and all other belts should be checked carefully.

4 Use only warm water and non-detergent soap to clean the belts. Never use any chemical cleaners, strong detergents, dyes or bleaches. Keep the belts fully extended until they have dried naturally - do not apply heat to dry them.

30 Hinge and lock lubrication

1 Work around the vehicle, and lubricate the hinges of the bonnet, doors, and tailgate, or boot lid, with a light machine oil.

2 Lightly lubricate the bonnet release mechanism and the exposed sections of the inner cable with a smear of grease. Similarly, lubricate the tailgate/boot lid/fuel filler flap release mechanisms, where accessible.

3 Check carefully the security and operation of all hinges, latches and locks, adjusting them where required (see Chapter 11). Check the operation of the central locking system.

4 Check the condition and operation of the tailgate/boot lid struts, renewing them if either is leaking or no longer able to support the tailgate securely when raised.

31 Road test

Instruments and electrical equipment

1 Check the operation of all instruments and electrical equipment.

2 Make sure that all instruments read correctly, and switch on all electrical equipment in turn to check that it functions properly.

Steering and suspension

3 Check for any abnormalities in the steering, suspension, handling or road feel.

4 Drive the vehicle, and check that there are no unusual vibrations or noises.
5 Check that the steering feels positive, with no excessive "sloppiness", or roughness, and check for any suspension noises when cornering and driving over bumps.

Drivetrain

6 Check the performance of the engine, clutch (where applicable), transmission and driveshafts.
7 Listen for any unusual noises from the engine, clutch and transmission.
8 Make sure that the engine runs smoothly when idling, and that there is no hesitation when accelerating.
9 Check that, where applicable, the clutch action is smooth and progressive, that the drive is taken up smoothly, and that the pedal travel is not excessive. Also listen for any noises when the clutch pedal is depressed.
10 On manual transmission models, check

that all gears can be engaged smoothly without noise, and that the gear lever action is not abnormally vague or "notchy".
11 On automatic transmission models, make sure that all the gearchanges occur smoothly, without snatching, and without an increase in engine speed between changes. Check that all the gear positions can be selected with the vehicle at rest. If any problems are found, they should be referred to a Nissan dealer.
12 Listen for a metallic clicking sound from the front of the vehicle as the vehicle is driven slowly in a circle with the steering on full lock. Carry out this check in both directions. If a clicking noise is heard, this indicates wear in a driveshaft joint, in which case, the complete driveshaft must be renewed (see Chapter 8).

Check the operation and performance of the braking system

13 Make sure that the vehicle does not pull to

one side when braking, and that the wheels do not lock prematurely when braking hard.
14 Check that there is no vibration through the steering when braking.
15 Check that the handbrake operates correctly without excessive movement of the lever, and that it holds the vehicle stationary on a slope.
16 Test the operation of the brake servo unit as follows. Depress the footbrake four or five times to exhaust the vacuum, then start the engine. As the engine starts, there should be a noticeable "give" in the brake pedal as vacuum builds up. Allow the engine to run for at least two minutes and then switch it off. If the brake pedal is depressed again, it should be possible to detect a hiss from the servo as the pedal is depressed. After about four or five applications, no further hissing should be heard, and the pedal should feel considerably harder.

Every 36 000 miles or 2 years - whichever comes first

32 Air filter renewal

1 Where necessary, unscrew the air cleaner housing lid retaining nut(s) and screw (as applicable) **(see illustrations)**.

2 Release the lid retaining clips, then lift off the lid and position it clear of the housing **(see illustration)**. If necessary, disconnect the inlet duct from the lid to allow the lid to be removed from the engine compartment.
3 Lift the air cleaner filter element out of the housing, noting which way around it is fitted **(see illustrations)**.

4 Wipe the inside of the air cleaner housing and lid with a clean cloth to remove all traces of dirt and debris.
5 Install the new filter element, ensuring that it is the right way up and is correctly seated in the housing.
6 Refit the air cleaner lid, and secure it in position with its retaining clips **(see**

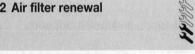

32.1a On 1.6 litre carburettor models, unscrew the retaining nut and bolt (arrowed) . . .

32.1b . . . then release the air cleaner lid retaining clips

32.2 Removing the air cleaner housing lid - 1.6 litre fuel injection models

32.3a Removing the air filter element - 1.6 litre carburettor models

32.3b Removing the air filter element - 1.6 litre fuel injection models

32.3c Removing the air filter element - 2.0 litre multi-point injection models

32.6 On refitting, ensure that the lid is securely held in position by all the relevant retaining clips

33.3 Ensure that the HT leads are clearly numbered before removing them

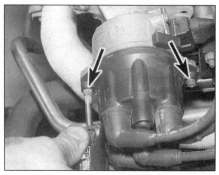

33.9a The distributor cap is retained by two screws (arrowed)

illustration). Where necessary, refit the lid retaining nut(s) and screw (as applicable), and tighten them securely.

33 Ignition system check

⚠️ **Warning: Voltages produced by an electronic ignition system are considerably higher than those produced by conventional ignition systems. Extreme care must be taken when working on the system with the ignition switched on. Persons with surgically-implanted cardiac pacemaker devices should keep well clear of the ignition circuits, components and test equipment**

1 The ignition system components should be checked for damage or deterioration as described under the relevant sub-heading.

General component check

2 The spark plug (HT) leads should be checked whenever new spark plugs are installed in the engine. Where necessary, unclip the cover from the distributor.
3 Ensure that the leads are numbered before removing them, to avoid confusion when refitting. Pull the leads from the plugs by gripping the end fitting, not the lead, otherwise the lead connection may be fractured **(see illustration)**.
4 Check inside the end fitting of each lead for signs of corrosion, which will look like a white crusty powder. Push the end fitting back onto the spark plug, ensuring that it is a tight fit on the plug. If not, remove the lead again and use pliers to carefully crimp the metal connector inside the end fitting until it fits securely on the end of the spark plug.
5 Using a clean rag, wipe the entire length of the lead, to remove any built-up dirt and grease. Once the lead is clean, check for burns, cracks and other damage. Do not bend the lead excessively, or pull the lead lengthwise - the conductor inside might break.
6 Disconnect the other end of the lead from the distributor cap. Again, pull only on the end

fitting. Check for corrosion and a tight fit in the same manner as the spark plug end. If an ohmmeter is available, check the resistance of the lead by connecting the meter between the spark plug end of the lead and the segment inside the distributor cap. Refit the lead securely on completion.
7 Check the remaining leads one at a time, in the same way.
8 If new spark plug (HT) leads are required, purchase a set for your specific car and engine.
9 Slacken and remove the distributor cap retaining screws. Remove the cap, and recover the cap seal. Wipe the cap clean, and carefully inspect it inside and out for signs of cracks, carbon tracks (tracking) and worn, burned or loose contacts. Check that the cap's carbon brush is unworn, free to move against spring pressure, and making good contact with the rotor arm. Also inspect the cap seal for signs of wear or damage, and renew if necessary. Slacken the retaining screw, remove the rotor arm from the distributor shaft, and inspect the rotor arm **(see illustrations)**. It is common practice to renew the cap and rotor arm whenever new spark plug (HT) leads are fitted. When fitting a new cap, remove the leads from the old cap one at a time, and fit them to the new cap in the exact same location - do not simultaneously remove all the leads from the old cap, or firing order confusion may occur. On refitting, ensure that the rotor arm is pressed securely onto the distributor shaft, and securely tighten its retaining screw. Ensure that

the cap seal is in position, then fit the cap and securely tighten its retaining screws. Where necessary, refit the cover to the distributor.
10 Even with the ignition system in first-class condition, some engines may still occasionally experience poor starting, attributable to damp ignition components. To disperse moisture, suitable aerosol products can be very effective. Products are also available to provide a sealing coat to exclude moisture from the ignition system, and in extreme difficulty will help to start a car when only a very poor spark occurs.

Ignition timing check and adjustment

11 Check the ignition timing as described in Chapter 5.

34 PCV filter renewal - 1.6 litre models and 2.0 litre single-point injection models

1.6 litre carburettor models

1 Undo the air cleaner housing lid retaining nut and screw, and release its retaining clips.
2 Lift the lid, and turn it over to gain access to the PCV filter which is screwed onto the underside of the lid.
3 Undo the two retaining screw and remove the filter assembly. Remove the filter element from the frame, and discard it **(see illustrations)**.

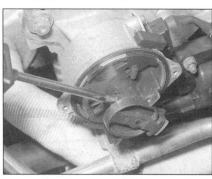

33.9b Slacken and remove the retaining screw, and pull the rotor arm off the shaft

34.3a On 1.6 litre carburettor models, undo the retaining screws . . .

1

34.3b . . . then remove the PCV filter assembly from the air cleaner lid

34.8 On 1.6 litre fuel-injected models, the PCV filter is fitted to the air cleaner housing base

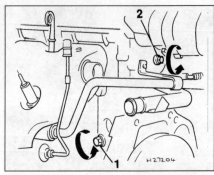

36.6a Coolant drain plug (1) and cylinder head air bleed screw (2) - 1.6 litre engine

4 Fit a new PCV filter element and refit the filter assembly to the air cleaner lid, tightening its retaining screws securely.

5 Refit the lid, and secure it in position with its retaining nut, screw and clips.

1.6 litre fuel-injected models

6 Release the retaining clips, and lift off the air cleaner housing lid.

7 Lift the filter element out from the housing to gain access to the PCV filter.

8 Remove the filter from the air cleaner housing, and wipe clean the area around the filter **(see illustration)**.

9 Fit a new PCV filter to the housing, and refit the air cleaner filter element.

10 Seat the air cleaner lid on the housing, and secure it in position with the retaining clips.

2.0 litre single-point injection models

11 Undo the air cleaner housing lid retaining nuts, and release its retaining clips.

12 Lift the lid to gain access to the PCV filter.

13 Undo the two retaining screws and remove the filter assembly. Remove the filter element from the frame, and discard it.

14 Fit a new PCV filter element and refit the filter assembly, tightening its retaining screws securely.

15 Refit the lid, and secure it in position with its retaining nuts and clips.

35 Braking system vacuum servo unit check

1 To test the operation of the servo unit, depress the footbrake several times to exhaust the vacuum, and check that there is no change in the pedal stroke.

2 Depress the brake pedal, then start the engine whilst keeping the pedal firmly depressed. As the engine starts, there should be a noticeable "give" in the brake pedal as the vacuum builds up. Allow the engine to run for at least two minutes, then switch it off. If the brake pedal is now depressed, it should feel normal, but further applications should result in the pedal feeling firmer, with the

pedal stroke decreasing with each application.

3 With the engine running, depress the brake pedal then, with the pedal still depressed, stop the engine. The pedal should not "give" for at least 30 seconds.

4 If the servo does not operate as described, first inspect the servo unit check-valve as described in Chapter 9.

5 If the servo unit still fails to operate satisfactorily, the fault lies within the unit itself. Repairs to the unit are not possible - if faulty, the servo unit must be renewed (see Chapter 9).

36 Coolant renewal

Cooling system draining

⚠ **Warning: Wait until the engine is cold before starting this procedure. Do not allow antifreeze to come in contact with your skin, or with the painted surfaces of the vehicle. Rinse off spills immediately with plenty of water. Never leave antifreeze lying around in an open container, or in a puddle in the driveway or garage floor. Children and pets are attracted by its sweet smell, but antifreeze can be fatal if ingested. Refer to the note at the beginning of the "Antifreeze mixtures" sub-Section before proceeding.**

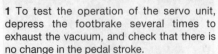

36.6b Coolant drain plug (arrowed) viewed from underneath vehicle - 2.0 litre engine

1 To drain the cooling system, first cover the radiator pressure tank cap with a wad of rag, and slowly turn the cap anti-clockwise to relieve the pressure in the cooling system (a hissing sound will normally be heard). Wait until any pressure remaining in the system is released, then continue to turn the cap until it can be removed.

2 Inside the car, move the heater temperature control lever fully to the "HOT" position.

3 Where applicable, remove the engine undershield, then check to see whether a radiator drain plug is fitted in the bottom of the radiator. If a drain plug is fitted, position a suitable container beneath drain plug. Loosen the drain plug, and allow the coolant to drain into the container.

4 On models without a radiator drain plug, position the container beneath the radiator bottom hose connection, then slacken the hose clip and ease the hose from the radiator stub. If the hose joint has not been disturbed for some time, it will be necessary to manipulate the hose to break the joint. Allow the coolant to drain into the container.

5 If necessary, remove the coolant expansion tank, drain out the coolant, then refit the tank, ensuring that the hoses are securely reconnected. Take care not to spill coolant on the surrounding components.

6 Re-position the container under the cylinder block drain plug. The drain plug is located at the front of the cylinder block, at the transmission end on 1.6 litre engines, and at the timing chain end on 2.0 litre engines **(see illustrations)**.

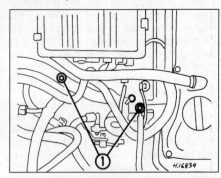

36.7a Cooling system air bleed screws (1) - 1.6 litre engine

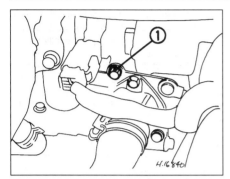

36.7b Cooling system cylinder head air bleed screw (1) - 2.0 litre engine

36.7c Alternative location (arrowed) for cylinder head air bleed screw - 2.0 litre engine

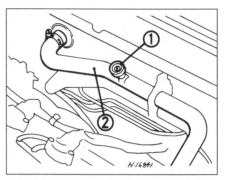

36.7d Cooling system heater hose air bleed screw - 2.0 litre engine

1 Air bleed screw   2 Heater hose

7 Remove the cylinder block drain plug, then unscrew the air bleed screws. The 1.6 litre engine has bleed screws located at the transmission end of the cylinder head, next to the distributor; at the rear timing belt end of the cylinder head; and/or in the heater hose at the rear of the engine. On 2.0 litre engines, the bleed screws are located in the front distributor end of the cylinder head (next to the thermostat housing), and in the heater hose at the rear of the engine **(see illustrations)**.

8 If the coolant has been drained for a reason other than renewal, then provided it is clean and less than two years old, it can be re-used.

Cooling system flushing

9 If coolant renewal has been neglected, or if the antifreeze mixture has become diluted, then in time, the cooling system may gradually lose efficiency, as the coolant passages become restricted due to rust, scale deposits, and other sediment. The cooling system efficiency can be restored by flushing the system clean.

10 The radiator should be flushed independently of the engine, to avoid unnecessary contamination.

11 To flush the radiator, fit and tighten the radiator pressure cap, and if the radiator is fitted to the vehicle, clamp the hose running from the top of the radiator to the coolant expansion tank.

12 Disconnect the top hose at the radiator, then insert a garden hose into the radiator top inlet. Direct a flow of clean water through the radiator, and continue flushing until clean water emerges from the radiator bottom outlet (the bottom radiator hose should have been disconnected to drain the system). If after a reasonable period, the water still does not run clear, the radiator can be flushed with a good proprietary cleaning agent. It is important that the cleaning agent manufacturer's instructions are followed carefully. If the contamination is particularly bad, insert the hose in the radiator bottom outlet, and flush the radiator in reverse ("reverse-flushing").

13 Remove the thermostat as described in Chapter 3, then temporarily refit the thermostat cover. Close the cooling system bleed screws if they have been opened.

14 With the radiator top and bottom hoses disconnected from the radiator, insert a hose into the radiator bottom hose. Direct a clean flow of water through the engine, and continue flushing until clean water emerges from the radiator top hose.

15 On completion of flushing, refit the thermostat with reference to Chapter 3, and reconnect the hoses.

Cooling system filling

16 Before attempting to fill the cooling system, make sure that all hoses and clips are in good condition, and that the clips are tight. Note that an antifreeze mixture must be used all year round, to prevent corrosion of the alloy engine components.

17 Ensure that the air bleed screws have been unscrewed (see paragraph 7), and reconnect the radiator bottom hose.

18 Position the container under the cylinder block drain plug, then refill the cooling system through the radiator filler neck, until coolant runs from the cylinder block drain plug aperture. Coat the threads of the drain plug with suitable sealant, then refit and tighten the plug.

19 Continue to fill the system through the radiator until coolant free from air bubbles emerges from the air bleed screws. Close the bleed screws once the coolant escaping is free from bubbles.

20 Continue to fill the radiator until the level reaches the filler opening, then fill the expansion tank until the coolant level reaches the "MAX" mark. Refit the radiator pressure cap, and the expansion tank cap.

21 Start the engine, and warm it up until it reaches normal operating temperature. Race the engine two or three times under no load, and check the coolant temperature gauge for signs of overheating.

22 Stop the engine, allow it to cool completely, then check for leaks, particularly around the disturbed components.

23 With the system cold (the system must be cold for an accurate coolant level indication), remove the radiator pressure cap (turn the pressure cap on the radiator anti-clockwise until it reaches the first stop; wait until any pressure remaining in the system is released, then push the cap down, turn it anti-clockwise to the second stop and lift off). The level should be up to the filler opening.

24 If necessary, top-up the coolant level in the radiator, then top-up the expansion tank to the "MAX" level mark. On completion, refit the radiator pressure cap (turn the cap clockwise as far as it will go to secure), and refit the expansion tank cap. Where applicable, refit the engine undershield.

Antifreeze mixture

25 Always use an ethylene-glycol based antifreeze which is suitable for use in mixed-metal cooling systems. The quantity of antifreeze and levels of protection are indicated in the Specifications.

26 Before adding antifreeze, the cooling system should be completely drained, preferably flushed, and all hoses and clips checked for condition and security.

27 After filling with antifreeze, a label should be attached to the radiator or expansion tank stating the type and concentration of antifreeze used, and the date installed. Any subsequent topping-up should be made with the same type and concentration of antifreeze.

28 Do not use engine antifreeze in the windscreen/tailgate/headlight washer system, as it will cause damage to the vehicle paintwork. A screenwash additive should be added to the washer system in the quantities recommended on the bottle.

37 Manual transmission oil renewal

1 This operation is much quicker and more efficient if the car is first taken on a journey of sufficient length to warm the engine/transmission up to normal operating temperature.

2 Park the car on level ground, switch off the ignition and apply the handbrake firmly. For

improved access, jack up the front of the car and support it securely on axle stands. Note that the car must be lowered to the ground and level, to ensure accuracy, when refilling and checking the oil level.

3 Wipe clean the area around the filler/level plug, which is on the front face of the transmission. Unscrew the plug and clean it.

4 Position a suitable container under the drain plug situated on the left-hand side of the transmission differential housing.

5 Allow the oil to drain completely into the container. If the oil is hot, take precautions against scalding. Clean both the filler/level and the drain plugs, being especially careful to wipe any metallic particles off the magnetic inserts.

6 When the oil has finished draining, clean the drain plug threads and those of the transmission casing, then refit the drain plug, tightening it to the specified torque wrench setting. If the car was raised for the draining operation, lower it to the ground.

7 Refilling the transmission is an extremely awkward operation. Above all, allow plenty of time for the oil level to settle properly before checking it. Note that the car must be parked on flat level ground when checking the oil level.

8 Refill the transmission with the exact amount of the specified type of oil, then check the oil level as described in Section 12; if the correct amount was poured into the transmission, and a large amount flows out on checking the level, refit the filler/level plug and take the car on a short journey so that the new oil is distributed fully around the transmission components, then check the level again on your return.

9 When the level is correct, refit the filler/level plug, tightening it to the specified torque wrench setting. Wash off any spilt oil.

38 Automatic transmission fluid renewal

1 Take the vehicle on a short run to warm the transmission up to normal operating temperature.

2 Park the car on level ground, switch off the ignition and apply the handbrake firmly. For improved access, jack up the front of the car and support it securely on axle stands. Note that the car must be lowered to the ground and level, to ensure accuracy, when refilling and checking the fluid level.

3 Remove the dipstick, then position a suitable container under the transmission.

4 Unscrew the drain plug from the transmission sump, and allow the fluid to drain completely into the container. If the fluid is hot, take precautions against scalding. Clean the drain plug, being especially careful to wipe any metallic particles off the magnetic insert. Discard the original sealing washer; it should be renewed whenever it is disturbed.

5 When the fluid has finished draining, clean the drain plug threads and those of the transmission. Fit a new sealing washer to the drain plug and refit it to the transmission, tightening it to the specified torque setting. If the car was raised for the draining operation, lower it to the ground.

6 Refilling the transmission is an extremely awkward operation, adding the specified type of fluid to the transmission a little at a time via the dipstick tube. Use a funnel with a fine mesh gauze, to avoid spillage and to ensure that no foreign matter enters the transmission. Allow plenty of time for the level to settle properly before checking it as described above. Note that the car must be parked on flat level ground when checking the level.

7 Once the level is up to the MAX mark on the dipstick, refit the dipstick then start the engine and allow it to idle for a few minutes. Switch the engine off and recheck the fluid level, topping-up if necessary. Take the car on a short run to fully distribute the new fluid around the transmission and recheck the fluid level as described in Section 24.

Chapter 2 Part A
1.6 litre engine in-car repair procedures

Contents

Degrees of difficulty

Easy, suitable for novice with little experience	**Fairly easy,** suitable for beginner with some experience	**Fairly difficult,** suitable for competent DIY mechanic 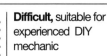

Difficult, suitable for experienced DIY mechanic	**Very difficult,** suitable for expert DIY or professional

Specifications

Engine (general)

Designation	GA
Engine code:	
Carburettor models	GA16DS
Fuel-injected models	GA16DE
Capacity	1597 cc
Bore	76.0 mm
Stroke	88.0 mm
Direction of crankshaft rotation	Clockwise (viewed from right-hand side of vehicle)
No 1 cylinder location	At timing chain end of block
Firing order	1-3-4-2
Compression ratio	9.8 : 1
Cylinder compression pressures:	
Standard:	
Carburettor models	13.7 bars
Fuel-injected models	13.2 bars
Minimum:	
Carburettor models	11.8 bars
Fuel-injected models	11.3 bars
Maximum difference between cylinders (all models)	1.0 bar

Valve clearances

Cold engine*:	
Inlet	0.25 to 0.33 mm
Exhaust	0.32 to 0.40 mm
Hot engine:	
For checking:	
Inlet	0.21 to 0.49 mm
Exhaust	0.30 to 0.58 mm
For adjusting:	
Inlet	0.32 to 0.40 mm
Exhaust	0.37 to 0.45 mm

*The valve clearances must always be checked with the engine "hot". Although Nissan quote valve clearances for a "hot" and "cold" engine, the valve clearances should only be checked "cold", prior to starting the engine after an overhaul. The valve clearances should then be checked with the engine "hot" once it has been warmed up to normal operating temperature.

2A

Camshaft and followers

Drive	Chain
Number of bearings	5
Endfloat:	
Standard:	
Carburettor models	0.115 to 0.188 mm
Fuel-injected models	0.070 to 0.143 mm
Service limit (all models)	0.20 mm
Camshaft lobe height:	
Inlet:	
Carburettor models	39.880 to 40.070 mm
Fuel-injected models	39.380 to 39.570 mm
Exhaust (all models)	39.880 to 40.070 mm
Bearing journal outer diameter:	
No 1 bearing	27.935 to 27.955 mm
Nos 2 to 5 bearings	23.935 to 23.955 mm
Camshaft cylinder head bearing journal internal diameter:	
No 1 bearing	28.000 to 28.021 mm
Nos 2 to 5 bearings	24.000 to 24.021 mm
Camshaft journal-to-bearing clearance:	
Standard	0.045 to 0.086 mm
Service limit	0.15 mm
Camshaft run-out:	
Standard	Less than 0.02 mm
Service limit	0.1 mm
Camshaft follower outer diameter	29.960 to 29.975 mm
Camshaft follower cylinder head bore internal diameter	30.000 to 30.021 mm
Camshaft follower-to-cylinder head bore clearance	0.025 to 0.061 mm

Lubrication system

Oil pump type	Gear-type, driven off crankshaft right-hand end
Minimum oil pressure at normal operating temperature:	
At idle	0.49 to 1.86 bars
At 3000 rpm	3.43 to 4.41 bars
Oil pump clearances:	
Outer gear-to-cover clearance	0.11 to 0.20 mm
Outer gear-to-crescent clearance	0.04 to 0.38 mm
Inner gear-to-crescent clearance	0.04 to 0.30 mm
Outer gear endfloat	0.05 to 0.11 mm
Inner gear endfloat	0.05 to 0.09 mm
Inner gear flange-to-cover bearing surface clearance	0.045 to 0.091 mm

Torque wrench settings

	Nm	lbf ft
Big-end bearing cap nuts:		
Stage 1	15	11
Stage 2 (if an angle tightening gauge is available)	Angle-tighten by 35 to 40°	
Stage 2 (if an angle-tightening gauge is not available)	25	18
Camshaft bearing cap bolts	11	8
Camshaft sprocket retaining bolts	115	84
Centre member bolts	88	65
Crankshaft pulley bolt	142	105
Cylinder head bolts:		
Main bolts:		
Stage 1	29	22
Stage 2	59	43
Fully slacken all the bolts, then tighten through		
Stage 3	29	22
Stage 4 (if an angle tightening gauge is available)	Angle-tighten by 50 to 55°	
Stage 4 (if an angle-tightening gauge is not available)	59 ± 5	43 ± 4
6 mm bolts (to timing chain cover)	8	6
Cylinder head camshaft sprocket access cover nuts/bolts	5	4
Cylinder head cover bolts	4	3
Engine-to-transmission fixing bolts:		
Bolts less than 30 mm in length	19	14
Bolts 30 mm in length and longer	35	26

Torque wrench settings (continued)

	Nm	lbf ft
Front engine/transmission mounting bolts:		
Mounting bracket-to-engine bolts:		
Carburettor models	55	41
Fuel-injected models	70	52
Mounting-to-centre member bolts - Estate models	55	41
Through-bolt	70	52
Flywheel bolts	88	65
Left-hand engine/transmission mounting:		
Through-bolt	49	37
Mounting-to-transmission bolts	49	37
Lower timing chain front guide bolts	16	12
Lower timing chain rear guide pivot bolt	16	12
Lower timing chain tensioner bolts	9	7
Main bearing cap bolts	50	37
Oil pump:		
Cover retaining screws	5	4
Cover retaining bolt	8	6
Regulator valve bolt	50	37
Rear engine/transmission mounting:		
Mounting-to-centre member bolts	55	41
Through-bolt	69	51
Mounting bracket retaining bolts	69	51
Rear oil seal housing bolts	8	6
Right-hand engine/transmission mounting:		
Mounting-to-engine mounting bracket bolts	55	41
Through-bolt	49	37
Mounting upper bracket bolts	49	37
Sump drain plug	35	26
Sump nuts and bolts	8	6
Timing chain idler sprocket centre bolt	50	37
Upper timing chain front guide bolts - early models	8	6
Upper timing chain tensioner bolts..........................	8	6
Upper timing chain top guide bolts - early models	11	8

2A

1 General information

How to use this Chapter

1 This Part of Chapter 2 describes those repair procedures that can reasonably be carried out on the 1.6 litre engine models while it remains in the car. If the engine has been removed from the car and is being dismantled as described in Part C, any preliminary dismantling procedures can be ignored.

2 Note that, while it may be possible physically to overhaul items such as the piston/connecting rod assemblies while the engine is in the car, such tasks are not normally carried out as separate operations. Usually, several additional procedures (not to mention the cleaning of components and of oilways) have to be carried out. For this reason, all such tasks are classed as major overhaul procedures, and are described in Part C of this Chapter.

3 Part C describes the removal of the engine/transmission unit from the vehicle, and the full overhaul procedures that can then be carried out.

Engine description

4 The 1.6 litre (1597 cc) engine is from the GA series of Nissan engines. It is of the sixteen-valve, in-line four-cylinder, double overhead camshaft (DOHC) type, mounted transversely at the front of the car with the transmission attached to its left-hand end.

5 The crankshaft runs in five main bearings. Thrustwashers are fitted to No 3 main bearing (upper half) to control crankshaft endfloat.

6 The connecting rods rotate on horizontally-split bearing shells at their big-ends. The pistons are attached to the connecting rods by gudgeon pins, which are a sliding fit in the connecting rod small-end eyes being retained by circlips. The aluminium-alloy pistons are fitted with three piston rings - two compression rings and an oil control ring.

7 The cylinder block is made of cast iron and the cylinder bores are an integral part of the block. On this type of engine the cylinder bores are sometimes referred to as having dry liners.

8 The inlet and exhaust valves are each closed by coil springs, and operate in guides pressed into the cylinder head; the valve seat inserts are also pressed into the cylinder head, and can be renewed separately if worn.

9 The camshaft is driven by a timing chain, and operates the sixteen valves via bucket-type followers. The followers are situated directly below the camshafts. Valve clearances are adjusted by shims. The camshafts rotate directly in the cylinder head.

10 Lubrication is by means of an oil pump, which is driven off the right-hand end of the crankshaft. It draws oil through a strainer located in the sump, and then forces it through an externally-mounted filter into galleries in the cylinder block/crankcase. From there, the oil is distributed to the crankshaft (main bearings) and camshaft. The big-end bearings are supplied with oil via internal drillings in the crankshaft, while the camshaft bearings also receive a pressurised supply. The camshaft lobes and valves are lubricated by splash, as are all other engine components.

Repair operations possible with the engine in the car

11 The following work can be carried out with the engine in the car:
a) Compression pressure - testing.
b) Cylinder head cover - removal and refitting.
c) Timing chain cover - removal and refitting.
d) Timing chains - removal and refitting.
e) Timing chain tensioners, guides and sprockets - removal and refitting.
f) Camshaft and followers - removal, inspection and refitting.
g) Valve clearances - adjustment.
h) Cylinder head - removal and refitting.
i) Cylinder head and pistons - decarbonising (refer to Part C of this Chapter).

j) Sump - removal and refitting.
k) Oil pump - removal, overhaul and refitting.
l) Crankshaft oil seals - renewal.
m) Engine/transmission mountings - inspection and renewal.
n) Flywheel - removal, inspection and refitting.

2 Compression test - description and interpretation

1 When engine performance is down, or if misfiring occurs which cannot be attributed to the ignition or fuel systems, a compression test can provide diagnostic clues as to the engine's condition. If the test is performed regularly, it can give warning of trouble before any other symptoms become apparent.
2 The engine must be fully warmed-up to normal operating temperature, the battery must be fully charged, and all the spark plugs must be removed (Chapter 1). The aid of an assistant will also be required.
3 Disable the ignition system by disconnecting the ignition coil HT lead from the distributor cap and earthing it on the cylinder block. Use a jumper lead or similar wire to make a good connection.
4 Fit a compression tester to the No 1 cylinder spark plug hole - the type of tester which screws into the plug thread is to be preferred.
5 Have the assistant hold the throttle wide open, and crank the engine on the starter motor; after one or two revolutions, the compression pressure should build up to a maximum figure, and then stabilise. Record the highest reading obtained.
6 Repeat the test on the remaining cylinders, recording the pressure in each.
7 All cylinders should produce very similar pressures; any difference greater than that specified indicates the existence of a fault. Note that the compression should build up quickly in a healthy engine; low compression on the first stroke, followed by gradually increasing pressure on successive strokes, indicates worn piston rings. A low compression reading on the first stroke, which

does not build up during successive strokes, indicates leaking valves or a blown head gasket (a cracked head could also be the cause). Deposits on the undersides of the valve heads can also cause low compression.
8 If the pressure in any cylinder is reduced to the specified minimum or less, carry out the following test to isolate the cause. Introduce a teaspoonful of clean oil into that cylinder through its spark plug hole and repeat the test.
9 If the addition of oil temporarily improves the compression pressure, this indicates that bore or piston wear is responsible for the pressure loss. No improvement suggests that leaking or burnt valves, or a blown head gasket, may be to blame.
10 A low reading from two adjacent cylinders is almost certainly due to the head gasket having blown between them; the presence of coolant in the engine oil will confirm this.
11 If one cylinder is about 20 percent lower than the others and the engine has a slightly rough idle, a worn camshaft lobe could be the cause.
12 If the compression reading is unusually high, the combustion chambers are probably coated with carbon deposits. If this is the case, the cylinder head should be removed and decarbonised.
13 On completion of the test, refit the spark plugs and reconnect the ignition HT coil lead.

3 Top dead centre (TDC) for No 1 piston - locating

1 Disconnect the battery negative lead and remove all the spark plugs as described in Chapter 1.
2 Trace No 1 spark plug (HT) lead from the plug back to the distributor cap, and use chalk or similar to mark the distributor body or engine casting nearest to the cap's No 1 terminal. Unclip the distributor cover (where fitted) then undo the cap retaining screws, remove the cap and recover the seal.
3 Apply the handbrake and ensure that the transmission is in neutral, then jack up the front of the vehicle and support it on axle

stands. Remove the right-hand roadwheel. Undo the retaining screws and remove the plastic cover from underneath the wing to gain access to the crankshaft pulley bolt; on some models, the bolt can be accessed via a small hole in the cover **(see illustrations)**.
4 The timing marks are in the form of notches on the crankshaft pulley rim which align with a pointer on the timing chain cover. The notches are spaced at intervals of 5°, and go from 20° before top dead centre (BTDC) to 5° after top dead centre (ATDC). The TDC mark is highlighted with yellow paint to aid identification.
5 Using a spanner (or socket and extension bar) applied to the crankshaft pulley bolt, rotate the crankshaft clockwise until the TDC notch on the crankshaft pulley rim is aligned with the pointer on the timing chain cover.
6 With the crankshaft in this position, Nos 1 and 4 cylinders are now at TDC, one of them on the compression stroke. If the distributor rotor arm is pointing at (the previously-marked) No 1 terminal, then No 1 cylinder is correctly positioned; if the rotor arm is pointing at No 4 terminal, rotate the crankshaft one full turn (360°) clockwise until the arm points at the marked terminal. No 1 cylinder will then be at TDC on the compression stroke.
7 Once No 1 cylinder has been positioned at TDC on the compression stroke, TDC for any of the other cylinders can then be located by rotating the crankshaft clockwise 180° at a time and following the firing order (see Specifications).

4 Cylinder head cover - removal and refitting

Removal

1 Disconnect the spark plug (HT) leads from the plugs, and free them from their retaining clips on the top of the cover.
2 Release the retaining clips and disconnect the breather hoses from the rear of the cover **(see illustrations)**.
3 Working in the **reverse** of the sequence

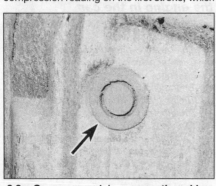

3.3a On some models, remove the rubber plug (arrowed) from the plastic cover . . .

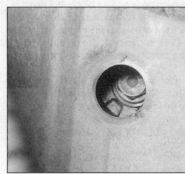

3.3b . . . to gain access to the crankshaft pulley bolt

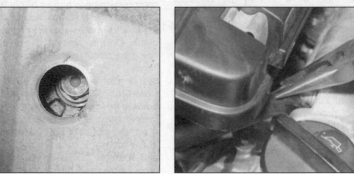

4.2a Release the retaining clips and disconnect the breather hoses from the right-hand . . .

4.2b . . . and left-hand end (arrowed) of the
cylinder head cover

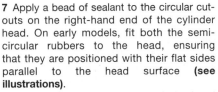

4.7a Apply a bead of sealant to the
cylinder head cut-outs

4.7b On early models, install both semi-
circular rubbers in the head cut-outs

shown in illustration 4.11a, slacken and remove the cylinder head cover retaining screws and washers.

4 Lift off the cylinder head cover, and recover the rubber seal from the outer edge of the cover, and the circular seal from each of the cover spark plug holes. On early models, also remove the two semi-circular rubbers from the cut-outs on the right-hand end of the cylinder head; on later models, the rubbers are an integral part of the cover seal.

5 Inspect the cover seals for signs of damage and deterioration, and renew as necessary.

Refitting

6 Carefully clean the cylinder head and cover mating surfaces, and remove all traces of oil.

7 Apply a bead of sealant to the circular cut-outs on the right-hand end of the cylinder head. On early models, fit both the semi-circular rubbers to the head, ensuring that they are positioned with their flat sides parallel to the head surface **(see illustrations)**.

8 Fit the rubber seal to the cylinder head cover groove, ensuring that it is correctly located along its entire length, and install the four spark plug hole seals, ensuring that they are the correct way around. If necessary, the seals can be held in position using a smear of suitable sealant **(see illustrations)**.

9 Apply a bead of sealant to the cover seal, approximately 1 cm either side of the left-

hand exhaust camshaft bearing cap circular cut-out edges **(see illustration)**.

10 Carefully refit the cylinder head cover to the engine, taking great care not to displace any of the rubber seals **(see illustration)**.

11 Make sure the cover is correctly seated, then install the retaining screws and washers. Working in the sequence shown, tighten all the cover screws to the specified torque **(see illustrations)**.

12 Reconnect the breather hoses to the cylinder head cover, and secure them in position with the retaining clips.

13 Connect the HT lead caps to the correct spark plugs, and clip the leads back into the retaining clips. Reconnect the battery negative lead.

2A

4.8a Fit the rubber seal to the cover
groove . . .

4.8b . . . and fit the spark plug hole seals

4.9 Apply a bead of sealant to the seal on
1 cm either side of the exhaust camshaft
bearing cap cut-out

4.10 Refit the head cover, ensuring that
the seals stay in position

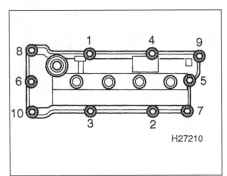

H27210

4.11a Cylinder head cover bolt tightening
sequence

4.11b Working in the specified sequence,
tighten the cover screws to the specified
torque

5.4 Unscrew the pulley bolt and washer, and withdraw the crankshaft pulley

5.6 Align the pulley groove (arrowed) with the key, and slide the pulley onto the crankshaft

5.7 Refit the retaining bolt (and washer) and tighten to the specified torque

5 Crankshaft pulley - removal and refitting

Removal

1 Remove the auxiliary drivebelt(s) as described in Chapter 1.

2 If necessary, position No 1 cylinder at TDC on its compression stroke as described in Section 3.

3 To prevent crankshaft rotation while the pulley bolt is unscrewed, select top gear and have an assistant apply the brakes firmly. If the engine has been removed from the car, lock the flywheel using a tool similar to the

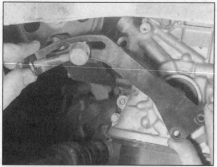

6.4 Removing the power steering pump mounting bracket

one shown in illustration 15.2 (see Section 15).

4 Unscrew the pulley bolt, along with its washer, and remove the pulley from the crankshaft (see illustration). If the pulley Woodruff key is a loose fit, remove it and store it with the pulley for safe-keeping.

Refitting

5 Refit the Woodruff key (where removed).

6 Align the crankshaft pulley groove with the key, then slide the sprocket onto the crankshaft, and refit the retaining bolt and washer (see illustration).

7 Lock the crankshaft by the method used on removal, and tighten the pulley retaining bolt to the specified torque setting (see illustration).

8 Refit the auxiliary drivebelt(s) and adjust them as described in Chapter 1.

6 Timing chain cover - removal and refitting

Note: *If the timing chain cover is to be removed without disturbing the cylinder head, there is a slight risk of oil leakage from chain cover-to-cylinder head joint after refitting. Bearing in mind this information, it is up to the individual owner to decide whether or not it is worth renewing the head gasket when the chain cover is removed.*

Removal

1 Remove the coolant pump as described in Chapter 3.

2 Remove the crankshaft pulley as described in Section 5.

3 Remove the sump and oil pump pick-up/strainer as described in Section 12.

4 Undo the two bolts securing the power steering pump mounting bracket to the front of the timing chain cover, then undo the nut/bolt securing the bracket to the pump and remove the bracket (see illustration).

5 Slacken and remove the three retaining bolts, and remove the mounting bracket from the top of the right-hand engine/transmission mounting; where necessary, free the wiring from its retaining clips on the bracket. Unscrew the retaining nuts and bolts, and remove the camshaft sprocket access cover from the right-hand end of the cylinder head. Recover the cover gasket (where fitted) (see illustrations).

6 Unscrew the two retaining bolts, and remove the lower timing chain tensioner from the rear of the chain cover. Recover the tensioner gasket, noting which way up its is fitted (see illustration). **Note:** *Do not rotate the engine whilst the chain tensioner is removed.*

7 Slacken and remove the four bolts securing the right-hand end of the cylinder head to the top of the timing chain cover. On early models, it will be necessary to remove the

6.5a Undo the three retaining bolts (arrowed) and remove the bracket from the engine mounting

6.5b Undo the retaining nuts and bolts . . .

6.5c . . . and remove the camshaft sprocket access cover (early model shown, complete with gasket)

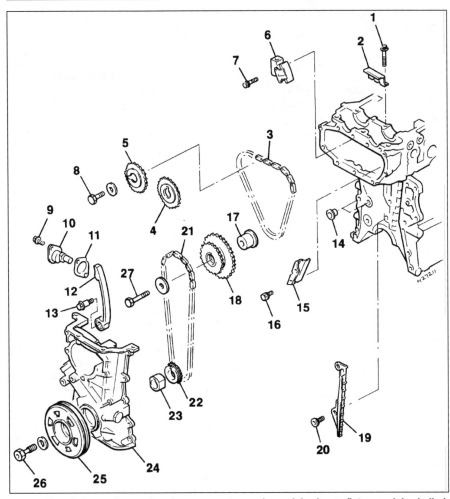

6.6 Timing chains and associated components - early models shown (later models similar)

1 Upper chain top guide bolt*
2 Upper chain top guide*
3 Upper timing chain
4 Exhaust camshaft sprocket
5 Inlet camshaft sprocket
6 Upper chain tensioner
7 Upper chain tensioner bolt
8 Camshaft sprocket bolt
9 Lower chain tensioner bolt
10 Lower chain tensioner

11 Lower chain tensioner gasket
12 Lower chain rear guide
13 Lower chain rear guide pivot bolt
14 Locating dowel and O-ring
15 Upper chain front guide*
16 Upper chain front guide bolt*
17 Idler sprocket shaft
18 Idler sprocket

19 Lower chain front guide
20 Lower chain front guide bolt
21 Lower timing chain
22 Crankshaft sprocket
23 Oil pump drive spacer
24 Timing chain cover
25 Crankshaft pulley
26 Crankshaft pulley bolt
27 Idler sprocket bolt
*Fitted to early models only

upper timing chain front guide to gain access to one of the bolts.

8 Place a jack with interposed block of wood beneath the engine to take the weight of the engine. Alternatively, attach a hoist or support bar to the engine lifting eyes, and take the weight of the engine.

9 Unscrew the through-bolt from the right-hand engine/transmission mounting, then undo the three retaining bolts and remove the mounting assembly from the engine compartment. Recover the rubbers fitted to the body mounting bracket, if they are loose **(see illustrations)**.

10 Undo the bracket retaining bolts and the bolt securing the alternator adjuster strap to the bracket, and remove the right-hand engine/transmission mounting bracket from the engine **(see illustration)**.

6.9a Slacken and remove the through bolt . . .

2A

6.9b . . . then undo the three retaining bolts (arrowed) . . .

6.9c . . . and remove the right-hand engine/transmission mounting

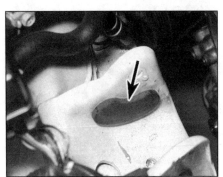

6.9d If the mounting rubbers (arrowed) are loose, remove them from the body

6.10 Undo the retaining bolts and remove the right-hand engine/transmission mounting bracket from the engine

6.12 Removing the timing chain cover

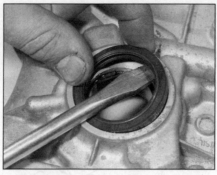

6.14a Lever out the crankshaft oil seal with a large screwdriver . . .

6.14b . . . and tap the new seal into position with a suitable socket

11 Slacken and remove the timing chain cover retaining bolts. Note the correct fitted location of each bolt, as the bolts are of different lengths.

12 Slide the timing chain cover off the end of the crankshaft, and manoeuvre it out of the engine compartment **(see illustration)**. Recover the special sealing collars from the oil galleries and discard them; new ones must be used on refitting. If the cover locating dowels are a loose fit, remove them and store them with the cover for safe-keeping.

13 Slide the oil pump drive spacer off the end of the crankshaft.

Refitting

14 Prior to refitting the cover, it is recommended that the crankshaft oil seal should be renewed. Carefully lever the old seal out of the cover using a large flat-bladed screwdriver. Fit the new seal to the cover, making sure its sealing lip is facing inwards. Drive the seal into position until it seats on its locating shoulder, using a suitable tubular drift, such as a socket, which bears only on the hard outer edge of the seal **(see illustrations)**.

15 Ensure that the cover and crankcase mating surfaces are clean and dry.

16 Fit the new special sealing collars to the cylinder block oil galleries **(see illustration)**.

17 Apply a thin coat of suitable sealant to the timing cover crankcase mating surface, not forgetting to apply sealant to the area around the coolant pump passage in the centre of the cover **(see illustration)**. If the cylinder head is in position, also apply sealant to the upper face of the cover.

18 Refit the cover locating dowels to the cylinder block (where removed).

19 Align the oil pump drive spacer groove with the key, then slide the spacer onto the crankshaft **(see illustration)**.

20 Offer up the cover, and position the oil pump inner rotor so that it will engage with the drive spacer as the cover is refitted **(see illustration)**. Slide the cover over the end of the crankshaft, taking great care not to damage the oil seal lip, and seat it on its locating dowels.

21 Refit the cover retaining bolts in their original locations and tighten them securely, working in several stages.

22 Fit the four 6 mm bolts securing the cylinder head to the chain cover, and tighten them to the specified torque setting. On early models, refit the upper timing chain front guide **(see illustrations)**.

23 Fit a new gasket to the lower chain tensioner, making sure it is fitted the correct way up so its cut-out is aligned with the tensioner oil hole. Install the tensioner and

6.16 Fit the new special sealing collars to the cylinder block oil galleries

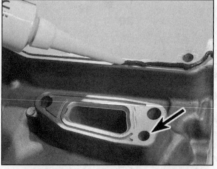

6.17 Apply sealant to the timing cover mating surface, not forgetting the area around the coolant pump passage (arrowed)

6.19 Align the oil pump drive spacer with the key, and slide it onto the crankshaft (cover locating dowel locations arrowed)

6.20 Engage the oil pump with the drive spacer, and slide the timing cover into position

6.22a Refit the bolts securing the cylinder head to the top of the timing cover, and tighten them to the specified torque

6.22b On early models, refit the upper timing chain front guide

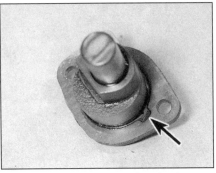

6.23a Fit the gasket, ensuring that its cut-out is correctly aligned with the tensioner oil hole (arrowed) . . .

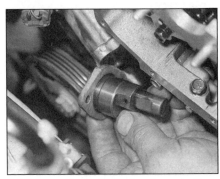

6.23b . . . then refit the tensioner to the engine

2A

gasket, and tighten its retaining bolts to the specified torque setting **(see illustrations)**.

24 Refit right-hand engine/transmission mounting bracket to the engine, and securely tighten its retaining bolts. Fit the rubbers to the body mounting bracket (where removed), ensuring that their pins are correctly seated in the bracket holes, and fit the mounting, tightening its retaining bolts to the specified torque setting.

25 Align the right-hand mounting with its body bracket, then insert the through-bolt and tighten its nut to the specified torque setting. Remove the jack from underneath the engine.

26 Ensure that the sprocket access cover and head mating surfaces are clean and dry. Where the cover was originally fitted with a gasket, fit a new gasket to the cylinder head; where the cover was originally fitted using sealant, apply a continuos bead of suitable sealant to the cover mating surface. Install the cover and tighten its retaining nuts and bolts to the specified torque setting.

27 Install the bracket to the top of the right-hand engine/transmission mounting, and tighten its bolts to the specified torque setting.

28 Refit the power steering pump to the engine, and securely tighten its mounting bracket bolts.

29 Install the oil pump pick-up/strainer and sump as described in Section 12.

30 Refit the crankshaft pulley as described in Section 5.

31 Refit the coolant pump as described in Chapter 3.

32 Replenish the engine oil and coolant as described in Chapter 1.

7 Timing chains - removal, inspection and refitting

Note: *The following section refers to "early" and "later" models. The two models can be distinguished from their upper timing chain components; early models have a top and front chain guide for the upper timing chain - these are omitted on later models.*

Removal

1 Position No 1 cylinder at TDC on its compression stroke, as described in Section 3.

2 Remove the cylinder head cover as described in Section 4.

3 Remove the timing chain cover as described in Section 6.

4 On early models, slacken and remove the bolts securing the upper chain top guide in position, and remove it from the head. Retract the upper chain tensioner, and retain it in the retracted position using the hook on the side of the tensioner. Undo the two retaining bolts,

and remove the tensioner from the end of the cylinder head **(see illustrations)**.

5 On later models, retract the upper chain tensioner, and hold it in position by inserting a small-diameter rod in front of the tensioner pad. Undo the two retaining bolts, and remove the tensioner from the end of the cylinder head.

6 Slacken the camshaft sprocket retaining bolts, whilst retaining the camshafts with a large open-ended spanner fitted to the flats on the right-hand end of each shaft. Remove each bolt along with its washer **(see illustrations)**.

7 Disengage each sprocket from the end of its respective camshaft, and manoeuvre them

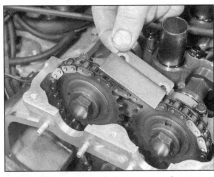

7.4a On early models, remove the top chain upper guide . . .

7.4b . . . then retract the tensioner as described in text and remove it from the head

7.6a Slacken the sprocket retaining bolt whilst holding the camshaft with an open-ended spanner . . .

7.6b . . . then remove the bolt along with its washer

7.8 Manoeuvre the upper timing chain out through the head aperture

7.9 Unscrew the pivot bolt, and remove the lower chain rear guide from the cylinder block

7.10 Unscrew the centre bolt and washer, and remove the idler sprocket from the engine

out from the cylinder head. If the sprocket locating pins are a loose fit in the camshaft ends, remove them and store them with the sprockets.

8 Disengage the upper timing chain from the idler sprocket, and manoeuvre it out of the cylinder head **(see illustration)**.

9 Unscrew the pivot bolt, and remove the lower chain rear guide from the crankcase **(see illustration)**.

10 Slacken and remove the idler sprocket centre bolt and washer, then lower the sprocket out of position and remove it from the bottom of the cylinder head **(see illustration)**. Recover the idler shaft from the rear of the sprocket.

11 Disengage the lower timing chain from the

crankshaft sprocket, and remove it from the engine.

12 Slide the crankshaft sprocket off the end of the crankshaft. Remove the Woodruff key (if loose) from the crankshaft, and store it with the sprocket for safe-keeping. **Note:** *Do not rotate the crankshaft or camshafts whilst the timing chains are removed.*

Inspection

13 Examine the teeth on the camshaft, idler and crankshaft sprockets for any sign of wear or damage such as chipped, hooked or missing teeth. If there is any sign of wear or damage on either sprocket, *all* sprockets and *both* timing chains should be renewed as a set.

14 Inspect the links of the timing chains for signs of wear or damage on the rollers. The extent of wear can be judged by checking the amount by which the chain can be bent sideways; a new chain will have very little sideways movement. If there is an excessive amount of side play in either timing chain, it must be renewed.

15 Note that it is a sensible precaution to renew the timing chains, regardless of their apparent condition, if the engine has covered a high mileage, or if it has been noted that the chain(s) have sounded noisy when the engine running. Although not strictly necessary, it is always worth renewing the chains and sprockets as a matched set, since it is false

economy to run a new chain on worn sprockets and vice-versa. If there is any doubt about the condition of the timing chains and sprockets, seek the advice of a Nissan dealer service department, who will be able to advise you as to the best course of action, based on their previous knowledge of the engine.

16 Examine the chain guides for signs of wear or damage to their chain contact faces, renewing any which are badly marked **(see illustration)**.

17 Check the upper chain tensioner pad for signs of wear, and check that the plunger is free to slide freely in the tensioner body. The condition of the tensioner spring can only be judged in comparison to a new component. Renew the tensioner if its pad is worn or there is any doubt about the condition of its tensioning spring.

Refitting

18 Check the crankshaft is still positioned at TDC (the keyway will be in the 12 o'clock position, seen from the right-hand end of the engine) and refit the Woodruff key to the crankshaft groove **(see illustration)**.

19 Ensure that the crankshaft sprocket is positioned the correct way around, with its timing mark facing away from the crankcase, then align its groove with the key, and slide the sprocket onto the crankshaft **(see illustration)**.

20 Apply a smear of clean engine oil to the idler sprocket shaft, and fit the shaft to the

7.16 Examine the chain guides for signs of wear such as that shown

7.18 Ensure that the crankshaft is correctly positioned, then fit the Woodruff key (arrowed) . . .

7.19 . . . and slide on the crankshaft sprocket

7.20a Fit the shaft to the rear of the idler sprocket . . .

7.20b ... then engage the sprocket with the timing chain, aligning its timing mark with one of the chain's coloured links (arrowed)

7.21 Engage the chain with the crankshaft sprocket so that its coloured link is correctly aligned with the sprocket timing mark (arrowed)

7.22 Check that the timing marks are correctly positioned then fit the idler sprocket bolt and washer, and tighten it to the specified torque

rear of the sprocket so that its flange is positioned between the sprocket and crankcase. Engage the idler sprocket with the lower timing chain, aligning its outer timing mark with one of the chain's coloured (silver) links **(see illustrations)**.

21 Manoeuvre the chain and idler sprocket assembly into position, engaging the chain with the crankshaft sprocket so that its second coloured (silver) link is aligned with the timing mark on the crankshaft sprocket; the timing mark is in the form of a small cut-out on the sprocket hub **(see illustration)**.

22 Check that the idler sprocket and crankshaft sprocket marks are still correctly aligned with the lower chain silver links, then install the idler sprocket centre bolt and washer, and tighten it to the specified torque setting **(see illustration)**.

23 The upper timing chain has three coloured links, one for each of the sprocket timing marks. Note, however, that the links are not spaced at regular intervals. On early models, all three links are silver; the first (inlet camshaft sprocket) link and second (exhaust camshaft sprocket) link are 16 rollers apart, the second and third (idler sprocket) link are also 16 rollers apart, but the gap between the third silver link and the first link is 22 rollers **(see illustration)**. On later models, the gaps between the links are the same, but the idler gear link is easily identified since it is gold in

colour (camshaft sprocket links remain silver).
24 Bearing in mind paragraph 23, lower the upper chain into position, making sure its coloured links are facing outwards. Engage the chain with the idler sprocket, aligning its appropriate link with the sprocket inner timing mark **(see illustration)**.

25 Manoeuvre both the inlet and exhaust camshaft sprockets into position, ensuring that their timing marks are facing outwards. **Note:** *Both sprockets are identical.* Engage them with the chain, aligning the inlet

sprocket timing mark with the first chain silver link and the exhaust timing mark with the second. Check that all the timing marks are correctly aligned with the upper chain links **(see illustrations)**.

26 Locate the sprockets on the camshafts, aligning their cut-outs with the locating pins. Check that the chain silver links are correctly aligned with each sprocket's timing mark. If not, disengage the sprocket(s) from the chain, and make the necessary adjustments **(see illustration)**.

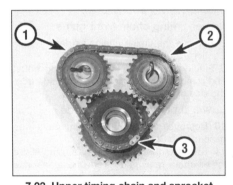

7.23 Upper timing chain and sprocket coloured links and timing marks

1 *Inlet camshaft sprocket link and mark*
2 *Exhaust camshaft sprocket link and mark*
3 *Idler sprocket link and mark*

7.24 Manoeuvre the upper chain into position, and engage it with the idler sprocket so that the relevant coloured link is correctly aligned with its timing mark (arrowed)

7.25a Engage the inlet camshaft sprocket with the chain, aligning its timing mark (arrowed) with the relevant coloured link ...

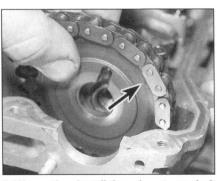

7.25b ... then install the exhaust camshaft sprocket and align its timing mark (arrowed) with the last coloured link

7.26 Locate the sprockets on the camshafts, and check that all the timing marks and coloured links are correctly aligned (arrowed)

2A

7.27 Refit the sprocket retaining bolts and washers, and tighten them to the specified torque setting

7.29a On early models, fit the tensioner with its plunger held in the retracted position, and securely tighten its bolts . . .

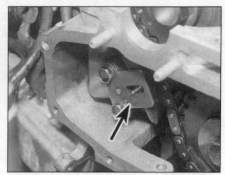

7.29b . . . then release the hook (arrowed) and check that the plunger extends from the body

27 With the timing marks correctly positioned, install the camshaft sprocket retaining bolts and washers, and tighten them both to the specified torque **(see illustration)**.
28 Fit the lower chain rear guide, and tighten its pivot bolt to the specified torque.
29 On early models, fit the upper chain top guide to the cylinder head, and tighten its retaining bolts to the specified torque setting. Ensure that the upper chain tensioner assembly is held in the retracted position by its hook, and fit the tensioner to the cylinder head. Tighten the tensioner retaining bolts to the specified torque, then release the hook and check that the tensioner pad is forced against the chain **(see illustrations)**.
30 On later models, retract the tensioner pad and hold it in position with a suitable rod. Fit the tensioner to the cylinder head, and tighten its retaining bolts to the specified torque. Withdraw the rod, and check that the tensioner pad is forced against the chain.
31 Refit the cylinder head cover as described in Section 3.
32 Refit the timing chain cover as described in Section 6.

8 Timing chain tensioners, guides and sprockets - removal, inspection and refitting

Removal

Lower timing chain tensioner

1 Firmly apply the handbrake, then jack up the front of the vehicle and support it on axle stands.
2 From underneath the vehicle, unscrew the two retaining bolts and remove the lower timing chain tensioner from the rear of the chain cover. Recover the tensioner gasket, noting which way up it is fitted. **Note:** *Do not rotate the engine whilst the chain tensioner is removed.*

Upper timing chain tensioner

3 Slacken and remove the three retaining bolts, and remove the mounting bracket from the top of the right-hand engine/transmission mounting.

4 Unscrew the retaining nuts and bolts, and remove the camshaft sprocket access cover from the right-hand end of the cylinder head. Recover the cover gasket (where fitted).
5 On early models, retract the chain tensioner, and retain it in the retracted position using the hook on the side of the tensioner.
6 On later models, retract the chain tensioner ,and hold it in position by inserting a small diameter rod in front of the tensioner pad.
7 Undo the two retaining bolts and remove the tensioner from the end of the cylinder head. **Note:** *Do not rotate the engine whilst the chain tensioner is removed.*

Lower timing chain front guide

8 Remove the timing chains as described in Section 7.
9 Slacken and remove the retaining bolts, and remove the lower chain front guide from the side of the crankcase.

Lower timing chain rear guide

10 Remove the timing chain cover as described in Section 6.
11 Unscrew the pivot bolt, and remove the lower chain rear guide from the crankcase **(see illustration)**.

Upper chain top guide (early models only)

12 Remove the cylinder head cover as described in Section 4.
13 Undo the two retaining bolts, and remove

the guide from the top of the camshaft bearing cap.

Upper chain front guide (early models only)

14 Remove the camshaft sprocket access cover from the cylinder head, as described in paragraphs 3 and 4.
15 Undo the two retaining bolts, and remove the guide from the cylinder head **(see illustration)**.

Camshaft sprockets

16 Position No 1 cylinder at TDC on its compression stroke as described in Section 3.
17 Remove the cylinder head cover as described in Section 4.
18 Remove the camshaft sprocket access cover as described in paragraphs 3 and 4 of this Section.
19 Remove both camshaft sprockets and the upper timing chain as described in paragraphs 4 to 7 of Section 7.

Idler sprocket and crankshaft sprocket

20 Remove the timing chains and sprockets as described in Section 7.

Inspection

21 Refer to Section 7.

Refitting

Lower timing chain tensioner

22 Ensure that the tensioner and cover mating surfaces are clean and dry.

8.11 Remove the pivot bolt, and withdraw the lower chain rear guide from the cylinder block

8.15 The upper chain front guide is retained by two bolts (arrowed) - early models only

8.25 On early models, prior to refitting retract the plunger and secure it in position with the hook (arrowed)

23 Fit a new tensioner gasket to the cover, making sure it is fitted the correct way up so its cut-out is aligned with the tensioner oil hole (see illustration 6.23a).

24 Install the chain tensioner, and tighten its retaining bolts to the specified torque setting.

Upper timing chain tensioner

25 On early models, ensure that the tensioner assembly is held in the retracted position by its hook, and fit it to the cylinder head. Tighten the tensioner retaining bolts to the specified torque, then release the hook and check that the tensioner pad is forced against the chain (see illustration).

26 On later models, retract the tensioner pad, and hold it in position with a suitable rod. Fit the tensioner to the head, and tighten its retaining bolts to the specified torque. Withdraw the rod, and check that the tensioner pad is forced against the chain.

27 Ensure that the sprocket access cover and head mating surfaces are clean and dry. Where the cover was originally fitted with a gasket, fit a new gasket to the cylinder head; where the cover was originally fitted using sealant, apply a continuous bead of suitable sealant to the cover mating surface. Install the cover, and tighten its retaining nuts and bolts to the specified torque setting.

28 Install the bracket to the top of the right-hand engine/transmission mounting, and tighten its bolts to the specified torque setting.

Lower timing chain front guide

29 Fit the guide to the crankcase, and tighten its retaining bolts to the specified torque.

30 Refit the timing chains as described in Section 7.

Lower timing chain rear guide

31 Fit the guide to the crankcase, and tighten its pivot bolt to the specified torque.

32 Refit the timing chain cover as described in Section 6.

Upper chain top guide (early models only)

33 Fit the guide to the top of the camshaft bearing cap, and tighten its retaining bolts to the specified torque.

34 Refit the cylinder head cover as described in Section 4.

Upper chain front guide (early models only)

35 Fit the guide to the cylinder head and tighten its retaining bolts to the specified torque.

36 Refit the sprocket access cover as described in paragraphs 27 and 28.

Camshaft sprockets

37 Refit the camshaft sprockets and upper timing chain as described in paragraphs 23 to 27 of Section 7.

38 On early models, refit the top and front upper chain guides, and tighten the retaining bolts to their specified torque setting.

39 Refit the upper chain tensioner as described in paragraphs 25 to 28.

40 Refit the cylinder head cover as described in Section 4.

Idler sprocket and crankshaft sprocket

41 Refit the timing chains and sprockets as described in Section 7.

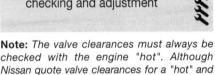

9 Valve clearances - checking and adjustment

Note: *The valve clearances must always be checked with the engine "hot". Although Nissan quote valve clearances for a "hot" and "cold" engine, the valve clearances should only be checked "cold", prior to starting the engine after an overhaul. The valve clearances should then be checked again once the engine has been warmed up to normal operating temperature.*

Note: *This is not a routine operation. It should only be necessary at high mileage, after overhaul, or when investigating noise or power loss which may be attributable to the valve gear.*

1 The importance of having the valve clearances correctly adjusted cannot be overstressed, as they vitally affect the performance of the engine. That being said, the check should not be regarded as routine maintenance, and should only be carried out when the valve gear has become noisy, after engine overhaul, or when trying to trace the cause of power loss which may be attributed to the valves. The clearances are checked as follows.

2 Draw the outline of the engine on a piece of paper, numbering the cylinders 1 to 4, with No 1 cylinder at the timing chain end of the engine. Show the position of each valve, together with the specified valve clearance. Above each valve, draw two lines for noting the actual clearance and the amount of adjustment required. **Note:** *Nissan quote two sets of clearance tolerances; one for **checking** the clearance, and a second one to use when **adjusting/setting** the clearance.*

The checking tolerance is exceptionally large and, although not strictly necessary, it is desirable to have all valve clearances within the adjusting/setting tolerances.

3 Warm the engine up to normal operating temperature, then switch off. Remove the cylinder head cover as described in Section 4.

4 Position No 1 cylinder at TDC on its compression stroke, as described in Section 3.

5 Using feeler gauges, measure the clearance between the base of the cam and the follower of the following valves, recording each clearance on the paper **(see illustration)**.
No 1 cylinder inlet and exhaust valves
No 2 cylinder inlet valves
No 3 cylinder exhaust valves

6 Rotate the crankshaft through one complete turn (360°) clockwise until the TDC notch on the crankshaft pulley is realigned with the pointer. No 4 cylinder is now at TDC on its compression stroke.

7 Check the clearances of the following valves, and record them on the paper.
No 2 cylinder exhaust valves
No 3 cylinder inlet valves
No 4 cylinder inlet and exhaust valves

8 Calculate the difference between each measured clearance and the desired value, and record it on the piece of paper. Where a valve clearance differs from the specified value, then the shim for that valve must be replaced with a thinner or thicker shim accordingly.

9 To remove the shim, the follower has to be pressed down against valve spring pressure just far enough to allow the shim to be slid out. To do this, make sure that the cam lobe of the valve on which the shim is to be removed is pointing away from the follower, then rotate the follower so that its notch is at a right-angle to the camshaft centre-line.

10 Using a suitable C-spanner or stout screwdriver, carefully lever down between the camshaft and the edge of the follower, until the follower is depressed sufficiently to allow the shim to be slid out of position. With the shim removed, slowly release the follower. If difficulty is experienced in removing the shims, it will be necessary to remove the camshaft(s) as described in Section 10.

11 The shim size is stamped on the bottom face of the shim (eg. 224 indicates the shim is

2A

9.5 Checking a valve clearance

2.24 mm thick), but it is advisable to use a micrometer to measure the true thickness of any shim removed, as it may have been reduced by wear. **Note:** *Shims are available in thicknesses between 2.00 mm and 2.98 mm, in steps of 0.02 mm.* The size of shim required is calculated as follows.

12 If the measured clearance is less than specified, subtract the measured clearance from the specified clearance, and subtract the result from the thickness of the existing shim. For example:

**Sample calculation -
inlet valve clearance too small**
Clearance measured = 0.26 mm
Desired clearance = 0.36 mm
                      (0.32 to 0.40 mm)
Difference = 0.10 mm
Shim thickness fitted = 2.50 mm
Shim thickness required =
                      2.50 - 0.10 = 2.40 mm

13 If the measured clearance is greater than specified, subtract the specified clearance from the measured clearance, and add the result to the thickness of the existing shim. For example:

**Sample calculation -
exhaust valve clearance too big**
Clearance measured = 0.51 mm
Desired clearance = 0.41 mm
                      (0.37 to 0.45 mm)
Difference = 0.10 mm
Shim thickness fitted = 2.76 mm
Shim thickness required =
                      2.76 + 0.10 = 2.86 mm

14 Depress the follower, then slide the required size of shim into position, so that it is fitted with its marked face facing downwards. Ensure that the shim is correctly seated, then repeat the procedure (as required) for the remaining valve(s) which require adjustment.

15 Once all valves have been adjusted, rotate the crankshaft through at least four complete turns in the correct direction of rotation, to settle all disturbed shims in position, then recheck the clearances as described above.

16 With all valve clearances correctly adjusted, refit the cylinder head cover as described in Section 4, and refit all components removed to gain access to the crankshaft pulley.

10 Camshafts and followers - removal, inspection and refitting

Removal

1 Remove the distributor as described in Chapter 5.

2 Remove the camshaft sprockets as described in Section 8.

3 The camshaft right- and left-hand end bearing caps are noticeably different to the others, however, the other bearing caps are all similar. On later models, the caps have identification markings cast into the top of

10.3 Inlet and exhaust camshaft bearing cap markings (arrowed)

each centre bearing cap; the exhaust camshaft caps are marked "E2" to "E5" and the inlet camshaft caps are marked "I2" to "I5"; the No 2 caps being fitted nearest the timing chain end of the engine **(see illustration)**. On early models, the caps may not be marked, and suitable identification marks should be made prior to removal. Using white paint or a suitable marker pen, mark each cap in some way to indicate its correct fitted orientation and position. This will avoid the possibility of installing the caps in the wrong positions and/or the wrong way around on refitting.

4 Working in the **reverse** of the sequence shown in illustration 10.23, evenly and progressively slacken the camshaft bearing cap retaining bolts by one turn at a time, to relieve the pressure of the valve springs on the bearing caps gradually and evenly. Once the valve spring pressure has been relieved, the bolts can be fully unscrewed and removed. Remove the end bearing caps first, then remove the exhaust camshaft caps followed by the inlet camshaft caps.

5 Lift the camshafts out of the cylinder head.

6 Obtain sixteen small, clean plastic containers, and number them 1 to 16. Alternatively, divide a larger container into sixteen compartments. Using a rubber sucker, withdraw each shim and follower in turn, and place it in its respective container. Do not interchange the cam followers, or the rate of wear will be increased.

Inspection

7 Inspect the cam bearing surfaces of the head and the bearing caps. Look for score marks and deep scratches. Check the camshaft lobes for heat discoloration (blue appearance), score marks, chipped areas or flat spots.

8 Camshaft run-out can be checked by supporting each end of the camshaft on V-blocks, and measuring any run-out at the centre of the shaft using a dial gauge. If the run-out exceeds the specified limit, a new camshaft will be required.

9 Measure the height of each lobe with a micrometer, and compare the results to the figures given in the Specifications at the start of this Chapter. If damage is noted or wear is

excessive, new camshaft(s) must be fitted.

10 The camshaft bearing oil clearance should now be checked. There are two possible ways of checking this; the first method is by direct measurement (see paragraphs 11 and 16) and the second by the use of a product called Plastigage (see paragraphs 12 to 16).

11 If the direct measurement method is to be used, fit the bearing caps to the head, using the marks made on removal to ensure that they are correctly positioned. Tighten the retaining bolts to the specified torque in the sequence shown in illustration 10.23. Measure the diameter of each bearing cap journal, and compare the measurements obtained with the results given in the Specifications at the start of this Chapter. If any journal is worn beyond the service limit, the cylinder head must be renewed. The camshaft bearing oil clearance can then calculated by subtracting the camshaft bearing journal diameter from the bearing cap journal diameter.

12 If the Plastigage method is to be used, clean the camshafts, the bearing surfaces in the cylinder head and the bearing caps with a clean, lint-free cloth, then lay the cams in place in the cylinder head.

13 Cut strips of Plastigage, and lay one piece on each bearing journal, parallel with the camshaft centreline. Ensuring that the camshafts are not rotated at all, refit both camshafts as described in paragraphs 19 to 23, ignoring the remark about applying sealant to the bearing cap.

14 Now unscrew the bolts as described in paragraph 4 and carefully lift off the bearing caps, again making sure the camshafts are not rotated.

15 To determine the oil clearance, compare the crushed Plastigage (at its widest point) on each journal to the scale printed on the Plastigage container.

16 Compare the results to this Chapter's Specifications. If the oil clearance is greater than specified, measure the diameter of the cam bearing journal with a micrometer. If the journal diameter is less than the specified limit, renew the camshaft and recheck the clearance. If the clearance is still too great, replace the cylinder head and bearing caps with new parts.

17 Check the cam follower and cylinder head bearing surfaces for signs of wear or damage. If the necessary measuring equipment is available, the amount of wear can be assessed by direct measurement. Compare the measurement of each follower and its cylinder head bore with the measurements given in the Specifications at the start of this Chapter. Renew worn components as necessary.

Refitting

18 Liberally oil the cylinder head cam follower bores and the followers. Carefully refit the followers to the cylinder head, ensuring that each follower is refitted to its original bore. Some care will be required to enter the followers squarely into their bores. Ensure that all the shims are correctly seated in the top of each follower, then liberally oil the camshaft bearing and lobe contact surfaces.

19 Refit the camshafts to their correct locations in the cylinder head. The exhaust camshaft is easily distinguished by the distributor drive slot on its left-hand end. On later models, the shafts also have identification markings - the inlet camshaft is marked "I" and the exhaust camshaft "E".

20 Check that the crankshaft pulley TDC notch is still aligned with the pointer on the timing chain cover. Position each camshaft so that its No 1 cylinder lobes are pointing away from their valves. With the shafts in this position, the sprocket locating pin in the inlet camshaft's right-hand end will be in the 9 o'clock position when viewed from the right-hand end of the engine, while that of the exhaust camshaft will be in the 12 o'clock position.

21 Ensure that the bearing cap and head mating surfaces are completely clean, unmarked and free from oil. Apply a smear of suitable sealant to the exhaust camshaft's left-hand end bearing cap mating surface.

22 Refit the bearing caps, using the identification marks made or noted on removal to ensure that each is installed the correct way round and in its original location.

23 Working in the sequence shown **(see illustration)**, evenly and progressively tighten the camshaft bearing cap bolts by one turn at a time until the caps touch the cylinder head. Then go round again and tighten all the bolts to the specified torque setting. Work only as described, to impose the pressure of the valve springs gradually and evenly on the bearing caps.

24 Refit the camshaft sprockets as described in Section 8. **Note:** *If the cylinder head/camshafts have been overhauled, check the valve clearances "cold" prior to refitting the cylinder head cover (see Section 9).*

25 Refit the distributor as described in Chapter 5.

26 Check the valve clearances as described in Section 9.

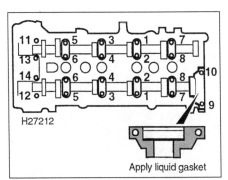

10.23 Camshaft bearing cap bolt tightening sequence. Apply sealant to the shaded area of the left-hand exhaust camshaft bearing (inset) cap prior to refitting

11 Cylinder head - removal and refitting

> **HAYNES HiNT**
>
> *To aid refitting, make notes on the locations of all relevant brackets and the routing of hoses and cables before removal.*

Removal

1 Disconnect the battery negative lead.

2 Remove the timing chains as described in Section 7.

3 Remove the camshafts as described in Section 10.

4 Note that the following text assumes that the cylinder head will be removed with both inlet and exhaust manifolds attached; this is easier, but makes it a bulky and heavy assembly to handle. If it is wished to remove the manifolds first, proceed as described in the relevant Part of Chapter 4.

5 Working as described in the relevant Part of Chapter 4, disconnect the exhaust system front pipe from the manifold.

6 Remove the air cleaner assembly as described in Chapter 4.

7 On carburettor engines, disconnect the following from the carburettor and inlet manifold, as described in Chapter 4A:

a) *Fuel feed hose and return hose from the fuel pump (plug all openings, to prevent loss of fuel and the entry of dirt into the system).*

b) *Accelerator cable.*

c) *Carburettor wiring connector(s).*

d) *Vacuum servo unit vacuum hose, coolant hose and all other relevant breather/vacuum hoses from the manifold and associated valves.*

e) *Remove the inlet manifold support bracket.*

f) *On models with a catalytic converter, disconnect the exhaust gas sensor wiring connector.*

8 On fuel-injected engines, carry out the following operations as described in the relevant Part of Chapter 4.

a) *Depressurise the fuel system, and disconnect the fuel feed and return hoses from the fuel rail (plug all openings, to prevent loss of fuel and entry of dirt into the fuel system).*

b) *Disconnect the accelerator cable.*

c) *Disconnect the relevant electrical connectors from the throttle housing, inlet manifold and associated components.*

d) *Disconnect the vacuum servo unit hose, coolant hose(s) and all the other relevant/breather hoses from the manifold and associated valves.*

e) *Remove the inlet manifold support brackets.*

f) *On models with a catalytic converter,*

disconnect the exhaust gas sensor wiring connector.

9 Slacken the retaining clip(s) and disconnect the coolant hose(s) from the cylinder head.

10 Slacken and remove the 6 mm bolt from the front, left-hand corner of the cylinder head.

11 Working in the **reverse** of the sequence shown in illustration 11.25, progressively slacken the ten main cylinder head bolts by half a turn at a time, until all bolts can be unscrewed by hand.

12 Lift out the cylinder head bolts and recover the washers, noting which way around they are fitted.

13 Lift the cylinder head away; seek assistance if possible, as it is a heavy assembly (especially if complete with manifolds). Remove the gasket from the top of the block, noting the two locating dowels and the oil jet fitted to the top of the cylinder block. If they are a loose fit in the block, remove the locating dowels and oil jet, noting which way round they are fitted, and store them with the head for safe-keeping.

14 If the cylinder head is to be dismantled for overhaul, then refer to Part C of this Chapter.

Preparation for refitting

15 Check the condition of the cylinder head bolts, and particularly their threads, whenever they are removed. Wash the bolts and wipe dry, then check each for any sign of visible wear or damage, renewing any bolt if necessary. Although Nissan do not actually specify that the bolts must be renewed, it is strongly recommended that the bolts should be renewed as a complete set whenever they are disturbed.

16 The mating faces of the cylinder head and cylinder block/crankcase must be perfectly clean before refitting the head. Use a hard plastic or wood scraper to remove all traces of gasket and carbon; also clean the piston crowns. Take particular care, as the surfaces are damaged easily. Also, make sure that the carbon is not allowed to enter the oil and water passages - this is particularly important for the lubrication system, as carbon could block the oil supply to any of the engine's components. Using adhesive tape and paper, seal the water, oil and bolt holes in the cylinder block/crankcase. To prevent carbon entering the gap between the pistons and bores, smear a little grease in the gap. After cleaning each piston, use a small brush to remove all traces of grease and carbon from the gap, then wipe away the remainder with a clean rag. Clean all the pistons in the same way.

17 Check the mating surfaces of the cylinder block/crankcase and the cylinder head for nicks, deep scratches and other damage. If slight, they may be removed carefully with a file, but if excessive, machining may be the only alternative to renewal.

18 If warpage of the cylinder head gasket surface is suspected, use a straight-edge to

2A

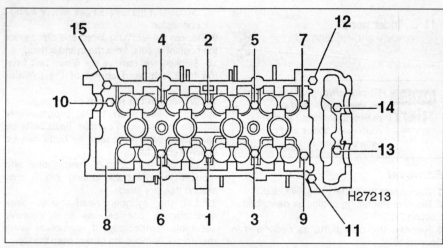

11.25 Cylinder head bolt tightening sequence

33 Refit the camshafts to the head as described in Section 10.

34 Fit the timing chains and sprockets as described in Section 7. **Note:** *If the cylinder head has been overhauled, check the valve clearances "cold" prior to refitting the cylinder head cover (see Section 9).*

35 Start the engine and warm it up to normal operating temperature, then check the valve clearances as described in Section 9.

12 Sump -
removal and refitting

Removal

1 Firmly apply the handbrake, then jack up the front of the vehicle and support it on axle stands. Disconnect the battery negative lead.

2 To improve access, slacken and remove the retaining screws and remove the plastic undershield(s) from beneath the engine.

3 Drain the engine oil, then clean and refit the engine oil drain plug, tightening it to the specified torque. If the engine is nearing its service interval when the oil and filter are due for renewal, it is recommended that the filter is also removed, and a new one fitted. After reassembly, the engine can then be refilled with fresh oil. Refer to Chapter 1 for further information.

4 Remove the exhaust system front pipe as described in the relevant Part of Chapter 4.

5 Undo the retaining bolts, and remove the small support bars linking the transmission to the cylinder block, from the front and rear of the block **(see illustration)**.

6 Progressively slacken and remove all the sump retaining nuts and bolts.

7 Break the joint by striking the sump with the palm of your hand, then lower the sump and withdraw it from underneath the vehicle **(see illustration)**.

8 While the sump is removed, undo the two retaining bolts and remove the oil pump pick-up/strainer and O-ring from the base of the timing cover **(see illustration)**.

9 Wash the strainer in a suitable solvent, and

check it for distortion. Refer to Part C of this Chapter if necessary.

Refitting

19 Wipe clean the mating surfaces of the cylinder head and cylinder block/crankcase. Check that the two locating dowels are in position at each end of the cylinder block/crankcase surface, and refit the oil jet to the centre of the block.

20 Fit a new gasket to the cylinder block/crankcase surface, aligning it with the oil jet and locating dowels.

21 With the aid of an assistant, carefully refit the cylinder head assembly to the block, aligning it with the locating dowels.

22 Apply a smear of clean oil to the threads, and to the underside of the heads, of the ten main cylinder head bolts.

23 Fit the washer to each head bolt, making sure it is fitted with its tapered edge uppermost.

24 Carefully enter each bolt into its relevant hole (*do not drop them in*) and screw in, by hand only, until finger-tight.

25 Working progressively and in the sequence shown, tighten the **ten main** cylinder head bolts (Nos 1 to 10 in the accompanying illustration) to their Stage 1 torque setting, using a torque wrench and suitable socket **(see illustration)**. **Note:** *Bolts 11 to 15 in the sequence (the 6 mm bolts) should not be tightened now, but only after the ten main bolts have been tightened to Stage 4.*

26 Once the ten main bolts have been tightened to their Stage 1 setting, go around again in the specified sequence and tighten them to the specified Stage 2 torque setting.

27 Leave the bolts a minute then, working in the **reverse** of the specified sequence, progressively slacken the head bolts by half a turn at a time, until all bolts can be unscrewed by hand.

28 Tighten the ten main bolts again by hand, then go around again in the specified

sequence and tighten these ten bolts to the specified Stage 3 torque setting.

29 Finally, go around again in the specified sequence and tighten the ten main head bolts either through the specified Stage 4 angle setting **or**, if an angle-measuring gauge is not available, to the specified Stage 4 torque setting.

30 With the main cylinder head bolts correctly tightened, fit the five 6 mm bolts (Nos 11 to 15 in the tightening sequence) and tighten them in sequence to their specified torque setting.

31 Reconnect the coolant hose to the cylinder head and securely tightening its retaining clip.

32 Working as described in the relevant Part of Chapter 4, carry out the following tasks:

a) Refit all disturbed wiring, hoses and control cable(s) to the inlet manifold and fuel system components.

b) Reconnect and adjust the accelerator cable.

c) Reconnect the exhaust system front pipe to the manifold. Where applicable, reconnect the exhaust gas sensor wiring connector.

d) Refit the air cleaner assembly and inlet duct.

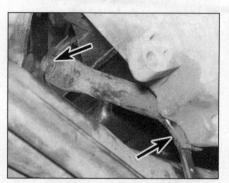

12.5 Engine/transmission front support bar fixings (arrowed)

12.7 Removing the sump from the engine

12.8 Undo the two bolts and remove the oil pump pick-up/strainer from the base of the timing chain cover

12.11 Fit a new O-ring (arrowed) to the oil pump pick-up/strainer recess

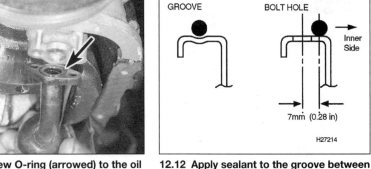

12.12 Apply sealant to the groove between the sump mounting bolt holes, and to the inner side of each hole

check it for signs of clogging or splitting. Renew it if the pick-up/strainer is damaged in any way.

Refitting

10 Clean all traces of sealant from the mating surfaces of the cylinder block/crankcase and sump, then use a clean rag to wipe out the sump and the engine's interior.

11 Fit a new O-ring to the recess in the top of the pick-up/strainer, and fit the strainer to the base of the timing cover **(see illustration)**. Securely tighten the strainer bolts.

12 Ensure that the sump and cylinder block/crankcase mating surfaces are clean and dry. Apply a continuous bead of suitable sealant to the mating surface of the sump. Apply the sealant to the groove in the centre of the mating surface between the holes, and around the inner edge of each bolt hole **(see illustration)**.

13 Offer up the sump, locating it on its retaining studs, and refit its retaining nuts and bolts. Tighten the nuts and bolts evenly and progressively to the specified torque.

14 Refit the support bars, tightening their retaining bolts securely.

15 Refit the exhaust front pipe as described in the relevant Part of Chapter 4.

16 Refit the undershields (if removed) and securely tighten their retaining screws.

17 Replenish the engine oil as described in Chapter 1.

13 Oil pump - removal, inspection and refitting

Removal

1 The oil pump is an integral part of the timing chain cover **(see illustration)**. Remove the cover as described in Section 6.

Inspection

2 Unscrew the retaining screws and bolt, and remove the pump cover from the rear of the timing chain cover **(see illustrations)**.

3 Remove both the oil pump gears from the cover **(see illustrations)**.

2A

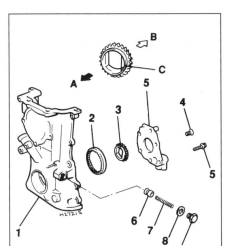

13.1 Exploded view of the oil pump components

1 *Timing chain cover*
2 *Outer gear*
3 *Inner gear*
4 *Pump cover screw*
5 *Pump cover bolt*
6 *Oil pressure regulator valve piston*
7 *Spring*
8 *Sealing washer*
9 *Oil pressure regulator valve bolt*

13.2a Undo the retaining screws and bolts . . .

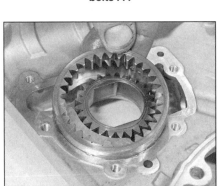

13.3a . . . then lift out the pump outer gear . . .

13.2b . . . and remove the pump cover from the rear of the timing chain cover

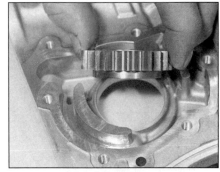

13.3b . . . and inner gear

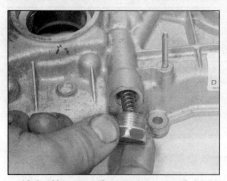

13.4a Unscrew the pressure regulator valve bolt and sealing washer . . .

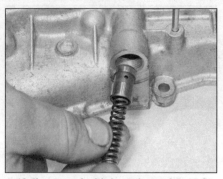

13.4b . . . and withdraw the spring and piston from the cover

4 Unscrew the oil pressure regulator valve bolt from the front edge of the cover, and recover its sealing washer. Withdraw the spring and the valve piston, noting which way around the piston is fitted **(see illustrations)**.
Note: *If necessary, the pressure regulator valve can be dismantled without removing the timing cover from the engine.*
5 Inspect the pump gears, regulator valve piston and the cover for obvious signs of wear or damage.
6 Fit the gears to the cover and, using feeler blades of the appropriate thickness, measure the clearance between the outer gear and cover, and between the tips of inner and outer gear teeth and the crescent which is positioned between them **(see illustrations)**.
7 Using feeler gauge blades and a straight-edge placed across the top of the cover and the gears, measure the inner and outer gear endfloat **(see illustration)**.
8 If access to the necessary measuring equipment can be gained, measure the diameter of the inner gear and cover bearing surfaces. Subtract the gear outer diameter from the cover inner diameter, and calculate the gear-to-housing clearance.
9 If any measurement is outside the specified limits, or the gears, valve or cover is damaged, the complete timing chain cover assembly should be renewed.
10 If the pump is found to be worn, also check the oil pressure relief valve. To gain access to the relief valve, unscrew the oil filter from the front of the cylinder block. Inspect the valve ball for signs of wear or damage.

Depress the valve ball, and check that it moves smoothly and easily, and returns quickly under spring pressure. If not the valve must be renewed. Pull the valve out from the cylinder block, noting which way round it is fitted. Press the new one into position using a suitable tubular spacer. Fit a new oil filter to the engine (see Chapter 1).
11 Lubricate the gears with clean engine oil, and refit them to the pump body. Ensure that the inner gear is fitted with its flange towards the cover.
12 Ensure that the mating surfaces are clean and dry, and refit the pump cover. Fit the cover retaining bolt and screws, and tighten them to the specified torque settings.
13 Fit the pressure regulator valve, piston ensuring it is the correct way around, and install the spring. Fit a new sealing washer to the valve bolt, and tighten the bolt to the specified torque setting.

Refitting

14 Refit the timing chain cover as described in Section 6.

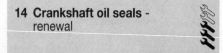

14 Crankshaft oil seals - renewal

Right-hand (timing chain cover) oil seal

1 Remove the crankshaft pulley as described in Section 5.
2 Carefully lever the oil seal out of position,

using a large flat-bladed screwdriver, taking care not to damage the oil pump gears or timing cover.
3 Clean the seal housing, and polish off any burrs or raised edges which may have caused the seal to fail in the first place.
4 Lubricate the lips of the new seal with a smear of grease and offer up the seal, ensuring its sealing lip is facing inwards. Carefully ease the seal into position, taking care not to damage its sealing lip. Drive the seal into position until it seats on its locating shoulder, using a suitable tubular drift, such as a socket, which bears only on the hard outer edge of the seal. Take care not to damage the seal lips during fitting. Note that the seal lips should face inwards.
5 Wash off any traces of oil, then refit the crankshaft pulley as described in Section 5.

Left-hand (flywheel) oil seal

6 Remove the flywheel as described in Section 15.
7 Taking care not to mark either the crankshaft or any part of the cylinder block/crankcase, lever the seal evenly out of its housing using a large flat-bladed screwdriver.
8 Clean the seal housing, and polish off any burrs or raised edges which may have caused the seal to fail in the first place.
9 Lubricate with grease the lips of the new seal and the crankshaft shoulder, then offer up the seal to the cylinder block/crankcase.
10 Ease the sealing lip of the seal over the crankshaft shoulder by hand only, and press the seal evenly into its housing until its outer flange seats evenly on the housing lip. If necessary, a soft-faced mallet can be used to tap the seal gently into place.
11 Wash off any traces of oil, then refit the flywheel as described in Section 15.

15 Flywheel - removal, inspection and refitting

Removal

1 Remove the transmission as described in Chapter 7A, then remove the clutch assembly as described in Chapter 6.

13.6a Measuring outer gear-to-cover clearance

13.6b Measuring outer gear-to-crescent clearance

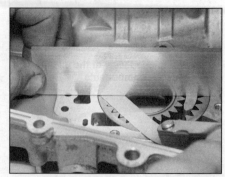

13.7 Checking gear endfloat with a straight edge and feeler gauge

2 Prevent the flywheel from turning by locking the ring gear teeth with a similar arrangement to that shown **(see illustration)**. Alternatively, bolt a strap between the flywheel and the cylinder block/crankcase.

3 Slacken and remove the flywheel retaining bolts, and remove the flywheel. Do not drop it, as it is very heavy.

4 If necessary, remove the cover plate from the cylinder block, noting which way round it is fitted. If the cover plate dowels are a loose fit in the block, remove them and store them with the plate for safe-keeping.

Inspection

5 If the flywheel's clutch mating surface is deeply scored, cracked or otherwise damaged, the flywheel must be renewed. However, it may be possible to have it surface-ground; seek the advice of a Nissan dealer or engine reconditioning specialist.

6 If the ring gear is badly worn or has missing teeth, it must be renewed. This job is best left to a Nissan dealer or engine reconditioning specialist. The temperature to which the new ring gear must be heated for installation is critical and, if not done accurately, the hardness of the teeth will be destroyed.

Refitting

7 Install the locating dowels (where removed) and refit the cover plate to the cylinder block.

8 Clean the mating surfaces of the flywheel and crankshaft.

9 Offer up the flywheel, and refit the retaining bolts.

10 Lock the flywheel using the method employed on dismantling, and tighten the retaining bolts to the specified torque.

11 Refit the clutch as described in Chapter 6. Remove the locking tool, and refit the transmission as described in Chapter 7A.

---

16 Engine/transmission mountings - inspection and renewal

Inspection

1 If improved access is required, raise the front of the car and support it securely on axle stands.

2 Check the mounting rubber to see if it is cracked, hardened or separated from the metal at any point; renew the mounting if any such damage or deterioration is evident.

3 Check that all the mounting's fasteners are securely tightened; use a torque wrench to check if possible.

4 Using a large screwdriver or a crowbar, check for wear in the mounting by carefully levering against it to check for free play. Where this is not possible, enlist the aid of an assistant to move the engine/transmission back and forth, or from side to side, while you watch the mounting. While some free play is to be expected even from new components,

15.2 Use the fabricated tool shown to lock the flywheel ring gear and prevent crankshaft rotation

excessive wear should be obvious. If excessive free play is found, check first that the fasteners are correctly secured, then renew any worn components as described below.

Renewal

Right-hand mounting

5 Disconnect the battery negative lead.

6 Place a jack beneath the engine, with a block of wood on the jack head. Raise the jack until it is supporting the weight of the engine.

7 Slacken and remove the three retaining bolts, and remove the mounting bracket from the top of the right-hand engine/transmission mounting.

8 Unscrew the nut and through-bolt, then undo the three retaining bolts and remove the right-hand mounting assembly from the engine compartment. Recover the rubbers which are fitted to each side of the body mounting bracket.

9 If necessary, undo the retaining bolts and remove the right-hand engine/transmission mounting bracket from the engine.

10 Check carefully for signs of wear or damage on all components, and renew them where necessary.

11 On refitting, fit the mounting bracket (where removed) to the engine, and securely tighten its retaining bolts.

12 Fit the rubbers to the body mounting bracket, ensuring that their pins are correctly seated in the bracket holes. Fit the mounting to the top of the engine bracket, tightening its retaining bolts to the specified torque setting.

13 Align the right-hand mounting with the body bracket, then insert the through-bolt and tighten its nut to the specified torque setting. Remove the jack from underneath the engine.

14 Refit the bracket to the top of the right-hand engine/transmission mounting, and tighten its bolts to the specified torque setting.

15 Reconnect the battery negative lead.

Left-hand mounting

16 Remove the battery as described in Chapter 5.

17 Place a jack and block of wood beneath the transmission, and raise the jack to take the weight of the transmission.

18 Slacken and remove the through-bolt, then undo the three bolts and remove the left-hand mounting from the transmission. Recover the rubbers from each side of the mounting bracket and, if necessary, unbolt the mounting bracket from the vehicle body.

19 Check carefully for signs of wear or damage on all components, and renew them where necessary.

20 On refitting, fit the mounting bracket (where removed) and securely tighten its retaining bolts.

21 Refit the rubbers to the mounting bracket, ensuring that their pins are correctly seated in the bracket holes, and manoeuvre the mounting into position. Fit the bolts securing the mounting to the transmission, and tighten them to the specified torque setting.

22 Align the left-hand mounting with its bracket, then insert the through-bolt and tighten its nut to the specified torque setting.

23 Remove the jack from underneath the engine, and reconnect the battery negative lead.

Front mounting - Saloon and Hatchback models

24 If not already done, firmly apply the handbrake, then jack up the front of the vehicle and support it securely on axle stands. Disconnect the battery negative lead. Undo the retaining screws and, if necessary, remove the engine undershields to improve access.

25 Using a suitable marker pen, mark the outline of the front engine/transmission through-bolt on the mounting bracket to use as a guide on refitting.

26 Place a jack beneath the engine, with a block of wood on the jack head. Raise the jack until it is supporting the weight of the engine.

27 Slacken and remove the nut and through-bolt from mounting.

28 Undo the retaining bolts, and remove the mounting bracket from the front of the engine.

29 Check carefully for signs of wear or damage on all components, and renew them where necessary. If renewal of the mounting rubber is necessary, press the original out from the centre member. Install the new rubber; coating the rubber with soapy water (or washing-up liquid) to ease installation.

30 On refitting, fit the mounting bracket to the engine, and tighten its retaining bolts to the specified torque.

31 Refit the through-bolt to the mounting, and lightly tighten its nut. Position the engine/transmission so that the front mounting through-bolt is correctly aligned with the mark made prior to removal, then tighten the through-bolt to the specified torque setting.

32 Remove the jack from underneath the transmission.

33 Refit the undershields, tighten their fasteners securely, then lower the vehicle to the ground and reconnect the battery.

2A

Front mounting - Estate models

34 Carry out the operations described above in paragraphs 24 to 27 **(see illustrations)**.

35 Undo the two retaining bolts, and remove the mounting and movement damper assembly from the centre member.

36 If necessary, undo the retaining bolts and remove the mounting bracket from the front of the engine.

37 Check carefully for signs of wear or damage on all components, and renew as necessary.

38 On refitting, where removed, fit the mounting bracket to the engine, and tighten its retaining bolts to the specified torque.

39 Fit the damper assembly to the centre member, and tighten its retaining bolts to the specified torque.

40 Fit the through-bolt to the mounting, ensuring that the bolt passes correctly through the damper and mounting rubber, and lightly tighten its nut.

41 Position the engine/transmission so that the front mounting through-bolt is correctly aligned with the mark made prior to removal, then tighten it to the specified torque setting.

42 Remove the jack from underneath the transmission.

43 Refit the undershields, tighten their fasteners securely, then lower the vehicle to the ground and reconnect the battery.

16.34a On Estate models, withdraw the front mounting through bolt . . .

Rear mounting

44 If not already done, firmly apply the handbrake, then jack up the front of the vehicle and support it securely on axle stands. Disconnect the battery negative lead.

45 Slacken and remove the through-bolt from the rear engine/transmission mounting.

46 Undo the bolts securing the mounting bracket in position, and manoeuvre it away from the engine/transmission.

47 Undo the two retaining bolts, and remove the mounting assembly from the centre member.

16.34b . . . then free the damper assembly from the mounting bracket

48 Check carefully for signs of wear or damage on all components, and renew them where necessary.

49 On reassembly, fit the rear mounting to the centre member, and tighten its retaining bolts to the specified torque.

50 Refit the mounting bracket and tighten its retaining bolts to the specified torque.

51 Align the rear mounting with its bracket, then insert the through-bolt and tighten its nut to the specified torque setting.

52 Remove the jack from underneath the engine, and reconnect the battery negative lead.

Chapter 2 Part B
2.0 litre engine in-car repair procedures

Contents

Degrees of difficulty

Easy, suitable for novice with little experience	Fairly easy, suitable for beginner with some experience	Fairly difficult, suitable for competent DIY mechanic	Difficult, suitable for experienced DIY mechanic	Very difficult, suitable for expert DIY or professional 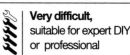

Specifications

Engine (general)

Designation .... SR
Engine code:
  Single-point injection models SR20Di
  Multi-point injection models:
    Phase I models SR20DE
    Phase II low-specification models SR20De
    Phase II high-specification models SR20DE
Capacity .... 1998 cc
Bore .... 86.0 mm
Stroke .... 86.0 mm
Direction of crankshaft rotation .... Clockwise (viewed from right-hand side of vehicle)
No 1 cylinder location .... At timing chain end of block
Firing order 1-3-4-2
Compression ratio .... 9.8 : 1
Cylinder compression pressures:
  Standard:
    SR20Di and SR20De engines .... 12.26 bars
    SR20DE engines .... 12.75 bars
  Minimum:
    SR20Di and SR20De engines .... 10.30 bars
    SR20DE engines .... 10.79 bars
  Maximum difference between cylinders (all models) .... 1.0 bar

Lubrication system

Oil pump type .... Gear-type, driven off crankshaft right-hand end
Minimum oil pressure at normal operating temperature:
  At idle .... Not less than 0.78 bars
  At 3000 rpm:
    SR20Di and SR20De engines .... 4.0 bars
    SR20DE engines .... 4.5 bars
Oil pump clearances:
  Outer rotor-to-cover clearance .... 0.11 to 0.20 mm
  Inner rotor tip-to-outer gear clearance .... Less than 0.18 mm
  Outer gear endfloat .... 0.05 to 0.11 mm
  Inner gear endfloat .... 0.05 to 0.09 mm
  Inner gear flange-to-cover bearing surface clearance .... 0.045 to 0.091 mm

Camshaft and hydraulic adjusters

Drive	Chain
Number of bearings	5
Endfloat:	
Standard	0.055 to 0.139 mm
Service limit	0.20 mm
Camshaft lobe height:	
Inlet:	
SR20Di and SR20De engines	37.920 to 38.110 mm
SR20DE engines	38.408 to 38.598 mm
Exhaust (all engines)	37.920 to 38.110 mm
Bearing journal outer diameter	27.935 to 27.955 mm
Camshaft cylinder head bearing journal internal diameter	28.000 to 28.021 mm
Camshaft journal-to-bearing clearance:	
Standard	0.045 to 0.086 mm
Service limit	0.12 mm
Camshaft run-out:	
Standard	Less than 0.02 mm
Service limit	0.1 mm
Hydraulic adjuster outer diameter	16.980 to 16.993 mm
Hydraulic adjuster cylinder head bore internal diameter	17.000 to 17.020 mm
Hydraulic adjuster-to-cylinder head clearance	0.007 to 0.040 mm

Torque wrench settings

	Nm	lbf ft
Big-end bearing cap nuts:		
Stage 1	15	11
Stage 2 (if an angle tightening gauge is available)	Angle-tighten by 60 to 65°	
Stage 2 (if an angle-tightening gauge is not available)	40	30
Camshaft bearing cap bolts:		
Exhaust camshaft left-hand end bearing cap bolts	22	16
All other bolts	11	8
Camshaft sprocket retaining bolts	147	109
Centre member bolts	88	65
Crankshaft pulley bolt	147	109
Cylinder head bolts:		
Main bolts:		
Stage 1	39	29
Stage 2	78	58
Fully slacken all the bolts, then tighten through:		
Stage 3	39 ± 5	29 ± 4
Stage 4	Angle-tighten by 90 to 100°	
Stage 5	Angle-tighten by a further 90 to 100°	
6 mm bolts	7	5
Cylinder head cover nuts	10	7
Engine-to-transmission fixing bolts:		
Bolts less than 45 mm in length	19	12
Bolts 55 mm in length and longer	75	55
Flywheel/driveplate bolts	88	65
Front engine/transmission mounting bolts:		
Mounting bracket-to-engine bolts	49	37
Mounting-to-centre member bolts - Estate models	55	41
Through-bolt	70	52
Left-hand engine/transmission mounting:		
Through-bolt	49	37
Mounting-to-transmission bolts	49	37
Main bearing cap bolts:		
Stage 1	35	26
Stage 2 (if an angle tightening gauge is available)	Angle-tighten by 45 to 50°	
Stage 2 (if an angle-tightening gauge is not available)	78	58
Oil cooler centre bolt	39	29
Oil pressure relief valve bolt	65	48
Oil pump:		
Cover retaining screws	5	4
Cover retaining bolt	8	6
Regulator valve bolt	60	44
Rear engine/transmission mounting:		
Mounting-to-centre member bolts	55	41
Through-bolt	79	58
Mounting bracket retaining bolts	69	51

Torque wrench settings (continued)	Nm	lbf ft
Rear oil seal housing bolts	8	6
Right-hand engine/transmission mounting:		
Mounting bracket-to-engine bolts	49	37
Mounting-to-engine mounting bracket bolts	55	41
Through-bolt	49	37
Sump drain plug	35	26
Sump nuts and bolts:		
Aluminium sump:		
Numbers 1 to 16 in tightening sequence	18	13
Numbers 17 and 18 in tightening sequence	7	5
Pressed-steel sump bolts	7	5
Timing chain cover bolts	7	5
Timing chain front guide bolts	16	12
Timing chain rear guide pivot bolt	16	12
Timing chain tensioner nuts	8	6
Timing chain top guide bolts	18	13

1 General information

How to use this Chapter

1 This Part of Chapter 2 describes those repair procedures that can reasonably be carried out on the 2.0 litre engine while it remains in the car. If the engine has been removed from the car and is being dismantled as described in Part C, any preliminary dismantling procedures can be ignored.

2 Note that, while it may be possible physically to overhaul items such as the piston/connecting rod assemblies while the engine is in the car, such tasks are not normally carried out as separate operations. Usually, several additional procedures (not to mention the cleaning of components and of oilways) have to be carried out. For this reason, all such tasks are classed as major overhaul procedures, and are described in Part C of this Chapter.

3 Part C describes the removal of the engine/transmission from the vehicle, and the full overhaul procedures that can then be carried out.

Engine description

4 The 2.0 litre (1998 cc) engine is from the SR series of Nissan engines. It is of the sixteen-valve, in-line four-cylinder, double overhead camshaft (DOHC) type, mounted transversely at the front of the car, with the transmission attached to its left-hand end.

5 The crankshaft runs in five main bearings. Thrustwashers are fitted to No 3 main bearing (upper half) to control crankshaft endfloat.

6 The connecting rods rotate on horizontally-split bearing shells at their big-ends. The pistons are attached to the connecting rods by gudgeon pins, which are an interference fit in the connecting rod small-end eyes, and retained by circlips. The aluminium-alloy pistons are fitted with three piston rings - two compression rings and an oil control ring.

7 The cylinder block is made of cast-iron, and the cylinder bores are an integral part of the block. On this type of engine, the cylinder bores are sometimes referred to as having "dry liners".

8 The inlet and exhaust valves are each closed by coil springs, and operate in guides pressed into the cylinder head; the valve seat inserts are also pressed into the cylinder head, and can be renewed separately if worn.

9 The camshaft is driven by a timing chain, and operates the sixteen valves via followers. The followers are situated directly below the camshafts. Valve clearances are adjusted automatically by hydraulic adjusters. The camshafts rotate directly in the cylinder head.

10 Lubrication is by means of an oil pump, which is driven off the right-hand end of the crankshaft. It draws oil through a strainer located in the sump, and then forces it through an externally-mounted filter into galleries in the cylinder block/crankcase. From there, the oil is distributed to the crankshaft (main bearings) and camshaft. The big-end bearings are supplied with oil via internal drillings in the crankshaft, while the camshaft bearings also receive a pressurised supply. The camshaft lobes and valves are lubricated by splash, as are all other engine components. On some models, an oil cooler is fitted, to help keep the oil temperature constant under arduous operating conditions.

Repair operations possible with the engine in the car

11 The following work can be carried out with the engine in the car:
a) *Compression pressure - testing.*
b) *Cylinder head cover - removal and refitting.*
c) *Timing chain cover - removal and refitting.*
d) *Timing chain - removal and refitting.*
e) *Timing chain tensioners, guides and sprockets - removal and refitting.*
f) *Camshaft and followers - removal, inspection and refitting.*
g) *Cylinder head - removal and refitting.*
h) *Cylinder head and pistons - decarbonising (refer to Part C of this Chapter).*
i) *Sump - removal and refitting.*
j) *Oil pump - removal, overhaul and refitting.*
k) *Crankshaft oil seals - renewal.*
l) *Engine/transmission mountings - inspection and renewal.*
m) *Flywheel/driveplate - removal, inspection and refitting.*

2 Compression test - description and interpretation

Refer to Chapter 2, Part A, Section 2.

3 Top dead centre (TDC) for No 1 piston - locating

Refer to Chapter 2, Part A, Section 3.

4 Cylinder head cover - removal and refitting

Removal

1 Disconnect the HT leads from the plugs, and free them from their retaining clips on the top of the cover **(see illustrations)**.

4.1a Disconnect the HT leads from the plugs . . .

4.1b . . . then free the leads from the clip, and position them clear of the cylinder head cover

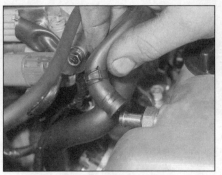

4.2a Release the retaining clips and disconnect the breather hoses from the right-hand . . .

4.2b . . . and left-hand end of the cover

2 Release the retaining clips, and disconnect the breather hoses from the rear of the cover **(see illustrations)**.

3 Slacken the retaining clips, and disconnect the oil separator hose from its union on the head cover, and the hose from the base of the separator. Undo the retaining bolts, and remove the separator from the front of the cylinder head **(see illustrations)**.

4 Work in the **reverse** of the sequence shown in illustration 4.11c, slacken and remove the cylinder head cover retaining nuts and washers.

5 Lift off the cylinder head cover. Recover the rubber seal from the outer edge of the cover, and the circular seal from each of the cover

spark plug holes and the centre cover stud hole.

6 Inspect the cover seals for signs of damage and deterioration, and renew as necessary.

Refitting

7 Carefully clean the cylinder head and cover mating surfaces, and remove all traces of oil. Apply a bead of sealant to the three semi-circular cut-outs in the cylinder head **(see illustration)**.

8 Fit the rubber seal to the cylinder head cover groove, ensuring that it is correctly located along its entire length, and install the four spark plug hole seals and the stud hole seal **(see illustrations)**. If necessary, the seals

can be held in position using a smear of suitable sealant.

9 Apply a bead of sealant to the cover seal, approximately 1 cm either side of the left-hand exhaust camshaft bearing cap circular cut-out edges **(see illustration)**.

10 Carefully refit the cylinder head cover to the engine, taking great care not to displace any of the rubber seals **(see illustration)**.

11 Make sure that the cover is correctly seated, then install the retaining nuts, washers and rubbers. Referring to illustration 4.11c, seat the cover in position, then lightly tighten the centre nut (No 1) and the four corner nuts in the following sequence; 10, 11, 13 and 8. Working in the specified sequence, tighten all

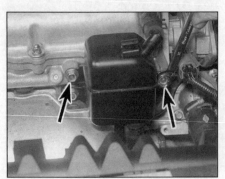

4.3a Undo the two retaining bolts (arrowed) . . .

4.3b . . . then detach the hoses and remove the oil separator from the front of the cylinder head

4.7 On refitting, apply sealant to the cylinder head semi-circular cut-outs (arrowed)

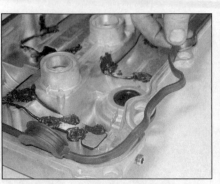

4.8a Fit the rubber seal to the head cover groove . . .

4.8b . . . and fit the seals to each of the spark plug holes and the centre stud hole

4.9 Apply sealant to the area each side of the seal around the camshaft bearing cap cut-out

4.10 Refit the cylinder head cover, taking care not to disturb the seals

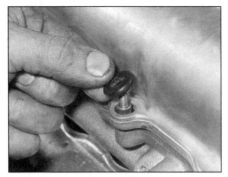

4.11a Fit the rubber seal to each stud . . .

4.11b . . . followed by the washer and nut

the retaining nuts to the specified torque **(see illustrations)**.

12 Reconnect the breather hoses to the cylinder head cover, and secure them in position with the retaining clips.

13 Reconnect the hose to the base of the separator, then refit the separator to the front of the cylinder head and securely tighten its retaining bolts. Connect the separator hose to the cover, and secure it in position with its retaining clip.

14 Connect the HT lead caps to the correct spark plugs, and clip the leads back into the retaining clips. Reconnect the battery negative lead.

5 Crankshaft pulley -
removal and refitting

Refer to Chapter 2, Part A, Section 5. If the pulley is a tight fit on the crankshaft, it may be necessary to use a puller to free it. The crankshaft pulley has threaded holes for the puller to be screwed into.

6 Timing chain cover -
removal and refitting

Note: *If the timing chain cover is to be removed without disturbing the cylinder head,*

there is a slight risk of oil leakage from chain cover-to-cylinder head joint after refitting. Bearing in mind this information, it is up to the individual owner to decide whether or not it is worth renewing the head gasket when the chain cover is removed.

Removal

1 Remove the crankshaft pulley as described in Section 5.
2 Remove both sumps and the oil pump pick-up/strainer as described in Section 12.
3 Remove the power steering pump as described in Chapter 10.
4 Remove the coolant pump pulley as described in Chapter 3.
5 Remove the alternator as described in Chapter 5.
6 Place a jack with interposed block of wood beneath the main bearing ladder to take the weight of the engine. Alternatively, attach a hoist or support bar to the engine lifting eyes and take the weight of the engine.
7 Unscrew the through-bolt from the right-hand engine/transmission mounting, then undo the retaining bolts and remove the mounting assembly from the engine compartment. Recover the rubbers fitted to the mounting bracket, if they are loose.
8 Undo the retaining bolts, and remove the right-hand engine/transmission mounting bracket from the engine **(see illustration)**.
9 Slacken and remove the timing chain cover retaining bolts, not forgetting the three top

bolts securing the cylinder head to the cover. Note the correct fitted location of each bolt, as the bolts are of different lengths.
10 Slide the timing chain cover off the end of the crankshaft, and manoeuvre it out of the engine compartment. Remove the O-ring from the oil gallery, and discard it.
11 If the cover locating dowels are a loose fit, remove them and store them with the cover for safe-keeping.
12 Note the correct fitted position of the timing chain oil jet in the cylinder block; if it is loose, remove it and store it with the cover.
13 Slide the oil pump drive spacer off the end of the crankshaft. If it is loose, remove the Woodruff key from the crankshaft, and store it with the spacer for safe-keeping.

Refitting

14 Prior to refitting, it is recommended that the crankshaft oil seal be renewed. Carefully lever the old seal out of the cover, using a large flat-bladed screwdriver. Fit the new seal to the cover, making sure that its sealing lip is facing inwards. Drive the seal into position until it seats on its locating shoulder, using a suitable tubular drift, such as a socket, which bears only on the hard outer edge of the seal **(see illustrations)**.
15 Ensure that the cover and crankcase mating surfaces are clean and dry.
16 Refit the Woodruff key (where removed) to the crankshaft groove.
17 Align the oil pump drive spacer groove

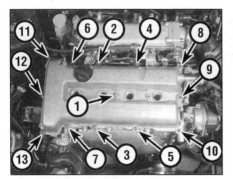

4.11c Tighten the cylinder head cover nuts in the specified sequence

6.8 Removing the right-hand engine/transmission mounting bracket from the engine

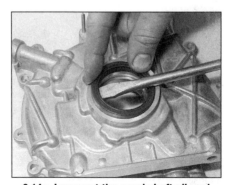

6.14a Lever out the crankshaft oil seal with a large flat-bladed screwdriver . . .

2B

6.14b . . . and tap the new one into position using a suitable socket

6.17 Align its slot with the Woodruff key, and slide on the oil pump drive spacer

6.18 Fit a new O-ring to the cylinder block oil gallery recess

with the key, then slide the spacer onto the crankshaft **(see illustration)**.

18 Ensure that the locating dowels are in position in the crankcase, and fit a new O-ring to the oil gallery recess **(see illustration)**. Also make sure that the timing chain oil jet is in position.

19 Apply a thin coat of suitable sealant to timing cover crankcase mating surface. **Note:** *Do not apply sealant to the area around the cover oil gallery and groove* **(see illustration)**. If the cylinder head is in position, also apply sealant to the upper face of the cover.

20 Offer up the cover, and position the oil pump inner rotor so that it will engage with the drive spacer as the cover is refitted. Slide the

cover over the end of the crankshaft, taking great care not to damage the oil seal lip, and seat it on its locating dowels.

21 Refit the cover retaining bolts in their original locations, and tighten them evenly and progressively to the specified torque setting.

22 Fit the three 6 mm bolts securing the cylinder head to the chain cover, and tighten them to the specified torque setting **(see illustration)**.

23 Refit the right-hand engine/transmission mounting bracket to the engine, and tighten its retaining bolts to the specified torque. Fit the rubbers to the body mounting bracket (where removed), ensuring that their pins are correctly seated in the bracket holes, and fit the mounting, tightening its retaining bolts to the specified torque setting.

24 Align the right-hand mounting with its body bracket, then insert the through-bolt and tighten its nut to the specified torque setting. Remove the jack from underneath the engine.

25 Refit the oil pump pick-up/strainer and sump as described in Section 12.

26 Refit the cylinder head cover as described in Section 4.

27 Refit the alternator as described in Chapter 5.

28 Refit the coolant pump pulley, and securely tighten its retaining bolts.

29 Refit the power steering pump as described in Chapter 10.

30 Refit the crankshaft pulley as described in Section 5.

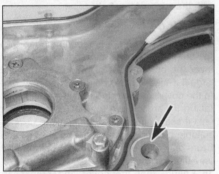

6.19 Apply a bead of sealant to the timing chain cover as shown. Do not apply sealant to the area around the cover oil gallery and groove (arrowed)

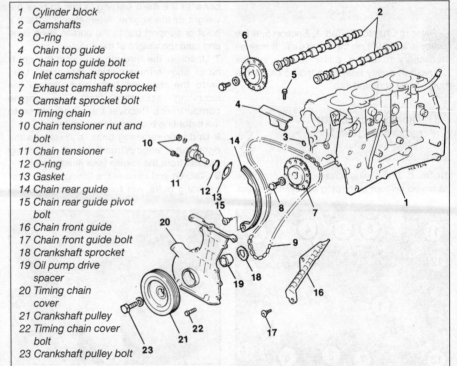

1 Cylinder block
2 Camshafts
3 O-ring
4 Chain top guide
5 Chain top guide bolt
6 Inlet camshaft sprocket
7 Exhaust camshaft sprocket
8 Camshaft sprocket bolt
9 Timing chain
10 Chain tensioner nut and bolt
11 Chain tensioner
12 O-ring
13 Gasket
14 Chain rear guide
15 Chain rear guide pivot bolt
16 Chain front guide
17 Chain front guide bolt
18 Crankshaft sprocket
19 Oil pump drive spacer
20 Timing chain cover
21 Crankshaft pulley
22 Timing chain cover bolt
23 Crankshaft pulley bolt

6.22 Refit the three bolts securing the cover to the cylinder head and tighten them to the specified torque

7.3 Exploded view of timing chain and associated components

7.6a Undo the two bolts . . .

7.6b . . . and remove the chain top guide from the cylinder head

7.7 Removing the chain rear guide

7 Timing chain - removal and refitting

Removal

1 Position No 1 cylinder at TDC on its compression stroke as described in Section 3.

2 Remove the cylinder head cover as described in Section 4.

3 Remove the timing chain cover as described in Section 6 **(see illustration)**.

4 Remove the oil filter as described in Chapter 1. If the filter is damaged during removal, a new one should be obtained for refitting.

5 Undo the retaining nuts/bolts, and withdraw the timing chain tensioner from the rear of the cylinder head. Recover the tensioner O-ring and gasket. **Note:** *Do not rotate the engine whilst the tensioner is removed.*

6 Undo the retaining bolts, and remove the chain top guide from the top of the cylinder head caps **(see illustrations)**.

7 Unscrew the pivot bolt and remove the chain rear guide from the crankcase **(see illustration)**.

8 Slacken and remove the retaining bolts, and remove the chain front guide from the side of the crankcase **(see illustrations)**.

9 Slacken the camshaft sprocket retaining bolts, whilst retaining the camshafts with a large open-ended spanner fitted to the flats

on the right-hand end of each shaft (see illustration 7.22b). Remove each bolt along with its washer. Disengage each sprocket from the end of its respective camshaft, and manoeuvre them out from the cylinder head. If the sprocket locating pins are a loose fit in the camshaft ends, remove them and store them with the sprockets.

10 Disengage the timing chain from the crankshaft sprocket, and remove it from the engine. **Note:** *Do not rotate the crankshaft or camshafts whilst the timing chain is removed.*

11 If necessary, slide the sprocket off the end of the crankshaft, noting which way round it is fitted, and remove the Woodruff key (if loose). Store the key with the sprocket for safe-keeping.

Inspection

12 Examine the teeth on the camshaft and crankshaft sprockets for any sign of wear or damage such as chipped, hooked or missing teeth. If there is any sign of wear or damage on either sprocket, all sprockets and both timing chains should be renewed as a set.

13 Inspect the links of the timing chain for signs of wear or damage on the rollers. The extent of wear can be judged by checking the amount by which the chain can be bent sideways; a new chain will have very little sideways movement. If there is an excessive amount of side play in the timing chain, it must be renewed. Note that it is a sensible precaution to renew the timing chain,

regardless of its apparent condition, if the engine has covered a high mileage, or if it has been noted that the chain has sounded noisy with the engine running. Although not strictly necessary, it is always worth renewing the chain and sprockets as a matched set, since it is false economy to run a new chain on worn sprockets, and vice-versa. If there is any doubt about the condition of the timing chains and sprockets, seek the advice of a Nissan dealer service department, who will be able to advise you as to the best course of action, based on their previous knowledge of the engine.

14 Examine the chain guides for signs of wear or damage to the their chain contact faces, renewing any which are badly marked.

15 The condition of the tensioner can only be judged in comparison to a new component. Renew the tensioner if there is any doubt about its condition.

Refitting

16 Check that the crankshaft is still positioned at TDC (the keyway will be in the 12 o'clock position, when viewed from the right-hand end of the engine) and refit the Woodruff key to the crankshaft groove.

17 Ensuring that the crankshaft sprocket is positioned the correct way round, with its timing mark facing away from the crankcase, then align its groove with the key, and slide the sprocket onto the crankshaft **(see illustration)**.

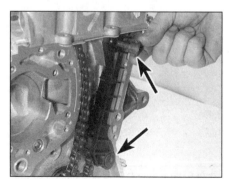

7.8a Undo the two retaining bolts (arrowed) . . .

7.8b . . . and remove the timing chain front guide

7.17 Slide the crankshaft sprocket into position, making sure that it is the correct way round

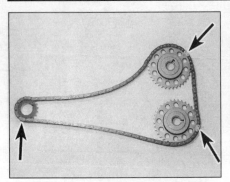

7.18 Timing chain and sprocket timing marks and coloured links (arrowed)

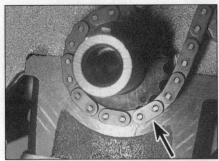

7.19 Engage the timing chain with the crankshaft sprocket, aligning the correct coloured link with its timing mark (arrowed)

7.20a Engage the exhaust camshaft sprocket with the chain, aligning its timing mark with the coloured link . . .

18 The timing chain has three coloured links, one for each of the sprocket timing marks. The two links which are closest together are the camshaft sprocket timing links; the third link should be aligned with the crankshaft sprocket timing mark **(see illustration)**. **Note:** *On some models, the camshaft sprocket timing links are also a different colour to the crankshaft sprocket timing link.*

19 Bearing in mind paragraph 18, making sure that the coloured links are facing outwards, engage the chain with the crankshaft sprocket, aligning its appropriate link with the sprocket timing mark **(see illustration)**.

20 Manoeuvre both the inlet and exhaust camshaft sprockets into position, ensuring

that their timing marks are facing outwards. **Note:** *Both sprockets are identical.* Engage them with the chain, aligning their timing marks with the coloured chain links. Check that all the timing marks are correctly aligned with the coloured chain links **(see illustrations)**.

21 Fit the locating pins (where removed) to the ends of the camshafts, and locate the sprockets on the camshafts, aligning their cut-outs with the locating pins. Check that the coloured chain links are correctly aligned with each sprocket's timing mark. If not, disengage the sprocket(s) from the chain, and make the necessary adjustments.

22 With the timing marks correctly positioned, install the camshaft sprocket

retaining bolts and washers, and tighten them both to the specified torque **(see illustrations)**. Prevent the camshafts from rotating as this is done by holding them with a spanner on the flats provided.

23 Fit the chain front guide to the crankcase, and tighten its retaining bolts to the specified torque setting.

24 Fit the chain rear guide, and tighten its pivot bolt to the specified torque **(see illustration)**.

25 Refit the chain top guide to the top of the cylinder head, and tighten its retaining bolts to the specified torque setting.

26 Release the plunger detent lever, then press the tensioner plunger into its housing, and hold it in the retracted position by

7.20b . . . then install the inlet camshaft sprocket, aligning its mark with the coloured link (arrowed)

7.22a Install the sprocket retaining bolts and washers . . .

7.22b . . . and tighten them to the specified torque setting - note the spanner holding the camshaft against rotation on the flats provided

7.24 Tighten the rear chain guide pivot bolt to the specified torque setting

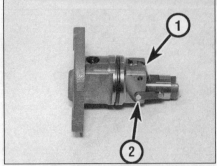

7.26a Depress the detent lever (1), then push the plunger back into its housing and hold it in position with the hook (2)

7.26b Fit a new O-ring and gasket to the tensioner, making sure that the gasket is fitted the correct way round

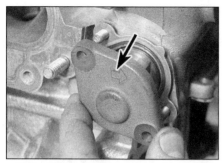

7.26c Fit the tensioner assembly to the cylinder head, making sure that its arrow (arrowed) is pointing away from the cylinder head

engaging the hook with the plunger pin. Fit a new gasket to the tensioner, making sure that it is the correct way round, then fit a new O-ring to the tensioner body groove. Install the tensioner, making sure that it is fitted with its arrow pointing away from the cylinder head **(see illustrations)**. Fit the tensioner nuts and washers, and tighten them to the specified torque setting. As the nuts are tightened, the hook will automatically disengage from the pin, and the plunger will be released.

27 Fit a new oil filter and replenish the engine oil as described in Chapter 1.

28 Refit the timing chain cover as described in Section 6.

29 Refit the cylinder head cover as described in Section 4.

---

8 Timing chain tensioner, guides and sprockets - removal, inspection and refitting

Removal

Timing chain tensioner

1 Drain the engine oil and remove the filter as described in Chapter 1. If the filter is damaged during removal, a new filter must be obtained for refitting.

2 Unscrew the two retaining nuts and washers, and remove the timing chain tensioner from the rear of the cylinder head. Recover the tensioner gasket and O-ring.
Note: *Do not rotate the engine whilst the chain tensioner is removed.*

Timing chain front guide

3 Remove the timing chain cover as described in Section 6.

4 Remove the timing chain tensioner as described in paragraphs 1 and 2.

5 Slacken and remove the retaining bolts, and remove the chain front guide from the side of the cylinder block.

Timing chain rear guide

6 Remove the timing chain cover as described in Section 6.

7 Remove the chain tensioner as described in paragraphs 1 and 2.

8 Unscrew the pivot bolt, and remove the chain rear guide from the cylinder block.

Timing chain top guide

9 Remove the cylinder head cover as described in Section 4.

10 Undo the two retaining bolts, and remove the guide from the top of the cylinder head.

Timing chain sprockets

Note: *Refer to the note at the start of Section 9.*

11 Remove the timing chain and camshaft sprockets as described in Section 7. If the chain is being left in position (see note at the start of Section 9), unbolt the sprockets from the camshafts as described in paragraph 9 of Section 7; mark each sprocket for identification purposes, to ensure that it is refitted in its original position.

Inspection

12 Refer to Section 7.

Refitting

Timing chain tensioner

13 Ensure that the tensioner and cover mating surfaces are clean and dry.

14 Release the plunger detent arm, then press the tensioner plunger into its housing and hold it in the retracted position by engaging the hook with the plunger pin (see illustration 7.26a).

15 Fit a new gasket to the tensioner, making sure that it is the correct way round, then fit a new O-ring to the tensioner groove (see illustration 7.26b).

16 Install the tensioner, making sure that it is fitted with its arrow pointing away from the cylinder head (see illustration 7.26c). Fit the tensioner nuts and washers, and tighten them to the specified torque setting. As the nuts are tightened, the hook will automatically disengage from the pin, and the plunger will be released.

Timing chain front guide

17 Fit the guide to the cylinder block, and tighten its retaining bolts to the specified torque.

18 Fit the chain tensioner as described in paragraphs 13 to 16.

19 Refit the timing chain cover as described in Section 6.

9.0a If the camshafts are to be removed without removing the timing chain, alignment marks must be made between the sprockets and chain . . .

Timing chain rear guide

20 Fit the guide to the crankcase, and tighten its pivot bolt to the specified torque.

21 Fit the chain tensioner as described in paragraphs 13 to 16.

22 Refit the timing chain cover as described in Section 6.

Timing chain top guide

23 Fit the guide to the top of the cylinder head, and tighten its retaining bolts to the specified torque.

24 Refit the cylinder head cover as described in Section 4.

Timing chain sprockets

25 Refit the timing chain and sprockets as described in Section 7.

26 If the chain was not removed, ensure that the sprockets are fitted to the relevant camshafts, and engage them with the chain so the marks made prior to removal are correctly aligned. Fit the sprocket retaining bolts and washers, and tighten them to the specified torque as described in Section 7.

---

9 Camshafts - removal, inspection and refitting

Note: *Although the following text recommends that the timing chain is removed, this is only necessary if the manufacturer's timing chain marks are to be used on refitting. If the engine is positioned with No.1 cylinder at TDC on compression (see Section 3) it will be seen that the camshaft sprocket timing marks are correctly positioned, although they will not be aligned with the timing chain coloured links (see Section 7). Alignment marks can be made between the camshaft sprocket marks and relevant chain links by the owner; these marks can be used on refitting to ensure that the camshaft sprockets and chain are correctly mated. If this method is to be used, great care must be taken to ensure that the camshaft sprockets are fitted in their original positions on refitting. As an extra precaution, to ensure that the sprockets and chain stay correctly mated, it would be wise to tie each sprocket to the chain (see illustrations).*

9.0b . . . as an added precaution, the sprockets can be tied to the chain (cable-tie used here, arrowed) to ensure that they stay correctly mated

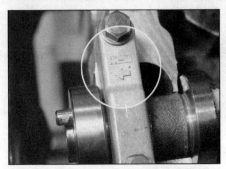

9.3 Camshaft bearing caps are each marked with an arrow (arrowed) to indicate their correct fitted direction

9.9 Measuring camshaft lobe height

9.11 Measuring camshaft bearing journal diameter

This method requires extra care and thought on behalf of the owner, but means that the timing chain cover can be left in position.

Removal

1 Remove the distributor as described in Chapter 5.

2 Remove the timing chain and camshaft sprockets as described in Section 7. If the chain is being left in position (see note at the start of this Section), make the alignment marks and unbolt the sprockets from the camshafts as described in paragraph 9 of Section 7.

3 With the exception of the exhaust camshaft right-hand end bearing cap, all other bearing caps are all similar and it will be necessary to make suitable identification marks on each cap prior to removal. The caps all have an arrow cast into their upper surface indicating their correct fitted direction (all arrows should point towards the timing chain end of the engine). The inlet camshaft caps are marked with a capital "I", to distinguish them from the exhaust camshaft caps **(see illustration)**. Using a scriber or a suitable marker pen, number each cap in some way as to indicate its correct fitted position, with No 1 at the timing chain end. This will avoid the possibility of installing the caps in the wrong positions on refitting.

4 Working in the **reverse** of the sequence shown in illustration 9.24, evenly and progressively slacken the exhaust camshaft bearing cap retaining bolts by one turn at a time, to relieve the pressure of the valve springs on the bearing caps gradually and evenly. Once the valve spring pressure has been relieved, the bolts can be fully unscrewed and removed. Note the correct fitted position of each bolt as it is removed, the bolts are of three different lengths.

5 Remove the oil pipe from the top of the bearing caps, and the baffle plate from the top of No 2 bearing cap. Lift off the camshaft bearing caps, and lift the exhaust camshaft out of the head.

6 Repeat paragraphs 4 and 5 and remove the inlet camshaft and bearing caps from the head (note that there is no baffle pate fitted).

Inspection

7 Inspect the cam bearing surfaces of the head and the bearing caps. Look for score marks and deep scratches. Check the camshaft lobes for heat discoloration (blue appearance), score marks, chipped areas or flat spots.

8 Camshaft run-out can be checked by supporting each end of the camshaft on V-blocks, and measuring any run-out at the centre of the shaft using a dial gauge. If the run-out exceeds the specified limit, a new camshaft will be required.

9 Measure the height of each lobe with a micrometer, and compare the results to the figures given in the Specifications at the start of this Chapter **(see illustration)**. If damage is noted or wear is excessive, new camshaft(s) must be fitted.

10 The camshaft bearing oil clearance should then be checked. There are two possible ways of checking this - the first method is by direct measurement (see paragraphs 11 and 16), and the second by the use of a product called Plastigage (see paragraphs 12 to 16).

11 If the direct measurement method is to be used, fit the bearing caps to the head, using the marks made on removal to ensure that they are correctly positioned. Fit the oil pipe to the top of the caps, and tighten the retaining bolts to the specified torque in the sequence shown in illustration 9.24. Measure the diameter of each bearing cap journal and compare the measurements obtained with the results given in the Specifications at the start of this Chapter. If any journal is worn beyond the service limit, the cylinder head must be renewed. The camshaft bearing oil clearance can then be calculated by subtracting the camshaft bearing journal diameter from the bearing cap journal diameter **(see illustration)**.

12 If the second method is to be used, clean the camshafts, the bearing surfaces in the cylinder head and the bearing caps with a clean, lint-free cloth, then lay the camshafts in place in the cylinder head.

13 Cut strips of Plastigage and lay one piece on each bearing journal, parallel with the camshaft centreline. Ensuring that the camshafts are not rotated at all, refit both

camshafts as described in paragraphs 19 to 25, ignoring the remark about applying sealant to the bearing cap.

14 Now unscrew the bolts as described in paragraph 4, and carefully lift off the oil pipe and bearing caps, again making sure that the camshafts are not rotated.

15 To determine the oil clearance, compare the crushed Plastigage (at its widest point) on each journal to the scale printed on the Plastigage container.

16 Compare the results to this Chapter's Specifications. If the oil clearance is greater than specified, measure the diameter of the cam bearing journal with a micrometer. If the journal diameter is less than the specified limit, renew the camshaft and recheck the clearance. If the clearance is still too great, replace the cylinder head and bearing caps with new parts.

Refitting

17 Ensure that each of the followers is correctly engaged with its hydraulic adjuster and guide plate which is fitted to one of its two valves.

18 Liberally oil the cylinder head camshaft bearings with clean engine oil.

19 Refit the camshafts to their correct locations in the cylinder head. The exhaust camshaft is easily distinguished by the distributor drive slot on its left-hand end.

9.20 Lay the camshafts in the cylinder head, positioning the locating pins (arrowed) as shown

9.21 Apply sealant to the exhaust camshaft bearing cap, as indicated by the shaded area

9.22 Fit the bearing caps, using the marks made prior to removal to ensure that each is correctly positioned

9.23a Fit the baffle plate to No 2 exhaust camshaft bearing cap . . .

9.23b . . . then install the oil pipes and bearing cap bolts

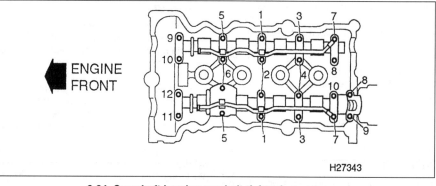

9.24 Camshaft bearing cap bolt tightening sequence

20 Check that the crankshaft is still positioned at TDC (the keyway will be in the 12 o'clock position, when viewed from the right-hand end of the engine). Position each camshaft so that its No 1 cylinder lobes are pointing away from their valves. With the shafts in this position, the sprocket locating pin in the inlet camshaft's right-hand end will be in the 10 o'clock position when viewed from the right-hand end of the engine, while that of the exhaust camshaft will be in the 12 o'clock position **(see illustration)**.

21 Ensure that the bearing cap and head mating surfaces are completely clean, unmarked and free from oil. Apply a smear of suitable sealant to exhaust camshaft left-hand end bearing cap mating surface as shown **(see illustration)**.

22 Using the marks made on removal, refit the bearing caps to their original locations, making sure that the arrow on each cap is pointing towards the timing chain end of the engine **(see illustration)**.

23 Fit the baffle plate to No 2 exhaust camshaft bearing cap, and refit the oil pipe to the top of each set of caps. Refit the bearing cap bolts to their original locations, and screw in all bolts by hand only **(see illustrations)**.

24 Working in the sequence shown, evenly and progressively tighten the inlet camshaft bearing cap bolts by one turn at a time until the caps touch the cylinder head **(see illustration)**. Then tighten all the bolts to the specified torque setting. Work only as

described to impose the pressure of the valve springs gradually and evenly on the bearing caps.

25 Repeat paragraph 24 and tighten the exhaust camshaft bearing cap bolts to the specified torque setting.

26 Refit the timing chain and sprockets as described in Section 7.

27 If the chain was not removed, ensure that the sprockets are fitted to the relevant camshafts, and engage them with the chain so the marks made prior to removal are correctly aligned. Fit the sprocket retaining bolts and washers, and tighten them to the specified torque as described in Section 7.

28 Refit the distributor as described in Chapter 5.

10.3a Lift out the follower . . .

10 Camshaft followers and hydraulic adjusters - removal, inspection and refitting

Removal

1 Remove the camshafts as described in Section 9.

2 Obtain sixteen small, clean plastic containers, and number them 1 to 16. Alternatively, divide a larger container into sixteen compartments.

3 Lift the first follower away from the head, withdraw the hydraulic adjuster from the cylinder head bore, and store the components in their respective positions in the container **(see illustrations)**. **Note:** *Ensure that each*

10.3b . . . and remove the hydraulic adjuster from the cylinder head

2B

10.9a Position a dial test indicator on the follower contact surface of the guide, and zero the gauge . . .

10.9b . . . then carefully pivot the indicator around to rest on the shim, and note the reading obtained

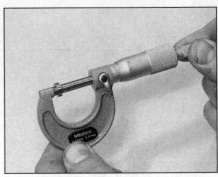

10.10 Using a micrometer to measure shim thickness

adjuster is stored the correct way up; if it is stored on its side or upside-down, air will enter the adjuster, making it necessary to bleed the adjuster prior to installation (see paragraphs 13 and 14). Remove the shim and follower guide from the top of the valves, and store each with its respective adjuster.

4 Repeat paragraph 3 and remove all the remaining followers, adjusters, follower guides and shims. Do not interchange the cam followers or adjusters, as the rate of wear on reassembly will be increased.

Inspection

5 Inspect the cam follower camshaft lobe contact surfaces for signs of wear or damage. If the followers are worn, it is likely that the camshaft lobes are also worn (see Section 9). Renew worn followers as necessary.

6 Check the hydraulic adjuster and cylinder head bearing surfaces for signs of wear or damage. If the necessary measuring equipment is available, the amount of wear can be assessed by direct measurement. Measure the outer diameter of each adjuster, and the internal diameter of its cylinder head bore. The adjuster-to-bore clearance can then be calculated by subtracting the adjuster diameter from the head bore. Compare all measurements with those given in the Specifications at the start of this Chapter, and renew worn components as necessary.

7 Inspect the follower guides for signs of wear or damage, and renew as necessary.

Refitting

8 Prior to refitting, the thickness of each shim should be checked for suitability. This is especially important if new valves and/or seats have been fitted, or if the valves have been reground. The shim thicknesses are checked as described in paragraphs 9 to 11. If no work has been carried out on the cylinder head, and it is not wished to check the shim thicknesses, proceed as described in paragraph 12 onwards.

9 Fit the follower guide to the top of its **original** valve (this is most important - see paragraph 16). Attach a dial test indicator to the cylinder head, and position its probe on the follower contact surface of the guide. Zero the dial test indicator, then carefully lift the probe, and swivel the indicator squarely around; position the probe so that it contacts the end of the other valve stem which the follower will act on, ie. the second valve from that cylinder **(see illustrations). Note:** *Ensure that the indicator is not tilted as it is moved, as this will affect the reading obtained.* Measure the height difference between the tip of the valve stem and the follower contact surface of the follower guide and note this down on a piece of paper. To check the indicator has not tilted as it is moved, swivel it back around and position its probe on the follower guide; the gauge reading should be zero. Repeat this

procedure for each pair of inlet and exhaust valves on each cylinder, and record the measurement obtained.

10 Using the above measurements, select a suitable thickness shim for each pair of valves. The shim should the same thickness as the measurement obtained, although Nissan do give a tolerance of ± 0.025 mm. **Note:** *Shims are available in thicknesses between 2.800 mm and 3.200 mm, in steps of 0.025 mm.* The shim size is stamped on the bottom face of the shim (eg. 2875 indicates the shim is 2.875 mm thick), but it is advisable to use a micrometer to measure the true thickness of any shim removed, as it may have been reduced by wear **(see illustration).**

11 Fit each shim to its respective valve, ensuring that it is fitted with its marked face facing downwards.

12 If the shim thicknesses are not being checked, refit the follower guides and shims to their original valves, making sure that the shims are fitted with their marked faces downwards **(see illustration).**

13 Prior to refitting the hydraulic adjusters, check that each one is free of air. To do this, with the adjuster standing upright, push down on the adjuster plunger and check that it does not move. If the plunger moves approximately 1 mm or more, this indicates the presence of air in the adjuster. If air is present in the adjuster, or if new adjusters are being fitted, the air must be bled from them as follows.

> ⚠ **Warning:** *The adjusters will not bleed themselves of air when the engine is running. If they are installed with air trapped in them, they will not function correctly, and will be noisy in operation.*

14 Obtain a small container which is taller than the adjuster, and a suitable length of welding rod which passes down through the hole in the adjuster plunger. Fill the container with clean engine oil of the specified type and grade (see Chapter 1), and stand the adjuster upright in the container so that it is completely submerged in the oil. Pass the rod down through the adjuster plunger hole, and gently depress the adjuster ball valve **(see illustration).** With the ball valve depressed, slowly move the adjuster plunger in and out;

10.12 Ensure that the shim and follower guide (arrowed) are correctly located in their respective valves

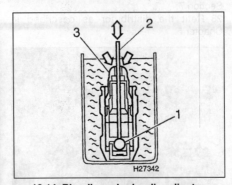

10.14 Bleeding a hydraulic adjuster. Submerge the adjuster in oil, then depress the ball valve (1) with a suitable rod (2) and slowly move the plunger (3) in and out until air bubbles cease to appear

this should bleed the trapped air from the ball valve chamber. When air bubbles cease to appear from the top of the adjuster, release the plunger then remove the rod and allow the ball valve to close. **Note:** *Ensure that the ball valve remains open whilst the plunger is released.* Remove the adjuster from the oil bath, and recheck it as described in paragraph 13.

15 Once all adjusters have been bled, install them in their original locations in the cylinder head.

16 Refit the camshaft followers in their original locations, ensuring that each one is correctly engaged with the hydraulic adjuster and its guide. **Note:** *The follower ends which rest on the top of the shim and guide are of different widths; the shim end is slightly wider than the guide end. If the follower guide is not fitted to the top of the correct valve, the follower will not seat correctly into the guide groove.*

17 Refit the camshafts as described in Section 9.

---

11 Cylinder head -
removal and refitting

Note: *Refer to the note at the start of Section 9.*

> **HAYNES HiNT**
> *To aid refitting, make notes on the locations of all relevant brackets and the routing of hoses and cables before removal.*

Removal

1 Disconnect the battery negative lead.
2 Drain the cooling system as described in Chapter 1.
3 Remove the camshafts as described in Section 9.
4 Note that the following text assumes that the cylinder head will be removed with both inlet and exhaust manifolds attached; this is easier, but makes it a bulky and heavy assembly to handle. If it is wished to remove the manifolds first, proceed as described in the relevant Part of Chapter 4.
5 On single-point injection engines, carry out the following operations as described in the Chapter 4B.
a) Remove the air cleaner housing.
b) Depressurise the fuel system, and disconnect the fuel feed and return hoses from the throttle body (plug all openings, to prevent loss of fuel and entry of dirt into the fuel system).
c) Disconnect the accelerator cable.
d) Disconnect the relevant electrical connectors from the throttle body, inlet manifold and associated components.
e) Disconnect the vacuum servo unit hose, coolant hose(s) and all the other

relevant/breather hoses from the manifold and associated valves.
f) Remove the inlet manifold support bracket(s).
g) Disconnect the exhaust front pipe from the manifold.
6 On multi-point injection engines, carry out the following operations as described in Chapter 4C.
a) Remove the air cleaner inlet duct.
b) Depressurise the fuel system, and disconnect the fuel feed and return hoses from the fuel rail (plug all openings, to prevent loss of fuel and entry of dirt into the fuel system).
c) Disconnect the accelerator cable.
d) Disconnect the relevant electrical connectors from the throttle housing, inlet manifold and associated components. Free the wiring from the manifold, and position it clear of the cylinder head so that it does not hinder removal.
e) Disconnect the vacuum servo unit hose, coolant hose(s) and all the other relevant/breather hoses from the manifold and associated valves.
f) Remove the inlet manifold support bracket(s).
g) Disconnect the exhaust front pipe from the manifold.
7 On automatic transmission models, disconnect the kickdown cable from the throttle body/housing as described in Chapter 7B.
8 Slacken the retaining clip and disconnect the coolant hoses from the back of the coolant pump, the heater matrix and, where necessary, the oil cooler. Also disconnect the radiator hoses from the front of the cylinder head.
9 On "Phase I" multi-point injection models, remove the starter motor as described in Chapter 5, then slacken and remove the bolt securing the cylinder head coolant pipes to the rear of the block.
10 Referring to Chapter 5, disconnect the wiring connectors from the distributor, ignition HT coil and the power transistor unit. Free the wiring loom from any relevant retaining clips, so that it is free from the cylinder head and will not hinder the removal procedure. Also undo the retaining bolts and disconnect all the relevant earth leads from the head and inlet manifold.
11 Undo the two retaining bolts, and free the alternator mounting bracket from the head.
12 Slacken and remove the 6 mm bolts from the timing chain end of the cylinder head (if not already done), and one from the front of the head **(see illustration)**.
13 Working in the **reverse** of the sequence shown in illustration 11.25a, progressively slacken the ten main cylinder head bolts by half a turn at a time, until all bolts can be unscrewed by hand.
14 Lift out the cylinder head bolts and recover the washers, noting which way round they are fitted.

15 Lift the cylinder head away; seek assistance if possible, as it is a heavy assembly (especially if complete with manifolds). Remove the gasket from the top of the block. If the locating dowels are a loose fit in the block, remove them and store them with the head for safe-keeping. Also note the correct fitted locations of the oil jets in the cylinder block; if they are loose, remove them and store them with the head.
16 If the cylinder head is to be dismantled for overhaul, refer to Part C of this Chapter.

Preparation for refitting

17 The manufacturers recommend that the cylinder head bolts are measured, to determine whether renewal is necessary. Measure the length of each bolt (without the washer fitted) from the base of the head to the end of the shank. If all of the bolts are less than 158.2 mm in length they may be re-used, however if any one bolt is greater than 158.2 mm in length, all of the bolts should be renewed as a complete set. Considering the stress which the cylinder head bolts are under, it is highly recommended that they are renewed, regardless of their apparent condition.
18 The mating faces of the cylinder head and cylinder block/crankcase must be perfectly clean before refitting the head. Use a hard plastic or wood scraper to remove all traces of gasket and carbon; also clean the piston crowns. Take particular care, as the surfaces are damaged easily. Also, make sure that the carbon is not allowed to enter the oil and water passages - this is particularly important for the lubrication system, as carbon could block the oil supply to any of the engine's components. Using adhesive tape and paper, seal the water, oil and bolt holes in the cylinder block/crankcase. To prevent carbon entering the gap between the pistons and bores, smear a little grease in the gap. After cleaning each piston, use a small brush to remove all traces of grease and carbon from the gap, then wipe away the remainder with a clean rag. Clean all the pistons in the same way.
19 Check the mating surfaces of the cylinder block/crankcase and the cylinder head for

11.12 Do not forget the small 6 mm bolts which are fitted to the front of the cylinder head

2B

11.22 Fit a new gasket to the cylinder block, aligning it with the locating dowels

11.24 Lubricate the threads and washers, and screw the head bolts into position

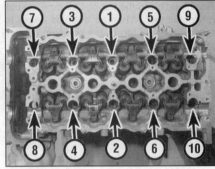

11.25a Working in the sequence shown . . .

nicks, deep scratches and other damage. If slight, they may be removed carefully with a file, but if excessive, machining may be the only alternative to renewal.

20 If warpage of the cylinder head gasket surface is suspected, use a straight-edge to check it for distortion. Refer to Part C of this Chapter if necessary.

Refitting

21 Wipe clean the mating surfaces of the cylinder head and cylinder block/crankcase. Check that the two locating dowels and oil jets are correctly fitted to the cylinder block.

22 Fit a new gasket to the cylinder block/crankcase surface, aligning it with the locating dowels **(see illustration)**.

23 With the aid of an assistant, carefully refit the cylinder head assembly to the block, aligning it with the locating dowels.

24 Apply a smear of clean oil to the threads, and to the underside of the heads, of the cylinder head bolts. Fit the washer to each head bolt, and carefully enter each bolt into its relevant hole (*do not drop them in*) and screw in, by hand only, until finger-tight **(see illustration)**.

25 Working progressively and in the sequence shown, tighten the ten main cylinder head bolts to their Stage 1 torque setting, using a torque wrench and suitable socket **(see illustrations)**.

26 Once all the bolts have been tightened to their Stage 1 setting, go around again in the

specified sequence and tighten them to the specified Stage 2 torque setting.

27 Leave the bolts a minute then, working in the **reverse** of the specified sequence, progressively slacken the head bolts by half a turn at a time, until all bolts can be unscrewed by hand.

28 Tighten all bolts again by hand, then go around again in the specified sequence and tighten the bolts to the specified Stage 3 torque setting.

29 Once all the bolts have been tightened to their Stage 3 setting, working again in the specified sequence, angle-tighten the bolts through the specified Stage 4 angle, using a socket and extension bar. It is recommended that an angle-measuring gauge is used during this stage of the tightening, to ensure accuracy **(see illustration)**. If a gauge is not available, use white paint to make alignment marks between the bolt head and cylinder head prior to tightening; the marks can then be used to check that the bolt has been rotated through the correct angle during tightening.

30 With all bolts tightened through the specified Stage 4 angle, tighten the bolts through the specified Stage 5 angle setting, working in the specified sequence.

31 With the main cylinder head bolts correctly tightened, fit the 6 mm bolt(s) to the front of the head, and tighten them to the specified torque setting.

32 Ensuring that the wiring is correctly

routed, reconnect the connectors to the distributor, coil and power transistor unit. Secure the harness in position with all the necessary clips and ties.

33 Reconnect the earth leads to the head and manifold, and securely tighten their retaining bolts.

34 On "Phase I" multi-point injection models, refit the bolt securing the coolant pipe to the cylinder block, and tighten it securely. Install the starter motor as described in Chapter 5.

35 Reconnect the coolant hoses to their original locations, and securely tighten their retaining clips.

36 Working as described in the relevant Part of Chapter 4, carry out the following tasks:

a) *Refit all disturbed wiring, hoses and control cable(s) to the inlet manifold and fuel system components.*

b) *Refit the inlet manifold support bracket(s).*

c) *Reconnect and adjust the accelerator cable.*

d) *Reconnect the exhaust system front pipe to the manifold.*

e) *Refit the air cleaner housing and/or inlet duct (as applicable).*

37 On automatic transmission models, reconnect and adjust the kickdown cable as described in Chapter 7B.

38 Refit the camshafts as described in Section 9.

12 Sump - removal and refitting

Removal

1 Firmly apply the handbrake, then jack up the front of the vehicle and support it on axle stands. Disconnect the battery negative lead.

2 Slacken and remove the retaining screws, and remove the plastic undershields from beneath the engine.

3 Drain the engine oil, then clean and refit the engine oil drain plug, tightening it to the specified torque. If the engine is nearing its service interval when the oil and filter are due for renewal, it is recommended that the filter is also removed, and a new one fitted. After

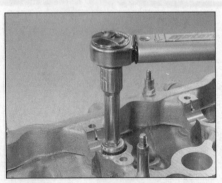

11.25b . . . tighten the cylinder head bolts through the specified torque settings . . .

11.29 . . . and then through the specified angle tightening stages as described in the text

12.5 Removing the small pressed-steel sump

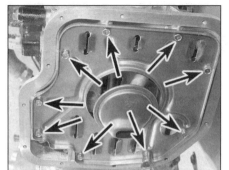

12.6a Unscrew the retaining bolts (arrowed) . . .

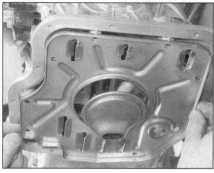

12.6b . . . and remove the baffle plate from the base of the aluminium sump

reassembly, the engine can then be refilled with fresh oil. Refer to Chapter 1 for further information.

4 Remove the exhaust system front pipe as described in the relevant Part of Chapter 4.

5 Working in the **reverse** of the sequence shown in illustration 12.31, progressively slacken and remove all the retaining bolts securing the small pressed-steel sump to the base of the main aluminium sump. Break the joint by striking the sump with the palm of your hand, and withdraw the steel sump from underneath the vehicle **(see illustration)**.

6 Undo the retaining bolts and remove the baffle plate from the base of the aluminium sump **(see illustrations)**.

7 Place a jack with interposed block of wood beneath the transmission to take the weight of the unit. Alternatively, attach a hoist or support bar to the engine, and take the weight of the engine.

8 On manual transmission models, using a suitable marker pen, mark the outline of the front engine/transmission through-bolt on the mounting bracket, to use as a guide on refitting. Slacken and remove the nut, and withdraw the through-bolt from the mounting.

9 On all models, slacken and remove the nut and through-bolt from the rear engine/transmission mounting.

10 Slacken and remove the four bolts and washers securing the centre member to the vehicle body, and lower the assembly away from the engine. Recover the stopper ring

which is fitted between the rear engine/transmission mounting and its bracket.

11 On models with air conditioning, slacken and remove the bolts securing the compressor lower mounting bracket to the aluminium sump. **Note:** *It is not necessary to remove the compressor.*

12 Undo the two bolts and remove the small cover plate from the sump flange, to gain access to two of the sump retaining nuts **(see illustrations)**.

13 Working in the **reverse** of the sequence shown in illustration 12.21, slacken and remove the nuts and bolts securing the aluminium sump to the base of the cylinder block.

14 Unscrew the two bolts securing the sump flange to the transmission housing. The bolts can then be screwed into the threaded holes directly above their original locations, and used as jacking bolts to release the sump from the cylinder block. Screw both bolts until they contact the cylinder block surface, then evenly and progressively tighten the bolts whilst ensuring that the sump comes squarely away from the base of the cylinder block **(see illustration)**.

15 Remove the aluminium sump, and unscrew the jacking bolts **(see illustration)**. **Note:** *On automatic transmission models, it may be necessary to disconnect the selector cable from the transmission to gain the necessary clearance required to allow the*

2B

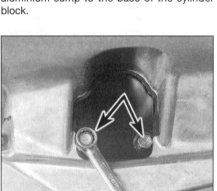

12.12a Undo the two retaining bolts (arrowed) . . .

12.12b . . . and remove the cover plate from the sump flange . . .

12.12c . . . to gain access to the two retaining nuts

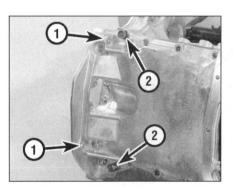

12.14 Unscrew the bolts from the sump flange holes (1) and screw them into the sump locations (2) . . .

12.15 . . . to release the aluminium sump from the base of the cylinder block

12.16a Undo the retaining bolts and remove the oil pump pick-up/strainer . . .

12.16b . . . and baffle plate from the engine

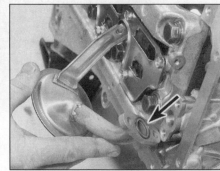

12.19 On refitting, fit a new O-ring (arrowed) to the oil pump pick-up/strainer

sump to be removed. See Chapter 7B for further information.

16 While the sump is removed, undo the retaining bolts and remove the oil pump pick-up/strainer and baffle plate from the base of the main bearing ladder casting **(see illustrations)**. Recover the O-ring fitted between the strainer and timing chain cover, and wash the strainer in a suitable solvent. Check the strainer mesh for signs of clogging or splitting, renewing the pick-up pipe/strainer assembly if it is damaged in any way.

17 Check the centre member mounting rubbers for signs of damage and deterioration, and renew if necessary.

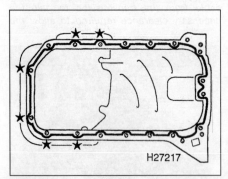

12.20 Apply a bead of sealant to the mating surface of the aluminium sump as shown. Note that the bead should go around the outside of all bolt holes marked with a star, and around the inside of all others

Refitting

18 Clean all traces of sealant from the mating surfaces of the cylinder block/crankcase and sumps, then use a clean rag to wipe out the sump and the engine's interior.

19 Fit a new O-ring to the recess in the top of the pick-up/strainer, and fit the strainer to the base of the timing cover **(see illustration)**. Securely tighten the strainer bolts. Refit the baffle plate to the main bearing ladder casting and securely tighten its retaining bolts

20 Ensure that the sump and cylinder block/crankcase mating surfaces are clean and dry. Apply a continuous bead of suitable sealant to the mating surface of the aluminium sump as shown **(see illustration)**.

21 Offer up the sump, and locate it on the cylinder block. Refit the sump retaining nuts and bolts, tightening them by hand only. Working in the sequence shown **(see illustration)**, tighten all the nuts and bolts to their specified torque settings.

22 Refit the two bolts securing the sump flange to the transmission housing, and tighten them securely. Where necessary, reconnect the selector cable to the automatic transmission as described in Chapter 7B.

23 Fit the small cover plate to the sump flange, and securely tighten its retaining bolts.

24 On models with air conditioning, refit the compressor mounting bolts and tighten them securely.

25 Ensure that all the mounting rubbers are

in position, and refit the stopper ring to the rear engine/transmission mounting bracket. Manoeuvre the centre member into position, aligning it with the engine mountings, and refit its mounting bolts and washers. Tighten the centre member mounting bolts to the specified torque.

26 On models with manual transmission, refit the through-bolt and nut to the front engine/transmission mounting. Position the engine/transmission so that the front mounting through-bolt is correctly aligned with the mark made prior to removal, then tighten the bolt to the specified torque setting.

27 Refit the through-bolt to the rear engine/transmission mounting, and tighten its nut to the specified torque setting.

28 Remove the jack from underneath the transmission.

29 Refit the baffle plate to the base of the aluminium sump, and securely tighten its retaining bolts.

30 Ensure that the sump mating surfaces are clean and dry. Apply a continuous bead of suitable sealant to the mating surface of the small pressed-steel sump **(see illustration)**. Apply the sealant to the groove in the centre of the mating surface between the holes, and around the inner edge of each bolt hole (see illustration 12.12 in Part A).

31 Offer up the sump and refit its retaining bolts, tightening them by hand only. Working

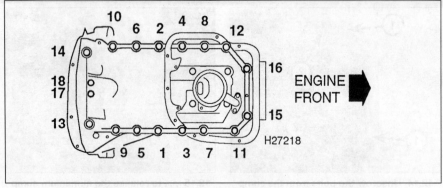

12.21 Aluminium sump retaining nuts and bolts tightening sequence

12.30 Apply a bead of sealant to the pressed-steel sump flange . . .

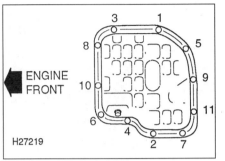

12.31 . . . then fit the sump and tighten its retaining bolts to the specified torque in the sequence shown

in the sequence shown **(see illustration)**, tighten the bolts to the specified torque.

32 Refit the exhaust system front pipe as described in the relevant Part of Chapter 4.

33 Refit the engine undershields, and securely tighten their retaining screws.

34 Replenish the engine oil as described in Chapter 1.

13 Oil pump - removal, inspection and refitting

Removal

1 The oil pump is an integral part of the timing chain cover **(see illustration)**. Remove the cover as described in Section 6.

1 Timing chain cover
2 Oil pump cover
3 Oil pump cover screw
4 Oil pump cover bolts
5 Pick-up/strainer nut
6 Pick-up/strainer bolts
7 Pick-up/strainer
8 O-ring
9 Inner rotor
10 Outer rotor
11 Oil pressure regulator valve piston
12 Spring
13 Sealing washer
14 Oil pressure regulator valve cap

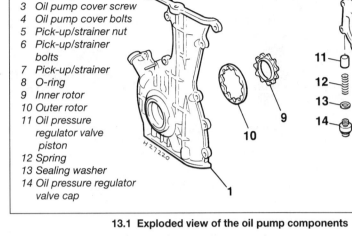

13.1 Exploded view of the oil pump components

Inspection

2 Unscrew the retaining screws and bolt, and remove the pump cover from the rear of the timing chain cover **(see illustration)**.

3 Remove both the oil pump rotors from the cover **(see illustrations)**.

4 Unscrew the oil pressure regulator valve cap from the base of the pump cover, and recover its sealing washer. Withdraw the spring and the valve piston, noting which way round the piston is fitted.

5 Inspect the pump rotors, regulator valve piston and the cover for obvious signs of wear or damage.

6 Fit the rotors to the cover and, using feeler blades of the appropriate thickness, measure the clearance between the outer rotor and cover, and between the tip of the inner and outer rotor **(see illustrations)**.

7 Using feeler blades and a straight-edge placed across the top of the cover and the rotors, measure the inner and outer gear endfloat **(see illustration)**.

8 If access to the necessary measuring

13.2 Remove the pump cover . . .

13.3a . . . and withdraw the outer . . .

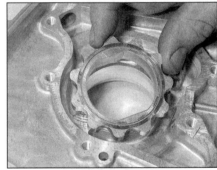

13.3b . . . and inner rotors from the timing chain cover

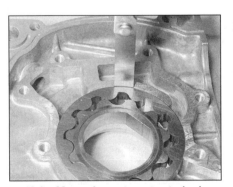

13.6a Measuring outer rotor-to-body clearance

13.6b Measuring inner rotor tip-to-outer rotor clearance

13.7 Measuring rotor endfloat

2B

13.12 Refit the pump cover, and tighten its bolts and screws to their specified torque settings

13.13a Refit the pressure regulator valve piston and spring . . .

13.13b . . then fit the valve bolt and sealing washer . . .

equipment can be gained, measure the diameter of the inner rotor and cover bearing surfaces. Subtract the rotor outer diameter from the cover inner diameter, and calculate the rotor-to-housing clearance.

9 If any measurement is outside the specified limits, or the rotors, valve or cover is damaged, the complete timing chain cover assembly should be renewed.

10 If the pump is found to be worn, also check the oil pressure relief valve. The valve is located in the oil filter housing, which is mounted onto the rear of the cylinder block. Unscrew the valve bolt from the top of the filter housing, and recover the sealing washer, spring and ball. Examine all components for signs of wear or damage, and renew as necessary. On refitting, fit the ball and spring to the housing. Fit a new sealing washer to the valve bolt, then refit the bolt, tightening it to the specified torque setting.

11 Lubricate the rotors with clean engine oil, and refit them to the pump body. Ensure that the inner rotor is fitted with its flange towards the cover.

12 Ensure that the mating surfaces are clean and dry, and refit the pump cover. Fit the cover retaining bolt and screws, and tighten them to the specified torque settings **(see illustration)**.

13 Fit the pressure regulator valve piston, ensuring that it is the correct way round, and install the spring. Fit a new sealing washer to

the valve bolt, and tighten the bolt to the specified torque setting **(see illustrations)**.

Refitting

14 Refit the timing chain cover as described in Section 6.

14 Oil cooler - removal and refitting

Removal

1 The oil cooler (where fitted) is mounted onto the oil filter housing, which is bolted to the rear of the block **(see illustration)**.

2 To gain access to the cooler, firmly apply the handbrake, then jack up the front of the vehicle and support it on axle stands. Disconnect the battery negative lead.

3 Drain the cooling system as described in Chapter 1. Alternatively, clamp the oil cooler coolant hoses directly above the cooler pipes, and be prepared for some coolant loss as the hoses are disconnected.

4 Release the hose clips, and disconnect the coolant hoses from the oil cooler.

5 Using a dab of paint or a suitable marker pen, make alignment marks between the cooler and oil filter housing.

6 Position a suitable container beneath the oil cooler, then unscrew the oil cooler centre bolt. Allow the oil to drain into the container, then remove the oil cooler from the engine. Recover the cooler sealing ring and the O-ring from the centre bolt. Discard both the O-ring and seal; new ones must be used on refitting.

7 Inspect the oil cooler for signs of damage, and check that it is free from obstructions by blowing down through its coolant unions. If the cooler is damaged or blocked, it must be renewed.

Refitting

8 Fit a new sealing ring to the rear of the cooler, and fit a new sealing ring to the centre bolt.

9 Refit the cooler to the oil filter housing, aligning the marks made prior to removal, and install the centre bolt. Tighten the centre bolt to the specified torque setting.

10 Reconnect the coolant hoses to the oil cooler, and secure them in position with their retaining clips.

11 Lower the vehicle to the ground, and refill/top-up the cooling system and engine oil as described in Chapter 1 (as applicable). Start the engine, and check the oil cooler for signs of leakage.

13.13c . . . and tighten it to the specified torque setting

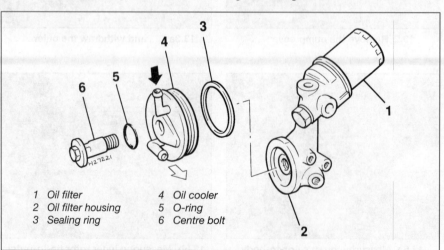

1 Oil filter
2 Oil filter housing
3 Sealing ring
4 Oil cooler
5 O-ring
6 Centre bolt

14.1 Oil cooler components (arrows indicate the flow of coolant through cooler)

15.7 Removing the crankshaft left-hand oil seal

16.3 Note the use of the home-made tool (arrowed) to prevent rotation as the flywheel bolts are slackened

16.4 Removing the cover plate from the end of the cylinder block

15 Crankshaft oil seals - renewal

Right-hand (timing chain cover) oil seal

1 Remove the crankshaft pulley as described in Section 5.

2 Carefully lever the oil seal out of position, using a large flat-bladed screwdriver, taking care not to damage the oil pump gears or timing cover.

3 Clean the seal housing, and polish off any burrs or raised edges which may have caused the seal to fail in the first place.

4 Lubricate the lips of the new seal with a smear of grease and offer up the seal, ensuring that its sealing lip is facing inwards. Carefully ease the seal into position, taking care not to damage its sealing lip. Drive the seal into position until it seats on its locating shoulder, using a suitable tubular drift, such as a socket, which bears only on the hard outer edge of the seal. Take care not to damage the seal lips during fitting. Note that the seal lips should face inwards.

5 Wash off any traces of oil, then refit the crankshaft pulley as described in Section 5.

Left-hand (flywheel/driveplate) oil seal

6 Remove the flywheel/driveplate as described in Section 16.

7 Taking care not to mark either the crankshaft or any part of the cylinder block/crankcase, lever the seal evenly out of its housing using a large flat-bladed screwdriver **(see illustration)**.

8 Clean the seal housing, and polish off any burrs or raised edges which may have caused the seal to fail in the first place.

9 Lubricate the lips of the new seal and the crankshaft shoulder with grease, then offer up the seal to the cylinder block/crankcase.

10 Ease the sealing lip of the seal over the crankshaft shoulder by hand only, and press the seal evenly into its housing until its outer flange seats evenly on the housing lip. If necessary, a soft-faced mallet can be used to tap the seal gently into place.

11 Wash off any traces of oil, then refit the flywheel/driveplate as described in Section 16.

16 Flywheel/driveplate - removal, inspection and refitting

Removal

Flywheel - manual transmission models

1 Remove the transmission as described in Chapter 7A, then remove the clutch assembly as described in Chapter 6.

2 Prevent the flywheel from turning by locking the ring gear teeth with a similar arrangement to that shown in illustration 16.3. Alternatively, bolt a strap between the flywheel and the cylinder block/crankcase.

3 Slacken and remove the flywheel retaining bolts, and remove the flywheel **(see illustration)**. Do not drop it, as it is very heavy.

4 If necessary, remove the cover plate from the cylinder block, noting which way round it is fitted **(see illustration)**. If the cover plate dowels are a loose fit in the block, remove them and store them with the plate for safe-keeping.

Driveplate - automatic transmission models

5 Remove the transmission as described in Chapter 7B.

6 Lock the driveplate as described in paragraph 2.

7 Slacken and remove the driveplate retaining bolts along with the driveplate retaining plate. Remove the driveplate, and recover the collar which is fitted between the driveplate and crankshaft.

8 If necessary, remove the cover plate from the cylinder block, noting which way round it is fitted. If the cover plate dowels are a loose fit in the block, remove them and store them with the plate for safe-keeping.

Inspection

9 On manual transmission models, examine the flywheel for scoring of the clutch face, and for wear or chipping of the ring gear teeth. If the

flywheel's clutch mating surface is deeply scored, cracked or otherwise damaged, the flywheel must be renewed. However, it may be possible to have it surface-ground; seek the advice of a Nissan dealer or engine reconditioning specialist. If the ring gear is badly worn or has missing teeth, it must be renewed. This job is best left to a Nissan dealer or engine reconditioning specialist. The temperature to which the new ring gear must be heated for installation is critical and, if not done accurately, the hardness of the teeth will be destroyed.

10 On automatic transmission models, check the torque converter driveplate carefully for signs of distortion, and for any hairline cracks around the bolt holes or radiating outwards from the centre. Inspect the ring gear teeth for signs of wear or chipping. If any sign of wear or damage is found, the driveplate must be renewed.

Refitting

Flywheel - manual transmission models

11 Install the locating dowels (where removed) and refit the cover plate to the cylinder block.

12 Clean the mating surfaces of the flywheel and crankshaft.

13 Offer up the flywheel, and refit the retaining bolts.

14 Lock the flywheel using the method employed on dismantling, and tighten the retaining bolts to the specified torque.

15 Refit the clutch as described in Chapter 6. Remove the locking tool, and refit the transmission as described in Chapter 7A.

Driveplate - automatic transmission models

16 Install the locating dowels (where removed) and refit the cover plate to the cylinder block.

17 Clean the mating surfaces of the driveplate and crankshaft.

18 Refit the collar to the rear of the driveplate, and position the assembly on the end of the crankshaft.

19 Install the retaining bolts and retaining plate.

20 Lock the driveplate using the method employed on dismantling, and tighten the retaining bolts to the specified torque.

21 Remove the locking tool, and refit the transmission as described in Chapter 7B.

2B

17 Engine/transmission mountings - inspection and renewal

Inspection

1 If improved access is required, raise the front of the car and support it securely on axle stands.

2 Check the mounting rubber to see if it is cracked, hardened or separated from the metal at any point; renew the mounting if any such damage or deterioration is evident.

3 Check that all the mounting's fasteners are securely tightened; use a torque wrench to check if possible.

4 Using a large screwdriver or a crowbar, check for wear in the mounting by carefully levering against it to check for free play. Where this is not possible, enlist the aid of an assistant to move the engine/transmission back and forth, or from side to side, while you watch the mounting. While some free play is to be expected even from new components, excessive wear should be obvious. If excessive free play is found, check first that the fasteners are correctly secured, then renew any worn components as described below.

Renewal

Right-hand mounting

5 Disconnect the battery negative lead.

6 Place a jack beneath the engine, with a block of wood on the jack head. Raise the jack until it is supporting the weight of the engine.

7 Unscrew the nut and through-bolt, then undo the retaining bolts and remove the right-hand mounting from the engine compartment. Recover the rubbers which are fitted to each side of the body mounting bracket.

8 If necessary, undo the retaining bolts and remove the mounting bracket from the engine.

9 Check carefully for signs of wear or damage on all components, and renew them where necessary.

10 On refitting, fit the mounting bracket (where removed) to the engine, and tighten its retaining bolts to the specified torque.

11 Fit the rubbers to the body mounting bracket, ensuring that their pins are correctly seated in the bracket holes. Fit the mounting to the top of the mounting bracket, and tighten its retaining bolts to the specified torque setting.

12 Insert the through-bolt, and tighten its nut to the specified torque setting. Remove the jack from underneath the engine.

13 Reconnect the battery negative lead.

Left-hand mounting

14 Remove the battery and tray as described in Chapter 5.

15 Place a jack and block of wood beneath the transmission, and raise the jack to take the weight of the transmission.

16 Slacken and remove the through-bolt, then undo the three bolts securing the mounting to the transmission and manoeuvre it out of position. Recover the rubbers from each side of the mounting bracket. If necessary, unbolt the mounting bracket from the engine compartment.

17 Check carefully for signs of wear or damage on all components, and renew them where necessary.

18 On refitting, fit the mounting bracket (where removed) and securely tighten its retaining bolts.

19 Refit the rubbers to the mounting bracket, ensuring that their pins are correctly seated in the bracket holes, and manoeuvre the mounting into position. Fit the bolts securing the mounting to the transmission, and tighten them to the specified torque setting.

20 Insert the through-bolt, and tighten its nut to the specified torque setting.

21 Remove the jack from underneath the engine, and refit the battery and tray as described in Chapter 5.

Front mounting - Saloon and Hatchback manual transmission models

22 If not already done, firmly apply the handbrake, then jack up the front of the vehicle and support it securely on axle stands. Disconnect the battery negative lead, then undo the retaining screws and remove the undershields from beneath the engine/transmission.

23 Using a suitable marker pen, mark the outline of the front engine/transmission through-bolt on the mounting bracket, to use as a guide on refitting.

24 Place a jack beneath the engine, with a block of wood on the jack head. Raise the jack until it is supporting the weight of the engine.

25 Slacken and remove the nut and through-bolt from mounting.

26 Undo the retaining bolts, and remove the mounting bracket from the front of the engine.

27 Check carefully for signs of wear or damage on all components, and renew them where necessary. If renewal of the mounting rubber is necessary, press the original out from the centre member, and install the new rubber; coat the rubber with soapy water (or washing-up liquid) to ease installation.

28 On refitting, fit the mounting bracket to the engine, and tighten its retaining bolts to the specified torque.

29 Refit the through-bolt to the mounting, and lightly tighten its nut. Position the engine/transmission so that the front mounting through-bolt is correctly aligned with the mark made prior to removal, then tighten it to the specified torque setting.

30 Remove the jack from underneath the transmission.

31 Refit the undershield, tighten its fasteners securely, then lower the vehicle to the ground and reconnect the battery.

Front mounting - Estate manual transmission models

32 Carry out the operations described above in paragraphs 22 to 25.

33 Undo the two retaining bolts, and remove the mounting assembly from the centre member.

34 If necessary, undo the retaining bolts and remove the mounting bracket from the front of the engine.

35 Check carefully for signs of wear or damage on all components, and renew them as necessary.

36 On refitting, where removed, fit the mounting bracket to the engine, and tighten its retaining bolts to the specified torque.

37 Fit the mounting to the centre member, and tighten its retaining bolts to the specified torque.

38 Fit the through-bolt to the mounting, and lightly tighten its nut.

39 Position the engine/transmission so that the front mounting through-bolt is correctly aligned with the mark made prior to removal, then tighten the through-bolt to the specified torque setting.

40 Remove the jack from underneath the transmission.

41 Refit the undershield, tighten its fasteners securely, then lower the vehicle to the ground and reconnect the battery.

Rear mounting

42 If not already done, firmly apply the handbrake, then jack up the front of the vehicle and support it securely on axle stands. Disconnect the battery negative lead.

43 Slacken and remove the through-bolt from the rear engine/transmission mounting.

44 Undo the bolts securing the mounting bracket in position, and manoeuvre it away from the engine/transmission. Recover the stopper ring which is fitted between the mounting bracket and mounting.

45 Undo the two retaining bolts, and remove the mounting assembly from the centre member.

46 Check carefully for signs of wear or damage on all components, and renew them where necessary.

47 On reassembly, fit the rear mounting to the centre member, and tighten its retaining bolts to the specified torque.

48 Refit the stopper ring, then install the mounting bracket and tighten its retaining bolts to the specified torque.

49 Align the rear mounting with its bracket, then insert the through-bolt and tighten its nut to the specified torque setting.

50 Remove the jack from underneath the engine, and reconnect the battery negative lead.

Chapter 2 Part C Engine removal and general overhaul procedures

Contents

2C

Degrees of difficulty

Easy, suitable for novice with little experience	**Fairly easy,** suitable for beginner with some experience	**Fairly difficult,** suitable for competent DIY mechanic	**Difficult,** suitable for experienced DIY mechanic	**Very difficult,** suitable for expert DIY or professional

Specifications

Cylinder head

Maximum gasket face distortion	0.1 mm
Cylinder head height:	
1.6 litre engines	117.0 to 118.0 mm
2.0 litre engines	136.9 to 137.1 mm

Cylinder block

Cylinder bore diameter:	
1.6 litre engine:	
Grade 1	76.000 to 76.010 mm
Grade 2	76.010 to 76.020 mm
Grade 3	76.020 to 76.030 mm
Oversizes available	0.5 mm and 1.0 mm
2.0 litre engine:	
Grade 1	86.000 to 86.010 mm
Grade 2	86.010 to 86.020 mm
Grade 3	86.020 to 86.030 mm
Oversize available	0.2 mm

Valves

Valve head diameter:
  Inlet:
    1.6 litre engine . . . . 29.9 to 30.1 mm
    2.0 litre engine . . . . 34.0 to 34.2 mm
  Exhaust:
    1.6 litre engine . . . . 23.9 to 24.1 mm
    2.0 litre engine . . . . 30.0 to 30.2 mm
Valve stem diameter:
  Inlet:
    1.6 litre engine . . . . 5.465 to 5.480 mm
    2.0 litre engine . . . . 5.965 to 5.980 mm
  Exhaust:
    1.6 litre engine . . . . 5.445 to 5.460 mm
    2.0 litre engine:
      SR20Di and SR20De engines . . . . 5.945 to 5.960 mm
      SR20DE engines . . . . 6.945 to 6.960 mm
Overall length:
  Inlet:
    1.6 litre engine . . . . 92.05 to 92.45 mm
    2.0 litre engine . . . . 101.19 to 101.61 mm
  Exhaust:
    1.6 litre engine . . . . 92.42 to 92.82 mm
    2.0 litre engine . . . . 102.11 to 102.53 mm
Valve guide inner diameter:
  Inlet:
    1.6 litre engine . . . . 5.500 to 5.515 mm
    2.0 litre engine . . . . 6.000 to 6.018 mm
  Exhaust:
    1.6 litre engine . . . . 5.500 to 5.515 mm
    2.0 litre engine:
      SR20Di and SR20De engines . . . . 6.000 to 6.018 mm
      SR20DE engine . . . . 7.000 to 7.018 mm
Valve stem-to-guide clearance:
  Inlet:
    1.6 litre engine . . . . 0.020 to 0.050 mm
    2.0 litre engine . . . . 0.020 to 0.053 mm
  Exhaust:
    1.6 litre engine . . . . 0.040 to 0.070 mm
    2.0 litre engine . . . . 0.040 to 0.073 mm
Valve spring free length:
  1.6 litre engine . . . . 40 00 mm
  2.0 litre engine . . . . 49 36 mm
Valve spring out-of-square limit:
  1.6 litre engine . . . . 1.74 mm
  2.0 litre engine . . . . 2.20 mm

Piston rings

Ring-to-groove clearance:
  Standard:
    Top compression ring . . . . 0.040 to 0.085 mm
    Second compression ring . . . . 0.030 to 0.070 mm
  Service limit . . . . 0.2 mm
End gaps:
  1.6 litre engine:
    Standard:
      Top compression ring . . . . 0.20 to 0.40 mm
      Second compression ring . . . . 0.35 to 0.55 mm
      Oil control ring . . . . 0.25 to 1.00 mm
    Service limit:
      Top compression ring . . . . 0.49 mm
      Second compression ring . . . . 0.64 mm
      Oil control ring . . . . 1.09 mm
  2.0 litre engine:
    Standard:
      Top compression ring . . . . 0.20 to 0.30 mm
      Second compression ring . . . . 0.35 to 0.55 mm
      Oil control ring . . . . 0.20 to 0.60 mm
    Service limit (all rings) . . . . 1.00 mm

Piston and connecting rod

Piston diameter:
  1.6 litre engine (measured 9.5 mm up from the base of skirt):
    Standard piston:
      Grade 1 . . . .   75.980 to 75.990 mm
      Grade 2 . . . .   75.990 to 76.000 mm
      Grade 3 . . . .   76.000 to 76.010 mm
    0.5 mm oversize piston . . . .   76.490 to 76.510 mm
    1.0 mm oversize piston . . . .   76.990 to 77.010 mm
  2.0 litre engine (measured 11.0 mm up from the base of skirt):
    Standard piston:
      Grade 1 . . . .   86.000 to 86.010 mm
      Grade 2 . . . .   86.010 to 86.020 mm
      Grade 3 . . . .   86.020 to 86.030 mm
    0.2 mm oversize piston . . . .   86.180 to 86.210 mm
Piston-to-bore clearance . . . .   0.010 to 0.030 mm
Piston gudgeon pin bore diameter:
  1.6 litre engine . . . .   18.987 to 18.999 mm
  2.0 litre engine . . . .   21.987 to 21.999 mm
Gudgeon pin outer diameter:
  1.6 litre engine . . . .   18.989 to 19.001 mm
  2.0 litre engine . . . .   21.989 to 22.001 mm
Piston-to-gudgeon pin clearance . . . .   -0.004 to 0.000 mm (ie. an interference fit)
Connecting rod small-end bush diameter:
  1.6 litre engine . . . .   19.000 to 19.012 mm
  2.0 litre engine . . . .   22.000 to 22.012 mm
Connecting rod small-end bush-to-gudgeon pin clearance:
  Standard . . . .   0.005 to 0.017 mm
  Service limit . . . .   0.023 mm
Connecting rod big-end bore diameter:
  1.6 litre engine . . . .   43.000 to 43.013 mm
  2.0 litre engine . . . .   51.000 to 51.013 mm
Connecting rod big-end bearing side clearance:
  Standard:
    1.6 litre engine . . . .   0.20 to 0.47 mm
    2.0 litre engine . . . .   0.20 to 0.35 mm
  Service limit . . . .   0.5 mm

Crankshaft

Endfloat:
  Standard:
    1.6 litre engine . . . .   0.06 to 0.18 mm
    2.0 litre engine . . . .   0.10 to 0.26 mm
  Service limit . . . .   0.3 mm
Run-out:
  Standard:
    1.6 litre engine . . . .   Less than 0.040 mm
    2.0 litre engine . . . .   Less than 0.025 mm
  Service limit . . . .   0.05 mm
Main bearing journal diameter:
  1.6 litre engine:
    Grade 0 . . . .   49.956 to 49.964 mm
    Grade 1 . . . .   49.948 to 49.956 mm
    Grade 2 . . . .   49.940 to 49.948 mm
  2.0 litre engine:
    Grade 0 . . . .   54.974 to 54.980 mm
    Grade 1 . . . .   54.968 to 54.974 mm
    Grade 2 . . . .   54.962 to 54.968 mm
    Grade 3 . . . .   54.956 to 54.962 mm
Journal ovality . . . .   Less than 0.005 mm
Journal taper:
  1.6 litre engine . . . .   Less than 0.002 mm
  2.0 litre engine . . . .   Less than 0.005 mm
Big-end bearing journal diameter:
  1.6 litre engine:
    Grade 0 . . . .   39.968 to 39.974 mm
    Grade 1 . . . .   39.962 to 39.968 mm
    Grade 2 . . . .   39.956 to 39.962 mm

2C

Crankshaft

Big-end bearing journal diameter: (continued)

2.0 litre engine:

Grade 0	47.968 to 47.974 mm
Grade 1	47.962 to 47.968 mm
Grade 2	47.956 to 47.962 mm

Journal ovality .... Less than 0.005 mm

Journal taper:

1.6 litre engine	Less than 0.002 mm
2.0 litre engine	Less than 0.005 mm

Main bearing running clearance:

1.6 litre engine:

Standard	0.020 to 0.044 mm
Service limit	0.064 mm

2.0 litre engine:

Standard	0.004 to 0.022 mm
Service limit	0.050 mm

Big-end bearing running clearance:

1.6 litre engine:

Standard	0.010 to 0.035 mm
Service limit	0.055 mm

2.0 litre engine:

Standard	0.020 to 0.045 mm
Service limit	0.090 mm

Main bearing shell thicknesses:

1.6 litre engine:

Standard:

Black	1.826 to 1.830 mm
Brown	1.830 to 1.834 mm
Green	1.834 to 1.838 mm
Yellow	1.838 to 1.842 mm
Blue	1.842 to 1.846 mm
0.25 mm undersize	1.960 to 1.964 mm
0.50 mm undersize	2.085 to 2.089 mm

2.0 litre engine:

Standard:

Black	1.977 to 1.980 mm
Brown	1.980 to 1.983 mm
Green	1.983 to 1.986 mm
Yellow	1.986 to 1.989 mm
Blue	1.989 to 1.992 mm
Pink	1.992 to 1.995 mm
White (or no colour)	1.995 to 1.998 mm
0.25 mm undersize	2.109 to 2.117 mm

Big-end bearing shell thicknesses:

1.6 litre engine:

Standard:

Black	1.505 to 1.508 mm
Brown	1.508 to 1.511 mm
Green	1.511 to 1.514 mm
0.08 mm undersize	1.540 to 1.548 mm
0.12 mm undersize	1.560 to 1.568 mm
0.25 mm undersize	1.625 to 1.633 mm

2.0 litre engine:

Standard:

White (or no colour)	1.500 to 1.503 mm
Black	1.503 to 1.506 mm
Brown	1.506 to 1.509 mm
0.08 mm undersize	1.541 to 1.549 mm
0.12 mm undersize	1.561 to 1.569 mm
0.25 mm undersize	1.626 to 1.634 mm

Torque wrench settings

1.6 litre engines

Refer to Chapter 2A Specifications.

2.0 litre engine

Refer to Chapter 2B Specifications.

1 General information

1 Included in this Part of Chapter 2 are details of removing the engine from the vehicle, and general overhaul procedures for the cylinder head, cylinder block/crankcase and all other engine internal components.

2 The information given ranges from advice concerning preparation for an overhaul and the purchase of replacement parts, to detailed step-by-step procedures covering removal, inspection, renovation and refitting of engine internal components.

3 After Section 6, all instructions are based on the assumption that the engine has been removed from the vehicle. For information concerning in-car engine repair, as well as the removal and refitting of those external components necessary for full overhaul, refer to Part A or B of this Chapter (as applicable) and to Section 6. Ignore any preliminary dismantling operations described in Part A (1.6 litre engine) or Part B (2.0 litre engine) that are no longer relevant once the engine has been removed from the vehicle.

4 Apart from torque wrench settings, which are given at the beginning of Part A or Part B, all specifications relating to engine overhaul are at the beginning of this Part of Chapter 2.

2 Engine overhaul - general information

1 It is not always easy to determine when, or if, an engine should be completely overhauled, as a number of factors must be considered.

2 High mileage is not necessarily an indication that an overhaul is needed, while low mileage does not preclude the need for an overhaul. Frequency of servicing is probably the most important consideration. An engine which has had regular and frequent oil and filter changes, as well as other required maintenance, should give many thousands of miles of reliable service. Conversely, a neglected engine may require an overhaul very early in its life.

3 Excessive oil consumption is an indication that piston rings, valve seals and/or valve guides are in need of attention. Make sure that oil leaks are not responsible before deciding that the rings and/or guides are worn. Perform a compression test, as described in Part A or B of this Chapter (as applicable), to determine the likely cause of the problem.

4 Check the oil pressure with a gauge fitted in place of the oil pressure switch, and compare it with that specified. If it is extremely low, the main and big-end bearings, and/or the oil pump, are probably worn out.

5 Loss of power, rough running, knocking or metallic engine noises, excessive valve gear noise, and high fuel consumption may also point to the need for an overhaul, especially if they are all present at the same time. If a complete service does not remedy the situation, major mechanical work is the only solution.

6 An engine overhaul involves restoring all internal parts to the specification of a new engine. During an overhaul, the pistons and the piston rings are renewed. New main and big-end bearings are generally fitted; if necessary, the crankshaft may be renewed, to restore the journals. The valves are also serviced as well, since they are usually in less-than-perfect condition at this point. While the engine is being overhauled, other components, such as the distributor, starter and alternator, can be overhauled as well. The end result should be an as-new engine that will give many trouble-free miles.

7 **Note:** *Critical cooling system components such as the hoses, thermostat and water pump should be renewed when an engine is overhauled. The radiator should be checked carefully, to ensure that it is not clogged or leaking. Also, it is a good idea to renew the oil pump whenever the engine is overhauled.*

8 Before beginning the engine overhaul, read through the entire procedure, to familiarise yourself with the scope and requirements of the job. Overhauling an engine is not difficult if you follow carefully all of the instructions, have the necessary tools and equipment, and pay close attention to all specifications. It can, however, be time-consuming. Plan on the car being off the road for a minimum of two weeks, especially if parts must be taken to an engineering works for repair or reconditioning. Check on the availability of parts, and make sure that any necessary special tools and equipment are obtained in advance. Most work can be done with typical hand tools, although a number of precision measuring tools are required for inspecting parts to determine if they must be renewed. Often, the engineering works will handle the inspection of parts, and can offer advice concerning reconditioning and renewal.

9 **Note:** *Always wait until the engine has been completely dismantled, and until all components (especially the cylinder block/ crankcase and the crankshaft) have been inspected, before deciding what service and repair operations must be performed by an engineering works. The condition of these components will be the major factor to consider when determining whether to overhaul the original engine, or to buy a reconditioned unit. Do not, therefore, purchase parts or have overhaul work done on other components until they have been thoroughly inspected. As a general rule, time is the primary cost of an overhaul, so it does not pay to fit worn or sub-standard parts.*

10 As a final note, to ensure maximum life and minimum trouble from a reconditioned engine, everything must be assembled with care, in a spotlessly-clean environment.

3 Engine removal - methods and precautions

1 If you have decided that the engine must be removed for overhaul or major repair work, several preliminary steps should be taken.

2 Locating a suitable place to work is extremely important. Adequate work space, along with storage space for the vehicle, will be needed. If a workshop or garage is not available, at the very least, a flat, level, clean work surface is required.

3 Cleaning the engine compartment and engine/transmission before beginning the removal procedure will help keep tools clean and organised.

4 An engine hoist or A-frame will also be necessary. Make sure that the equipment is rated in excess of the combined weight of the engine and transmission. Safety is of primary importance, considering the potential hazards involved in removing the engine/transmission from the vehicle.

5 If this is the first time you have removed an engine, an assistant should ideally be available. Advice and aid from someone more experienced would also be helpful. There are many instances when one person cannot simultaneously perform all of the operations required when lifting the engine out of the vehicle.

6 Plan the operation ahead of time. Before starting work, arrange for the hire of, or obtain, all of the tools and equipment you will need. Some of the equipment necessary to perform engine/transmission removal and installation safely and with relative ease (in addition to an engine hoist) is as follows: a heavy-duty trolley jack, complete sets of spanners and sockets as described in the front of this manual, wooden blocks, and plenty of rags and cleaning solvent for mopping up spilled oil, coolant and fuel. If the hoist must be hired, make sure that you arrange for it in advance, and perform all of the operations possible without it beforehand. This will save you money and time.

7 Plan for the vehicle to be out of use for quite a while. An engineering works will be required to perform some of the work which the do-it-yourselfer cannot accomplish without special equipment. These places often have a busy schedule, so it would be a good idea to consult them before removing the engine, in order to accurately estimate the amount of time required to rebuild or repair components that may need work.

8 Always be extremely careful when removing and refitting the engine/transmission. Serious injury can result from careless actions. Plan ahead and take your time, and a job of this nature, although major, can be accomplished successfully.

9 The engine and transmission is removed from under the vehicle on all models described in this manual.

2C

4 Engine and manual transmission - removal, separation and refitting

Removal

Note: *The engine can be removed from the car only as a complete unit with the transmission; the two are then separated for overhaul. The engine/transmission unit is lowered out of position, and withdrawn from under the vehicle. To allow adequate clearance underneath the vehicle, there should be at least 75 cm between the front bumper and the ground when the vehicle is raised and supported.*

1 Park the vehicle on firm, level ground. Chock the rear wheels, then firmly apply the handbrake. Apply the handbrake, then jack up the front of the vehicle. Securely support it on axle stands, bearing in mind the note at the start of this Section.

2 Remove both front roadwheels.

3 Undo all the retaining screws, and remove the undershields from underneath and around the engine.

4 Remove the bonnet as described in Chapter 11.

5 Drain the cooling system (see Chapter 1), saving the coolant if it is fit for re-use.

6 Drain the transmission oil as described in Chapter 1. Refit the drain and filler plugs, and tighten them to their specified torque settings.

7 If the engine is to be dismantled, working as described in Chapter 1, drain the oil and if required remove the oil filter. Clean and refit the drain plug, tightening it to the specified torque.

8 Remove the radiator, complete with hoses and cooling fans, as described in Chapter 3.

9 Working as described in Chapter 5, remove the alternator and disconnect the wiring from the starter motor.

10 Remove the power steering pump as described in Chapter 10.

11 On carburettor engines, disconnect the following from the carburettor and inlet manifold, as described in Chapter 4A:

a) Air cleaner housing.
b) Fuel feed hose and return hose from the fuel pump (plug all openings, to prevent loss of fuel and the entry of dirt into the system).
c) Accelerator cable.
d) Carburettor wiring connector(s).
e) Vacuum servo unit vacuum hose, coolant hose, and all other relevant breather/vacuum hoses from the manifold and associated valves.
f) Remove the inlet manifold support bracket.
g) Remove the exhaust system front pipe.
h) On models with a catalytic converter, disconnect the exhaust gas sensor wiring connector.

12 On single-point injection engines, carry out the following operations as described in the Chapter 4B.

a) Remove the air cleaner housing.
b) Depressurise the fuel system, and disconnect the fuel feed and return hoses from the throttle body (plug all openings, to prevent loss of fuel and entry of dirt into the fuel system).
c) Disconnect the accelerator cable.
d) Disconnect the relevant electrical connectors from the throttle body, inlet manifold and associated components.
e) Disconnect the vacuum servo unit hose, coolant hose(s), and all the other relevant/breather hoses from the manifold and associated valves.
f) Remove the inlet manifold support bracket(s).
g) Remove the exhaust front pipe.

13 On multi-point injection engines, carry out the following operations as described in Chapter 4C.

a) Remove the air cleaner inlet duct.
b) Depressurise the fuel system, and disconnect the fuel feed and return hoses from the fuel rail (plug all openings, to prevent loss of fuel and entry of dirt into the fuel system).
c) Disconnect the accelerator cable.
d) Disconnect the relevant electrical connectors from the throttle housing, inlet manifold and associated components.

Free the wiring from the manifold, and position it clear of the cylinder head so that it does not hinder removal **(see illustration)**.
e) Disconnect the vacuum servo unit hose, coolant hose(s), and all the other relevant/breather hoses from the manifold and associated valves **(see illustration)**.
f) Remove the inlet manifold support bracket(s).
g) Remove the exhaust front pipe.

14 Slacken the retaining clips, and disconnect the heater hoses and all other relevant cooling system hoses from the engine, noting each hose's correct fitted location.

15 On models with air conditioning, unbolt the compressor and position it clear of the engine. Support the weight of the compressor by tying it to the vehicle body, to prevent any excess strain being placed on the compressor lines whilst the engine is removed. **Do not** disconnect the refrigerant lines from the compressor (see the warnings given in Chapter 3, Section 10).

16 Referring to Chapter 5, disconnect the wiring connectors from the distributor, ignition HT coil and the power transistor unit. Free the wiring loom from any relevant retaining clips, so that it is free from the cylinder head and will not hinder the removal procedure. Also undo the retaining bolts, and disconnect all the relevant earth leads from the head and inlet manifold **(see illustration)**.

17 Working as described in Chapter 8, remove the driveshafts.

18 Disconnect the clutch cable from the transmission as described in Chapter 6.

19 Working as described in Chapter 7A, disconnect the gearchange linkage link rods, the speedometer cable and the wiring connector(s) from the transmission **(see illustration)**.

20 Manoeuvre the engine hoist into position, and attach it to the cylinder head using suitable lifting brackets. Raise the hoist until it is supporting the weight of the engine.

21 Using a suitable marker pen, mark the outline of the front engine/transmission through-bolt on the mounting bracket to use

4.13a Disconnect all the relevant fuel system wiring, and free it from the inlet manifold (2.0 litre "Phase II" model shown)

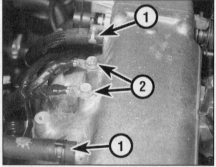

4.13b Inlet manifold vacuum hoses (1) and earth leads (2) - 2.0 litre "Phase II" model

4.16 Unscrew the bolt(s) and free all earth lead(s) from the cylinder head

4.19 Disconnect the gearchange linkage support rod (1) and selector rod (2) from the transmission

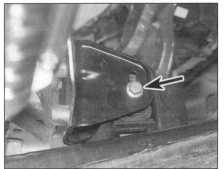

4.21a Prior to removal, mark the position of the front engine/transmission mounting through-bolt (arrowed) on its bracket

4.21b Slacken and remove the rear engine/transmission mounting through-bolt (arrowed)

as a guide on refitting. Slacken and remove the nut and withdraw the through-bolt from the mounting. Slacken and remove the nut and through-bolt from the rear engine/transmission mounting **(see illustrations)**.

22 Slacken and remove the four bolts and washers securing the centre member to the vehicle body, and lower the assembly away from the engine **(see illustrations)**. On 2.0 litre models, recover the stopper ring which is fitted between the rear engine/transmission mounting and its bracket.

23 On 1.6 litre models, undo the three retaining bolts and remove the mounting bracket from the top of the right-hand engine/transmission mounting.

24 On all models, unscrew the nut and through-bolt from the right-hand engine/transmission mounting, then undo the retaining bolts and remove the mounting assembly from the engine compartment. Recover the rubbers which are fitted to each side of the body mounting bracket, if they are loose.

25 Slacken and remove the through-bolt from the left-hand engine/transmission mounting. Undo the three bolts securing the mounting to the transmission, and manoeuvre the mounting out of position. Recover the rubbers from each side of the mounting bracket, if they are loose.

26 Make a final check that any components which would prevent the removal of the engine/transmission from the car have been

removed or disconnected. Ensure that components such as the gearchange link rods are secured so that they cannot be damaged on removal.

27 If available, a low trolley should be placed under the engine/transmission assembly, to facilitate its easy removal from under the vehicle. Lower the engine/transmission assembly, making sure that nothing is trapped or damaged. Enlist the help of an assistant during this procedure, as it may be necessary to tilt the assembly slightly to clear the body panels **(see illustration)**. Great care must be taken to ensure that no components are trapped and damaged during the removal procedure.

28 Withdraw the assembly from under the vehicle.

Separation

29 With the engine/transmission assembly removed, support the assembly on suitable blocks of wood, on a workbench (or failing that, on a clean area of the workshop floor).

30 Unscrew the retaining bolts, and remove the starter motor from the transmission.

31 Ensure that both engine and transmission are adequately supported, then slacken and remove the bolts securing the transmission housing to the engine. Note the correct fitted positions of each bolt (and, where fitted, the relevant brackets) as they are removed, to use as a reference on refitting.

32 Carefully withdraw the transmission from the engine, ensuring that the weight of the transmission is not allowed to hang on the input shaft while it is engaged with the clutch friction disc.

33 If they are loose, remove the locating dowels from the engine or transmission, and keep them in a safe place.

Refitting

34 If the engine and transmission have been separated, perform the operations described below in paragraphs 35 to 39. If not, proceed as described from paragraph 40 onwards.

35 Apply a smear of high-melting-point grease to the splines of the transmission input shaft. Do not apply too much, otherwise there is a possibility of the grease contaminating the clutch friction plate.

36 Ensure that the locating dowels are correctly positioned in the engine or transmission, and that the release bearing is correctly engaged with the fork.

37 Carefully offer the transmission to the engine, until the locating dowels are engaged. Ensure that the weight of the transmission is not allowed to hang on the input shaft as it is engaged with the clutch friction plate.

38 Refit the transmission housing-to-engine bolts, ensuring that all the necessary brackets are correctly positioned, and tighten them to the specified torque setting.

39 Refit the starter motor and tighten the retaining bolts.

2C

4.22a Undo the four bolts and washers . . .

4.22b . . . and remove the centre member from underneath the engine/transmission

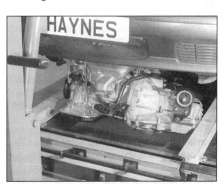

4.27 Carefully lower the engine/transmission downwards and out of position

4.44 Tighten the centre member mounting bolts to the specified torque

40 Position the engine/transmission assembly under the vehicle, then reconnect the hoist and lifting tackle to the engine lifting brackets.

41 With the aid of an assistant, lift the assembly up into the engine compartment, making sure that it clears the surrounding components.

42 Refit the rubbers to the left-hand engine/transmission mounting bracket, ensuring that their pins are correctly seated in the bracket holes. Manoeuvre the mounting into position, then fit the bolts securing it to the transmission and tighten them to the specified torque setting. Insert the through-bolt and nut, tightening it by hand only at this stage.

43 Fit the rubbers to the right-hand body mounting bracket, ensuring that their pins are correctly seated in the bracket holes. Refit the mounting to the top of its bracket, and tighten its retaining bolts to the specified torque setting. Insert the through-bolt and nut, tightening it by hand only at this stage.

44 Ensure that all the mounting rubbers are in position. On 2.0 litre models, refit the stopper ring to the rear engine/transmission mounting. Manoeuvre the centre member into position, aligning it with the engine mountings, and refit its mounting bolts and washers. Tighten the centre member mounting bolts to the specified torque **(see illustration)**.

45 Refit the through-bolt and nut to the rear engine/transmission mounting, tightening it by hand only.

46 Refit the through-bolt and nut to the front engine/transmission mounting. Position the engine/transmission so that the front mounting through-bolt is correctly aligned with the mark made prior to removal, then tighten to the specified torque setting.

47 Rock the engine/transmission to settle it in position, then tighten the front, right- and left-hand mounting through-bolts to their specified torque settings.

48 On 1.6 litre models, refit the mounting bracket to the top of the right-hand mounting, and tighten its retaining bolts to the specified torque.

49 The remainder of the refitting procedure is a direct reversal of the removal sequence, noting the following points:

a) Ensuring that the wiring harness is correctly routed and retained by all the relevant retaining clips, and all connectors are correctly and securely reconnected.
b) Prior to refitting the driveshafts to the transmission, renew the driveshaft oil seals as described in Chapter 7A.
c) Ensure that all coolant hoses are correctly reconnected and securely retained by their retaining clips.
d) Adjust the accelerator cable as described in the relevant Part of Chapter 4.
e) Connect and adjust the clutch cable as described in Chapter 6.
f) Refit and adjust the auxiliary drivebelt(s) as described in Chapter 1.
g) Refill the engine and transmission unit with correct quantity and type of lubricant, as described in the relevant Sections of Chapter 1.
h) Refill the cooling system as described in Chapter 1.
i) On completion, start the engine and check for leaks.

5 Engine and automatic transmission - removal, separation and refitting

Removal

Note: *The engine can be removed from the car only as a complete unit with the transmission; the two are then separated for overhaul. The engine/transmission is lowered out of position, and withdrawn from under the front of the vehicle. To allow adequate clearance underneath the vehicle, there should be at least 75 cm between the front bumper and the ground when the vehicle is raised and supported.*

1 Carry out the operations described in paragraphs 1 to 10 of Section 4.

2 On single-point injection engines, carry out the following operations as described in the Chapter 4B.
a) Remove the air cleaner housing.
b) Depressurise the fuel system, and disconnect the fuel feed and return hoses from the throttle body (plug all openings, to prevent loss of fuel and entry of dirt into the fuel system).
c) Disconnect the accelerator cable.
d) Disconnect the relevant electrical connectors from the throttle body, inlet manifold and associated components.
e) Disconnect the vacuum servo unit hose, coolant hose(s) and all the other relevant/breather hoses from the manifold and associated valves.
f) Remove the inlet manifold support bracket(s).
g) Remove the exhaust front pipe.

3 On multi-point injection engines, carry out the following operations as described in Chapter 4C.

a) Remove the air cleaner inlet duct.
b) Depressurise the fuel system, and disconnect the fuel feed and return hoses from the fuel rail (plug all openings, to prevent loss of fuel and entry of dirt into the fuel system).
c) Disconnect the accelerator cable.
d) Disconnect the relevant electrical connectors from the throttle housing, inlet manifold and associated components. Free the wiring from the manifold, and position it clear of the cylinder head so that it does not hinder removal.
e) Disconnect the vacuum servo unit hose, coolant hose(s) and all the other relevant/breather hoses from the manifold and associated valves.
f) Remove the inlet manifold support bracket(s).
g) Remove the exhaust front pipe.

4 Slacken the retaining clips, and disconnect the heater hoses and all other relevant cooling system hoses from the engine, noting each hose's correct fitted location.

5 On models with air conditioning, unbolt the compressor and position it clear of the engine. Support the weight of the compressor by tying it to the vehicle body, to prevent any excess strain being placed on the compressor lines whilst the engine is removed. **Do not** disconnect the refrigerant lines from the compressor (see the warnings given in Chapter 3).

6 Working as described in Chapter 8, remove both driveshafts.

7 Carry out the following operations as described in Chapter 7B.
a) Disconnect the selector cable from the transmission.
b) Disconnect the kickdown cable from the throttle body/housing.
c) Disconnect the transmission wiring connectors.
d) Disconnect the fluid cooler hoses from the transmission.
e) Disconnect the speedometer cable.

8 Manoeuvre the engine hoist into position, and attach it to the cylinder head using suitable lifting brackets bolted. Raise the hoist until it is supporting the weight of the engine.

9 Slacken and remove the nut and through-bolt from the rear engine/transmission mounting.

10 Slacken and remove the four bolts and washers securing the centre member to the vehicle body, and lower the assembly away from the engine. Recover the stopper ring which is fitted between the rear engine/transmission mounting and its bracket.

11 Unscrew the nut and through-bolt from the right-hand engine/transmission mounting, then undo the retaining bolts and remove the mounting assembly from the engine compartment. Recover the rubbers which are fitted to each side of the body mounting bracket.

12 Slacken and remove the through-bolt

from the left-hand engine/transmission mounting. Undo the three bolts securing the mounting to the transmission, and manoeuvre the mounting out of position. Recover the rubbers from each side of the mounting bracket.

13 Make a final check that any components which would prevent the removal of the engine/transmission from the car have been removed or disconnected. Ensure that components such as the driveshafts are secured so that they cannot be damaged on removal.

14 If available, a low trolley should be placed under the engine/transmission assembly to facilitate its easy removal from under the vehicle. Lower the engine/transmission assembly, making sure that nothing is trapped or damaged. Enlist the help of an assistant during this procedure, as it may be necessary to tilt the assembly slightly to clear the body panels. Great care must be taken to ensure that no components are trapped and damaged during the removal procedure.

15 Withdraw the assembly from under the vehicle.

Separation

16 With the engine/transmission assembly removed, support the assembly on suitable blocks of wood, on a workbench (or failing that, on a clean area of the workshop floor).

17 Unscrew the retaining bolts, and remove the starter motor from the transmission.

18 Undo the retaining bolts, and remove the cover plate from the sump flange to gain access to the torque converter retaining bolts. Slacken and remove the visible bolt then, using a socket and extension bar to rotate the crankshaft pulley, undo the remaining bolts securing the torque converter to the driveplate as they become accessible. There are four bolts in total.

19 To ensure that the torque converter does not fall out as the transmission is removed, secure it in position using a length of metal strip bolted to one of the starter motor bolt holes.

20 Ensure that both engine and transmission are adequately supported, then slacken and remove the bolts securing the transmission housing to the engine. Note the correct fitted positions of each bolt (and, where fitted, the relevant brackets) as they are removed, to use as a reference on refitting.

21 Carefully withdraw the transmission from the engine. If they are loose, remove the locating dowels from the engine or transmission, and keep them in a safe place.

Refitting

22 If the engine and transmission have been separated, perform the operations described below in paragraphs 23 to 28. If not, proceed as described from paragraph 29 onwards.

23 Prior to joining, ensure that the torque converter is correctly engaged with the transmission. This can be checked by

measuring the distance from the converter mounting bolt holes to the transmission mating surface; if the converter is correctly seated, this distance will be at least 15.9 mm.

24 Ensure that the locating dowels are correctly positioned in the engine or transmission.

25 Carefully offer the transmission to the engine, and engage it on the locating dowels. Refit the transmission housing-to-engine bolts, ensuring that all the necessary brackets are correctly positioned, and tighten them to the specified torque settings.

26 Remove the torque converter retaining strap (where fitted) installed prior to removal. Align the torque converter holes with the those in the driveplate, and install the retaining bolts.

27 Tighten the torque converter retaining bolts to the specified torque setting, then refit the cover plate to the sump and securely tighten its retaining bolts.

28 Refit the starter motor and tighten the retaining bolts.

29 Position the engine/transmission assembly under the vehicle, then reconnect the hoist and lifting tackle to the engine lifting brackets.

30 With the aid of an assistant, lift the assembly up into the engine compartment, making sure that it clears the surrounding components.

31 Refit the rubbers to the left-hand engine/transmission mounting bracket, ensuring that their pins are correctly seated in the bracket holes. Manoeuvre the mounting into position, then fit the bolts securing it to the transmission and tighten them to the specified torque setting. Insert the through-bolt and nut, tightening it by hand only at this stage.

32 Fit the rubbers to the right-hand body mounting bracket, ensuring that their pins are correctly seated in the bracket holes. Refit the mounting to the top of its bracket, and tighten its retaining bolts to the specified torque setting. Insert the through-bolt and nut, tightening it by hand only at this stage.

33 Ensure that all the mounting rubbers are in position, and refit the stopper ring to the rear engine/transmission mounting. Manoeuvre the centre member into position, aligning it with the engine mounting, and refit its mounting bolts and washers. Tighten the mounting bolts to the specified torque.

34 Refit the through-bolt and nut to the rear engine/transmission mounting, tightening it by hand only.

35 Rock the engine/transmission to settle it in position, then tighten the front, right- and left-hand mounting through-bolts to their specified torque settings.

36 The remainder of the refitting procedure is a direct reversal of the removal sequence, noting the following points:

a) Ensuring that the wiring harness is correctly routed and retained by all the relevant retaining clips, and all connectors are correctly and securely reconnected.

b) Prior to refitting the driveshafts to the transmission, renew the driveshaft oil seals as described in Chapter 7B.

c) Ensure that all coolant hoses are correctly reconnected and securely retained by their retaining clips.

d) Adjust the accelerator cable as described in the relevant Part of Chapter 4.

e) Connect and adjust the selector and kick-down cables as described in Chapter 7B.

f) Refit and adjust the auxiliary drivebelt(s) as described in Chapter 1.

g) Refill the engine and transmission with correct quantity and type of lubricant, as described in the relevant Sections of Chapter 1.

h) Refill the cooling system as described in Chapter 1.

i) On completion, start the engine and check for leaks.

6 Engine overhaul - dismantling sequence

1 It is much easier to dismantle and work on the engine if it is mounted on a portable engine stand. These stands can often be hired from a tool hire shop. Before the engine is mounted on a stand, the flywheel should be removed, so that the stand bolts can be tightened into the end of the cylinder block/crankcase.

2 If a stand is not available, it is possible to dismantle the engine with it blocked up on a sturdy workbench, or on the floor. Be extra-careful not to tip or drop the engine when working without a stand.

3 If you are going to obtain a reconditioned engine, all the external components must be removed first, to be transferred to the replacement engine (just as they will if you are doing a complete engine overhaul yourself). These components include the following **(see illustrations)**:

a) Alternator, power steering pump and/or air conditioning compressor mounting brackets (as applicable).

b) Distributor, HT leads and spark plugs (Chapters 1 and 5).

c) Coolant pump and thermostat/coolant outlet housing(s) (Chapter 3).

d) The carburettor/fuel injection system components (see relevant Part of Chapter 4).

e) All electrical switches and sensors, and the engine wiring harness.

f) Inlet and exhaust manifolds (see relevant Part of Chapter 4).

g) Oil filter housing - 2.0 litre models only.

h) Fuel pump - carburettor models (Chapter 4A).

i) Engine mountings (Part A or B of this Chapter).

j) Flywheel/driveplate (Part A or B of this Chapter).

Note: When removing the external components from the engine, pay close attention to details that may be helpful or

2C

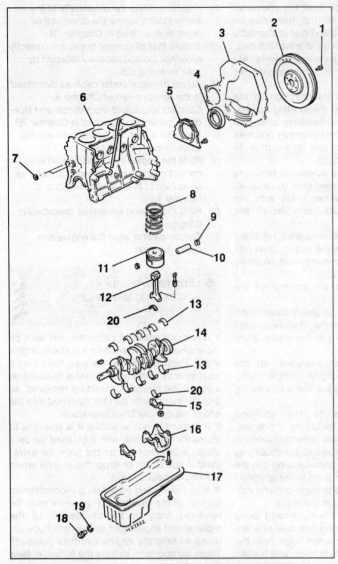

6.3a Exploded view of the cylinder block and associated components - 1.6 litre engine

1 Flywheel retaining bolt
2 Flywheel
3 Cover plate
4 Oil seal
5 Oil seal housing
6 Cylinder block
7 Locating dowels and O-rings
8 Piston rings
9 Circlips
10 Gudgeon pin
11 Piston
12 Connecting rod
13 Main bearing inserts and thrustwashers
14 Crankshaft
15 Connecting rod big-end cap
16 Main bearing caps
17 Sump
18 Drain plug
19 Sealing washer
20 Big-end bearing inserts

6.3b Exploded view of the cylinder block and associated components - 2.0 litre engine

1 Oil seal housing
2 Cylinder block
3 Coolant pump
4 Alternator bracket
5 Timing chain cover
6 O-ring
7 Oil pump pick-up/strainer
8 Flywheel/driveplate
9 Cover plate
10 Main bearing inserts
11 Crankshaft thrustwashers
12 Crankshaft
13 Main bearing caps
14 Main bearing ladder
15 Piston rings
16 Piston
17 Gudgeon pin
18 Circlips
19 Small-end bush
20 Connecting rod and big-end cap
21 Big-end bearing inserts
22 Oil baffle plate
23 Oil baffle plate
24 Aluminium sump
25 Baffle plate
26 Pressed-steel sump
27 Drain plug
28 Cover plate

important during refitting. Note the fitted position of gaskets, seals, spacers, pins, washers, bolts, and other small items.

4 If you are obtaining a "short" engine (which consists of the engine cylinder block/crankcase, crankshaft, pistons and connecting rods all assembled), then the cylinder head, sump, oil pump, and timing chains will have to be removed also.

5 If you are planning a complete overhaul, the engine can be dismantled, and the internal components removed, in the order given below, referring to Part A or B of this Chapter unless otherwise stated.

a) *Inlet and exhaust manifolds (Chapter 4A, 4B or 4C).*
b) *Sump.*
c) *Timing chain(s) and sprockets.*

d) *Cylinder head.*
e) *Flywheel.*
f) *Piston/connecting rod assemblies.*
g) *Crankshaft.*

6 Before beginning the dismantling and overhaul procedures, make sure that you have all of the correct tools necessary. Refer to *"Tools and working facilities"* at the end of this manual for further information.

6.3c On 2.0 litre models, remove the oil filter housing . . .

7 Cylinder head - dismantling

Note: *New and reconditioned cylinder heads are available from the manufacturer, and from engine overhaul specialists. Be aware that some specialist tools are required for the dismantling and inspection procedures, and new components may not be readily available. It may therefore be more practical and economical for the home mechanic to purchase a reconditioned head, rather than dismantle, inspect and recondition the original head.*

1 Remove the cylinder head as described in Part A or B of this Chapter (as applicable).
2 If not already done, remove the inlet and exhaust manifolds with reference to the relevant Part of Chapter 4.
3 On 1.6 litre engines, if not already done, remove the camshaft followers and shims as described in Part A.
4 On 2.0 litre engines, if not already done, remove the camshaft followers and hydraulic adjusters as described in Part B. Undo the retaining bolts, and remove the coolant pipe assembly from the cylinder head.
5 On all models, using a valve spring compressor, compress each valve spring in turn until the split collets can be removed. Release the compressor, and lift off the spring retainer, spring and spring seat. Using a pair of pliers, carefully extract the valve stem seal from the top of the guide **(see illustration)**.

7.8 Place each valve and its associated components in a labelled polythene bag

6.3d . . . and recover the special sealing collars from the cylinder block oil galleries

6 If, when the valve spring compressor is screwed down, the spring retainer refuses to free and expose the split collets, gently tap the top of the tool, directly over the retainer, with a light hammer. This will free the retainer.
7 Withdraw the valve through the combustion chamber.
8 It is essential that each valve is stored together with its collets, retainer, spring, and spring seat. The valves should also be kept in their correct sequence, unless they are so badly worn that they are to be renewed. If they are going to be kept and used again, place each valve assembly in a labelled polythene bag or similar small container **(see illustration)**. Note that No 1 valve is nearest to the timing chain end of the engine.

8 Cylinder head and valves - cleaning and inspection

1 Thorough cleaning of the cylinder head and valve components, followed by a detailed inspection, will enable you to decide how much valve service work must be carried out during the engine overhaul. **Note:** *If the engine has been severely overheated, it is best to assume that the cylinder head is warped - check carefully for signs of this.*

Cleaning

2 Scrape away all traces of old gasket material from the cylinder head.
3 Scrape away the carbon from the

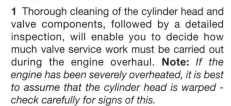

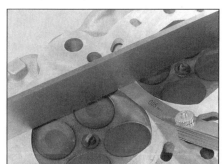

8.6 Using a straight edge and feeler blade to measure cylinder head gasket face distortion

7.5 Pull the valve stem oil seal off the guide using a pair of pliers

combustion chambers and ports, then wash the cylinder head thoroughly with paraffin or a suitable solvent.
4 Scrape off any heavy carbon deposits that may have formed on the valves, then use a power-operated wire brush to remove deposits from the valve heads and stems.

Inspection

Note: *Be sure to perform all the following inspection procedures before concluding that the services of a machine shop or engine overhaul specialist are required. Make a list of all items that require attention.*

Cylinder head

5 Inspect the head very carefully for cracks, evidence of coolant leakage, and other damage. If cracks are found, a new cylinder head should be obtained.
6 Use a straight-edge and feeler blade to check that the cylinder head surface is not distorted **(see illustration)**. If it is, it may be possible to have it machined, provided that the cylinder head is not reduced to less than the specified height.
7 Examine the valve seats in each of the combustion chambers. If they are severely pitted, cracked, or burned, they will need to be renewed or re-cut by an engine overhaul specialist. If they are only slightly pitted, this can be removed by grinding-in the valve heads and seats with fine valve-grinding compound, as described below.
8 Check the valve guides for wear by inserting the relevant valve, and checking for side-to-side motion of the valve. A very small amount of movement is acceptable. If the movement seems excessive, remove the valve. Measure the valve stem diameter (see below), and renew the valve if it is worn. If the valve stem is not worn, the wear must be in the valve guide, and the guide must be renewed. The renewal of valve guides is best carried out by a Nissan dealer or engine overhaul specialist, who will have the necessary tools available.
9 If renewing the valve guides, the valve seats are to be re-cut or re-ground only *after* the guides have been fitted.

Valves

10 Examine the head of each valve for pitting, burning, cracks, and general wear.

2C

8.11 Measuring a valve stem diameter

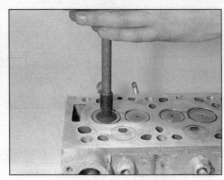

8.14 Grinding-in a valve

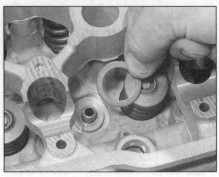

9.1a Fit the spring seat . . .

Check the valve stem for scoring and wear ridges. Rotate the valve, and check for any obvious indication that it is bent. Look for pits and excessive wear on the tip of each valve stem. Renew any valve that shows any such signs of wear or damage.

11 If the valve appears satisfactory at this stage, measure the valve stem diameter at several points using a micrometer **(see illustration)**. Any significant difference in the readings obtained indicates wear of the valve stem. Should any of these conditions be apparent, the valve(s) must be renewed.

12 If the valves are in satisfactory condition, they should be ground (lapped) into their respective seats, to ensure a smooth, gas-tight seal. If the seat is only lightly pitted, or if it has been re-cut, fine grinding compound *only* should be used to produce the required finish. Coarse valve-grinding compound should *not* be used, unless a seat is badly burned or deeply pitted. If this is the case, the cylinder head and valves should be inspected by an expert, to decide whether seat re-cutting, or even the renewal of the valve or seat insert (where possible) is required.

13 Valve grinding is carried out as follows. Place the cylinder head upside-down on a bench.

14 Smear a trace of (the appropriate grade of) valve-grinding compound on the seat face, and press a suction grinding tool onto the valve head. With a semi-rotary action, grind the valve head to its seat, lifting the valve occasionally to redistribute the grinding

compound **(see illustration)**. A light spring placed under the valve head will greatly ease this operation.

15 If coarse grinding compound is being used, work only until a dull, matt even surface is produced on both the valve seat and the valve, then wipe off the used compound, and repeat the process with fine compound. When a smooth unbroken ring of light grey matt finish is produced on both the valve and seat, the grinding operation is complete. *Do not* grind-in the valves any further than absolutely necessary, or the seat will be prematurely sunk into the cylinder head.

16 When all the valves have been ground-in, carefully wash off *all* traces of grinding compound using paraffin or a suitable solvent, before reassembling the cylinder head.

Valve components

17 Examine the valve springs for signs of damage and discoloration. The specified Nissan procedure for checking the condition of valve springs involves measuring the force necessary to compress each spring to a specified height. This is not possible without the use of the Nissan special test equipment, and therefore spring checking must be entrusted to a Nissan dealer. A rough idea of the condition of the spring can be gained by measuring the spring free length, and comparing it to the length given in this Chapter's Specifications.

18 Stand each spring on a flat surface, and position a square alongside the edge of the

spring. Measure the gap between the upper edge of the spring and the square, and compare it to the out-of-square limit given in the Specifications.

19 If any of the springs are damaged, distorted or have lost their tension, obtain a complete new set of springs. It is normal to renew the valve springs as a matter of course if a major overhaul is being carried out.

20 Renew the valve stem oil seals regardless of their apparent condition.

9 Cylinder head - reassembly

1 Refit the spring seat then, working on the first valve, dip the new valve stem seal in fresh engine oil. Carefully locate it over the valve and onto the guide. Take care not to damage the seal as it is passed over the valve stem. Use a suitable socket or metal tube to press the seal firmly onto the guide **(see illustrations)**.

2 Lubricate the stems of the valves, and insert the valves into their original locations **(see illustration)**. If new valves are being fitted, insert them into the locations to which they have been ground.

3 Locate the valve spring on top of its seat, ensuring that the spring is fitted with its closer-pitched coils at the bottom, then refit the spring retainer **(see illustrations)**.

4 Compress the valve spring, and locate the

9.1b . . . and press a new oil seal onto the valve guide using a suitable socket

9.2 Lubricate the valve stem, and slide the valve into its respective guide

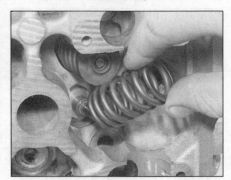

9.3a Fit the spring with its closer-pitched coils at the bottom . . .

9.3b ... and fit the spring retainer

9.4 Install the collets, noting the use of grease to help keep the collets in position

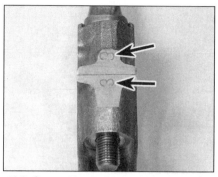

10.3 Connecting rods should be stamped with their relevant cylinder number (arrowed)

split collets in the recess in the valve stem (see illustration). Release the compressor, then repeat the procedure on the remaining valves.

HAYNES HINT *Use a little dab of grease to hold the collets in position on the valve stem while the spring compressor is released.*

5 With all the valves installed, place the cylinder head flat on the bench and, using a hammer and interposed block of wood, tap the end of each valve stem to settle the components.

6 On 2.0 litre models, ensure that the coolant pipe and head mating surfaces are clean and dry. Apply a bead of suitable sealant to the pipe mating surfaces and refit the pipe assembly, tightening its retaining bolts securely.

7 The cylinder head and associated components may now be refitted as described in Part A or B of this Chapter (as applicable).

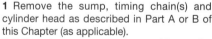

10 Piston/connecting rod assembly - removal

1 Remove the sump, timing chain(s) and cylinder head as described in Part A or B of this Chapter (as applicable).

2 If there is a pronounced wear ridge at the top of any bore, it may be necessary to remove it with a scraper or ridge reamer, to avoid piston damage during removal. Such a ridge indicates excessive wear of the cylinder bore.

3 Each connecting rod and bearing cap should be stamped with its respective cylinder number, No 1 cylinder being at the timing chain end of the engine **(see illustration)**. If no markings are visible, using a hammer and centre-punch, paint or similar, mark each connecting rod and big-end bearing cap with its respective cylinder number on the flat machined surface provided.

4 Turn the crankshaft to bring pistons 1 and 4 to BDC (bottom dead centre).

5 Unscrew the nuts from No 1 piston big-end bearing cap. Take off the cap, and recover the bottom half bearing shell **(see illustration)**. If the bearing shells are to be re-used, tape the cap and the shell together.

6 To prevent the possibility of damage to the crankshaft bearing journals, tape over the connecting rod bolt threads.

7 Using a hammer handle, push the piston up through the bore, and remove it from the top of the cylinder block. Recover the bearing shell, and tape it to the connecting rod for safe-keeping.

8 Loosely refit the big-end cap to the connecting rod, and secure with the nuts - this will help to keep the components in their correct order.

9 Remove No 4 piston assembly in the same way.

10 Turn the crankshaft through 180° to bring pistons 2 and 3 to BDC (bottom dead centre), and remove them in the same way.

11 Crankshaft - removal

1 Remove the sump, timing chain(s) and flywheel as described in Part A or B of this Chapter (as applicable).

2 Remove the pistons and connecting rods,

as described in Section 10. **Note:** *If no work is to be done on the pistons and connecting rods, there is no need to remove the cylinder head, or to push the pistons out of the cylinder bores. The pistons should just be pushed far enough up the bores that they are positioned clear of the crankshaft journals.*

3 Check the crankshaft endfloat as described in Section 14, then proceed as follows.

1.6 litre engines

4 Undo the retaining bolts, and remove the rear oil seal housing from the left-hand (flywheel) end of the cylinder block. If the locating dowels are a loose fit, remove them and store them with the housing for safe-keeping.

5 The main bearing caps should be numbered 1 to 5 from the timing chain end of the engine **(see illustration)**. If not, using white paint or a suitable marker pen, mark each cap in some way as to indicate its correct fitted orientation and position. This will avoid the possibility of installing the caps in the wrong positions and/or the wrong way around on refitting.

6 Working in the **reverse** of the sequence shown in illustration 18.27, slacken the main bearing cap retaining bolts by a turn at a time. Once all bolts are loose, unscrew and remove them from the cylinder block.

7 Withdraw the bearing caps, and recover the lower main bearing shells. Tape each shell to its respective cap for safe-keeping.

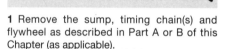

10.5 Removing a big-end cap and shell (2.0 litre engine shown)

11.5 Main bearing cap identification numbers (arrowed) - 1.6 litre engine

2C

11.12 Removing the main bearing ladder - 2.0 litre engine

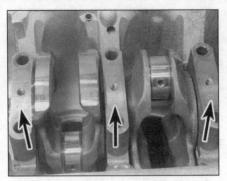

11.13 On 2.0 litre engines, the main bearing caps should be numbered 1 to 5 (arrowed)

6 If the castings are not very dirty, you can do an adequate cleaning job with hot (as hot as you can stand!), soapy water and a stiff brush. Take plenty of time, and do a thorough job. Regardless of the cleaning method used, be sure to clean all oil holes and galleries very thoroughly, and to dry all components well. Protect the cylinder bores as described above, to prevent rusting.

7 All threaded holes must be clean, to ensure accurate torque readings during reassembly. To clean the threads, run the correct-size tap into each of the holes to remove rust, corrosion, thread sealant or sludge, and to restore damaged threads **(see illustration)**. If possible, use compressed air to clear the holes of debris produced by this operation.

11.15 Lifting the crankshaft out of position

8 Carefully lift out the crankshaft, taking care not to displace the upper main bearing shells.
9 Recover the upper bearing shells from the cylinder block, and tape them to their respective caps for safe-keeping. Remove the thrustwasher halves from the side of No 3 main bearing, and store them with the bearing cap.

2.0 litre models

10 Undo the retaining bolts, and remove the rear oil seal housing from the left-hand (flywheel) end of the cylinder block. If the locating dowels are a loose fit, remove them and store them with the housing for safe-keeping.
11 Working in the **reverse** of the sequence shown in illustration 18.35a, slacken the main bearing cap retaining bolts by a turn at a time. Once all bolts are loose, unscrew and remove them from the cylinder block.
12 Lift the main bearing ladder off the main bearing caps, noting which way around it is fitted **(see illustration)**.
13 The main bearing caps should be numbered 1 to 5 from the timing chain end of the engine **(see illustration)**. If not, using white paint or a suitable marker pen, mark each cap in some way as to indicate its correct fitted orientation and position. This will avoid the possibility of installing the caps in the wrong positions and/or the wrong way around on refitting.
14 Withdraw the bearing caps, and recover

the lower main bearing shells. Tape each shell to its respective cap for safe-keeping.
15 Carefully lift out the crankshaft, taking care not to displace the upper main bearing shells **(see illustration)**.
16 Recover the upper bearing shells from the cylinder block, and tape them to their respective caps for safe-keeping. Remove the thrustwasher halves from the side of No 3 main bearing, and store them with the bearing cap.

12 Cylinder block/crankcase - cleaning and inspection

Cleaning

1 Remove all external components and electrical switches/sensors from the block. For complete cleaning, the core plugs should ideally be removed. Drill a small hole in the plugs, then insert a self-tapping screw into the hole. Pull out the plugs by pulling on the screw with a pair of grips, or by using a slide hammer.
2 Scrape all traces of sealant from the cylinder block/crankcase, and from the main bearing ladder (where fitted), taking care not to damage the gasket/sealing surfaces.
3 Remove all oil gallery plugs (where fitted). The plugs are usually very tight - they may have to be drilled out, and the holes re-tapped. Use new plugs when the engine is reassembled.
4 If any of the castings are extremely dirty, all should be steam-cleaned.
5 After the castings are returned, clean all oil holes and oil galleries one more time. Flush all internal passages with warm water until the water runs clear. Dry thoroughly, and apply a light film of oil to all mating surfaces and the cylinder bores, to prevent rusting. If you have access to compressed air, use it to speed up the drying process, and to blow out all the oil holes and galleries.

 Warning: Wear eye protection when using compressed air!

 A good alternative is to inject an aerosol water-dispersant lubricant into each hole, using the long tube usually supplied.

⚠ **Warning: Wear eye protection when cleaning out these holes in this way!**

8 Apply suitable sealant to the new oil gallery plugs, and insert them into the holes in the block. Tighten them securely.
9 If the engine is not going to be reassembled right away, cover it with a large plastic bag to keep it clean; protect all mating surfaces and the cylinder bores as described above, to prevent rusting.

Inspection

10 Visually check the casting for cracks and corrosion. Look for stripped threads in the threaded holes. If there has been any history of internal water leakage, it may be worthwhile having an engine overhaul specialist check the cylinder block/crankcase with special equipment. If defects are found, have them repaired if possible, or obtain a new block.
11 Check each cylinder bore for scuffing and scoring. Check for signs of a wear ridge at the top of the cylinder, indicating that the bore is excessively worn.
12 Check the bore of each cylinder for scuffing and scoring.

12.7 Cleaning a cylinder block threaded hole using a suitable tap

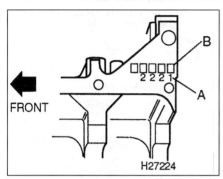

12.13a On 1.6 litre models, cylinder bore grades can be determined from the four-digit code (A) stamped on the base of the block. The five-digit code (B) is for the main bearing bores

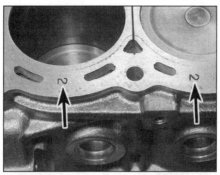

12.13b On 2.0 litre models, the cylinder bore grades (arrowed) are stamped on the cylinder head mating surface

13.2 Using a feeler blade to ease piston ring removal

13 Measure the diameter of each cylinder bore 10 mm from the top of the bore, both parallel to the crankshaft axis and at right-angles to it. Repeat the procedure measuring the bore diameter 60 mm from the top, and then 100 mm from the top, so that a total of six measurements are taken. Using the measurements obtained, calculate the cylinder taper and cylinder out-of-round dimensions. **Note:** *The cylinder bore grades are stamped on the cylinder block. On 1.6 litre engines, the grades are stamped on the flywheel end of the cylinder block base; there are two sets of codes - the four-digit code is for the cylinder bores, the first number in the sequence is for No 1 cylinder and the last for No 4 (the five-digit code is for the cylinder block main bearing bores - see Section 18). On 2.0 litre engines, the grades are stamped on the cylinder block upper gasket face, at the front of each bore* **(see illustrations).**

14 Check the pistons and rings as described in Section 13. The piston-to-bore clearance can be calculated by subtracting the piston diameter from the cylinder bore diameter measurement.

15 Compare all results with the Specifications at the beginning of this Chapter. If any measurement exceeds the service limit specified, the cylinder must be rebored, where possible, to the next oversize and new pistons fitted, or the cylinder block must be renewed. Seek the advice of an engine overhaul specialist as to the best course of action. On 1.6 litre engines, pistons are available in two oversizes - 0.5 mm and 1.0 mm; on 2.0 litre engines, pistons are available in only one oversize - 0.2 mm.

16 If the cylinder bores and pistons are in reasonably good condition, and not worn to the specified limits, and if the piston-to-bore clearances can be maintained properly, then it may only be necessary to renew the piston rings.

17 If this is the case, the bores should be honed, to allow the new rings to bed in correctly and provide the best possible seal. The conventional type of hone has spring-loaded stones, and is used with a power drill.

You will also need some paraffin or honing oil and rags. The hone should be moved up and down the bore to produce a cross-hatch pattern, and plenty of honing oil should be used. Ideally the cross-hatch lines should intersect at approximately a 60° angle. Do not take off more material than is necessary to produce the required finish. If new pistons are being fitted, the piston manufacturers may specify a finish with a different angle, so their instructions should be followed. Do not withdraw the hone from the bore while it is still being turned - stop it first. After honing a bore, wipe out all traces of the honing oil. If equipment of this type is not available, or if you are not sure whether you are competent to undertake the task yourself, an engine overhaul specialist will carry out the work at moderate cost.

13 Piston/connecting rod assembly - inspection

1 Before the inspection process can begin, the piston/connecting rod assemblies must be cleaned, and the original piston rings removed from the pistons.

2 Carefully expand the old rings over the top of the pistons. The use of two or three old feeler blades will be helpful in preventing the rings dropping into empty grooves **(see illustration).** Be careful not to scratch the piston with the ends of the ring. The rings are brittle, and will snap if they are spread too far. They're also very sharp - protect your hands and fingers. Always remove the rings from the top of the piston. Keep each set of rings with its piston if the old rings are to be re-used.

3 Scrape away all traces of carbon from the top of the piston. A hand-held wire brush (or a piece of fine emery cloth) can be used, once the majority of the deposits have been scraped away.

4 Remove the carbon from the ring grooves in the piston, using an old ring. Break the ring in half to do this (be careful not to cut your fingers - piston rings are sharp). Be careful to remove only the carbon deposits - do not

remove any metal, and do not nick or scratch the sides of the ring grooves.

5 Once the deposits have been removed, clean the piston/connecting rod assembly with paraffin or a suitable solvent, and dry thoroughly. Make sure that the oil return holes in the ring grooves are clear.

6 Using a micrometer, measure the piston diameter at right-angles to the gudgeon pin axis (at the specified distance up from the bottom of the skirt), and compare the results with the Specifications at the beginning of this Chapter. The piston size grade is stamped onto the piston crown. Renew any piston which has worn beyond its specified limits.

7 Check the ring-to-groove clearance by inserting each ring from the outside, together with a feeler blade between the ring's top surface and the piston land. If the ring-to-groove clearance is excessive, renew the rings and recheck the clearance. If the clearance is still excessive, even with new piston rings, then the piston must be renewed.

8 Check the ring end gaps by inserting each ring into the cylinder bore and pushing it in with the piston crown to ensure that it is square in the bore. Push the ring down into the bore until the piston skirt is level with the block mating surface, then withdraw the piston. Using feeler blades, measure the piston ring end gap. If the ring end gap is excessive, renew the rings and repeat the checking procedure. If the clearance is still excessive, even with new piston rings, then the cylinder bores must be rebored/renewed (see Section 12).

9 Carefully inspect each piston for cracks around the skirt, around the gudgeon pin holes, and at the piston ring "lands" (between the ring grooves).

10 Look for scoring and scuffing on the piston skirt, holes in the piston crown, or burned areas at the edge of the crown. If the skirt is scored or scuffed, the engine may have been suffering from overheating, and/or abnormal combustion which caused excessively-high operating temperatures. The cooling and lubrication systems should be checked thoroughly. Scorch marks on the

2C

sides of the pistons show that blow-by has occurred. A hole in the piston crown, or burned areas at the edge of the piston crown, indicates that abnormal combustion (pre-ignition, knocking, or detonation) has been occurring. If any of the above problems exist, the causes must be investigated and corrected, or the damage will occur again. The causes may include incorrect ignition timing, inlet air leaks, or a faulty injector (as applicable).

11 Corrosion of the piston, in the form of pitting, indicates that coolant has been leaking into the combustion chamber and/or the crankcase. Again, the cause must be corrected, or the problem may persist in the rebuilt engine.

12 Examine each connecting rod carefully for signs of damage, such as cracks around the big-end and small-end bearings. Check that the rod is not bent or distorted. Damage is highly unlikely, unless the engine has been seized or badly overheated. Detailed checking of the connecting rod assembly can only be carried out by a Nissan dealer or engine repair specialist with the necessary equipment.

13 If necessary, the piston and connecting rods can be separated and reassembled as follows.

14 Using a small flat-bladed screwdriver, prise out the circlips, and push out the gudgeon pin **(see illustration)**. If necessary, support the piston, and tap the pin out using a suitable hammer and punch, taking great care not to mark the piston/connecting rod bores.

Gudgeon pin removal will be considerably eased if the piston is warmed (to approximately 60 to 70ºC) first. Warm the piston by submerging it in a pan of hot water, then remove the assembly and press the gudgeon pin out, taking great care not to burn your hands.

Identify the piston, gudgeon pin and rod to ensure correct reassembly. Discard the circlips - new ones *must* be used on refitting.

15 Examine the gudgeon pin, piston bore and connecting rod small-end bearing for signs of wear or damage. If the necessary measuring equipment is available, the amount of wear can be assessed by direct measurement, and the piston-to-gudgeon pin, and gudgeon pin-to-small-end clearances can be calculated.

16 If the gudgeon pin and connecting rod small-end bush are worn or the specified clearance is exceeded, this can be cured by renewing both the pin and bush. Bush renewal, however, is a specialist job - press facilities are required, and the new bush must be reamed accurately.

17 If the gudgeon pin-to-piston clearance is greatly exceeded, both the piston and pin

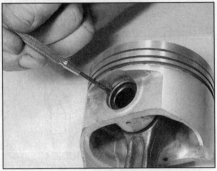

13.14 Prise out the circlips, then press the gudgeon pin out of the piston

should be renewed as a matched pair. Note that this clearance is not as critical as the gudgeon pin-to-small-end clearance, since the pin is retained by circlips.

18 The connecting rods themselves should not need renewal, unless seizure or some other major mechanical failure has occurred. Check the alignment of the connecting rods visually, and if the rods are not straight, take them to an engine overhaul specialist for a more detailed check.

19 Examine all components, and obtain any new parts from your Nissan dealer.

20 Position the piston so that the front marking on the piston crown (either in the form of an arrow or a dot) is positioned correctly in relation to the oil hole in the connecting rod shaft **(see illustrations)**. With the piston and rod correctly mated, the piston front marking will face towards the timing chain end of the engine, and the connecting rod oil hole will face the rear of the cylinder block.

21 Apply a smear of clean engine oil to the gudgeon pin. Slide it into the piston and through the connecting rod small-end **(see illustration)**. **Note:** *Gudgeon pin installation will be greatly eased if the piston is first warmed (see paragraph 14).* If necessary, tap the pin into position using a hammer and suitable punch, whilst ensuring that the piston is securely supported.

22 Check that the piston pivots freely on the rod, then secure the gudgeon pin in position

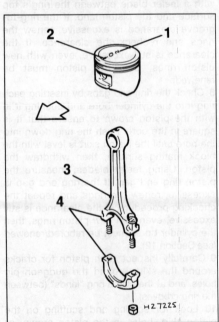

13.20a Correct connecting rod/piston fitting orientation - 1.6 litre models

1 *Piston grade number*
2 *Front marking (arrowed)*
3 *Connecting rod oil hole*
4 *Connecting rod cylinder number marking (maybe on opposite side of rod)*

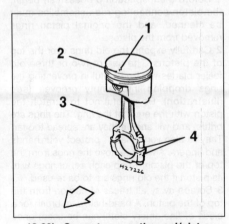

13.20b Correct connecting rod/piston fitting orientation - 2.0 litre models

1 *Piston grade number*
2 *Front marking (arrowed)*
3 *Connecting rod oil hole*
4 *Connecting rod cylinder number marking (maybe on opposite side of rod)*

13.21 Ensure that the piston and connecting rod are correctly mated, then press the gudgeon pin into position . . .

13.22 . . . and secure it in position with two new circlips

14.2 Using a dial gauge to measure crankshaft endfloat

14.3 Using a feeler blade (arrowed) to measure crankshaft endfloat

with two new circlips **(see illustration)**. Ensure that each circlip is correctly located in its groove in the piston.

14 Crankshaft - inspection

Checking crankshaft endfloat

1 If the crankshaft endfloat is to be checked, this must be done when the crankshaft is still installed in the cylinder block/crankcase, but is free to move (see Section 11).

2 Check the endfloat using a dial gauge in contact with the end of the crankshaft. Push the crankshaft fully one way, and then zero the gauge. Push the crankshaft fully the other way, and check the endfloat **(see illustration)**. The result can be compared with the specified amount, and will give an indication as to whether new thrustwashers are required.

3 If a dial gauge is not available, feeler blades can be used. First push the crankshaft fully towards the flywheel end of the engine, then use feeler blades to measure the gap between the No 4 crankpin web and No 3 main bearing thrustwasher **(see illustration)**.

Inspection

4 Clean the crankshaft using paraffin or a suitable solvent, and dry it, preferably with compressed air if available.

⚠ *Warning: Wear eye protection when using compressed air! Be sure to clean the oil holes with a pipe cleaner or similar probe, to ensure that they are not obstructed.*

5 Check the main and big-end bearing journals for uneven wear, scoring, pitting and cracking.

6 Big-end bearing wear is accompanied by distinct metallic knocking when the engine is running (particularly noticeable when the engine is pulling from low speed) and some loss of oil pressure.

7 Main bearing wear is accompanied by severe engine vibration and rumble - getting progressively worse as engine speed increases - and again by loss of oil pressure.

8 Check the bearing journal for roughness by running a finger lightly over the bearing surface. Any roughness (which will be accompanied by obvious bearing wear) indicates that the crankshaft requires regrinding (where possible) or renewal.

9 Crankshaft run-out can be checked by supporting each end of the crankshaft on V-blocks, and measuring any run-out at the centre of the shaft using a dial gauge. If the run-out exceeds the specified limit, a new crankshaft will be required.

10 If the crankshaft has been reground, check for burrs around the crankshaft oil holes (the holes are usually chamfered, so burrs should not be a problem unless regrinding has been carried out carelessly). Remove any burrs with a fine file or scraper, and thoroughly clean the oil holes as described previously.

11 Using a micrometer, measure the diameter of the main and big-end bearing journals, and compare the results with the Specifications **(see illustrations)**. By measuring the diameter at a number of points around each journal's circumference, you will be able to determine whether or not the journal is out-of-round. Take the measurement at each end of the journal, near the webs, to determine if the journal is tapered. Compare the results obtained with those given in the Specifications.

12 Check the oil seal contact surfaces at each end of the crankshaft for wear and

damage. If the seal has worn a deep groove in the surface of the crankshaft, consult an engine overhaul specialist. Repair may be possible, but otherwise a new crankshaft will be required.

13 Nissan produce undersize bearing shells for both the main bearings and big-end bearings. On the 1.6 litre engine, there are two undersizes of main bearing shells (0.25 and 0.50 mm) and three undersizes of big-end bearing shells (0.08, 0.12 and 0.25 mm). On the 2.0 litre engine, there is only one undersize of main bearing shell (0.25 mm) but there are three undersizes of big-end bearing shell available (0.08, 0.12 and 0.25 mm). Refer to your Nissan dealer for further information on parts availability. If undersize bearing shells are available, and the crankshaft has worn beyond the specified limits, providing that the crankshaft journals have not already been reground, it may be possible to have the crankshaft reconditioned, and to fit the undersize shells. Seek the advice of your Nissan dealer or engine specialist on the best course of action.

2C

15 Main and big-end bearings - inspection

1 Even though the main and big-end bearings should be renewed during the engine overhaul, the old bearings should be retained

14.11a Using a micrometer to measure a crankshaft main bearing journal diameter

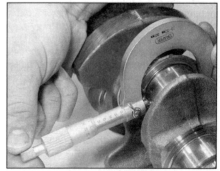

14.11b Using a micrometer to measure a crankshaft big-end bearing journal diameter

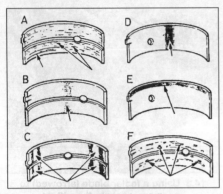

15.2 Typical bearing failures

A Scratched by dirt; dirt embedded in bearing material
B Lack of oil; overlay wiped out
C Improper seating; bright (polished) sections
D Tapered journal; overlay gone from entire surface
E Radius ride
F Fatigue failure; craters or pockets

for close examination, as they may reveal valuable information about the condition of the engine. The bearing shells are graded by thickness, the grade of each shell being indicated by the colour code marked on it.

2 Bearing failure can occur due to lack of lubrication, the presence of dirt or other foreign particles, overloading the engine, or corrosion. Regardless of the cause of bearing failure, the cause must be corrected (where applicable) before the engine is reassembled, to prevent it from happening again **(see illustration)**.

3 When examining the bearing shells, remove them from the cylinder block/crankcase, the main bearing caps, the connecting rods and the connecting rod big-end bearing caps. Lay them out on a clean surface in the same general position as their location in the engine. This will enable you to match any bearing problems with the corresponding crankshaft journal. *Do not* touch any shell's bearing surface with your fingers while checking it, or the delicate surface may be scratched.

4 Dirt and other foreign matter gets into the engine in a variety of ways. It may be left in the engine during assembly, or it may pass through filters or the crankcase ventilation system. It may get into the oil, and from there into the bearings. Metal chips from machining operations and normal engine wear are often present. Abrasives are sometimes left in engine components after reconditioning, especially when parts are not thoroughly cleaned using the proper cleaning methods. Whatever the source, these foreign objects often end up embedded in the soft bearing material, and are easily recognised. Large particles will not embed in the bearing, and will score or gouge the bearing and journal. The best prevention for this cause of bearing

failure is to clean all parts thoroughly, and keep everything spotlessly-clean during engine assembly. Frequent and regular engine oil and filter changes are also recommended.

5 Lack of lubrication (or lubrication breakdown) has a number of interrelated causes. Excessive heat (which thins the oil), overloading (which squeezes the oil from the bearing face) and oil leakage (from excessive bearing clearances, worn oil pump or high engine speeds) all contribute to lubrication breakdown. Blocked oil passages, which usually are the result of misaligned oil holes in a bearing shell, will also oil-starve a bearing, and destroy it. When lack of lubrication is the cause of bearing failure, the bearing material is wiped or extruded from the steel backing of the bearing. Temperatures may increase to the point where the steel backing turns blue from overheating.

6 Driving habits can have a definite effect on bearing life. Full-throttle, low-speed operation (labouring the engine) puts very high loads on bearings, tending to squeeze out the oil film. These loads cause the bearings to flex, which produces fine cracks in the bearing face (fatigue failure). Eventually, the bearing material will loosen in pieces, and tear away from the steel backing.

7 Short-distance driving leads to corrosion of bearings, because insufficient engine heat is produced to drive off the condensed water and corrosive gases. These products collect in the engine oil, forming acid and sludge. As the oil is carried to the engine bearings, the acid attacks and corrodes the bearing material.

8 Incorrect bearing installation during engine assembly will lead to bearing failure as well. Tight-fitting bearings leave insufficient bearing running clearance, and will result in oil starvation. Dirt or foreign particles trapped behind a bearing shell result in high spots on the bearing, which lead to failure.

9 *Do not* touch any shell's bearing surface with your fingers during reassembly; there is a risk of scratching the delicate surface, or of depositing particles of dirt on it.

10 As mentioned at the beginning of this Section, the bearing shells should be renewed as a matter of course during engine overhaul; to do otherwise is false economy. Refer to Section 17 for details of bearing shell selection.

16 Engine overhaul - reassembly sequence

1 Before reassembly begins, ensure that all new parts have been obtained, and that all necessary tools are available. Read through the entire procedure, to familiarise yourself with the work involved, and to ensure that all items necessary for reassembly of the engine are at hand. In addition to all normal tools and materials, thread-locking compound will be

needed. A suitable tube of liquid sealant will also be required for the joint faces that are fitted without gaskets; it is recommended that Nissan's Genuine Liquid Gasket (available from your Nissan dealer) is used.

2 In order to save time and avoid problems, engine reassembly can be carried out in the following order:

a) Crankshaft (Section 18).
b) Piston/connecting rod assemblies (Section 19).
c) Cylinder head (See Part A or B as applicable).
d) Timing chain(s) and cover (See Part A or B - as applicable).
e) Sump (See Part A or B - as applicable).
f) Flywheel (See Part A or B - as applicable).
g) Engine external components.

3 At this stage, all engine components should be absolutely clean and dry, with all faults repaired. The components should be laid out (or in individual containers) on a completely clean work surface.

17 Piston rings - refitting

1 Before fitting new piston rings, the ring end gaps must be checked as follows.

2 Lay out the piston/connecting rod assemblies and the new piston ring sets, so that the ring sets will be matched with the same piston and cylinder during the end gap measurement and subsequent engine reassembly.

3 Insert the top ring into the first cylinder, and push it down the bore using the top of the piston. This will ensure that the ring remains square with the cylinder walls. Push the ring down into the bore until the piston skirt is level with the block mating surface, then withdraw the piston.

4 Measure the end gap using feeler gauges, and compare the measurements with the figures given in the Specifications **(see illustration)**.

5 If the gap is too small (unlikely if genuine Nissan parts are used), it must be enlarged, or the ring ends may contact each other during engine operation, causing serious damage. Ideally, new piston rings providing the correct

17.4 Measuring a piston ring end gap

17.9a Fit the oil control ring expander . . .

17.9b . . . then install the side rails as described in text

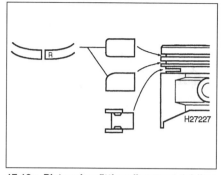

17.10a Piston ring fitting diagram - 1.6 litre engine

end gap should be fitted. As a last resort, the end gap can be increased by filing the ring ends very carefully with a fine file. Mount the file in a vice with soft jaws, slip the ring over the file with the ends contacting the file face, and slowly move the ring to remove material from the ends. Take care, as piston rings are sharp, and are easily broken.

6 With new piston rings, it is unlikely that the end gap will be too large. If the gaps are too large, check that you have the correct rings for your engine and for the particular cylinder bore size.

7 Repeat the checking procedure for each ring in the first cylinder, and then for the rings in the remaining cylinders. Remember to keep rings, pistons and cylinders matched up.

8 Once the ring end gaps have been checked and if necessary corrected, the rings can be fitted to the pistons. **Note:** *Always follow any instructions supplied with the new piston ring sets - different manufacturers may specify different procedures. Do not mix up the top and second compression rings, as they have different cross-sections.*

9 The oil control ring (lowest on the piston) is installed first. It is composed of three separate components. Slip the expander into the groove, then install the upper side rail into the groove between the expander and the ring land, then install the lower side rail in the same manner **(see illustrations)**.

10 Install the second ring next. **Note:** *The*

second ring and top ring are different, and can be identified by their cross-sections. Making sure the ring is the correct way up (on 2.0 litre models, the ring identification marking should be facing upwards), fit the ring into the middle groove on the piston, taking care not to expand the ring any more than is necessary **(see illustrations)**.

11 Install the top ring in the same way, making sure the ring is the correct way up. Where the ring is symmetrical, fit it with its identification marking facing upwards.

12 With all the rings in position on the piston, space the ring end gaps as shown **(see illustration)**.

13 Repeat the above procedure for the remaining pistons and rings.

---

18 Crankshaft - refitting and main bearing running clearance check

Selection of new bearing shells

Note: *This information applies only to standard size bearing shells. Undersize shells are not graded.*

1 New bearing shells are selected using the identification marks on the crankshaft and cylinder block.

2 The crankshaft markings are stamped on the side of No 1 cylinder crankweb (at the

17.10b Piston ring fitting diagram - 2.0 litre engine

1 SR20DE engine
2 SR20Di and SR20De engines

timing chain end of the crankshaft). The five-digit code refers to the main bearing journal diameters - the first number in the sequence is for No 1 bearing journal, and the last for No 5 journal **(see illustration)**. **Note:** *On some models, there is also a four-digit code stamped on the web; these numbers are for the big-end bearing (crankpin) journals (see Section 19).*

3 The cylinder block markings are stamped on the flywheel end of the cylinder block base. On 1.6 litre engines, there are two sets of codes; the five-digit code is for the main bearing bores - the first number in the sequence is for No 1 main bearing journal,

2C

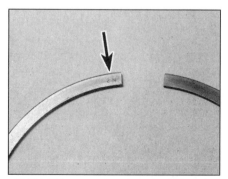

17.10c Where necessary, ensure that the rings are installed with their identification marking (arrowed) uppermost

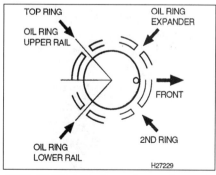

17.12 Position the piston ring end gaps as shown

18.2 Crankshaft main bearing journal codes (1) and big-end bearing journal codes (2)

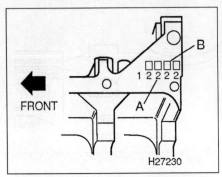

18.3a On 1.6 litre models, cylinder block main bearing bore grades can be determined from the five-digit code (A) stamped on the base of the block. The four-digit code (B) is for the cylinder bore grades

18.3b On 2.0 litre models, the cylinder block main bearing bore grades are stamped on the base of the block (arrowed)

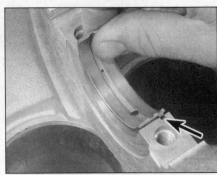

18.6a Fit the upper grooved bearing shells, aligning their tabs with the crankcase cut-outs (arrowed) . . .

and the last for No 5 journal (the four-digit code is for the cylinder bore size grades). On 2.0 litre engines, there is only one five-digit code, the first number in the sequence is for No 1 bearing journal, and the last for No 5 journal (see illustrations).

4 Obtain the identification number of both the relevant crankshaft journal and the cylinder block bearing bore, and select the correct grade of main bearing shell required for each journal, using the relevant following table. The grade of each shell is indicated by a dab of paint on the side of the shell.

Crankshaft code	Block code	Bearing shell grade
1.6 litre engine		
0	0	Black
0	1	Brown
0	2	Green
1	0	Brown
1	1	Green
1	2	Yellow
2	0	Green
2	1	Yellow
2	2	Blue
2.0 litre engine		
0	0	Black
0	1	Brown
0	2	Green
0	3	Yellow
1	0	Brown
1	1	Green
1	2	Yellow
1	3	Blue
2	0	Green
2	1	Yellow
2	2	Blue
2	3	Pink
3	0	Yellow
3	1	Blue
3	2	Pink
3	3	White (or no colour)

Main bearing running clearance check

5 Clean the backs of the bearing shells, and the bearing locations in both the cylinder block and the main bearing caps.

6 Press the bearing shells into their locations, ensuring that the tab on each shell engages in the notch in the cylinder block/crankcase or main bearing ladder location. Take care not to touch any shell's bearing surface with your fingers. Note that all the upper bearing shells are grooved, and have oil holes in them; the lower shells are plain (see illustrations). If the original bearing shells are being used for the check, ensure that they are refitted in their original locations. The clearance can be checked in either of two ways.

7 One method (which will be difficult to achieve without a range of internal micrometers or internal/external expanding calipers) is to refit the main bearing caps/ladder (as applicable) to the cylinder block, with the bearing shells in place. With the casting retaining bolts correctly tightened, measure the internal diameter of each assembled pair of bearing shells. If the diameter of each corresponding crankshaft journal is measured and then subtracted from the bearing internal diameter, the result will be the main bearing running clearance.

8 The second (and more accurate) method is to use an American product called Plastigage.

This consists of a fine thread of perfectly-round plastic, which is compressed between the bearing shell and the journal. When the shell is removed, the plastic is deformed, and can be measured with a special card gauge supplied with the kit. The running clearance is determined from this gauge. Plastigage should be available from your Nissan dealer; otherwise, enquiries at one of the larger specialist motor factors should produce the name of a stockist in your area. The procedure for using Plastigage is as follows.

9 With the main bearing upper shells in place, carefully lay the crankshaft in position. Do not use any lubricant; the crankshaft journals and bearing shells must be perfectly clean and dry.

10 Cut several lengths of the appropriate-size Plastigage (they should be slightly shorter than the width of the main bearings), and place one length on each crankshaft journal axis (see illustration).

11 On 1.6 litre engines, with the main bearing lower shells in position, refit the main bearing caps using the identification markings to ensure each cap is fitted correctly. Refit the main bearing cap bolts and, working in the sequence shown in illustration 18.27, tighten them evenly and progressively to the specified torque setting. Take care not to disturb the Plastigage, and *do not* rotate the crankshaft at any time during this operation.

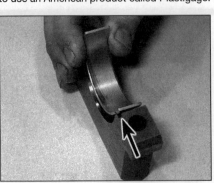

18.6b . . . and fit the lower plain shells to the caps, also aligning their tabs with the cap cut-outs (arrowed)

18.10 Plastigage in place on a crankshaft journal main bearing

18.15 Measuring the width of the deformed Plastigage using the scale on the card provided

18.21 Lubricate the main bearing shells with clean engine oil . . .

18.22 . . . then fit the thrustwasher halves, making sure that their grooved faces are facing away from the crankcase

12 On 2.0 litre engines, with the main bearing lower shells in position, refit the main bearing caps using the identification markings to ensure each cap is fitted correctly. Fit the main bearing ladder casting, then install the retaining bolts and tighten them as described in paragraphs 35 and 36. Take care not to disturb the Plastigage, and *do not* rotate the crankshaft at any time during this operation.

13 On all models, working in **reverse** to the sequence shown in illustration 18.27 or 18.35a (as applicable), progressively slacken the bearing cap retaining bolts by one turn at a time. Once all bolts are loose, unscrew them and remove them from the cylinder block.

14 Remove the main bearing ladder/caps (as applicable), again taking great care not to disturb the Plastigage, nor to rotate the crankshaft.

15 Compare the width of the crushed Plastigage on each journal to the scale printed on the Plastigage envelope, to obtain the main bearing running clearance. Compare the clearance measured with that given in the Specifications at the start of this Chapter **(see illustration)**.

16 If the clearance is not as specified, the bearing shells may be the wrong size (or excessively worn, if the original shells are being re-used). Before deciding that different-size shells are required, make sure that no dirt or oil was trapped between the bearing shells and the main bearing ladder or block when the clearance was measured. If the Plastigage was wider at one end than at the other, the crankshaft journal may be tapered.

17 If the clearance is not as specified with the original bearing shells, repeat the checking procedure using new bearing shells. If the clearance is not as specified even with new bearing shells, then seek the advice of a Nissan dealer or suitable engine overhaul specialist. They will be able to advise you on the best course of action, and whether or not it will be necessary to have the crankshaft journals reground and fit undersize shells.

18 Where necessary, obtain the required grades of bearing shell, and repeat the running clearance checking procedure as described above.

19 On completion, carefully scrape away all traces of the Plastigage material from the crankshaft and bearing shells. Use your fingernail, or a wooden or plastic scraper which is unlikely to score the bearing surfaces.

Final crankshaft refitting

1.6 litre engine

20 Carefully lift the crankshaft out of the cylinder block once more.

21 Place the bearing shells in their locations as described in paragraph 5 and 6. If new shells are being fitted, ensure that all traces of protective grease are cleaned off using paraffin. Wipe dry the shells and connecting rods with a lint-free cloth. Liberally lubricate each bearing shell in the cylinder block/crankcase with clean engine oil **(see illustration)**.

22 Using a little grease, stick the upper thrustwashers to each side of the No 3 main bearing upper location; ensure that the oilway grooves on each thrustwasher face outwards (away from the cylinder block) **(see illustration)**.

23 Lower the crankshaft into position, and check the crankshaft endfloat as described in Section 14.

24 Thoroughly degrease the mating surfaces of the cylinder block and the main bearing caps.

25 Lubricate the lower bearing shells in the main bearing caps with clean engine oil. Make sure that the locating lugs on the shells engage with the corresponding recesses in the caps.

26 Fit the main bearing caps, using the identification marks to ensure that they are installed in the correct locations and are fitted the correct way round. Insert the retaining bolts, tightening them by hand only.

27 Working in the sequence shown, tighten the bearing cap retaining bolts to approximately half the specified torque setting **(see illustration)**. Then go around in the same sequence and tighten the bolts to the full specified torque setting. Check that the crankshaft rotates freely before proceeding any further.

28 Fit the piston/connecting rod assemblies as described in Section 19.

29 Ensure that the mating surfaces of the rear oil seal housing and cylinder block are clean and dry. Note the correct fitted depth of the oil seal then, using a large flat-bladed screwdriver, lever the seal out of the housing.

30 Fit the new crankshaft seal to the housing,

2C

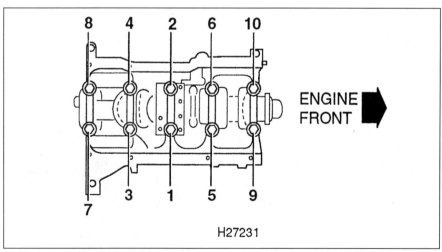

18.27 Main bearing cap bolt tightening sequence - 1.6 litre engine

18.34a On 2.0 litre engines, fit the main bearing caps using their markings to ensure each is correctly positioned . . .

18.34b . . . then refit the main bearing ladder, and install the retaining bolts and washers

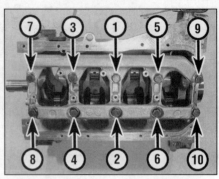

18.35a Working in the sequence shown . . .

making sure that its sealing lip is facing inwards. Tap the seal squarely into the housing until it is positioned at the same depth as the original was noted prior to removal.

31 Apply a bead of suitable sealant to the oil seal housing mating surface, and make sure that the locating dowels are in position. Slide the housing over the end of the crankshaft, and into position on the cylinder block. Tighten the housing retaining bolts to the specified torque setting.

32 Refit the flywheel, timing chains and sump as described in Part A of this Chapter.

2.0 litre engine

33 Carry out the operations described above in paragraphs 20 to 25.

34 Fit the main bearing caps, using the identification marks to ensure that they are installed in the correct locations and are fitted the correct way round. Refit the main bearing ladder casting, and install the retaining bolts, tightening them by hand only at this stage **(see illustrations)**.

35 Working progressively and in the sequence shown, tighten the main bearing retaining bolts to their Stage 1 torque setting, using a torque wrench and suitable socket **(see illustrations)**.

36 Working again in the specified sequence, tighten the main bearing cap bolts either through the specified Stage 2 angle setting

(see illustration). If an angle-measuring gauge is not available, tighten the bolts in sequence to the specified Stage 2 torque setting.

37 Check that the crankshaft rotates freely before proceeding, then install the remaining components as described in paragraphs 28 to 32.

---

19 Piston/connecting rod assembly - refitting and big-end bearing running clearance check

Note: This information applies only to standard size bearing shells. Undersize shells are not graded.

Selection of new bearing shells

1 New bearing shells are selected using the identification marks on the crankshaft.

2 The crankshaft markings are stamped either on the side of No 1 cylinder crankweb (at the timing chain end of the crankshaft) or on the side of No 4 cylinder crankweb (at the flywheel/driveplate end of the crankshaft). The four-digit code refers to the big-end (crankpin) journal diameters - the first number in the sequence is for No 1 crankpin, and the last for No 4 crankpin. The five-digit code stamped on No 1 cylinder crankweb refers to main bearing journal sizes (see Section 18).

3 Obtain the identification number of both the relevant crankshaft journal and the cylinder block bearing bore, and select the correct grade of main bearing shell required for each journal using the relevant following table. The grade of each shell is indicated by a dab of paint on the side of the shell.

Crankshaft code	Bearing shell grade
1.6 litre engine	
0	White (or no colour)
1	Black
2	Brown
2.0 litre engine	
0	Black
1	Brown
2	Green

Big-end bearing running clearance check

4 Clean the backs of the bearing shells, and the bearing locations in both the connecting rod and bearing cap.

5 Press the bearing shells into their locations, ensuring that the tab on each shell engages in the recess in the connecting rod and cap **(see illustration)**. Take care not to touch any shell's bearing surface with your fingers, and ensure that the shells are correctly installed so that the upper shell oil hole is correctly aligned with connecting rod oil hole. If the original bearing shells are being used for the check, ensure that they are refitted in their original

18.35b . . . tighten the main bearing cap bolts to the Stage 1 torque setting . . .

18.36 . . . and then tighten them through the specified Stage 2 angle setting as described in text

19.5 Fit each bearing shell to its connecting rod, aligning its tab with the rod cut-out (arrowed)

locations. The clearance can be checked in either of two ways.

6 One method is to refit the big-end bearing cap to the connecting rod, ensuring that they are fitted the correct way round, with the bearing shells in place. With the cap retaining nuts correctly tightened, use an internal micrometer or vernier caliper to measure the internal diameter of each assembled pair of bearing shells. If the diameter of each corresponding crankshaft journal is measured and then subtracted from the bearing internal diameter, the result will be the big-end bearing running clearance.

7 The second, and more accurate, method is to use Plastigage (see Section 18).

8 Ensure that the bearing shells are correctly fitted. Place a strand of Plastigage on each (cleaned) crankpin journal.

9 Refit the (clean) piston/connecting rod assemblies to the crankshaft, and refit the big-end bearing caps, using the marks made or noted on removal to ensure that they are fitted the correct way round.

10 Tighten the bearing cap nuts as described below in paragraph 22. Take care not to disturb the Plastigage, nor to rotate the connecting rod during the tightening sequence.

11 Dismantle the assemblies without rotating the connecting rods. Use the scale printed on the Plastigage envelope to obtain the big-end bearing running clearance.

12 If the clearance is not as specified, the bearing shells may be the wrong size (or excessively worn, if the original shells are being re-used). Make sure that no dirt or oil was trapped between the bearing shells and the caps or connecting rods when the clearance was measured. If the Plastigage was wider at one end than at the other, the crankpins may be tapered.

13 If the clearance is not as specified with the original bearing shells, repeat the checking procedure using new bearing shells. If the clearance is not as specified even with new bearing shells, then seek the advice of a Nissan dealer or suitable engine overhaul specialist. They will be able to advise you on the best course of action, and whether or not it will be necessary to have the crankpin journals reground and fit undersize shells.

14 Where necessary, obtain the required grades of bearing shell, and repeat the running clearance checking procedure as described above.

15 On completion, carefully scrape away all traces of the Plastigage material from the crankshaft and bearing shells. Use your fingernail, or a wooden or plastic scraper which is unlikely to score the bearing surfaces.

Final piston/connecting rod refitting

16 Note that the following procedure assumes that the crankshaft and main bearing ladder/caps are in place (see Section 18).

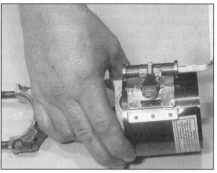

19.19 Ensure that the piston rings end gaps are correctly spaced, then clamp them in position with piston ring compressor

17 Ensure that the bearing shells are correctly fitted as described in paragraphs 4 and 5. If new shells are being fitted, ensure that all traces of the protective grease are cleaned off using paraffin. Wipe dry the shells and connecting rods with a lint-free cloth.

18 Lubricate the cylinder bores, the pistons, and piston rings, then lay out each piston/connecting rod assembly in its respective position.

19 Start with assembly No 1. Make sure that the piston rings are still spaced as described in Section 17, then clamp them in position with a piston ring compressor **(see illustration)**.

20 Insert the piston/connecting rod assembly into the top of cylinder No 1. Ensure that the piston front marking (in the form of either an arrow or a dot) on the piston crown is on the timing chain side of the bore. Using a block of wood or hammer handle against the piston crown, tap the assembly into the cylinder until the piston crown is flush with the top of the cylinder **(see illustration)**.

21 Ensure that the bearing shell is still correctly installed. Liberally lubricate the crankpin and both bearing shells. Taking care not to mark the cylinder bores, tap the piston/connecting rod assembly down the bore and onto the crankpin. Refit the big-end bearing cap, tightening its retaining nuts finger-tight at first. Note that the faces with the identification marks must match (which

19.20 Insert the piston/connecting rod assembly into its respective cylinder, and gently tap it into position

means that the bearing shell locating tabs abut each other).

22 Tighten the bearing cap retaining nuts to their Stage 1 torque setting, using a torque wrench and suitable socket. Then tighten them either through the specified Stage 2 angle setting or, if an angle-measuring gauge is not available, to the specified Stage 2 torque setting **(see illustrations)**.

23 Rotate the crankshaft. Check that it turns freely; some stiffness is to be expected if new components have been fitted, but there should be no signs of binding or tight spots.

24 Refit the remaining three piston/connecting rod assemblies in the same way.

25 Refit the cylinder head, timing chain(s) and sump as described in Part A or B of this Chapter (as applicable).

20 Engine -
initial start-up after overhaul

1 With the engine refitted in the vehicle, double-check the engine oil and coolant levels. Make a final check that everything has been reconnected, and that there are no tools or rags left in the engine compartment.

2 Remove the spark plugs, and disable the ignition system by disconnecting the ignition HT coil lead from the distributor cap, and earthing it on the cylinder block. Use a jumper

19.22a Evenly and progressively tighten the big-end bearing cap retaining nuts to the specified Stage 1 torque setting . . .

19.22b . . . and then through the specified Stage 2 angle setting

2C

lead or similar wire to make a good connection.

3 Turn the engine on the starter until the oil pressure warning light goes out. Refit the spark plugs, and reconnect the spark plug (HT) leads, referring to Chapter 1 for further information. Reconnect the HT leads to the distributor.

4 Start the engine, noting that this may take a little longer than usual, due to the fuel system components having been disturbed.

5 While the engine is idling, check for fuel, water and oil leaks. Don't be alarmed if there are some odd smells and smoke from parts getting hot and burning off oil deposits.

6 Assuming all is well, keep the engine idling until hot water is felt circulating through the top hose, then switch off the engine.

7 Check the ignition timing and the idle speed settings (as appropriate), then switch the engine off.

8 After a few minutes, recheck the oil and coolant levels as described in Chapter 1, and top-up as necessary.

9 If they were tightened as described, there is no need to re-tighten the cylinder head bolts once the engine has first run after reassembly.

10 If new pistons, rings or crankshaft bearings have been fitted, the engine must be treated as new, and run-in for the first 500 miles (800 km). *Do not* operate the engine at full-throttle, or allow it to labour at low engine speeds in any gear. It is recommended that the oil and filter be changed at the end of this period.

Chapter 3
Cooling, heating and ventilation systems

Contents

Degrees of difficulty

Easy, suitable for novice with little experience		Fairly easy, suitable for beginner with some experience		Fairly difficult, suitable for competent DIY mechanic		Difficult, suitable for experienced DIY mechanic		Very difficult, suitable for expert DIY or professional	

Specifications

General

Radiator cap opening pressure .... 0.78 to 0.98 bars (11.0 to 14.0 psi)

Thermostat

Opening temperature:
  Starts to open:
    All except 1.6 litre fuel injection engines .... 76.5°C
    1.6 litre fuel injection engines .... 82°C
  Fully open:
    All except 1.6 litre fuel injection engines .... 90°C
    1.6 litre fuel injection engines .... 95°C
Maximum valve lift (approximate) .... 8.0 mm

Electric cooling fan

Cut-in temperature .... 82 to 88°C

Engine temperature sensor

Resistance:
  20°C .... 2.10 to 2.90 kilohms
  50°C .... 0.68 to 1.00 kilohms
  80°C .... 0.30 to 0.33 kilohms

Torque wrench settings	Nm	lbf ft
Coolant pump pulley securing bolts	7	5
Coolant pump securing bolts:		
1.6 litre engine	7	5
2.0 litre engine	18	13
Thermostat cover securing bolts	7	5
Thermostat housing securing bolts:		
1.6 litre engine	7	5
2.0 litre engine	18	13

3

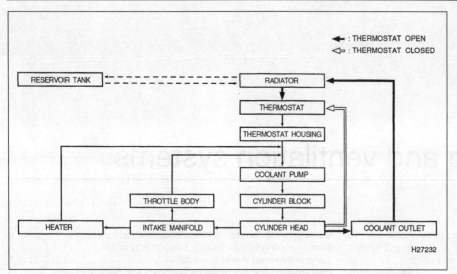

: THERMOSTAT OPEN
: THERMOSTAT CLOSED

RESERVOIR TANK

RADIATOR

THERMOSTAT

THERMOSTAT HOUSING

COOLANT PUMP

THROTTLE BODY

CYLINDER BLOCK

HEATER

INTAKE MANIFOLD

CYLINDER HEAD

COOLANT OUTLET

H27232

1.1 Typical cooling system layout - 2.0 litre engine shown, 1.6 litre engine similar

1 General information and precautions

General information

1 The cooling system is of pressurised type, comprising a coolant pump driven by a V-belt from the crankshaft pulley, a crossflow radiator, a coolant expansion tank, an electric cooling fan, a thermostat, heater matrix, and all associated hoses and switches (see illustration).

2 The system functions as follows. The coolant pump pumps cold water around the cylinder block and head passages, and through the inlet manifold, heater and carburettor/ throttle body to the thermostat housing.

3 When the engine is cold, the coolant is returned from the thermostat housing to the coolant pump. When the coolant reaches a predetermined temperature, the thermostat opens, and the coolant passes through the top hose to the radiator. As the coolant circulates through the radiator, it is cooled by the inrush of air when the car is in forward motion. The airflow is supplemented by the action of the electric cooling fan when necessary. Upon reaching the bottom of the radiator, the coolant has now cooled, and the cycle is repeated.

4 When the engine is at normal operating temperature, the coolant expands, and some of it is released through the valve in the radiator pressure cap into the expansion tank. Coolant collects in the tank, and is returned to the radiator when the system cools.

5 On some models, the coolant is also passed through the engine oil cooler.

6 The electric cooling fan(s) mounted in front of the radiator are controlled by a thermostatic switch. At a predetermined coolant temperature, the switch/sensor actuates the fan.

Precautions

 Warning: Do not attempt to remove the radiator pressure cap, or to disturb any part of the cooling system, while the engine is hot, as there is a high risk of scalding. If the radiator pressure cap must be removed before the engine and radiator have fully cooled (even though this is not recommended), the pressure in the cooling system must first be relieved. Cover the cap with a thick layer of cloth, to avoid scalding, and slowly unscrew the pressure cap until a hissing sound is heard. When the hissing has stopped, indicating that the pressure has reduced, slowly unscrew the pressure cap until it can be removed; if more hissing sounds are heard, wait until they have stopped before unscrewing the cap completely. At all times, keep your face well away from the pressure cap opening, and protect your hands.

 Warning: Do not allow antifreeze to come into contact with your skin, or with the painted surfaces of the vehicle. Rinse off spills immediately, with plenty of water. Never leave antifreeze lying around in an open container, or in a puddle in the driveway or on the garage floor. Children and pets are attracted by its sweet smell, but antifreeze can be fatal if ingested.

 Warning: If the engine is hot, the electric cooling fan may start rotating even if the engine is not running. Be careful to keep your hands, hair, and any loose clothing well clear when working in the engine compartment.

 Warning: Refer to Section 10 for precautions to be observed when working on models equipped with air conditioning.

2 Cooling system hoses - disconnection and renewal

1 The number, routing and pattern of hoses will vary according to model, but the same basic procedure applies. Before commencing work, make sure that the new hoses are to hand, along with new hose clips if needed. It is good practice to renew the hose clips at the same time as the hoses.

2 Drain the cooling system, as described in Chapter 1, saving the coolant if it is fit for re-use. Squirt a little penetrating oil onto the hose clips if they are corroded.

3 Release the hose clips from the hose concerned. Three types of clip are used; worm-drive, spring and "sardine-can". The worm-drive clip is released by turning its screw anti-clockwise. The spring clip is released by squeezing its tags together with pliers, at the same time working the clip away from the hose stub. The "sardine-can" clip is not re-usable, and is best cut off with snips or side cutters.

4 Unclip any wires, cables or other hoses which may be attached to the hose being removed. Make notes for reference when reassembling if necessary.

5 Release the hose from its stubs with a twisting motion. Be careful not to damage the stubs on delicate components such as the radiator. If the hose is stuck fast, the best course is often to cut it off using a sharp knife, but again be careful not to damage the stubs.

6 Before fitting the new hose, smear the stubs with washing-up liquid or a suitable rubber lubricant to aid fitting. Do not use oil or grease, which may attack the rubber.

7 Fit the hose clips over the ends of the hose, then fit the hose over its stubs. Work the hose into position. When satisfied, locate and tighten the hose clips.

8 Refill the cooling system as described in Chapter 1. Run the engine, and check that there are no leaks.

9 Recheck the tightness of the hose clips on any new hoses after a few hundred miles.

10 Top-up the coolant level if necessary.

3 Radiator - removal, inspection and refitting

Removal

Note: *If leakage is the reason for removing the radiator, bear in mind that minor leaks can often be cured using a radiator sealant with the radiator in situ.*

1 Disconnect the battery negative lead.

2 Drain the cooling system as described in Chapter 1.

3 Disconnect the remaining coolant hose(s) from the radiator (on models with automatic transmission, the fluid cooler hoses are

3.3 Disconnecting the radiator top hose

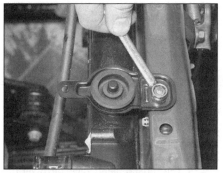

3.5 Unscrew the radiator top mounting bracket securing bolts

3.7 Lifting out the radiator

connected to the bottom of the radiator) **(see illustration)**.

4 To improve the clearance available, remove the cooling fan(s) and shroud assembly, as described in Section 5.

5 Working at the top of the radiator, unscrew the bolts securing the radiator mounting brackets to the upper body panel **(see illustration)**.

6 Withdraw the mounting brackets, and recover the upper mounting rubbers if they are loose.

7 Carefully tilt the radiator back towards the engine, then lift the radiator from the engine compartment **(see illustration)**. Recover the lower mounting rubbers if they are loose.

Inspection

8 If the radiator has been removed due to suspected blockage, reverse-flush it as described in Chapter 1. Clean dirt and debris from the radiator fins, using an air line (in which case, wear eye protection) or a soft brush. Be careful, as the fins are sharp, and easily damaged.

9 If necessary, a radiator specialist can perform a "flow test" on the radiator, to establish whether an internal blockage exists.

10 A leaking radiator must be referred to a specialist for permanent repair. Do not attempt to weld or solder a leaking radiator, as damage to the plastic components may result. In an emergency, minor leaks from the radiator can be cured by using a suitable radiator sealant, in accordance with its manufacturer's instructions, with the radiator *in situ*. If the radiator is to be sent for repair, or is to be renewed, remove all hoses, and the cooling fan switch.

11 Inspect the condition of the radiator mounting rubbers, and renew them if necessary.

Refitting

12 Refitting is a reversal of removal, bearing in mind the following points:

a) *Ensure that the radiator lower lugs engage correctly with the lower mounting rubbers.*

b) *On completion, refill the cooling system as described in Chapter 1.*

4 Thermostat - removal, testing and refitting

Removal

Note: *Suitable sealant (liquid gasket) will be required when refitting the thermostat housing.*

1 On 1.6 litre engine models, the thermostat is located in a housing bolted to the side of the coolant pump, at the timing chain end of the engine **(see illustration)**.

2 On 2.0 litre engine models, the thermostat is located in a housing bolted to the transmission end of the cylinder head **(see illustration)**.

3 Disconnect the battery negative lead.

4 Drain the cooling system as described in Chapter 1.

5 Disconnect the coolant hose from the thermostat cover **(see illustration)**.

6 On 1.6 litre engine models, disconnect the wiring plug from the cooling fan switch located in the thermostat cover.

3

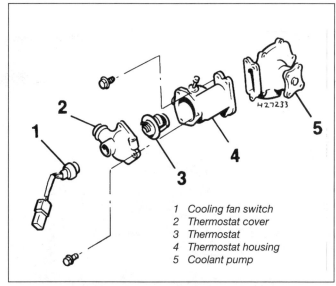

**4.1 Thermostat housing and coolant pump components -
1.6 litre engine**

1 Cooling fan switch
2 Thermostat cover
3 Thermostat
4 Thermostat housing
5 Coolant pump

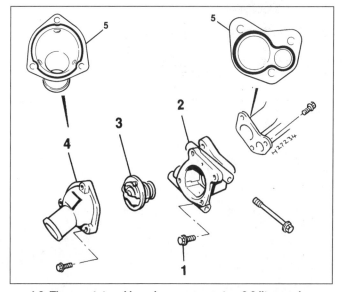

4.2 Thermostat and housing components - 2.0 litre engine

1 Air bleed screw   3 Thermostat   5 Sealant (liquid gasket)
2 Thermostat housing   4 Thermostat cover

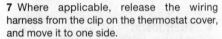

4.5 Disconnecting the coolant hose from the thermostat housing

4.14 Thermostat bleed valve (arrowed) must be uppermost

4.15 Apply a bead of sealant to the thermostat cover

7 Where applicable, release the wiring harness from the clip on the thermostat cover, and move it to one side.

8 Unscrew the securing bolts, and remove the thermostat cover from the housing. If the cover is stuck to the housing, tap it gently, or rock it back and forth to free it - **do not** lever between the mating faces.

9 Lift the thermostat from the housing, noting that the bleed valve is located at the top.

Testing

10 A rough test of the thermostat may be made by suspending it with a piece of string in a container full of water. Heat the water to bring it to the boil - the thermostat must open by the time the water boils. If not, renew it.

11 If a thermometer is available, the precise opening temperature of the thermostat may be determined; compare with the figures given in the Specifications. The opening temperature is also marked on the thermostat.

12 A thermostat which fails to close as the water cools must also be renewed.

Refitting

13 Commence refitting by thoroughly cleaning the mating faces of the cover and the housing.

14 Refit the thermostat to the housing, noting that it should fit with the bleed valve uppermost **(see illustration)**.

15 Apply a continuous bead of sealant (liquid gasket) to the housing mating face of the thermostat cover, taking care not to apply excess sealant, which may enter the cooling system **(see illustration)**.

16 Fit the cover to the thermostat housing, then refit the securing bolts, and tighten to the specified torque.

17 Where applicable, fit the wiring harness to the clip on the thermostat cover, and on 1.6 litre engine models, reconnect the wiring plug to the cooling fan switch.

18 Reconnect the coolant hose to the thermostat cover.

19 Refill the cooling system as described in Chapter 1.

20 Reconnect the battery negative lead.

5 Electric cooling fan(s) - testing, removal and refitting

Testing

1 Current supply to the cooling fan(s) is via the ignition switch (see Chapter 5) and a fuse (see Chapter 12). On all except 1.6 litre carburettor models, the circuit is completed by the engine temperature sensor, via the engine management electronic control unit. The sensor is located in the inlet manifold, at the rear (timing chain end) of the cylinder head. On 1.6 litre carburettor engine models, the circuit is completed by the cooling fan switch, which is located in the thermostat cover, bolted to the coolant pump at the timing chain end of the engine. On models with air conditioning and/or automatic transmission, two cooling fans are fitted.

2 Detailed fault diagnosis can be carried out by a Nissan dealer using suitable test equipment, but basic diagnosis can be carried out as follows.

3 If the fan does not appear to work, run the engine until normal operating temperature is reached, then allow it to idle. The fan should cut in within a few minutes (before the temperature gauge needle enters the red section). If not, switch off the ignition and disconnect the cooling fan motor wiring connector.

4 The motor can be tested by disconnecting it from the wiring loom, and connecting a 12-volt supply directly to it. The motor should operate - if not, the motor, or the motor wiring, is faulty.

5 If the motor operates when tested as described in paragraph 4, the fault must lie in the engine wiring harness, the engine management electronic control unit, or the temperature sensor. The temperature sensor/switch can be tested as described in Section 6. Any further fault diagnosis should be referred to a suitably-equipped Nissan dealer - **do not** attempt to test the electronic control unit.

Removal

6 Disconnect the battery negative lead.

7 Disconnect the motor wiring connector(s) **(see illustration)**.

8 Unscrew the two securing screws from the top of the shroud, then lift out the assembly to release the lower clips **(see illustrations)**.

Refitting

9 Refitting is a reversal of removal.

5.7 Disconnecting a cooling fan motor wiring connector

5.8a Remove the two securing screws . . .

5.8b . . . and lift out the cooling fan assembly

6.13 Engine temperature sensor (arrowed) - 1.6 litre fuel injection engine

6.19a Coolant temperature gauge sender (arrowed) - 1.6 litre fuel injection engine

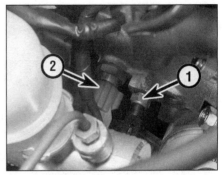

6.19b Coolant temperature gauge sender (1) and engine temperature sensor (2) - 2.0 litre engine

6 Cooling system electrical switches - testing, removal and refitting

Cooling fan switch - 1.6 litre carburettor models

Testing

1 The switch is located in the end of the thermostat cover, on the end of the coolant pump, at the timing chain end of the engine.
2 The switch can be tested by removing it, and checking that the switching action occurs at the correct temperature (heat the sensor in a container of water, and monitor the temperature with a thermometer).
3 There should be no continuity between the switch terminals, until the specified cooling fan cut-in temperature is reached, when continuity (and zero resistance) should exist between the terminals.

Removal

4 Disconnect the battery negative lead.
5 Partially drain the cooling system to just below the level of the sensor (as described in Chapter 1). Alternatively, have ready a suitable bung to plug the aperture in the housing when the sensor is removed.
6 Disconnect the wiring plug from the sensor.
7 Carefully unscrew the sensor and, where applicable, recover the sealing ring. If the system has not been drained, plug the sensor aperture to prevent further coolant loss.

Refitting

8 If the sensor was originally fitted using sealing compound, clean the sensor threads thoroughly, and coat them with fresh sealing compound.
9 If the sensor was originally fitted using a sealing ring, use a new sealing ring on refitting.
10 Refitting is a reversal of removal, but refill (or top-up) the cooling system as described in Chapter 1.
11 On completion, start the engine and run it until it reaches normal operating temperature. Continue to run the engine until the cooling fan cuts in and out correctly.

Engine temperature sensor

General

12 The engine temperature sensor provides information to the engine management electronic control unit to control the fuel and ignition systems, and the radiator cooling fan (except on 1.6 litre carburettor engines).

Testing

13 On all models, the sensor is located in the inlet manifold, at the rear (timing chain end) of the cylinder head **(see illustration)**.
14 The sensor contains a thermistor - an electronic component whose electrical resistance decreases at a predetermined rate as its temperature rises.
15 The fuel injection/engine management ECU supplies the sensor with a set voltage and then, by measuring the current flowing in the sensor circuit, it determines the engine temperature. This information is then used, in conjunction with other inputs, to control the fuel injection/engine management system, and the engine cooling fan.
16 If the sensor circuit should fail to provide adequate information, the ECU back-up facility will override the sensor signal. In this event, the ECU assumes a predetermined setting which will allow the fuel injection/ engine management system to run, albeit at reduced efficiency. When this occurs, the engine warning light on the instrument panel will come on, and the advice of a Nissan dealer should be sought. The sensor itself can be tested by removing it, and checking the resistances at various temperatures using an ohmmeter (heat the sensor in a container of water, and monitor the temperature with a thermometer). The resistance values are given in the Specifications. *Do not* attempt to test the circuit with the sensor fitted to the engine, and the wiring connector fitted, as there is a high risk of damaging the ECU.
17 Refer to the relevant Part of Chapter 4 for further details of the fuel injection/engine management system.

Removal and refitting

18 Proceed as described previously for the cooling fan switch on 1.6 litre carburettor models.

Coolant temperature gauge sender

Testing

19 On 1.6 litre engine models, the sender is located in the rear of the cylinder head, at the flywheel end of the engine. On 2.0 litre engine models, the sender is located in the inlet manifold, at the rear (timing chain end) of the cylinder head **(see illustrations)**. The sender is the smaller of the two (where applicable).
20 The temperature gauge is fed with a stabilised voltage from the instrument panel feed (via the ignition switch and a fuse). The gauge earth is controlled by the sender. The sender contains a thermistor - an electronic component whose electrical resistance decreases at a predetermined rate as its temperature rises. When the coolant is cold, the sender resistance is high, current flow through the gauge is reduced, and the gauge needle points towards the blue (cold) end of the scale. As the coolant temperature rises and the sender resistance falls, current flow increases, and the gauge needle moves towards the upper end of the scale. If the sender is faulty, it must be renewed.
21 If the gauge develops a fault, first check the other instruments; if they do not work at all, check the instrument panel electrical feed. If the readings are erratic, there may be a fault in the voltage stabiliser, which will necessitate renewal of the stabiliser (the stabiliser is integral with the instrument panel printed circuit board - see Chapter 12). If the fault lies in the temperature gauge alone, check it as follows.
22 If the gauge needle remains at the "cold" end of the scale when the engine is hot, disconnect the sender wiring plug, and earth the relevant wire to the cylinder head. If the needle then deflects when the ignition is switched on, the sender unit is proved faulty, and should be renewed. If the needle still does not move, remove the instrument panel (Chapter 12) and check the continuity of the wire between the sender unit and the gauge, and the feed to the gauge unit. If continuity is shown, and the fault still exists, then the gauge is faulty, and the gauge should be renewed.

3

7.4 Removing the coolant pump pulley - 1.6 litre engine

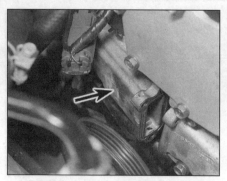

7.5 Unbolt the thermostat housing (arrowed) from the coolant pump - 1.6 litre engine

7.10a Apply sealant to the coolant pump's cylinder block mating face . . .

23 If the gauge needle remains at the "hot" end of the scale when the engine is cold, disconnect the sender wire. If the needle then returns to the "cold" end of the scale when the ignition is switched on, the sender unit is proved faulty, and should be renewed. If the needle still does not move, check the remainder of the circuit as described previously.

Removal and refitting

24 The procedure is similar to that described previously in this Section for the engine temperature sensor. On some models, access to the switch is poor, and other components may need to be removed (or hoses, wiring, etc moved to one side) before the sender unit can be reached.

Air conditioning system temperature sensor

Testing

25 The sensor is integral with the air conditioning temperature control unit, located on the side of the heater/air conditioning unit behind the facia. Testing should be entrusted to a Nissan dealer.

Removal and refitting

26 Removal and refitting should be entrusted to a Nissan dealer suitably equipped to test the unit.

---

7 Coolant pump - removal, inspection and refitting

1.6 litre engine models

Removal

1 Disconnect the battery negative lead.
2 Drain the cooling system as described in Chapter 1.
3 Remove the auxiliary drivebelt(s) as described in Chapter 1.
4 Unscrew the securing bolts, and remove the coolant pump pulley **(see illustration)**. It will be necessary to counterhold the pulley in order to unscrew the bolts, and this is most easily achieved by wrapping an old drivebelt tightly around the pulley to act in a similar manner to a strap wrench.
5 Unbolt the thermostat housing from the stub on the coolant pump, and move the housing to one side, taking care not to strain the sensor/switch wiring **(see illustration)**. If the housing is stuck, tap it gently with a soft-faced mallet - **do not** lever between the mating faces. If necessary to improve access, disconnect the wiring and the coolant hose, and remove the housing.
6 Unscrew the securing bolts, and withdraw the coolant pump. If the pump is stuck, tap it gently using a soft-faced mallet - **do not** lever

between the pump and cylinder block mating faces.

Inspection

7 Check the pump body and impeller for signs of excessive corrosion. Turn the impeller, and check for stiffness due to corrosion, or roughness due to excessive end play.
8 No spare parts are available for the pump, and if faulty, worn or corroded, a new pump should be fitted.

Refitting

9 Commence refitting by thoroughly cleaning all traces of sealant from the mating faces of the pump and cylinder block, and from the thermostat housing.
10 Apply a continuous bead of sealant (liquid gasket) to the cylinder block mating face of the pump, taking care not to apply excessive sealant, which may enter the pump itself. Similarly, apply a bead of sealant to the thermostat housing mating face of the pump **(see illustrations)**.
11 Place the pump in position in the cylinder block, then refit and tighten the bolts. Note that the threads of the two lower bolts should be coated with thread-locking compound **(see illustrations)**.
12 Refit the pump pulley, then refit the securing bolts and tighten to the specified torque. Counterhold the pulley using an old drivebelt as during removal.

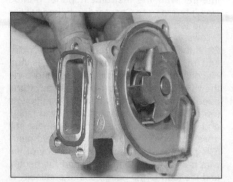

7.10b . . . and thermostat housing mating face - 1.6 litre engine

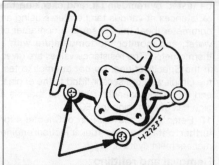

7.11a Apply thread-locking compound to the two coolant pump lower securing bolts (arrowed) - 1.6 litre engine

7.11b Refitting the coolant pump - 1.6 litre engine

13 Apply a continuous bead of sealant (liquid gasket) to the coolant pump mating face of the thermostat housing, again taking care not to apply excessive sealant.

14 Place the thermostat housing in position on the pump stub, then refit the securing bolts, and tighten to the specified torque.

15 Refit and tension the auxiliary drivebelt(s) as described in Chapter 1.

16 Refill the cooling system as described in Chapter 1.

17 Reconnect the battery negative lead.

2.0 litre engine models

18 The procedures are as described previously in this Section for 1.6 litre engine models, noting the following differences:

a) *Remove the power steering pump as described in Chapter 10.*

b) *Ignore the references to unbolting the thermostat housing from the pump, which is not applicable to the 2.0 litre engine.*

c) *There is no need to apply sealant to the lower coolant pump securing bolts on 2.0 litre engines.*

8 Heater/ventilation system - general information

1 The heater/ventilation system consists of a four-speed blower motor (housed behind the facia), face level vents in the centre and at each end of the facia, and air ducts to the front footwells.

2 The control unit is located in the facia, and the controls operate flap valves to deflect and mix the air flowing through the various parts of the heating/ventilation system. The flap valves are contained in the air distribution housing, which acts as a central distribution unit, passing air to the various ducts and vents.

3 Cold air enters the system through the grille at the rear of the engine compartment. If required, the airflow is boosted by the blower fan, and then flows through the various ducts, according to the settings of the controls. Stale air is expelled through ducts at the rear of the vehicle. If warm air is required, the cold air is passed over the heater matrix, which is heated by the engine coolant.

4 On models fitted with air conditioning, a recirculation switch enables the outside air supply to be closed off, while the air inside the vehicle is recirculated. This can be useful to prevent unpleasant odours entering from outside the vehicle, but should only be used briefly, as the recirculated air inside the vehicle will soon become stale.

9 Heater/ventilation components - removal and refitting

Heater/ventilation control unit
Removal

1 Disconnect the battery negative lead.

2 Remove the facia lower centre panel, as described in Chapter 11.

3 Withdraw the control unit forwards from the facia, and disconnect the wiring plugs from the rear of the unit **(see illustration)**.

4 Pull out the securing clip, and disconnect the temperature control cable from the lever on the rear of the unit, then withdraw the unit **(see illustrations)**.

Refitting

5 Refitting is a reversal of removal, but reconnect the temperature control cable as follows:

a) *Move the temperature control lever on the control unit to the fully hot position.*

b) *Move the air mix door lever on the heater unit to the fully hot position.*

c) *Reconnect the end of the cable to the lever on the heater unit, then push the securing clip over the cable.*

Temperature control cable

6 Removal of the control cable is described previously in this Section as part of the heater/ventilation control unit removal and refitting procedure.

Complete heater assembly

⚠️ **Warning: On models fitted with air conditioning, do not attempt to remove the cooling unit, which is located between the heater blower motor casing and the main heater assembly. Removal of the cooling unit entails disconnection of refrigerant lines - refer to Section 10 for precautions to be observed. If in any doubt as to the procedure to follow on models with air conditioning, consult a Nissan dealer for advice.**

Note: *This is an involved procedure, and it is recommended that the following Section is read thoroughly before commencing work. Plenty of time should be allowed to complete the operation. During dismantling, make notes on the routing of all wiring and cables, and the locations of all fixings, to aid reassembly.*

Removal

7 Disconnect the battery negative lead.

8 Drain the cooling system as described in Chapter 1.

9 Working inside the vehicle, under the glovebox, remove the two securing screws (one on each side of the glovebox), then lower the glovebox from the facia.

10 Remove the three securing screws, and withdraw the passenger's side lower facia panel from the facia **(see illustration)**.

11 Remove the securing screws, and withdraw the metal reinforcing bracket which fits across the glovebox aperture **(see illustration)**.

12 Open the passenger's door (if not already done), and pull the weatherstrip and the sill trim panel from the edge of the footwell trim panel.

13 Remove the upper securing nut and the lower screw, then pull the footwell trim panel

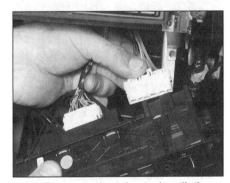

9.3 Disconnecting a heater/ventilation control unit wiring plug

9.4a Pull out the securing clip . . .

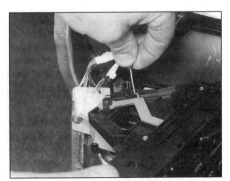

9.4b . . . then disconnect the control cable from the rear of the unit

9.10 Removing the passenger's side lower facia panel

3

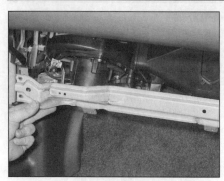

9.11 Removing the metal reinforcing bracket

9.13 Remove the upper securing nut (arrowed) and the screw from the footwell trim panel

9.17a Disconnecting the wiring plug from the blower motor resistor . . .

9.17b . . . and the air flap motor

9.18a Unscrew the upper bolt and the two lower nuts (arrowed) securing the motor casing . . .

from the footwell to release the securing clip **(see illustration)**.

14 Disconnect the wiring connector from the now-exposed ABS electronic control unit.

15 Pull back the carpet trim panel to expose the ABS control unit bracket.

16 Unscrew the two securing screws, and withdraw the ABS control unit, complete with the bracket (see Chapter 9).

17 Working at the passenger's side of the car, disconnect the wiring plugs from the heater blower motor, the blower motor resistor, and the air flap motor **(see illustrations)**.

18 Unscrew the upper bolt, and the two lower nuts, securing the heater motor casing, then remove the two screws securing the motor unit ducting to the main heater unit, and withdraw the heater blower motor casing from the scuttle **(see illustrations)**.

19 Remove the complete facia assembly as described in Chapter 11.

20 Withdraw the heater/ventilation control unit forwards from the facia, and disconnect the wiring plugs from the rear of the unit.

21 Pull out the securing clip, and disconnect the temperature control cable from the lever on the rear of the heater/ventilation control unit, then withdraw the unit.

22 Working at the centre of the facia, remove the securing screws, and withdraw the electronic control unit from the facia centre brackets **(see illustrations)**. Disconnect the wiring plug and withdraw the control unit.

9.18b . . . and the two screws (arrowed) securing the motor unit ducting . . .

9.18c . . . and withdraw the motor casing

9.22a Remove the securing screws . . .

9.22b . . . and withdraw the electronic control unit

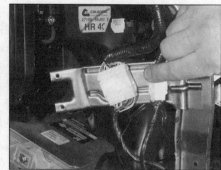

9.23 Unclip the wiring connectors . . .

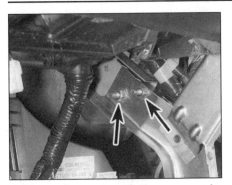

9.24a . . . then remove the two upper nuts (arrowed) . . .

9.24b . . . and the two lower screws (arrowed) . . .

9.24c . . . and withdraw the left-hand metal bracket

23 Unclip and wiring plugs, connectors, and/or harnesses from the left-hand facia metal centre bracket, noting their locations **(see illustration)**.

24 Remove the two upper nuts, and the two lower screws, and withdraw the left-hand facia centre bracket **(see illustrations)**.

25 Similarly, remove the right-hand facia metal centre bracket **(see illustration)**.

26 Unclip the air ducting connecting the bottom of the heater assembly to the floor vents under the centre of the facia **(see illustration)**.

27 Unscrew the two front securing bolts, then withdraw the engine management electronic control unit, and disconnect the wiring plug **(see illustration)**.

28 Where applicable, remove the securing screws, then disconnect the side air ducts from the heater unit. Withdraw the left-hand duct, manipulating it around the facia cross-tube. Pull the right-hand duct away from the heater assembly (the duct cannot be removed due to the proximity of the steering column **(see illustrations)**.

29 Unclip the air ducting connector from the top of the heater unit **(see illustration)**.

30 Working in the engine compartment, slacken the hose clips, and disconnect the coolant hoses from the heater matrix pipes at the bulkhead.

31 If not already done, disconnect the wiring plug from the air flap motor on the heater unit.

32 Working inside the vehicle, unscrew the

9.25 Removing the screw securing the wiring bracket to the right-hand metal bracket

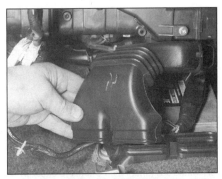

9.26 Unclip the air ducting from the centre of the heater assembly

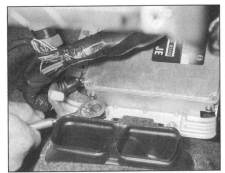

9.27 Unscrewing an engine management electronic control unit securing bolt

9.28a Removing the left-hand side air duct

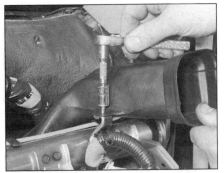

9.28b Unscrewing the right-hand side air duct securing screw

9.29 Unclip the air ducting from the top of the heater unit

9.32a Heater assembly lower securing nut (arrowed)

3

9.32b Heater assembly upper securing bolt (arrowed)

9.32c Withdraw the heater assembly . . .

9.32d . . . and pass the heater matrix pipes (arrowed) through the bulkhead

two lower nuts, and the upper bolt, securing the heater assembly to the bulkhead. Manipulate the assembly past the facia cross-tube, passing the heater matrix pipes through the bulkhead as the assembly is removed **(see illustrations)**.

Refitting

33 To refit the assembly, reverse the steps described for removal, bearing in mind the following points:
a) *Make sure that all wiring and cables are routed as noted during dismantling.*
b) *Make sure that all air ducts are securely reconnected.*
c) *Refit the facia components with reference to Chapter 11.*

d) *On completion, refill and bleed the cooling system as described in Chapter 1.*

Heater matrix

Removal

34 Remove the complete heater assembly as described previously in this Section.
35 Remove the plastic heater matrix retaining clip from the end of the heater assembly **(see illustration)**.
36 Release the securing clip, and disconnect the actuating rod from the lever on the heater assembly air flap **(see illustration)**.
37 Unhook the actuating rod spring from the water valve lever on the heater matrix, and withdraw the actuating rod.

38 Withdraw the heater matrix from the heater assembly casing **(see illustration)**.

Refitting

39 Refitting is a reversal of removal, but refit the heater assembly as described previously in this Section.

Heater blower motor

Removal

40 Disconnect the battery negative lead.
41 Working under the glovebox, remove the two securing screws (one on each side of the glovebox), then lower the glovebox from the facia.
42 Remove the three securing screws, and withdraw the passenger's side lower facia panel from the facia.
43 Remove the securing screws, and withdraw the metal reinforcing bracket which fits across the glovebox aperture.
44 Disconnect the cooling air hose from the bottom of the motor casing **(see illustration)**.
45 Remove the two securing screws, noting the locations of any brackets secured by the screws, then withdraw the motor assembly from the heater casing **(see illustrations)**.

Refitting

46 Refitting is a reversal of removal, but ensure that any brackets are positioned as noted before removal, and make sure that the cooling air hose is reconnected.

9.35 Remove the heater matrix retaining clip

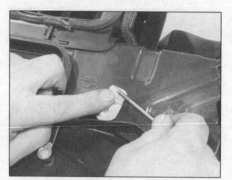

9.36 Disconnect the actuating rod from the lever on the heater assembly air flap

9.38 Withdrawing the heater matrix

9.44 Disconnect the air hose from the motor casing . . .

9.45a . . . then remove the securing screws . . .

9.45b ... and withdraw the motor assembly

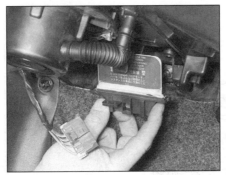

9.52 Removing the heater blower motor resistor

9.58a Removing the inlet air flap actuator motor

Heater blower motor resistor

Removal

47 The resistor is located at the bottom of the heater casing, behind the blower motor.

48 Disconnect the battery negative lead.

49 Working under the glovebox, remove the two securing screws (one on each side of the glovebox), then lower the glovebox from the facia.

50 For improved access, proceed as described in paragraphs 42 and 43.

51 Disconnect the wiring plug from the resistor.

52 Remove the two securing screws, and withdraw the resistor from the heater unit **(see illustration)**.

Refitting

53 Refitting is a reversal of removal.

Heater air flap motors

Removal

54 Two air flap motors are fitted, one in the air inlet ducting next to the blower motor, and one on the right-hand side of the main heater casing.

55 For access to the motor in the air inlet ducting, proceed as described in paragraphs 41 to 43 inclusive.

56 For access to the motor on the main heater casing, remove the driver's side lower facia panel, as described in Chapter 11.

57 Disconnect the battery negative lead.

58 To remove a motor, disconnect the wiring plug and the actuator rod from the motor

9.58b Disconnecting the wiring plug from the main heater casing air flap motor

assembly, then unscrew the two securing nuts, and withdraw the motor complete with its mounting bracket **(see illustrations)**.

Refitting

59 Refitting is a reversal of removal, but make sure that the actuating rod is correctly reconnected to the motor.

10 Air conditioning system - general information and precautions

General information

1 An air conditioning system is available on certain models **(see illustration)**. It enables the temperature of incoming air to be lowered, and also dehumidifies the air, which makes for rapid demisting and increased comfort.

2 The cooling side of the system works in the same way as a domestic refrigerator.

Refrigerant gas is drawn into a belt-driven compressor, and passes into a condenser mounted on the front of the radiator, where it loses heat and becomes liquid. The liquid passes through an expansion valve to an evaporator, where it changes from liquid under high pressure to gas under low pressure. This change is accompanied by a drop in temperature, which cools the evaporator. The refrigerant returns to the compressor, and the cycle begins again.

3 Air blown through the evaporator passes to the air distribution unit, where it is mixed with hot air blown through the heater matrix to achieve the desired temperature in the passenger compartment.

4 The heating side of the system works in the same way as on models without air conditioning (see Section 8).

5 The system is electronically-controlled. Any problems with the system should be referred to a Nissan dealer.

3

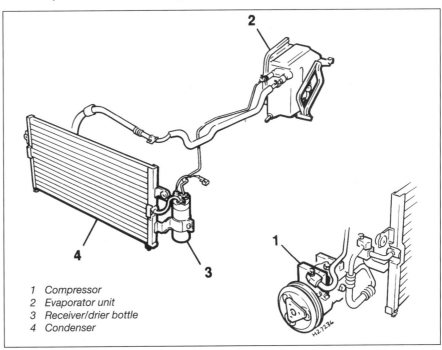

1 Compressor
2 Evaporator unit
3 Receiver/drier bottle
4 Condenser

10.1 Air conditioning system components

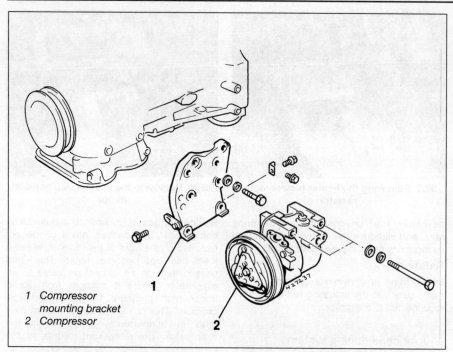

1 Compressor
  mounting bracket
2 Compressor

11.2 Air conditioning compressor mounting details - do not disconnect refrigerant lines

Precautions

6 With an air conditioning system, it is necessary to observe special precautions whenever dealing with any part of the system, or its associated components. If for any reason the system must be disconnected,

entrust this task to your Peugeot dealer or a refrigeration engineer.

> ⚠ **Warning: The refrigeration circuit contains a liquid refrigerant (Freon). The refrigerant is potentially**

dangerous, and should only be handled by qualified persons. If it is splashed onto the skin, it can cause frostbite. It is not itself poisonous, but in the presence of a naked flame (including a cigarette), it forms a poisonous gas. Uncontrolled discharging of the refrigerant is dangerous, and potentially damaging to the environment. For all these reasons, it is dangerous to disconnect any part of the system without specialised knowledge and equipment.

7 Do not operate the air conditioning system if it is known to be short of refrigerant, as this may damage the compressor.

11 Air conditioning components - removal and refitting

> ⚠ **Warning: Do not attempt to open the refrigerant circuit. Refer to the precautions given in Section 10.**

1 The only operation which can be carried out easily without discharging the refrigerant is renewal of the compressor drivebelt. This is described in Chapter 1, Section 21. All other operations must be referred to a Nissan dealer or an air conditioning specialist.

2 If necessary for access to other components, the compressor can be unbolted and moved aside, *without disconnecting its flexible hoses*, after removing the drivebelt **(see illustration)**.

Chapter 4 Part A
Fuel/exhaust systems - carburettor models

Contents

Degrees of difficulty

| Easy, suitable for novice with little experience | | Fairly easy, suitable for beginner with some experience | | Fairly difficult, suitable for competent DIY mechanic | | Difficult, suitable for experienced DIY mechanic | | Very difficult, suitable for expert DIY or professional | |

Specifications

4A

General

Engine code:
  1.6 litre models GA16DS
Fuel pump type .... Mechanical, driven by eccentric on inlet camshaft
Carburettor type .... Nikki 21L
  Designation:
    Models without a catalytic converter 21L304-05
    Models with a catalytic converter 21L304-06
Choke type .... Automatic

Carburettor data

For idle speed and mixture settings, refer to Chapter 1 Specifications.

	Primary	Secondary
Models without a catalytic converter:		
Throttle chamber bore	30 mm	34 mm
Venturi diameter	22 mm	30 mm
Main jet	100	135
Main air bleed	80	60
Slow jet	40	80
Slow air bleed	80	80
Power jet	55	
Float height setting:		
Float upper edge to carburettor body (carburettor inverted)	10 ± 0.5 mm	
Float lower edge to carburettor body (carburettor upright)	43.5 ± 0.5 mm	
Throttle valve fast idle setting	0.63 ± 0.07 mm	
Choke pull-down setting:		
Stage 1	1.27 ± 0.14 mm	
Stage 2	2.02 ± 0.32 mm	

Carburettor data (continued)

	Primary	Secondary
Models with a catalytic converter:		
Throttle chamber bore	30 mm	34 mm
Venturi diameter	22 mm	30 mm
Main jet	92	135
Main air bleed	70	60
Slow jet	50	80
Slow air bleed	80	80
Float height setting:		
Float upper edge to carburettor body (carburettor inverted)	10 ± 0.5 mm	
Float lower edge to carburettor body (carburettor upright)	43.5 ± 0.5 mm	
Throttle valve fast idle setting	0.63 ± 0.07 mm	
Choke pull-down setting:		
Stage 1	1.49 ± 0.14 mm	
Stage 2	2.26 ± 0.32 mm	

Fuel system component test data - non-catalyst models

Idle cut-off solenoid (see illustration SPEC 1):	
Apply 12 volts across terminal "E" (+) and solenoid body(-)	Solenoid should click, indicating correct operation
Accelerator pump solenoid (see illustration SPEC 1):	
Apply 12 volts across terminal "A" (+ supply) and "B" (- supply)	Solenoid should click, indicating correct operation
Idle-up solenoid (see illustration SPEC 1):	
Apply 12 volts across terminal "C" (+ supply) and "D" (- supply)	Solenoid should click, indicating correct operation
Accelerator pump solenoid coolant temperature switch:	
Meter connected across switch terminals:	
Below 70°C (158°F)	Continuity between terminals
Above 70°C (158°F)	Open-circuit between terminals
Power steering pressure switch:	
Steering wheel being turned	Continuity between switch terminals
Steering wheel stationary	Open-circuit between switch terminals

Note: *All resistance readings given are approximate values, which should be used as a guide only. Before condemning a component as faulty, have your findings confirmed by a Nissan dealer.*

Fuel system (ECC) component test data - catalyst models

Throttle valve switch resistances (see illustration SPEC 2):	
Meter connected between terminals "C" and "D":	
Throttle valve fully closed	Open-circuit between terminals
Throttle valve open	Continuity between terminals
Idle cut-off solenoid (see illustration SPEC 2):	
Apply 12 volts across terminal "G" (+ supply) and "H" (- supply)	Solenoid should click, indicating correct operation
Accelerator pump solenoid (see illustration SPEC 2):	
Apply 12 volts across terminal "A" (+ supply) and "B" (- supply)	Solenoid should click, indicating correct operation
Idle-up solenoid (see illustration SPEC 3):	
Apply 12 volts across terminal "C" (+ supply) and "D" (- supply)	Solenoid should click, indicating correct operation
Air/fuel ratio solenoid valve (see illustration SPEC 3):	
Meter connected between terminals "A" and "B"	Continuity should exist
Throttle switch	See Section 13
Mixture heater	Continuity should exist between heater terminals
Clutch switch:	
Clutch pedal released	Continuity between switch terminals
Clutch pedal depressed	Open-circuit between switch terminals
Power steering pressure switch:	
Steering wheel being turned	Continuity between switch terminals
Steering wheel stationary	Open-circuit between switch terminals

Note: *All resistance readings given are approximate values, which should be used as a guide only. Before condemning a component as faulty, have your findings confirmed by a Nissan dealer.*

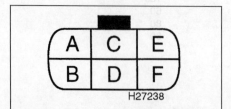

**SPEC 1 Carburettor wiring connector -
non-catalyst models**

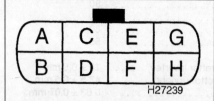

**SPEC 2 Carburettor 8-pin wiring
connector - catalyst models**

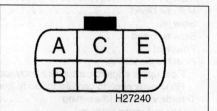

**SPEC 3 Carburettor 6-pin wiring
connector - catalyst models**

Recommended fuel

Models without a catalytic converter ("non-catalyst" models)	95 RON unleaded or 97 RON leaded (eg UK "4-star")
Models with a catalytic converter ("catalyst" models)	95 RON unleaded. Leaded fuel (eg UK "4-star") must **not** be used

Torque wrench settings

	Nm	lbf ft
Exhaust manifold retaining nuts and bolts	19	14
Exhaust system fasteners:		
Front pipe-to-manifold nut	31	23
Front pipe mounting bolt	23	17
Front pipe-to-intermediate pipe/catalytic converter nuts	49	36
Catalytic converter-to-tailpipe bolts	49	36
Intermediate pipe-to-tailpipe bolts	49	36
Fuel pump retaining bolts	19	14
Fuel tank retaining bolts	34	24
Inlet manifold retaining nuts and bolts	19	14

---

1 General information and precautions

1 The fuel system consists of a fuel tank mounted under the rear of the car, a mechanical fuel pump, and a carburettor. The fuel pump is operated by an eccentric on the inlet camshaft, and is mounted on the rear of the cylinder head. The air cleaner contains a disposable paper filter element, and incorporates a flap valve air temperature control system which allows cold air from the outside of the car and warm air from the exhaust manifold to enter the air cleaner in the correct proportions.

2 The fuel pump lifts fuel from the fuel tank via a filter, which is mounted onto the engine compartment bulkhead, and supplies it to the carburettor. Excess fuel is returned from the pump to the fuel tank. Further details on the carburettor and exhaust system can be found in Sections 10 and 16.

⚠️ *Warning: Many of the procedures in this Chapter require the removal of fuel lines and connections, which may result in some fuel spillage. Before carrying out any operation on the fuel system, refer to the precautions given in "Safety first!" at the beginning of this manual, and follow them implicitly. Petrol is a highly-dangerous and volatile liquid, and the precautions necessary when handling it cannot be overstressed.*

2 Air cleaner assembly - removal and refitting

Removal

1 Release the retaining clips, then slacken and remove the air cleaner housing lid retaining nut and screw. Free the lid from the inlet duct, then slacken the retaining clip and disconnect the hot-air inlet hose from the base of the lid. Position the lid clear of the base **(see illustrations)**.

2 Lift out the filter element and remove the mounting frame **(see illustration)**.

3 Undo the retaining bolt, and disconnect the breather hose from the front of the air cleaner

housing base. Lift up the base, then disconnect the necessary vacuum hose(s) (noting their correct fitted locations) from the hot idle compensator and air temperature control valve switch, as they become accessible. On models with a catalytic converter, also disconnect the air induction valve (AIV) hose **(see illustrations)**.

4 Remove the housing lid and base as an assembly, and recover the housing seal from the top of the carburettor.

5 To remove the inlet duct, undo the two retaining bolts and free it from the resonator. If necessary, the resonator box can then be unbolted and removed from the vehicle.

Refitting

6 Refitting is a reverse of the removal procedure, ensuring that all ducts and hoses

2.1a Release the air cleaner housing lid from the inlet duct . . .

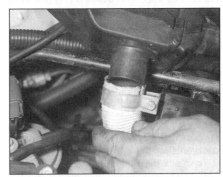

2.1b . . . then disconnect the hot-air inlet hose

2.2 Remove the filter element and lift off the mounting frame

2.3a Disconnect the breather hose (arrowed), and undo the mounting bolt . . .

2.3b . . . then lift up the housing base and disconnect the various vacuum hoses . . .

4A

2.3c . . . and on catalyst models, the air induction valve (AIV) hose (arrowed)

are securely reconnected to their original locations, and do not become trapped as the housing is refitted.

3 Air cleaner air temperature control (ATC) system

General information

1 The system is controlled by a heat-sensitive vacuum switch mounted in the base of the air cleaner housing. When the engine is started from cold, the switch is open, and allows inlet manifold depression to act on the air temperature control valve diaphragm in the air inlet nozzle. This vacuum causes the diaphragm to rise, drawing a flap valve across the cold air inlet, thus allowing only (warmed) air from around the exhaust manifold to enter the air cleaner.

2 As the temperature of the exhaust-warmed air in the air cleaner rises, the bi-metallic strip in the vacuum switch deforms, closing the switch to shut off vacuum supply to the air temperature control valve assembly. As the vacuum supply is cut, the flap is gradually lowered across the hot-air inlet until, when the engine is fully warmed up to normal operating temperature, only cold air from the front of the car is entering the air cleaner.

3 To check the system, allow the engine to cool down completely, then disconnect the inlet duct from the front of the air cleaner inlet nozzle; the flap valve in the nozzle should be securely seated across the hot-air inlet. Start the engine; the flap should immediately rise to close off the cold air inlet, and should then lower steadily as the engine warms up until it is eventually seated across the hot-air inlet again.

4 To check the vacuum switch, disconnect the vacuum pipe from the control valve when the engine is running, and place a finger over the pipe end. When the engine is cold, full inlet manifold vacuum should be present in the pipe; when the engine is at normal operating temperature, there should be no vacuum in the pipe.

5 To check the air temperature control valve assembly, remove the valve assembly from the air cleaner lid (see below). Disconnect the vacuum pipe, and suck hard at the control valve stub; the flap should rise to shut off the cold air inlet.

6 If either component is faulty, it must be renewed.

Vacuum switch - renewal

7 Remove the air cleaner housing as described in Section 2.

8 Bend up the tangs on the switch retaining clip, and remove the clip (see illustration). Withdraw the switch and seal from the housing. Examine the seal for signs of damage or deterioration, and renew if necessary.

9 Fit the seal to the switch, and install the assembly in the housing. Ensure that the switch is pressed firmly against the housing, and refit the retaining clip, securing it in position by bending down the clip tangs.

10 Refit the air cleaner housing as described in Section 2.

Air temperature control valve - renewal

11 Remove the air cleaner housing as described in Section 2.

12 Undo the three screws, and remove the air temperature control valve from the housing lid (see illustration). Disconnect the vacuum hose and remove the valve assembly.

13 Undo the retaining screw, then free the vacuum diaphragm unit from the flap valve and remove it from the duct.

14 Fit the new diaphragm unit, attach it to the flap valve, and securely tighten its retaining screw.

15 Connect the vacuum hose and refit the valve assembly to the housing lid, tightening its retaining screws securely.

16 Refit the air cleaner as described in Section 2.

4 Fuel pump - testing, removal and refitting

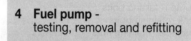
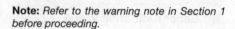

Note: *Refer to the warning note in Section 1 before proceeding.*

Testing

1 To test the fuel pump without removing it from the engine (see illustration), disconnect the outlet pipe which leads to the carburettor, and hold a wad of rag over the pump outlet while an assistant spins the engine on the starter. *Keep the hands away from the electric cooling fan.* Regular spurts of fuel should be ejected as the engine turns.

2 The pump can also be tested after it has been removed. With the pump outlet pipe disconnected but the inlet pipe still connected, hold a wad of rag by the outlet. Operate the pump lever by hand, moving it in and out; if the pump is in a satisfactory condition, the lever should move and return smoothly, and a strong jet of fuel should be ejected.

Removal

3 Identify the pump inlet, outlet and return hoses, and slacken the retaining clips. Place wads of rag beneath the hose unions to catch any spilled fuel, then disconnect both hoses from the pump, and plug the hose ends to minimise fuel loss. If necessary, remove the air cleaner housing to improve access to the pump.

4 Slacken and remove the bolts securing the pump to the rear of the cylinder head.

3.8 Air temperature control valve vacuum switch (arrowed). Hot idle compensator valve is also shown

3.12 Removing the air temperature control valve assembly from the air cleaner lid

4.1 The fuel pump is mounted on the left-hand end of the cylinder head

Remove the pump along with its insulating spacer; discard the spacer, a new one must be used on refitting.

Refitting

5 Ensure that the pump and cylinder head mating surfaces are clean and dry, then offer up the new insulating spacer. Refit the pump to the cylinder head, and tighten the pump retaining bolts to the specified torque setting.
6 Reconnect the inlet, outlet and return hoses to their relevant pump unions, and securely tighten their retaining clips.

5 Fuel gauge sender unit - removal and refitting

Note: *Refer to the warning note in Section 1 before proceeding.*

Removal

1 Disconnect the battery negative lead.
2 To gain access to the sender unit, remove the rear seat back as described in Chapter 11.
3 Undo the retaining screws, and lift up the access cover to expose the sender unit.
4 Disconnect the wiring connector from the sender unit, and tape the connector to the vehicle body to prevent it disappearing behind the tank.
5 Mark the hoses for identification purposes, then slacken the feed and return hose retaining clips. Disconnect both hoses from the top of the sender unit, and plug the hose ends. Tape the hoses to the vehicle body to prevent them disappearing behind the tank.
6 Note the alignment marks on the sender unit and tank - if no marks exist, make some.
7 On models where the sender unit is retained by a large ring, unscrew the locking ring and remove it from the tank. This is best accomplished by using a screwdriver on the raised ribs of the locking ring. Carefully tap the screwdriver to turn the ring anti-clockwise until it can be unscrewed by hand.
8 On models where the sender unit is bolted to the tank, slacken and remove all the retaining bolts and washers.
9 On all models, carefully lift the sender unit from the top of the fuel tank, taking great care not to bend the sender unit float arm, or to spill fuel onto the interior of the vehicle. As the sender unit is being removed, unclip the fuel filter from the base of the tank, and remove the sender unit and filter as an assembly.
10 Recover the rubber sealing ring and discard it; a new one must be used on refitting.
11 Wash the filter assembly in a high flash-point solvent. Examine the filter for signs of clogging or splitting, and renew if necessary.

Refitting

12 Refitting is a reversal of the removal procedure, noting the following points:

a) *Fit a new rubber sealing ring to the fuel tank.*
b) *Ensure that the filter is clipped securely in position before seating the sender unit in the tank.*
c) *Where the unit is retained by a locking ring, align the sender unit arrow with the mark on the tank, and securely tighten the locking ring.*
d) *Where the unit is retained by bolts, align the marks made on removal, and securely tighten all the bolts.*
e) *Ensure that the feed and return hoses are correctly reconnected, and are securely retained by their clips.*

6 Fuel tank - removal and refitting

Note: *Refer to the warning note in Section 1 before proceeding.*

Removal

1 Before removing the fuel tank, all fuel must be drained from the tank. Since a fuel tank drain plug is not provided, it is therefore preferable to carry out the removal operation when the tank is nearly empty. Before proceeding, disconnect the battery negative lead, and syphon or hand-pump the remaining fuel from the tank.
2 Remove the exhaust system as described in Section 16.
3 Free both handbrake cables from their retaining clips on the base of the fuel tank.
4 Disconnect the wiring connector and fuel hoses from the fuel gauge sender unit, as described in paragraphs 1 to 5 of Section 5.
5 Working at the left-hand side of the rear of the fuel tank, release the retaining clips, then disconnect the filler neck vent pipe and main filler neck hose from the fuel tank.
6 Place a trolley jack with an interposed block of wood beneath the tank, then raise the jack until it is supporting the weight of the tank.
7 Slacken and remove the three bolts securing the rear of the fuel tank retaining straps to the vehicle body, then pivot each strap away from the tank.
8 Slowly lower the fuel tank out of position, disconnecting any other relevant vent pipes as they become accessible (where necessary). Remove the tank from underneath the vehicle, and recover the tank mounting rubbers, noting their correct fitted positions.
9 If the tank is contaminated with sediment or water, remove the sender unit (Section 5) and swill the tank out with clean fuel. The tank is injection-moulded from a synthetic material, and if damaged, it should be renewed. However, in certain cases, it may be possible to have small leaks or minor damage repaired. Seek the advice of a suitable specialist before attempting to repair the fuel tank.

Refitting

10 Refitting is the reverse of the removal procedure, noting the following points:
a) *When lifting the tank back into position, reconnect all the relevant breather hoses, and take great care to ensure that none of the hoses become trapped between the tank and vehicle body. Tighten the fuel tank mounting bolts to the specified torque setting.*
b) *Ensure that all pipes and hoses are correctly routed,. and securely held in position with their retaining clips.*
c) *On completion, refill the tank with fuel, and check for signs of leakage prior to taking the vehicle out on the road.*

7 Accelerator cable - removal, refitting and adjustment

Removal

1 Free the accelerator inner cable from the carburettor throttle cam.
2 Slacken the outer cable locknut and adjuster nut, then free the outer cable from its mounting bracket **(see illustration)**.
3 Working back along the length of the cable, free it from any relevant retaining clips or ties, whilst noting its correct routing.
4 Working inside the vehicle, remove the lower facia panel from the driver's side of the facia, as described in Chapter 11.
5 Reach up behind the facia, and detach the inner cable from the top of the accelerator pedal.
6 Undo the bolts securing the outer cable end fitting to the bulkhead, then withdraw the cable through the bulkhead and into the passenger compartment.

Refitting

7 From inside the vehicle, feed the cable through the hole in the bulkhead.
8 When the end of the cable appears in the engine compartment, pull the cable through

7.2 Slacken the locknut (arrowed) and free the accelerator cable from its mounting bracket

4A

the bulkhead, and route it correctly around the engine compartment.

9 Return to the inside of the vehicle, and secure the outer cable end fitting to the bulkhead by securely tightening its retaining bolts. Clip the inner cable into position on the top of the accelerator pedal.

10 Make sure that the cable is securely retained, then refit the lower panel to the facia (see Chapter 11).

11 From within the engine compartment, work along the cable, and ensure that it is secured in position with all the relevant retaining clips and ties, and correctly routed.

12 Locate the outer cable in its mounting bracket, and reconnect the inner cable to the throttle cam. Adjust the cable as described below.

Adjustment

13 With the throttle cam resting against its stop, slacken the accelerator cable locknut, and position the adjuster nut so that only a slight amount of free play is present in the inner cable. Hold the adjuster nut stationary, and securely tighten the locknut.

14 Have an assistant depress the accelerator pedal, and check that the throttle cam opens fully and returns smoothly to its stop. If necessary, readjust the cable as described above.

8 Accelerator pedal - removal and refitting

Removal

1 Remove the lower facia panel from the driver's side of the facia, as described in Chapter 11.

2 Reach up behind the facia, and detach the inner cable from the top of the accelerator pedal.

3 Undo the two mounting bolts securing the pedal mounting bracket to the bulkhead, and remove the pedal assembly from underneath the facia.

4 If necessary, remove the retaining clip from the end of the accelerator pedal pivot shaft, then slide the pedal out of position and recover the return spring from the mounting bracket.

5 Examine the mounting bracket and pedal pivot points for signs of wear, and renew as necessary.

Refitting

6 Refitting is a reversal of the removal procedure, applying a little multi-purpose grease to the pedal pivot shaft. On completion, adjust the accelerator cable as described in Section 7.

9 Unleaded petrol - general information and usage

Note: *The information given in this Chapter is correct at the time of writing, and applies only to petrols currently available in the UK. If updated information is thought to be required, check with a Nissan dealer. If travelling abroad, consult one of the motoring organisations (or a similar authority) for advice on the petrols available, and their suitability for your vehicle.*

1 The fuel recommended by Nissan is given in the Specifications Section of this Chapter.

2 RON and MON are different testing standards; RON stands for Research Octane Number (also written as RM), while MON stands for Motor Octane Number (also written as MM).

3 All Nissan Primera carburettor models are designed to run on fuel with a minimum octane rating of 95 (RON). All models with a catalytic converter must be run on unleaded fuel **only**. Under no circumstances should leaded fuel be used, as this may damage the catalyst. On models without a catalytic converter, either unleaded or leaded fuel can be used without modification.

10 Carburettor - general information

Models without a catalytic converter

1 The Nikki 21 L series carburettor is a downdraught progressive twin venturi instrument, with a vacuum-controlled secondary throttle **(see illustration)**. The choke control is semi-automatic in operation.

2 The carburettor is constructed in three main bodies; these are the upper body, the main body, and the throttle body (which contains the throttle assembly). An insulating block, placed between the main carburettor body and the throttle body, prevents excess heat transference to the main body.

3 During slow running and at idle, fuel sourced from the float chamber passes into the idle channel through a metered idle jet. Here it is mixed with a small amount of air from a calibrated air bleed. The resulting mixture is drawn through a channel, to be discharged from the idle orifice under the throttle valve. A tapered mixture screw is used to vary the outlet, and this ensures fine control of the idle mixture. An idle cut-off valve is used to prevent run-on when the engine is shut down. It utilises a 12-volt solenoid plunger to block the idle channel when the ignition is switched off.

4 A progression slot provides extra enrichment as it is uncovered by the opening of the throttle valve during initial acceleration.

5 Under normal operating conditions, fuel is drawn through a calibrated main jet, into the base of the auxiliary venturi. An emulsion tube is placed in the auxiliary venturi, capped with a main air bleed. The fuel is mixed with air, drawn in through the holes in the emulsion tube. The resulting mixture is discharged into the main airstream via the main nozzle.

6 The carburettor is also equipped with an accelerator pump, to provide an initial spurt of extra fuel during sudden acceleration. The accelerator pump is mechanically operated by a lever which is connected to the throttle linkage. A solenoid valve, controlled by a thermostatic switch, is fitted to the accelerator pump circuit to vary the pump output. With the engine cold, the solenoid valve is opened, and the pump gives maximum output. Once the engine reaches operating temperature, the solenoid valve closes, and the pump output is reduced.

7 The idle speed is set by an adjustable screw. The adjustable mixture screw is sealed during production with a tamperproof plug to prevent unnecessary adjustment.

8 When an electrical load is placed on the alternator (or the power steering is in operation), the idle speed will tend to drop, since both the alternator and the power steering pump are engine-driven. To counteract this stalling tendency, an idle-up solenoid is fitted to the carburettor. The solenoid opens a bypass fuel-and-air channel to increase the idle speed.

9 The choke is controlled by an electrically-heated bi-metallic coil spring which is linked to the choke valve. The choke is operated by slowly depressing the accelerator pedal. Once the engine is running, an electrical supply is applied to the bi-metallic coil. This heats the bi-metallic coil, causing it to unwind and open up the choke valve.

Models with a catalytic converter

10 The Nikki carburettor fitted to models with a catalytic converter is basically the same as that fitted to non-catalytic converter models described above. The only major difference is that the carburettor is electronically controlled by the ECC (electronically controlled carburettor) control unit (which also controls the ignition system - see Chapter 5). This is made possible by the fitting of an air/fuel ratio solenoid valve to the carburettor, this is opened and closed rapidly under the control of the ECC control unit, to richen or weaken the air/fuel mixture ratio by opening or closing the compensating air bleed and main jet.

11 The electrical side of the system consists of the ECC control unit, and all the sensors that provide it with information.

12 The principal information required by the control unit is provided by the boost pressure sensor and the crank angle sensor (which is housed in the distributor). The boost pressure sensor informs the ECC unit of the load on the

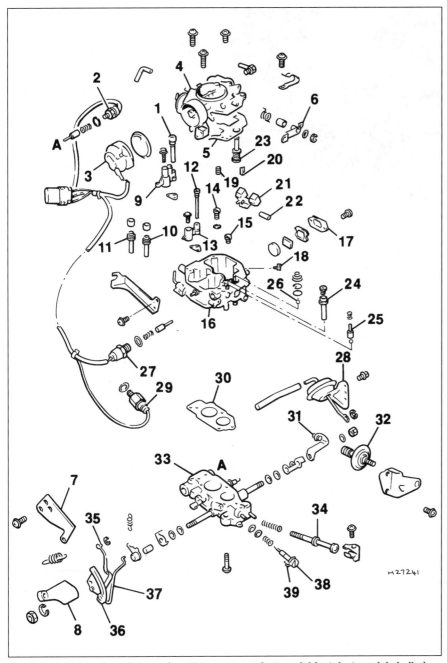

10.1 Exploded view of the carburettor - non-catalyst model (catalyst model similar)

1 Secondary emulsion tube	15 Primary main jet	28 Secondary throttle valve
2 Idle-up control solenoid	16 Main body	diaphragm
3 Choke bi-metallic coil	17 Float level inspection	29 Accelerator pump control
cover	window	solenoid
4 Upper body	18 Secondary main jet	30 Gasket
5 Float chamber gasket	19 Primary idle jet	31 Adjustment screw
6 Accelerator pump lever	20 Needle valve	32 Throttle damper
7 Bracket	21 Float	33 Throttle body
8 Bracket	22 Float pivot pin	34 Idle speed adjusting screw
9 Secondary venturi	23 Accelerator pump piston	35 Choke link rod
10 Secondary progression jet	24 Primary idle fuel jet	36 Throttle lever
11 Idle-up jet	25 Accelerator pump weight	37 Accelerator pump link rod
12 Primary main air bleed	26 Accelerator pump ball	38 Idle mixture (exhaust gas
13 Primary auxiliary venturi	valve	CO) adjustment screw
14 Part-load enrichment valve	27 Idle cut-off valve solenoid	39 Tamperproof cap

engine, and the crank angle sensor informs the unit of the engine speed and crankshaft position (see Chapter 5 for further information).

13 Additional information to refine air/fuel mixture control comes from the following sensors:

a) *Coolant temperature sensor - informs control unit of the engine temperature.*

b) *Throttle valve switch - informs control unit whether the throttle is closed or open.*

c) *Ignition switch - informs the control unit when the engine is being started.*

d) *Neutral switch - informs the control unit when the transmission is in neutral.*

e) *Clutch switch - informs the control unit when the clutch is engaged/disengaged.*

f) *Vehicle speed sensor (mounted in the speedometer) - informs the control unit of the vehicle speed.*

g) *The exhaust gas sensor - sends the control unit information on the amount of oxygen in the exhaust gases (see Part D of this Chapter).*

14 All the signals received by the control unit are compared with set values pre-programmed (mapped) into its memory; based on this information, the control unit selects the response appropriate to those values, and accordingly controls the ignition coil (via the power transistor, varying the ignition timing as required), the air/fuel ratio solenoid valve, the accelerator pump, idle-up and idle cut-off solenoid valves, and the exhaust gas sensor. The mixture, idle speed and ignition timing are constantly varied by the control unit, to provide the best settings for starting (with either a hot or cold engine), engine warm-up, idle, cruising and acceleration.

15 To reduce emissions and improve driveability when the engine is cold, an electrical heating element (controlled by the ECC unit) is fitted between the carburettor and inlet manifold to quickly warm-up the carburettor on cold starts. When the engine is up to normal operating temperature, the ECC unit closes the idle cut-off valve when the engine is on the overrun (effectively cutting off the fuel supply to the engine) to improve fuel economy and reduce exhaust emissions.

16 In order to further reduce exhaust emissions, an exhaust gas recirculation (EGR) system and air induction system is fitted. Refer to Part D of this Chapter for further information on these systems.

4A

11 Carburettor -
removal and refitting

Note: *Refer to the warning note in Section 1 before proceeding.*

Removal

1 Disconnect the battery negative terminal. Partially drain the cooling system as described in Chapter 1.

11.4 Carburettor wiring connectors

11.5 Slacken the retaining clip (arrowed) and disconnect the fuel hose from the carburettor

2 Remove the air cleaner housing as described in Section 2.

3 Free the accelerator inner cable from the carburettor throttle cam, then slacken the outer cable locknut and adjuster nut, and free the outer cable from its mounting bracket.

4 Trace the wiring back from the carburettor electrical components to its wiring connector(s), and disconnect them from the main wiring harness **(see illustration)**. On models with a catalytic converter, also disconnect the mixture heater connector situated at the front of the manifold.

5 Slacken the retaining clip, and disconnect the fuel feed hose from the carburettor **(see illustration)**. Place wads of rag around the union to catch any spilled fuel. Plug the hose as soon as it is disconnected, to minimise fuel loss and prevent dirt entry into the system.

6 Make a note of the correct fitted positions of all the relevant vacuum pipes and breather hoses, to ensure that they are correctly positioned on refitting, then release the retaining clips (where fitted) and disconnect them from the carburettor.

7 Slacken and remove the four retaining bolts securing the carburettor to the manifold, and remove the carburettor assembly from the car. Remove the insulating spacer (non-catalyst models) or heating element (catalyst models), and plug the inlet manifold port with a wad of clean cloth to prevent the possible entry of foreign matter.

Refitting

8 Refitting is the reverse of the removal procedure, noting the following points:

a) *Prior to refitting, ensure that the carburettor, inlet manifold and insulating spacer/heating element sealing faces are clean and flat. Refit them to the manifold, and securely tighten the carburettor retaining bolts.*

b) *Use the notes made on dismantling to ensure that all hoses are refitted to their original positions and, where necessary, are securely held by their retaining clips.*

c) *Ensure that all wiring is correctly routed and securely reconnected.*

d) *Reconnect and adjust the accelerator*

cable as described in Section 7.

e) *Refit the air cleaner housing as described in Section 2.*

f) *On completion, top-up the cooling system then check and, if necessary, adjust the idle speed and mixture settings as described in Chapter 1.*

12 Carburettor - fault diagnosis, overhaul and adjustments

Diagnosis

1 If a carburettor fault is suspected, always check first that the ignition timing is accurate, that the spark plugs are in good condition and correctly gapped, that the accelerator and choke cables are correctly adjusted, and that the air cleaner filter element is clean; see the relevant Sections of Chapter 1 or of this Chapter. If the engine is running very roughly, first check the valve clearances and the compression pressures as described in Chapter 2A.

2 If careful checking of all of the above produces no improvement, the carburettor must be removed for cleaning and overhaul.

3 Note that in the rare event of a complete carburettor overhaul being necessary, it may prove more economical to renew the carburettor as a complete unit. Check the price and availability of a replacement carburettor and of its component parts before starting work; note that most sealing washers, screws and gaskets are available in kits, as are some of the major sub-assemblies. In most cases, it will be sufficient to dismantle the carburettor and to clean the jets and passages.

Overhaul

Note: *Refer to the warning note in Section 1 before proceeding.*

4 Disconnect the throttle return spring, and inspect the accelerator pump operating lever for wear. Remove the accelerator pump lever retaining spring, circlip and clip, and disconnect the pump lever and spring assembly.

5 Remove the clip, and disconnect the choke connecting rod.

6 Remove the retaining screws, and detach the carburettor upper body. If the top is tight, a gentle tap with a plastic hammer is usually sufficient to free it. Do not lever the assemblies apart, as there is a risk of damaging the mating surfaces.

7 Inspect the float chamber for corrosion and calcium build-up.

8 Remove the accelerator pump inlet spring, retaining clip, strainer and ball; invert the carburettor over a cupped hand to catch these parts.

9 Unscrew the brass plug, and remove the accelerator pump outlet spring, weight and ball; invert the carburettor over a cupped hand to catch these parts.

10 Remove the accelerator pump bellows and piston assembly from the upper body, and check the assembly for fatigue and damage.

11 Tap out the float pin, and remove the float, needle valve and float chamber gasket. **Note:** *In some instances, the needle valve seat Is not removable.*

12 Note the correct location of all the jets and air bleeds prior to removal; these notes can then be used to ensure that the jets are correctly positioned on refitting.

13 Where necessary, remove all primary and secondary jets and air bleeds, using a close-fitting screwdriver. **Note:** *Do not attempt to remove the secondary slow air bleeds from the carburettor.*

14 Remove each plug, and unscrew the primary idle-up and secondary slow jets from the main body. Unscrew the primary idle air bleed.

15 Remove the two screws, and detach the auxiliary venturis. Unscrew the primary and secondary combined air corrector and emulsion tubes from the auxiliary venturis.

16 Remove the float chamber plug, and unscrew the primary main jet from its place in the side of the float chamber. Unscrew the secondary main jet, and remove it from the bottom of the float chamber.

17 Remove the idle mixture adjustment screw tamperproof cap. Turn the screw in until it seats lightly, counting the **exact** number of turns required to do this, then unscrew it. On refitting, turn the screw in until it seats lightly, then back the screw off by the number of turns noted on removal, to return the screw to its original location. **Note:** *special tool is required to remove the mixture screw.*

18 If necessary, the various solenoids can be unscrewed and removed from the carburettor body, noting their correct fitted positions. As each solenoid is removed, recover its spring and plunger and, where fitted, the solenoid sealing washer. Each solenoid can be tested by applying 12 volts across its terminals - as the voltage is applied, the solenoid plunger should be drawn into the solenoid body.

19 On models with a catalytic converter, if

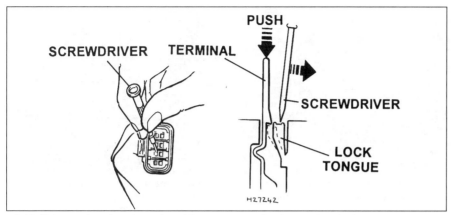

12.22 Release the wires from the wiring connector by depressing the lock tongue with a small, flat-bladed screwdriver as shown

12.26 Float height setting can be checked as described in text using the inspection window (arrowed)

the fuel/air ratio solenoid is to be removed, free its wiring from the connector as described in paragraph 22. Remove the two retaining screws, and withdraw the solenoid valve. Recover the sealing rings from the solenoid and discard them; new ones must be used on refitting.

20 Clean the jets, carburettor body assemblies, float chamber and internal drillings. An air line may be used to clear the internal passages once the carburettor is fully dismantled.

> ⚠ **Warning: If high-pressure air is directed into drillings and passages where a diaphragm is fitted, the diaphragm is likely to be damaged. Aerosol cans of carburettor cleaner are widely available, and can prove very useful in helping to clear internal passages of stubborn obstructions.**

21 Use a straight edge to check all carburettor body assembly mating surfaces for distortion.

22 Although all electrical components are connected to the same wiring connectors, each one can be renewed individually once its wiring has been released from the relevant connector. To free the wiring, lift the tangs on the side of the wiring connector, and free the retaining clip from the rear of the connector. Using a small, flat-bladed screwdriver, free the relevant wires of the component to be removed, and push them out of the connector **(see illustration)**. Note the correct fitted location of each wire, and take great care not to damage the wiring terminals as they are removed. Slide the wires of the new component into position in the connector, check they are securely retained, then clip the retaining clip into position on the rear of the connector. **Note:** *Ensure that the wires are correctly seated in the connector. If they are not, a poor electrical connection will be made when the two halves of the connector are joined, which could result in the carburettor electrical components not functioning correctly.*

23 On reassembly, renew any worn components, and fit a complete set of new

gaskets and seals. A gasket and seal kit is available from your Nissan dealer.

24 Reassembly is a reversal of the dismantling procedure. Ensure that all jets are securely locked in position, but do not overtighten them. Ensure that all mating surfaces are clean and dry, and that all body sections are correctly assembled with their fuel and air passages correctly aligned. Check the float height when reassembling the carburettor. Prior to refitting the carburettor, set the throttle valve fast idle and choke pull-down settings as described below.

Adjustments

Idle speed and mixture settings

25 Refer to Chapter 1.

Float height (fuel level) setting

Note: *The float height setting can be checked without removing the carburettor, by checking the fuel level in the inspection window on the carburettor body. With the car parked on level ground, and the engine idling at the specified speed, the fuel level should be between the marks on each side of the inspection window (see illustration). If not, the float height must be adjusted as described below.*

26 Invert the carburettor body so that the float is at the top.

27 Raise the float fully, then lower it slowly

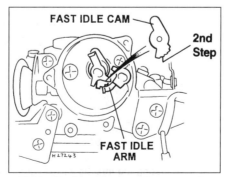

12.31a Position the fast idle arm on the second step of the cam as shown . . .

until it contacts the needle valve tip. Hold the float in this position, and measure the distance between the upper edge of the float and the sealing face of the upper body. This should be as given in the Specifications at the start of this Chapter. To adjust the setting, **carefully** bend the pivot arm.

28 Turn the carburettor body the correct way up, then measure the distance between the lower edge of the float and the sealing face of the upper body. This should be as given in the Specifications at the start of this Chapter. To adjust the setting, **carefully** bend the float stopper arm.

Throttle valve fast idle setting

29 Remove the three screws, and detach the bi-metallic cover assembly and fixing ring.

30 Invert the carburettor, then open the throttle slightly and place the fast idle arm against the second step of the fast idle cam. The adjustment screw will force open the throttle plate, to leave a small clearance.

31 Ensure that the choke flap is fully closed, then use the shank of a twist drill to measure the clearance "A" between the wall of the throttle bore and the throttle valve **(see illustration)**. Refer to the Specifications at the start of this Chapter for the required drill size.

32 Adjust as necessary by turning the fast idle adjustment screw in the appropriate direction.

33 Refit the fixing ring and bi-metallic coil housing, ensuring that the spring locates in

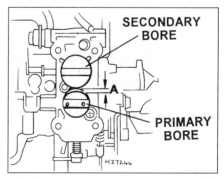

12.31b . . . then measure the clearance (A) between the primary throttle valve and bore

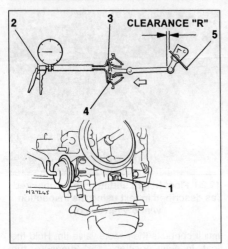

12.38 Choke pull-down setting

1 *Pull-down adjustment tongue*
2 *Vacuum pump*
3 *Pull-down vacuum unit*
4 *Diaphragm*
5 *Choke valve-to-bore clearance*

the slot of the choke lever. Secure loosely with the three screws.

34 Align the cut mark on the bi-metallic cover with the correct mark on the choke assembly housing, and tighten the three screws.

Choke pull-down setting

35 Operate the carburettor choke linkage to fully close the choke valve, and hold the linkage in this position.

36 Attach a hand-held vacuum pump to the choke pull-down diaphragm, and apply a vacuum to the diaphragm so that the diaphragm rod is pulled fully into the diaphragm body. In the absence of a vacuum pump, the rod can be pushed into the diaphragm using a small screwdriver.

37 With the rod fully retracted, use the shank of a suitable twist drill to measure the clearance between the edge of the choke valve and bore, and compare this to the clearance given in the Specifications. **Note:** *If the carburettor temperature is below 5°C (41 °F), use the stage 1 clearance; above 16.5°C (62°F), refer to the stage 2 clearance.*

38 If necessary, adjust the clearance by **carefully** bending the pull-down tongue in the appropriate direction **(see illustration)**.

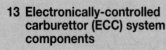

13 Electronically-controlled carburettor (ECC) system components

Boost pressure sensor

1 The boost pressure sensor is mounted onto the left-hand front suspension mounting turret, where it is located next to the power transistor.

2 To remove the sensor, first disconnect the battery negative terminal.

3 Undo the two retaining screws and remove

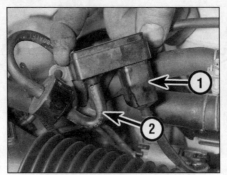

13.3 Boost pressure sensor wiring connector (1) and vacuum hose (2)

the boost pressure sensor, disconnecting its wiring connector and vacuum hose as they become accessible **(see illustration)**.

4 Refitting is the reverse of removal.

Power transistor

5 See Chapter 5.

Fuel/air ratio solenoid valve

6 Refer to Section 12.

Carburettor solenoid valves

7 Refer to Section 12, paragraphs 18 and 22. It is not necessary to remove the carburettor from the vehicle, but access can be considerably improved by removing the air cleaner housing as described in Section 2.

Throttle valve switch

8 Undo the two screws, and free the switch from the right-hand side of the carburettor **(see illustration)**. If necessary, remove the air cleaner housing to improve access to the switch.

9 Free the switch wiring from the connector as described in paragraph 22 of Section 12, and remove the switch.

10 Refitting is the reverse of removal. On completion, adjust the switch as follows.

11 Warm the engine up to normal operating temperature, then stop it and disconnect the carburettor wiring connector containing the throttle switch wiring connectors. Referring to

13.8 Throttle valve switch (arrowed) is mounted on the right-hand side of the carburettor

the accompanying illustration, use two pieces of wire to connect the terminals of the idle cut-off valve solenoid; this is necessary to allow the engine to start. Connect a multimeter set to its resistance across the switch terminals.

12 Start the engine, and allow it to idle. Slowly increase the engine speed to approximately 2000 rpm; continuity should exist between the switch terminals. Slowly decrease the engine speed whilst observing the meter; at 1200 rpm the switch should operate, and an open-circuit will be present between the switch terminals. If adjustment is necessary, carefully bend the tang until the switch operates as described.

13 Once the switch is correctly adjusted, stop the engine and reconnect the wiring connector.

Coolant temperature sensor

14 Refer to Chapter 3.

ECC control unit

15 The ECC control unit is situated just in front of the centre console, mounted onto the transmission tunnel floor. Prior to removal, disconnect the battery negative terminal.

16 To gain access to the control unit, undo the retaining screws and release the retaining clips, then remove the small trim panel from each side of the front of the centre console (see Chapter 11).

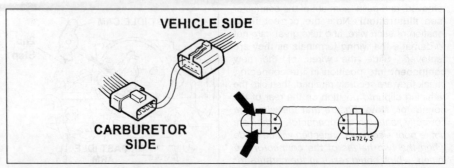

13.11 Adjusting the throttle valve switch. Disconnect the wiring connector, and bridge the idle cut-off solenoid wiring connectors with two pieces of wire. Connect the multimeter to the arrowed terminals of the carburettor side of the connector, and adjust the switch as described in text

17 Undo the retaining screws, and release the control unit from its mounting bracket. Disconnect the wiring connector(s) and remove the unit from the vehicle.

18 Refitting is the reverse of removal, ensuring that the wiring connector is securely reconnected.

Crank angle sensor

19 The crank angle sensor is an integral part of the distributor, and cannot be renewed separately. If the sensor is faulty, the complete distributor body assembly must be renewed. Refer to Chapter 5 for further information.

Clutch switch

20 The clutch switch is located on the pedal bracket behind the facia. To remove the switch, first disconnect the battery negative lead. If necessary, to improve access, remove the driver's side lower facia panel as described in Chapter 11.

21 Disconnect the wiring plug from the switch, then slacken the locknut and unscrew the switch from its mounting bracket.

22 Refitting is a reversal of removal. Ensure that the clutch is correctly adjusted (see Chapter 6) then adjust the switch as follows.

23 Connect a multi-meter, set to its resistance function, across the switch terminals. Position the switch so there is continuity between the terminals when the pedal is in the at-rest position, and an open-circuit when the pedal is lightly depressed. Once the switch is correctly adjusted, securely tighten the locknut and reconnect the wiring.

Neutral switch

24 Refer to Chapter 7A.

Power steering idle-up switch

25 The power steering idle-up switch is screwed into the power steering feed pipe, in the right-hand rear corner of the engine

15.1 Exhaust manifold and associated components - models with a catalytic converter

1 Hot-air inlet hose
2 EGR pipe
3 Exhaust gas sensor wiring connector
4 Exhaust gas sampling pipe

compartment. Prior to removal, position the front wheels in the straight-ahead position, then disconnect the battery negative terminal.

26 Locate the switch and disconnect its wiring connector.

27 Unscrew the switch and plug its opening in the pipe, working quickly to minimise fluid loss and prevent dirt entering into the hydraulic system. Recover the switch sealing washer.

28 Refitting is the reverse of removal, using a new sealing washer.

Vehicle speed sensor

29 The vehicle speed sensor is an integral part of the speedometer. Refer to Chapter 12 for removal and refitting details.

14 Inlet manifold - removal and refitting

Note: *Refer to the warning note in Section 1 before proceeding.*

Removal

1 Remove the carburettor as described in Section 11.

2 Drain the cooling system as described in Chapter 1.

3 Make a note of the correct fitted locations of all the relevant inlet manifold vacuum and coolant hose connections. Disconnect them from the manifold and, where necessary, from the associated vacuum valves. To avoid confusion on refitting, it may be wise to label each hose as it is disconnected.

4 On models with a catalytic converter, unscrew the union nut and free the EGR pipe, linking the inlet and exhaust manifolds, from the control valve on the left-hand end of the inlet manifold.

5 Disconnect the wiring connector from the coolant temperature sensor on the right-hand end of the manifold. Where necessary, undo the retaining bolt and free the earth lead from the manifold.

6 Undo the retaining bolts and remove the support bracket from the underside of the manifold.

7 Make a final check that all the relevant vacuum/breather hoses have been disconnected from the manifold.

8 Unscrew the retaining nuts and bolts, then manoeuvre the manifold away from the head and out of the engine compartment.

9 Remove the manifold gasket and discard it.

Refitting

10 Refitting is the reverse of the removal procedure, noting the following points:

a) *Ensure that the manifold and cylinder head mating surfaces are clean and dry, and fit the new gasket to the head studs. Install the manifold, and tighten its retaining nuts and bolts to the specified torque setting.*

b) *Ensure that all relevant hoses are reconnected to their original positions, and are securely held (where necessary) by their retaining clips.*

c) *Refit the carburettor as described in Section 11.*

d) *On completion, refill the cooling system as described in Chapter 1.*

15 Exhaust manifold - removal and refitting

Removal

1 Disconnect the hot-air inlet hose from the manifold shroud, and remove it from the vehicle **(see illustration)**.

2 On models with a catalytic converter, trace the wiring back from the exhaust gas sensor to its wiring connector, and disconnect it from the main wiring harness. Also unscrew the union nuts and free the EGR pipe, air induction pipe and the exhaust gas sampling pipe from the side of the manifold.

3 On all models, slacken and remove the retaining screws, and remove the shroud from the top of the exhaust manifold.

4 Firmly apply the handbrake, then jack up the front of the vehicle and support it on axle stands.

5 Undo the nuts securing the exhaust front pipe to the manifold, and the bolt securing the front pipe to its mounting bracket. Free the front pipe from the manifold, and recover the gasket.

6 Undo the retaining nuts and bolts securing the manifold to the head. Manoeuvre the manifold out of the engine compartment, and discard the manifold gaskets.

Refitting

7 Refitting is the reverse of the removal procedure, noting the following points:

a) *Examine all the exhaust manifold studs for signs of damage and corrosion; remove all traces of corrosion, and repair or renew any damaged studs.*

b) *Ensure that the manifold and cylinder head sealing faces are clean and flat, and fit the new manifold gaskets. Tighten the manifold retaining nuts and bolts to the specified torque.*

c) *Reconnect the front pipe to the manifold using the information given in Section 16.*

16 Exhaust system - general information and component removal

General information

1 On models without a catalytic converter, the exhaust system consists of three sections; the front pipe, the intermediate pipe and silencer box, and the tailpipe and main silencer box.

4A

16.6a Undo the three nuts securing the front pipe to the manifold . . .

16.6b . . . and the bolt securing the front pipe to its mounting bracket

16.7 Slacken and remove the bolts and springs securing the front pipe to the intermediate pipe/catalytic converter

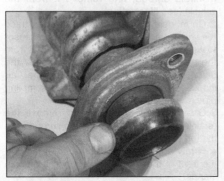

16.20 Renew all gaskets (front pipe shown)

2 On models with a catalytic converter, the exhaust system consists of four sections, the front pipe, the catalytic converter, the intermediate pipe and silencer box, and the tailpipe and main silencer box.

3 The system is suspended throughout its entire length by rubber mountings, and all exhaust sections are joined by flanged joints which are secured together by nuts and/or bolts.

Removal

4 Each exhaust section can be removed individually, or the complete system can be removed as a unit.

5 To remove the system or part of the system, first jack up the front or rear of the car, and support it on axle stands. Alternatively, position the car over an inspection pit or on car ramps.

Front pipe

6 Undo the nuts securing the front pipe to the manifold, and the bolt securing the front pipe

to its mounting bracket **(see illustrations)**. Separate the front pipe from the manifold and collect the gasket.

7 Slacken and remove the two nuts/bolts and springs securing the front pipe flange joint to the intermediate pipe/catalytic converter (as applicable) **(see illustration)**. Withdraw the front pipe from underneath the vehicle, and recover the gasket from the joint.

Catalytic converter (where fitted)

8 Slacken and remove the two nuts/bolts and springs (as applicable) securing the front pipe flange joint to the catalytic converter.

9 Unscrew the two bolts securing the intermediate pipe to the catalytic converter, and recover the gasket from between the two.

10 Free the catalytic converter from the front pipe, and recover the gasket.

Intermediate pipe

11 On models with a catalytic converter, unscrew the two bolts securing the intermediate pipe to the catalytic converter, and recover the gasket from between the two.

12 On models without a catalytic converter, undo the two nuts/bolts and springs (as applicable) securing the front pipe flange joint to the intermediate pipe, then separate the joint and recover the gasket.

13 On all models, slacken and remove the bolt securing the mounting rubber to the rear of the intermediate pipe.

14 Undo the two bolts securing the tailpipe to the intermediate pipe, then manoeuvre the intermediate pipe out from underneath the vehicle. Recover the gasket from the tailpipe joint.

Tailpipe

15 Slacken and remove the two bolts

securing the tailpipe to the intermediate pipe.

16 Unhook the tailpipe from its mounting rubbers, then remove it from the vehicle and recover the gasket.

Complete system

17 Undo the nuts securing the front pipe to the manifold, and the bolt securing the front pipe to its mounting bracket. Separate the front pipe from the manifold, and collect the gasket.

18 With the aid of an assistant, free the system from all its mounting rubbers, and manoeuvre it out from underneath the vehicle.

Heat shield(s)

19 The heat shields (where fitted) are secured in position by a mixture of nuts, bolts and clamps. When an exhaust section is renewed, transfer any relevant heat shields from the original over to the new section before installing the exhaust section on the vehicle.

Refitting

20 Each section is refitted by a reverse of the removal sequence, noting the following points:

a) *Ensure that all traces of corrosion have been removed from the flanges, and renew all necessary gaskets (see illustration).*

b) *Inspect the rubber mountings for signs of damage or deterioration, and renew as necessary.*

c) *Prior to tightening the exhaust system fasteners to the specified torque, ensure that all rubber mountings are correctly located, and that there is adequate clearance between the exhaust system and vehicle underbody.*

Chapter 4 Part B Fuel/exhaust systems - single-point fuel injection models

Contents

Degrees of difficulty

Easy, suitable for novice with little experience	**Fairly easy,** suitable for beginner with some experience	**Fairly difficult,** suitable for competent DIY mechanic 	**Difficult,** suitable for experienced DIY mechanic	**Very difficult,** suitable for expert DIY or professional 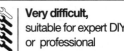

Specifications

General

System type . . . . Nissan Electronic Concentrated Control System (ECCS) single-point injection

Engine code:
2.0 litre models SR20Di

Fuel system data

For idle speed and mixture settings, refer to Chapter 1 Specifications.
Fuel pump type . . . . Electric, immersed in tank
Fuel pump regulated constant pressure (approximate) . . . . 2.5 bars

Fuel system component test data

Fuel pump resistance (at fuel gauge sender unit connection) . . . . 0.7 ohms
Throttle potentiometer resistances **(see illustration SPEC 1):**
  Meter connected between terminals "A" and "B":
    Throttle valve closed . . . . 1 kilohm
    Throttle valve partially open . . . . 1 to 9 kilohms
    Throttle valve fully open . . . . 9 kilohms
Fuel injector resistance **(see illustration SPEC 2):**
  Meter connected between terminals "A" and "D" . . . . 1 to 2 ohms
Auxiliary air control (AAC) valve resistance **(see illustration SPEC 2):**
  Meter connected between terminals "B" and "E" . . . . 10 ohms
Fast idle control (FICD) solenoid valve **(see illustration SPEC 2):**
  Apply 12 volts across terminals "C" (+ supply) and "F" (- supply) . . . Solenoid should click, indicating correct operation
Knock sensor **(see illustration SPEC 3):**
  Meter connected between terminal "A" and a suitable earth . . . . Continuity should exist (meter must be able to read more than 10 megohms)

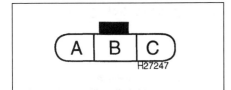
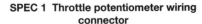

SPEC 1 Throttle potentiometer wiring connector

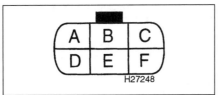

SPEC 2 Throttle body wiring connector

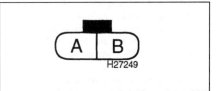

SPEC 3 Knock sensor wiring connector

4B

Fuel system component test data (continued)

Mixture heater	Continuity should exist between heater terminals
Power steering pressure switch:	
Steering wheel being turned	Continuity between switch terminals
Steering wheel stationary	Open-circuit between switch terminals
Coolant temperature sensor resistances:	
At 20ºC (68ºF)	2.1 to 2.9 kilohms
At 50ºC (122ºF)	0.68 to 1 kilohms
At 80ºC (176ºF)	0.30 to 0.33 kilohms

Note: *All resistance readings given are approximate values, which should be used as a guide only. Before condemning a component as faulty, have your findings confirmed by a Nissan dealer.*

Recommended fuel

Models without a catalytic converter ("non-catalyst" models)	95 RON unleaded or 97 RON leaded (eg UK "4-star")
Models with a catalytic converter ("catalyst" models)	95 RON unleaded. Leaded fuel (eg UK "4-star") must **not** be used

Torque wrench settings

	Nm	lbf ft
Dashpot retaining nut	29	21
Exhaust manifold nuts and bolts	43	31
Exhaust system fasteners:		
Front pipe-to-manifold nut	45	33
Front pipe mounting bolt	23	17
Front pipe-to-intermediate pipe/catalytic converter nuts	49	36
Catalytic converter-to-tailpipe bolts	49	36
Intermediate pipe-to-tailpipe bolts	49	36
Inlet manifold nuts and bolts	20	15
Knock sensor bolt	24	18
Throttle body retaining bolts:		
Stage 1	10	7
Stage 2	20	15

1 General information and precautions

1 The fuel system consists of a fuel tank mounted under the rear of the car, with an electric fuel pump immersed in it, a fuel filter, fuel feed and return lines, and the throttle body assembly (which incorporates the single fuel injector). Additionally, there is the ECCS (Electronic Concentrated Control System) control unit and its various sensors, electrical components and related wiring. The air cleaner is mounted on top of the throttle body, and contains a disposable paper filter element.

2 Refer to Section 6 for further information on the operation of the fuel injection system, and to Section 16 for information on the exhaust system.

 Warning: Many of the procedures in this Chapter require the removal of fuel lines and connections, which may result in some fuel spillage. Before carrying out any operation on the fuel system, refer to the precautions given in "Safety first!" at the beginning of this manual, and follow them implicitly. Petrol is a highly-dangerous and volatile liquid, and the precautions necessary when handling it cannot be overstressed.
Note: *Residual pressure will remain in the fuel lines long after the vehicle was last used.*

Before disconnecting any fuel line, depressurise the fuel system as described in Section 7.

2 Air cleaner assembly - removal and refitting

Removal

1 Slacken and remove the bolt, and free the inlet duct from the side of the air cleaner housing.

2 Unscrew the air cleaner cover nuts, then release the retaining clips and lift off the cover.

3 Withdraw the filter element.

4 Slide the spacers and rubbers off the air cleaner housing studs, then lift off the retaining plate and seal.

5 Slacken and remove the remaining air cleaner housing retaining bolts, and remove the housing from the engine compartment. Disconnect any relevant vacuum and breather hoses from the housing, noting each one's correct fitted location, as they become accessible.

6 The inlet duct and resonator assembly can then be removed, once all its retaining bolts have been removed. If necessary, the two can then be separated.

7 Inspect the mounting rubbers and seals for signs of damage or deterioration, and renew if necessary.

Refitting

8 Refitting is a reverse of the removal procedure, ensuring that all ducts and hoses are securely control reconnected to their original locations, and do not become trapped as the housing is refitted.

3 Accelerator cable - removal, refitting and adjustment

Refer to Chapter 4A, Section 7, substituting "throttle body" for all references to the carburettor.

4 Accelerator pedal - removal and refitting

Refer to Chapter 4A, Section 8, substituting "throttle body" for all references to the carburettor.

5 Unleaded petrol - general information and usage

Note: *The information given in this Chapter is correct at the time of writing, and applies only to petrols currently available in the UK. If updated information is thought to be required, check with a Nissan dealer. If travelling* abroad, consult one of the motoring organisations (or a similar authority) for advice on the petrols available, and their suitability for your vehicle.

1 The fuel recommended by Nissan is given in the Specifications Section of this Chapter.

2 RON and MON are different testing standards; RON stands for Research Octane Number (also written as RM), while MON stands for Motor Octane Number (also written as MM).

3 All Nissan Primera models are designed to run on fuel with a minimum octane rating of 95 (RON). All models with a catalytic converter must be run on unleaded fuel **only**. Under no circumstances should leaded fuel be used, as this may damage the catalyst. On models without a catalytic converter, either unleaded or leaded fuel can be used without modification.

6 Fuel injection system - general information

1 All single-point injection models are fitted with a combined fuel injection/ignition (engine management) system, otherwise known as the Electronic Concentrated Control System (ECCS). Refer to Chapter 5 for information on the ignition side of the system; the fuel injection side of the system operates as follows.

2 The fuel pump, immersed in the fuel tank, supplies fuel from the fuel tank to the throttle body via a filter mounted on the engine compartment bulkhead. Fuel supply pressure is controlled by the pressure regulator, on the side of the throttle body assembly, which lifts to allow excess fuel to return to the tank when the optimum operating pressure of the fuel system is exceeded. To reduce emissions and to improve driveability when the engine is cold, an electrical heating element is fitted between the throttle body and inlet manifold, to quickly warm it up on cold starts.

3 The electrical control system consists of the ECCS control unit, along with the following sensors:

a) *Throttle potentiometer - informs the ECCS control unit of the throttle valve position, and the rate of throttle opening/closing.*

b) *Coolant temperature sensor - informs the ECCS control unit of engine temperature.*

c) *Airflow meter - informs the ECCS control unit of the mass and temperature of the air entering the throttle body.*

d) *Crank angle sensor (housed in the distributor) - informs the ECCS control unit of the engine speed and crankshaft position (see Chapter 5 for further information).*

e) *Vehicle speed sensor (built into the speedometer) - informs the ECCS control unit of the vehicle speed.*

f) *Power steering and air conditioning*

system switches - informs the ECCS control unit if the system(s) are in operation, to allow it to adjust the idle speed to compensate for the extra load on the engine.

g) *Exhaust gas sensor (catalyst models only) - informs the ECCS control unit of the oxygen content of the exhaust gases (see Part D of this Chapter for further information).*

4 All the above signals are analysed by the ECCS control unit. Based on this information, the ECCS control unit selects the response appropriate to those values, and controls the fuel injector (varying its pulse width - the length of time the injector is held open - to provide a richer or weaker mixture, as appropriate). The mixture and idle speed are constantly varied by the ECCS control unit, to provide the best settings for cranking, starting (with either a hot or cold engine) and engine warm-up, idle, cruising and acceleration.

5 The ECCS control unit also has full control over the engine idle speed, via the auxiliary air control (AAC) valve. The valve, which is fitted to the throttle body, controls the opening of an air passage which bypasses the throttle valve. When the throttle valve is closed, the ECCS control unit controls the opening of the valve, which regulates the amount of air which flows through the throttle body passage, and so controls the idle speed.

6 The throttle body has a built-in fast idle facility, which is controlled by a thermostatic valve. When the engine is cold, the wax capsule in the valve (which is fitted to the throttle body), is at its smallest, and the fast idle cam holds the throttle valve slightly open. As the engine warms up, the wax capsule expands, forcing the valve plunger upwards, which in turn rotates the fast idle cam to the required position. In addition to this, there is also a fast idle control device (FICD) solenoid valve, which is controlled by the ECCS control unit. The solenoid valve controls the opening of an air passage which bypasses the throttle valve, and this is used to raise the idle speed when either the power steering and/or air conditioning systems are in operation.

7 On models with a catalytic converter, the ECCS control unit also controls the exhaust and evaporative emission control systems, which are described in detail in Chapter 4D.

8 If there is an abnormality in any of the readings obtained from sensors, the ECCS control unit switches to its back-up mode. If this happens, it ignores the abnormal sensor signal, and assumes a pre-programmed value which will allow the engine to continue running, albeit at reduced efficiency. If the ECCS control unit enters its back-up mode, the warning light on the instrument panel will come on, and the relevant fault code will be stored in the ECCS control unit memory.

9 If the warning light comes on, the vehicle should be taken to a Nissan dealer at the earliest opportunity. Once there, a complete test of the engine management system can be carried out,

using a special electronic diagnostic test unit which is simply plugged into the system's diagnostic connector. **Note:** *The ECCS control unit also has a self-diagnostic mode which can be accessed by the DIY mechanic. See Section 12 for further information.*

7 Fuel system - depressurisation

Note: *Refer to the warning note in Section 1 before proceeding.*

 Warning: The following procedure will merely relieve the pressure in the fuel system - remember that fuel will still be present in the system components, and take precautions accordingly before disconnecting any of them. Use clean rags wrapped around the connections to catch escaping fuel, and dispose of any fuel-soaked rags with care. Plug or tape over any open fuel lines, to prevent further loss of fuel or ingress of dirt.

1 The fuel system referred to in this Section is defined as the tank-mounted fuel pump, the fuel filter, the fuel injector and the pressure regulator, and the metal pipes and flexible hoses of the fuel lines between these components. All these contain fuel which will be under pressure while the engine is running and/or while the ignition is switched on. The pressure will remain for some time after the ignition has been switched off, and must be relieved before any of these components are disturbed for servicing work.

2 Identify and remove the fuel pump fuse from the vehicle fusebox - the fuses are not numbered as such, but can be identified from the label inside the fusebox cover, or from the wiring diagrams at the end of this manual.

3 Start the engine, and allow it to run until it stalls.

4 Try to start the engine at least twice more, to ensure that all residual pressure has been relieved.

5 Disconnect the battery negative terminal.

6 For safety, the fuel pump fuse should not be refitted until all work on the fuel system has been completed. If you refit the fuse now, **do not** switch on the ignition until completion of work.

8 Fuel pump - removal and refitting

Note: *Refer to the warning note in Section 1 before proceeding.*

Removal

1 The pump is removed as an assembly along with the fuel gauge sender unit. Remove the sender unit, and separate it from the fuel pump as described in Section 9.

4B

2 If necessary, unclip the filter element from the base of the fuel pump, then release the retaining clips, and separate the fuel pump from its plastic covers.

3 Wash the pump filter in a high flash-point solvent. Examine the filter for signs of clogging or splitting, and renew if necessary.

Refitting

4 Where necessary, reassemble the pump and covers, and refit the filter.

5 Ensure that the covers are clipped securely onto the pump, then join the pump to the sender unit and install the assembly as described in Section 9.

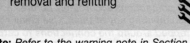

9 Fuel gauge sender unit - removal and refitting

Note: *Refer to the warning note in Section 1 before proceeding.*

Removal

1 Disconnect the battery negative lead.

2 To gain access to the sender unit, remove the rear seat cushion as described in Chapter 11.

3 Undo the retaining screws, and lift up the access cover to expose the sender unit.

4 Disconnect the wiring connector(s) from the fuel gauge sender unit, and tape the connector to the vehicle body to prevent it disappearing behind the tank.

5 Depressurise the fuel system as described in Section 7. Mark the hoses for identification purposes, then slacken the feed and return hose retaining clips. Disconnect both hoses from the top of the sender unit, and plug the hose ends.

6 Note the correct fitted position of the alignment mark on the sender unit (the arrow should be pointing towards the front of the vehicle). If no alignment mark exists, make one.

7 On models where the sender unit is retained by a large ring, unscrew the locking ring and remove it from the tank. This is best accomplished by using a screwdriver on the raised ribs of the locking ring. Carefully tap the screwdriver to turn the ring anti-clockwise until it can be unscrewed by hand.

8 On models where the sender unit is bolted to the tank, slacken and remove all the retaining bolts and washers.

9 On all models, carefully lift the sender unit from the top of the fuel tank, taking great care not to bend the sender unit float arm, or to spill fuel onto the interior of the vehicle. As the sender unit is being removed, disconnect the pump wiring connector from its base; reach into the tank, and depress the retaining clip to release the fuel pump from the base of the tank. The fuel pump and sender unit can then be removed as an assembly.

10 Recover the rubber sealing ring and

discard it; a new one must be used on refitting.

11 Slacken the retaining clip, then disconnect the fuel pump hose from the underside of the sender unit, and separate pump and sender unit.

12 Wash the pump filter in a high flash-point solvent. Examine the filter for signs of clogging or splitting, and renew if necessary.

Refitting

13 Refitting is a reversal of the removal procedure, noting the following points:

a) *Reassemble the fuel pump and sender unit, ensuring that the hoses are correctly reconnected to their original locations, and are securely held by their retaining clips.*

b) *Fit a new rubber sealing ring to the fuel tank.*

c) *Ensure that the fuel pump is clipped securely into position before seating the sender unit in the tank.*

d) *Where the unit is retained by a locking ring, align the sender unit arrow with the mark on the tank, and securely tighten the locking ring.*

e) *Where the unit is retained by bolts, align the marks made on removal, and securely tighten all the bolts.*

f) *Ensure that the fuel pump is clipped securely in position before seating the sender unit in the tank.*

g) *Ensure that the feed and return hoses are correctly reconnected, and are securely retained by their clips.*

h) *Prior to refitting the access cover, reconnect the battery, then start the engine and check the fuel hoses for signs of leaks.*

10 Fuel tank - removal and refitting

1 Refer to Chapter 4A, Section 6, noting that it will be necessary to depressurise the fuel system before the feed and return hoses are disconnected from the fuel sender unit (see Section 9).

11 Throttle body - removal and refitting

Note: *Refer to the warning note in Section 1 before proceeding.*

Removal

1 Disconnect the battery negative terminal.

2 Remove the air cleaner housing as described in Section 2.

3 Depress the retaining clips, and disconnect

the wiring connectors from the throttle potentiometer, the auxiliary air control valve, the airflow meter, and the injector wiring loom connector. Also disconnect the wiring connector from the heating element fitted between the throttle body and manifold.

4 Depressurise the fuel system as described in Section 7, then release the retaining clips and disconnect the fuel feed and return hoses from the throttle body assembly.

5 Free the accelerator inner cable from the throttle cam, then slacken the outer cable locknut and adjuster nut, then free the outer cable from its mounting bracket. On automatic transmission models, also disconnect the kickdown cable as described in Chapter 7B.

6 Release the retaining clips, then disconnect the coolant hoses from the rear of the throttle body, and plug the hose ends. Work quickly, to minimise coolant loss.

7 Make a note of the correct fitted positions of all the relevant vacuum pipes and breather hoses, to ensure that they are correctly positioned on refitting, then release the retaining clips (where fitted) and disconnect them from the throttle body.

8 Slacken and remove the bolts securing the throttle body assembly to the inlet manifold, and remove it from the engine compartment. Remove the heating element. Plug the inlet manifold port with a wad of clean cloth, to prevent the possible entry of foreign matter.

9 If necessary, with the throttle body removed, undo the retaining screws and separate the upper and lower sections, noting the gasket which is fitted between the two.

Refitting

10 Refitting is a reverse of the removal procedure, bearing in mind the following points:

a) *Where necessary, ensure that the mating surfaces of the upper and lower throttle body sections are clean and dry, then fit a new gasket and reassemble the two, tightening the retaining screws securely.*

b) *Ensure that the mating surfaces of the manifold, throttle body and heating element are clean and dry. Fit the heating element and throttle body. Working in a diagonal sequence, tighten all the retaining bolts first to the specified Stage 1 torque setting, then go around again and tighten them to the specified Stage 2 torque setting.*

c) *Ensure that all hoses are correctly reconnected and, where necessary, that their retaining clips are securely tightened.*

d) *On completion, adjust the accelerator cable using the information given in Section 3. On automatic transmission models, adjust the kickdown cable as described in Chapter 7B.*

12 Fuel injection/ignition system - general diagnosis and adjustment

General diagnosis

General information

1 If a fault appears in the fuel injection/ ignition system, first ensure that all the system wiring connectors are securely connected and free of corrosion. Then ensure that the fault is not due to poor maintenance - ie, check that the air cleaner filter element is clean, that the spark plugs are in good condition and correctly gapped, that the valve clearances are correctly adjusted, the cylinder compression pressures are correct, the ignition timing is correct, and that the emission control systems are operating correctly, referring to Chapters 1, 2, 4 and 5 for further information.

2 If these checks fail to reveal the cause of the problem, a quick check of the fuel injection/ignition circuits can be performed by setting the ECCS control unit to its self-diagnostic mode "2". In mode "2", the ECCS control unit will reveal any fault codes stored in its memory, using the engine check light in the instrument panel and the red LED on the right-hand side of the control unit.

3 Faults detected by ECCS control unit are stored in its memory, until the starter motor has been operated 50 times. If the fault is not detected again within this period, it will automatically be erased from the memory. Fault codes can also be erased from the memory by setting the control unit to self-diagnostic mode "2" and then switching it back to mode "1", as described below, or by leaving the battery disconnected for more than 24 hours.

Setting the self-diagnostic modes

4 Remove the fusebox cover, to gain access to the diagnostic connector which is clipped to the base of the fusebox.

5 Turn the ignition switch to the "ON" position, but do not start the engine. The ECCS control unit is now in self-diagnostic mode "1".

6 Using a spare piece of wire, connect the "IGN" terminal of the diagnostic connector to the "CHK" terminal **(see illustration)**. Keep

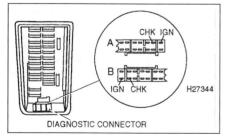

12.6 Diagnostic wiring connector and terminal identification

A 1.6 litre models   B 2.0 litre models

the terminals connected for at least 2 seconds, then disconnect the wire. The ECCS control unit is now in self-diagnostic mode "2".

7 In mode "2", the control unit will reveal any fault codes stored in its memory.

8 The code is revealed using a series of long (0.6 second) and short (0.3 second) flashes of the instrument panel engine check light and the red LED on the right-hand side of the control unit. The long flashes, which indicate the first digit of the fault code, will be given out first, then after a gap of approximately 0.9 seconds, the short flashes, which indicate the second digit of the fault code, will follow. There will be a gap of 2.1 seconds before any other codes are revealed. Once all codes have been revealed, the ECU will continuously run through the code(s) stored in its memory, revealing each one in turn with a gap of 2.1 seconds between each code. The fault codes are as follows.

Code number	Faulty circuit
11	Crank angle sensor circuit
12	Airflow meter circuit
13	Coolant temperature sensor circuit
21	Ignition signal circuit
34	Knock sensor circuit
43	Throttle potentiometer circuit
55	All circuits operating correctly

Note: *If both codes 11 and 21 are displayed, check the crank angle sensor circuit before checking the rest of the ignition circuit.*

9 On models with a catalytic converter, with the control unit in mode "2", if the engine is started it will automatically enter its exhaust gas sensor check mode. In this mode, the light and LED indicate the condition of the exhaust gases. When the light and LED are illuminated, the exhaust gas mixture is lean, and when they are off, the mixture is rich. To check the sensor, with the control unit in self-diagnostic mode "2", start the engine and warm it up to normal operating temperature. Once it is warm, raise the engine speed to approximately 2000 rpm, and hold it there for approximately 2 minutes whilst observing the instrument panel light or control unit LED. If the exhaust gas sensor is functioning correctly, the light/LED should flash on and off at least 5 times every 10 seconds.

10 When all the checks are complete, exit the self-diagnostic mode "2". If the engine has not been started, this can be achieved by reconnecting the "IGN" and "CHK" terminals of the diagnostic connector again for at least two seconds. If the engine is running, exit mode "2" by switching the ignition switch to the "OFF" position and disconnecting the battery negative terminal.

11 If a more detailed check of the fuel injection/ignition system is required, take the vehicle to a Nissan dealer. They will have access to the special electronic diagnostic test unit which is plugged into the system's diagnostic connector, and can carry out a full check of the system components.

Adjustment

12 On models without a catalytic converter, both the base idle speed and the mixture setting (exhaust gas CO level) are adjustable. On models with a catalytic converter, only the base idle speed is adjustable. Refer to Chapter 1 for the adjustment procedures.

13 Fuel injection system components - removal and refitting

Fuel injector

Note: *Refer to the warning note in Section 1 before proceeding. If a faulty injector is suspected, before condemning the injector, it is worth trying the effect of one of the proprietary injector-cleaning treatments.*

1 Disconnect the battery negative terminal.

2 Remove the air cleaner housing as described in Section 2.

3 Trace the wiring back from the injector, and disconnect it at the wiring connector.

4 Refer to Section 7 and depressurise the fuel system.

5 Undo the two injector cap retaining screws then lift off the cap and recover the gaskets.

6 Lift the injector out of the throttle body, and recover the injector sealing washer and seals. **Note:** *The injector may be a tight fit in the throttle body - if this is the case, do not try and pull it out using the wiring. Removal will require the upper half of the throttle body to be removed, so that the injector can be pushed out of position.*

7 If the injector is to be renewed, it will be necessary to free its wiring from the wiring connector. To do this, slide out the retaining clip from the rear of the connector then, using a small, flat-bladed screwdriver, free the relevant wires of the component to be removed, and push them out of the connector (see illustration 12.22 in Part A). Note the correct fitted location of each wire, and take great care not to damage the wiring terminals as they are removed.

8 Alternatively, if it is not wished to disturb the wiring connector, the injector can be removed complete with the fast idle control device (FICD) solenoid valve and auxiliary air control (AAC) valve. Refer to the relevant sub-headings of this Section for further information.

9 Refitting is a reverse of the removal procedure, noting the following points:
a) *Fit a new injector sealing washer and seals, and injector cap gaskets.*
b) *Where a new injector is being fitted, slide its wires into the correct positions in the connector. Check they are securely retained, then refit the retaining clip to the rear of the connector. Ensure that the wires are correctly seated in the connector. If they are not, a poor electrical connection will be made when*

4B

the two halves of the connector are joined, which could result in the injector not functioning correctly.

Fuel pressure regulator

Note: *Refer to the warning note in Section 1 before proceeding.*

10 The fuel pressure regulator is mounted onto the right-hand side of the throttle body. Prior to removal, disconnect the battery negative terminal. Note that access to the fuel pressure regulator is greatly improved if the air cleaner housing is removed (see Section 2).

11 Depressurise the fuel system as described in Section 7. Slacken the retaining clip and disconnect the fuel hose from the fuel pressure regulator.

12 Disconnect the vacuum hose from the regulator.

13 Slacken and remove the two retaining screws, then remove the regulator from the throttle body, and recover both of its sealing rings.

14 Refitting is the reverse of removal, using new sealing rings.

Auxiliary air control (AAC) valve

15 The auxiliary air control (AAC) valve is mounted onto the front of the throttle body. Prior to removal, disconnect the battery negative terminal.

16 Trace the wiring back from the injector, and disconnect it at the wiring connector.

17 Undo the two retaining screws, then remove the valve from the throttle body and recover the gasket.

18 If the valve is to be renewed, it will be necessary to free its wiring from the wiring connector as described in paragraph 7.

19 Alternatively, if it is not wished to disturb the wiring connector, the valve can be removed complete with the fast idle control device (FICD) solenoid valve and fuel injector. Refer to the relevant sub-headings of this Section for further information.

20 If necessary, with the valve removed, undo the retaining screws, and separate the two halves of the valve. Check that the valve plunger is free to move easily, and returns quickly under spring pressure. If not, the valve assembly must be renewed.

21 Refitting is the reverse of removal using a new gasket.

Throttle potentiometer

22 The throttle potentiometer is mounted onto the right-hand side of the throttle body. Prior to removal, disconnect the battery negative terminal. Note that access to the throttle potentiometer is greatly improved if the air cleaner housing is removed (see Section 2).

23 Disconnect the wiring connector from the throttle potentiometer.

24 Using a dab of white paint or a suitable marker pen, make alignment marks between the potentiometer and the throttle body.

25 Slacken and remove the two retaining screws, then remove the retaining plate and potentiometer.

26 On refitting, offer up the potentiometer, making sure its lever is correctly positioned on the top of the throttle valve spindle lever.

27 Install the retaining plate, then align the marks made prior to removal, and lightly tighten the retaining screws. Adjust the potentiometer as follows.

28 Using a multi-meter set to the resistance scale, check that the potentiometer resistance readings are as given in the Specifications at the start of this Chapter. If necessary, slacken the retaining screws and reposition the potentiometer until its resistances are as specified.

29 When the potentiometer is correctly positioned, securely tighten its retaining screws and reconnect the wiring connector.

30 Connect the battery and, where necessary, refit the air cleaner housing.

Airflow meter

31 The airflow meter is mounted onto the rear of the throttle body. Prior to removal, disconnect the battery negative terminal. Note that access to the airflow meter is greatly improved if the air cleaner housing is removed (see Section 2).

32 Disconnect the wiring connector from the airflow meter.

33 Undo the three retaining screws, then remove the meter from the throttle body, and recover its sealing ring.

34 Refitting is the reverse of removal, using a new sealing ring and tightening its retaining screws securely.

Fast idle control device (FICD) solenoid valve

35 The fast idle control device (FICD) solenoid valve is screwed into the right-hand side of the throttle body. Prior to removal, disconnect the battery negative terminal. If necessary, remove the air cleaner housing as described in Section 2 to improve access to the valve.

36 Trace the wiring back from the solenoid to its wiring connector, and disconnect it from the main wiring harness.

37 Unscrew the solenoid valve from the body, and recover the plunger, spring and sealing washer.

38 If the solenoid is to be renewed, it will be necessary to free its wiring from the wiring connector as described in paragraph 7.

39 Alternatively, if it is not wished to disturb the wiring connector, the solenoid valve can be removed complete with the fuel injector and auxiliary air control (AAC) valve. Refer to the relevant sub-headings of this Section for further information.

40 Refitting is the reverse of removal, ensuring that the solenoid plunger and spring are fitted in the correct order and the correct way round.

Fast idle thermostatic valve

41 The fast idle thermostatic valve is fitted to the left-hand side of the throttle body, sandwiched between the upper and lower halves of the body. Prior to removal, disconnect the battery negative terminal.

42 Remove the air cleaner housing as described in Section 2.

43 Rotate the fast idle cam to disengage it from the throttle linkage. Align its hole with the hole in the throttle body, and lock the cam in position by inserting a 3 mm diameter rod or drill.

44 Undo the upper throttle body retaining screws, then carefully disengage the upper body assembly from the lower body, and position it clear of the fast idle valve. Recover the gasket and discard it; a new one must be used on refitting.

45 Undo the two retaining screws, and remove the fast idle valve retaining plate from the lower throttle body. Lift the valve out of position, and recover its sealing ring.

46 Refitting is the reverse of removal, using a new sealing ring and throttle body gasket.

Dashpot

47 The dashpot is fitted to the left-hand side of the throttle body. The dashpot can be checked as described in Part D of this Chapter.

48 To remove it, unscrew its retaining nut, and lift the dashpot out of its retaining bracket.

49 To refit, install the dashpot and tighten its retaining nut to the specified torque.

Crank angle sensor

50 The crank angle sensor is an integral part of the distributor, and cannot be renewed separately. If the sensor is faulty, the complete distributor body assembly must be renewed. Refer to Chapter 5 for further information.

Power transistor

51 Refer to Chapter 5.

Coolant temperature sensor

52 Refer to Chapter 3.

Knock sensor

Note: *The knock sensor is delicate, and will not work correctly if it is dropped or knocked.*

53 The knock sensor is mounted onto the rear face of the cylinder block.

54 To gain access to the sensor, firmly apply the handbrake then jack up the front of the vehicle and support it on axle stands. Access to the sensor can then be gained from underneath the vehicle.

55 Disconnect the battery negative terminal, then disconnect the wiring connector from the sensor.

56 Slacken and remove the bolt securing the sensor to the cylinder block, and remove it from underneath the vehicle.

57 On refitting, ensure that the sensor and

block mating surfaces are clean and dry. Position the sensor so that its wiring connector is facing the right-hand end of the engine, then fit the mounting bolt and tighten it to the specified torque. Ensure that no other component is contacting the sensor, then lower the vehicle to the ground and reconnect the battery.

ECCS control unit

58 The ECCS control unit is situated just in front of the centre console, mounted onto the transmission tunnel floor. Prior to removal, disconnect the battery negative terminal.

59 To gain access to the control unit, undo the retaining screws and release the retaining clips, then remove the small trim panel from each side of the front of the centre console (see Chapter 11).

60 Undo the retaining screws and release the control unit from its mounting bracket, then disconnect the wiring connector(s) and remove the unit from the vehicle.

61 Refitting is the reverse of removal, ensuring that the wiring connector is securely reconnected.

Mixture heater

62 Refer to Section 11.

Neutral switch - manual transmission models

63 Refer to Chapter 7A.

Starter inhibitor/reversing light switch - automatic transmission models

64 Refer to Chapter 7B.

ECCS control unit, mixture heater and fuel pump relays

65 Refer to Chapter 12.

Power steering idle-up switch

66 The power steering idle-up switch is screwed into the power steering feed pipe, in the right-hand rear corner of the engine compartment. Prior to removal, set the front wheels in the straight-ahead position, then disconnect the battery negative terminal.

67 Locate the switch, and disconnect its wiring connector.

68 Unscrew the switch, recover its sealing washer, and plug its opening in the pipe. Work quickly, to minimise fluid loss and prevent dirt entering the hydraulic system.

69 Refitting is the reverse of removal, using a new sealing washer.

Air conditioning system idle-up switch

70 The air conditioning switch is screwed into the air conditioning pipe, in the left-hand front corner of the engine compartment. Removal and refitting of the switch requires the air conditioning system to be discharged and recharged (see Chapter 3, Section 10), and should not be attempted by the home mechanic.

14 Inlet manifold - removal and refitting

Removal

1 Remove the throttle body as described in Section 11.

2 Drain the cooling system as described in Chapter 1.

3 Make a note of the correct fitted locations of all the relevant inlet manifold vacuum hose connections, and disconnect them from the manifold and, where necessary, the associated vacuum valves. To avoid confusion on refitting, it may be wise to label each hose as it is disconnected.

4 On models with a catalytic converter, unscrew the union nut and free the EGR pipe, linking the inlet and exhaust manifolds, from the control valve on the left-hand end of the inlet manifold.

5 Disconnect the wiring connector from the coolant temperature sensor on the right-hand end of the manifold. Where necessary, undo the retaining bolt and free the earth lead from the manifold.

6 Undo the retaining bolts and remove the support bracket from the rear of the manifold.

7 Make a final check that all the necessary vacuum/breather hoses have been disconnected from the manifold.

8 Working in the **reverse** of the sequence shown in illustration 14.10, slacken and remove the manifold retaining nuts and bolts.

9 Manoeuvre the manifold away from the head and out of the engine compartment, then remove the manifold gasket and discard it.

Refitting

10 Refitting is the reverse of the removal procedure, noting the following points:

a) Ensure that the manifold and cylinder head mating surfaces are clean and dry, and fit the new gasket to the head studs. Install the manifold, and tighten its retaining nuts and bolts to the specified torque setting in the order shown **(see illustration)**.

b) Ensure that all relevant hoses are reconnected to their original positions, and are securely held (where necessary) by their retaining clips.

c) Refit the throttle body as described in Section 11.

d) On completion, refill the cooling system as described in Chapter 1.

15 Exhaust manifold - removal and refitting

Removal

1 Disconnect the hot-air inlet hose from the manifold shroud, and remove it from the vehicle.

2 On models with a catalytic converter, unscrew the union nut and free the EGR pipe from the side of the manifold.

3 On all models, slacken and remove the retaining screws, and remove the shroud from the top of the exhaust manifold.

4 Firmly apply the handbrake, then jack up the front of the vehicle and support it on axle stands.

5 Undo the nuts securing the exhaust front pipe to the manifold, and the bolt securing the front pipe to its mounting bracket. Free the front pipe from the manifold, and recover the gaskets. Either disconnect the exhaust gas sensor wiring connector, or support the pipe to ensure that no strain is placed on the wiring.

6 Working in the **reverse** of the sequence shown in illustration 15.8, slacken and remove the manifold retaining nuts and bolts.

7 Manoeuvre the manifold away from the head, and out of the engine compartment. Remove the manifold gasket and discard it.

Refitting

8 Refitting is the reverse of the removal procedure, noting the following points:

a) Examine all the exhaust manifold studs for signs of damage and corrosion; remove all traces of corrosion, and repair or renew any damaged studs.

b) Ensure that the manifold and cylinder head sealing faces are clean and flat, and fit a new manifold gasket. Tighten the manifold retaining nuts and bolts to the specified torque in the order shown **(see illustration)**.

c) Reconnect the front pipe to the manifold using the information given in Section 16.

4B

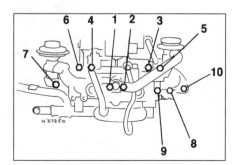

14.10 Inlet manifold nut and bolt tightening sequence

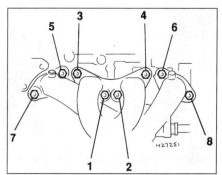

15.8 Exhaust manifold nut and bolt tightening sequence

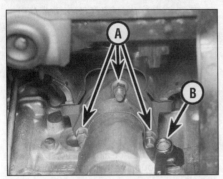

16.7 Front pipe-to-manifold nuts (A) and front pipe mounting bolt (B)

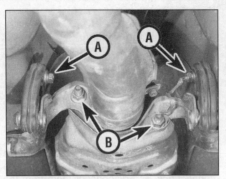

16.8a Undo the mounting bracket retaining bolts (A) (where fitted), noting the earth lead fitted to right-hand bolt, and the front pipe nuts (B) . . .

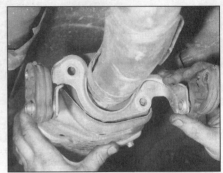

16.8b . . . then remove the mounting bracket assembly and front pipe

16 Exhaust system - general information and component removal

General information

1 On models without a catalytic converter, the exhaust system consists of three sections; the front pipe, the intermediate pipe and silencer box, and the tailpipe and main silencer box.

2 On models with a catalytic converter, the exhaust system consists of four sections, the front pipe, the catalytic converter, the intermediate pipe and silencer box, and the tailpipe and main silencer box.

3 The system is suspended throughout its entire length by rubber mountings, and all exhaust sections are joined by flanged joints which are secured together by nuts and/or bolts.

Removal

4 Each exhaust section can be removed individually or, alternatively, the complete system can be removed as a unit.

5 To remove the system or part of the system, first jack up the front or rear of the car, and support it on axle stands. Alternatively, position the car over an inspection pit, or on car ramps.

Front pipe

6 On models with a catalytic converter, trace the wiring back from the exhaust gas sensor to its wiring connector. Disconnect the connector, and free the wiring from any relevant retaining clips so that it is free to be removed with the front pipe.

7 On all models, undo the nuts securing the front pipe to the manifold, and the bolt securing the front pipe to its mounting bracket. Separate the front pipe from the manifold, and collect the gaskets **(see illustration)**.

8 Slacken and remove the two nuts/bolts and springs (as applicable) securing the front pipe flange joint to the intermediate pipe/catalytic converter (as applicable). Withdraw the front pipe from underneath the vehicle, and recover the gasket from the joint. Note that it may be necessary to undo the bolts and release the mounting bracket from the vehicle body to allow the front pipe to be withdrawn **(see illustrations)**.

Catalytic converter (where fitted)

9 Slacken and remove the two nuts/bolts and springs (as applicable) securing the front pipe flange joint to the catalytic converter.

10 Unscrew the two nuts/bolts securing the intermediate pipe to the catalytic converter, and recover the gasket from between the two **(see illustration)**.

11 Free the catalytic converter from the front pipe, and recover the gasket.

Intermediate pipe

12 On models with a catalytic converter, unscrew the two bolts securing the intermediate pipe to the catalytic converter, and recover the gasket from between the two.

13 On models without a catalytic converter, undo the two nuts securing the front pipe flange joint to the intermediate pipe, then separate the joint and recover the gasket.

14 On all models, slacken and remove the bolt securing the mounting rubber to the rear of the intermediate pipe.

15 Undo the two bolts securing the tailpipe to the intermediate pipe **(see illustration)**, then manoeuvre the intermediate pipe out from underneath the vehicle. Recover the gasket from the tailpipe joint.

Tailpipe

16 Slacken and remove the two bolts securing the tailpipe to the intermediate pipe.

17 Unhook the tailpipe from its mounting rubbers, then remove it from the vehicle and recover the gasket.

Complete system

18 On models with a catalytic converter, trace the wiring back from the exhaust gas sensor to its wiring connector. Disconnect the connector, and free the wiring from any

16.8c On some models, the front pipe is secured to the intermediate pipe by bolts and springs (arrowed)

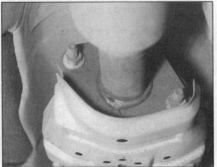

16.10 Catalytic converter-to-intermediate pipe joint

16.15 Intermediate pipe-to-tailpipe joint

relevant retaining clips so that it is free to be removed with the exhaust system.

19 Undo the nuts securing the front pipe to the manifold, and the bolt securing the front pipe to its mounting bracket. Separate the front pipe from the manifold, and collect the gaskets.

20 With the aid of an assistant, free the system from all its mounting rubbers, and manoeuvre it out from underneath the vehicle.

Heat shield(s)

21 The heat shields (where fitted) are secured in position by a mixture of nuts, bolts and clamps. When an exhaust section is renewed, transfer any relevant heat shields from the original over to the new section before installing the exhaust section on the vehicle.

Refitting

22 Each section is refitted by a reverse of the removal sequence, noting the following points:

a) *Ensure that all traces of corrosion have been removed from the flanges, and renew all necessary gaskets* **(see illustration)**.

b) *Inspect the rubber mountings for signs of damage or deterioration, and renew as necessary.*

c) *Prior to tightening the exhaust system fasteners to the specified torque, ensure that all rubber mountings are correctly located, and that there is adequate clearance between the exhaust system and vehicle underbody/suspension components, etc.*

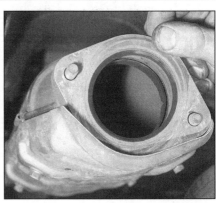

16.22 Renew all exhaust gaskets on refitting

4B

Notes

Chapter 4 Part C Fuel/exhaust systems - multi-point fuel injection models

Contents

Degrees of difficulty

Easy, suitable for novice with little experience	Fairly easy, suitable for beginner with some experience	Fairly difficult, suitable for competent DIY mechanic	Difficult, suitable for experienced DIY mechanic	Very difficult, suitable for expert DIY or professional

Specifications

General

System type	Nissan Electronic Concentrated Control System (ECCS) multi-point injection

Engine codes:
1.6 litre models	GA16DE
2.0 litre models	SR20De and SR20DE

Fuel system data

For idle speed and mixture settings, refer to Chapter 1 Specifications.

Fuel pump type	Electric, immersed in tank
Fuel pump regulated constant pressure (approximate):	
1.6 litre models	2.5 bars
2.0 litre models	3.0 bars

Fuel system component test data

1.6 litre models

Fuel pump resistance (at fuel gauge sender unit connection)	0.7 ohms
Throttle potentiometer resistances **(see illustration SPEC 1 overleaf)**:	
Meter connected between terminals "A" and "B":	
Throttle valve closed	0.5 kilohm
Throttle valve partially open	0.5 to 4 kilohms
Throttle valve fully open	4 kilohm
Fuel injector resistance	10 ohms
Auxiliary air control (AAC) valve resistance	10 ohms
Fast idle control device (FICD) solenoid valve:	
Apply 12 volts across solenoid terminals	Solenoid should click, indicating correct operation
Power steering pressure switch:	
Steering wheel being turned	Continuity between switch terminals
Steering wheel stationary	Open-circuit between switch terminals
Coolant temperature sensor resistances:	
At 20°C (68°F)	2.1 to 2.9 kilohms
At 90°C (194°F)	0.24 to 0.26 kilohms
At 110°C (230°F)	0.14 to 0.15 kilohms

4C

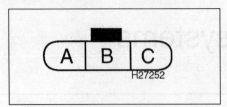

SPEC 1 Throttle potentiometer wiring connector - manual transmission models

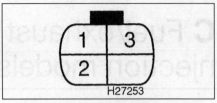

SPEC 2 Throttle potentiometer wiring connector - automatic transmission models

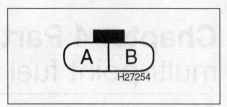

SPEC 3 Knock sensor wiring connector

2.0 litre models

Fuel pump resistance (at fuel gauge sender unit connection) . . . . 0.7 ohms
Manual transmission model throttle potentiometer resistances **(see illustration SPEC 1):**
  Meter connected between terminals "A" and "B":
    Throttle valve closed . . . . 2 kilohms
    Throttle valve partially open . . . . 2 to 11 kilohms
    Throttle valve fully open . . . . 11 kilohms
Automatic transmission model throttle potentiometer resistances **(see illustration SPEC 2):**
  Meter connected between terminals "1" and "2":
    Throttle valve fully closed . . . . Continuity between terminals
    Throttle valve open . . . . Open-circuit between terminals
  Meter connected between terminals "2" and "3":
    Throttle valve fully closed . . . . Open-circuit between terminals
    Throttle valve open . . . . Continuity between terminals
Fuel injector resistance . . . . 10 to 14 ohms
Auxiliary air control (AAC) valve resistance . . . . 10 ohms
Fast idle control (FICD) solenoid valve:
  Apply 12 volts across solenoid terminals . . . . Solenoid should click, indicating correct operation
Air regulator valve resistance . . . . 70 to 80 ohms
Knock sensor **(see illustration SPEC 3):**
  Meter connected between terminal "A" and earth . . . . Continuity should exist (meter must be able to read more than 10 megohms)
Power steering pressure switch:
  Steering wheel being turned . . . . Continuity between switch terminals
  Steering wheel stationary . . . . Open-circuit between switch terminals
Coolant temperature sensor resistances:
  At 20°C (68°F) . . . . 2.1 to 2.9 kilohms
  At 50°C (122°F) . . . . 0.68 to 1.0 kilohms
  At 80°C (176°F) . . . . 0.30 to 0.33 kilohms
Note: *All resistance readings given are approximate values, which should be used as a guide only. Before condemning a component as faulty, have your findings confirmed by a Nissan dealer.*

Recommended fuel

Models without a catalytic converter ("non-catalyst" models) . . . . 95 RON unleaded or 97 RON leaded (eg UK "4-star")
Models with a catalytic converter ("catalyst" models) . . . . 95 RON unleaded. Leaded fuel (eg UK "4-star") must **not** be used

Torque wrench settings	Nm	lbf ft
Exhaust manifold nuts and bolts:		
1.6 litre models	21	16
2.0 litre models	43	31
Exhaust system fasteners:		
Front pipe-to-manifold nuts:		
1.6 litre models	32	24
2.0 litre "Phase I" (pre-June 1993) models	45	33
2.0 litre "Phase II" (June 1993 onwards) models	65	48
Front pipe mounting bolt	23	18
Front pipe-to-intermediate pipe/catalytic converter nuts	49	36
Catalytic converter-to-tailpipe bolts	49	36
Intermediate pipe-to-tailpipe bolts	49	36
Fuel rail retaining bolts:		
Stage 1	10	7
Stage 2	24	18
Inlet manifold nuts and bolts	20	15
Knock sensor bolt - 2.0 litre models	24	18
Throttle housing retaining bolts:		
Stage 1	10	7
Stage 2	20	15

2.3 On 1.6 litre models, disconnect the inlet duct . . .

2.4a . . . then slacken the retaining clip securing the air cleaner housing to the throttle housing

2.4b Disconnect the breather hose then undo the retaining bolt (arrowed) . . .

1 General information and precautions

1 The fuel system consists of a fuel tank mounted under the rear of the car with an electric fuel pump immersed in it, a fuel filter, fuel feed and return lines. The fuel pump supplies fuel to the fuel rail which acts as a reservoir for the four fuel injectors which inject fuel into the inlet tracts. A fuel filter is incorporated in the feed line from the pump to the fuel rail to ensure that the fuel supplied to the injectors is clean.

2 Refer to Section 6 for further information on the operation of the fuel injection system, and Section 17 for information on the exhaust system.

Note: *Throughout this Chapter, references are made to "Phase I" models (up to June 1993) and "Phase II" models (June 1993 on). In the case of 1.6 litre models, distinction is easy - only "Phase II" models were fitted with multi-point fuel injection (engine code GA16DE). On 2.0 litre models, the "Phases" can be distinguished from the shape of the inlet manifold. On "Phase I" models, the throttle body is mounted onto the base of the manifold, and the manifold curves upwards towards the cylinder head; the fuel injectors are easily accessible, on the top of the manifold. On "Phase II" models, the throttle*

body is mounted on the top of the manifold, and the inlet manifold curves downwards towards the cylinder head; the fuel injectors are not so easily accessible.

> **Warning:** *Many of the procedures in this Chapter require the removal of fuel lines and connections which may result in some fuel spillage. Before carrying out any operation on the fuel system refer to the precautions given in Safety first! at the beginning of this Manual and follow them implicitly. Petrol is a highly dangerous and volatile liquid and the precautions necessary when handling it cannot be overstressed. Residual pressure will remain in the fuel lines long after the vehicle was last used, when disconnecting any fuel line, depressurise the fuel system as described in Section 7.*

2 Air cleaner assembly - removal and refitting

Removal

1.6 litre models

1 Release the retaining clips, then lift off the air cleaner housing lid along with its seal.

2 Lift out the filter element, noting which way around it is fitted.

3 Disconnect the inlet duct from the left-hand end of the air cleaner housing **(see illustration)**.

4 Slacken and remove the housing retaining bolt and retaining clip, then free the housing from the top of the throttle housing. Disconnect all the relevant vacuum/breather hoses from the base of the housing, noting their correct fitted positions, and remove the housing. Remove the sealing ring from the top of the throttle housing **(see illustrations)**.

5 If necessary, undo the two retaining bolts, then free the inlet duct from the top of the resonator and remove it from the engine compartment. The resonator can then be lifted out of position.

2.0 litre models

6 Slacken the retaining clip, and free the inlet duct from the airflow meter.

7 Disconnect the wiring connector from the airflow meter, then release the retaining clips and lift the lid off the air cleaner housing.

8 Lift out the filter element, noting which way around it is fitted.

9 Disconnect the inlet duct from the front of the housing, then undo the housing retaining bolts and lift the housing out of the engine compartment.

10 With the housing removed, the various ducts and resonator boxes can then be removed once their retaining bolts have been undone and hoses have been disconnected **(see illustrations)**.

4C

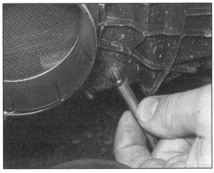

2.4c . . . and lift off the housing, disconnecting the vacuum hose as it becomes accessible

2.4d Recover the sealing ring from the throttle housing and store it with the air cleaner housing

2.10a On 2.0 litre "Phase II" models, disconnect the hoses (arrowed) and slacken the duct retaining clips . . .

2.10b . . . then lift up the duct and disconnect its lower breather hose (arrowed)

Refitting

11 Refitting is a reversal of the relevant removal procedure, ensuring that all hoses are properly reconnected, and that all ducts are correctly seated and securely held by their retaining clips.

3 Accelerator cable - removal, refitting and adjustment

1 Refer to Chapter 4A, Section 7, substituting "throttle body" for all references to the carburettor. On 1.6 litre models, remove the air cleaner housing (see Section 2) to improve access to the throttle body end of the cable.
2 On 2.0 litre "Phase I" models, the throttle valve is operated via an intermediate cam which is mounted onto the top of the inlet manifold; once the accelerator cable is correctly adjusted, adjust the cam setting as follows. Slacken the locknut, and unscrew the intermediate cam stopper screw. Hold the cam fully open, then lightly tighten the screw until it is just contacting the stopper lever. From this point, release the cam, then rotate the screw three complete turns clockwise. Hold the screw stationary, and securely tighten its locknut. Fully open the cam, and check that its stopper arm contacts the screw.

4 Accelerator pedal - removal and refitting

Refer to Chapter 4A, Section 8, substituting "throttle body" for all references to the carburettor.

5 Unleaded petrol - general information and usage

Note: *The information given in this Chapter is correct at the time of writing, and applies only to petrols currently available in the UK. If updated information is thought to be required,* check with a Nissan dealer. If travelling abroad, consult one of the motoring organisations (or a similar authority) for advice on the petrols available, and their suitability for your vehicle.

1 The fuel recommended by Nissan is given in the Specifications Section of this Chapter.
2 RON and MON are different testing standards; RON stands for Research Octane Number (also written as RM), while MON stands for Motor Octane Number (also written as MM).
3 All Nissan Primera models are designed to run on fuel with a minimum octane rating of 95 (RON). All models with a catalytic converter must be run on unleaded fuel **only**. Under no circumstances should leaded fuel be used, as this may damage the catalyst. On models without a catalytic converter, either unleaded or leaded fuel can be used without modification.

6 Fuel injection system - general information

1 All multi-point injection models are fitted with a combined fuel injection/ignition (engine management) system, otherwise known as the Electronic Concentrated Control System (ECCS). Refer to Chapter 5 for information on the ignition side of the system, the fuel injection side of the system operates as follows.
2 The fuel pump, immersed in the fuel tank, supplies fuel from the fuel tank to the fuel rail, via a filter mounted on the engine compartment bulkhead. Fuel supply pressure is controlled by the pressure regulator, on the end of the fuel rail, which lifts to allow excess fuel to return to the tank when the optimum operating pressure of the fuel system is exceeded.
3 The electrical control system consists of the ECCS control unit, along with the following sensors:
a) *Throttle potentiometer - informs the ECCS control unit of the throttle valve position, and the rate of throttle opening/closing.*
b) *Coolant temperature sensor - informs the ECCS control unit of engine temperature.*
c) *Airflow meter - informs the ECCS control unit of the mass and temperature of the air passing through the inlet duct.*
d) *Crank angle sensor (housed in the distributor) - informs the ECCS control unit of the engine speed and crankshaft position (see Chapter 5 for further information).*
e) *Vehicle speed sensor (built into the speedometer) - informs the ECCS control unit of the vehicle speed.*
f) *Power steering and air conditioning system switches (where fitted) - informs the ECCS control unit if the system(s) are in operation, to allow it to adjust the idle speed to compensate for the extra load on the engine.*

g) *Exhaust gas sensor (catalyst models only) - informs the ECCS control unit of the oxygen content of the exhaust gases (see Part D of this Chapter for further information).*

4 All the above signals are analysed by the ECCS control unit. Based on this information, the ECCS control unit selects the response appropriate to those values, and controls the fuel injectors (varying their pulse width - the length of time each injector is held open - to provide a richer or weaker mixture, as appropriate). The mixture and idle speed are constantly varied by the ECCS control unit to provide the best settings for cranking, starting (with either a hot or cold engine) and engine warm-up, idle, cruising, and acceleration.
5 The ECCS control unit also has full control over the engine idle speed via the auxiliary air control (AAC) valve. The valve, which is fitted to the throttle housing (1.6 litre models) or inlet manifold (2.0 litre models), controls the opening of an air passage which bypasses the throttle valve. When the throttle valve is closed, the ECCS control unit controls the opening of the valve, which regulates the amount of air which flows through the valve, and so controls the idle speed.
6 On 1.6 litre models, the throttle housing has a built-in fast idle facility, which is controlled by a thermostatic valve. When the engine is cold, the wax capsule in the valve (which is fitted to the throttle housing), is at its smallest, and the fast idle cam holds the throttle valve slightly open. As the engine warms up, the wax capsule expands, forcing the valve plunger upwards, which in turn rotates the fast idle cam to the required position.
7 On 2.0 litre models, the fast idle facility is controlled by the air regulator valve, which contains a bi-metallic strip and shutter valve. When the valve is cold, the bi-metallic strip in the valve holds the shutter valve open. Air then passes through the valve, allowing an additional supply of air to enter the inlet manifold. With the engine running, the valve bi-metallic strip is supplied with current, which gradually increases its temperature. As the temperature increases, the bi-metallic strip deforms and closes the shutter valve, so cutting off the additional air supply to the engine.
8 On all models, there is also a fast idle control (FICD) solenoid valve which is controlled by the ECCS control unit. The solenoid valve controls the opening of an air passage which bypasses the throttle valve, and this is used to raise the idle speed when either the power steering and/or air conditioning systems are in operation. **Note:** *On some models, the valve may be fitted but will not be operational.*
9 On models with a catalytic converter, the ECCS control unit also controls the exhaust and evaporative emission control systems, which are described in detail in Chapter 4D.
10 If there is an abnormality in any of the readings obtained from sensors, the ECCS

control unit switches to its back-up mode. If this happens, it ignores the abnormal sensor signal, and assumes a pre-programmed value which will allow the engine to continue running, albeit at reduced efficiency. If the ECCS control unit enters its back-up mode, the warning light on the instrument panel will come on, and the relevant fault code will be stored in the ECCS control unit memory.

11 If the warning light comes on, the vehicle should be taken to a Nissan dealer at the earliest opportunity. Once there, a complete test of the engine management system can be carried out, using a special electronic diagnostic test unit which is simply plugged into the system's diagnostic connector. **Note:** *The ECCS control unit also has a self-diagnostic mode which can be accessed by the DIY mechanic. See Part B, Section 12 for further information.*

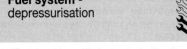

7 Fuel system - depressurisation

Note: *Refer to the warning note in Section 1 before proceeding.*

⚠️ *Warning: The following procedure will merely relieve the pressure in the fuel system - remember that fuel will still be present in the system components, and take precautions accordingly before disconnecting any of them. Use clean rags wrapped around the connections to catch escaping fuel, and dispose of any fuel-soaked rags with care. Plug or tape over any open fuel lines, to prevent further loss of fuel or ingress of dirt.*

1 The fuel system referred to in this Section is defined as the tank-mounted fuel pump, the fuel filter, the fuel rail and injectors, the pressure regulator, and the metal pipes and flexible hoses of the fuel lines between these components. All these contain fuel which will be under pressure while the engine is running and/or while the ignition is switched on. The pressure will remain for some time after the ignition has been switched off, and must be relieved before any of these components are disturbed for servicing work.

2 Identify and remove the fuel pump fuse from the vehicle fusebox - the fuses are not numbered as such, but can be identified from the label inside the fusebox cover, or from the wiring diagrams at the end of this manual.

3 Start the engine, and allow it to run until it stalls.

4 Try to start the engine at least twice more, to ensure that all residual pressure has been relieved.

5 Disconnect the battery negative terminal.

6 For safety, the fuel pump fuse should not be refitted until all work on the fuel system has been completed. If you refit the fuse now, **do not** switch on the ignition until completion of work.

8 Fuel pump - removal and refitting

Refer to Chapter 4B, Section 8.

9 Fuel gauge sender unit - removal and refitting

Refer to Chapter 4B, Section 9.

10 Fuel tank - removal and refitting

Refer to Chapter 4A, Section 6, noting that it will be necessary to depressurise the fuel system as the feed and return hoses are disconnected from the fuel gauge sender unit (see Section 9).

11 Fuel injection system - general diagnosis and adjustment

Refer to Chapter 4B, Section 12.

12 Throttle housing - removal and refitting

1.6 litre models

1 Disconnect the battery negative terminal.

2 Remove the air cleaner housing as described in Section 2.

3 Depress the retaining clips and disconnect the wiring connectors from the throttle potentiometer, the auxiliary air control valve, the airflow meter and the fast idle control device (FICD) solenoid valve.

4 Free the accelerator inner cable from the throttle cam. Slacken the outer cable locknut and adjuster nut, then free the outer cable from its mounting bracket.

5 Make a note of the correct fitted positions of all the relevant vacuum pipes and breather hoses, to ensure that they are correctly positioned on refitting, then release the retaining clips (where fitted) and disconnect them from the throttle housing.

6 Release the retaining clips, disconnect the coolant hoses from each side of the throttle housing, and plug the hose ends. Work quickly, to minimise coolant loss.

7 Slacken and remove the bolts securing the throttle housing assembly to the inlet manifold, and remove it from the engine compartment **(see illustration)**. Remove the gasket and discard it; a new one must be used on refitting. Plug the inlet manifold port with a wad of clean cloth, to prevent the possible entry of foreign matter.

2.0 litre models

8 Slacken the retaining clip, and disconnect the inlet duct from the throttle housing.

9 Disconnect the wiring connector from the throttle potentiometer.

10 On "Phase I" models, carefully prise the accelerator linkage rod off its throttle housing balljoint.

11 On "Phase II" models, free the accelerator inner cable from the throttle cam. On automatic transmission models, also disconnect the kickdown cable as described in Chapter 7B.

12 On all models, release the retaining clip(s), disconnect the coolant hose(s) from the throttle housing, and plug the hose end(s). Work quickly, to minimise coolant loss.

13 On all models, make a note of the correct fitted positions of all the relevant vacuum pipes and breather hoses, to ensure that they are correctly positioned on refitting, then release the retaining clips (where fitted) and disconnect them from the throttle housing.

14 Where necessary, unbolt the inlet manifold support bracket to gain access to the throttle housing bolts.

15 Slacken and remove the bolts securing the throttle housing assembly to the inlet manifold, and remove it from the engine compartment. Remove the gasket and discard it; a new one must be used on refitting. Plug the inlet manifold port with a wad of clean cloth, to prevent the possible entry of foreign matter.

Refitting

16 Refitting is a reverse of the removal procedure, bearing in mind the following points:
a) *Ensure that the mating surfaces of the manifold and throttle housing are clean and dry, and fit a new gasket to the manifold. Fit the throttle body then, working in a diagonal sequence, tighten the retaining bolts to the specified Stage 1 torque setting. Go around again in sequence, and tighten them to the specified Stage 2 torque setting.*
b) *Ensure that all hoses are correctly reconnected and, where necessary, that their retaining clips are securely tightened.*

4C

12.7 Throttle housing retaining bolts (arrowed) - 1.6 litre models

c) On completion, adjust the accelerator cable using the information given in Section 3. On automatic transmission models, also check the kickdown cable adjustment as described in Chapter 7B.

13 Fuel injection system components (1.6 litre models) - removal and refitting

Fuel rail and injectors

Note: *Refer to the warning note in Section 1 before proceeding.*

Note: *If a faulty injector is suspected, before condemning the injector, it is worth trying the effect of one of the proprietary injector-cleaning treatments.*

1 Disconnect the battery negative terminal. To improve access to the fuel rail, remove the air cleaner housing as described in Section 2.
2 Disconnect the vacuum pipe from the fuel pressure regulator.
3 Depressurise the fuel system as described in Section 7, then slacken the retaining clips and disconnect the fuel feed and return hoses from the left-hand end of the fuel rail **(see illustration)**. Label the hoses if wished, to avoid confusion on refitting.
4 Depress the retaining tangs, and disconnect the wiring connectors from the four injectors.
5 Slacken and remove the fuel rail retaining bolts, then carefully ease the fuel rail and injector assembly out from the inlet manifold, and remove it from the vehicle. Recover the spacers fitted between the rail and manifold, and remove each injector seal from the manifold.
6 Undo the two retaining bolts, and remove the retaining plate from the relevant injector. Push the injector out of position, and recover the sealing rings. Repeat the procedure as required to remove any other injectors.
7 Discard the seals and sealing rings; new ones must be used on refitting.
8 Refitting is a reversal of the removal procedure, noting the following points:
a) *Fit new O-rings to all disturbed injectors,*

13.3 Fuel rail feed and return hoses (arrowed) - 1.6 litre models

and fit new injector seals to the manifold.
b) *Apply a smear of engine oil to the O-rings to aid installation, then ease the injectors into the fuel rail.*
c) *Fit a new seal to each injector, and ease the fuel rail assembly into position in the manifold. Fit the spacers between the rail and manifold then, working in a diagonal sequence from the centre outwards, tighten the bolts to their specified Stage 1 torque setting. Go around again in sequence, and tighten them to the specified Stage 2 torque.*
d) *On completion, start the engine and check for fuel leaks.*

Fuel pressure regulator

Note: *Refer to the warning note in Section 1 before proceeding.*

9 Disconnect the battery negative terminal.
10 Disconnect the vacuum hose from the fuel pressure regulator, which is mounted on the left-hand end of the fuel rail **(see illustration)**.
11 Depressurise the fuel system as described in Section 7, then slacken the retaining clips and disconnect the fuel hose from base of the regulator.
12 Undo the two retaining bolts, and remove the regulator from the end of the fuel rail. Recover the sealing ring fitted to the regulator and discard it; a new one must be used on refitting.
13 Refitting is the reverse of removal, using a new sealing ring. On completion, start the engine and check for fuel leaks.

Throttle potentiometer

14 The throttle potentiometer is mounted onto the right-hand side of the throttle housing **(see illustration)**. Prior to removal, disconnect the battery negative terminal.
15 Disconnect the wiring connector from the throttle potentiometer.
16 Using a dab of white paint or a suitable marker pen, make alignment marks between the potentiometer and the throttle housing.
17 Undo the two retaining screws, and remove the potentiometer.
18 On refitting, offer up the potentiometer, making sure its lever is correctly engaged with the throttle valve spindle lever.
19 Align the marks made prior to removal, and lightly tighten the retaining screws. Adjust the potentiometer as follows.
20 Using a multi-meter set to the resistance scale, check that the potentiometer resistance readings are as given in the Specifications at the start of this Chapter. If necessary, slacken the retaining screws and reposition the potentiometer until its resistances are as specified.
21 When the potentiometer is correctly positioned, securely tighten its retaining screws and reconnect the wiring connector.
22 Reconnect the battery negative terminal.

Auxiliary air control (AAC) valve

23 The auxiliary air control (AAC) valve is mounted onto the front of the throttle body. Prior to removal, disconnect the battery negative terminal.
24 Disconnect the wiring connector from the control valve **(see illustration)**.
25 Undo the retaining screws, then remove the valve from the throttle body and recover the gasket.
26 If necessary, with the valve removed, separate the two halves of the valve by removing the retaining screws, then recover the sealing ring. Check that the valve plunger is free to move easily, and returns quickly under spring pressure. If not, the valve assembly must be renewed.
27 Refitting is the reverse of removal, using a new gasket.

13.10 Fuel pressure regulator (arrowed) is mounted on the left-hand end of the fuel rail

13.14 Throttle potentiometer (arrowed) is mounted on the right-hand side of the throttle housing

13.24 Auxiliary air control (AAC) valve wiring connector (1) and retaining screws (2)

13.29 Disconnect the wiring connector . . .

13.30 . . . then undo the retaining screws (arrowed) and remove the airflow meter

13.32 The fast idle control device (FICD) (arrowed) is screwed into the front of the throttle housing

Airflow meter

28 The airflow meter is mounted onto the right-hand side of the throttle body. Prior to removal, disconnect the battery negative terminal.

29 Disconnect the wiring connector from the airflow meter **(see illustration)**.

30 Undo the retaining screws, then remove the meter from the throttle body **(see illustration)**. Recover its sealing ring (where fitted).

31 Refitting is the reverse of removal, using a new sealing ring (where applicable) and tightening its retaining screws securely.

Fast idle control device (FICD) solenoid valve

32 The fast idle control device (FICD) solenoid valve is screwed into the front of the throttle body **(see illustration)**. Prior to removal, disconnect the battery negative terminal. If necessary, remove the air cleaner housing as described in Section 2 to improve access to the valve.

33 Disconnect the wiring connector from the solenoid.

34 Unscrew the solenoid valve from the body, and recover the plunger, spring and sealing washer.

35 Refitting is the reverse of removal, using a new sealing washer. Ensure that the solenoid plunger and spring are fitted in the correct order, and the correct way around.

Fast idle thermostatic valve

36 The fast idle thermostatic valve is fitted to the left-hand side of the throttle body. Prior to removal, disconnect the battery negative terminal.

37 Remove the air cleaner housing as described in Section 2.

38 Unscrew the nut and washer, then withdraw the fast idle cam retaining plate, spring, spacer and lever, noting each component's correct fitted position.

39 Undo the retaining screw, and remove the fast idle valve retaining plate. Lift the valve out of position, and recover its sealing ring.

40 Refitting is the reverse of removal. Use a new sealing ring, and ensure that all the fast idle cam components are refitted in their original positions.

Crank angle sensor and power transistor

41 The crank angle sensor and power transistor are integral parts of the distributor, and cannot be renewed separately. If either is faulty, the complete distributor body assembly must be renewed. Refer to Chapter 5 for further information.

Coolant temperature sensor

42 Refer to Chapter 3.

ECCS control unit

43 The ECCS control unit is situated just in front of the centre console, mounted onto the transmission tunnel floor. Prior to removal, disconnect the battery negative terminal.

44 To gain access to the control unit, undo the retaining screws and release the retaining clips, then remove the small trim panel from each side of the front of the centre console.

45 Undo the retaining screws, and release the control unit from its mounting bracket. Disconnect the wiring connector(s), and remove the unit from the vehicle.

46 Refitting is the reverse of removal, ensuring that the wiring connector is securely reconnected.

Neutral switch - manual transmission models

47 Refer to Chapter 7A.

Starter inhibitor/reversing light switch - automatic transmission models

48 Refer to Chapter 7B.

ECCS control unit and fuel pump relays

49 Refer to Chapter 12.

Power steering idle-up switch

50 The power steering idle-up switch is screwed into the power steering feed pipe, in the right-hand rear corner of the engine compartment. Prior to removal, set the front wheels in the straight-ahead position, then disconnect the battery negative terminal.

51 Locate the switch and disconnect its wiring connector.

52 Unscrew the switch, recover its sealing washer, and plug the opening in the pipe. Work quickly, to minimise fluid loss and to prevent dirt entering the hydraulic system.

53 Refitting is the reverse of removal, using a new sealing washer.

Air conditioning system idle-up switch

54 The air conditioning switch is screwed into the air conditioning pipe, in the left-hand front corner of the engine compartment. Removal and refitting of the switch requires the air conditioning system to be discharged and recharged (see Chapter 3, Section 10), and this should not be attempted by the home mechanic.

Vehicle speed sensor

55 The vehicle speed sensor is an integral part of the speedometer. Refer to Chapter 12 for removal and refitting details.

4C

14 Fuel injection system components (2.0 litre models) - removal and refitting

Note: "Phase I" models (up to June 1993) and "Phase II" models (June 1993 on) are easily identified from the shape of their inlet manifold. On "Phase I" models, the throttle body is mounted onto the base of the manifold, and the manifold curves upwards towards the cylinder head; the fuel injectors are easily accessible, on the top of the manifold. On "Phase II" models, the throttle body is mounted on the top of the manifold, and the inlet manifold curves downwards towards the cylinder head; the fuel injectors are not so easily accessible.

Fuel rail and injectors

Note: Refer to the warning note in Section 1 before proceeding.

Note: If a faulty injector is suspected, before condemning the injector, it is worth trying the effect of one of the proprietary injector-cleaning treatments.

14.6a On 2.0 litre "Phase II" models, remove the fuel rail . . .

14.6b . . . and recover its spacers from the manifold

14.7a Remove the retaining plate . . .

"Phase I" models

1 Refer to Section 13, noting that additional insulators are fitted between the top of each injector and the retaining plate.

"Phase II" models

2 Remove the upper section of the inlet manifold as described in paragraphs 20 to 25 of Section 15.

3 Disconnect the vacuum pipe from the fuel pressure regulator.

4 Depressurise the fuel system as described in Section 7, then slacken the retaining clips and disconnect the fuel feed and return hoses from the left-hand end of the fuel rail.

5 Release the retaining clips, and disconnect the wiring connectors from the four injectors.

6 Slacken and remove the fuel rail retaining

bolts, then carefully ease the fuel rail and injector assembly out from the inlet manifold, and remove it from the vehicle. Recover the spacers fitted between the rail and manifold, and remove the injector seals from the manifold **(see illustrations)**.

7 Undo the two retaining screws, then remove the retaining plate and recover the insulator from the top of the each injector, noting which way round it is fitted. Withdraw the injector, and recover its sealing rings **(see illustrations)**.

8 Discard the seals and sealing rings; new ones must be used on refitting.

9 Refitting is a reversal of the removal procedure, noting the following points:

a) Fit new O-rings to all disturbed injectors **(see illustration)**.

b) Apply a smear of engine oil to the O-rings to aid installation, then ease the injectors into the fuel rail. Ensure that the insulator is fitted the correct way round, then refit the retaining plate and securely tighten its retaining screws.

c) Fit new injector seals to the manifold **(see illustration)**, and fit the fuel rail spacers to the manifold. Ease the fuel rail assembly into position in the manifold, and fit its retaining bolts. Working from the centre outwards, tighten the bolts first to their specified Stage 1 torque, then go around again and tighten them to the specified Stage 2 torque.

d) Install the upper section of the manifold as described in Section 15.

e) Ensure that all hoses are reconnected to their original locations and, where necessary, are securely held with the retaining clips.

f) Adjust the accelerator cable as described in Section 3.

g) On completion, start the engine and check for fuel leaks.

Fuel pressure regulator

Note: Refer to the warning note in Section 1 before proceeding.

10 Refer to Section 13 **(see illustration)**.

Throttle potentiometer

11 The throttle potentiometer is mounted onto the rear of the throttle housing **(see illustration)**. Prior to removal, disconnect the battery negative terminal.

14.7b . . . and withdraw the injector from the fuel rail

14.9a Prior to installation, fit new O-rings (arrowed) to each disturbed injector . . .

14.9b . . . and fit new injector seals to the manifold

14.10 Slacken the retaining clip and disconnect the return hose from the pressure regulator (arrowed)

14.11 Throttle potentiometer location (arrowed) - "Phase II" models

14.22 Disconnect the wiring connector . . .

14.23 . . . then undo the retaining bolts (three arrowed) and remove the airflow meter from the air cleaner housing

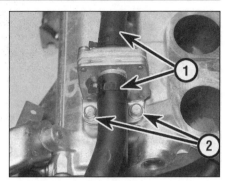

14.45 Air regulator valve vacuum hoses (1) and retaining bolts (2) - "Phase II" models

12 Disconnect the wiring connector from the throttle potentiometer.

13 Using a dab of white paint or a suitable marker pen, make alignment marks between the potentiometer and the throttle housing.

14 Undo the two retaining screws and remove the potentiometer.

15 On refitting, offer up the potentiometer, making sure that its lever is correctly engaged with the throttle valve spindle lever.

16 Align the marks made prior to removal, and lightly tighten the retaining screws. Adjust the potentiometer as follows.

17 Using a multi-meter set to the resistance scale, check that the potentiometer resistance readings are as given in the Specifications at the start of this Chapter. If necessary, slacken the retaining screws and reposition the potentiometer until its resistances are as specified.

18 When the potentiometer is correctly positioned, securely tighten its retaining screws, and reconnect the wiring connector.

19 Reconnect the battery on completion.

Airflow meter

20 The airflow meter is mounted onto the air cleaner housing lid. Prior to removal, disconnect the battery negative terminal.

21 Slacken the retaining clip, and disconnect the inlet duct from the airflow meter.

22 Disconnect the wiring connector from the airflow meter **(see illustration)**.

23 Undo the four bolts, and remove the meter from the air cleaner housing **(see illustration)**. Recover the sealing ring and discard it; a new one must be used on refitting.

24 Refitting is the reverse of removal, using a new sealing ring.

Auxiliary air control (AAC) valve

Note: *The auxiliary air valve is not available separately. If the valve is faulty, the complete idle air adjusting (IAA) unit must be renewed. The idle air adjusting unit is the cast housing which is bolted to the end of the manifold, containing the auxiliary air control (AAC) valve, the fast idle control device (FICD) solenoid valve, and the base idle speed adjusting screw.*

25 The auxiliary air control (AAC) valve is mounted onto the right-hand end of the inlet manifold. Prior to removal, disconnect the battery negative terminal.

26 Disconnect the wiring connector from the control valve.

27 Undo the retaining screws, then remove the valve from the manifold, along with its plunger and spring.

28 Check the valve plunger and spring for signs of wear or damage, and renew if necessary.

29 Refitting is the reverse of removal. Ensure that the plunger and spring are fitted in the correct order, and that the plunger is installed the correct way round.

Fast idle control device (FICD) solenoid valve

Note: *The fast idle control device (FICD) solenoid valve is not available separately. If the valve is faulty, the complete idle air adjusting (IAA) unit must be renewed. The idle air adjusting (IAA) unit is the cast housing which is bolted to the end of the manifold, containing the auxiliary air control (AAC) valve, the fast idle control device (FICD) solenoid valve, and the base idle speed adjusting screw.*

30 The fast idle control device (FICD) solenoid valve is screwed into the right-hand end of the inlet manifold. Prior to removal, disconnect the battery negative terminal.

31 Trace the wiring back from the solenoid to its wiring connector, and disconnect it from the main wiring harness.

32 Unscrew the solenoid valve from the manifold, and recover the plunger, spring, and sealing washer.

33 Refitting is the reverse of removal, ensuring that the solenoid plunger and spring are fitted in the correct order, and that the plunger is installed the correct way round.

Idle air adjusting (IAA) unit

34 The idle air adjusting unit is bolted to the right-hand end of the inlet manifold. Prior to removal, disconnect the battery negative terminal.

35 Disconnect the wiring connectors from the auxiliary air control (AAC) valve and the fast idle control device (FICD) solenoid valve,

and free the wiring from any relevant retaining clips.

36 Undo the retaining bolts, and remove the unit from the end of the manifold. Recover the gasket and discard it; a new one must be used on refitting.

37 On refitting, ensure that the unit and manifold faces are clean and dry, then offer up the new gasket. Fit the idle air adjusting unit, and securely tighten its mounting bolts. Reconnect the wiring connectors and the battery negative terminal.

Air regulator valve

"Phase I" models

38 The air regulator valve is located underneath the inlet manifold. Prior to removal, disconnect the battery negative terminal.

39 To improve access, firmly apply the handbrake, then jack up the front of the vehicle and support it on axle stands. Access to the valve can then be gained from both above and below.

40 Disconnect the wiring connector from the valve, then release the retaining clips and disconnect both the vacuum and coolant hoses. Plug the coolant hose ends, working quickly to minimise coolant loss.

41 Slacken and remove the mounting bolts, then release the valve from the manifold and remove it from the engine.

42 Refitting is the reverse of removal.

"Phase II" models

43 The air regulator valve is located on the left-hand end of the manifold, directly beneath the idle air adjusting (IAA) unit. Prior to removal, disconnect the battery negative terminal.

44 Remove the upper section of the inlet manifold as described in paragraphs 20 to 25 of Section 15.

45 Release the retaining clips, and disconnect both vacuum hoses from the valve **(see illustration)**.

46 Undo the two retaining bolts, and remove the valve from the manifold.

47 Refitting is the reverse of removal.

4C

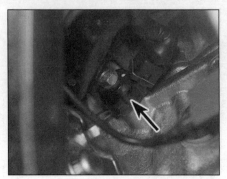

14.50 Knock sensor (arrowed) is situated directly beneath the inlet manifold

15.4 Unscrew the union nut (arrowed) and disconnect the EGR pipe from the valve

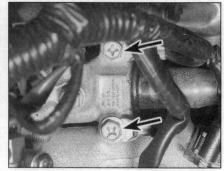

15.5 Undo the bolts, and free the earth leads (arrowed) from the right-hand end of the manifold

Crank angle sensor

48 The crank angle sensor is an integral part of the distributor. Refer to Chapter 5.

Power transistor

49 Refer to Chapter 5.

Knock sensor

50 Refer to Section 13 of Part B of this Chapter, noting that access to the knock sensor is very poor **(see illustration)**.

ECCS control unit

51 Refer to Section 13.

Neutral switch - manual transmission models

52 Refer to Chapter 7A.

Starter inhibitor/reversing light switch - automatic transmission models

53 Refer to Chapter 7B.

ECCS control unit and fuel pump relays

54 Refer to Chapter 12.

Power steering idle-up switch

55 Refer to Section 13.

Air conditioning system idle-up switch

56 The air conditioning switch is screwed into the air conditioning pipe, in the left-hand front corner of the engine compartment. Removal and refitting of the switch requires the air conditioning system to be discharged and recharged (see Chapter 3, Section 10), and this should not be attempted by the home mechanic.

Vehicle speed sensor

57 The vehicle speed sensor is an integral part of the speedometer. Refer to Chapter 12 for removal and refitting details.

15 Inlet manifold - removal and refitting

Note: *On 2.0 litre models, "Phase I" and "Phase II" models are easily distinguished by the shape of their inlet manifold. On "Phase I" models, the throttle body is mounted onto the base of the manifold, and the manifold curves upwards towards the cylinder head; the fuel injectors are easily accessible on the top of the manifold. On "Phase II" models, the throttle body is mounted on the top of the manifold, and the inlet manifold curves downwards towards the cylinder head; the fuel injectors are not so easily accessible.*

Removal

1.6 litre models

1 Drain the cooling system as described in Chapter 1.
2 Carry out the operations described in paragraphs 1 to 6 of Section 12, and disconnect all components from the throttle housing.
3 Make a note of the correct fitted locations of all the relevant inlet manifold vacuum hose connections, and disconnect them from the manifold and (where necessary) from the associated vacuum valves. To avoid confusion on refitting, it may be wise to label each hose as it is disconnected.
4 Unscrew the union nut and free the EGR pipe linking the inlet and exhaust manifolds, from the control valve on the left-hand end of the inlet manifold **(see illustration)**.
5 Disconnect the wiring connectors from the injectors and the engine coolant temperature sensor. Free the wiring from any relevant retaining clips, and position it clear of the manifold. Where necessary, also undo the retaining bolt(s) and free the earth lead(s) from the manifold **(see illustration)**.
6 Undo the retaining bolts and remove the support bracket from the underside of the manifold.
7 Depressurise the fuel system as described in Section 7, then slacken the retaining clips and disconnect the fuel feed and return hoses

from the left-hand end of the fuel rail. Plug the hose and rail unions, to minimise fuel loss and to prevent dirt entering the system.
8 Make a final check that all the necessary vacuum/breather hoses have been disconnected from the manifold then, working in the **reverse** of the sequence shown in illustration 15.33, slacken and remove the manifold retaining nuts and bolts.
9 Manoeuvre the manifold away from the head, and out of the engine compartment. Remove the manifold gasket and discard it.

2.0 litre "Phase I" models

10 To improve access, firmly apply the handbrake, then jack up the front of the vehicle and support it on axle stands. Access to the manifold and associated components can then be gained from above and below.
11 Slacken the retaining clip, and disconnect the inlet duct from the throttle housing. Free the accelerator cable from the throttle cam, then slacken the locknut and adjuster nut, and free the outer cable from its mounting bracket.
12 Depressurise the fuel system as described in Section 7, then slacken the retaining clips and disconnect the fuel feed and return hoses from the left-hand end of the fuel rail. Plug the hose and rail unions, to minimise fuel loss and to prevent dirt entering the system.
13 Release the retaining clip(s), then disconnect the coolant hose(s) from the throttle housing and manifold. Plug the hose end(s), working quickly to minimise coolant loss.
14 Make a note of the correct fitted locations of all the relevant inlet manifold vacuum hose connections, and disconnect them from the manifold and (where necessary) from the associated vacuum valves. To avoid confusion on refitting, it may be wise to label each hose as it is disconnected.
15 Disconnect the wiring connectors from the throttle potentiometer, the air regulator valve, the injectors, the coolant temperature sensor, and the idle air adjusting (IAA) unit. Free the wiring from any relevant retaining clips, and position it clear of the manifold.
16 Undo the retaining bolts, and remove the support brackets from the left- and right-hand ends of the manifold.

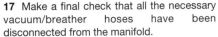

15.21 Fuel rail feed and return hoses (arrowed) - 2.0 litre "Phase II" models

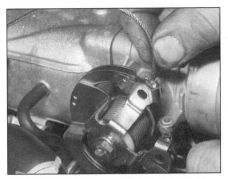

15.22a Free the accelerator inner cable from the throttle cam . . .

15.22b . . . and release the outer cable from its mounting bracket

17 Make a final check that all the necessary vacuum/breather hoses have been disconnected from the manifold.

18 Working in the **reverse** of the sequence shown in illustration 15.34, slacken and remove the manifold retaining nuts and bolts. Note that it may be necessary to remove the oil filter and/or oil filter housing from the rear of the block to gain access to the lower manifold nuts and bolts (refer to Chapters 1 and 2 for further information).

19 Manoeuvre the manifold away from the head, and out of the engine compartment. Remove the manifold gasket, and discard it.

2.0 litre "Phase II" models

20 To improve access, firmly apply the handbrake, then jack up the front of the vehicle and support it on axle stands. Access to the manifold and associated components can then be gained from above and below.

21 Depressurise the fuel system as described in Section 7, then slacken the retaining clips and disconnect the fuel feed and return hoses from the left-hand end of the fuel rail **(see illustration)**. Plug the hose and rail unions, to minimise fuel loss and to prevent dirt entering the system. Label the hoses if wished, to avoid confusion when refitting.

22 Slacken the retaining clip, and disconnect the inlet duct from the throttle housing. Free the accelerator inner cable from the throttle cam. Slacken the outer cable locknut and adjuster nut, then free the outer cable from its mounting bracket **(see illustrations)**.

23 Make a note of the correct fitted locations of all the relevant hose connections, and disconnect them from the throttle housing and inlet manifold upper section. Plug the coolant hose ends, working quickly to minimise coolant loss. To avoid confusion on refitting, it may be wise to label each hose as it is disconnected.

24 Disconnect the wiring connectors from the throttle potentiometer, auxiliary air control (AAC) valve, the fast idle control device (FICD) solenoid valve, and the coolant temperature sensors on the right-hand end of the manifold. Free the wiring from all its relevant retaining clips, and position the loom clear of the manifold.

25 Slacken and remove the eight retaining bolts (see illustration 15.35b) and the upper support bracket bolts **(see illustration)**, then lift off the upper section of inlet manifold complete with the throttle housing. Recover the gasket and discard it.

26 Disconnect the wiring connectors from the air regulator valve and the injectors. Free the wiring from any relevant retaining clips, and position it clear of the manifold.

27 Release the retaining clip(s), then disconnect the coolant hose(s) from the throttle housing and manifold. Plug the hose end(s), working quickly to minimise coolant loss.

28 Undo the retaining bolts and remove the support brackets from the rear of the manifold.

29 Unscrew the union nut and free the EGR

pipe linking the inlet and exhaust manifolds, from the control valve on the left-hand end of the inlet manifold **(see illustration)**.

30 Make a note of the correct fitted locations of all the relevant hose connections, and disconnect them from the lower section of the manifold. Plug the coolant hose ends, working quickly to minimise coolant loss. To avoid confusion on refitting, it may be wise to label each hose as it is disconnected. Make a final check that all the necessary vacuum/breather hoses have been disconnected from the manifold.

31 Drain the engine oil and remove the oil filter as described in Chapter 1. If the filter is damaged during removal, a new filter must be used on refitting.

32 Working in the **reverse** of the sequence shown in illustration 15.35a, slacken and remove the manifold retaining nuts and bolts. Note that it may be necessary to remove the oil filter housing from the rear of the block to gain access to the manifold right-hand end nuts and bolts (refer to Chapter 2B for further information). Manoeuvre the manifold away from the head, and out of the engine compartment. Remove the manifold gasket and discard it **(see illustrations)**.

Refitting

1.6 litre models

33 Refitting is the reverse of the removal procedure, noting the following points:
a) *Ensure that the manifold and cylinder*

15.25 Inlet manifold upper support brackets (arrowed)

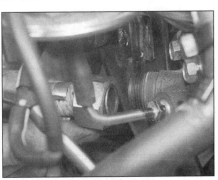

15.29 Undo the retaining nut, and free the EGR pipe from the valve

15.32a Remove the inlet manifold lower section . . .

4C

15.32b ... and recover the gasket

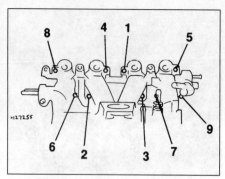

15.33 Inlet manifold nut and bolt tightening sequence - 1.6 litre models

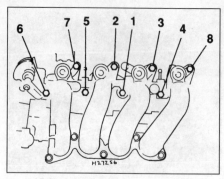

15.34 Inlet manifold nut and bolt tightening sequence - 2.0 litre "Phase I" models

head mating surfaces are clean and dry, and fit the new gasket to the head studs. Install the manifold, and tighten its retaining nuts and bolts to the specified torque setting in the order shown **(see illustration)**.
b) Ensure that all relevant hoses are reconnected to their original positions, and are securely held (where necessary) by their retaining clips.
c) Adjust the accelerator cable as described in Section 3.
d) On completion, refill the cooling system as described in Chapter 1.

2.0 litre "Phase I" models

34 Refitting is the reverse of the removal procedure, noting the following points:
a) Ensure that the manifold and cylinder head mating surfaces are clean and dry, and fit the new gasket to the head studs. Install the manifold, and tighten its retaining nuts and bolts to the specified torque setting in the order shown **(see illustration)**.
b) Ensure that all relevant hoses are reconnected to their original positions, and are securely held (where necessary) by their retaining clips.
c) Ensure that the fuel injection system wiring is correctly routed, and retained by

all the necessary clips.
d) Adjust the accelerator cable as described in Section 3.
e) Where necessary, fit new O-rings to the oil filter housing recesses, and refit the housing to the cylinder block, tightening its retaining bolts securely.
f) Fit the oil filter, and refill the engine with oil as described in Chapter 1.

2.0 litre "Phase II" models

35 Refitting is the reverse of the removal procedure, noting the following points:
a) Ensure that the manifold lower section and cylinder head mating surfaces are clean and dry, and fit the new gasket to the head studs. Install the manifold lower section, and tighten its retaining nuts and bolts to the specified torque setting in the order shown **(see illustration 15.35a)**.
b) Fit a new gasket to the lower section, then install the manifold upper section, and lightly tighten all its retaining bolts. Tighten the rear retaining bolts securely in

the order shown **(see illustration 15.35b)**, then securely tighten the three front retaining bolts.
c) Ensure that all relevant hoses are reconnected to their original positions, and are securely held (where necessary) by their retaining clips.
d) Ensure that the fuel injection system wiring is correctly routed, and retained by all the necessary clips.
e) Adjust the accelerator cable as described in Section 3.
f) Where necessary, fit new O-rings to the oil filter housing recesses, and refit the housing to the cylinder block, tightening its retaining bolts securely.
g) Fit the oil filter, and refill the engine with oil as described in Chapter 1.

16 Exhaust manifold - removal and refitting

Removal

1 On 1.6 litre models, trace the wiring back from the exhaust gas sensor to its wiring connector, and disconnect it from the main wiring harness.
2 On all models, slacken and remove the retaining screws, and remove the shroud from the top of the exhaust manifold **(see illustration)**.

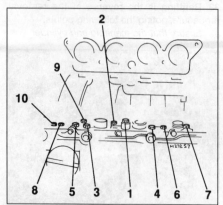

15.35a Inlet manifold lower section nut and bolt tightening sequence - 2.0 litre "Phase II" models

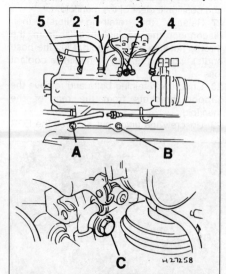

15.35b Inlet manifold upper section nut and bolt tightening sequence - 2.0 litre "Phase II" models

1 to 5 Rear bolts   a to c Front bolts

16.2 Removing the exhaust manifold shroud

16.3 Unscrew the union nut, and free the EGR pipe from the side of the manifold

16.7a Remove the exhaust manifold . . .

16.7b . . . and recover its gasket (2.0 litre model shown)

3 Where necessary, unscrew the union nut, and free the EGR pipe from the side of the manifold **(see illustration)**. Note that it may be necessary to slacken the inlet manifold end of the pipe, and the pipe mounting bolts (where fitted), in order to free the pipe from the manifold.

4 Firmly apply the handbrake, then jack up the front of the vehicle and support it on axle stands.

5 Undo the nuts securing the exhaust front pipe to the manifold, and the bolt securing the front pipe to its mounting bracket. Free the front pipe from the manifold, and recover the gasket(s). On 2.0 litre models fitted with a catalytic converter, either disconnect the exhaust gas sensor wiring connector, or support the pipe to ensure that no strain is placed on the wiring.

6 Working in the **reverse** of the sequence shown in illustration 16.8a or 16.8b, slacken and remove the manifold retaining nuts and bolts.

7 Manoeuvre the manifold out of the engine compartment, and discard the manifold gasket(s) **(see illustrations)**..

Refitting

8 Refitting is the reverse of the removal procedure, noting the following points:
a) *Examine all the exhaust manifold studs for signs of damage and corrosion; remove all traces of corrosion, and repair or renew any damaged studs.*
b) *Ensure that the manifold and cylinder head sealing faces are clean and flat, and fit the new manifold gasket(s). Tighten the manifold retaining nuts and bolts to the*

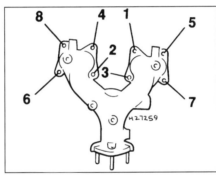

16.8a Exhaust manifold nut and bolt tightening sequence - 1.6 litre models

specified torque in the order shown **(see illustrations)**.
c) *Reconnect the front pipe to the manifold, using the information given in Section 17.*

17 Exhaust system - general information and component removal

Refer to Chapter 4B, Section 16.

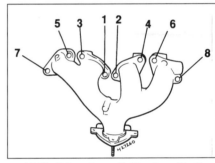

16.8b Exhaust manifold nut and bolt tightening sequence - 2.0 litre models (SR20De engine shown - DE model similar)

4C

Notes

Chapter 4 Part D Emissions control systems

Contents

Degrees of difficulty

Easy, suitable for novice with little experience	**Fairly easy,** suitable for beginner with some experience	**Fairly difficult,** suitable for competent DIY mechanic	**Difficult,** suitable for experienced DIY mechanic	**Very difficult,** suitable for expert DIY or professional

1 General information

1 All Nissan Primera models covered in this manual are capable of using unleaded petrol, and also have various other features built into the fuel system to help minimise harmful emissions.
2 All models are fitted with a crankcase emissions control system, along with the following systems, according to model:
1.6 litre non-catalyst carburettor models - idle compensator system and a dashpot.
1.6 litre catalyst carburettor models - catalytic converter, exhaust gas recirculation (EGR) system, evaporative emissions control system, air induction system, idle compensator system, and a dashpot.
1.6 litre multi-point injection models - catalytic converter, exhaust gas recirculation (EGR) system, and evaporative emissions control system.
2.0 litre single-point injection non-catalyst models - anti-afterburn system and a dashpot
2.0 litre single-point injection catalyst models - catalytic converter, exhaust gas recirculation (EGR) system, evaporative emissions control system, anti-afterburn system, and a dashpot.
2.0 litre multi-point injection non-catalyst models - no other emissions control systems fitted.
2.0 litre multi-point injection "Phase I" (pre-June 1993) catalyst models - catalytic converter and evaporative emissions control system.
2.0 litre multi-point injection "Phase II" (June 1993 on) models - catalytic converter, evaporative emissions control system, and an exhaust gas recirculation (EGR) system.
3 The various emissions control systems operate as follows.

Crankcase emissions control

4 To reduce the emission of unburned hydrocarbons from the crankcase into the atmosphere, the engine is sealed, and the blow-by gases and oil vapour are drawn from inside the crankcase, through the PCV valve, into the inlet tract, to be burned by the engine during normal combustion.
5 Under conditions of high manifold vacuum, the gases will be sucked positively out of the crankcase. Under conditions of low manifold vacuum, the gases are forced out of the crankcase by the (relatively) higher crankcase pressure; if the engine is worn, the raised crankcase pressure (due to increased blow-by) will cause some of the flow to return under all manifold conditions.

Catalytic converter

6 To minimise the amount of pollutants which escape into the atmosphere, some models are fitted with a catalytic converter in the exhaust system. On all models where a catalytic converter is fitted, the system is of the "closed-loop" type, in which an exhaust gas sensor provides the fuel system control unit constant feedback, enabling the unit to adjust the mixture to provide the best possible conditions for the converter to operate.
7 The sensor's tip is sensitive to oxygen, and sends the control unit a varying voltage depending on the amount of oxygen in the exhaust gases; if the intake air/fuel mixture is too rich, the sensor sends a high-voltage signal. The voltage falls as the mixture weakens. Peak conversion efficiency of all major pollutants occurs if the intake air/fuel mixture is maintained at the chemically-correct ratio for the complete combustion of petrol - 14.7 parts (by weight) of air to 1 part of fuel (the "stoichiometric" ratio). The sensor output voltage alters in a large step at this point, the control unit using the signal change as a reference point, and correcting the intake air/fuel mixture accordingly by altering the fuel injector pulse width (injector opening time). On later models, the sensor has a built-in heating element (controlled by the control unit), to quickly bring the sensor's tip to an efficient operating temperature.

Evaporative emissions control system

8 To minimise the escape of unburned hydrocarbons into the atmosphere, an evaporative emissions control system is fitted to models with a catalytic converter. The fuel tank filler cap is sealed, and a carbon canister collects the petrol vapours generated in the tank (fuel-injected models) or tank and carburettor float chamber (carburettor models) when the car is parked. It stores them until the vapours can be cleared into the inlet tract when the engine is running.
9 On carburettor models, the system is controlled by a thermal vacuum valve (TVV) which is screwed into the manifold; the TVV also controls the EGR system. When the engine is cold, the TVV cuts off the vacuum supply to the canister vacuum diaphragm valve, and the canister remains closed. When the engine reaches operating temperature (approximately 70°C), the TVV opens, and allows the vacuum (depression) present in the inlet manifold to act on the canister diaphragm. The diaphragm valve then opens, and all the vapours stored in the canister are drawn into the inlet tract to be burned during normal combustion.
10 On "Phase I" (pre-June 1993) 2.0 litre multi-point injection models, the canister is connected directly to the manifold, and the system is controlled by means of a restrictor valve on the canister vacuum diaphragm valve. When the engine is started, the vacuum present in the inlet manifold acts on the diaphragm, via the restrictor. At idle, the valve remains closed, but as the engine speed increases, so does the inlet manifold vacuum (depression). The restrictor governs the vacuum acting on the diaphragm, and so controls the valve opening in relation to engine speed - ie the valve is only slightly open at low engine speeds, but fully open at high engine speeds.

4D

11 On all other fuel-injected models, the system is controlled by the ECCS control unit via a solenoid valve; the same solenoid valve also operates the EGR system. To ensure that the engine runs correctly when it is cold and/or idling, and to protect the catalytic converter from the effects of an over-rich mixture, the solenoid valve is not opened by the control unit until the engine has warmed up and is under load. Once these conditions are met, the valve solenoid is modulated on and off to allow the stored vapour to pass into the inlet tract.

Exhaust gas recirculation (EGR) system

12 This system reduces the amount of unburnt hydrocarbons in the exhaust gases before the gases reach the catalytic converter. This is achieved by taking some of the exhaust gases from the exhaust manifold and recirculating them back into the inlet manifold, via a pipe linking the two, where they are burned again during normal combustion. The exhaust gas recirculation (EGR) valve is fitted to the inlet manifold end of the pipe.

13 On carburettor models, the system is controlled by the thermal vacuum valve (TVV) and the back-pressure transducer (BPT) valve; the TVV also controls the evaporative emission system. When the engine is cold, the TVV cuts off the vacuum supply to the EGR valve, and the valve remains closed. When the engine reaches operating temperature (approximately 70°C), the TVV opens, allowing the vacuum supply to act on the EGR valve, via the BPT valve. The BPT valve is sensitive to the exhaust gas back pressure, and regulates the EGR valve on and off accordingly. When the back pressure is high, the BPT valve closes, allowing the vacuum supply to act on the EGR valve, opening the valve. When the back pressure drops, the BPT valve opens, cutting off the vacuum supply to the EGR valve, and so closing the valve.

14 On fuel-injected models, the system is controlled by the ECCS control unit, via a solenoid valve and the back-pressure transducer (BPT) valve; the solenoid valve also operates the evaporative emissions control system. When the engine is cold, the ECCS control unit keeps the solenoid valve closed, cutting off the vacuum supply to the EGR valve. When the engine reaches operating temperature, the ECCS control unit opens the solenoid valve, allowing the vacuum supply to act on the EGR valve, via the BPT valve. The BPT valve is sensitive to the exhaust gas back pressure, and regulates the EGR valve on and off accordingly. When the back pressure is high, the BPT valve closes, allowing the vacuum supply to act on the EGR valve, opening the valve. When the back pressure drops, the BPT valve opens, cutting off the vacuum supply to the EGR valve, and so closing the valve.

Anti-afterburn (AB) system

15 This system prevents excessive hydrocarbon emissions in the exhaust gases, by stopping the exhaust gases from becoming excessively rich. This is achieved by supplying additional air into the manifold when the inlet manifold vacuum is high. The system consists solely of the anti-afterburn (AB) valve.

16 The anti-afterburn (AB) valve is sensitive to inlet manifold vacuum. Under cases of high inlet manifold vacuum (ie. when the throttle valve is shut at high engine speeds), the AB valve diaphragm opens, and the valve allows a charge of fresh filtered air from the air cleaner housing, to enter the manifold.

Air induction system

17 The air induction system reduces emissions of unburned hydrocarbon particles (HC) and carbon monoxide (CO) by passing filtered air directly into the exhaust manifold, so that a considerable proportion of these substances remaining in the exhaust gases after combustion are burned up in the manifold before reaching the catalytic converter. The system consists of the air induction valve (AIV) and a solenoid valve, and is controlled by the ECCS control unit.

18 To ensure that the engine runs correctly when it is cold and/or idling, the solenoid valve is not opened by the control unit until the engine has warmed up and is under load. When both these conditions are met, the valve solenoid is then modulated on and off to allow the fresh, filtered air to enter the exhaust manifold. The system functions by using the pressure variations in the exhaust gases to draw air through from the filter housing, so that there is no need for a separate air pump. The AIV only allows gases to flow only one way, so that there is no risk of hot exhaust gases flowing back into the filter.

Idle compensator system

19 The idle compensator system prevents the idle mixture becoming excessively rich at high engine temperatures. This is achieved by supplying additional air into the manifold when the engine temperature is high. The system consists solely of the idle compensator valve which is fitted to the air cleaner housing.

20 The compensator valve has a bi-metallic strip which is sensitive to temperature. At low temperatures, the valve is closed. As the temperature in the air cleaner housing increases, the bi-metallic strip in the valve deforms, and the valve gradually opens. This allows a charge of fresh, filtered air from the air cleaner housing to enter the manifold, and so weakens the idle mixture.

Dashpot

21 The dashpot is fitted to reduce the amount of unburnt hydrocarbons in the exhaust gases on the overrun. It does this by preventing the throttle valve from being snapped shut, such as when the driver lifts off suddenly at high engine speeds. The dashpot acts as a damper, and slowly closes throttle valve during its final stages. This reduces the amount of unburnt hydrocarbons in the exhaust gases by preventing the excessively-high inlet manifold vacuum which would otherwise draw unburnt fuel into the exhaust.

2 Emissions control systems - testing and component renewal

Note: *Refer to Section 1 for information on which systems are fitted to each relevant model.*

Crankcase emissions control

1 This system requires no attention, other than to check that the hose(s) are clear and undamaged, and to renew the PCV filter (where fitted) at the intervals given in Chapter 1.

Evaporative emissions control system

Testing - carburettor models

2 If the system is thought to be faulty, disconnect the hoses from the carbon canister and thermal vacuum valve (TVV), and check that they are clear by blowing through them.

3 To check the TVV, which is screwed into the right-hand end of the inlet manifold, with the engine cold, disconnect both hoses from the valve. Connect a length of hose to one of the valve ports, and blow down it; the valve should be closed to the passage of air. Start the engine and warm it up to normal operating temperature. With the engine warm, again blow down the valve ports; the valve should now be open, and allow air to pass freely. If the valve does not perform as expected, it is faulty and must be renewed.

4 The carbon canister and associated valves can be tested as follows (see illustration). The canister is located in the right-hand rear corner of the engine compartment.

5 Trace hose "a" back from the canister, and

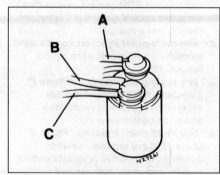

2.4 Carbon canister hose union identification - carburettor models

For A, B and C, refer to text

disconnect it from the T-piece connector. Start the engine and suck on the hose; there should be no sign of leakage, and the engine speed should increase slightly. Reconnect the hose to the T-piece.

6 Trace hose "c" back from the canister, and disconnect it from the carburettor float chamber. Start the engine and blow down the hose; there should be no sign of leakage. Reconnect the hose to the carburettor.

7 Trace hose "b" back from the canister, and disconnect it from the inlet manifold. With the engine stopped, blow and suck on the hose; there should be no sign of leakage. Reconnect the hose to the manifold.

8 If any trace of leakage is found whilst performing the checks described in paragraphs 5 to 7, the canister and valve assembly is faulty, and must be renewed.

Testing - "Phase I" (pre-June 1993) 2.0 litre multi-point injection models

9 If the system is thought to be faulty, disconnect the hoses from the carbon canister, which is mounted in the right-hand rear corner of the engine compartment, and check that they are clear by blowing through them.

10 The carbon canister and valve can be tested as follows **(see illustration)**. Disconnect the hoses from the canister, and blow down port "A" of the canister; there should be no sign of leakage. Blow down each of the ports "B" in turn. Both ports should be clear, and should freely pass air. If the checks do not give the expected results, the canister and valve assembly is faulty and must be renewed.

Testing - all other fuel-injected models

11 If the system is thought to be faulty, disconnect the hoses from the carbon canister and solenoid control valve, and check that they are clear by blowing through them. On 1.6 models, the canister is located in the left-hand rear corner of the engine compartment, and the solenoid valve is mounted onto the rear of the inlet manifold. On 2.0 litre models, the canister is located on the left-hand side of the engine compartment,

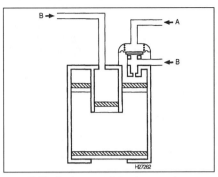

2.10 Carbon canister hose union identification - "Phase I" 2.0 litre multi-point injection models

For A and B, refer to text

and the solenoid valve is mounted on the left-hand end or underside of the inlet manifold.

12 The solenoid valve can be checked as follows, referring to illustration 2.14. If necessary, remove the valve as described in paragraphs 28 to 31 to improve access.

13 Blow down port "A", and check that no air flows through the valve. Blow down port "B", and check that air passes through the valve and flows out of port "C".

14 Connect a fused 12-volt supply to the solenoid valve as shown **(see illustration)**. With the voltage applied, blow down port "A", and check that air passes through the valve and flows out of port "B". Blow down port "B", and check that no air flows through the valve.

15 If the solenoid valve does not perform as expected, it is faulty and must be renewed.

16 The carbon canister and valve assembly can be checked as described in paragraph 10.

Carbon canister - renewal

17 The carbon canister is located either in right-hand rear corner of the engine compartment or on the left-hand side of the engine compartment, depending on model **(see illustration)**.

18 Make a note of the correct fitted location of each hose on the canister. To avoid the possibility of connecting the hoses incorrectly on refitting, make identification marks

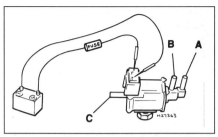

2.14 Evaporative emission control system solenoid valve test details - fuel-injected models

For A, B and C, refer to text

between each hose and its canister union.

19 Release the retaining clips (where fitted) and disconnect the hoses from the top of the canister.

20 Free the canister from its mounting bracket, and remove it from the engine compartment.

21 Refitting is a reverse of the removal procedure, ensuring that the hoses are correctly reconnected.

Thermal vacuum valve (TVV) renewal - carburettor models

22 The thermal vacuum valve (TVV) is screwed into the right-hand end of the inlet manifold **(see illustration)**. The engine and manifold should be cold before removing the valve.

23 Either partially drain the cooling system (as described in Chapter 1) to just below the level of the valve, or have ready a suitable plug which can be used to plug the valve aperture in the manifold whilst it is removed. If a plug is used, take great care not to damage the manifold, and do not use anything which will allow foreign matter to enter the cooling system.

24 Disconnect both hoses from the valve.

25 Carefully unscrew the valve from the manifold, and recover the sealing ring (where applicable).

26 Refitting is the reverse of removal, using a new sealing ring (where fitted). If a sealing ring was not fitted to the valve, apply a smear of sealing compound to its threads prior to refitting.

4D

2.17 Carbon canister assembly - 1.6 litre fuel-injected model

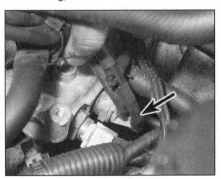

2.22 On carburettor models, the TVV valve (arrowed) is screwed into the right-hand end of the inlet manifold

2.27 On "Phase II" 2.0 litre multi-point models, the solenoid control valve is mounted onto the inlet manifold main support bracket

Solenoid control valve renewal - fuel-injected models (except 2.0 litre "Phase I" multi-point injection models)

27 The solenoid control valve is mounted onto the rear of the inlet manifold on 1.6 litre models, and on the left-hand end or underside of the inlet manifold on 2.0 litre models **(see illustration)**. To improve access on 1.6 litre models, remove the air cleaner housing (see Section 2). On 2.0 litre models, raise the vehicle and support it on axle stands so access can be gained from underneath the vehicle (where necessary).

28 To renew the solenoid valve, disconnect the battery negative terminal, then depress the retaining clip and disconnect the wiring connector from the valve.

29 Make a note of the correct fitted location of each hose on the valve. To avoid the possibility of connecting the hoses incorrectly on refitting, make identification marks between each hose and its valve union.

30 Release the retaining clips (where fitted) then disconnect the hoses from the valve, and free the valve from its mounting bracket.

31 Refitting is a reverse of the removal procedure, ensuring that the hoses are correctly reconnected.

Exhaust gas recirculation (EGR) system

Testing - carburettor models

32 If the system is thought to be faulty, disconnect the hoses from the exhaust gas recirculation (EGR) valve, the back-pressure transducer (BPT) valve and thermal vacuum valve (TVV), and check that they are clear by blowing through them. If all is well, reconnect all hoses.

33 The thermal vacuum valve can be checked as described in paragraph 3.

34 To check the operation of the EGR valve, disconnect the vacuum hose from the top of the valve, and fit a length of hose to the valve union. Suck on the hose end; check that the valve diaphragm is pulled up, and returns quickly when the vacuum is released. This can be checked by placing a finger lightly against

the underside of the valve where the movement of the diaphragm can be felt. If the valve operation is sticky or the diaphragm does not move at all, the EGR valve must be renewed.

35 If the TVV is known to be operating correctly, the BPT valve can be checked as follows. Warm the engine up to normal operating temperature, and disconnect the vacuum hose from the EGR valve. Place a finger over the end of the disconnected hose, and rev the engine in short bursts. As the engine speed (and exhaust gas pressure) increases, a vacuum should be felt in the pipe. As the engine speed falls, the vacuum should be switched off by the BPT valve. If this is not the case, the BPT valve is faulty and should be renewed.

Testing - fuel-injected models

36 The system can be tested as described above in paragraphs 32 to 35, ignoring the information about the TVV. Instead of the TVV, a solenoid control valve is fitted. The solenoid valve is the same valve as controls the evaporative emissions control system, and can be tested as described above in paragraphs 12 to 15.

Exhaust gas recirculation (EGR) valve - renewal

37 Disconnect the vacuum hose from the EGR valve, which is mounted on the left-hand end of the inlet manifold **(see illustration)**. Where necessary, remove the air cleaner housing to improve access to the valve. On some models, access can be further improved by first removing the BPT valve (see below).

38 Slacken the union nuts, and disconnect the EGR pipe and BPT valve pipe from the EGR valve.

39 Unscrew the two retaining nuts/bolts and washers, and remove the valve from the manifold. Remove the gasket and discard it.

40 Refitting is the reverse of removal, using a new gasket.

Back-pressure transducer (BPT) valve - renewal

41 The BPT valve is mounted on the left-hand side of the inlet manifold **(see**

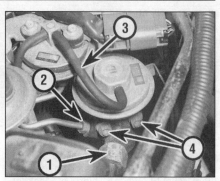

2.37 EGR valve details - 1.6 litre carburettor model (other models similar)

1 EGR pipe
2 BPT valve pipe
3 Vacuum pipe
4 Retaining nuts

illustration). Where necessary, remove the air cleaner housing to improve access to the valve.

42 Disconnect both vacuum hoses from the top of the valve.

43 Undo the two retaining bolts and remove the valve from the manifold, disconnecting it from the exhaust gas pipe.

44 Refitting is the reverse of removal

Thermal vacuum valve renewal - carburettor models

45 Refer to paragraphs 22 to 26 of this Section.

Solenoid control valve renewal - fuel-injected models

46 Refer to paragraphs 27 to 31 of this Section.

Exhaust emissions control system

Testing - carburettor models

47 Adjust the idle mixture (exhaust gas CO content) as described in Chapter 1.

48 Remove the fusebox cover, to gain access to the diagnostic connector which is clipped to the base of the fusebox.

49 Using multi-meter set to its voltage function, connect the probes of the meter to the check connector as shown **(see illustration)**

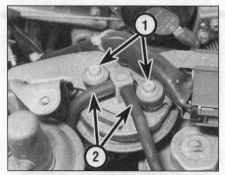

2.41 BPT valve details - 1.6 litre carburettor model (other models similar)

1 Retaining screws   2 Vacuum pipes

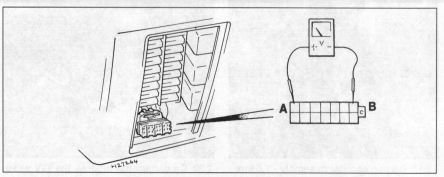

2.49 On carburettor models with a catalyst, connect the multi-meter to the fusebox check connector as shown, and test the exhaust gas sensor as described in text

2.53 On 1.6 litre models, the exhaust gas sensor is screwed into the manifold

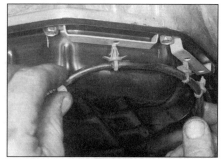
2.54a On 2.0 litre models, free the exhaust gas sensor wiring from its retaining clips . . .

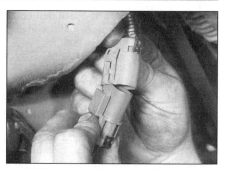
2.54b . . . then disconnect its wiring connector

50 Start the engine, raise the engine speed to approximately 2000 rpm, and hold it there for approximately 2 minutes whilst observing the meter. If the exhaust gas sensor is functioning correctly, the meter reading should switch from 0 volts to approximately 12 volts at least 5 times every 10 seconds. If not, the sensor is probably faulty. A more detailed check of the sensor and catalytic converter can be carried out by a Nissan dealer.

Testing - fuel-injected models

51 If the CO level at the tailpipe is too high, the operation of the exhaust gas sensor should be tested using the ECCS control unit self-diagnosis facility as described in Chapter 4B, Section 12. Detailed testing of the sensor and catalytic converter must be left to a Nissan dealer.

Catalytic converter - renewal

52 Refer to Part A, B or C of this Chapter (as applicable).

Exhaust gas sensor - renewal

Note: *The exhaust gas sensor is delicate, and it will not work if it is dropped or knocked, if its power supply is disrupted, or if any cleaning materials are used on it.*

53 On 1.6 litre models, trace the wiring back from the exhaust gas sensor, which is screwed into the exhaust manifold **(see illustration)**. Disconnect the wiring connector, and free the wiring from any relevant retaining clips or ties.

54 On 2.0 litre models, firmly apply the handbrake, then jack up the front of the vehicle and support it on axle stands. Trace the wiring back from the sensor (which is

screwed into the front pipe), freeing it from any relevant retaining clips. Disconnect the wiring at the connector **(see illustrations)**.

55 Unscrew the sensor, and remove it along with its sealing washer **(see illustration)**.

56 Refitting is a reverse of the removal procedure, using a new sealing washer. Prior to installing the sensor, apply a smear of high-temperature grease to the sensor threads. Ensure that the sensor is securely tightened. Check that the wiring is correctly routed, and in no danger of contacting either the exhaust system or the engine.

Anti-afterburn (AB) system
Testing

57 Remove the air cleaner lid and filter as described in Chapter 1.

58 Start the engine, steadily increase the engine speed, and hold it at approximately 3000 rpm. Place a finger over the anti-afterburn (AB) valve vacuum hose union in the base of the air cleaner housing, then quickly release the throttle valve so that the engine returns to its normal idle speed. As the throttle valve is released and the engine speed falls, a vacuum should be felt in the AB valve hose. If this is not the case, the AB valve is faulty and must be renewed.

Anti-afterburn (AB) valve - renewal

59 The valve is located on the top of the manifold, on the right-hand side of the throttle body.

60 Release the valve from its retaining clip, then disconnect the three hoses from the valve, noting each one's correct fitted location.

61 Refitting is the reverse of removal, ensuring that the hoses are correctly reconnected.

Air induction system
Testing

62 If the system is thought to be faulty, disconnect the hoses from the air induction solenoid control valve and the air induction valve (AIV), and check that they are clear by blowing through them. The solenoid valve is located on the left-hand end of the inlet manifold, and the air induction valve (AIV) is mounted on the left-hand suspension mounting turret.

63 The solenoid valve can be checked as follows. If preferred, remove the valve as described in paragraphs 69 to 73 to improve access.

64 Connect a 12-volt supply to the solenoid valve as shown **(see illustration)**. Blow down port "A" - air should pass through the valve, and flow out of port "B". Blow down port "B", and check that no air flows through the valve.

65 If the solenoid valve does not perform as expected, it is faulty and must be renewed.

66 To check the AIV, first remove it as described in paragraphs 75 to 77 then check it as follows.

67 Blow down port "B" **(see illustration)**, and check that no air passes through the valve. Apply a vacuum to port "A" of the valve, then blow down port "B" - air should pass through the valve, and flow out of port "C".

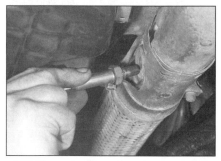
2.55 Removing the exhaust gas sensor - 2.0 litre models

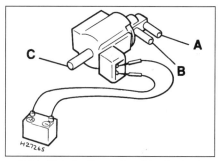
2.64 Air induction solenoid valve test details - carburettor models with a catalyst

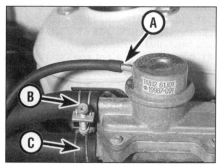
2.67 Air induction valve (AIV) port details - carburettor catalyst models

A *Vacuum pipe from solenoid valve*
B *From air cleaner housing*
C *To exhaust manifold*

4D

Blow down port "C", and check that no air passes through the valve, both with and without a vacuum applied to port "A".

68 If the AIV does not perform as expected, it is faulty and must be renewed.

Air induction solenoid control valve - renewal

69 The solenoid control valve is mounted on the left-hand end of the inlet manifold.

70 To renew the solenoid valve, disconnect the battery negative terminal. then depress the retaining clip and disconnect the wiring connector from the valve.

71 Make a note of the correct fitted location of each hose on the valve. To avoid the possibility of connecting the hoses incorrectly on refitting, make identification marks between each hose and its valve union.

72 Release the retaining clips (where fitted), and disconnect the hoses from the valve.

73 Free the valve from its mounting bracket, and remove it from the engine compartment.

74 Refitting is a reverse of the removal procedure, ensuring that the hoses are correctly reconnected.

Air induction valve (AIV) - renewal

75 The AIV is mounted on the left-hand suspension turret.

76 To renew the valve, slacken the retaining clips (where fitted), and disconnect the hoses from the valve **(see illustration)**.

77 Undo the mounting bolts and remove the valve from the engine compartment.

78 Refitting is the reverse of removal, ensuring that the hoses are correctly reconnected and securely retained by their clips.

Idle compensator system

Testing

79 Remove the air cleaner housing lid and filter as described in Chapter 1 for access to the valve **(see illustration)**.

80 The operation of the valve can be checked using a thermometer and a hairdryer. Position the thermometer as close as possible to the valve, then gently heat the valve using the hairdryer. The valve should remain closed below 38°C (100°F), start to open between 38° and 48°C (100 and 118°F), and be fully open at 48°C (118°F). Allow the valve to cool, and check that it closes fully.

81 If the valve does not open and close as specified; it is faulty and must be renewed.

Idle compensator valve - renewal

82 Remove the air cleaner filter element as described in Chapter 1.

83 Disconnect the hose from the base of the

2.76 Air induction valve (AIV) is secured to the body by two bolts (arrowed)

valve, then undo the retaining screws and remove it from the air cleaner housing.

84 Refitting is the reverse of removal.

Dashpot

Testing

85 Push the dashpot rod into the dashpot, making sure that the rod enters the dashpot slowly, then release the rod and check that it returns quickly. If not, the dashpot must be renewed.

Dashpot - renewal

86 On carburettor models, undo the two retaining screws, and remove the dashpot assembly from the side of the carburettor.

87 On fuel-injected models, unscrew the retaining nut, and lift the dashpot out of its throttle body mounting bracket.

88 Refitting is the reverse of removal. On completion, start the engine and warm it up to normal operating temperature. With the engine idling, have an assistant slowly depress the accelerator pedal, while you observe the dashpot. Note the engine speed at which the adjustment screw comes into contact with the end of the dashpot rod. This should happen at 2500 ± 200 rpm. If adjustment is necessary, slacken the locknut and rotate the screw as required. Recheck the dashpot contact speed, tightening the locknut securely when the screw is correctly adjusted.

---

3 Catalytic converter - general information and precautions

1 The catalytic converter is a reliable and simple device which needs no maintenance in itself, but there are some facts of which an owner should be aware if the converter is to function properly for its full service life.

2.79 Idle compensator valve (arrowed) is mounted onto the base of the air cleaner housing

a) DO NOT use leaded petrol in a car with a catalytic converter - the lead will coat the precious metals, reducing their converting efficiency, and will eventually destroy the converter.

b) Always keep the ignition and fuel systems well-maintained in accordance with the manufacturer's schedule (see Chapter 1).

c) If the engine develops a misfire, do not drive the car at all (or at least as little as possible) until the fault is cured.

d) DO NOT push- or tow-start the car - this will soak the catalytic converter in unburned fuel, causing it to overheat when the engine does start.

e) DO NOT switch off the ignition at high engine speeds - ie do not "blip" the throttle immediately before switching off.

f) DO NOT use fuel or engine oil additives - these may contain substances harmful to the catalytic converter.

g) DO NOT continue to use the car if the engine burns oil to the extent of leaving a visible trail of blue smoke.

h) Remember that the catalytic converter operates at very high temperatures. DO NOT, therefore, park the car in dry undergrowth, over long grass, or over piles of dead leaves, after a long run.

i) Remember that the catalytic converter is FRAGILE - do not strike it with tools during servicing work.

j) In some cases, a sulphurous smell (like that of rotten eggs) may be noticed from the exhaust. This is common to many catalytic converter-equipped cars when new - once the car has covered a few thousand miles, the problem should disappear.

k) The catalytic converter, used on a well-maintained and well-driven car, should last for between 50 000 and 100 000 miles, but if the converter is no longer effective, it must be renewed.

Chapter 5 Engine electrical systems

Contents

Degrees of difficulty

Easy, suitable for novice with little experience		Fairly easy, suitable for beginner with some experience		Fairly difficult, suitable for competent DIY mechanic		Difficult, suitable for experienced DIY mechanic		Very difficult, suitable for expert DIY or professional	

Specifications

System type . . . . 12-volt, negative earth

Battery
Type . . .Low-maintenance or maintenance-free, depending on model
Charge condition:
   Poor . . . . 12.5 volts
   Normal . . . . 12.6 volts
   Good . . . . 12.7 volts

Ignition system
System type:*
   Carburettor models without a catalytic
   converter ("non-catalyst" models) . . . . Breakerless electronic ignition
   Carburettor models with a catalytic converter ("catalyst" models) .. Breakerless electronic ignition controlled by ECC control unit
   Fuel-injected models . . . . Breakerless electronic ignition controlled by ECCS control unit
*Refer to text for further information on each relevant system
Firing order . . . . 1-3-4-2 (No 1 cylinder at timing chain end)
Ignition timing (at specified idle speed):
   Carburettor non-catalyst models:
      Distributor vacuum hose disconnected and plugged . . . . 2° ± 2° BTDC
      Distributor vacuum hose connected . . . . 10° ± 5° BTDC
   Carburettor catalyst models:
      Boost pressure sensor hose disconnected and plugged . . . . 2° ± 2° BTDC
      Boost pressure sensor hose connected . . . . 10° ± 2° BTDC
   1.6 litre fuel-injected models . . . . 10° ± 2° BTDC
   2.0 litre models . . . . 15° ± 2° BTDC
Ignition HT coil resistances:*
   1.6 litre fuel-injected models:
      Primary windings . . . . 2 ohms
      Secondary windings . . . . 12 kilohms
   All other models:
      Primary windings . . . . 1 ohm
      Secondary windings . . . . 10 kilohms
*The above results are approximate values, and are accurate only when the coil is at 20°C. See text for further information.

5

Alternator

Type	Bosch, Magneti Marelli, Mitsubishi or Hitachi (depending on model)

Minimum brush length:

Bosch	10.0 mm
Magneti Marelli	5.0 mm
Mitsubishi	8.0 mm
Hitachi	6.0 mm

Starter motor

Type . . . .Magneti Marelli, Mitsubishi or Hitachi (depending on model)	

Minimum brush length:

Magneti Marelli	5.0 mm
Mitsubishi	12.0 mm
Hitachi	11.0 mm

Torque wrench settings

	Nm	lbf ft
Distributor mounting bolts:		
1.6 litre models	8	5
2.0 litre models	15	11

1 General information and precautions

General information

1 The "engine" electrical system includes all charging, starting and ignition system components. Because of their engine-related functions, these components are covered separately from the "body" electrical devices such as the lights, instruments, etc (which are covered in Chapter 12).

2 The electrical system is of the 12-volt negative earth type.

3 The battery is of the low-maintenance or "maintenance-free" (sealed for life) type, and is charged by the alternator, which is belt-driven from the crankshaft pulley.

4 The starter motor is of the pre-engaged type, incorporating an integral solenoid. On starting, the solenoid moves the drive pinion into engagement with the flywheel ring gear before the starter motor is energised. Once the engine has started, a one-way clutch prevents the motor armature being driven by the engine until the pinion disengages from the flywheel.

5 Refer to Section 5 for further information on the various ignition systems.

Precautions

6 Further details of the various systems are given in the relevant Sections of this Chapter. While some repair procedures are given, the usual course of action is to renew the component concerned. The owner whose interest extends beyond mere component renewal should obtain a copy of the "*Automobile Electrical & Electronic Systems Manual*", available from the publishers of this manual.

7 It is necessary to take extra care when working on the electrical system, to avoid damage to semi-conductor devices (diodes and transistors), and to avoid the risk of personal injury. In addition to the precautions given in "*Safety first!*" at the beginning of this manual, observe the following when working on the system:

8 *Always remove rings, watches, etc before working on the electrical system.* Even with the battery disconnected, capacitive discharge could occur if a component's live terminal is earthed through a metal object. This could cause a shock or nasty burn.

9 *Do not reverse the battery connections.* Components such as the alternator, ECCS control unit (where applicable), or any other components having semi-conductor circuitry, could be irreparably damaged.

10 If the engine is being started using jump leads and a slave battery, connect the batteries *positive-to-positive* and *negative-to-negative* (see "*Jump starting*"). This also applies when connecting a battery charger.

11 Never disconnect the battery terminals, the alternator, any electrical wiring, or any test instruments, when the engine is running.

12 Do not allow the engine to turn the alternator when the alternator is not connected.

13 Never "test" for alternator output by "flashing" the output lead to earth.

14 Never use an ohmmeter of the type incorporating a hand-cranked generator for circuit or continuity testing.

15 Always ensure that the battery negative lead is disconnected when working on the electrical system.

16 Before using electric-arc welding equipment on the car, disconnect the battery, alternator and components such as electronic control units, to protect them from the risk of damage.

17 The radio/cassette unit fitted as standard equipment by Nissan has a built-in security code, to deter thieves. If the power source to the unit is cut, the anti-theft system will activate. Even if the power source is immediately reconnected, the radio/cassette unit will not function until the correct security code has been entered. Therefore, if you do not know the correct security code for the radio/cassette unit, **do not** disconnect the battery negative terminal, or remove the radio/cassette unit from the vehicle. Refer to "*Radio/cassette unit anti-theft system - precaution*" Section at the beginning of this manual.

2 Electrical fault-finding - general information

Refer to Chapter 12.

3 Battery - testing and charging

Standard and low-maintenance battery - testing

1 If the vehicle covers a small annual mileage, it is worthwhile checking the specific gravity of the electrolyte every three months, to determine the state of charge of the battery. Use a hydrometer to make the check, and compare the results with the following table. Note that the specific gravity readings assume an electrolyte temperature of 15°C (60°F); for every 10°C (18°F) below 15°C (60°F), subtract 0.007. For every 10°C (18°F) above 15°C (60°F), add 0.007. However, for convenience, the temperatures quoted in the following table are **ambient** (outdoor air) temperatures, above or below 25°C (77°F):

	Above 25°C (77°F)	Below 25°C (77°F)
Fully-charged	1.210 to 1.230	1.270 to 1.290
70% charged	1.170 to 1.190	1.230 to 1.250
Fully-discharged	1.050 to 1.070	1.110 to 1.130

2 If the battery condition is suspect, first check the specific gravity of electrolyte in each cell. A variation of 0.040 or more between any cells indicates loss of electrolyte, or deterioration of the internal plates.

3 If the specific gravity variation is 0.040 or more, a new battery should be fitted. If the cell variation is satisfactory but the battery is discharged, it should be charged as described later in this Section.

Maintenance-free battery - testing

4 In cases where a "sealed for life" maintenance-free battery is fitted, topping-up and testing of the electrolyte in each cell is not possible. The condition of the battery can therefore only be tested using a battery condition indicator or a voltmeter.

5 One type of maintenance-free battery which may be fitted is the "Delco" type maintenance-free battery, with a built-in charge condition indicator. The indicator is located in the top of the battery casing, and indicates the condition of the battery from its colour. If the indicator shows green, then the battery is in a good state of charge. If the indicator turns darker, eventually to black, then the battery requires charging, as described later in this Section. If the indicator shows clear/yellow, then the electrolyte level in the battery is too low to allow further use, and the battery should be renewed. **Do not** attempt to charge, load or jump start a battery when the indicator shows clear/yellow.

6 If testing the battery using a voltmeter, connect the voltmeter across the battery, and compare the result with those given in the Specifications under "charge condition". The test is only accurate if the battery has not been subjected to any kind of charge for the previous six hours. If this is not the case, switch on the headlights for 30 seconds, then wait four to five minutes before testing the battery after switching off the headlights. All other electrical circuits must be switched off, so check that the doors and tailgate are fully shut when making the test.

7 If the voltage reading is less than 12.2 volts, then the battery is discharged, whilst a reading of 12.2 to 12.4 volts indicates a partially-discharged condition.

8 If the battery is to be charged, remove it from the vehicle (Section 4) and charge it as described later in this Section.

Standard and low-maintenance battery - charging

Note: The following is intended as a guide only. Always refer to the manufacturer's recommendations (often printed on a label attached to the battery) before charging a battery.

9 Charge the battery at a rate of 3.5 to 4 amps, and continue to charge the battery at this rate until no further rise in specific gravity is noted over a four-hour period.

10 Alternatively, a trickle charger charging at the rate of 1.5 amps can safely be used overnight.

11 Specially rapid "boost" charges which are claimed to restore the power of the battery in 1 to 2 hours are not recommended, as they can cause serious damage to the battery plates through overheating.

12 While charging the battery, note that the temperature of the electrolyte should never exceed 37.8°C (100°F).

Maintenance-free battery - charging

Note: The following is intended as a guide only. Always refer to the manufacturer's recommendations (often printed on a label attached to the battery) before charging a battery.

13 This battery type takes considerably longer to fully recharge than the standard type, the time taken being dependent on the extent of discharge, but it can take anything up to three days.

14 A constant-voltage type charger is required, to be set, when connected, to 13.9 to 14.9 volts, with a charger current below 25 amps. Using this method, the battery should be usable within three hours, giving a voltage reading of 12.5 volts, but this is for a partially-discharged battery and, as mentioned, full charging can take considerably longer.

15 If the battery is to be charged from a fully-discharged state (condition reading less than 12.2 volts), have it recharged by your Nissan dealer or local automotive electrician, as the charge rate is higher, and constant supervision during charging is necessary.

4 Battery - removal and refitting

Removal

1 The battery is located on the left-hand side of the engine compartment.

2 Slacken the clamp nut/bolt, and disconnect the clamp from the battery negative terminal.

3 Remove the insulation cover (where fitted) and disconnect the positive clamp in the same way.

4 Unscrew the nuts, and remove the battery retaining clamp.

5 Lift the battery out of the engine compartment and, where necessary, remove the plastic battery tray. If necessary, the battery mounting bracket can also be unbolted and removed from the engine compartment.

Refitting

6 Refitting is a reversal of removal, but smear petroleum jelly on the terminals when reconnecting the leads, and always reconnect the positive lead first, and the negative lead last.

5 Ignition system - general information

Carburettor models without a catalytic converter

1 On these models, a breakerless electronic ignition system is used. The system comprises solely of the HT ignition coil and the distributor, both of which are mounted on the left-hand end of the cylinder head, the distributor being driven off the end of the exhaust camshaft.

2 The distributor contains a toothed reluctor mounted onto its shaft, and the IC ignition unit which is fixed to its body. The system operates as follows.

3 When the ignition is switched on but the engine is stationary, the IC ignition unit prevents current flowing through the ignition system primary (LT) circuit.

4 As the crankshaft rotates, the reluctor moves through the magnetic field created by the IC ignition unit. When the reluctor teeth are correctly positioned, a small AC voltage is created. The IC ignition unit uses this voltage to switch and complete the ignition system primary (LT) circuit.

5 As the reluctor teeth move out of alignment, the AC voltage changes, and the IC ignition unit switches again to interrupt the primary (LT) circuit. This causes a high voltage to be induced in the coil secondary (HT) windings, which then travels down the HT lead to the distributor and onto the relevant spark plug.

6 In addition to system components described above, the system has an ignition timing retard system. The system is controlled by the thermal vacuum valve (TVV) which is screwed into the right-hand end of the inlet manifold. The TVV is fitted in the vacuum pipe linking the distributor vacuum diaphragm unit to the inlet manifold. When the engine is cold (coolant temperature below 40°C), the TVV cuts off the main vacuum supply. The only vacuum supply to the distributor diaphragm is through the vacuum delay valve (VDV), which contains a restrictor, and therefore the ignition advance is reduced. When engine has warmed up (coolant temperature between 40° and 50°C) the TVV opens the main vacuum supply to the diaphragm

Carburettor models with a catalytic converter, and all fuel-injected models

7 On these models, the ignition system is integrated with the fuel system, to form a combined fuel/ignition system which is controlled by the ECC control unit (carburettor models) or ECCS control unit (fuel-injected models) (see the relevant Part of Chapter 4 for further information on the fuelling side of the system).

8 The distributor contains a crank angle sensor, which informs the control unit of engine

5

speed and crankshaft position. Based on this information, and the information received from its other sensors, the control unit then calculates the correct ignition timing setting, and switches the power transistor unit on and off accordingly. This causes a high voltage to be induced in the coil secondary (HT) windings, which then travels down the HT lead to the distributor and onto the relevant spark plug.

9 On 2.0 litre models, a knock sensor is incorporated into the ignition system. The sensor is mounted onto the rear of the cylinder block, and prevents the engine "pinking" under load. The sensor is sensitive to vibration, and detects the knocking which occurs when the engine starts to "pink" (pre-ignite). The knock sensor sends an electrical signal to the control unit, which in turn retards the ignition advance setting until the "pinking" ceases.

6 Ignition system - testing

Warning: Voltages produced by an electronic ignition system are considerably higher than those produced by conventional ignition systems. Extreme care must be taken when working on the system with the ignition switched on. Persons with surgically-implanted cardiac pacemaker devices should keep well clear of the ignition circuits, components and test equipment

Carburettor models without a catalytic converter

Note: *Refer to the warning given in Section 1 before starting work. Always switch off the ignition before disconnecting or connecting any component, and when using a multi-meter to check resistances.*

General

1 The components of electronic ignition systems are normally very reliable; most faults are far more likely to be due to loose or dirty connections, or to "tracking" of HT voltage due to dirt, dampness or damaged insulation, than to the failure of any of the system's components. **Always** check all wiring thoroughly before condemning an electrical component, and work methodically to eliminate all other possibilities before deciding that a particular component is faulty.

2 The old practice of checking for a spark by holding the live end of an HT lead a short distance away from the engine is **not** recommended; not only is there a high risk of a powerful electric shock, but the HT coil or power transistor unit will very likely be damaged. Similarly, **never** try to "diagnose" misfires by pulling off one HT lead at a time.

Engine will not start

3 If the engine either will not turn over at all, or only turns very slowly, check the battery

and starter motor. Connect a voltmeter across the battery terminals (meter positive probe to battery positive terminal), then disconnect the ignition coil HT lead from the distributor cap and earth it. Note the voltage reading obtained while turning over the engine on the starter for (no more than) ten seconds. If the reading obtained is less than approximately 9.5 volts, first check the battery, starter motor and charging system as described in the relevant Sections of this Chapter.

4 If the engine turns over at normal speed but will not start, check the HT circuit by connecting a timing light (following the equipment manufacturer's instructions) and turning the engine over on the starter motor; if the light flashes, voltage is reaching the spark plugs, so these should be checked first. If the light does not flash, check the HT leads themselves, followed by the distributor cap, carbon brush and rotor arm using the information given in Chapter 1.

5 If there is a spark, check the carburettor, referring to Chapter 4A for further information.

6 If there is still no spark, check the voltage at the ignition HT coil "+" terminal; it should be the same as the battery voltage (ie, at least 11.7 volts). If the voltage at the coil is more than 1 volt less than that at the battery, check the feed back through the fusebox and ignition switch to the battery and its earth until the fault is found.

7 If the feed to the HT coil is sound, check the coil's primary and secondary winding resistance as described later in this Section; renew the coil if faulty, but be careful to check carefully the condition of the LT connections themselves before doing so, to ensure that the fault is not due to dirty or poorly-fastened connectors.

8 If the HT coil is in good condition, the fault is probably within the IC ignition unit. Testing of the unit should be entrusted to a Nissan dealer.

9 The ignition timing retard system thermal vacuum valve (TVV) can be checked as described for similar components in Part D of Chapter 4. Check the vacuum delay valve (VDV) by blowing through it from both sides of the valve. The valve should pass air freely when blown through from the distributor side of the valve, but resistance should be felt when air is blown through from the carburettor side of the valve; if not, renew the VDV. On refitting, ensure that the valve is installed the correct way round, with its brown side facing the carburettor.

Engine misfires

10 An irregular misfire suggests either a loose connection or intermittent fault on the primary circuit, or an HT fault on the coil side of the rotor arm.

11 With the ignition switched off, check carefully through the system, ensuring that all connections are clean and securely fastened. If the equipment is available, check the LT circuit as described above.

12 Check that the HT coil, the distributor cap and the HT leads are clean and dry. Check the leads themselves and the spark plugs (by substitution, if necessary), then check the distributor cap, carbon brush and rotor arm as described in Chapter 1.

13 Regular misfiring is almost certainly due to a fault in the distributor cap, HT leads or spark plugs. Use a timing light (paragraph 4 above) to check whether HT voltage is present at all leads.

14 If HT voltage is not present on any particular lead, the fault will be in that lead, or in the distributor cap. If HT is present on all leads, the fault will be in the spark plugs; check and renew them if there is any doubt about their condition.

15 If no HT is present, check the HT coil; its secondary windings may be breaking down under load.

Carburettor models with a catalytic converter, and all fuel-injected models

16 If a fault appears in the ignition system, first ensure that the fault is not due to a poor electrical connection or poor maintenance; ie, check that the air cleaner filter element is clean, that the spark plugs are in good condition and correctly gapped, that the engine breather hoses are clear and undamaged, referring to Chapter 1 for further information. Also check that the accelerator cable is correctly adjusted, as described in the relevant Part of Chapter 4. If the engine is running very roughly, check the compression pressures and, where possible, the valve clearances, as described in the relevant Part of Chapter 2.

17 The only ignition system checks which can be carried out by the home mechanic are those described in Chapter 1, relating to the spark plugs, and the ignition coil test described in this Chapter. If necessary, the system wiring and wiring connectors can be checked as described in Chapter 12, ensuring that the control unit wiring connector(s) have first been disconnected.

18 On fuel-injected models, a quick check of the system can be carried out using the control unit self-diagnosis mode (see Chapter 4B, Section 12).

19 If the above checks fail to reveal the cause of the problem, the vehicle should be taken to a suitably-equipped Nissan dealer for testing.

7 Ignition HT coil - removal, testing and refitting

Removal

1 The ignition coil is mounted on the left-hand end of the cylinder head. Prior to removal, disconnect the battery negative terminal.

2 Disconnect the HT lead from the coil, then

7.2a Disconnect the HT lead . . .

7.2b . . . and wiring connector from the ignition coil . . .

7.3 . . . then undo the two bolts (arrowed) and remove the coil from its mounting bracket (2.0 litre model shown)

depress the retaining clip and disconnect the coil wiring connector **(see illustrations)**.

3 Slacken and remove the two retaining bolts, and remove the coil from its mounting bracket on the cylinder head **(see illustration)**.

Testing

4 Testing of the coil consists of using a multimeter set to its resistance function, to check the primary (LT "+" to "-" terminals) and secondary (LT "+" to HT lead terminal) windings for continuity. Compare the results obtained to those given in the Specifications at the start of this Chapter. Note that the resistance of the coil windings will vary slightly according to the coil temperature - the results in the Specifications are approximate values for when the coil is at 20ºC.

5 Check that there is no continuity between the HT lead terminal and the coil body.

6 If the coil is thought to be faulty, have your findings confirmed by a Nissan dealer before renewing the coil.

Refitting

7 Refitting is a reversal of the relevant removal procedure, ensuring that the wiring connector and HT lead are securely reconnected.

8 Distributor - removal and refitting

Removal

1 Disconnect the battery negative terminal.

2 Unclip the cover (where fitted), then slacken and remove the distributor cap retaining screws. Remove the cap, position it clear of the distributor body, and recover the cap seal.

3 Depress the retaining clip, and disconnect the wiring connector(s) from the distributor.

4 Where necessary, disconnect the hose from the vacuum diaphragm unit.

5 Check the cylinder head and distributor flange for signs of alignment marks. If no marks are visible, using a scriber or suitable marker pen, mark the relationship of the

distributor body to the cylinder head. Slacken and remove the two mounting bolts, and withdraw the distributor from the cylinder head. Remove the O-ring from the end of the distributor body and discard it; a new one must be used on refitting.

Refitting

6 Lubricate the new O-ring with a smear of engine oil, and fit it to the groove in the distributor body. Examine the distributor cap seal for wear or damage, and renew if necessary.

7 Align the distributor rotor shaft drive coupling key with the slots in the camshaft end, noting that the slots are offset to ensure

8.7 Fit a new O-ring (arrowed) and refit the distributor, aligning its drive coupling with the camshaft slot

8.9a Fit the seal to the distributor body . . .

that the distributor can only be fitted in one position. Carefully insert the distributor into the cylinder head, whilst rotating the rotor arm slightly to ensure that the coupling is correctly engaged **(see illustration)**.

8 Align the marks noted or made on removal, and install the distributor retaining nuts/bolts (as applicable), tightening them lightly only **(see illustration)**.

9 Ensure that the seal is correctly located in its groove, then refit the cap assembly to the distributor and tighten its retaining screws securely **(see illustrations)**. Fold the waterproof cover back over the distributor cap, ensuring that it is correctly located.

10 Reconnect the distributor wiring

8.8 Align the marks made prior to removal (arrowed), and refit the distributor mounting bolts

8.9b . . . then refit the cap and securely tighten its retaining screws

5

8.10 Connecting the distributor wiring connector

10.7 Disconnecting the power transistor wiring connector - 2.0 litre models

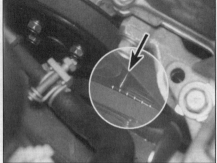

11.2 Crankshaft pulley TDC notch aligned with timing chain cover pointer (arrowed) - 2.0 litre model shown

connector **(see illustration)**and, where necessary, the vacuum hose to the diaphragm unit.

11 Check and, if necessary, adjust the ignition timing as described in Section 11, then tighten the distributor mounting bolts to the specified torque.

9 IC ignition unit (carburettor models without a catalytic converter) - removal and refitting

Removal

1 Remove the distributor as described in Section 8.

2 Undo the retaining screw and remove the rotor arm.

3 Using a dab of paint or suitable marker pen, make an identification mark on the top of the distributor toothed reluctor. The mark can then be used to ensure that the reluctor is installed the right way up.

4 Slide the reluctor off the distributor shaft, and recover the roll pin. If necessary, the rotor can be drawn off using a suitable legged puller.

5 Carefully disconnect the wiring connectors from the ignition unit, noting each wire's correct fitted position.

6 Undo the retaining screws, and remove the IC ignition unit from the distributor.

Refitting

7 Install the IC ignition unit, and securely tighten its retaining screws.

8 Connect the wires to their original locations, taking care not to damage the unit terminals.

9 Using the mark made on removal, ensure that the toothed reluctor is positioned the correct way up, and slide it onto the distributor shaft. Align it with the shaft, and secure the reluctor in position with the roll pin.

10 Refit the rotor arm, and securely tighten its retaining screw.

11 Refit the distributor as described in Section 8.

10 Ignition power transistor unit - removal and refitting

Carburettor models with a catalytic converter

1 The power transistor unit is situated in the engine compartment, mounted onto the left-hand suspension mounting turret.

2 Disconnect the battery negative terminal, then disconnect the wiring connector from the power transistor.

3 Undo the retaining bolts, and remove the power transistor from the vehicle.

4 Refitting is the reverse of removal.

1.6 litre fuel-injected models

5 On 1.6 litre fuel-injected models, the power transistor is an integral part of the distributor, and cannot be renewed separately. If the unit is faulty, the complete distributor body assembly must be renewed.

2.0 litre models

6 The power transistor is mounted on the left-hand end of the cylinder head.

7 Disconnect the battery negative terminal, then disconnect the wiring connector from the power transistor **(see illustration)**.

8 Undo the retaining bolts, and remove the power transistor from the vehicle.

9 Refitting is the reverse of removal.

11 Ignition timing - checking and adjustment

1 To check the ignition timing, a stroboscopic timing light will be required.

2 The timing marks are in the form of notches on the crankshaft pulley rim, which align with a pointer on the timing chain cover. The notches are spaced at intervals of 5°, and go from 20° before top dead centre (BTDC) to 5° after top dead centre (ATDC). The TDC mark is highlighted with paint to aid identification **(see illustration)**.

3 Start the engine, warm it up to normal operating temperature, and then switch off. Check the ignition timing as described under the relevant sub-heading.

Carburettor models

4 Disconnect the vacuum hose from the distributor vacuum diaphragm unit (non-catalyst models) or the boost pressure sensor (catalyst models), which is mounted on the left-hand suspension mounting turret. Plug the hose end.

5 Connect the timing light to No 1 cylinder (nearest the timing chain) plug lead as described in the timing light manufacturer's instructions.

6 Start the engine, allowing it to idle at the specified speed, and point the timing light at the crankshaft pulley. The relevant timing mark should be aligned with the pointer on the timing chain cover (see Specifications for the correct timing setting).

7 If adjustment is necessary, slacken the two distributor mounting bolts, then slowly rotate the distributor body as required until the crankshaft pulley marks are correctly positioned.

⚠ *Warning: At all times, avoid touching the HT leads, and keep loose clothing, long hair, etc, well away from the moving parts of the engine. Once the marks are correctly aligned, hold the distributor stationary, and tighten its mounting bolts to the specified torque. Recheck that the timing marks are still correctly aligned and, if necessary, repeat the adjustment procedure.*

8 When the timing is correctly set, increase the engine speed, and check that the pulley mark advances to beyond the beginning of the timing plate reference marks, returning to close to the specified mark when the engine is allowed to idle; this shows that the centrifugal advance mechanism is functioning, but a detailed check must be left to a Nissan dealer.

9 Reconnect the vacuum hose to the distributor (non-catalyst models) or boost pressure sensor (catalyst models). Check that the timing advances by the correct amount, so that the crankshaft pulley timing marks are

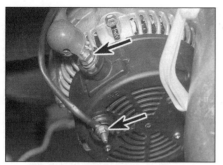

14.3 Alternator wiring connections (arrowed) - 2.0 litre Phase II models

14.4 Removing the alternator (2.0 litre model shown)

correctly positioned (refer to the Specifications for the correct timing setting). If not, it is likely that the vacuum diaphragm unit/boost pressure sensor (as applicable) is faulty, or that the vacuum hose is leaking.

10 When the ignition timing is correct, stop the engine and disconnect the timing light.

Fuel-injected models

11 Disconnect the wiring connector from the throttle potentiometer (see the relevant Part of Chapter 4).

12 Check and adjust the ignition timing as described above in paragraphs 5 to 7.

13 When the ignition timing is correctly set, stop the engine and disconnect the timing light.

14 Reconnect the throttle potentiometer wiring connector.

12 Charging system - testing

Note: *Refer to the warnings given in "Safety first!" and in Section 1 of this Chapter before starting work.*

1 If the ignition/no-charge warning light fails to come on when the ignition is switched on, first check the alternator wiring connections for security. If satisfactory, check that the warning light bulb has not blown, and that the bulbholder is secure in its location in the instrument panel. If the light still fails to come on, check the continuity of the warning light feed wire from the alternator to the bulbholder. If all is satisfactory, the alternator is at fault, and should be taken to an auto-electrician for testing and repair.

2 If the ignition warning light comes on when the engine is running, stop the engine as soon as possible. Check that the drivebelt is correctly tensioned (see Chapter 1), that the drivebelt is not contaminated (with oil or water, for example), and that the alternator connections are secure. If all is so far satisfactory, check the alternator brushes and slip-rings as described in Section 15. If the fault persists, the alternator should be taken to an auto-electrician for testing and repair.

3 If the alternator output is suspect, even though the warning light functions correctly,

the regulated voltage may be checked as follows.

4 Connect a voltmeter across the battery terminals, and start the engine.

5 Increase the engine speed until the voltmeter reading remains steady; the reading should be approximately 12 to 13 volts, and no more than 14 volts.

6 Switch on as many electrical accessories (eg, the headlights, heated rear window and heater blower) as possible, and check that the alternator maintains the regulated voltage at around 13 to 14 volts.

7 If the regulated voltage is not as stated, the fault may be due to worn brushes, weak brush springs, a faulty voltage regulator, a faulty diode, a severed phase winding, or worn or damaged slip-rings. The brushes and slip-rings may be checked (see Section 15), but if the fault persists, the alternator should taken to an auto-electrician for testing and repair.

13 Alternator drivebelt - removal, refitting and tensioning

1 Refer to the procedure given for the auxiliary drivebelt in Chapter 1.

14 Alternator - removal and refitting

Removal

1 Disconnect the battery negative lead.

2 Slacken the auxiliary drivebelt as described in Chapter 1, and disengage it from the alternator pulley.

3 Remove the rubber covers (where fitted) from the alternator terminals, then unscrew the retaining nut(s) and disconnect the wiring from the rear of the alternator. Where necessary, also undo the retaining screw and disconnect the earth lead **(see illustration)**

4 Unscrew the alternator upper and lower mounting bolts and washers, then manoeuvre the alternator away from its mounting brackets and out of position **(see illustration)**. On 1.6 litre models, recover the spacer (where fitted) from between the alternator and the adjuster strap.

On 2.0 litre models with ABS, in order to gain the clearance required to remove the alternator, it may be necessary to drain the cooling system (see Chapter 1) and remove the radiator top hose. Additional clearance can also be gained by unbolting the ABS wiring connector and air conditioning pipe support brackets.

Refitting

5 Refitting is a reversal of removal, tensioning the auxiliary drivebelt as described in Chapter 1, and ensuring that the alternator mountings are securely tightened.

15 Alternator brushes and regulator - inspection and renewal

1 Remove the alternator as described in Section 14. Proceed as described below the relevant sub-heading.

HAYNES HINT *Consult your dealer or an auto electrician on the cost and availability of spare parts before stripping the alternator, as some parts for certain alternators may either be unavailable or more expensive than an exchange unit.*

Bosch alternator

2 Unscrew the retaining screws and terminal nut (where necessary), and unclip the cover from the rear of the alternator **(see illustrations)**.

15.2a Unscrew the terminal nut (A), then undo the three retaining screws (B) . . .

15.2b . . . and remove the rear cover from the alternator

15.3a Undo the two screws . . .

15.3b . . . and remove the regulator/brush holder assembly

15.4 Brush wear markings are in the form of a line (arrowed) on each brush

3 If necessary, scrape the sealing compound from the rear of the alternator, to expose the regulator/brush holder assembly retaining screws. Slacken and remove the retaining screws, and remove the regulator/brush holder from the rear of the alternator **(see illustrations)**.

4 Note the length of each brush. If either brush is worn down to, or close to, its wear marking (in the form of a line on the brush), the complete regulator/brush holder assembly must be renewed **(see illustration)**. It is not possible to renew the brushes separately.

5 If the brushes are still serviceable, clean them with a petrol-moistened cloth. Check that the brush spring tension is equal for both brushes, and that it provides a reasonable pressure. The brushes must move freely in their holders.

6 Clean the alternator slip-rings with a petrol-moistened cloth. Check for signs of scoring, burning or severe pitting on the surface of the slip-rings **(see illustration)**. It may be possible to have the slip-rings renovated by an electrical specialist.

7 Refit the regulator/brush holder assembly, and securely tighten its retaining screws.

8 Clip the rear cover onto the alternator, and refit the alternator as described in Section 14.

Magneti Marelli alternator

9 Refer to the information given above in paragraphs 3 to 7.

Mitsubishi alternator

10 Make alignment marks between the stator coil and the front and rear covers.

11 Undo the four screws securing the front cover to the rear cover.

12 Carefully prise the stator coil away from the front cover, and remove the rear cover and stator assembly from the alternator. If difficulty is encountered, heat the rear cover bearing box for a few minutes with a large soldering iron - this will expand the cover, and help to release it from the rotor.

⚠️ *Warning: Do attempt to heat the cover with any other source of heat, such as a welding torch or heat gun, as the diode assembly will almost certainly be damaged.*

13 Note the length of each brush. If either brush is worn down to, or close to, its wear marking (in the form of a line on the brush), both brushes and their springs should be renewed.

14 If the brushes are still serviceable, clean them with a petrol-moistened cloth. Check that the brush spring tension is equal for both brushes, and that it provides a reasonable pressure. The brushes must move freely in their holders.

15 Clean the alternator slip-rings with a petrol-moistened cloth. Check for signs of scoring, burning or severe pitting on the surface of the slip-rings. It may be possible to have the slip-rings renovated by an electrical specialist.

16 To remove the regulator/brush holder assembly, unsolder the wires, noting their correct fitted positions, whilst using a pair of pointed-nose pliers as a heat sink. **Note:** *Work quickly to ensure excess heat is not*

transferred to the other components, as this could damage them. Slacken and remove the retaining screws and plate, and remove the regulator/brush holder assembly.

17 To renew the brushes individually, remove the small insulator (where fitted) from the base of regulator/brush holder assembly, to expose the brush leads. Then, using a pair of pointed-nose pliers as a heat sink, unsolder the leads. **Note:** *Work quickly to ensure excess heat is not transferred to the other components, as this could damage them.* With the leads unsoldered, slide the brushes out of position, and recover the springs. Insert the new brushes and springs into the holder, and solder the leads onto their terminals. Each brush should be positioned so that its wear mark is 2 mm above the regulator/brush holder surface **(see illustration)**. Work quickly again, to avoid excess heat affecting the other components - use a pair of pliers as a heat sink. Check that the wires are securely retained, then (where necessary) clip the insulator into position.

18 Fit the regulator/brush holder assembly, and solder on the wires to the correct terminals. Work quickly, to avoid excess heat affecting the other components - use a pair of pliers as a heat sink.

19 Push the brushes fully into their holders, and retain them there by inserting a length of wire through the hole in the rear cover to hold them in position.

20 Fit the retaining clip to the rear bearing groove. Noting that the groove is eccentric, position the clip so that it protrudes above the outer race surface by the minimum possible amount **(see illustration)**.

15.6 Examine the alternator slip-rings (arrowed) for sign of wear or damage

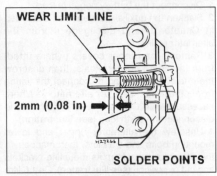

WEAR LIMIT LINE

2mm (0.08 in)

SOLDER POINTS

15.17 On Mitsubishi alternator, position the brushes as shown on refitting

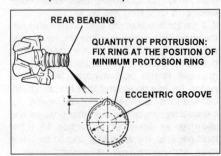

REAR BEARING

QUANTITY OF PROTRUSION: FIX RING AT THE POSITION OF MINIMUM PROTOSION RING

ECCENTRIC GROOVE

15.20 Alternator rear bearing retaining clip fitting position - Mitsubishi alternator

21 Align the marks made on removal, and refit the stator and rear cover assembly to the rotor and front cover. If necessary, heat the rear cover bearing box (see paragraph 12) to ease installation.

22 Refit the screws to the front cover, and tighten them securely.

23 Withdraw the wire from the rear cover, so that the brushes contact the slip-rings, and refit the alternator as described in Section 14.

Hitachi alternator

24 Refer to the information given above in paragraphs 10 to 23, noting that the regulator and brush holder are separate components. If the brushes are to renewed individually, solder their leads into position so that the brushes protrude from the holder by 10.5 to 11.5 mm.

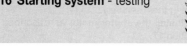

16 Starting system - testing

Note: *Refer to the precautions given in "Safety first!" and in Section 1 of this Chapter before starting work.*

1 If the starter motor fails to operate when the ignition key is turned to the appropriate position, the following may be to blame:
a) The battery is faulty.
b) The electrical connections between the switch, solenoid, battery and starter motor are somewhere failing to pass the necessary current from the battery through the starter to earth.
c) The solenoid is faulty.
d) The starter motor is mechanically or electrically defective.

2 To check the battery, switch on the headlights. If they dim after a few seconds, this indicates that the battery is discharged - recharge (see Section 3) or renew the battery. If the headlights glow brightly, operate the ignition switch and observe the lights. If they dim, then this indicates that current is reaching the starter motor, therefore the fault must lie in the starter motor. If the lights continue to glow brightly (and no clicking sound can be heard from the starter motor solenoid), this indicates that there is a fault in the circuit or solenoid - see following paragraphs. If the starter motor turns slowly when operated, but the battery is in good condition, then this indicates that either the starter motor is faulty, or there is considerable resistance somewhere in the circuit.

3 If a fault in the circuit is suspected, disconnect the battery leads (including the earth connection to the body), the starter/solenoid wiring and the engine/transmission earth strap. Thoroughly clean the connections, reconnect the leads and wiring, then use a voltmeter or test light to check that full battery voltage is available at the battery positive lead connection to the solenoid, and that the earth is sound. Smear petroleum jelly around the battery

17.5a Peel back the rubber cover, then unscrew the nut (arrowed) and disconnect the main battery cable from the starter solenoid

terminals to prevent corrosion - corroded connections are amongst the most frequent causes of electrical system faults.

4 If the battery and all connections are in good condition, check the circuit by disconnecting the wire from the solenoid blade terminal. Connect a voltmeter or test light between the wire end and a good earth (such as the battery negative terminal), and check that the wire is live when the ignition switch is turned to the "start" position. If it is, then the circuit is sound - if not, the circuit wiring can be checked as described in Chapter 12.

5 The solenoid contacts can be checked by connecting a voltmeter or test light between the battery positive feed connection on the starter side of the solenoid, and earth. When the ignition switch is turned to the "start" position, there should be a reading or lighted bulb, as applicable. If there is no reading or lighted bulb, the solenoid is faulty and should be renewed.

6 If the circuit and solenoid are proved sound, the fault must lie in the starter motor. Begin checking the starter motor by removing it (see Section 17), and checking the brushes (see Section 18). If the fault does not lie in the brushes, the motor windings must be faulty. In this event, it may be possible to have the starter motor overhauled by a specialist, but check on the availability and cost of spares before proceeding, as it may prove more economical to obtain a new or exchange motor.

17 Starter motor - removal and refitting

Removal

1 Disconnect the battery negative lead.

2 So that access to the motor can be gained both from above and below, firmly apply the handbrake, then jack up the front of the vehicle and support it on axle stands.

3 Remove the exhaust front pipe as described in the relevant Part of Chapter 4.

4 To improve access to the starter motor, undo the bolts securing the inlet manifold support bracket(s), and move the bracket(s) clear of the starter motor. Note that it is not

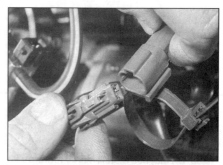

17.5b Disconnecting the solenoid wiring connector

17.6 Removing the starter motor assembly

necessary to remove the brackets completely.

5 Slacken and remove the retaining nut, and disconnect the main battery cable from the starter motor solenoid. Also disconnect the wiring connector from the solenoid **(see illustrations)**.

6 Unscrew the starter motor mounting bolts, supporting the motor as the bolts are withdrawn, and manoeuvre the starter motor out from underneath the engine **(see illustration)**.

Refitting

7 Refitting is a reversal of removal.

18 Starter motor - brush renewal

1 Remove the starter motor as described in Section 17. Proceed as described below the relevant sub-heading.

 HAYNES HiNT *Consult your dealer on the cost and availability of spare parts before stripping the starter motor, as some parts for certain starter motors may not be available.*

Magneti Marelli starter

2 On motors where a small centre cover is fitted to the rear cover, undo the two screws, and remove the centre cover and gasket from the end cover. Prise out the C-clip, and withdraw any shims fitted to the armature end. Make alignment marks between the end cover and yoke, then unscrew the two through-bolts and withdraw the end cover.

5

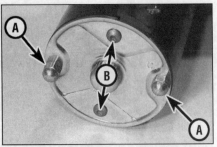

18.3a On Magneti Marelli starter motors with a one-piece end cover, undo the cover retaining nuts (A) and brush holder screws ...

3 On motors with a one piece end cover, undo the end cover retaining nuts and the brush holder assembly screws, and remove the end cover from the motor **(see illustrations)**.

4 Remove the nut and spring washer securing the positive brush lead to the solenoid terminal, and slide the brush holder assembly off the end of the commutator **(see illustration)**.

5 Withdraw the plastic insulating plate from the brush holder, then carefully prise off the brush retaining caps, and remove the springs and brushes.

6 Measure the length of each brush. If any brush is worn to less than, or close to, the minimum specified length, then all the brushes should be renewed as a complete set.

7 Clean the commutator with a solvent-moistened cloth, then check for signs of scoring, burning, excessive wear or severe pitting. If worn or damaged, the commutator should be attended to by an auto-electrician.

18.4 Undo the retaining nut, then disconnect the lead from the solenoid and remove the brush holder assembly

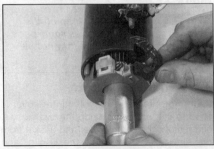

18.9 Refitting the brush holder assembly. Note the use of the socket to help keep the brushes in their holders as the assembly is engaged with the commutator

18.3b ... then remove the end cover

8 On refitting, slot the brushes into position in the holder, ensuring that the small threaded brackets are correctly positioned on the brush holder, then refit the springs and brush retaining caps. Check that each brush is free to move smoothly in its holder.

9 Clip the insulating plate onto the rear of the brush holder, and fit the brush holder assembly to the commutator **(see illustration)**. Check that the brushes are pressed firmly against the commutator by spring pressure.

10 On motors with a one-piece end cover, ensure that the rubber grommet is correctly seated, then install the cover and refit the retaining nuts and brush holder screws, tightening them securely.

11 On motors where a small end cover is fitted to the rear cover, fit the end cover, engaging it with the grommet, and align the marks noted on removal. Tighten the cover through-bolts securely. Refit any necessary thrustwashers to the end of the armature, and secure them in position with the C-clip. Refit the gasket and small cover to the end cover, and tighten its retaining screws securely.

12 On all motors, fit the brush holder lead to the solenoid terminal, then fit the washer and retaining nut, tightening it securely. Refit the starter motor as described in Section 17.

Hitachi and Mitsubishi starters

13 Where necessary, undo the retaining screws and remove the centre cap from the starter motor end cover. Recover any shims which are fitted to the end of the armature.

14 Undo the two small screws securing the brushplate assembly to the rear cover, and remove the two starter motor through-bolts.

20.1 On 2.0 litre models, the oil pressure switch (arrowed) is screwed into the oil filter housing assembly, which is mounted on the rear of the cylinder block

Withdraw the rear cover, and release it from the rubber grommet. Remove any shim(s) from the armature shaft.

15 Disconnect the brushes from their holders by lifting the springs with a screwdriver, then remove the brush plate assembly.

16 Check the brushes and commutator as described above in paragraphs 6 and 7.

17 On refitting, fit the brushes into their holders, and check that they are able to slide freely.

18 Fit the brush plate assembly over the commutator, and make sure that all springs are correctly located in the brush slots.

19 Refit any relevant shims to the armature shaft.

20 Engage the rear cover with the grommet, and fit it to the motor. Align the cover holes with those of the brushplate, and install the brushplate retaining screws, tightening them securely.

21 Refit the starter motor through-bolts and tighten them securely.

22 Install the starter motor as described in Section 17.

19 Ignition switch - removal and refitting

The ignition switch is integral with the steering column lock, and can be removed as described in Chapter 10.

20 Oil pressure warning light switch - removal and refitting

Removal

1 The switch is located at the rear of the cylinder block, towards its right-hand end **(see illustration)**. Access to the switch is improved if the vehicle is jacked up and supported on axle stands, so that the switch can be reached from underneath.

2 Disconnect the battery negative lead.

3 Remove the protective sleeve from the wiring plug (where applicable), then disconnect the wiring from the switch.

4 Unscrew the switch and recover the sealing washer (where fitted). Be prepared for oil spillage. If the switch is to be left removed from the engine for any length of time, plug the hole to prevent excessive oil loss.

Refitting

5 Where the switch was fitted with a sealing washer, examine the sealing washer for signs of damage or deterioration, and if necessary renew it. Where no sealing washer was fitted, clean the switch and apply a smear of sealant to its threads.

6 Refit the switch, tightening it securely, and reconnect the wiring connector.

7 Lower the vehicle to the ground, then check and if necessary, top-up the engine oil as described in Chapter 1.

Chapter 6 Clutch

Contents

Degrees of difficulty

Easy, suitable for novice with little experience	**Fairly easy,** suitable for beginner with some experience	**Fairly difficult,** suitable for competent DIY mechanic	**Difficult,** suitable for experienced DIY mechanic	**Very difficult,** suitable for expert DIY or professional

Specifications

Type . . . . Single dry plate with diaphragm spring. Cable-operated release mechanism

Adjustment data
Clutch pedal height:
  Right-hand drive models . . . . 171 to 181 mm
  Left-hand drive models . . . . 159.5 to 169.5 mm
Clutch pedal free play (measured at pedal pad) . . . . 10.8 to 15.1 mm

Friction plate
Diameter:
  1.6 litre models . . . . 200 mm
  2.0 litre models . . . . 215 mm
Friction material thickness (new) . . . . 7.7 to 8.3 mm
Minimum friction material-to-rivet head depth . . . . 0.3 mm
Maximum friction plate run-out:
  1.6 litre models (measured 95 mm out from plate centre) . . . . 1.0 mm
  2.0 litre models (measured 102.5 mm out from the plate centre) . . . . 1.0 mm

Torque wrench settings

	Nm	lbf ft
Clutch cable retainer-to-bulkhead nuts	10	7
Clutch pedal height adjustment bolt locknut	19	14
Clutch pedal pivot bolt	19	14
Pressure plate retaining bolts	25	18

6

1 General information

1 The clutch consists of a friction plate, a pressure plate assembly, a release bearing and the release mechanism. All of these components are contained in the large cast-aluminium alloy bellhousing, sandwiched between the engine and the transmission. The release mechanism is mechanical, being operated by a cable **(see illustration)**.

2 The friction plate is fitted between the engine flywheel and the clutch pressure plate, and is allowed to slide on the transmission input shaft splines. It consists of two circular facings of friction material riveted in position to provide the clutch bearing surface, and a spring-cushioned hub to damp out transmission shocks.

3 The pressure plate assembly is bolted to the engine flywheel, and is located by three dowel pins. When the engine is running, drive is transmitted from the crankshaft via the flywheel to the friction plate (these components being clamped securely together by the pressure plate assembly), and from the friction plate to the transmission input shaft.

4 To interrupt the drive, the spring pressure must be relaxed. This is achieved by a sealed release bearing fitted concentrically around the transmission input shaft; when the driver depresses the clutch pedal, the release bearing is pressed against the fingers at the centre of the diaphragm spring. Since the spring is held by rivets between two annular fulcrum rings, the pressure at its centre causes it to deform, so that it flattens and thus releases the clamping force it exerts, at its periphery, on the pressure plate.

5 Depressing the clutch pedal pulls the control cable inner wire, and this in turn rotates the release fork by acting on the lever at the fork's upper end, above the bellhousing. The fork itself is clipped to the left of the release bearing.

6 As the friction plate facings wear, the pressure plate moves towards the flywheel; this causes the diaphragm spring fingers to push against the release bearing, thus reducing the clearance which must be present in the mechanism. To ensure correct operation, the clutch cable must be regularly adjusted.

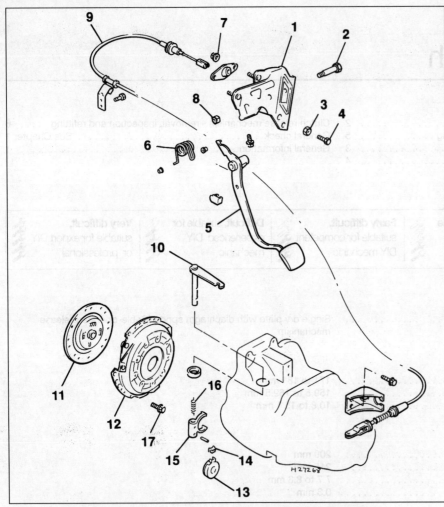

1.1 Exploded view of the clutch and associated components

1 Pedal mounting bracket	6 Assist spring	12 Pressure plate
2 Pedal pivot bolt	7 Cable-to-bulkhead nut	13 Release bearing
3 Pedal height adjusting bolt locknut	8 Pedal pivot bolt nut	14 Retaining clip
4 Pedal height adjusting bolt	9 Cable	15 Release fork
5 Clutch pedal	10 Release lever	16 Return spring
	11 Friction plate	17 Pressure plate bolt

2.2 Clutch pedal height adjustment details

Dimension "H" - pedal height measurement
Dimension "A" - pedal free play measurement
1 Pedal mounting bracket
2 Locknut
3 Pedal height adjustment bolt
4 Carpet
5 Insulator sheet
6 Insulator sheet
7 Floor panel

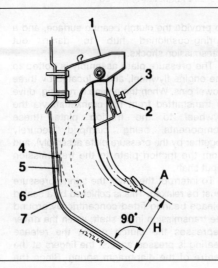

2 Clutch - adjustment

1 The clutch adjustment is checked by first by setting the clutch pedal height, and then by adjusting the pedal free play.

2 Peel back the carpet from underneath the clutch pedal, and ensure that there are no obstructions between the pedal and floor panel. Measure the distance from the centre of the clutch pedal pad to the floor **(see illustration)**. Note: *This measurement can be taken with the carpet in position, so long as the thickness of the carpet is added onto the pedal height measurement.* The pedal height should be within the range given in the Specifications at the start of this Chapter.

3 If height adjustment is necessary, reach up behind the facia, and slacken the pedal height adjusting bolt locknut. If necessary, remove the lower facia panel (see Chapter 11, Section 30) to improve access to the bolt. Position the bolt as required, so that the pedal height is correctly set, then tighten the locknut to the specified torque.

4 With the pedal height correctly set, check the pedal free play as follows.

5 Slowly depress the clutch pedal, and measure the distance that the clutch pedal pad travels from the at-rest position to the point where resistance is felt (see illustration 2.2). This is the pedal free play, and should be within the range given in this Chapter's Specifications.

6 If free play adjustment is necessary, working within the engine compartment, locate the clutch release lever, which is situated on the top of the transmission. Slacken the cable locknut, then rotate the knurled adjusting nut until the release lever travel from the at-rest position to the position where resistance is felt is approximately 2.5 to 3.5 mm **(see illustration)**. Recheck the clutch pedal free play as described in paragraph 5, and readjust if necessary. Once the pedal free play is correctly set, securely tighten the cable locknut.

7 With the pedal height and free play correctly adjusted, refit all components removed for access.

2.6 Slacken the locknut, and adjust the clutch cable by rotating the knurled adjusting nut (arrowed)

3.2 Detach the clutch inner cable from the release lever, then free the outer cable from its mounting bracket

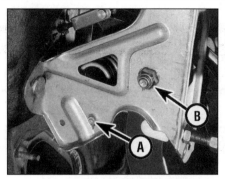

4.3 Clutch pedal assist spring end (A) and pivot bolt nut (B) (shown with facia removed)

5.2 Prior to removal, make alignment marks between the clutch pressure plate and flywheel

3 Clutch cable - removal and refitting

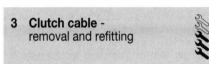

Removal

1 Working in the engine compartment, locate the clutch release lever which is situated on the top of the transmission, then slacken the locknut and knurled adjuster nut situated on the cable end fitting.

2 Release the inner cable end fitting from the release lever, and the outer cable fitting from its mounting bracket on the transmission **(see illustration)**.

3 Working inside the vehicle, remove the lower facia panel from the driver's side of the facia as described in Chapter 11, Section 30. Unhook the clutch inner cable from the top of the clutch pedal. Note that access to the top of the pedal is very poor, but can only be significantly improved by removing the complete facia.

4 Return to the engine compartment, and withdraw the cable from the engine compartment bulkhead. If necessary, undo the two nuts securing the cable retainer to the bulkhead, and remove the retainer along with the cable.

5 Work back along the cable, releasing it from any relevant retaining clips and guides, and noting its correct routing, and remove it from the vehicle.

6 Examine the cable, looking for worn end fittings or a damaged outer casing, and for signs of fraying of the inner wire. Check the cable's operation; the inner wire should move smoothly and easily through the outer casing. Remember that a cable that appears serviceable when tested off the car may well be much heavier in operation, when compressed into its working position. Renew the cable if it shows any signs of excessive wear or damage. If the cable has seen several years' service, it would be best to renew it anyway, as a precaution against it breaking in service.

Refitting

7 Apply a thin smear of multi-purpose grease to the cable end fittings, then pass the cable through the engine compartment bulkhead. Locate the cable retainer on its studs (where removed), and tighten its retaining nuts to the specified torque.

8 From inside the vehicle, hook the inner cable over the clutch pedal end, and check that it is securely retained.

9 Work along the cable, ensuring that it is correctly routed, and retained by all the relevant retaining clips and guides. Clip the outer cable into its mounting bracket on the transmission.

10 Hook the inner cable end fitting over the end of the clutch release lever, and adjust the clutch pedal settings as described in Section 2.

4 Clutch pedal - removal and refitting

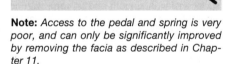

Note: *Access to the pedal and spring is very poor, and can only be significantly improved by removing the facia as described in Chapter 11.*

Removal

1 Working as described in Section 2, slacken the clutch cable locknut and knurled adjuster nut, to obtain maximum free play in the cable.

2 Working inside the vehicle, remove the lower facia panel from the driver's side of the facia (see Chapter 11, Section 30). Unhook the clutch inner cable from the top of the clutch pedal; access to the top of the pedal is very poor.

3 Carefully unhook the ends of the clutch pedal assist spring from its locations in the pedal mounting bracket, and recover the spring seats **(see illustration)**.

4 Slacken and remove the nut and pivot bolt, then withdraw the clutch pedal and assist spring from the mounting bracket. If necessary, the pedal and spring can then be separated.

5 Carefully clean all components, and renew any that are worn or damaged. Check the bearing surfaces of the pivot bushes and bolt with particular care; the bushes can be renewed separately if worn.

Refitting

6 Press the pivot bushes into the pedal bore, then apply a smear of multi-purpose grease to their bearing surfaces. Ensure that the clutch pedal and assist spring are correctly mated.

7 Refit the spring seats to the pedal mounting bracket, and install the pedal assembly. Refit the pivot bolt and nut, and tighten it to the specified torque setting.

8 Locate each end of the assist spring in its relevant seat.

9 Hook the clutch cable onto the end of the pedal, then adjust the clutch pedal settings as described in Section 2.

5 Clutch assembly - removal, inspection and refitting

 Warning: Dust created by clutch wear and deposited on the clutch components may contain asbestos, which is a health hazard. DO NOT blow it out with compressed air, or inhale any of it. DO NOT use petrol or petroleum-based solvents to clean off the dust. Brake system cleaner or methylated spirit should be used to flush the dust into a suitable receptacle. After the clutch components are wiped clean with rags, dispose of the contaminated rags and cleaner in a sealed, marked container.

Note: *Although some friction materials may no longer contain asbestos, it is safest to assume that they DO, and to take precautions accordingly*

Removal

1 Unless the complete engine/transmission is to be removed from the car, and separated for major overhaul (see Chapter 2C), the clutch can be reached by removing the transmission as described in Chapter 7A.

2 Before disturbing the clutch, use chalk or a marker pen to mark the relationship of the pressure plate assembly to the flywheel **(see illustration)**.

3 Working in a diagonal sequence, slacken the pressure plate bolts by half a turn at a

6

5.14 Fit the friction plate with its spring hub assembly facing away from the flywheel, and install the pressure plate

5.17 Using a clutch-aligning tool to centralise the friction plate

5.18 Once the friction plate is correctly centralised, tighten the pressure plate retaining bolts to the specified torque

time, until the spring pressure is released and the bolts can be unscrewed by hand.

4 Prise the pressure plate assembly off its locating dowels, and collect the friction plate, noting which way round the friction plate is fitted.

Inspection

Note: *Due to the amount of work necessary to remove and refit clutch components, it is usually considered good practice to renew the clutch friction plate, pressure plate assembly and release bearing as a matched set, even if only one of these is actually worn enough to require renewal.*

5 Remove the clutch assembly.

6 When cleaning clutch components, first read the warning at the beginning of this Section. Remove the dust only as described - working with dampened cloths will help to keep dust levels to a minimum. Wherever possible, work in a well-ventilated atmosphere.

7 Check the friction plate facings for signs of wear, damage or oil contamination. If the friction material is cracked, burnt, scored or damaged, or if it is contaminated with oil or grease (shown by shiny black patches), the friction plate must be renewed. Measure the depth of the rivets below the friction material surface. If depth of any rivet is equal to, or less than, the service limit given in the Specifications, then the friction plate must be renewed.

8 If the friction material is still serviceable, check that the centre boss splines are unworn, that the torsion springs are in good condition and securely fastened, and that all the rivets are tightly fastened. If excessive wear or damage is found, the friction plate must be renewed.

9 If the friction material is fouled with oil, this must be due to an oil leak from the crankshaft left-hand oil seal, from the sump-to-cylinder block joint, or from the transmission input shaft. Renew the seal or repair the joint, as appropriate, as described in Chapter 2 or 7 before installing the new friction plate, or the new plate will quickly go the same way.

10 Check the pressure plate assembly for

obvious signs of wear or damage; shake it to check for loose rivets, or worn or damaged fulcrum rings. Check that the drive straps securing the pressure plate to the cover do not show signs (such as a deep yellow or blue discoloration) of overheating. If the diaphragm spring is worn or damaged, or if its pressure is in any way suspect, the pressure plate assembly should be renewed.

11 Examine the machined bearing surfaces of the pressure plate and of the flywheel; they should be clean, completely flat, and free from scratches or scoring. If either is discoloured from excessive heat, or shows signs of cracks, it should be renewed; however, minor damage of this nature can sometimes be polished away using emery paper.

12 Check that the release bearing contact surface rotates smoothly and easily, with no sign of noise or roughness, and that the surface itself is smooth and unworn, with no signs of cracks, pitting or scoring. If there is any doubt about its condition, the bearing must be renewed

Refitting

13 On reassembly, ensure that the bearing surfaces of the flywheel and pressure plate are completely clean, smooth, and free from oil or grease. Use solvent to remove any protective grease from new components.

14 Fit the friction plate so that its spring hub assembly faces away from the flywheel; there may also be a marking showing which way round the plate is to be refitted **(see illustration)**.

15 Refit the pressure plate assembly, aligning the marks made on dismantling (if the original pressure plate is re-used), and locating the pressure plate on its three locating dowels. Fit the pressure plate bolts, but tighten them only finger-tight so that the friction plate can still be moved.

16 The friction plate must now be centralised, so that when the transmission is refitted, its input shaft will pass through the splines at the centre of the friction plate.

17 Centralisation can be achieved by passing a screwdriver or other long bar through the friction plate, and into the hole in the

crankshaft. The friction plate can then be moved around until it is centred on the crankshaft hole. Alternatively, a clutch-aligning tool can be used to eliminate the guesswork. These can be obtained from most accessory shops, or can be made up from a length of metal rod or wooden dowel which fits closely inside the crankshaft hole, and has insulating tape wound around it to match the diameter of the friction plate splined hole **(see illustration)**.

18 When the friction plate is centralised, tighten the pressure plate bolts evenly and in a diagonal sequence to the specified torque setting **(see illustration)**.

19 Apply a thin smear of high-melting point grease to the splines of the friction plate and the transmission input shaft, also to the release bearing bore and release fork shaft.

20 Refit the transmission as described in Chapter 7A.

6 Clutch release mechanism - removal, inspection and refitting

Note: *Refer to the warning concerning the dangers of asbestos dust at the beginning of Section 5*

Removal

1 Unless the complete engine/transmission is to be removed from the car, and separated for major overhaul (see Chapter 2C), the clutch release mechanism can be reached by removing the transmission as described in Chapter 7A.

2 Lift the retaining clips, then slide the release bearing from the fork and remove it from the transmission. Note the correct fitted direction of each clip on the bearing.

3 Rotate the release fork then, using a hammer and suitable punch, drive out the roll pins securing the release fork to the shaft (drive out the small inner pins first, then remove the outer pins) **(see illustration)**. Discard the roll pins; new ones should be used on refitting.

4 Note the correct fitted position of the return

6.3 Clutch release fork is secured to the release lever shaft by two dual-roll pin arrangements (arrowed)

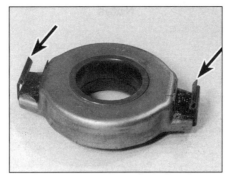

6.12a Ensure that the retaining clips (arrowed) are correctly fitted to the release bearing . . .

6.12b . . . then fit the bearing to the transmission, making sure the clips are correctly engaged with the release fork ends

spring, then withdraw the release lever; recover the release fork and spring from the transmission housing.

Inspection

5 Check the release mechanism, renewing any component which is worn or damaged. Carefully check all bearing surfaces and points of contact.

6 Inspect the bush and dust seal fitted to the transmission housing for signs of damage and deterioration, and renew if necessary. The old bush can be tapped out of position, and the new one installed using a hammer and suitable tubular socket.

7 When checking the release bearing itself, note that it is often considered worthwhile to renew it as a matter of course, given that a significant amount of work is required to gain access to it. Check that the contact surface rotates smoothly and easily, with no sign of noise or roughness. Also check that the surface itself is smooth and unworn, with no signs of cracks, pitting or scoring. If there is any doubt about its condition, the bearing must be renewed.

Refitting

8 Apply a smear of high-melting point grease to the shaft pivot points and the contact surfaces of the release fork.

9 Slide the release lever partially into position in the transmission.

10 Offer up the release fork and spring, aligning them with the lever shaft, and push the release lever fully into position.

11 Align the release fork holes with the holes in the lever shaft, and drive the two new roll pins into position.

12 Fit the retaining clips (where removed) to the release bearing, making sure that they are fitted the correct way round. Apply a smear of high-melting point grease to the contact surfaces of the bearing and input shaft, then slide the bearing along the shaft and clip it onto the release fork (see illustrations).

13 Check the operation of the release mechanism, ensuring that it moves smoothly, and returns easily under the pressure of the return spring, then refit the transmission as described in Chapter 7A.

6

Notes

Chapter 7 Part A Manual transmission

Contents

Degrees of difficulty

Easy, suitable for novice with little experience		Fairly easy, suitable for beginner with some experience		Fairly difficult, suitable for competent DIY mechanic	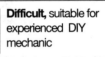	Difficult, suitable for experienced DIY mechanic		Very difficult, suitable for expert DIY or professional	

Specifications

General

Type . . . .   Manual, five forward speeds and reverse. Synchromesh on all forward speeds

Designation:
1.6 litre models RS5F31A
2.0 litre models RS5F32A

Gear ratios

1.6 litre models:
1st . . . .   3.333 : 1
2nd . . . .   1.954 : 1
3rd . . . .   1.286 : 1
4th . . . .   0.902 : 1
5th . . . .   0.733 : 1
Reverse . . . .   3.417 : 1
Final drive . . . .   4.056 : 1
2.0 litre models:
1st . . . .   3.063 : 1
2nd . . . .   1.826 : 1
3rd . . . .   1.207 : 1
4th . . . .   0.927 : 1
5th . . . .   0.756 : 1
Reverse . . . .   3.154 : 1
Final drive . . . .   4.177 : 1

Torque wrench settings

	Nm	lbf ft
Engine-to-transmission fixing bolts:		
1.6 litre models:		
Bolts less than 30 mm long	19	14
Bolts 30 mm long, and longer	35	26
2.0 litre models:		
Bolts less than 45 mm long	19	12
Bolts 55 mm long, and longer	75	55
Gearchange linkage components:		
Selector rod front pivot bolt	16	12
Selector rod rear pivot bolt	21	15
Support rod-to-transmission bolt	42	32
Support rod-to-gear lever retaining plate nuts	14	10
Support rod rear mounting bracket nuts	14	10
Support rod-to-rear mounting bracket nut	25	18
Gaiter retaining plate nuts	5	4

7A

Torque wrench settings (continued)

	Nm	lbf ft
Left-hand engine/transmission mounting:		
Through-bolt	49	37
Mounting-to-transmission bolts	49	37
Neutral switch	19	14
Oil drain plug	29	22
Oil filler/level plug:		
1.6 litre models	29	22
2.0 litre models	15	11
Rear engine/transmission mounting:		
Through-bolt	69	51
Mounting bracket retaining bolts	69	51
Reversing light switch	19	14

1 General information

1 The transmission is contained in a cast-aluminium alloy casing bolted to the engine's left-hand end, and consists of the gearbox and final drive differential, often called a transaxle.

2 Drive is transmitted from the crankshaft via the clutch to the input shaft, which has a splined extension to accept the clutch friction plate, and rotates in sealed ball-bearings. From the input shaft, drive is transmitted to the output shaft, which rotates in a roller bearing at its right-hand end, and a sealed ball-bearing at its left-hand end. From the output shaft, the drive is transmitted to the differential crownwheel, which rotates with the differential case and planetary gears, thus driving the sun gears and driveshafts. The rotation of the planetary gears on their shaft allows the inner roadwheel to rotate at a slower speed than the outer roadwheel when the car is cornering.

3 The input and output shafts are arranged side by side, parallel to the crankshaft and driveshafts, so that their gear pinion teeth are in constant mesh. In the neutral position, the output shaft gear pinions rotate freely, so that drive cannot be transmitted to the crownwheel.

4 Gear selection is via a floor-mounted lever and selector rod mechanism. The selector rod causes the appropriate selector fork to move its respective synchro-sleeve along the shaft, to lock the gear pinion to the synchro-hub. Since the synchro-hubs are splined to the output shaft, this locks the pinion to the shaft so that drive can be transmitted. To ensure that gearchanging can be made quickly and quietly, a synchromesh system is fitted to all forward gears, consisting of baulk rings and spring-loaded fingers, as well as the gear pinions and synchro-hubs; the synchromesh cones are formed on the mating faces of the baulk rings and gear pinions.

2 Gearchange linkage - general information

1 If a stiff, sloppy or imprecise gearchange leads you to suspect that a fault exists within the linkage, first remove and dismantle it completely. Check it for wear or damage as described in Section 3, then reassemble it, applying a smear of multi-purpose grease to all bearing surfaces.

2 If this does not cure the fault, the car should be examined by an expert, as the fault must lie within the transmission itself. No adjustment of the linkage is possible.

3 Gearchange linkage - removal and refitting

Removal

1 Remove the centre console as described in Chapter 11.

2 Firmly apply the handbrake, then jack up the front of the vehicle and support it on axle stands.

3 From underneath the vehicle, using a pair of pliers, unhook the spring securing the rear of the selector rod to the support rod (see illustration).

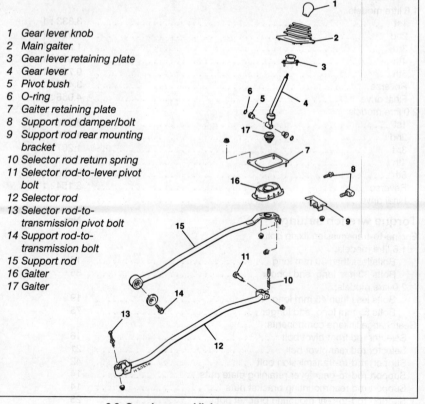

1 Gear lever knob
2 Main gaiter
3 Gear lever retaining plate
4 Gear lever
5 Pivot bush
6 O-ring
7 Gaiter retaining plate
8 Support rod damper/bolt
9 Support rod rear mounting bracket
10 Selector rod return spring
11 Selector rod-to-lever pivot bolt
12 Selector rod
13 Selector rod-to-transmission pivot bolt
14 Support rod-to-transmission bolt
15 Support rod
16 Gaiter
17 Gaiter

3.3 Gear lever and linkage components

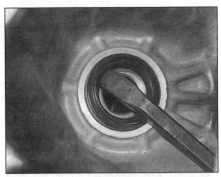

4.4 Using a large flat-bladed screwdriver to lever out a driveshaft oil seal

4.5a Tap the new seal into position using a suitable tubular drift, such as a large socket

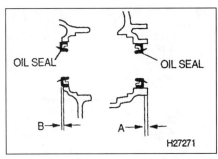

4.5b On 2.0 litre models, ensure that the oil seals are positioned as shown

Right-hand side seal (A) - 5.9 to 6.1 mm
Left-hand side seal (B) - 0.5 mm or less

4 Slacken and remove the nuts, and withdraw the pivot bolts securing the selector rod to the gear lever and transmission. Remove the selector rod from underneath the vehicle, and recover the O-rings and bushes from the base of the gear lever.

5 Unscrew the bolt and washer securing the support rod to the transmission housing. Slacken and remove the nuts securing the rear of the support rod and the support rod bracket to the underside of the vehicle, and manoeuvre the rod and bracket assembly out of position. If necessary, undo the retaining nut, and separate the support rod and mounting bracket.

6 From inside the vehicle, lift out the gear lever and retaining plate, and recover the small rubber gaiter from the base of the lever.

7 If necessary, slacken and remove the retaining nuts, then lift off the retaining plate and remove the main gear lever gaiter from the vehicle.

8 Inspect all the linkage components for signs of wear or damage, paying particular attention to the pivot bushes and selector rod universal joint, and renew worn components as necessary. Renew the rubber gaiters if they are split or badly perished.

Refitting

9 Refitting is a reversal of the removal procedure, applying a smear of multi-purpose grease to the gear lever pivot ball and bushes, and to the selector rod rear pivot bolt. Tighten all the linkage nuts and bolts to their specified torque settings (where given).

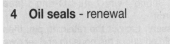

4   Oil seals - renewal

Driveshaft oil seal

1 Chock the rear wheels of the car, firmly apply the handbrake, then jack up the front of the car and support it on axle stands. Remove the appropriate front roadwheel.

2 Drain the transmission oil as described in Chapter 1.

3 Working as described in Chapter 8, free the

inner end of the driveshaft from the transmission, and place it clear of the seal, noting that there is no need to unscrew the driveshaft retaining nut; the driveshaft can be left secured to the hub. Support the driveshaft, to avoid placing any strain on the driveshaft joints or gaiters.

4 Carefully prise the oil seal out of the transmission using a large flat-bladed screwdriver **(see illustration)**.

5 Remove all traces of dirt from the area around the oil seal aperture, then apply a smear of grease to the outer lip of the new oil seal, and locate it in its aperture. Drive the seal squarely into position, using a suitable tubular drift (such as a socket) which bears only on the hard outer edge of the seal. On 1.6 litre models, drive the seal into position until it seats against its locating shoulder. On 2.0 litre models, position the seal as shown in the accompanying illustration **(see illustrations)**.

6 Refit the driveshaft as described in Chapter 8.

7 Refill the transmission with the specified type and amount of oil, as described in Chapter 1.

Input shaft oil seal

8 To renew the input shaft seal, the transmission must be dismantled. This task should therefore be entrusted to a Nissan dealer.

Selector shaft oil seal

9 Chock the rear wheels of the car, firmly

4.10 Selector rod end fitting is retained by a dual-roll pin arrangement (arrowed)

apply the handbrake, then jack up the front of the car and support it on axle stands. Drain the transmission oil as described in Chapter 1, or be prepared for some oil loss as the seal is removed.

10 Slide back the transmission selector rod rubber gaiter, to reveal the roll pin **(see illustration)**.

11 Using a hammer and suitable punch, tap out the roll pin (tap out the small inner pin first, followed by the larger outer pin) then free the selector rod from the transmission. Discard the roll pin; a new one should be used on refitting.

12 Remove the rubber gaiter, then carefully lever the selector shaft oil seal out of position and slide it off the shaft.

13 Before fitting a new seal, check the selector shaft's seal rubbing surface for signs of burrs, scratches or other damage which may have caused the seal to fail in the first place. It may be possible to polish away minor faults of this sort using fine abrasive paper, but more serious defects will require the renewal of the selector shaft.

14 Apply a smear of grease to the new seal's outer edge and sealing lip, then carefully slide the seal along the selector rod. Press the seal fully into position in the transmission housing.

15 Refit the rubber gaiter, making sure that it is correctly seated on the seal.

16 Engage the selector rod with the shaft. Align the pin holes, and tap the new roll pins into position.

17 Lower the vehicle to the ground, and top-up/refill (as applicable) the transmission oil as described in Chapter 1.

5   Neutral switch - testing, removal and refitting

Testing

1 A neutral switch is fitted to all models with a catalytic converter, the switch is one of the many fuel system switches/sender units (see relevant Part of Chapter 4), and is screwed into the base of the transmission on its right-

7A

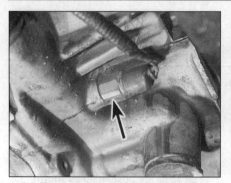

5.1 The neutral switch (where fitted) is screwed into the right-hand side of the transmission (arrowed)

hand side **(see illustration)**. **Note:** *Do not confuse the neutral switch with the reversing light switch, which is screwed in to the left-hand side of the transmission.*

2 To test the switch, trace the wiring back from the switch to its connector, which is on top of the transmission. Disconnect the wiring connector, and use a multi-meter (set to the resistance function) or a battery-and-bulb test circuit to check that there is continuity between the switch terminals only when the transmission is in neutral. If this is not the case, and there are no obvious breaks or other damage to the wires, the switch is faulty and must be renewed.

Removal

3 Chock the rear wheels of the car, firmly apply the handbrake, then jack up the front of the car and support it on axle stands. Drain the transmission oil as described in Chapter 1, or be prepared for some oil loss as the switch is removed.

4 Trace the switch wiring back to its connector, and disconnect it from the main harness.

5 Unscrew the switch from the transmission, and remove it. Plug the transmission housing aperture, to minimise oil loss (if the transmission has not been drained) and to prevent dirt entry.

Refitting

6 Remove all traces of sealant from the

7.3a Unscrew the retaining bolt . . .

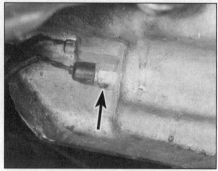

6.1 The reversing light switch (arrowed) is screwed into the left-hand side of the transmission

threads of the switch, and apply a smear of fresh sealant to them.

7 Remove the plug from the switch aperture in the transmission, and screw the switch into position.

8 Tighten the switch to the specified torque, and reconnect the wiring connector.

9 Lower the vehicle to the ground, and top-up/refill the transmission oil (as applicable) as described in Chapter 1.

---

6 Reversing light switch -
  testing, removal and refitting

Testing

1 The reversing light circuit is controlled by a plunger-type switch that is screwed into the base of the transmission on its left-hand side **(see illustration)**. **Note:** *Do not confuse the reversing light switch with the neutral switch, which is screwed in to the right-hand side of the transmission.* If a fault develops in the circuit, first ensure that the circuit fuse has not blown.

2 To test the switch, trace the wiring back from the switch to its connector, which is on top of the transmission. Disconnect the wiring connector, and use a multi-meter (set to the resistance function) or a battery-and-bulb test circuit to check that there is continuity between the switch terminals only when

7.3b . . . and withdraw the speedometer drive assembly (shown with transmission removed for clarity)

reverse gear is selected. If this is not the case, and there are no obvious breaks or other damage to the wires, the switch is faulty and must be renewed.

Removal

3 Chock the rear wheels of the car, firmly apply the handbrake, then jack up the front of the car and support it on axle stands. Drain the transmission oil as described in Chapter 1, or be prepared for some oil loss as the switch is removed.

4 Trace the switch wiring back to its connector, and disconnect it from the main harness.

5 Unscrew the switch from the transmission, and remove it. Plug the transmission housing aperture, to minimise oil loss (if the transmission has not been drained), and to prevent dirt entry.

Refitting

6 Remove all traces of sealant from the threads of the switch, and apply a smear of fresh sealant to them.

7 Remove the plug from the switch aperture in the transmission, and screw the switch into position.

8 Tighten the switch to the specified torque, then reconnect the wiring connector and check the operation of the circuit.

9 Lower the vehicle to the ground, and top-up/refill the transmission oil (as applicable) as described in Chapter 1.

---

7 Speedometer drive -
  removal and refitting

Removal

1 Chock the rear wheels of the car, firmly apply the handbrake, then jack up the front of the car and support it on axle stands. The speedometer drive is situated on the rear of the transmission housing, next to the inner end of the right-hand driveshaft.

2 Unscrew the knurled retaining ring, and disconnect the speedometer cable from the speedometer drive.

3 Slacken and remove the retaining bolt, and withdraw the speedometer drive and driven pinion assembly from the transmission housing, along with its O-ring **(see illustrations)**.

4 If necessary, tap out the retaining pin, then slide the pinion out of the housing and recover the thrustwasher **(see illustration)**. The oil seal can then be removed from the housing.

5 Examine all components for signs of damage, and renew if necessary. Renew the housing O-ring as a matter of course. Note that the thrustwasher is available in various thicknesses - measure the thickness of the original, and quote this when ordering a new one.

6 If the driven pinion is worn or damaged,

7.4 Speedometer drive pinion roll pin and housing O-ring (arrowed)

also examine the drive pinion in the transmission housing for signs of wear or damage. To renew the drive pinion, the transmission must be dismantled and the differential gear removed. This task should therefore be entrusted to a Nissan dealer.

Refitting

7 Where necessary, press the new seal into the housing. Apply a smear of multi-purpose grease to the driven pinion shaft, and slide on the thrustwasher. Insert the driven pinion into the housing, and secure it in position with the retaining pin.

8 Fit a new O-ring to the speedometer drive, and refit it to the transmission, ensuring that the drive and driven pinions are correctly engaged. Securely tighten the housing retaining bolt.

9 Reconnect the speedometer cable, and securely tighten its retaining ring. Lower the vehicle to the ground.

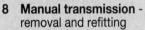

8 Manual transmission - removal and refitting

Removal

1 Chock the rear wheels, then firmly apply the handbrake. Apply the handbrake, then jack up the front of the vehicle and securely support it on axle stands. Remove both front roadwheels. Undo the retaining screws, and remove the plastic undershields from beneath

8.8b Unscrew the nut, then withdraw the pivot bolt . . .

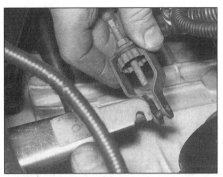

8.6 Free the clutch cable from the release lever, and position it clear of the transmission

the engine/transmission, and the covers from underneath both wheel arches.

2 Drain the transmission oil as described in Chapter 1, then refit the drain and filler/level plugs and tighten them to their specified torque settings.

3 Remove the battery as described in Chapter 5.

4 If necessary, to improve access to the top of the transmission, remove the air cleaner housing inlet duct as described in the relevant Part of Chapter 4.

5 Remove the starter motor as described in Chapter 5.

6 Slacken the clutch cable locknut and knurled adjuster nut, then free the cable end fitting from the release lever, and the outer

8.7b . . . and neutral switch connector (where fitted) then detach the earth lead(s) from the transmission housing (arrowed)

8.8c . . . and free the selector rod from the transmission

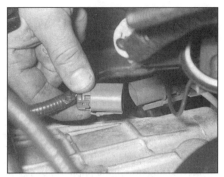

8.7a Disconnect the reversing light switch wiring connector . . .

cable fitting from its mounting bracket **(see illustration)**.

7 Disconnect the wiring connectors from the reversing light switch and, where applicable, from the neutral switch. Disconnect the earth lead(s) from the top of the transmission housing **(see illustrations)**. Free the wiring from any relevant retaining clips, and position it clear of the transmission.

8 Slacken and remove the nut and pivot bolt securing the gearchange linkage selector rod to the transmission, and the bolt and washer securing the support rod in position. Free both rods, and position them clear of the transmission **(see illustrations)**.

9 Disconnect the breather pipe from the top of the transmission housing **(see illustration)**.

8.8a Unscrew the bolt and recover the washer securing the gearchange linkage support rod to the mounting bracket

8.9 Disconnect the breather hose from the top of the transmission

7A

8.12 Using an engine support bar to support the engine whilst the transmission is removed

8.14a Slacken and remove the through-bolt, then undo the three mounting retaining bolts (two arrowed) . . .

8.14b . . . and remove the left-hand mounting assembly from the transmission

10 Unscrew the knurled retaining ring, and disconnect the speedometer cable from the transmission.

11 Working as described in Chapter 8, free the inner end of each driveshaft from the transmission, and place the ends clear of the transmission. Note that there is no need to unscrew the driveshaft retaining nuts - each driveshaft can be left secured to the hub. Support the driveshafts, to avoid placing any strain on the driveshaft joints or gaiters.

12 Place a jack with interposed block of wood beneath the engine, to take the weight of the engine. Alternatively, attach a hoist or support bar to the engine and take the weight of the engine **(see illustration)**.

13 Place a jack and block of wood beneath the transmission, and raise the jack to take the weight of the transmission.

14 Slacken and remove the through-bolt from the left-hand engine/transmission mounting. Undo the three bolts securing the mounting to the transmission, and manoeuvre the mounting out of position. Recover the rubbers from each side of the mounting bracket, if they are loose **(see illustrations)**.

15 Slacken and remove the through-bolt from the rear engine/transmission mounting. Undo the bolts securing the mounting bracket in position, and manoeuvre it away from the engine/transmission. On 2.0 litre models, recover the stopper ring which is fitted between the mounting bracket and mounting **(see illustrations)**.

16 With the jack positioned beneath the

transmission taking the weight, slacken and remove the remaining bolts securing the transmission housing to the engine. Note the correct fitted positions of each bolt (and the relevant brackets) as they are removed, to use as a reference on refitting - the bolts are of different lengths. Note that it may be necessary to raise the transmission slightly to gain access to the lower bolts.

17 Make a final check that all necessary components have been disconnected, and are positioned clear of the transmission so that they will not hinder the removal procedure.

18 Move the trolley jack and transmission to the left to free it from its locating dowels. Keep the transmission fully supported until the input shaft is free of the engine.

19 Once the transmission is free, lower the jack and manoeuvre the unit out from under the car. If they are loose, remove the locating dowels from the transmission or engine, and keep them in a safe place.

Refitting

20 The transmission is refitted by a reversal of the removal procedure, bearing in mind the following points:

a) *Apply a little high-melting point grease to the splines of the transmission input shaft. Do not apply too much, otherwise there is a possibility of the grease contaminating the clutch friction plate.*

b) *Ensure that the locating dowels are correctly positioned prior to installation.*

c) *Insert the transmission-to-engine bolts into their original locations, as noted on removal. Tighten all nuts and bolts to the specified torque (where given).*

d) *Renew the driveshaft oil seals using the information given in Section 4.*

e) *On completion, refill the transmission with the specified type and quantity of lubricant as described in Chapter 1.*

---

9 Manual transmission overhaul - general information

1 Overhauling a manual transmission is a difficult and involved job for the DIY home mechanic. In addition to dismantling and reassembling many small parts, clearances must be precisely measured and, if necessary, changed by selecting shims and spacers. Internal transmission components are also often difficult to obtain, and in many instances, extremely expensive. Because of this, if the transmission develops a fault or becomes noisy, the best course of action is to have the unit overhauled by a specialist repairer, or to obtain an exchange reconditioned unit.

2 Nevertheless, it is not impossible for the more experienced mechanic to overhaul the transmission, if the special tools are available, and the job is done in a deliberate step-by-step manner so that nothing is overlooked.

3 The tools necessary for an overhaul include internal and external circlip pliers, bearing pullers, a slide hammer, a set of pin punches, a dial test indicator, and possibly a hydraulic press. In addition, a large, sturdy workbench and a vice will be required.

4 During dismantling of the transmission, make careful notes of how each component is fitted, to make reassembly easier and accurate.

5 Before dismantling the transmission, it will help if you have some idea which area is malfunctioning. Certain problems can be closely related to specific areas in the transmission, which can make component examination and replacement easier. Refer to the *"Fault finding"* Section at the rear of this manual for more information.

8.15a Remove the rear engine/transmission mounting bracket . . .

8.15b . . . and, on 2.0 litre models, recover the rubber stopper ring from the mounting

Chapter 7 Part B Automatic transmission

Contents

Degrees of difficulty

Easy, suitable for novice with little experience	**Fairly easy,** suitable for beginner with some experience	**Fairly difficult,** suitable for competent DIY mechanic	**Difficult,** suitable for experienced DIY mechanic	**Very difficult,** suitable for expert DIY or professional 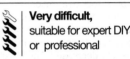

Specifications

General

Type	Automatic, four forward speeds and reverse
Designation	RL4F03A

Gear ratios

1st	2.861
2nd	1.562
3rd	1.000
4th	0.697
Reverse	2.310
Final drive	4.072

7B

Torque wrench settings

	Nm	lbf ft
Drain plug	34	26
Engine-to-transmission fixing bolts:		
Bolts less than 45 mm long	18	13
Bolts 55 mm long, and longer	75	55
Left-hand engine/transmission mounting:		
Through-bolt	49	37
Mounting-to-transmission bolts	49	37
Rear engine/transmission mounting:		
Through-bolt	69	51
Mounting bracket retaining bolts	69	51
Selector cable fixings:		
Cable-to-transmission lever nut	21	15
Cable-to-selector lever nut	5	4
Outer cable-to-floor bolts	5	4
Torque converter-to-driveplate bolts	51	38

1 General information

1 Most 2.0 litre models covered in this manual were offered with the option of a four-speed fully automatic transmission, consisting of a torque converter, an epicyclic geartrain, and hydraulically-operated clutches and brakes.

2 The torque converter provides a fluid coupling between engine and transmission which acts as an automatic clutch, and also provides a degree of torque multiplication when accelerating.

3 The epicyclic geartrain provides either of the four forward or one reverse gear ratios, according to which of its component parts are held stationary, or are allowed to turn. The components of the geartrain are held or released by brakes and clutches which are activated by a hydraulic control unit. A fluid pump within the transmission provides the necessary hydraulic pressure to operate the brakes and clutches.

4 Driver control of the transmission is by a seven-position selector lever. The transmission has "drive" option, and a "hold" facility on the first three gear ratios. The drive option "A" provides automatic changing throughout the range of all four gear ratios, and is the one to select for normal driving. An automatic kickdown facility will automatically shift the transmission down a gear if the accelerator pedal is fully depressed. The "hold" options are very similar, but they limit the gear ratios available - ie, when the selector lever is in the "2" position, only the first two ratios can be selected, and in the "1" position, only the first ratio can be selected. The lower ratios can be

used to provide engine braking whilst travelling down steep gradients. Note, however, that the transmission should **never** be shifted down into position "2" whilst the vehicle is travelling at 68 mph (110 km/h) or more, or into position "1" whilst travelling at 56 mph (90 km/h) or more.

5 Due to the complexity of the automatic transmission, any repair or overhaul work must be left to a Nissan dealer with the necessary special equipment for fault diagnosis and repair. The contents of the following Sections are therefore confined to supplying general information, and any service information and instructions that can be used by the owner.

2 Selector cable - adjustment

1 Position the selector lever firmly against its detent mechanism in the "N" position.

2 Apply the handbrake, then jack up the front of the vehicle and support it on axle stands.

3 Working underneath the vehicle, slacken the nut securing the cable end fitting to the transmission selector lever.

4 Hook a spring balance into the slot in the cable end fitting, and pull the cable forwards with a force of 6.9 N (0.7 kg, or 1.5 lbs) **(see illustration)**.

5 From this position, remove the spring balance, and move the cable end fitting backwards by 1.0 mm. Hold the cable in this position, and tighten its retaining nut to the specified torque setting.

6 Check the operation of the selector lever, ensuring that it moves smoothly and easily, without any sign of the cable binding. If not, repeat the operations in paragraphs 3 to 5.

7 Once the selector lever is operating correctly, apply multi-purpose grease to the

contact surfaces of the transmission selector lever and cable, and lower the vehicle to the ground.

3 Selector cable - removal and refitting

Removal

1 Firmly apply the handbrake, then jack up the front of the vehicle and support it on axle stands. Position the selector lever in the "P" position.

2 Remove the centre console as described in Chapter 11.

3 Unscrew the nut securing the selector cable to the lever. Slide out the clip securing the outer cable to its mounting bracket, and free the selector cable from the selector lever **(see illustration)**.

4 From underneath the vehicle, undo the two bolts securing the cable to the vehicle body.

5 Withdraw the rear end of the cable from the vehicle. Work along the cable, freeing it from any relevant ties and clips, whilst noting its correct routing.

6 Slacken and remove the nut and washer securing the cable to the transmission selector lever. Slide out the clip securing the outer cable to its mounting bracket, then free the cable from the transmission and remove it from underneath the vehicle. Note that the transmission selector lever must not be disturbed until the cable is refitted. As a precaution, mark the position of the lever in relation to the transmission housing.

7 Examine the cable, looking for worn end fittings or a damaged outer casing. Check for signs of fraying of the inner cable. Check the cable's operation; the inner cable should move smoothly and easily through the outer casing. Remember, however, that a cable that appears serviceable when tested off the car

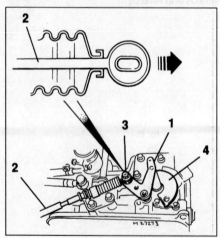

2.4 Selector cable adjustment details. Pull cable end fitting in the direction of the arrow with the specified force

1 Transmission selector lever
2 Selector cable
3 Cable retaining nut
4 Starter/inhibitor switch

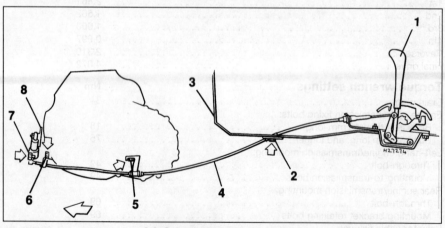

3.3 Selector cable fixing details

1 Selector lever	3 Vehicle floorpan	6 Mounting bracket
2 Selector cable-to-vehicle body fixing	4 Selector cable	7 Selector cable retaining nut
	5 Mounting bracket	8 Transmission selector lever

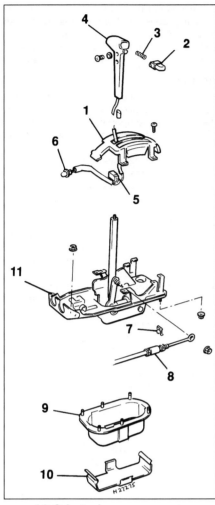

4.3 Selector lever components

1   Gear indicator panel
2   Detent button
3   Spring
4   Selector lever handle
5   Wiring connector
6   Gear indicator light bulb
7   Cable clip
8   Selector cable
9   Dust cover
10   Dust cover support
11   Selector lever assembly

may well be much heavier in operation, when compressed into its working position. Renew the cable if it shows any signs of excessive wear or of damage.

Refitting

8 Feed the cable up into position from underneath the vehicle. Refit the two bolts securing the cable to the floor, and tighten them to the specified torque setting.

9 From inside the vehicle, connect the cable to the selector lever, and clip the outer cable into its mounting bracket. Tighten the cable retaining nut to the specified torque setting, and secure the outer cable in position with the retaining clip.

10 From underneath the vehicle, work along the cable, securing it in position with all the relevant clips and ties, whilst ensuring that it is correctly routed.

11 Ensuring that the selector lever is in the "P" position, and that the transmission selector lever is still in the "Park" position, hook the inner cable onto the transmission selector lever. Clip the outer cable into position in its mounting bracket, and secure it in position with the retaining clip.

12 Hook a spring balance into the slot in the cable end fitting, and pull the cable forwards with a force of 6.9 N (0.7 kg, or 1.5 lbs).

13 From this position, remove the spring balance, and move the cable end fitting backwards by 1.0 mm. Hold the cable in this position, and tighten its retaining nut to the specified torque setting.

14 Check the operation of the selector lever, ensuring that it moves smoothly and easily, without any sign of the cable binding. If not, repeat the operations in paragraphs 12 and 13.

15 Once the selector lever is operating correctly, apply multi-purpose grease to the contact surfaces of the selector levers and cable, and lower the vehicle to the ground.

16 Refit the centre console as described in Chapter 11.

4   Selector lever assembly - removal and refitting

Removal

1 Firmly apply the handbrake, then jack up the front of the vehicle and support it on axle stands. Position the selector lever in the "N" position.

2 Remove the centre console as described in Chapter 11.

3 Unscrew the nut securing the selector cable to the lever. Slide out the clip securing the outer cable to its mounting bracket, and free the selector cable from the selector lever **(see illustration)**.

4 Disconnect the wiring from the overdrive switch and gear indicator light bulb.

5 Undo the two retaining screws, depress the detent button, and slide the handle off the top of the selector lever. If necessary, the detent button and spring can then be withdrawn from the handle, as can the overdrive switch.

6 Undo the nuts, accessed both from inside and underneath the vehicle, securing the selector lever to the floor, and lift the lever assembly out of the vehicle. Do not attempt to dismantle the selector lever components; the lever assembly is a sealed unit, with no individual components being available separately.

Refitting

7 Refit the selector lever assembly to the vehicle, and securely tighten its retaining nuts.

8 Clip the overdrive switch, detent button and spring back into position in the selector lever handle (where removed).

9 Ensure that the switch wiring is correctly routed down through the handle, and refit the handle to the selector lever. Securely tighten its retaining screws, then check the operation of the lever detent mechanism.

10 Connect the overdrive switch and gear indicator light wiring connector.

11 Connect the cable to the selector lever, and clip the outer cable into its mounting bracket. Tighten the cable retaining nut to the specified torque setting, and secure the outer cable in position with the retaining clip.

12 Adjust the selector cable as described in Section 2, then refit the centre console as described in Chapter 11.

5   Kickdown cable - adjustment

1 Ensure that the accelerator cable is correctly adjusted as described in the relevant Part of Chapter 4.

2 Depress the adjuster to release the outer cable locking mechanism, and move the outer cable fully towards the mounting bracket. Release the adjuster, so that the outer cable is locked in position.

3 Using a dab of white paint or a suitable marker pen, make a mark on the kickdown inner cable. This mark can then be used for measuring the cable travel.

4 Position a ruler next to the mark on the inner cable, then quickly move the throttle cam from its fully closed position to its fully open position, whilst measuring the travel of the kickdown cable. This should be within the range quoted **(see illustration)**.

5 If adjustment is necessary, depress the adjuster, then reposition the outer cable and repeat the procedure described in paragraph 4.

6 Repeat the procedure as necessary, until the kickdown cable travel is within the specified range.

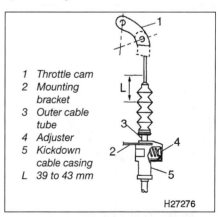

1   Throttle cam
2   Mounting bracket
3   Outer cable tube
4   Adjuster
5   Kickdown cable casing
L   39 to 43 mm

5.4 Adjust the kickdown cable so dimension "L" is as specified

7B

6 Kickdown cable - removal and refitting

1 Renewal of the kickdown cable is complex task, which should be entrusted to a Nissan dealer. To detach the cable at the transmission end first requires the removal of the hydraulic control valve assembly, which is a task that should not be undertaken by the home mechanic.

7 Speedometer drive - removal and refitting

Refer to Chapter 7A, Section 7.

8 Fluid seals - renewal

Driveshaft seals

1 Refer to the information given in Section 4 of Chapter 7A, noting that the seals must be positioned as shown (see illustration).

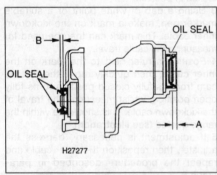

8.1 Correct fitted positions of driveshaft seals

Right-hand side seal (A) - 5.5 to 6.5 mm
Left-hand side seal (B) - 0.5 mm or less

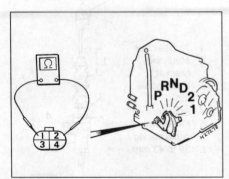

9.4 Starter/inhibitor switch terminal identification. Test switch as described in text

Selector shaft seal

2 Renewal of the selector shaft seal is complex task, requiring much dismantling of the transmission, and should therefore be entrusted to a Nissan dealer.

9 Starter inhibitor/reversing light switch - testing, removal and refitting

Testing

1 The starter inhibitor/reversing light switch is a dual-function switch which is screwed onto the front of the transmission housing. The inhibitor function of the switch ensures that the engine can only be started whilst the selector lever is in either the "N" or "P" positions, therefore preventing the engine being started whilst the transmission is in gear. If at any time it is noted that the engine can be started whilst the selector lever is in any position other than "P" or "N", then it is likely that the inhibitor function of the switch is incorrectly adjusted or faulty. The switch also performs the function of the reversing light switch, illuminating the reversing lights whenever the selector lever is in the "R" position. If either function of the switch is faulty, the switch must be tested as follows.
2 To improve access to the switch, firmly apply the handbrake, then jack up the front of the vehicle and support it on axle stands.
3 Disconnect the wiring connector from the switch.
4 Measure the resistances between the various terminals of the switch (see illustration) with the selector lever in the "P", "N" and "R" positions. If the switch is functioning correctly, there should be continuity between terminals 1 and 2 in the "P" and "N" positions, and continuity between terminals 3 and 4 in the "R" position.

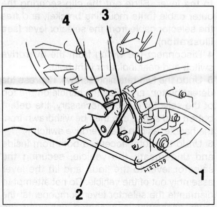

9.11 Adjust the switch using a drill/rod as described in text

1 *Starter/inhibitor switch*
2 *Transmission selector lever*
3 *Adjustment holes*
4 *4 mm diameter drill/rod*

5 If this is not the case, slacken the switch retaining bolts, and adjust the switch as described in paragraphs 10 and 11. If the switch still fails to function properly after adjustment, it is faulty and must be renewed.

Removal

6 To improve access to the switch, firmly apply the handbrake, then jack up the front of the vehicle and support it on axle stands.
7 Disconnect the wiring connector from the switch.
8 Slacken and remove the three retaining bolts, then free the switch from the transmission selector mechanism and remove it from the vehicle.

Refitting

9 Manoeuvre the switch into position, and engage it with the selector mechanism. Install the switch retaining bolts, tightening them loosely at this stage.
10 Position the selector lever in the "N" position, and obtain a 4 mm diameter twist drill or rod.
11 Insert the drill/rod through the hole in the top of the selector lever, and also through the hole in the top of the switch lever (see illustration). With the holes aligned, securely tighten the switch retaining bolts, then withdraw the drill/rod.
12 Reconnect the switch wiring, and check the operation of the switch.

10 Overdrive switch - testing, removal and refitting

Testing

1 Remove the centre console as described in Chapter 11.
2 Disconnect the wiring from the overdrive switch and gear indicator light.
3 Measure the resistance between terminals 1 and 2 of the connector (see illustration). If the switch is functioning correctly, there should be continuity between the terminals only when the switch is "on". If not, the switch must be renewed.

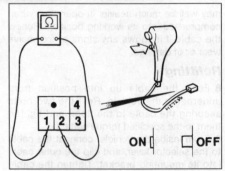

10.3 Overdrive switch terminal identification. Test switch as described in text

Removal

4 Remove the centre console as described in Chapter 11.

5 Disconnect the wiring from the overdrive switch and gear indicator light.

6 Undo the two retaining screws, depress the detent button, and slide the handle off the top of the selector lever.

7 Unclip the overdrive switch, and remove it from the handle.

Refitting

8 Clip the overdrive switch back into position in the selector lever handle.

9 Ensure that the switch wiring is correctly routed down through the handle, and refit the handle to the selector lever. Securely tighten its retaining screws, then check the operation of the lever detent mechanism.

10 Connect the overdrive switch and gear indicator light wiring, then refit the centre console as described in Chapter 11.

11 Automatic transmission - removal and refitting

Removal

1 Chock the rear wheels, then firmly apply the handbrake and position the selector lever in the "N" (neutral) position. Jack up the front of the vehicle, and securely support it on axle stands. Remove both front roadwheels.

2 Drain the transmission fluid as described in Chapter 1, then refit the drain plug and tighten it to the specified torque.

3 Remove the battery and battery tray as described in Chapter 5.

4 Remove the starter motor as described in Chapter 5.

5 Remove the air cleaner housing inlet duct as described in the relevant Part of Chapter 4.

6 Remove the driveshafts as described in Chapter 8.

7 Disconnect the wiring connectors from the starter inhibitor/reversing light switch and the transmission solenoid wiring.

8 Slacken and remove the nut and washer securing the selector cable to the transmission selector lever. Slide out the clip securing the outer cable to its mounting bracket, then free the cable from the transmission.

9 Using a hose clamp or similar, clamp both the fluid cooler hoses to minimise coolant loss. Slacken the retaining clips, and disconnect both hoses from the transmission - be prepared for some spillage. Wipe up any spilt fluid immediately.

10 Detach the kickdown inner cable from the throttle body cam. Slacken the outer cable locknuts, and unbolt the cable mounting bracket. Release the kickdown cable from any

relevant retaining clips, so that it is free to be removed with the transmission.

11 Undo the retaining bolts, and remove the cover plate from the sump flange to gain access to the torque converter retaining bolts. Slacken and remove the visible bolt then, using a socket and extension bar to rotate the crankshaft pulley, undo the remaining bolts securing the torque converter to the driveplate as they become accessible. There are four bolts in total.

12 Place a jack with interposed block of wood beneath the engine, to take the weight of the engine. Alternatively, attach a hoist or support bar to the engine lifting eyes, and take the weight of the engine.

13 Place a jack and block of wood beneath the transmission, and raise the jack to take the weight of the transmission.

14 Slacken and remove the through-bolt from the rear engine/transmission mounting. Undo the bolts securing the mounting bracket in position, and manoeuvre it away from the engine/transmission. Recover the stopper ring which is fitted between the mounting bracket and mounting.

15 To improve access, undo the four bolts and washers and remove the front crossmember from underneath the engine/transmission.

16 Slacken and remove the through-bolt from the left-hand engine/transmission mounting. Undo the three bolts securing the mounting to the transmission, and manoeuvre the mounting out of position. Recover the rubbers from each side of the mounting bracket.

17 To ensure that the torque converter does not fall out as the transmission is removed, secure it in position using a length of metal strip bolted to one of the starter motor bolt holes.

18 With the jack positioned beneath the transmission taking the weight, slacken and remove the remaining bolts securing the transmission housing to the engine. Note the correct fitted positions of each bolt (and any relevant brackets) as they are removed, to use as a reference on refitting.

19 Make a final check that all necessary components have been disconnected, and are positioned clear of the transmission so that they will not hinder the removal procedure.

20 With the bolts removed, move the trolley jack and transmission to the left, to free it from its locating dowels.

21 Once the transmission is completely free from the engine, lower the jack and manoeuvre the unit out from under the car. If they are loose, remove the locating dowels from the transmission or engine, and keep them in a safe place.

Refitting

22 The transmission is refitted by a reversal of the removal procedure, bearing in mind the following points:

a) Prior to installing the transmission, ensure that the torque converter is correctly engaged with the transmission. This can be checked by measuring the distance from the converter mounting bolt holes to the transmission mating surface; if the converter is correctly seated, this distance will be at least 15.9 mm **(see illustration)**.

b) Ensure that the locating dowels are correctly positioned prior to installation.

c) Tighten all nuts and bolts to the specified torque (where given).

d) Inspect the crossmember mounting rubbers for signs of damage or deterioration, and renew if necessary.

e) Prior to refitting the driveshafts, renew the driveshaft seals using the information given in Section 8.

f) Adjust the selector cable and kickdown cable as described in Sections 2 and 5 of this Chapter.

g) On completion, refill the transmission with the specified type and quantity of lubricant, as described in Chapter 1.

12 Automatic transmission overhaul - general information

1 In the event of a fault occurring on the transmission, it is first necessary to determine whether it is of an electrical, mechanical or hydraulic nature, and to do this, special test equipment is required. It is therefore essential to have the work carried out by a Nissan dealer if a transmission fault is suspected.

2 Do not remove the transmission from the car for possible repair before professional fault diagnosis has been carried out, since most tests require the transmission to be in the vehicle.

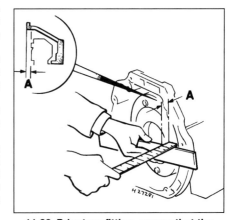

11.22 Prior to refitting, ensure that the distance (A) from the torque converter bolt holes to the transmission mating surface is at least 15.9 mm, indicating that the converter is correctly seated

7B

Notes

Chapter 8 Driveshafts

Contents

Degrees of difficulty

Easy, suitable for novice with little experience	**Fairly easy,** suitable for beginner with some experience	**Fairly difficult,** suitable for competent DIY mechanic	**Difficult,** suitable for experienced DIY mechanic	**Very difficult,** suitable for expert DIY or professional

Specifications

General

Type . . . . Unequal-length, solid steel shafts, splined to inner and outer constant velocity joints. Intermediate support bearing on right-hand driveshaft on 2.0 litre engine models

Lubrication

Lubricant type . . . . Nissan grease supplied with gaiter repair kit

Torque wrench settings

	Nm	lbf ft
Brake caliper guide pin bolts:		
Bendix caliper	35	26
Girling caliper	25	18
Driveshaft nut*	300	221
Hub carrier-to-suspension centre link nut*		
(Saloon and Hatchback models)	110	81
Lower arm balljoint-to-lower arm nuts* (Estate models)	90	66
Right-hand driveshaft intermediate bearing housing-to-support		
bracket bolts	15	11
Roadwheel nuts	110	81
Track-rod end-to-steering arm nut:		
Recommended torque	35	26
Maximum permissible torque	49	36

*Use a new nut.

1 General information

1 Drive is transmitted from the differential to the front wheels by means of two solid-steel driveshafts of unequal length **(see illustration)**.
2 Both driveshafts are splined at their outer ends, to accept the wheel hubs, and are threaded so that each hub can be fastened to the driveshaft by a large nut. The inner end of each driveshaft is splined, to accept the differential sun gear.
3 Constant velocity (CV) joints are fitted to each end of the driveshafts, to ensure the smooth and efficient transmission of power at all suspension and steering angles. The outer constant velocity joints are of the ball-and-cage type, and the inner joints may be of the ball-and-cage or tripod type, depending on model.
4 On 2.0 litre engine models, due to the length of the right-hand driveshaft, the inner constant velocity joint is situated approximately halfway along the length of the shaft, and an intermediate bearing is mounted in a bracket bolted to the rear of the cylinder block. The inner section of the driveshaft passes through the bearing, which prevents lateral flexing of the driveshaft.

2 Driveshafts - removal and refitting
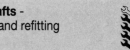

Note: *A balljoint separator tool will be required for this operation. A new driveshaft nut, new driveshaft inner joint retaining clip (where applicable), and new driveshaft nut and track-rod end nut split-pins must be used on refitting. On Saloon and Hatchback models, a new suspension centre link-to-hub carrier nut should be used on refitting, and on Estate models, new lower arm balljoint nuts should be used.*

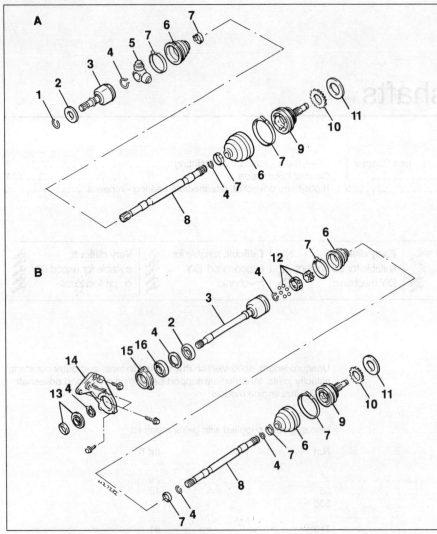

1.1 Typical driveshaft components

A All except right-hand
   driveshaft on 2.0 litre
   engine models
B Right-hand driveshaft on
   2.0 litre engine models
1 Inner joint retaining clip
2 Oil seal
3 Inner joint body

4 Circlip
5 Tripod
6 Gaiter
7 Gaiter clips
8 Driveshaft
9 Outer joint body
10 ABS wheel sensor rotor
11 Washer

12 Ball-and-cage inner joint
   components
13 Dust shield
14 Intermediate bearing
   support bracket
15 Intermediate bearing
   housing
16 Intermediate bearing

Removal

1 Chock the rear wheels, apply the handbrake, then jack up the front of the vehicle and support on axle stands (see "*Jacking, towing and wheel changing*"). Remove the appropriate roadwheel(s).

2 To reduce spillage when the inner end of the driveshaft is withdrawn from the transmission, drain the transmission oil/fluid as described in Chapter 7A or 7B, as applicable.

3 Remove the split-pin from the outer end of the driveshaft, then withdraw the castellated locking plate and the spacer. Discard the split-pin - a new one must be used on refitting **(see illustrations)**.

4 The front hub must now be held stationary in order to loosen the driveshaft nut. Ideally, the hub should be held by a suitable tool bolted into place using two of the roadwheel nuts. Alternatively, have an assistant firmly apply the brake pedal to prevent the hub from rotating. Using a socket and extension bar, slacken and remove the driveshaft nut **(see illustration)**. Remove the washer.

> ⚠️ **Warning: Take care, the nut is very tight! Discard the nut - a new one must be used on refitting.**

5 Unscrew the guide pin bolts, and withdraw the brake caliper from the hub carrier as described in Chapter 9. Note that there is no need to disconnect the brake fluid hose. Suspend the caliper from the body using wire or string. **Do not** depress the brake pedal

2.3a Remove the split-pin . . .

2.3b . . . then withdraw the locking plate . . .

2.3c . . . and the spacer

2.4 Removing the driveshaft nut

2.6 Using a balljoint separator tool to disconnect the track-rod end from the steering arm

2.7a Prise the dust cap from the nut securing the hub carrier to the centre link assembly - Saloon and Hatchback models

2.7b Remove the nut . . .

whilst the caliper is removed, as this will cause the piston to be ejected.

6 Remove the split-pin, then partially unscrew the castellated nut securing the track-rod end to the steering arm. Using a balljoint separator tool, separate the track-rod end from the steering arm **(see illustration)**. Remove the nut. Discard the split-pin - a new one must be used on refitting.

7 On Saloon and Hatchback models, prise off the dust cap, then unscrew the nut securing the hub carrier to the suspension centre link assembly. Recover the washer. Pull the hub carrier downwards to separate it from the centre link assembly. Discard the nut - a new one should be used on refitting. On models with ABS, take care not to strain the ABS sensor wiring - if necessary, remove the screws securing the wiring brackets to the hub carrier and the wing panel **(see illustrations)**.

8 On Estate models, unscrew the nuts securing the lower arm balljoint to the lower arm, and remove the mounting plate to free the hub carrier from the lower arm. Discard the nuts - new ones should be used on refitting.

9 Temporarily refit the driveshaft nut to the end of the driveshaft, to prevent damage to the driveshaft threads, then using a soft-faced mallet, carefully tap the driveshaft from the hub carrier **(see illustration)**. If the shaft is a tight fit, a suitable puller can be used to force

the end of the shaft from the hub. Support the end of the driveshaft - do not allow the end of the driveshaft to hang down.

10 Proceed as follows, according to which driveshaft is to be removed.

Right-hand driveshaft - 1.6 litre engine models

11 Separate the driveshaft from the transmission, using a suitable lever inserted between the casing of the inner constant velocity joint and the transmission casing. Prise out the driveshaft until the retaining clip compresses into its groove, and is released from the differential sun gear. Discard the retaining clip - a new clip must be used on refitting.

2.7c . . . and the washer . . .

12 Withdraw the driveshaft assembly.

Right-hand driveshaft - 2.0 litre engine models

13 Unscrew the three bolts securing the intermediate bearing housing to the support bracket **(see illustration)**.

14 Separate the housing from the bracket by rotating it (using both hands!) until a gap has opened into which a suitable lever can be inserted **(see illustration)**. **Do not** lever against the seal on the inner end of the driveshaft, or attempt to separate the intermediate bearing from its housing.

15 Withdraw the driveshaft assembly, complete with the intermediate bearing and housing.

2.7d . . . then pull the hub carrier down from the centre link

2.9 Withdraw the driveshaft from the hub carrier

2.13 Unscrew the bolts (arrowed) securing the intermediate bearing housing to the support bracket - 2.0 litre engine model

2.14 Separate the bearing housing from the bracket - 2.0 litre engine model

8

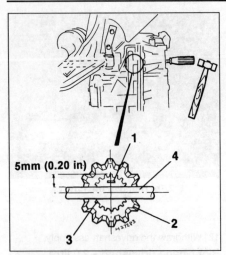

5mm (0.20 in)

2.18 Using a screwdriver to release the inner end of the left-hand driveshaft from the differential - 2.0 litre engine models with automatic transmission

1 *Screwdriver tip*   3 *Driveshaft*
2 *Sun gear*   4 *Planet gear shaft*

Left-hand driveshaft - all except 2.0 litre engine models with automatic transmission

16 The procedure is as described for the right-hand driveshaft in paragraphs 11 and 12, but take care not to damage the oil seal when prising the driveshaft from the transmission.

Left-hand driveshaft - 2.0 litre engine models with automatic transmission

17 To remove the left-hand driveshaft, the right-hand driveshaft **must** be removed first, as described previously in paragraphs 13 to 15.
18 Working through the aperture in the right-hand side of the differential created by removal of the right-hand driveshaft, pass a suitable long-bladed screwdriver or a similar drift into the differential until it rests against the inner end of the left-hand driveshaft. Take care not to damage the planet gear shaft or the sun gear **(see illustration)**.
19 Tap the end of the driveshaft until the retaining clip compressed into its groove, and is released from the differential sun gear.
20 Withdraw the driveshaft assembly. Discard the retaining clip - a new clip must be used on refitting.

Refitting

21 Before installing a driveshaft, examine the driveshaft oil seal in the transmission for signs of damage or deterioration and, if necessary, renew it, referring to Chapter 7A or 7B for further information (it is advisable to renew the seal as a matter of course).
22 Thoroughly clean the driveshaft splines, and the apertures in the transmission and hub assembly. Apply a thin film of grease to the oil seal lips, and to the driveshaft splines and shoulders. Check that all driveshaft gaiter clips are securely fastened.

23 Note that the retaining clip at the inner end of the driveshaft (all except right-hand driveshaft on 2.0 litre engine models) **must** be renewed on refitting.
24 When refitting a driveshaft, great care must be taken to prevent damage to the driveshaft oil seals. Nissan specify the use of special tools which guide the shafts through the seal lips on refitting. Provided that the seal lips and the shaft ends are lightly greased, and that care is taken on refitting, these tools should not be necessary.

Right-hand driveshaft - 1.6 litre engine models

25 Insert the inner end of the driveshaft into the transmission, taking care not to damage the oil seal.
26 Engage the driveshaft splines with those of the differential sun gear, and press the driveshaft into place until the retaining clip (a new clip should be fitted) engages correctly behind (inboard of) the sun gear.
27 Grasp the inner joint body firmly, and check that the clip is correctly engaged by attempting to pull the driveshaft from the transmission.
28 Proceed to paragraph 35.

Right-hand driveshaft - 2.0 litre engine models

29 Insert the inner end of the driveshaft through the intermediate bearing bracket, and engage the driveshaft splines with those of the differential sun gear, taking care not to damage the oil seal.
30 Manipulate the bearing housing into position in the bracket, ensuring that the bolt holes are aligned.
31 Refit the bolts securing the bearing housing to the support bracket, and tighten them to the specified torque.
32 Proceed to paragraph 35.

Left-hand driveshaft - all except 2.0 litre engine models with automatic transmission

33 Proceed as described in paragraphs 25 to 28.

Left-hand driveshaft - 2.0 litre models with automatic transmission

34 Proceed as described in paragraphs 25 to 27, then refit the right-hand driveshaft with reference to paragraphs 29 to 32.

All models

35 Apply a thin film of grease to the outer driveshaft joint splines, then engage the outer end of the driveshaft with the hub, ensuring that the splines engage correctly.
36 Refit the washer and a new driveshaft nut, but do not tighten the nut at this stage.
37 On Saloon and Hatchback models, engage the hub carrier with the suspension centre link assembly, then refit the washer and new nut. Tighten the nut to the specified torque, and refit the dust cap (fit a new dust cap of the original cap was damaged during removal).

38 On Estate models, refit the mounting plate (engage the studs with the lower arm balljoint, which is still attached to the hub carrier), then fit new nuts to secure the balljoint to the lower arm. Tighten the nuts to the specified torque.
39 Reconnect the track-rod end to the steering arm, then refit the castellated nut, and tighten to the specified torque.
40 If necessary, tighten the nut further (ensure that the maximum torque for the nut is not exceeded) until the nearest grooves in the nut are aligned with the split-pin hole in the track-rod end, then fit a new split-pin.
41 Refit the brake caliper as described in Chapter 9. Where applicable, refit the screws securing the ABS sensor wiring brackets.
42 Hold the front hub stationary as during removal, then tighten the new driveshaft nut to the specified torque.
43 Fit the spacer and the castellated locking plate (ensure that the grooves in the locking plate are aligned with the split-pin hole in the end of the driveshaft, then fit a new split-pin.
44 Refit the roadwheel(s), and lower the vehicle to the ground.
45 Refill the transmission with oil/fluid as described in Chapter 1.

3 Driveshaft rubber gaiters - renewal

Outer joint

Note: *New gaiter securing clips and a new joint retaining clip must be used on refitting.*
1 Remove the driveshaft as described in Section 2.
2 Measure the length of the gaiter, so that the new gaiter can be set to the same length before securing it in position **(see illustration)**.
3 Remove the rubber gaiter securing clips, then slide the gaiter away from the joint towards the centre of the driveshaft.
4 If the original joint is to be re-used, make alignment marks between the joint and the driveshaft.
5 The joint must now be pulled from the end of the driveshaft. Clamp the driveshaft in a vice.
6 To remove the joint, temporarily refit the driveshaft nut to the end of the driveshaft,

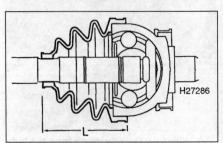

3.2 Measure the length (L) of the outer joint gaiter

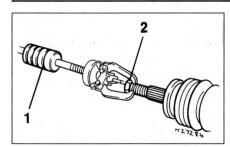

3.6 Using a slide hammer to remove the outer driveshaft joint

1 Slide hammer   2 Driveshaft nut

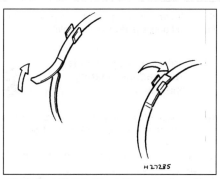

3.15 Bend back the gaiter securing clip, and secure it under the tags

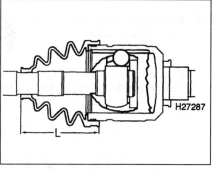

3.20 Measure the length (L) of the inner joint gaiter - ball-and-cage type joint

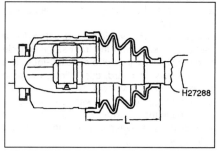

3.22 Measure the length (L) of the inner joint gaiter - tripod type joint

then attach a slide hammer with a suitable puller adapter to act on the driveshaft nut **(see illustration)**. Take great care not to damage the threads on the end of the driveshaft. Alternatively, tap the driveshaft joint outwards using a mallet, to force the retaining clip to contract into its groove, thus releasing the joint from the shaft.

7 Slide the gaiter from the end of the shaft, then remove the joint retaining clip. Discard the clip - a new clip must be used on refitting.

8 Thoroughly clean the outer constant velocity joint and the end of the driveshaft using paraffin, or a suitable solvent, and dry thoroughly. Carry out a visual inspection of the joint. If any of the joint components are worn, it will be necessary to renew the joint complete, as no spare parts are available.

9 Commence refitting by winding a thin layer of tape around the end of the shaft, to protect the gaiter from the shaft splines.

10 Slide the smaller gaiter securing clip onto the shaft, followed by the gaiter.

11 Remove the tape from the end of the shaft, then fit a new joint retaining clip to the end of the shaft.

12 Fit the outer joint to the shaft, and engage it with the shaft splines. If the original joint is re-used, align the marks made on the joint and the end of the driveshaft before dismantling.

13 Temporarily refit the driveshaft nut to protect the joint threaded end, then clamp the driveshaft in a vice, and use a mallet to tap the joint onto the shaft until the retaining clip engages correctly behind the joint cage.

14 Pack the joint with the correct amount of the specified grease (supplied with the gaiter kit), then twist the joint to ensure that all the recesses are filled. Pack any surplus grease into the gaiter.

15 Slide the gaiter onto the outer joint, then fit the new outer gaiter securing clip, and tighten as shown. Bend back the end of the clip, and secure it under the tags as shown **(see illustration)**.

16 Set the gaiter so that the length is as measured in paragraph 2.

17 Check that the smaller end of the gaiter is located in the driveshaft groove, and ensure that the gaiter is not trapped or deformed.

18 Slide the smaller securing clip onto the gaiter, and tighten and secure it as described previously.

19 Refit the driveshaft as described in Section 2.

Inner joint

Ball-and-cage type joint

Note: *New gaiter securing clips and a new joint retaining clip must be used on refitting.*

20 The procedure is as described for the outer joint in paragraphs 1 to 18 inclusive, bearing in mind the following points:

a) *Ignore the reference to refitting the driveshaft nut and using a slide hammer to remove the joint - the joint must be tapped off using a mallet.*

b) *Measure the length of the gaiter at the points shown* **(see illustration)**.

Tripod joint

Note: *New gaiter securing clips and a new joint spider circlip must be used on refitting.*

21 Remove the driveshaft as described in Section 2.

22 Measure the length of the gaiter, so that the new gaiter can be set to the same length before securing it in position **(see illustration)**.

23 Remove the gaiter securing clips, and slide the gaiter off the joint towards the middle of the driveshaft.

24 If the original joint is to be re-used, make alignment marks between the joint and the driveshaft.

25 Pull the joint body from the spider, ensuring that the rollers remain in place on the spider.

26 If the original spider is to be re-used, mark the relationship of the spider and the driveshaft, then using circlip pliers, remove the circlip securing the spider to the end of the shaft. Discard the circlip - a new one should be used on refitting.

27 Withdraw the spider and the gaiter from the end of the shaft.

28 Thoroughly clean the constant velocity joint components and the end of the driveshaft using paraffin, or a suitable solvent, and dry thoroughly. Carry out a visual inspection of the joint. If any of the joint

components are worn, the spider assembly or the joint body can be renewed separately as complete units, but no other spare parts are available.

29 Commence refitting by winding a thin layer of tape around the end of the shaft, to protect the gaiter from the shaft splines.

30 Slide the smaller gaiter securing clip onto the shaft, followed by the gaiter.

31 Remove the tape from the end of the shaft, then refit the spider. If the original spider is being refitted, align the marks made on the spider and the driveshaft before removal.

32 Fit a new circlip to secure the spider.

33 Pack the correct amount of the specified grease (supplied with the gaiter kit), around the spider rollers and into the joint body.

34 Fit the joint body over the spider. If the original body is being refitted, align the marks made between the body and the driveshaft before removal.

35 Slide the gaiter onto the joint body, expelling any trapped air, then fit a new outer gaiter securing clip, and tighten it. Bend back the end of the clip, and secure it under the tags as shown in illustration 3.15.

36 Set the gaiter so that the length is as measured in paragraph 22, then check that the smaller end of the gaiter is located in the driveshaft groove, and that the gaiter is not stretched or deformed when at this length.

37 Locate the smaller gaiter securing clip on the end of the gaiter, and secure it as described previously.

38 Refit the driveshaft as described in Section 2.

4 Driveshaft overhaul - general information

1 If any of the checks described in Chapter 1 reveal wear in any driveshaft joint, first remove the roadwheel trim or centre cap (as appropriate).
2 Check that the driveshaft nut is correctly tightened; if in doubt, remove the split pin and the castellated locking plate and spacer. Check that the nut is tightened to the specified torque, then refit the spacer, the locking plate, and a new split-pin. Refit the roadwheel trim or centre cap (as applicable), and repeat the check on the remaining driveshaft nut.
3 Road test the vehicle, and listen for a metallic clicking from the front as the vehicle is driven slowly in a circle on full-lock. If a clicking noise is heard, this indicates wear in the outer constant velocity joint.
4 If vibration, consistent with road speed, is felt through the car when accelerating, there is a possibility of wear in the inner constant velocity joints.
5 To check the joints for wear, remove the driveshafts, then dismantle them as described in Section 3. If any wear or free play is found, components are worn, the spacer assembly of the joint body can be renewed separately as complete units, but no other spare parts are available.

the relevant joint must be renewed (no individual spare parts are available).

5 Right-hand driveshaft intermediate bearing - renewal

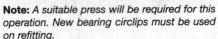

Note: *A suitable press will be required for this operation. New bearing circlips must be used on refitting.*
1 Remove the right-hand driveshaft as described in Section 2.
2 To ease the operation, remove the inner constant velocity joint, complete with intermediate bearing and housing, from the driveshaft as described in Section 3.
3 Clamp the joint in a vice, then tap the dust shield from the inner end of the shaft, using a suitable drift.
4 Using a suitable screwdriver, prise the bearing dust shield from the inboard end of the bearing housing.
5 Using circlip pliers, remove the bearing circlip. Discard the circlip - a new one should be used on refitting.
6 Using a suitable press, remove the bearing/housing assembly from the end of the shaft. It should be possible to tap the bearing from the end of the shaft, if the bearing inner race is supported adequately, but this is not

recommended if the bearing is to be re-used, as damage to the bearing is likely to result.
7 Invert the bearing/housing assembly, and use circlip pliers to remove the large circlip from the outboard end of the bearing. Discard the circlip - a new one should be used on refitting. Prise off the dust seal.
8 Support the bearing housing, then using a suitable tube or socket, which bears only on the bearing outer race, tap the bearing from the housing.
9 Commence refitting by packing the bearing with grease.
10 Using a suitable tube or socket which bears only on the bearing outer race, tap the bearing into the housing until the outboard dust shield and the large circlip can be refitted.
11 Ensure that the bearing inner race is adequately supported, then using a suitable tool (a block of wood should serve) to bear across the end of the driveshaft joint, press the shaft into the bearing until the inboard circlip can be refitted.
12 Carefully tap the bearing dust seal into position against the bearing, then tap the dust seal into position on the inboard end of the driveshaft.
13 Refit the inner constant velocity joint as described in Section 3.
14 Refit the driveshaft as described in Section 2.

Chapter 9 Braking system

Contents

Degrees of difficulty

Easy, suitable for novice with little experience	Fairly easy, suitable for beginner with some experience	Fairly difficult, suitable for competent DIY mechanic 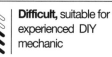	Difficult, suitable for experienced DIY mechanic	Very difficult, suitable for expert DIY or professional

Specifications

General

System type .... Dual hydraulic circuit. Anti-lock braking system fitted to certain "Phase I" and all "Phase II" models. Front ventilated disc brakes on all models. Rear drum brakes on 1.6 litre engine models without ABS, rear disc brakes on all other models. Vacuum servo-assistance on all models. Cable-operated handbrake acting on rear wheels.

Front brakes

Type .... Ventilated disc, with single-piston sliding caliper
Disc diameter:
  Saloon and Hatchback models:
    All except 1.6 litre models without ABS .... 257.0 mm
    1.6 litre models without ABS .... 242.0 mm
  Estate models .... 257.0 mm
Disc thickness:
  New:
    257.0 mm diameter disc .... 22.0 mm
    242.0 mm diameter disc .... 20.0 mm
  Minimum thickness (0.02 mm maximum variation between sides):
    257.0 mm diameter disc .... 20.0 mm
    242.0 mm diameter disc .... 18.0 mm
Maximum disc run-out .... 0.07 mm
Minimum pad friction material thickness .... 2.0 mm

9

Rear disc brakes

Type .... Solid disc with single-piston sliding caliper
Disc diameter .... 258.0 mm
Disc thickness:
  New:
    Saloon and Hatchback models .... 10.0 mm
    Estate models .... 9.0 mm
  Minimum thickness (0.02 mm maximum variation between sides):
    Saloon and Hatchback models .... 9.0 mm
    Estate models .... 8.0 mm
Maximum disc run-out .... 0.07 mm
Minimum pad friction material thickness .... 2.0 mm

Rear drum brakes

Type .... Drum, with leading and trailing shoes operated by twin-piston wheel cylinder

Drum inner diameter:
  New:
    Saloon and Hatchback models .... 203.2 mm
    Estate models .... 228.6 mm
  Maximum diameter after machining:
    Saloon and Hatchback models .... 204.5 mm
    Estate models .... 230.0 mm
Maximum out-of-round .... 0.03 mm
Minimum shoe lining thickness .... 1.5 mm

Brake pedal

Free height:
  Right-hand-drive models:
    Saloon and Hatchback models:
      Manual transmission .... 162.0 to 172.0 mm
      Automatic transmission .... 170.5 to 180.5 mm
    Estate models:
      Manual transmission .... 153.0 to 163.0 mm
      Automatic transmission .... 162.0 to 172.0 mm
  Left-hand-drive models:
    Saloon and Hatchback models:
      Manual transmission .... 151.0 to 161.0 mm
      Automatic transmission .... 159.0 to 169.0 mm
    Estate models:
      Manual transmission .... 143.0 to 153.0 mm
      Automatic transmission .... 151.5 to 161.5 mm
Pedal free-play .... 1.0 to 3.0 mm

Vacuum servo

Pushrod length:
  Models without ABS .... 125.0 mm
  Models with ABS .... 10.3 to 10.5 mm

Rear brake pressure-regulating valve

Valve spring length:
  Saloon and Hatchback models .... 86.0 to 90.0 mm
  Estate models .... 157.7 to 160.7 mm

Handbrake

Number of handbrake clicks required to operate handbrake "on" warning light:
  Saloon and Hatchback models .... 1 to 2 clicks
  Estate models .... 0 to 1 click

Torque wrench settings

	Nm	lbf ft
ABS modulator securing nuts	15	11
ABS wheel sensor securing bolts*:		
Front sensor	12	9
Rear sensor:		
Saloon and Hatchback models	12	9
Estate models	20	15
Brake fluid hose union banjo bolts	20	15
Brake fluid pipe union nuts	18	13

Torque wrench settings (continued)

	Nm	lbf ft
Brake hydraulic system bleed screws	10	7
Brake servo/pedal bracket securing nuts	15	11
Front brake caliper guide pin bolts*:		
Saloon and Hatchback models:		
Bendix caliper	35	26
Lucas Girling caliper	25	18
Estate models	25	18
Front brake caliper mounting bracket bolts	80	59
Handbrake lever mounting bolts	10	7
Master cylinder securing nuts	15	11
Master cylinder stop-bolt	2	1
Rear brake backplate bolts (drum brake models):		
Saloon and Hatchback models	45	33
Estate models	90	66
Rear brake caliper guide pin bolts*	25	18
Rear brake caliper mounting bracket bolts	45	33
Rear brake caliper handbrake lever cam nut (Estate models)	25	18
Rear brake caliper handbrake lever stop-bolt (Saloon and Hatchback models)	10	7
Rear brake pressure-regulating valve securing bolts	18	13
Rear wheel cylinder mounting bolts	10	7

*Use locking compound on the bolt threads.

1 General information

1 The braking system is of the servo-assisted, dual-circuit hydraulic type. The arrangement of the hydraulic system is such that each circuit operates one front and one rear brake from a tandem master cylinder. Under normal circumstances, both circuits operate in unison. However, in the event of hydraulic failure in one circuit, full braking force will still be available at two diagonally-opposite wheels. An anti-lock braking system (ABS) is available as on option on certain early models, and is standard equipment on all later "Phase II" models (refer to Section 21 for further details of the ABS system).

2 1.6 litre engine models with a conventional braking system are fitted with front disc brakes and rear drum brakes. 2.0 litre engine models, and all models with ABS, are fitted with front and rear disc brakes **(see illustrations)**.

3 The front disc brakes are actuated by single-piston sliding type calipers, which ensure that equal pressure is applied to each disc pad.

4 The rear drum brakes incorporate leading and trailing shoes, which are actuated by twin-piston wheel cylinders. A self-adjust mechanism is incorporated, to automatically compensate for brake shoe wear. As the brake shoe linings wear, the footbrake operation automatically operates the adjuster mechanism, which effectively lengthens the shoe strut and repositions the brake shoes, to remove the lining-to-drum clearance. The mechanical handbrake linkage operates the brake shoes via a lever attached to the trailing brake shoe.

5 The rear disc brakes are actuated by single-piston sliding type calipers, and incorporate a mechanical handbrake mechanism.

6 Models with rear disc brakes, and Estate models with rear drum brakes, are fitted with a load-sensitive dual rear pressure-regulating valve, to prevent the possibility of the rear wheels locking before the front wheels under heavy braking. On Saloon and Hatchback models with rear drum brakes, the pressure-regulating valves are integral with the rear wheel cylinders.

Note: *When servicing any part of the system, work carefully and methodically; also observe scrupulous cleanliness when overhauling any*

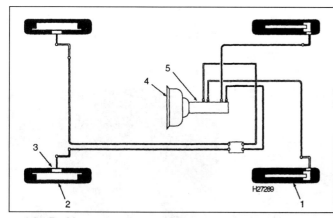

1.2a Braking system layout - Saloon and Hatchback models without ABS

1 *Front disc brake*
2 *Rear drum brake*
3 *Rear brake pressure-regulating valve (in wheel cylinder)*
4 *Vacuum servo*
5 *Master cylinder*

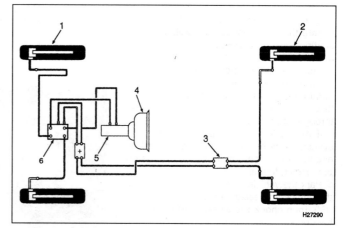

1.2b Braking system layout - models with ABS

1 *Front disc brake*
2 *Rear disc brake*
3 *Rear brake pressure-regulating valves*
4 *Vacuum servo*
5 *Master cylinder*
6 *Modulator assembly*

part of the hydraulic system. Always renew components (in axle sets, where applicable) if in doubt about their condition, and use only genuine Nissan replacement parts, or at least those of known good quality. Note the warnings given in "Safety first" and at relevant points in this Chapter concerning the dangers of asbestos dust and hydraulic fluid.

2 Hydraulic system - bleeding

Warning: Hydraulic fluid is poisonous; wash off immediately and thoroughly in the case of skin contact, and seek immediate medical advice if any fluid is swallowed, or gets into the eyes. Certain types of hydraulic fluid are inflammable, and may ignite when allowed into contact with hot components. When servicing any hydraulic system, it is safest to assume that the fluid IS inflammable, and to take precautions against the risk of fire as though it is petrol that is being handled. Hydraulic fluid is also an effective paint stripper, and will attack plastics; if any is spilt, it should be washed off immediately, using copious quantities of fresh water. Finally, it is hygroscopic (it absorbs moisture from the air) - old fluid may be contaminated and unfit for further use. When topping-up or renewing the fluid, always use the recommended type, and ensure that it comes from a freshly-opened sealed container.

General

1 The correct operation of any hydraulic system is only possible after removing all air from the components and circuit; and this is achieved by bleeding the system.
2 During the bleeding procedure, add only clean, unused hydraulic fluid of the recommended type; never re-use fluid that has already been bled from the system. Ensure that sufficient fluid is available before starting work.
3 If there is any possibility of incorrect fluid being already in the system, the brake components and circuit must be flushed completely with uncontaminated, correct fluid, and new seals should be fitted throughout the system.
4 If hydraulic fluid has been lost from the system, or air has entered because of a leak, ensure that the fault is cured before proceeding further.
5 Park the vehicle on level ground, switch off the engine and select first or reverse gear (or "P"), then chock the wheels and release the handbrake.
6 Check that all pipes and hoses are secure, unions tight and bleed screws closed. Remove the dust caps (where applicable), and clean any dirt from around the bleed screws.

7 Unscrew the master cylinder reservoir cap, and top the master cylinder reservoir up to the "MAX" level line; refit the cap loosely. Remember to maintain the fluid level at least above the "MIN" level line throughout the procedure, otherwise there is a risk of further air entering the system.
8 There are a number of one-man, do-it-yourself brake bleeding kits currently available from motor accessory shops. It is recommended that one of these kits is used whenever possible, as they greatly simplify the bleeding operation, and also reduce the risk of expelled air and fluid being drawn back into the system. If such a kit is not available, the basic (two-man) method must be used, which is described in detail below.
9 If a kit is to be used, prepare the vehicle as described previously, and follow the kit manufacturer's instructions, as the procedure may vary slightly according to the type being used; generally, they are as outlined below in the relevant sub-section.
10 Whichever method is used, the same sequence must be followed (paragraphs 11 and 12) to ensure that the removal of all air from the system.

Bleeding sequence

11 If the system has been only partially disconnected, and suitable precautions were taken to minimise fluid loss, it should be necessary to bleed only that part of the system (ie the primary or secondary circuit).
12 If the complete system is to be bled, then it should be done working in the following sequence:
a) Left-hand rear wheel.
b) Right-hand front wheel.
c) Right-hand rear wheel.
d) Left-hand front wheel.

Bleeding - basic (two-man) method

13 Collect a clean glass jar, a suitable length of plastic or rubber tubing which is a tight fit over the bleed screw, and a ring spanner to fit the screw. The help of an assistant will also be required.
14 Remove the dust cap from the first screw in the sequence (if not already done) **(see illustrations)**. Fit a suitable spanner and tube

to the screw, place the other end of the tube in the jar, and pour in sufficient fluid to cover the end of the tube.
15 Ensure that the master cylinder reservoir fluid level is maintained at least above the "MIN" level line throughout the procedure.
16 Have the assistant fully depress the brake pedal several times to build up pressure, then maintain it on the final downstroke.
17 While pedal pressure is maintained, unscrew the bleed screw (approximately one turn) and allow the compressed fluid and air to flow into the jar. The assistant should maintain pedal pressure, following the pedal down to the floor if necessary, and should not release the pedal until instructed to do so. When the flow stops, tighten the bleed screw again, have the assistant release the pedal slowly, and recheck the reservoir fluid level.
18 Repeat the steps given in paragraphs 16 and 17 until the fluid emerging from the bleed screw is free from air bubbles. If the master cylinder has been drained and refilled, and air is being bled from the first screw in the sequence, allow approximately five seconds between cycles for the master cylinder passages to refill.
19 When no more air bubbles appear, tighten the bleed screw securely, remove the tube and spanner, and refit the dust cap (where applicable). Do not overtighten the bleed screw.
20 Repeat the procedure on the remaining screws in the sequence, until all air is removed from the system, and the brake pedal feels firm again.

Bleeding - using a one-way valve kit

21 As their name implies, these kits consist of a length of tubing with a one-way valve fitted, to prevent expelled air and fluid being drawn back into the system; some kits include a translucent container, which can be positioned so that the air bubbles can be more easily seen flowing from the end of the tube.
22 The kit is connected to the bleed screw, which is then opened. The user returns to the

2.14a Bleed screw dust cap (arrowed) - rear drum brake shown

2.14b Removing the dust cap from a front caliper bleed screw

2.22 One-way valve brake bleeding kit connected to a front caliper

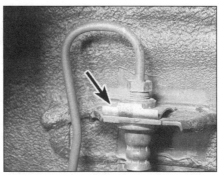

3.2a Brake pipe union-to-bracket securing clip (arrowed)

3.2b Removing a front brake hose-to-bracket securing clip

driver's seat, depresses the brake pedal with a smooth, steady stroke, and slowly releases it; this is repeated until the expelled fluid is clear of air bubbles **(see illustration)**.

23 Note that these kits simplify work so much that it is easy to forget the master cylinder reservoir fluid level; ensure that this is maintained at least above the "MIN" level line at all times.

Bleeding - using a pressure-bleeding kit

24 These kits are usually operated by the reservoir of pressurised air contained in the spare tyre. However, note that it will probably be necessary to reduce the pressure to a lower level than normal; refer to the instructions supplied with the kit.

25 By connecting a pressurised, fluid-filled container to the master cylinder reservoir, bleeding can be carried out simply by opening each screw in turn (in the specified sequence), and allowing the fluid to flow out until no more air bubbles can be seen in the expelled fluid.

26 This method has the advantage that the large reservoir of fluid provides an additional safeguard against air being drawn into the system during bleeding.

27 Pressure-bleeding is particularly effective when bleeding "difficult" systems, or when bleeding the complete system at the time of routine fluid renewal.

All methods

28 When bleeding is complete, and firm pedal feel is restored, wash off any spilt fluid, tighten the bleed screws securely, and refit their dust caps (where applicable).

29 Check the hydraulic fluid level in the master cylinder reservoir, and top-up if necessary (Chapter 1).

30 Discard any hydraulic fluid that has been bled from the system; it will not be fit for re-use.

31 Check the feel of the brake pedal. If it feels at all spongy, air must still be present in the system, and further bleeding is required. Failure to bleed satisfactorily after a reasonable repetition of the bleeding procedure may be due to worn master cylinder seals.

3 Hydraulic pipes and hoses - renewal

Note: *Before starting work, refer to the note at the beginning of Section 2 concerning the dangers of hydraulic fluid.*

1 If any pipe or hose is to be renewed, minimise fluid loss by first removing the master cylinder reservoir cap, then tighten the cap down onto a piece of polythene to obtain an airtight seal. Alternatively, flexible hoses can be sealed, if required, using a proprietary brake hose clamp; metal brake pipe unions can be plugged (if care is taken not to allow dirt into the system) or capped immediately they are disconnected. Place a wad of rag under any union that is to be disconnected, to catch any spilt fluid.

2 If a flexible hose is to be disconnected, unscrew the brake pipe union nut before removing the spring clip which secures the hose to its mounting bracket **(see illustrations)**.

3 To unscrew the union nuts, it is preferable to obtain a brake pipe spanner of the correct size; these are available from most large motor accessory shops. Failing this, a close-fitting open-ended spanner will be required, though if the nuts are tight or corroded, their flats may be rounded-off if the spanner slips. In such a case, a self-locking wrench is often the only way to unscrew a stubborn union, but it follows that the pipe and the damaged nuts must be renewed on reassembly. Always clean a union and surrounding area before disconnecting it. If disconnecting a component with more than one union, make a careful note of the connections before disturbing any of them.

4 If a brake pipe is to be renewed, it can be obtained, cut to length and with the union nuts and end flares in place, from Nissan dealers. All that is then necessary is to bend it to shape, following the line of the original, before fitting it to the vehicle. Alternatively, most motor accessory shops can make up brake pipes from kits, but this requires very careful measurement of the original, to ensure that the replacement is of the correct length.

The safest answer is usually to take the original to the shop as a pattern.

5 On refitting, do not overtighten the union nuts. It is not necessary to exercise brute force to obtain a sound joint.

6 Ensure that the pipes and hoses are correctly routed, with no kinks, and that they are secured in the clips or brackets provided. After fitting, remove the polythene from the reservoir, and bleed the hydraulic system as described in Section 2. Wash off any spilt fluid, and check carefully for fluid leaks.

4 Front brake pads - renewal

Warning: Renew BOTH sets of front brake pads at the same time - NEVER renew the pads on only one wheel, as uneven braking may result.

Warning: Note that the dust created by wear of the pads may contain asbestos, which is a health hazard. Never blow it out with compressed air, and don't inhale any of it. An approved filtering mask should be worn when working on the brakes. DO NOT use petrol or petroleum-based solvents to clean brake parts; use brake cleaner or methylated spirit only.

Note: *Suitable locking compound will be required to coat the threads of the caliper guide pin bolt(s) on refitting.*

1 Chock the rear wheels, apply the handbrake, then jack up the front of the vehicle and support it on axle stands (see *"Jacking, towing and wheel changing"*). Remove the front roadwheels. (Note the white paint blob on one of the roadwheel studs - for wheel alignment on refitting.)

2 Working on one side of the vehicle, push the caliper piston into its bore by pulling the caliper outwards.

Models with Girling-type front caliper

3 Unscrew the upper and lower caliper guide pin bolts (if necessary, use a slim open-ended

9

4.3 Removing the caliper lower guide pin bolt (arrowed) - Girling-type caliper

4.12a Refit the anti-rattle clips to the caliper mounting bracket - Girling-type caliper

4.12b Refit the inboard pad to the caliper mounting bracket . . .

spanner to counterhold the head of the guide pin), then lift the caliper from the hub/disc assembly (see illustration). Note that the outboard pad may be retained in the caliper bracket. Do not depress the brake pedal until the caliper is refitted.

4 Ensure that the caliper is adequately supported (do not allow the caliper to hang from the brake hose), then withdraw the brake pads. Note that the inboard pad is clipped into the caliper piston.

5 Where applicable, recover the shims from the rear of the pads.

6 First measure the thickness of each brake pad's friction material. If either pad is worn at any point to the specified minimum thickness or less, all four pads must be renewed. Also, the pads should be renewed if any are fouled with oil or grease; there is no satisfactory way of degreasing friction material, once contaminated. If any of the brake pads are worn unevenly, or are fouled with oil or grease, trace and rectify the cause before reassembly. New brake pads and shim/clip kits are available from Nissan dealers. Do not be tempted to swap brake pads over to compensate for uneven wear.

7 If the brake pads are still serviceable, carefully clean them using a clean, fine wire brush or similar, paying particular attention to the sides and back of the metal backing. Where applicable, clean out the grooves in the friction material, and pick out any large embedded particles of dirt or debris.

8 Remove the anti-rattle clips from the caliper bracket, and clean the surfaces of the bracket, clips, and the pad locations in the caliper body/mounting bracket.

9 Prior to fitting the pads, check that the guide pins are free to slide easily in the caliper body/mounting bracket, and check that the rubber guide pin gaiters are undamaged. Brush the dust and dirt from the caliper and piston, but do not inhale it, as it is a health hazard. Inspect the dust seal around the piston for damage, and the piston for evidence of fluid leaks, corrosion or damage. If attention to any of these components is necessary, refer to Section 9.

10 If new brake pads are to be fitted, the caliper piston must be pushed back into the cylinder, to make room for them. Either use a G-clamp or similar tool, or use suitable pieces of wood as levers. Provided that the master cylinder reservoir has not been overfilled with hydraulic fluid, there should be no spillage, but keep a careful watch on the fluid level while retracting the piston. If the fluid level rises above the "MAX" level line at any time, the surplus should be siphoned off or ejected via a plastic tube connected to the bleed screw (see Section 2). Note: Do not syphon the fluid by mouth, as it is poisonous; use a syringe or an old poultry baster.

11 Apply a little anti-squeal brake grease to the contact surfaces of the pad backing plates and the shims (where applicable), but take great care not to allow any grease onto the

pad friction linings. Similarly, apply brake grease to the contact surfaces of the anti-rattle clips - again take care not to apply excess grease, which may contaminate the pads.

12 Refit the anti-rattle clips to the caliper mounting bracket, then refit the pads and shims (where applicable), in the positions noted before removal, ensuring that the pad friction material is against the disc. Note that the outboard pad should be fitted to the caliper mounting bracket, and the inboard pad should be fitted to the caliper. Ensure that the inboard pad retaining clip is securely engaged with the caliper piston (see illustrations).

13 Slide the caliper into position on the mounting bracket, then apply a little locking fluid to the threads of the caliper guide pin bolts, and refit the bolts (see illustrations). Tighten the bolts to the specified torque wrench setting.

14 Check that the caliper body slides smoothly on the guide pins.

15 Repeat the procedure on the remaining front caliper.

16 With both sets of front brake pads refitted, depress the brake pedal repeatedly until the pads are pressed into firm contact with the brake disc, and normal pedal pressure is restored.

17 Refit the roadwheels, and lower the vehicle to the ground.

18 Finally, check the hydraulic fluid level as described in Chapter 1.

4 12c . . . and engage the outboard pad with the caliper piston - Girling-type caliper

4.13a Sliding the caliper into position on the mounting bracket - Girling-type caliper

4.13b Apply locking fluid to the threads of the caliper guide pin bolts - Girling caliper

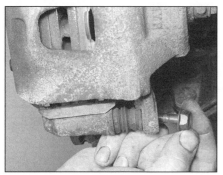

4.19 Removing the caliper lower guide pin bolt - Bendix-type caliper

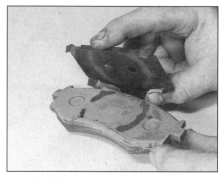

4.20 Pivot the caliper body upwards to expose the brake pads - Bendix caliper

4.22 Withdraw the pads and shims - Bendix caliper

Models with Bendix-type front caliper

19 Unscrew the caliper lower guide pin bolt (if necessary, use a slim open-ended spanner to counterhold the head of the guide pin), then remove the bolt **(see illustration)**.

20 Pivot the caliper body upwards to expose the brake pads **(see illustration)**. **Do not depress the brake pedal until the caliper is refitted.** Take care not to strain the brake fluid hose.

21 Note the locations and orientation of the shims fitted to the rear of each pad, and the anti-rattle clips fitted to the top and bottom of the pads.

22 Withdraw the pads and shims **(see illustration)**.

23 Proceed as described in paragraphs 6 to 11 inclusive.

24 Refit the anti-rattle clips to the caliper mounting bracket, then refit the pads and shims, in the positions noted before removal, ensuring that the pad friction material is against the disc **(see illustrations)**.

25 Pivot the caliper back into position, over the pads and mounting bracket.

26 Apply a little locking fluid to the threads of the caliper lower guide pin bolt, then refit the bolt and tighten to the specified torque.

27 Proceed as described in paragraphs 14 to 18 inclusive.

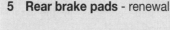

5 Rear brake pads - renewal

Warning: Renew BOTH sets of rear brake pads at the same time - NEVER renew the pads on only one wheel, as uneven braking may result.

Warning: Before starting work, refer to the warning given at the beginning of Section 4, concerning the dangers of asbestos dust.

Note: *Suitable locking compound will be required to coat the threads of the caliper guide pin bolt(s) on refitting.*

1 Chock the front wheels, then jack up the rear of the vehicle, and support on axle stands (see *"Jacking, towing and wheel changing"*). Remove the rear roadwheels, and release the handbrake fully.

2 Working on one side of the vehicle, release the spring clip securing the handbrake cable to the bracket on the brake caliper, then release the cable from the bracket, and disconnect the end of the cable from the lever on the caliper **(see illustrations)**.

3 Push the caliper piston into its bore by pulling the caliper outwards.

4.24a Refit the anti-rattle clips to the caliper mounting bracket - Bendix caliper

4.24b Refit the outboard . . .

4.24c . . . and inboard pads - Bendix caliper

5.2a Release the spring clip . . .

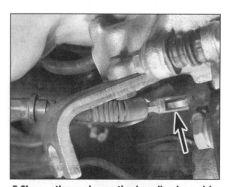

5.2b . . . then release the handbrake cable from the bracket and the lever on the caliper (arrowed)

9

5.4 Removing the caliper lower guide pin bolt

5.10a Using a retractor tool to retract a rear caliper piston

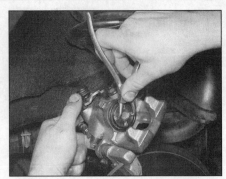

5.10b Using a pair of long-nosed pliers (circlip pliers shown) to retract a rear caliper piston

4 Unscrew the caliper lower guide pin bolt **(see illustration)**. If necessary, use a slim open-ended spanner to counterhold the head of the guide pin.

5 Pivot the caliper body upwards to expose the brake pads. **Do not** depress the brake pedal until the caliper is refitted. Take care not to strain the brake fluid hose. Where applicable, note the locations and orientation of the shims fitted to the rear of each pad and, where applicable, the anti-rattle shims fitted to the top and bottom of the pads.

6 Withdraw the pads, and where applicable, the shims and the anti-rattle springs.

7 First measure the thickness of each brake pad's friction material. If either pad is worn at any point to the specified minimum thickness or less, all four pads must be renewed. Also, the pads should be renewed if any are fouled with oil or grease; there is no satisfactory way of degreasing friction material, once contaminated. If any of the brake pads are worn unevenly, or are fouled with oil or grease, trace and rectify the cause before reassembly. New brake pads and shim/spring kits are available from Nissan dealers. Do not be tempted to swap brake pads over to compensate for uneven wear.

8 If the brake pads are still serviceable, carefully clean them using a clean, fine wire brush or similar, paying particular attention to the sides and back of the metal backing. Where applicable, clean out the grooves in the friction material, and pick out any large

embedded particles of dirt or debris. Carefully clean the pad locations in the caliper body/mounting bracket.

9 Prior to fitting the pads, check that the guide pins are free to slide easily in the caliper body/mounting bracket, and check that the rubber guide pin gaiters are undamaged. Brush the dust and dirt from the caliper and piston, but *do not* inhale it, as it is a health hazard. Inspect the dust seal around the piston for damage, and the piston for evidence of fluid leaks, corrosion or damage. If attention to any of these components is necessary, refer to Section 5.

10 If new brake pads are to be fitted, the caliper piston must be pushed back into the cylinder, to make room for them. To retract the piston, ideally a suitable retractor tool should be used (available from motor factors). Alternatively, engage a suitable pair of long-nosed pliers with the notches in the piston, then turn the piston clockwise (viewed from the outboard end of the caliper), whilst simultaneously pushing it into the caliper **(see illustrations)**. Take care not to damage the surface of the piston, or twist the dust seal. Provided that the master cylinder reservoir has not been overfilled with hydraulic fluid, there should be no spillage, but keep a careful watch on the fluid level while retracting the piston. If the fluid level rises above the "MAX" level line at any time, the surplus should be siphoned off or ejected via a plastic tube connected to the bleed screw (see Section 2).

Note: *Do not syphon the fluid by mouth, as it is poisonous; use a syringe or an old poultry baster.*

11 Apply a little anti-squeal brake grease to the contact surfaces of the pad backing plates and the shims (where applicable), but take great care not to allow any grease onto the pad friction linings. Similarly, where applicable, apply brake grease to the contact surfaces of the anti-rattle springs - again take care not to apply excess grease, which may contaminate the pads. Note that new pads may be supplied with an anti-squeal coating on their contact faces, in which case there is no need to apply brake grease.

12 Where applicable, refit the anti-rattle springs to the caliper mounting bracket, then refit the pads and the shims (where applicable), in the positions noted before removal **(see illustrations)**. Ensure that the pad friction material is against the disc.

13 Pivot the caliper body downwards over the brake pads. Ensure that the peg on the back of the inboard pad engages with the nearest notch in the piston. It may be necessary to rotate the piston as described in paragraph 10 to align the nearest notch with the peg.

14 Coat the threads of the caliper lower guide pin bolt with locking fluid, then refit the bolt, and tighten it to the specified torque.

15 Check that the caliper body slides smoothly on the guide pins.

16 Reconnect the end of the handbrake cable to the lever. Refit the cable mounting bracket, and where applicable, the spring clip. Where applicable, ensure that the locating peg on the mounting bracket engages with the corresponding hole in the caliper body.

17 Repeat the procedure on the remaining rear caliper.

18 With both sets of rear brake pads refitted, operate the handbrake repeatedly until the correct brake pad-to-disc clearance is established (adjustment occurs automatically when the handbrake is operated).

19 Depress the brake pedal repeatedly to ensure that normal pedal pressure is restored.

20 Refit the roadwheels, and lower the vehicle to the ground.

21 Finally check the hydraulic fluid level as described in Chapter 1.

5.12a Refit the inboard . . .

5.12b . . . and outboard pads to the caliper

6 Rear brake shoes - renewal

 Warning: Renew BOTH sets of rear brake shoes at the same time - NEVER renew the shoes on only one wheel, as uneven braking may result.

 Warning: Before starting work, refer to the warning given at the beginning of Section 4, concerning the dangers of asbestos dust.

1 Remove the rear brake drums, as described in Section 8.

2 Working on one side of the vehicle, brush the dirt and dust from the brake backplate and drum. **Do not** inhale the dust, as it may be a health hazard.

3 Note the position of each shoe, and the location of the return and steady springs. Also make a note of the adjuster component locations, in case the components are disturbed during the removal procedure **(see illustrations)**.

4 Remove the shoe hold-down springs **(see illustration)**. Use pliers to depress the outer spring cups, and turn them through 90°.

5 Recover the springs and cups (and where applicable, the spring seats), and remove the spring retainer pins from the backplate.

6 Carefully pull the leading brake shoe forwards from the backplate, and using a suitable pair of pliers, unhook and remove the lower return spring.

7 Disengage the lower ends of the shoes from the bottom anchor, and the pull the upper ends of the shoes from the wheel cylinder, then withdraw the shoe assembly, complete with the adjuster and handbrake operating components, and unhook the handbrake cable from the lever on the trailing brake shoe. Where applicable, recover the return spring fitted over the cable.

8 If necessary, position a rubber band or a cable-tie over the wheel cylinder, to prevent the pistons from being ejected. If there is any evidence of fluid leakage from the wheel cylinder, renew it or overhaul it as described in Section 11.

9 Unhook the upper return spring from the shoes, then withdraw the adjuster strut components, noting their locations and orientation. Unhook the adjuster spring.

10 If desired, the return spring can be withdrawn from the handbrake cable **(see illustration)**.

11 Working on the trailing brake shoe, prise off the retaining clip, then remove the pivot pin and withdraw the handbrake operating lever, and where applicable, the adjuster operating lever.

12 Transfer the handbrake operating lever, and where applicable, the adjuster operating lever, to the new trailing shoe as required, and secure with a new retaining clip. Note that the

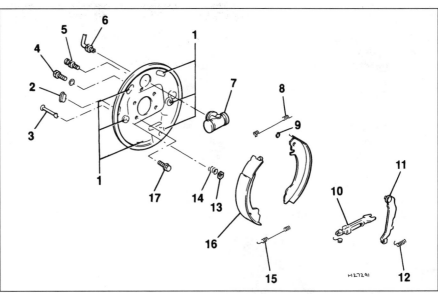

6.3a Rear brake shoe components - Saloon and Hatchback models

1 Brake grease application points	6 Brake fluid pipe	13 Hold-down spring cup
2 Rubber grommet	7 Wheel cylinder	14 Hold-down spring
3 Shoe hold-down pin	8 Shoe upper return spring	15 Shoe lower return spring
4 Wheel cylinder securing bolt	9 Spring clip	16 Brake shoe
5 Bleed screw	10 Adjuster strut assembly	17 Brake backplate securing bolt
	11 Handbrake operating lever	
	12 Adjuster spring	

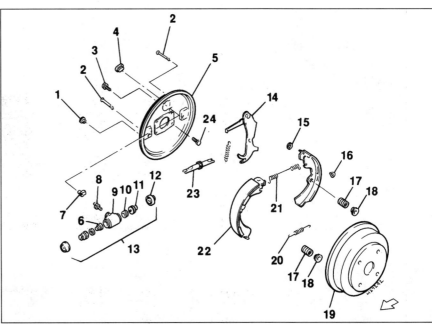

6.3b Rear brake shoe components - Estate models

1 Rubber grommet	9 Wheel cylinder body	17 Hold-down spring
2 Shoe hold-down pin	10 Piston cup	18 Hold-down spring cup
3 Wheel cylinder securing bolt	11 Piston	19 Brake drum
4 Rubber grommet	12 Dust cover	20 Shoe lower return spring
5 Brake backplate	13 Wheel cylinder assembly	21 Shoe upper return spring
6 Spring	14 Adjuster/handbrake operating lever assembly	22 Brake shoe
7 Bleed screw dust cover	15 Washer	23 Adjuster strut assembly
8 Bleed screw	16 Spring clip	24 Brake backplate securing bolt

9

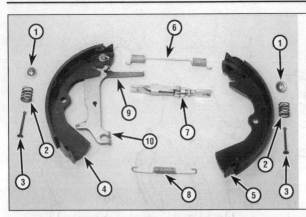

1 Hold-down spring cup
2 Hold-down spring
3 Hold-down spring retainer pin
4 Trailing brake shoe
5 Leading brake shoe
6 Upper return spring
7 Adjuster strut
8 Lower return spring
9 Adjuster operating lever
10 Handbrake operating lever

6.3c Exploded view of rear drum brake components - right-hand side shown

6.4 Removing a brake shoe hold-down spring

6.10 The return spring can be withdrawn from the handbrake cable

levers and adjuster strut components are different on each side of the vehicle - take care not to mix up the components. Make sure that the handbrake operating lever spring is correctly located **(see illustrations)**.

13 Shorten the adjuster strut to its minimum length by turning the toothed wheel, and apply a small amount of brake grease to the contact faces of the adjuster strut and handbrake operating lever/adjuster operating lever, as applicable.

14 Where applicable, fit the return spring over the handbrake cable.

15 Apply brake grease sparingly to the shoe

contact surfaces of the brake backplate **(see illustration)**.

16 Offer up the trailing shoe to the backplate, then engage the handbrake cable with the operating lever on the shoe. Manipulate the shoe into position, and secure with the hold-down pin, spring and cup **(see illustrations)**.

17 Engage the adjuster strut with the relevant cut-out in the trailing shoe. Ensure that the adjuster strut is fitted the correct way round. Where applicable, refit the adjuster spring, and on Estate models, ensure that the adjuster lever engages with the toothed wheel **(see illustrations)**.

18 Engage the upper return spring with the trailing shoe, noting that where applicable, the paint mark on the spring should be positioned

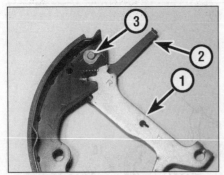

6.12a Front view of trailing shoe components

1 Handbrake operating lever
2 Adjuster operating lever
3 Retaining clip

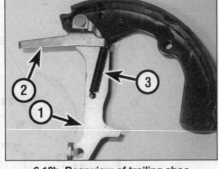

6.12b Rear view of trailing shoe components

1 Handbrake operating lever
2 Adjuster operating lever
3 Handbrake operating lever spring

6.15 Apply brake grease to the shoe contact faces of the backplate

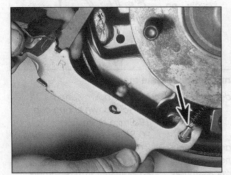

6.16a Engage the handbrake cable (arrowed) with the operating lever . . .

6.16b . . . then manipulate the shoe into position . . .

6.16c . . . and secure with the hold-down pin, spring . . .

6.16d . . . and cup

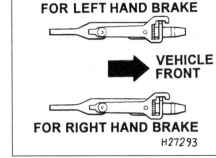

6.17a Adjuster strut orientation - Saloon and Hatchback models

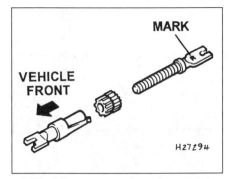

6.17b Adjuster strut orientation - Estate models

downwards on the leading shoe side (see illustration).

19 Engage the free end of the upper return spring with the leading shoe, then manipulate the leading shoe into position against the lower anchor, and fit the lower return spring (see illustrations).

20 Refit the hold-down pin, spring and cup to secure the leading shoe (see illustration).

21 Check that all components have been correctly refitted, and check that the adjuster mechanism operates correctly.

22 Turn the adjuster wheel to ensure that the diameter of the shoes is less than that of the drum.

23 Repeat the procedure on the remaining side of the vehicle, then refit the brake drums as described in Section 8.

---

7 Brake disc - inspection, removal and refitting

 Warning: Before starting work, refer to the warning at the beginning of Section 4 concerning the dangers of asbestos dust.

Front disc

Inspection

Note: *If either disc requires renewal, BOTH should be renewed at the same time, to ensure even and consistent braking. New brake pads should also be fitted.*

1 Chock the rear wheels, apply the handbrake, then jack up the front of the vehicle and support it on axle stands (see *"Jacking, towing and wheel changing"*). Remove the appropriate front roadwheel.

2 Slowly rotate the brake disc so that the full area of both sides can be checked; remove the brake pads (see Section 4) if better access is required to the inboard surface. Light scoring is normal in the area swept by the brake pads, but if heavy scoring or cracks are found, the disc must be renewed.

3 It is normal to find a lip of rust and brake dust around the disc's perimeter; this can be scraped off if required. If, however, a lip has formed due to excessive wear of the brake pad swept area, then the disc's thickness must be measured using a micrometer. Take measurements at several places around the disc, at the inside and outside of the pad swept area; if the disc has worn at any point to the specified minimum thickness or less, the disc must be renewed.

4 If the disc is thought to be warped, it can be checked for run-out. Either use a dial gauge mounted on any convenient fixed point, while the disc is slowly rotated, or use feeler blades to measure (at several points all around the disc) the clearance between the disc and a fixed point, such as the caliper mounting bracket. If the measurements obtained are at the specified maximum or beyond, the disc is excessively warped, and must be renewed; however, it is worth checking first that the hub bearing is in good condition (Chapters 1

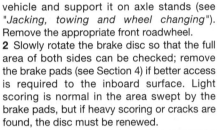

6.17c Engaging the adjuster strut with the trailing shoe - Estate model

6.18 Engage the upper return spring with the trailing shoe

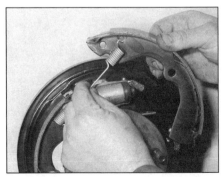

6.19a Engage the return spring with the leading shoe . . .

6.19b . . . then fit the lower return spring

6.20 Refitting the leading shoe hold-down spring

9

7.8 Removing a front brake disc

and/or 10). Also try the effect of removing the disc and turning it through 180°, to reposition it on the hub; if the run-out is still excessive, the disc must be renewed.

5 Check the disc for cracks, especially around the wheel stud holes, and any other wear or damage, and renew if necessary.

Removal

6 If not already done, chock the rear wheels, apply the handbrake, then jack up the front of the vehicle and support it on axle stands (see *"Jacking, towing and wheel changing"*). Remove the appropriate front roadwheel.

7 Unscrew the two bolts securing the caliper mounting bracket to the hub carrier. Withdraw the caliper assembly, and suspend it using wire or string. Take care not to strain the brake fluid hose - if necessary release the hose from the securing clip(s).

 HAYNES HiNT *Place a clean spacer (of the same thickness as the disc) between the pads, to prevent them from being dislodged.*

8 If the original disc is to be refitted, mark the relationship between the disc and the hub, then pull the disc from the roadwheel studs **(see illustration)**.

9 If the disc is stuck, it can be pushed off by screwing two M8 bolts into the holes provided in the disc, and evenly tightening the bolts to push the disc from the hub.

Refitting

10 Ensure that the mating faces of the disc and the hub are clean and flat. If necessary, wipe the mating surfaces clean.

11 If the original disc is being refitted, align the marks made on the disc and hub before removal, then refit the disc.

12 If a new disc has been fitted, use a suitable solvent to wipe any preservative coating from the disc.

13 Refit the caliper, ensuring that the pads locate correctly over the disc, then tighten the caliper bracket securing bolts to the specified torque. Where applicable, refit the brake fluid hose to the clip(s).

14 Depress the brake pedal repeatedly until the pads are pressed into firm contact with the brake disc, and normal pedal pressure is restored.

15 Refit the roadwheel, and lower the vehicle to the ground.

Rear disc

Inspection

Note: *If either disc requires renewal, BOTH should be renewed at the same time, to ensure even and consistent braking. New brake pads should also be fitted.*

16 Chock the front wheels, then jack up the rear of the vehicle and support it on axle stands (see *"Jacking, towing and wheel changing"*). Remove the appropriate rear roadwheel.

17 Fully release the handbrake.

18 Proceed as described for the front disc in paragraphs 2 to 5, but refer to Section 5 if the brake pads are to be removed.

Removal

19 If not already done, chock the front wheels, then jack up the rear of the vehicle, and support securely on axle stands (see *"Jacking, towing and wheel changing"*). Remove the appropriate rear roadwheel.

20 Unbolt the handbrake cable mounting bracket from the caliper, then disconnect the end of the cable from the lever on the caliper. It may be necessary to release the spring clip securing the cable to the mounting bracket to enable the cable to be disconnected.

21 Proceed as described for the front brake disc in paragraphs 7 to 9.

Refitting

22 Proceed as described for the front brake disc in paragraphs 10 to 13.

23 Reconnect the handbrake cable to the lever on the caliper, then refit the cable mounting bracket, and where applicable, the spring clip. Where applicable, ensure that the locating peg on the mounting bracket engages with the corresponding hole in the caliper body.

24 Operate the handbrake repeatedly until the correct brake pad-to-disc clearance is established (adjustment occurs automatically when the handbrake is operated).

25 Depress the brake pedal repeatedly to ensure that normal pedal pressure is restored.

26 Refit the roadwheel, and lower the vehicle to the ground.

8 Rear brake drum - removal, inspection and refitting

⚠ *Warning: Before starting work, refer to the warning at the beginning of Section 4 concerning the dangers of asbestos dust.*

Removal

1 Chock the front wheels, then jack up the rear of the vehicle and support it on axle stands (see *"Jacking, towing and wheel changing"*). Remove the appropriate rear roadwheel.

2 Fully release the handbrake.

3 If the drum cannot easily be pulled from the wheel studs, retract the brake shoes as follows.

4 Remove the blanking plug from the rear of the brake backplate. Insert a suitable tool through the hole in the backplate and through the hole in the shoe, until the tool contacts the handbrake operating lever. Lightly tap the tool in order to free the adjuster mechanism and retract the shoes **(see illustrations)**.

5 If the original drum is to be refitted, mark the relationship between the drum and the hub, then pull the drum from the roadwheel studs.

6 If the drum is still tight, it can be pushed off by screwing two M8 bolts into the holes provided in the drum, and evenly tightening the bolts to push the drum from the hub **(see illustration)**.

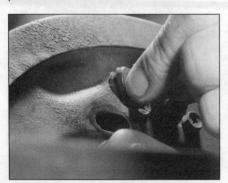

8.4a Remove the blanking plug from the brake backplate . . .

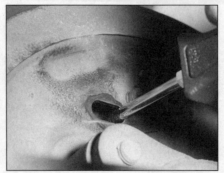

8.4b . . . and use a screwdriver to free the handbrake adjuster mechanism

8.6 Using two M8 bolts to remove a brake drum

Inspection

Note: *If either drum requires renewal, BOTH should be renewed at the same time, to ensure even and consistent braking. New brake shoes should also be fitted.*

7 Working carefully, remove all traces of brake dust from the drum, but *avoid inhaling the dust, as it is a health hazard.*

8 Clean the outside of the drum, and check it for obvious signs of wear or damage, such as cracks around the roadwheel stud holes; renew the drum if necessary.

9 Carefully examine the inside of the drum. Light scoring of the friction surface is normal, but if heavy scoring is found, the drum must be renewed.

10 It is usual to find a lip on the drum's inboard edge which consists of a mixture of rust and brake dust; this should be scraped away, to leave a smooth surface which can be polished with fine (120- to 150-grade) emery paper. If, however, the lip is due to the friction surface being recessed by excessive wear, then the drum must be renewed.

11 If the drum is thought to be excessively worn, or oval, its internal diameter must be measured at several points using an internal micrometer. Take measurements in pairs, the second at right-angles to the first, and compare the two, to check for signs of ovality. Provided that it does not enlarge the drum to beyond the specified maximum diameter, it may be possible to have the drum refinished by skimming or grinding; if this is not possible, the drums on both sides must be renewed. Note that if the drum is to be skimmed, BOTH drums must be refinished, to maintain a consistent internal diameter on both sides.

Refitting

12 If a new brake drum is to be installed, use a suitable solvent to remove any preservative coating that may have been applied to its internal friction surfaces. Note that it may also be necessary to shorten the adjuster strut length, by rotating the strut wheel, to allow the drum to pass over the brake shoes.

13 If the original drum is being refitted, align the marks made on the drum and hub before removal, then fit the drum over the wheel studs.

14 Depress the footbrake repeatedly to expand the brake shoes against the drum, and ensure that normal pedal pressure is restored.

15 Check and if necessary adjust the handbrake cable as described in Chapter 1.

16 Refit the roadwheel, and lower the vehicle to the ground.

9 Front brake caliper -
removal, overhaul and refitting

⚠ *Warning: Before starting work, refer to the note at the beginning of Section 2 concerning the dangers of hydraulic fluid, and to the warning at the beginning of Section 4 concerning the dangers of asbestos dust.*

Note: *Suitable locking compound will be required to coat the threads of the caliper guide pin bolts on refitting.*

Removal

1 Chock the rear wheels, apply the handbrake, then jack up the front of the vehicle and support it on axle stands (see *"Jacking, towing and wheel changing"*). Remove the appropriate front roadwheel.

2 To minimise fluid loss during the following operations, remove the master cylinder reservoir cap, then tighten it down onto a piece of polythene, to obtain an airtight seal. Alternatively, use a brake hose clamp, a G-clamp or a similar tool to clamp the flexible hose running to the caliper.

3 Clean the area around the fluid hose union on the caliper, then unscrew the hose union banjo bolt. Recover the two sealing washers. Cover the open ends of the banjo and the caliper, to prevent dirt ingress.

4 Remove the brake pads as described in Section 4.

5 Unscrew the caliper upper guide pin bolt. If necessary, use a slim open-ended spanner to counterhold the head of the guide pin.

6 Withdraw the caliper.

7 If desired, the caliper mounting bracket can be unbolted from the hub carrier.

Overhaul

HAYNES HiNT *Before commencing work, ensure that the appropriate caliper overhaul kit is obtained.*

8 With the caliper on the bench, wipe away all traces of dust and dirt, but *avoid inhaling the dust, as it is a health hazard.*

9 Extract the caliper guide pins, if necessary by screwing the bolts into the pins, and pulling on the bolts to withdraw the pins. Peel off the rubber dust cover from each guide pin **(see illustrations)**.

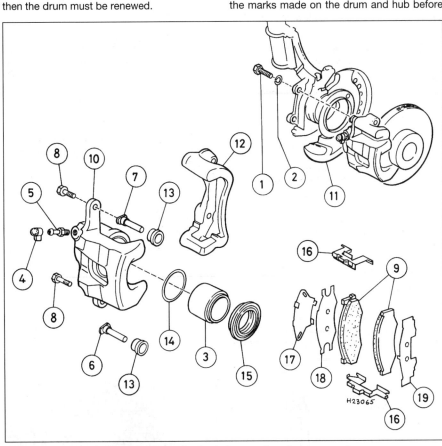

9.9a Girling front brake caliper and pad components

1 *Caliper mounting bracket bolt*	8 *Guide pin bolt*	16 *Anti-rattle spring*
2 *Washer*	9 *Brake pads*	17 *Inboard pad shim retainer (where applicable)*
3 *Piston*	10 *Caliper body*	18 *Inboard pad shim (where applicable)*
4 *Bleed screw dust cap*	11 *Brake disc shield*	19 *Outboard pad shim (where applicable)*
5 *Bleed screw*	12 *Caliper mounting bracket*	
6 *Lower guide pin*	13 *Guide pin dust cover*	
7 *Upper guide pin*	14 *Piston seal*	
	15 *Dust seal*	

9

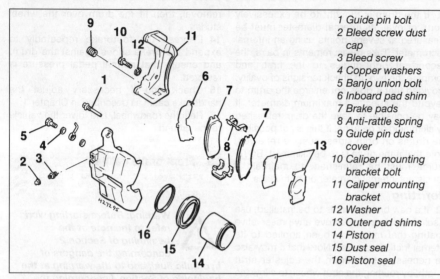

1 Guide pin bolt
2 Bleed screw dust cap
3 Bleed screw
4 Copper washers
5 Banjo union bolt
6 Inboard pad shim
7 Brake pads
8 Anti-rattle spring
9 Guide pin dust cover
10 Caliper mounting bracket bolt
11 Caliper mounting bracket
12 Washer
13 Outer pad shims
14 Piston
15 Dust seal
16 Piston seal

9.9b Bendix front brake caliper and pad components

10 Place a small block of wood between the caliper body and the piston. Remove the piston, including the dust seal, by applying a jet of low-pressure compressed air, such as that from a tyre pump, to the fluid inlet port.

11 Peel the dust seal off the piston, and use a blunt instrument, such as a knitting needle, to extract the piston seal from the caliper cylinder bore.

12 Thoroughly clean all components, using only methylated spirit or clean hydraulic fluid. Never use mineral-based solvents such as petrol or paraffin, which will attack the hydraulic system rubber components.

13 The caliper piston seal and the dust seal, the guide pin dust covers, and the bleed nipple dust cap, are only available as part of a seal kit. Since the manufacturers recommend that the piston seal and dust seal are renewed whenever they are disturbed, all of these components should be discarded, and new ones fitted on reassembly as a matter of course.

14 Carefully examine all parts of the caliper assembly, looking for signs of wear or damage. In particular, the cylinder bore and piston must be free from any signs of scratches, corrosion or wear. If there is any doubt about the condition of any part of the caliper, the relevant part should be renewed; note that if the caliper body or the mounting bracket are to be renewed, they are available only as part of the complete assembly.

15 The manufacturers recommend that minor scratches, rust, etc, may be polished away from the cylinder bore using fine emery paper, but the piston must be renewed to cure such defects. The piston surface is plated, and **must not** be polished with emery or similar abrasives.

16 Check that the threads in the caliper body and the mounting bracket are in good condition. Check that both guide pins are undamaged, and (when cleaned) a reasonably

tight sliding fit in the mounting bracket bores.

17 Use compressed air to blow clear the fluid passages.

Warning: Wear eye protection when using compressed air.

18 Before commencing reassembly, ensure that all components are spotlessly-clean and dry.

19 Soak the new piston seal in clean hydraulic fluid, and fit it to the groove in the cylinder bore, using your fingers only (no tools) to manipulate it into place.

20 Fit the new dust seal to the piston groove, smear clean hydraulic fluid over the piston and caliper cylinder bore, and refit the piston. Press the piston fully into the caliper body, then fit the dust seal to the groove in the caliper body **(see illustration)**.

21 Fit a new rubber dust cover to each guide pin, and apply a smear of brake grease to the guide pins before refitting them to their bores.

Refitting

22 Where applicable, refit the caliper mounting bracket to the hub carrier, and tighten the mounting bolts to the specified torque.

23 Place the caliper in position, then coat the threads of the caliper upper guide pin bolt

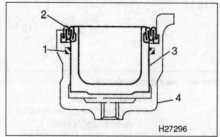

9.20 Correct fitting of caliper piston seal and dust seal

1 Piston seal	3 Piston
2 Dust seal	4 Caliper body

with locking compound, refit the bolt, and tighten it to the specified torque.

24 Refit the brake pads as described in Section 4.

25 Check that the caliper slides smoothly on the mounting bracket.

26 Check that the brake fluid hose is correctly routed, without being twisted, then reconnect the union to the caliper, using two new sealing washers. Refit the union banjo bolt, and tighten to the specified torque.

27 Remove the polythene from the master cylinder reservoir cap, or remove the clamp from the fluid hose, as applicable.

28 Bleed the hydraulic fluid circuit as described in Section 2. Note that if no other part of the system has been disturbed, it should only be necessary to bleed the relevant front circuit.

29 Depress the brake pedal repeatedly to bring the pads into contact with the brake disc, and ensure that normal pedal pressure is restored.

30 Refit the roadwheel, and lower the vehicle to the ground.

10 Rear brake caliper - removal, overhaul and refitting

Warning: Before starting work, refer to the note at the beginning of Section 2 concerning the dangers of hydraulic fluid, and to the warning at the beginning of Section 4 concerning the dangers of asbestos dust.

Note: Suitable locking compound will be required to coat the threads of the caliper guide pin bolts on refitting.

Removal

1 Chock the front wheels, then jack up the rear of the vehicle and support securely on axle stands (see "Jacking, towing and wheel changing"). Remove the appropriate rear roadwheel.

2 Release the spring clip securing the handbrake cable to the mounting bracket, then disconnect the end of the cable from the lever on the caliper **(see illustration)**.

10.2 Disconnecting the handbrake cable from the bracket on the rear caliper

3 To minimise fluid loss during the following operations, remove the master cylinder reservoir cap, then tighten it down onto a piece of polythene, to obtain an airtight seal. Alternatively, use a brake hose clamp, a G-clamp or a similar tool to clamp the flexible hose running to the caliper.

4 Clean the area around the fluid hose union on the caliper, then unscrew the hose union banjo bolt. Recover the two sealing washers. Cover the open ends of the banjo and the caliper, to prevent dirt ingress.

5 Remove the brake pads as described in Section 5.

6 Unscrew the caliper upper guide pin bolt. If necessary, use a slim open-ended spanner to counterhold the head of the guide pin.

7 Withdraw the caliper.

8 If desired, the caliper mounting bracket can be unbolted from the hub carrier.

Overhaul

Note: *Before commencing work, ensure that the appropriate caliper overhaul kit is obtained.*

9 With the caliper on the bench, wipe away all traces of dust and dirt, but *avoid inhaling the dust, as it is a health hazard.*

10 Extract the caliper guide pins by screwing the bolts into the pins, and pulling on the bolts to withdraw the pins. Peel off the rubber dust cover from each guide pin, and the rubber sleeve which may be fitted to the upper guide pin of some models **(see illustration)**.

11 Engage a suitable pair of long-nosed pliers with the notches in the piston, then turn the piston anti-clockwise (viewed from the outboard end of the caliper), to unscrew it from the caliper. Withdraw the piston from the caliper body, and peel off the dust seal.

12 Working inside the rear of the piston, use circlip pliers to extract the circlip, then remove the first spacer, the wave washer, the second spacer, the ball bearing, and the adjusting nut. Prise the cup seal off the adjusting nut.

13 Working inside the caliper cylinder bore, use circlip pliers to extract the circlip, whilst using a suitable length of tubing to compress the spring cap against the spring pressure.

14 With the circlip removed from its groove, allow the spring to push out the components until pressure is relaxed, then withdraw the circlip, the spring cap, the spring and the spring seat.

15 Use circlip pliers to extract the remaining circlip, then withdraw the key plate, the pushrod and the plunger. Prise the sealing O-ring off the pushrod.

16 Using a blunt instrument such as a knitting needle, extract the piston seal from the caliper cylinder bore.

17 Ensure that the pushrod and plunger have been removed (paragraph 15), then unhook the return spring from the handbrake lever, and prise the lever and, where applicable, the cam assembly from the caliper body. On Saloon and Hatchback models, it will be necessary to unscrew the stop-bolt before the lever can be withdrawn.

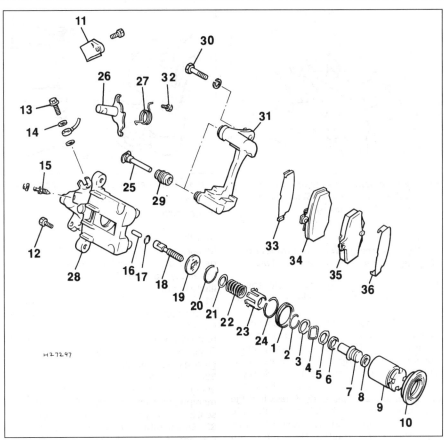

10.10 Rear brake caliper and pad components

1 Piston seal	13 Banjo union bolt	26 Handbrake lever
2 Circlip	14 Copper washers	27 Return spring
3 Spacer	15 Bleed screw	28 Caliper body
4 Wave washer	16 Plunger	29 Guide pin dust cover
5 Spacer	17 O-ring	30 Caliper mounting bracket
6 Ball bearing	18 Pushrod	bolt
7 Adjusting nut	19 Key plate	31 Caliper mounting bracket
8 Cup seal	20 Circlip	32 Stop-bolt
9 Piston	21 Spring seat	33 Inboard pad shim
10 Dust seal	22 Spring	34 Inboard pad
11 Handbrake cable mounting	23 Spring cap	35 Outboard pad
bracket	24 Circlip	36 Outboard pad shim
12 Guide pin bolts	25 Guide pin	

18 On Estate models, clamp the cam gently in a soft-jawed vice, then unscrew the retaining nut, and withdraw the spring washer, the return spring, the lever, and the dust cover, from the cam.

19 Thoroughly clean all components, using only methylated spirit or clean hydraulic fluid. Never use mineral-based solvents such as petrol or paraffin, which will attack the hydraulic system rubber components.

20 Discard all seals, cups, dust covers and other rubber components. These are available as part of a caliper seal kit, and should be renewed as a matter of course whenever they are disturbed.

21 Carefully examine all parts of the caliper assembly, looking for signs of wear or damage. In particular, the cylinder bore and piston must be free from any signs of

scratches, corrosion or wear. If there is any doubt about the condition of any part of the caliper, the relevant part should be renewed. Note that if the caliper body or the mounting bracket are to be renewed, they are available only as part of the complete assembly.

22 Minor scratches, rust, etc, may be polished away from the cylinder bore using fine emery paper, but the piston must be renewed to cure such defects. The piston surface is plated, and **must not** be polished with emery or similar abrasives.

23 Check that the threads in the caliper body and the mounting bracket are in good condition. Check that both guide pins are undamaged, and (when cleaned) a reasonably tight sliding fit in the mounting bracket bores.

24 Use compressed air to blow clear the fluid passages.

9

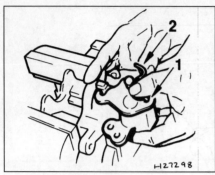

10.27 Fit the handbrake lever return spring in the order shown - Saloon and Hatchback models

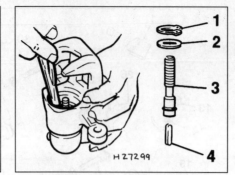

10.30 Rear caliper pushrod components

1	Circlip	3	Pushrod
2	Key plate	4	Plunger

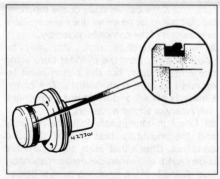

 Warning: Wear eye protection when using compressed air.

25 Before commencing reassembly, ensure that all components are spotlessly-clean and dry.

26 On Estate models, fit the new dust seal to the handbrake lever cam, and locate the lever on the cam flats. Refit the return spring, spring washer, and nut. Tighten the nut securely, taking care not to overtighten it. Apply a smear of brake grease to the cam, then slide the cam into the caliper body. Check that the assembly is correctly installed, and that the cam cut-out aligns with the pushrod aperture when the lever is rotated. Hook the return spring over its stop and into the lever.

27 On Saloon and Hatchback models, slide the handbrake lever into the caliper body, ensuring that the lever cam cut-out aligns with the pushrod aperture when the lever is rotated. Refit and tighten the stop-bolt, then refit the return spring, hooking it into position as shown **(see illustration)**.

28 Soak the new piston seal in clean hydraulic fluid, and fit it to the groove in the cylinder bore, using your fingers only (no tools) to manipulate it into position.

29 Fit a new O-ring to the pushrod, and apply a smear of rubber grease to the plunger and the pushrod. Assemble the plunger and pushrod, and fit them to the caliper body.

30 Refit the key plate so that its cut-out fits

over the squared section of the pushrod, and its convex locating pip matches the concave depression in the caliper body. Secure the assembly by refitting the circlip **(see illustration)**.

31 Refit the spring seat, the spring and the spring cap, then compress the spring cap (using a suitable length of tubing as during removal) while refitting the securing circlip. Check that the circlip is correctly seated in its groove **(see illustration)**.

32 Fit the new cup seal to the adjusting nut, using only your fingers (no tools) to manipulate it into position. Ensure that the seal is correctly fitted **(see illustration)**.

33 Smear rubber grease over the cup seal lips, and fit the adjusting nut into the piston.

34 Pack the ball bearing with brake grease and refit it, followed by the spacer, the wave washer, and the remaining spacer. Secure the components with the remaining circlip **(see illustration)**.

35 Apply a smear of rubber grease to the inner and outer lips of the new dust seal, then fit it to the piston.

36 Smear clean hydraulic fluid over the

piston and the caliper cylinder bore, then refit the piston assembly, and screw it in clockwise (using a retractor tool or long-nosed pliers if necessary - see Section 5) until it seats.

37 Engage the dust seal with the caliper body.

38 Fit a new rubber dust cover to each guide pin (also fit a new rubber sleeve to the upper guide pin, where applicable). Apply a smear of brake grease to the guide pins before refitting them to their bores.

Refitting

39 Where applicable, refit the caliper mounting bracket to the hub carrier, and tighten the mounting bolts to the specified torque.

40 Place the caliper in position, coat the threads of the caliper upper guide pin bolt with locking compound, refit the bolt, and tighten it to the specified torque.

41 Refit the brake pads as described in Section 5.

42 Check that the caliper slides smoothly on the mounting bracket.

43 Check that the brake fluid hose is correctly routed, without being twisted, then reconnect the union to the caliper, using two new sealing washers. Refit the union banjo bolt, and tighten to the specified torque.

44 Reconnect the end of the handbrake cable to the lever. Refit the cable mounting bracket, and where applicable, the spring clip. Where applicable, ensure that the locating peg on the mounting bracket engages with the corresponding hole in the caliper body.

45 Remove the polythene from the master cylinder reservoir cap, or remove the clamp from the fluid hose, as applicable.

46 Bleed the hydraulic fluid circuit as described in Section 2. Note that if no other part of the system has been disturbed, it should only be necessary to bleed the relevant rear circuit.

47 Depress the brake pedal repeatedly to bring the pads into contact with the brake disc, and ensure that normal pedal pressure is restored.

48 Refit the roadwheel, and lower the vehicle to the ground.

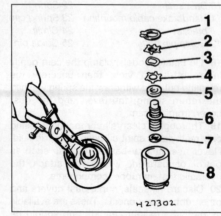

10.34 Rear caliper adjuster nut components

1	Circlip	5	Ball bearing
2	Spacer	6	Adjuster nut
3	Wave washer	7	Cup seal
4	Spacer	8	Piston

10.31 Rear caliper spring components

1	Circlip	3	Spring	5	Tube
2	Spring cap	4	Spring seat		

10.32 Ensure that the seal is correctly fitted to the rear brake caliper adjuster nut

11 Rear wheel cylinder - removal, overhaul and refitting

⚠️ **Warning: Before starting work, refer to the note at the beginning of Section 2 concerning the dangers of hydraulic fluid, and to the warning at the beginning of Section 4 concerning the dangers of asbestos dust.**

Removal

1 Remove the brake drum as described in Section 8.
2 Remove the brake shoes as described in Section 6.
3 To minimise fluid loss during the following operations, remove the master cylinder reservoir cap, then tighten it down onto a piece of polythene, to obtain an airtight seal.
4 Clean the brake backplate around the wheel cylinder mounting bolts and the hydraulic pipe union, then unscrew the union nut and disconnect the hydraulic pipe. Cover the open ends of the pipe and the master cylinder to prevent dirt ingress.
5 Remove the securing bolts, then withdraw the wheel cylinder from the backplate.

Overhaul

Saloon and Hatchback models

6 The rear brake pressure-regulating valves are integral with the rear wheel cylinders, and the cylinders **must not** be dismantled. No spare parts are available, and if a cylinder is faulty or damaged, the complete assembly must be renewed.

Estate models

Note: *Before commencing work, ensure that the appropriate wheel cylinder overhaul kit is obtained.*
7 Clean the assembly thoroughly, using only methylated spirit or clean brake fluid.
8 Peel off both rubber dust covers, then use paint or similar to mark one of the pistons so that the pistons are not interchanged on reassembly.
9 Withdraw both pistons and the spring.

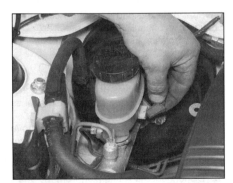

12.1 Disconnecting the brake fluid level sender wiring connector - Estate model

10 Discard the rubber piston cups and the dust covers. These components should be renewed as a matter of course, and are available as part of an overhaul kit, which also includes the bleed nipple dust cap.
11 Check the condition of the cylinder bore and the piston - the surfaces must be perfect and free from scratches, scoring and corrosion. It is advisable to renew the complete wheel cylinder if there is any doubt as to the condition of the cylinder bore or piston.
12 Ensure that all components are clean and dry. The pistons, spring and cups should be fitted wet, using hydraulic fluid as a lubricant - soak them in clean fluid before installation.
13 Fit the cups to the pistons, ensuring that they are the correct way round. Use only your fingers (no tools) to manipulate the cups into position.
14 Fit the first piston to the cylinder, taking care not to distort the cup. If the original pistons are being re-used, the marks made on dismantling should be used to ensure that the pistons are refitted to their original bores.
15 Refit the spring and the second piston.
16 Apply a smear of rubber grease to the exposed end of each piston and to the dust cover sealing lips, then fit the dust covers to each end of the wheel cylinder.

Refitting

17 Refitting is a reversal of removal, bearing in mind the following points:
a) Tighten the mounting bolts to the specified torque.
b) Refit the brake shoes as described in Section 6, and refit the brake drum as described in Section 8.
c) Before refitting the roadwheel and lowering the vehicle to the ground, remove the polythene from the fluid

reservoir, and bleed the hydraulic system as described in Section 2. Note that if no other part of the system has been disturbed, it should only be necessary to bleed the relevant rear circuit.

12 Master cylinder - removal, overhaul and refitting

Note: *Before starting work, refer to the warning at the beginning of Section 2 concerning the dangers of hydraulic fluid.*

Removal

1 Remove the master cylinder fluid reservoir cap, and syphon the hydraulic fluid from the reservoir. **Note:** *Do not syphon the fluid by mouth, as it is poisonous; use a syringe or an old poultry baster.* Alternatively, open any convenient bleed screw in the system, and gently pump the brake pedal to expel the fluid through a tube connected to the screw (see Section 2). Disconnect the wiring connector from the brake fluid level sender unit **(see illustration)**.
2 Wipe clean the area around the brake pipe unions on the side of the master cylinder, and place absorbent rags beneath the pipe unions to catch any surplus fluid. Make a note of the correct fitted positions of the unions, then unscrew the union nuts and carefully withdraw the pipes. Plug or tape over the pipe ends and master cylinder orifices, to minimise the loss of brake fluid, and to prevent the entry of dirt into the system. Wash off any spilt fluid immediately with cold water.
3 Slacken and remove the two nuts securing the master cylinder to the vacuum servo unit, then withdraw the unit from the engine compartment.

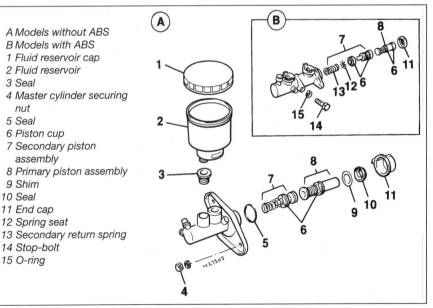

A Models without ABS
B Models with ABS
1 Fluid reservoir cap
2 Fluid reservoir
3 Seal
4 Master cylinder securing nut
5 Seal
6 Piston cup
7 Secondary piston assembly
8 Primary piston assembly
9 Shim
10 Seal
11 End cap
12 Spring seat
13 Secondary return spring
14 Stop-bolt
15 O-ring

12.6 Master cylinder components

9

4 Where applicable, recover the seal from the rear of the master cylinder, and discard it.

Overhaul

Note: *Before attempting overhaul of the master cylinder, ensure that the appropriate overhaul kit is obtained - a number of different master cylinder assemblies may be fitted, depending on model.*

5 Pull the fluid reservoir from the top of the master cylinder. Prise the reservoir seals from the reservoir or the master cylinder, as applicable.

6 Using a suitable screwdriver, bend back the tangs securing the master cylinder end cap, then withdraw the end cap **(see illustration)**.

7 On models with ABS, push on the end of the primary piston assembly using a suitable wooden dowel to compress the primary and secondary piston assemblies, then unscrew the stop-bolt from the side of the master cylinder.

8 Noting the order of removal, and the direction of fitting of each component, withdraw the washer and the piston assemblies with their springs and seals, tapping the body onto a clean wooden surface to dislodge them. If necessary, clamp the master cylinder body in a vice (fitted with soft jaw covers) and use compressed air (applied through the secondary circuit fluid port) to assist the removal of the secondary piston assembly.

> ⚠️ **Warning: Wear eye protection when working with compressed air.**

9 Thoroughly clean all components, using only methylated spirit, isopropyl alcohol or clean hydraulic fluid as a cleaning medium. Never use mineral-based solvents such as petrol or paraffin, as they will attack the hydraulic system rubber components. Dry the components immediately, using compressed air or a clean, lint-free cloth.

10 Check all components, and renew any that are worn or damaged (note that individual seal components are not available - the overhaul kit will contain complete primary and secondary piston assemblies, complete with all seals, washers, etc). Check particularly the cylinder bores and pistons; the complete assembly should be renewed if these are scratched, worn or corroded. If there is any doubt about the condition of the assembly or of any of its components, renew it. Check that the cylinder body fluid passages are clear.

11 Before reassembly, soak the pistons and the new seals in clean hydraulic fluid. Smear clean fluid into the cylinder bore.

12 Insert the piston assemblies into the cylinder bore (make sure that the assemblies are inserted squarely), using a twisting motion to avoid trapping the seal lips. Ensure that all components are refitted in the correct order and the right way round, then fit the washer to the end of the primary piston. Where applicable, follow the assembly instructions supplied with the repair kit. On models with ABS, ensure that the slot in the secondary piston assembly aligns with the stop-bolt hole in the side of the master cylinder.

13 On models with ABS, compress the piston assemblies into the cylinder bore, using a clean wooden dowel as during removal, then refit the stop-bolt, ensuring that it engages with the slot in the secondary piston assembly **(see illustration)**.

14 Press the piston assemblies fully into the bore using a clean wooden dowel, and secure them in position with the new end cap (supplied in the overhaul kit). Bend the tangs into position to secure the end cap.

15 Examine the fluid reservoir seals, and if necessary renew them. Fit the reservoir seals to the master cylinder body, then refit the reservoir.

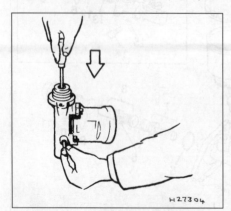

12.13 Compress the piston assemblies into the cylinder bore, and refit the stop-bolt - models with ABS

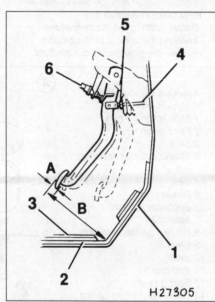

13.4 Brake pedal free height adjustment

A	Pedal free play	
H	Pedal free height	
1	Floor reinforcement panel	
2	Sound insulation	
3	Carpet panel	
4	Servo pushrod	
5	Locknut	
6	Stop-light switch	

Refitting

16 Remove all traces of dirt from the master cylinder and servo unit mating surfaces, and where applicable, fit a new seal between the master cylinder body and the servo.

17 Fit the master cylinder to the servo unit, ensuring that the servo unit pushrod enters the master cylinder bore centrally. Refit the master cylinder mounting nuts, and tighten them to the specified torque.

18 Wipe clean the brake pipe unions, then refit them to the correct master cylinder ports, as noted before removal, and tighten the union nuts securely.

19 Refill the master cylinder reservoir with new fluid, and bleed the complete hydraulic system as described in Section 2.

13 Brake pedal - adjustment, removal and refitting

Adjustment

1 The pedal free height should be measured from the top face of the pedal to the floor reinforcement panel.

2 If desired, to improve access, remove the driver's side lower facia panel, as described in Chapter 11, Section 30.

3 To take the measurement, remove the driver's side footwell trim panel, with reference to Chapter 11, Section 28 if necessary, then release the securing clip(s) and lift the carpet trim panel to expose the flap in the floor insulation.

4 Lift the flap in the floor insulation, and measure the pedal free height as shown **(see illustration)**. Check the measured height against the value given in the Specifications.

5 If the height of the pedal requires adjustment, proceed as follows.

6 Loosen the locknut on the servo pushrod, and turn the pushrod as required until the specified height is achieved. Retighten the locknut on completion.

7 Check the free play of the pedal by pressing the pedal slowly until resistance is felt. The free play should be as specified.

8 Check that the stop-lights go out when the pedal is released. Note that the switch (a bayonet fit in the pedal bracket) cannot be adjusted, and if faulty must be renewed.

9 On completion, refit the carpet and the trim panel(s).

Removal

10 To improve access, if not already done, remove the driver's side lower facia panel as described in Chapter 11, Section 30.

11 Working in the driver's footwell, remove the split-pin from the end of the servo pushrod clevis pin, then withdraw the clevis pin.

12 Disconnect the wiring plug from the stop-light switch.

13 Unscrew the four nuts securing the pedal

13.13 Brake pedal bracket securing nuts (1) and bolt (2)

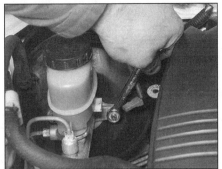

14.6a Unscrew the securing nuts . . .

14.6b . . . and pull the master cylinder from the servo

bracket to the bulkhead (note that these nuts also secure the vacuum servo) **(see illustration)**.

14 Unscrew the pedal bracket upper securing bolt, then withdraw the pedal/bracket assembly from the footwell.

15 The brake pedal is integral with the bracket assembly, and cannot be renewed individually.

Refitting

16 Refitting is a reversal of removal but, on completion, check the pedal height as described previously in this Section.

14 Vacuum servo unit - removal and refitting

Removal

1 Disconnect the battery negative lead.

2 On carburettor and single-point fuel injection models, it should be possible to remove the servo unit without removing the inlet manifold or the master cylinder.

3 On multi-point fuel injection models, it may be necessary to remove the inlet manifold (see Chapter 4C) to gain sufficient clearance to remove the servo unit.

4 On carburettor models, to improve access, remove the air cleaner as described in Chapter 4A.

5 Where applicable, disconnect the power

steering fluid pressure switch wiring plug, and/or unbolt the power steering fluid hose bracket from the body for improved access.

6 Disconnect the wiring plug from the brake fluid level sensor, then remove the two nuts securing the master cylinder to the servo. Release the master cylinder fluid pipes from any securing clips, then pull the master cylinder forwards from the servo **(see illustrations)**.

7 If this does not provide sufficient clearance to remove the servo, the master cylinder must be removed completely with reference to Section 12.

8 Disconnect the vacuum hose from the servo **(see illustration)**.

9 Working in the driver's footwell, remove the spring clip from the end of the servo pushrod clevis pin, then withdraw the clevis pin **(see illustration)**. If desired, remove the driver's side lower facia panel, as described in Chapter 11, Section 30, to improve access.

10 Again working in the driver's footwell, unscrew the four nuts securing the brake pedal mounting bracket to the servo studs.

11 Working in the engine compartment, withdraw the servo.

Refitting

12 Refitting is a reversal of removal, bearing in mind the following points:

a) *Before refitting the servo, check that the length of the pushrod is as specified (see Specifications), and adjust if necessary by*

loosening the locknut and turning the pushrod (see illustration).

b) *Where applicable, tighten all fixings to the specified torque.*

c) *Where applicable, refit the master cylinder as described in Section 12.*

d) *Where applicable, refit the inlet manifold as described in the relevant Part of Chapter 4.*

e) *On completion, check the brake pedal height as described in Section 13.*

15 Vacuum servo unit check valve - removal, testing and refitting

Models with servo-mounted valve

Removal

1 The valve is a push-fit in the front of the servo unit.

2 Release the securing clip, and disconnect the vacuum hose from the valve.

3 Withdraw the valve from its rubber sealing grommet, using a pulling and twisting motion. Remove the grommet from the servo.

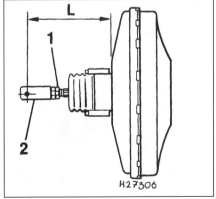

14.12 Ensure that the vacuum servo pushrod length is as specified

L   Approx 125.0 mm   2   Pushrod clevis
1   Locknut

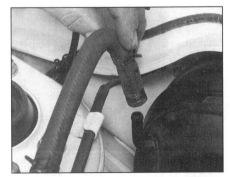

14.8 Disconnecting the vacuum hose from the servo

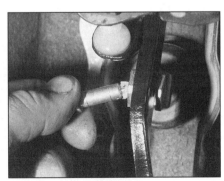

14.9 Removing the servo pushrod clevis pin

9

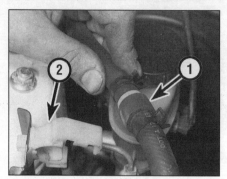

15.10 Removing the non-return valve (1) from the securing clip (2)

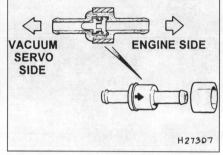

15.13 The arrow on the vacuum servo unit check valve must point towards the engine - models with ABS

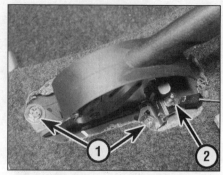

16.6 Handbrake lever securing bolts (1) and handbrake "on" warning light switch (2)

Testing

4 Examine the check valve for signs of damage, and renew if necessary. The valve may be tested by blowing through it in both directions. Air should flow through the valve in one direction only - when blown through from the servo unit end of the valve. Renew the valve if this is not the case.
5 Examine the rubber sealing grommet and flexible vacuum hose for signs of damage or deterioration, and renew as necessary.

Refitting

6 Fit the sealing grommet into position in the servo unit.
7 Carefully ease the check valve into position, taking great care not to displace or damage the grommet. Reconnect the vacuum hose to the valve and, where necessary, securely tighten its retaining clip.
8 On completion, start the engine, and check the check valve-to-servo unit connection for signs of air leaks.

Models with vacuum-hose mounted valve

Removal

9 The valve is located in the vacuum hose leading to the servo, and is secured to the body panel by a clip.
10 Release the valve from the securing clip **(see illustration)**. Take note of the direction of the arrow on the valve body, which should

point in the direction of the hose connected to the engine.
11 Release the retaining clips (where fitted), and disconnect the vacuum hoses from the valve, then withdraw the valve.

Testing

12 Proceed as described in paragraph 4.

Refitting

13 Refitting is a reversal of removal, ensuring that the arrow on the valve body points towards the engine **(see illustration)**.
14 On completion, start the engine and check the hose connections to the valve for air leaks.

16 Handbrake lever - removal and refitting

Removal

1 Disconnect the battery negative lead.
2 Remove the centre console as described in Chapter 11.
3 Chock the wheels, and fully release the handbrake.
4 Disconnect the wiring plug from the handbrake "on" warning light switch.
5 Count the number of exposed threads on the cable adjuster rod (to ease adjustment on refitting), then unscrew the adjuster nut, and disconnect adjuster rod from the handbrake lever.

6 Remove the two securing bolts, and withdraw the handbrake lever assembly **(see illustration)**.

Refitting

7 Refitting is a reversal of removal, bearing in mind the following point:
a) Screw the adjuster nut onto the cable adjuster rod to give the number of exposed threads noted before removal, then check the handbrake operation, and adjust if necessary, as described in Chapter 1.
b) Before refitting the centre console, check the operation of the handbrake "on" warning light.

17 Handbrake cables - removal and refitting

Rear cables

Removal

1 There are two rear handbrake cables, one on each side of the vehicle. To renew either rear cable, proceed as follows.
2 Chock the front wheels, then jack up the front of the vehicle and support securely on axle stands (see "Jacking, towing and wheel changing"). Release the handbrake fully.
3 On models with rear drum brakes, remove the brake shoes, and disconnect the end of the handbrake cable from the lever on the trailing shoe, as described in Section 6. Recover the return spring from the end of the cable, then unbolt the cable bracket from the brake backplate **(see illustration)**.
4 On models with rear disc brakes, release the spring clip securing the cable to the mounting bracket, then disconnect the end of the cable from the lever on the caliper.
5 Unscrew the nuts and bolts securing the handbrake cable brackets to the underbody, and to the suspension, where applicable.
6 On Estate models, unbolt the bracket securing the cable grommet to the trailing arm **(see illustration)**.
7 Disconnect the front of the cable from the

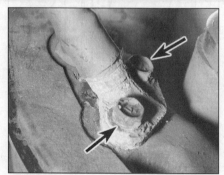

17.3 Handbrake cable bracket-to-brake backplate securing bolts (arrowed)

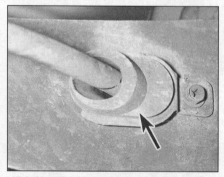

17.6 Handbrake cable grommet in trailing arm (arrowed) - Estate model

17.7a Exhaust heat shield removed to expose handbrake cable equaliser (arrowed)

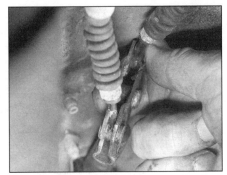

17.7b Disconnecting a front handbrake cable from the equaliser

17.13 Unscrewing the handbrake cable adjuster nut

cable equaliser at the front of the vehicle, then withdraw the cable **(see illustrations)**. Note that on certain models, it will be necessary to remove the exhaust heat shield for access to the handbrake cable equaliser.

Refitting

8 Refitting is a reversal of removal, bearing in mind the following points:
a) *On models with rear disc brakes, where applicable, when refitting the cable mounting bracket to the caliper, ensure that the locating peg on the bracket engages with the corresponding hole in the caliper body.*
b) *On models with rear drum brakes, reconnect the cable end to the lever on the trailing shoe, and refit the brake shoes, as described in Section 6.*
c) *On completion, check the handbrake adjustment, as described in Chapter 1.*

Front cable

Removal

9 Disconnect the battery negative lead.
10 Chock the rear wheels and fully release the handbrake.
11 Working inside the vehicle, remove the centre console as described in Chapter 11.
12 Disconnect the wiring plug from the handbrake "on" warning light switch.
13 Count the number of exposed threads on the cable adjuster rod (to ease adjustment on refitting), then unscrew the adjuster nut, and disconnect adjuster rod from the handbrake lever **(see illustration)**.
14 For improved access, ensure that the rear wheels are chocked, then jack up the front of the vehicle and support securely on axle stands (see "*Jacking, towing and wheel changing*").
15 Working under the vehicle, disconnect the two rear cables from the cable equaliser, then withdraw the front section of the cable (which includes the cable equaliser and the adjuster rod) down through the floor panel. Note that on certain models, it will be necessary to remove the exhaust heat shield for access to the handbrake cable equaliser.

Refitting

16 Refitting is a reversal of removal, bearing in mind the following points.

a) *Screw the adjuster nut onto the cable adjuster rod to give the number of exposed threads noted before removal, then check the handbrake adjustment as described in Chapter 1.*
b) *Before refitting the centre console, check the operation of the handbrake "on" warning light.*

18 Rear brake pressure-regulating valves - adjustment, removal and refitting

Saloon and Hatchback models with rear disc brakes

Adjustment

Note: *Two valves are fitted, and the two valve spring lengths **must** be the same.*

1 Twin valves are fitted on the right- and left-hand sides, between the rear suspension parallel links and the body **(see illustration)**. Note that on certain models, it will be necessary to remove the exhaust heat shield for access to the handbrake cable equaliser.
2 To check the adjustment of the valves, the following conditions must be met:

a) *A full fuel tank.*
b) *Engine oil and coolant levels normal.*
c) *Spare wheel, jack and tools fitted in correct positions.*

3 With the vehicle parked on flat ground, release the handbrake, then roll the vehicle backwards and forwards, and bounce the vehicle to settle the suspension.
4 Working under the rear of the vehicle,

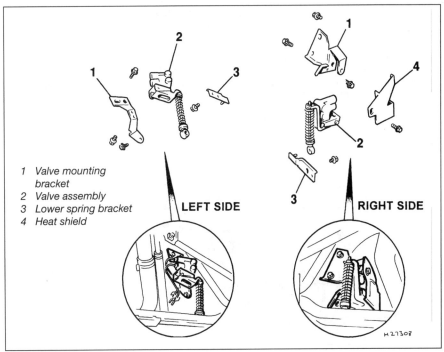

1 Valve mounting bracket
2 Valve assembly
3 Lower spring bracket
4 Heat shield

LEFT SIDE **RIGHT SIDE**

18.1 Rear brake pressure-regulating valve components - Saloon and Hatchback models with rear disc brakes

9

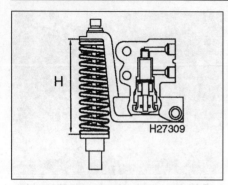

18.4 Rear brake pressure-regulating valve spring length measurement - Saloon and Hatchback models with rear disc brakes

H = 86.0 to 90.0 mm

measure the length of the relevant valve spring as shown **(see illustration)**.

5 If adjustment is required, loosen the two spring bracket lower mounting bolts, and rotate the bracket as necessary (the mounting bolt hole nearest the spring is elongated) to bring the spring length within the specified limits.

6 Tighten the bracket mounting bolts on completion.

7 Check the length of the spring on the remaining valve, and if necessary adjust as described previously so that both spring lengths are equal.

8 To check the operation of the valves, special pressure-testing equipment is required, and this task should be entrusted to a Nissan dealer.

Removal

Note: *If one of the valves is faulty or damaged, the manufacturers recommend that BOTH valves should be renewed as a pair.*

9 To improve access, chock the front wheels, then jack up the rear of the vehicle and support securely on axle stands (see *"Jacking, towing and wheel changing"*).

10 Before proceeding, place a suitable container under the valve, to collect the brake fluid which will escape as the fluid pipes are disconnected.

11 Unscrew the fluid pipe unions from the

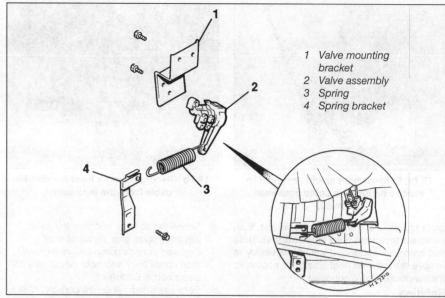

1 Valve mounting bracket
2 Valve assembly
3 Spring
4 Spring bracket

18.16 Rear brake pressure-regulating valve components - Estate models

valve body, and disconnect the pipes from the valve, taking care not to strain them. Note the locations of the pipes, to ensure correct refitting. Plug or cover the open ends of the pipes and valve, to reduce fluid spillage and to prevent dirt ingress. **Do not** depress the brake pedal whilst the valve is removed.

12 Unscrew the bolts securing the valve to its mounting bracket, and withdraw the valve.

13 Removal and refitting of the valve brackets is self-explanatory.

14 Note that the valve spring cannot be renewed independently of the valve - the components are only available as an assembly.

Refitting

15 Refitting is a reversal of removal, bearing in mind the following points:

a) *After refitting all the components, bleed the brake hydraulic circuit as described in Section 2.*

b) *On completion, check the adjustment of both valves as described previously in this Section.*

Estate models

Adjustment

16 A single valve is fitted between the rear axle and the body **(see illustration)**.

17 The procedure is as described previously in this Section for Saloon and Hatchback models, noting that only one valve is fitted. Note also that the valve operating lever should be pushed towards the spring bracket when measuring the spring length **(see illustration)**.

Removal and refitting

18 The procedure is as described previously for Saloon and Hatchback models, noting that only one valve is fitted.

Saloon and Hatchback models with rear drum brakes

Adjustment

19 The valves are integral with the rear wheel cylinders, and no adjustment is possible.

Removal and refitting

20 Removal and refitting of the rear wheel cylinders is described in Section 11. The valves are integral with the rear wheel cylinders, and the cylinders **must not** be dismantled. No spare parts are available, and if a pressure-regulating valve is faulty or damaged, the complete assembly must be renewed.

19 Stop-light switch -
adjustment, removal and refitting

Adjustment

1 The switch plunger operates on a ratchet.

2 If adjustment is required, pull the plunger fully out - the switch is then self-adjusting.

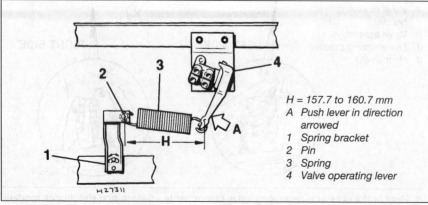

H = 157.7 to 160.7 mm
A Push lever in direction arrowed
1 Spring bracket
2 Pin
3 Spring
4 Valve operating lever

18.17 Rear brake pressure-regulating valve spring length measurement - Estate models

20.3 Disconnecting the handbrake "on" warning light switch wiring

Removal

3 Disconnect the battery negative lead.

4 For improved access, remove the driver's side lower facia panel, as described in Chapter 11, Section 30.

5 Disconnect the wiring plug from the switch.

6 Twist the switch anti-clockwise, and withdraw the switch from the pedal bracket.

Refitting

7 Refitting is a reversal of removal, but pull the switch plunger fully out before refitting (see paragraph 2).

20 Handbrake "on" warning light switch - removal and refitting

Removal

1 Disconnect the battery negative lead.

2 Remove the centre console as described in Chapter 11.

3 Disconnect the wiring plug from the switch **(see illustration)**.

4 Remove the securing screw, and withdraw the switch.

Refitting

5 Refitting is a reversal of removal, but before refitting the centre console, check that the warning light comes on after the specified number of handbrake clicks (see Specifications). If necessary, bend the switch bracket to give the correct adjustment.

21 Anti-lock braking system (ABS) - general information

1 ABS is fitted to certain "Phase I" models (up to June 1993), and to all "Phase II" models (June 1993 on).

2 The system is fail-safe, and is fitted in addition to the conventional braking system, meaning that the vehicle retains conventional braking in the event of an ABS failure.

3 To prevent wheel locking, the system provides a means of modulating (varying) the hydraulic pressure in the braking circuits, to control the amount of braking effort at each wheel. To achieve this, sensors mounted at all four wheels monitor the rotational speeds of the wheels, and are this able to detect when there is a risk of wheel locking (low rotational speed, relative to vehicle speed). Solenoid valves are positioned in the brake circuits to each wheel, and the solenoid valves are incorporated in a modulator assembly, which is controlled by an electronic control unit. The electronic control unit controls the braking effort applied to each wheel, according to the information supplied by the wheel sensors **(see illustration)**.

4 The braking system components used on models fitted with ABS are similar to those used on models with a conventional braking system. Rear disc brakes are fitted to all models with ABS.

5 Should a fault develop in the system, the system can be tested using specialist diagnostic equipment available to a Nissan dealer.

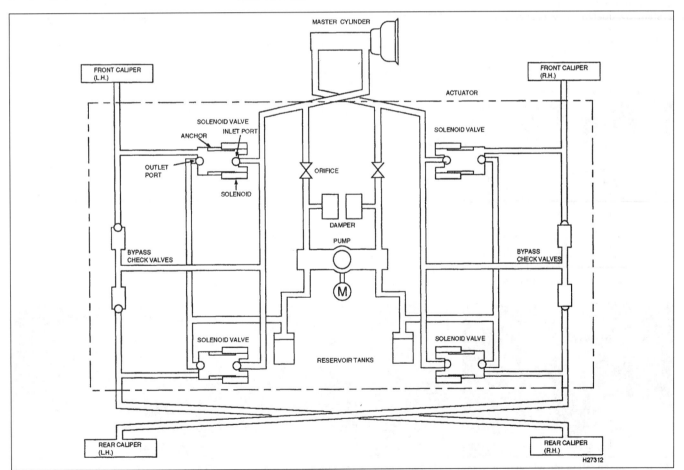

21.3 Schematic layout of ABS hydraulic system components

22.5 ABS modulator earth cable securing screw (arrowed) - Hatchback model

22.6 ABS modulator securing nut (arrowed) - Hatchback model

22.11 ABS modulator relay cover securing screw (arrowed)

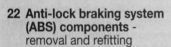

22 Anti-lock braking system (ABS) components - removal and refitting

Modulator assembly

Note: *Before starting work, refer to the warning at the beginning of Section 2 concerning the dangers of hydraulic fluid.*

Removal

1 Disconnect the battery negative lead.
2 Drain the brake fluid from the hydraulic system by opening any convenient bleed screw in the system, and gently pumping the brake pedal to expel the fluid through a tube connected to the screw (see Section 2).
3 Identify each fluid pipe connected to the

22.17 Removing the footwell trim panel - shown with glovebox removed

modulator assembly, to ensure correct refitting.
4 Unscrew the union nuts, and disconnect the fluid pipes from the modulator. Plug or cover the open ends of the pipes and modulator, to reduce fluid spillage and to prevent dirt ingress.
5 Disconnect the modulator wiring connector, and the earth cable (where applicable, remove the earth cable securing screw) **(see illustration)**.
6 Unscrew the three securing nuts, and withdraw the modulator assembly **(see illustration)**.

Refitting

7 Refitting is a reversal of removal, bearing in mind the following points:
a) *Ensure that the fluid pipes are correctly reconnected to the modulator, as noted before removal.*
b) *On completion, bleed the brake hydraulic system as described in Section 2.*

Modulator relays

Removal

8 The relays are mounted on the modulator assembly.
9 Disconnect the battery negative lead.
10 To provide sufficient clearance to remove the relay cover, it will be necessary to release the modulator assembly from its mountings, and move it away from the wing panel (see paragraph 6).
11 Remove the securing screw **(see**

illustration), and withdraw the cover to expose the relays.
12 Pull the relevant relay from its location. Note that the black relay controls the modulator motor, and the silver relay controls the solenoid valves.

Refitting

13 Refitting is a reversal of removal, but ensure that the modulator mounting nuts are securely tightened.

Electronic control unit

Removal

14 The unit is located under the passenger's side lower facia.
15 Disconnect the battery negative lead.
16 Working in the passenger's footwell, using a screwdriver, carefully prise out the trim plate to reveal the trim panel securing screw. Remove the screw.
17 Twist the rear securing nut to release it, then withdraw the clip, and pull the trim panel from the footwell **(see illustration)**.
18 Depress the securing clip, and disconnect the wiring plug from the control unit **(see illustration)**.
19 Reach up under the facia, and remove the two bolts securing the control unit bracket to the footwell (pull back the carpet panel for access to the lower bolt), then withdraw the unit, complete with the bracket, from the footwell **(see illustrations)**.

Refitting

20 Refitting is a reversal of removal.

22.18 Disconnecting the wiring plug from the ABS control unit

22.19a Unscrew the two securing bolts (arrowed) . . .

22.19b . . . and withdraw the ABS control unit

22.24 Removing an ABS front wheel sensor

22.27 ABS rear wheel sensor mounting bolt (arrowed)

22.29 Rear ABS sensor rotor (1) and sensor (2)

Front wheel sensor

Note: *Suitable thread-locking compound must be applied to the sensor securing bolt on refitting.*

Removal

21 To improve access, chock the rear wheels, apply the handbrake, then jack up the front of the vehicle and support securely on axle stands (see *"Jacking, towing and wheel changing"*). Remove the relevant roadwheel.
22 Trace the wiring back from the sensor, and remove the screws securing the wiring brackets to the suspension and/or body.
23 Locate the wiring connector, and separate the two halves of the connector (where applicable, feed the wiring through the grommet in the wheel arch, noting its routing).
24 Unscrew the bolt securing the sensor to the hub carrier, and withdraw the sensor complete with the wiring and brackets **(see illustration)**.

Refitting

25 Refitting is a reversal of removal, but ensure that the faces of the sensor and hub carrier are clean, and tighten the securing bolt to the specified torque.

Rear wheel sensor

Removal

26 To improve access, chock the front wheels, then jack up the rear of the vehicle and support securely on axle stands (see *"Jacking, towing and wheel changing"*).
27 Proceed as described for the front wheel sensor in paragraphs 22 to 24 **(see illustration)**.

Refitting

28 Proceed as described in paragraph 25.

Sensor rotors

29 The sensor rotors are integral with the driveshafts (front) and the hubs (rear), and cannot be removed independently **(see illustration)**. Removal and refitting details for the driveshafts and rear hubs are given in Chapters 8 and 10 respectively.

9

Notes

Chapter 10 Suspension and steering

Contents

Degrees of difficulty

Easy, suitable for novice with little experience		Fairly easy, suitable for beginner with some experience		Fairly difficult, suitable for competent DIY mechanic		Difficult, suitable for experienced DIY mechanic		Very difficult, suitable for expert DIY or professional	

Specifications

Front suspension

Type:

Saloon and Hatchback models .... Independent multi-link, incorporating upper and lower arms and coil spring-over-damper strut units. Anti-roll bar fitted to all models.

Estate models .... Independent by MacPherson struts, with coil springs and integral shock absorbers, and lower arms. Anti-roll bar fitted to all models.

Rear suspension

Type:

Saloon and Hatchback models .... Independent by MacPherson struts, with coil springs and integral shock absorbers, and parallel links with radius rods. Anti-roll bar fitted to all models.

Estate models .... Semi-independent by trailing arms linked by tubular crossmember, and located by Panhard rod. Coil springs and telescopic shock absorbers.

Wheel bearings

Maximum endfloat at hub (front and rear) .... 0.05 mm

Steering

Type .... Rack-and-pinion, manual or power-assisted, depending on model
Maximum steering wheel free play .... 35.0 mm
Steering column length (see Section 13) .... 556.2 to 557.8 mm

Tyres

Size:

5J x 13 wheels .... 165 R13 82T or 165 R13 84T (depending on model)
5.5JJ x 14 wheels .... 175/70 R14 84T, 185/65 R14 85H, 185/65 R14 87H, or 195/65 R14 89H (depending on model)
6J x 14 wheels .... 185/65 R14 87H, 195/65 R14 89H, 195/60 R14 85V, or 195/60 R14 86V (depending on model)

Tyre pressures .... Refer to manufacturer's tyre specification plate fitted to driver's door rear pillar

Roadwheels

Type . . . . Pressed-steel or aluminium alloy (depending on model)
Size . . . . 5J x 13, 5.5JJ x 14, or 6J x 14 (depending on model)

Wheel alignment and steering angles*

Front wheel camber angle:
    Saloon and Hatchback models . . . . 0°45' negative to 0°45' positive
    Estate models . . . . 0°05' negative to 1°25' positive
Front wheel castor angle:
    Saloon and Hatchback models . . . . 1°00' to 2°30' positive
    Estate models . . . . 1°15' to 2°45' positive
Kingpin inclination:
    Saloon and Hatchback models . . . . 13°45' to 15°15'
    Estate models . . . . 13°15' to 14°45'
Front wheel toe setting:
    Saloon and Hatchback models . . . . Parallel to 2.0 mm (0°12') toe-in
    Estate models . . . . 1.0 to 3.0 mm (0°6' to 0°17') toe-in
Rear wheel camber angle:
    Saloon and Hatchback models:
        "Phase I" models . . . . 1°45' to 0°15' negative
        "Phase II" models . . . . 2°15' to 0°45' negative
    Estate models . . . . 2°15' to °45' negative
Rear wheel toe-setting:
    Saloon and Hatchback models:
        "Phase I" models . . . . 2.0 mm (0°12') toe-out to 2.0 mm (0°12') toe-in
        "Phase II" models . . . . 1.0 mm (0°6') toe-out to 3.0 mm (0°18') toe-in

Note: *All specifications given are for an unladen vehicle - ie, no driver or passengers, fuel tank full, engine coolant and oil levels normal, and spare wheel, jack and tools fitted in normal locations.*

Torque wrench settings

	Nm	lbf ft
Front suspension - Saloon and Hatchback models		
Anti-roll bar clamp mounting bolts	45	33
Anti-roll bar drop link-to-anti-roll bar nuts*	45	33
Anti-roll bar drop link-to-centre link nuts (2.0 litre engine models)	20	15
Anti-roll bar drop link-to-lower arm nuts (1.6 litre engine models)*	25	18
Centre link-to-upper suspension link nut*	120	89
Driveshaft nut*	300	221
Hub carrier-to-centre link nut*	110	81
Hub carrier-to-lower arm balljoint nut	80	59
Lower arm front mounting nut*	100	74
Lower arm rear mounting clamp bolts	130	96
Lower arm front mounting pin-to-body bolts	100	74
Suspension strut damper rod top nut*	20	15
Suspension strut upper mounting nuts*	50	37
Suspension strut-to-centre link nut and bolt*	120	89
Track-rod end-to-steering arm nut:		
Recommended torque	35	26
Maximum permissible torque	49	36
Upper suspension link-to-mounting bracket nut*	110	81
Upper suspension link mounting bracket-to-body nuts* and bolts	110	81
Front suspension - Estate models		
Anti-roll bar drop link-to-anti-roll bar nuts*	45	33
Anti-roll bar drop link-to-lower arm nuts*	20	15
Anti-roll bar mounting clamp bolts	35	26
Anti-roll bar mounting clamp nuts*	45	33
Hub carrier-to-suspension strut nuts and bolts*	170	125
Lower arm balljoint-to-hub carrier nut	80	59
Lower arm balljoint-to-lower arm nuts*	90	66
Lower arm front mounting nut*	110	81
Lower arm rear mounting clamp bolts	130	96
Suspension strut damper rod top nut*	70	52
Suspension strut upper mounting nuts*	50	37
Track-rod end-to-steering arm nut:		
Recommended torque	35	26
Maximum permissible torque	49	36

Torque wrench settings (continued)

	Nm	lbf ft
Rear suspension - Saloon and Hatchback models		
Anti-roll bar clamp nut* and bolt	35	26
Anti-roll bar drop link-to-anti-roll bar nuts*	45	33
Anti-roll bar drop link-to-suspension strut nuts*	45	33
Anti-roll bar mounting bracket-to-body bolts	35	26
Parallel link mounting nuts*	120	89
Radius rod front mounting nut	100	74
Radius rod-to-hub carrier nut*	100	74
Rear hub nut	230	170
Suspension strut damper rod top nut	70	52
Suspension strut upper mounting nuts*	50	37
Suspension strut-to-hub carrier nuts*	100	74
Rear suspension - Estate models		
Bump rubber seat securing bolts	25	18
Bump rubber securing nut*	60	44
Panhard rod lower securing nut*	65	48
Panhard rod upper securing nut*	110	81
Shock absorber lower mounting nut*	110	81
Shock absorber upper mounting nut*	65	48
Trailing arm securing nuts (or pins)*	110	81
Steering		
Air bag securing bolts (Torx type)*	20	15
Power steering fluid pipe union banjo-to-pump bolt	60	44
Power steering pump-to-bracket bolts	30	22
Steering column securing nuts and bolts	15	11
Steering column universal joint clamp bolts	25	18
Steering gear mounting clamp bolts	90	66
Steering wheel securing nut	35	26
Track-rod end locknut	45	33
Track-rod end-to-steering arm nut:		
Recommended torque	35	26
Maximum permissible torque	49	36
Roadwheels		
Roadwheel nuts	110	81

Use new nut(s)/bolt(s).

1 General information

1 The suspension layout differs between Saloon and Hatchback, and Estate models, as explained below.

Front suspension

2 On Saloon and Hatchback models, the independent front suspension is of a unique Nissan multi-link type, comprising high-mounted upper arms, lower arms, and centre links which connect the upper arms to the hub carriers. The hub carriers are located at their lower ends by the transverse lower arms. The coil spring-over-damper strut units are connected to the bodyshell front suspension turrets at their top ends, and the centre links at their lower ends. A front anti-roll bar is fitted to all models **(see illustration)**.

3 On Estate models, the independent front suspension is of the MacPherson strut type, incorporating coil springs and integral telescopic shock absorbers. The upper ends of the MacPherson struts are connected to the bodyshell front suspension turrets; the

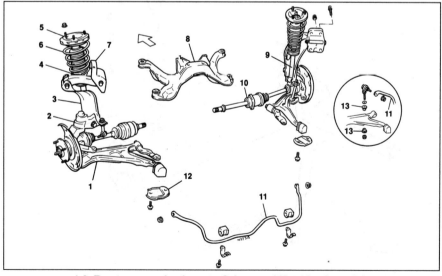

1.2 Front suspension layout - Saloon and Hatchback models

1 Lower arm	6 Coil spring	10 Driveshaft
2 Hub carrier	7 Upper link mounting	11 Anti-roll bar
3 Centre link	bracket	12 Lower arm rear mounting
4 Upper link	8 Front crossmember	clamp
5 Suspension strut top	9 Suspension strut	13 Rubber bushes
mounting		

Inset – Anti-roll bar mounting - 1.6 litre engine models

10

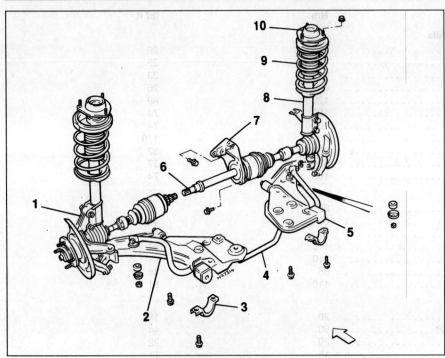

1.3 Front suspension layout - Estate models

1 Hub carrier	5 Lower arm mounting	8 Suspension strut
2 Lower arm	bracket	9 Coil spring
3 Lower arm front mounting	6 Driveshaft	10 Suspension strut top
bracket	7 Driveshaft intermediate	mounting
4 Anti-roll bar	bearing bracket	

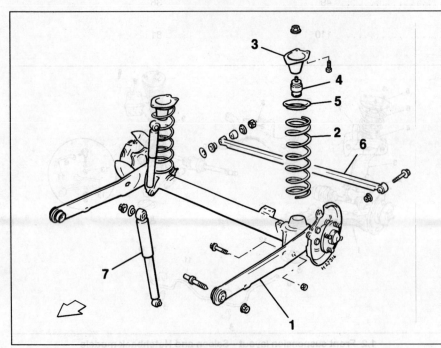

1.4 Rear suspension layout - Saloon and Hatchback models

1 Coil spring	5 Parallel link inboard	9 Anti-roll bar
2 Gasket	securing (adjuster) bolt	A Models with rear disc
3 Suspension strut top	6 Radius rod	brakes
mounting	7 Suspension strut	B Models with rear drum
4 Parallel links	8 Hub carrier	brakes

lower ends are bolted to the hub carriers, which carry the wheel bearings, brake calipers and hub/disc assemblies. The hub carriers are located at their lower ends by transverse lower arms. A front anti-roll bar is fitted to all models **(see illustration)**.

Rear suspension

4 On Saloon and Hatchback models, the independent rear suspension is of the MacPherson strut type, incorporating coil springs and integral telescopic shock absorbers. The upper ends of the MacPherson struts are connected to the bodyshell front suspension turrets, and the lower ends are bolted to the hub carriers, which carry the wheel bearings, brake calipers and hub/disc assemblies. The hub carriers are located at their lower ends by transverse parallel links. A rear anti-roll bar is fitted to all models **(see illustration)**.

5 On Estate models, the rear suspension is of the semi-independent trailing arm type, with two trailing arms, linked by a tubular crossmember. Separate coil springs and telescopic shock absorbers are fitted between the tubular crossmember and the vehicle body. The rear of the tubular crossmember is located by a transverse Panhard rod connected between the crossmember and the body **(see illustration)**.

Steering

6 The one-piece steering shaft has a universal joint fitted at its lower end, which is clamped to both the steering shaft and the steering gear pinion by means of clamp bolts.
7 The steering gear is mounted on the engine compartment bulkhead, and is connected to the steering arms projecting rearwards from the hub carriers. The track-rods are fitted with balljoints at their inner and outer ends, to allow for suspension movement, and are threaded to facilitate adjustment.
8 Power steering is fitted as standard on some models. The hydraulic system is powered by a belt-driven pump, which is driven from the crankshaft pulley.

---

2 Front hub bearings - renewal

Note: A balljoint separator tool, and a press or suitable alternative tools (see text) will be required for this operation. The bearing will be destroyed during the removal procedure.
Note: A new lower arm balljoint split pin will be required on refitting, On Estate models, the manufacturers recommend that the suspension strut-to-hub carrier bolts and nuts are renewed. New bearing oil seals should be used, and it is also advisable to renew the bearing retaining circlips.

Removal

1 Chock the rear wheels, apply the handbrake, then jack up the front of the vehicle and support on axle stands (see *"Jacking, towing and wheel changing"*). Remove the appropriate roadwheel.

2 Remove the brake disc, with reference to Chapter 9.

3 On models with ABS, unbolt the ABS wheel sensor, and remove the screw securing the ABS sensor wiring to the hub carrier. Suspend the sensor away from the working area, to avoid the possibility of damage.

Saloon and Hatchback models

4 Remove the split pin, then unscrew the nut securing the lower end of the hub carrier to the lower arm balljoint **(see illustration)**. Discard the split pin - a new one must be used on refitting.

5 Separate the hub carrier from the lower arm balljoint. If necessary, use a balljoint separator tool. Remove the nut, then withdraw the hub carrier.

6 Disconnect the outboard end of the driveshaft from the hub, as described during the driveshaft removal and refitting procedure in Chapter 8 **(see illustration)**. Note that there is no need to disconnect the inboard end of the driveshaft from the transmission. **Do not** allow the end of the driveshaft to hang down under its own weight - support the end of the driveshaft using wire or string.

7 Proceed to paragraph 10.

Estate models

8 Disconnect the outboard end of the driveshaft from the hub, as described during the driveshaft removal and refitting procedure in Chapter 8. Note that there is no need to disconnect the inboard end of the driveshaft from the transmission. **Do not** allow the end of the driveshaft to hang down under its own weight - support the end of the driveshaft using wire or string.

9 Remove the two nuts from the bolts securing the hub carrier to the suspension strut **(see illustration)**. Withdraw the bolts and remove the hub carrier assembly. Discard

2.4 Removing the split pin from the lower arm balljoint - Saloon/Hatchback model

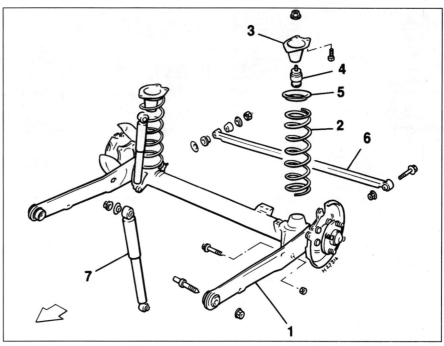

1.5 Rear suspension layout - Estate models

1 Trailing arm	4 Bump rubber	6 Panhard rod
2 Coil spring	5 Upper spring seat	7 Shock absorber
3 Bump rubber mounting		

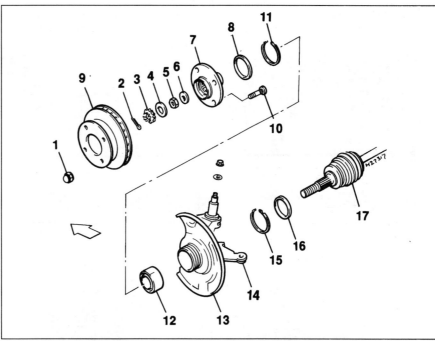

2.6 Front hub and bearing components - Saloon/Hatchback model shown

1 Roadwheel nut	8 Outer oil seal	13 Brake disc shield
2 Split pin	9 Brake disc	14 Hub carrier
3 Castellated locking plate	10 Roadwheel stud	15 Inner bearing retaining
4 Spacer	11 Outer bearing retaining	circlip
5 Driveshaft nut	circlip	16 Inner oil seal
6 Washer	12 Wheel bearing assembly	17 Driveshaft
7 Hub		

10

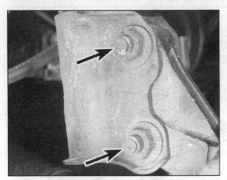

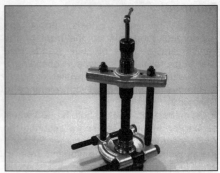

2.9 Remove the two nuts (arrowed) from the bolts securing the hub carrier to the suspension strut - Estate model

2.10 Removing the hub from the wheel bearing. Note bearing inner race (arrowed)

2.11 Using a puller to remove the bearing race from the hub

the nuts and bolts - new ones must be used on refitting.

All models

10 Support the outer face of the hub carrier on two metal bars, ensuring that the hub is free (take care not to damage the brake disc shield). Using a metal bar or tube of suitable diameter, press or drive the hub from the wheel bearing. Note that one half of the inner bearing race will remain on the hub **(see illustration)**.

11 Support the inner bearing race which is still attached to the hub, then press or drive the hub from the race. Alternatively, pull the bearing race from the hub using a suitable puller **(see illustration)**.

12 Recover the outer oil seal from the hub.

13 Working at the rear of the hub carrier, prise out the inner oil seal **(see illustration)**.

14 Using a suitable screwdriver, extract the inner and outer bearing retaining circlips from the hub carrier. Recover the remaining inner bearing race if it is loose **(see illustrations)**.

15 Support the inner face of the hub carrier, then using a suitable metal tube which bears only on the outer bearing race, press or drive the bearing from the hub carrier. Alternatively, temporarily refit the bearing inner race, and drive out the bearing using a tube or bar bearing on the inner race **(see illustration)**.

Refitting

16 Before installing the new bearing, thoroughly clean the bearing location in the

hub carrier, then fit the outer bearing retaining circlip to its groove in hub carrier.

17 Fit the new bearing from the rear of the hub, and press or drive the bearing into position until it contacts the outer circlip, applying pressure only to the bearing outer race. This can be achieved using suitable tools, and the old outer bearing race **(see illustration)** - *grind the outer surface of the old bearing race (to reduce its diameter) before use, to ensure that the race does not stick in the hub carrier*.

18 Fit the inner bearing retaining circlip to its groove in the hub carrier.

19 Pack the lips of the new outer oil seal with grease then, using a tube of suitable diameter, carefully press or tap the seal into position in the outer face of the hub carrier **(see illustration)**.

2.13 Prising the oil seal from the rear of the hub carrier

2.14a Removing the outer bearing circlip from the hub carrier

2.14b Recover the remaining inner bearing race from the rear of the hub

2.15 Driving the bearing from the hub carrier

2.17 Fitting the new bearing using improvised tools, and the old bearing outer race

2.19 Fit the outer oil seal

2.22 Fitting the hub using improvised tools

3.2 Remove the screw securing the ABS sensor wiring bracket - Hatchback model

3.3 Unbolt the brake fluid line connector block - Hatchback model

20 Support the outer face of the hub carrier on its periphery, taking care not to damage the outer oil seal.

21 Pack the lips of the new inner oil seal with grease then, using a tube of suitable diameter, carefully press or tap the seal into position in the inner face of the hub carrier.

22 Support the inner face of the hub carrier, using a suitable diameter metal bar or tube, which will just pass through the inner oil seal to support the wheel bearing inner race. Carefully press or draw the hub into the bearing, noting that the bearing inner race **must** be supported during this operation, as described previously. This can be achieved using a suitable socket, threaded rod, washers and a length of bar as shown **(see illustration)**. Check that the hub rotates freely in the hub carrier.

Saloon and Hatchback models

23 Reconnect the outboard end of the driveshaft to the hub as described in Chapter 8, noting that the brake disc must be refitted before refitting the brake caliper (see Chapter 9).

24 Reconnect the hub carrier to the lower arm balljoint, then refit the balljoint nut. Tighten the nut to the specified torque, then fit a new split pin.

25 Refit the roadwheel, and lower the vehicle to the ground.

Estate models

26 Engage the hub carrier with the

suspension strut, then refit the new securing bolts, noting that they should be fitted from the front of the strut. Fit new nuts to the bolts, and tighten to the specified torque.

27 Reconnect the outboard end of the driveshaft to the hub as described in Chapter 8, noting that the brake disc must be refitted before refitting the brake caliper (see Chapter 9).

28 Refit the roadwheel, and lower the vehicle to the ground.

3 Front suspension strut - removal, overhaul and refitting

Saloon and Hatchback models

Removal

Note: *The manufacturers recommend that the suspension strut-to-centre link bolt and nut, the centre link-to-upper link nut, and the suspension strut top mounting nuts and gasket, are renewed on refitting.*

1 Chock the rear wheels, apply the handbrake, then jack up the front of the vehicle and support securely on axle stands (see *"Jacking, towing and wheel changing"*). Remove the relevant roadwheel.

2 On models with ABS, remove the screws securing the ABS sensor wiring bracket to the inner wing panel **(see illustration)**.

3 Unbolt the brake fluid line connector block

from the suspension centre link **(see illustration)**.

4 Unscrew and remove the nut and bolt securing the suspension centre link to the upper link, then pivot the centre link and the upper link as necessary to allow sufficient clearance to remove the strut **(see illustration)**. Discard the nut - a new one should be used on refitting.

5 Remove the nut from the bolt securing the lower end of the strut to the suspension centre link, then withdraw the bolt **(see illustration)**. Discard the nut and bolt - new ones should be used on refitting.

6 Have an assistant support the strut from underneath the wheel arch then, working in the engine compartment, unscrew the three nuts securing the top of the strut to the suspension turret.

⚠ *Warning: Do not unscrew the centre damper rod nut. Lower the strut, and withdraw the assembly from under the wheel arch (see illustrations).*

Overhaul

Note: *Suitable coil spring compressor tools will be required for this operation, and a new damper rod top nut must be used on reassembly.*

7 Clamp the lower end of the strut in a vice fitted with jaw protectors.

8 Temporarily refit two of the strut upper securing nuts to their studs. Using a suitable bar inserted between the upper mounting

3.4 Removing the centre link-to-upper link bolt - Hatchback model

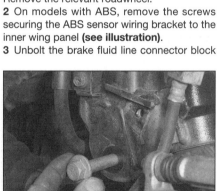

3.5 Removing the suspension strut-to-centre link bolt - Hatchback model

3.6a Unscrew the suspension strut top nuts (arrowed) . . .

10

3.6b . . . then manipulate the strut from behind the centre link . . .

3.6c . . . and withdraw the strut

studs, counterhold the upper strut mounting whilst loosening the damper rod top nut. **Do not** remove the nut **(see illustration)**.

9 Fit suitable spring compressors to the spring, and compress the spring sufficiently to enable the upper spring seat to be turned by hand **(see illustration)**.

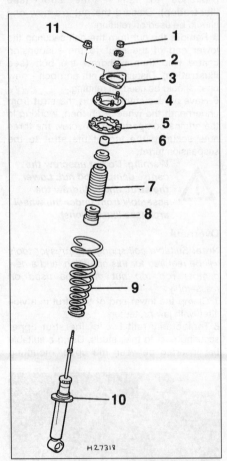

3.8 Front suspension strut components - Saloon and Hatchback models

1	Damper rod top nut	6	Bush
2	Bush	7	Rubber gaiter
3	Gasket	8	Bump rubber
4	Top mounting	9	Coil spring
5	Upper spring seat	10	Damper
		11	Top mounting nut

10 Fully unscrew and remove the damper rod top nut. Note that it will be necessary to counterhold the damper rod, using a suitable spanner, as the nut is unscrewed **(see illustration)**. Discard the nut - a new one must be used on reassembly.

11 Withdraw the washer, bush, gasket, top mounting, and upper spring seat.

12 Withdraw the spring, complete with the compressors, then lift the bush, rubber gaiter cap and rubber gaiter, and bump rubber, from the damper rod.

13 With the strut assembly now dismantled, examine all the components for wear, damage or deformation. Check the rubber components for deterioration. Renew any of the components as necessary.

14 Examine the damper for signs of fluid leakage. Check the damper rod for signs of

3.9 Fit suitable spring compressors to the suspension strut

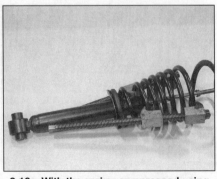

3.16a With the spring compressed using the spring compressor tools . . .

pitting along its entire length, and check the strut body for signs of damage. While holding it in an upright position, test the operation of the strut by moving the damper rod through a full stroke, and then through short strokes of 50 to 100 mm. In both cases, the resistance felt should be smooth and continuous. If the resistance is jerky, or uneven, or if there is any visible sign of wear or damage to the strut, renewal is necessary. Note that the damper cannot be renewed independently, and if leakage or damage is evident, the complete strut/damper assembly must be renewed (in which case, the spring, upper mounting components, bushes, and associated components can be transferred to the new strut).

15 If any doubt exists about the condition of the coil spring, carefully remove the spring compressors, and check the spring for distortion and signs of cracking. Renew the spring if it is damaged or distorted, or if there is any doubt as to its condition.

16 To reassemble the strut, follow the accompanying photo sequence, beginning with **illustration 3.16a**. Be sure to follow each step in sequence, and carefully read the caption underneath each photo **(see illustrations)**. Compress the spring sufficiently to allow the top mounting components to be refitted, and if necessary, pull on the end of the piston rod to extend the damper. **Note:** *There are two cut-outs in the strut top mounting, marked "R" and "L". When reassembling the components, note that on*

3.10 Unscrewing the damper rod top nut

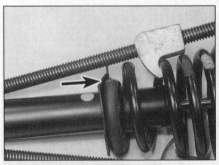

3.16b . . . fit the spring to the strut, ensuring that the lower end of the spring rests against the spring seat (arrowed)

3.16c Fit the bump stop . . .

3.16d . . . against the seat on the piston rod

3.16e Ensure that the gaiter cap is correctly engaged with the rubber gaiter . . .

3.16f . . . then fit the gaiter and cap . . .

3.16g . . . and the bush

3.16h Fit the upper spring seat to the top mounting . . .

3.16i . . . then refit the spring seat/top mounting assembly . . .

3.16j . . . noting that the cut-out marked "L" must be positioned nearest the inner edge of the suspension turret when the strut is refitted

3.16k . . . and the spring stop (arrowed) on the lower spring seat must be point towards the rear of the vehicle - left-hand strut shown, see text

3.16l Fit the bush . . .

3.16m . . . the washer . . .

3.16n . . . and the damper rod top nut (arrowed)

10

3.17 Fit a new gasket to the strut top mounting

3.24 Remove the securing clip (arrowed) to release the brake line from the hub carrier - Estate model

the left-hand strut, when the strut is refitted, the cut-out marked "L" must be positioned nearest the inner edge of the suspension turret (ie, the side nearest the engine), and the spring stop on the lower spring seat must point towards the rear of the vehicle. On the right-hand strut, the cut-out marked "R" must be positioned nearest the inner edge of the suspension turret (ie, nearest the engine), and the spring stop on the lower spring seat must point towards the front of the vehicle. Also note that a suitable crows-foot adapter will be required to tighten the piston top nut to the specified torque.

Refitting

17 Fit a new gasket to the top mounting, then manoeuvre the strut assembly into position under the wheel arch, behind the suspension centre link, passing the mounting studs through the holes in the body turret **(see illustration)**. Note that the relevant cut-out in the upper spring seat, and the arrow on the lower spring seat, must be positioned as described in the note at the end of paragraph 16. Fit the new upper mounting nuts, and tighten them to the specified torque.

18 Engage the lower end of the strut with the suspension centre link, then fit the new bolt and nut, noting that the nut should be positioned on the rear side of the strut, and tighten to the specified torque.

19 Reconnect the suspension centre link to the top link, then refit the bolt and a new nut, and tighten to the specified torque.

20 Refit the brake fluid line connector block to the suspension centre link, and tighten the securing bolt.

21 On models with ABS, refit the ABS wheel sensor wiring bracket to the inner wing panel.

22 Refit the roadwheel, and lower the vehicle to the ground.

Estate models

Removal

Note: The manufacturers recommend that the suspension strut-to-hub carrier bolts and nuts, and the suspension strut top mounting nuts and gasket, are renewed on refitting.

23 Chock the rear wheels, apply the handbrake, then jack up the front of the

vehicle and support securely on axle stands (see "Jacking, towing and wheel changing"). Remove the relevant roadwheel.

24 Release the brake fluid line from the bracket on the hub carrier **(see illustration)**.

25 Remove the two nuts from the bolts securing the lower end of the strut to the hub carrier, noting that the nuts fit on the rear side of the strut. Withdraw the bolts, and support the hub carrier. Discard the bolts and nuts - new ones should be used on refitting.

26 Have an assistant support the strut from underneath the wheel arch then, working in the engine compartment, unscrew the three nuts securing the top of the strut to the suspension turret.

> ⚠ **Warning: Do not unscrew the centre damper rod nut. Release the lower end of the strut from the hub carrier, then withdraw the assembly from under the wheel arch.**

Overhaul

Note: Suitable coil spring compressor tools will be required for this operation, and a new damper rod top nut must be used on reassembly.

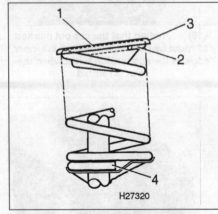

3.33a Top end of spring correctly located on upper spring seat - Estate models

1 Upper spring seat
2 Upper spring end
3 Spring locating shoulder
4 Lower spring end

27 Proceed as described for Saloon and Hatchback models in paragraphs 7 to 10 inclusive, noting that a plastic cap must be prised off for access to the damper rod top nut.

28 Withdraw the washer, gasket, top mounting, lockwasher, upper spring seat, and upper spring seat rubber.

29 Withdraw the spring, complete with the compressors, then withdraw the bump rubber and the lower spring seat rubber.

30 Proceed as described for Saloon and Hatchback models in paragraphs 13 to 15 inclusive.

31 Clamp the strut body in a vice, as during dismantling, then refit the lower spring seat rubber, and the bump rubber.

32 Ensure that the coil spring is compressed sufficiently to enable the upper mounting components to be fitted, then fit the spring over the damper rod, ensuring that the lower end of the spring is correctly located on the lower spring seat.

33 Refit the upper spring seat rubber, and the upper spring seat, ensuring that the top end of the spring is correctly located on the upper spring seat. Note that when the strut is refitted, the cut-out and arrow on the upper spring seat must be positioned nearest the outer edge of the suspension turret (ie, the side nearest the roadwheel) **(see illustrations)**. If there are two cut-outs in the strut top mounting, marked "R" and "L", proceed as follows.

a) On the left-hand strut, when the strut is refitted, the cut-out marked "L" must be positioned nearest the inner edge of the suspension turret (ie, the side nearest the engine), and the arrow on the lower spring seat must point towards the rear of the vehicle.

b) On the right-hand strut, when the strut is refitted, the cut-out marked "R" must be positioned nearest the inner edge of the suspension turret (ie, nearest the engine), and the arrow on the lower spring seat must point towards the front of the vehicle.

34 Refit the lockwasher, top mounting, washer and a new damper rod top nut, then

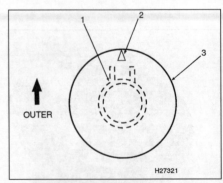

3.33b Upper spring seat orientation - Estate models

1 Strut position   2 Arrow   3 Spring seat

4.3 Lower arm rear mounting clamp bolts (arrowed) - Hatchback model

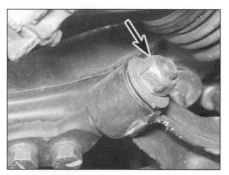

4.4 Lower arm-to-mounting pin nut (arrowed) - Hatchback model

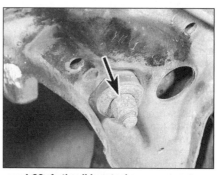

4.22 Anti-roll bar-to-lower arm nut (arrowed) - Estate model

tighten the top nut to the specified torque, counterholding the damper rod as during dismantling. Note that a suitable crows-foot adapter will be required to tighten the piston top nut to the specified torque.

35 Remove the spring compressors.

36 Refit the plastic cap to the damper rod top nut.

Refitting

37 Fit a new gasket to the top mounting, then manoeuvre the strut assembly into position under the wheel arch, passing the mounting studs through the holes in the body turret. Note that the cut-out and arrow on the upper spring seat must be positioned nearest the outer edge of the suspension turret (ie, the side nearest the roadwheel). Fit the new upper mounting nuts, and tighten them to the specified torque.

38 Engage the lower end of the strut with the hub carrier, then fit the new securing bolts and nuts, noting that the nuts fit on the rear side of the strut, and tighten to the specified torque.

39 Refit the brake fluid line to the bracket on the hub carrier.

40 Refit the roadwheel, and lower the vehicle to the ground.

---

4 Front suspension lower arm - removal, overhaul and refitting

Saloon and Hatchback models
Removal

Note: *A balljoint separator tool may be required for this operation. The lower arm balljoint split pin, lower arm front mounting nut, and on 1.6 litre engine models, the anti-roll bar drop link nut, must be renewed on refitting.*

1 Chock the rear wheels, apply the handbrake, then jack up the front of the vehicle and support securely on axle stands (see *"Jacking, towing and wheel changing"*). Remove the relevant roadwheel.

2 On 1.6 litre engine models, unscrew the nut securing the anti-roll bar drop link to the lower arm, and recover the washer and bush. Note that it may be necessary to counterhold the

drop link pin in order to unscrew the nut. Discard the nut - a new one should be used on refitting.

3 Unscrew the two bolts securing the lower arm rear mounting clamp to the vehicle floor, and remove the clamp **(see illustration)**.

4 Slacken the nut securing the front of the lower arm to the mounting pin. Do not remove the nut at this stage **(see illustration)**.

5 Remove the split pin, then unscrew the nut securing the lower end of the hub carrier to the lower arm balljoint. Discard the split pin - a new one must be used on refitting.

6 Separate the hub carrier from the lower arm. If necessary, use a balljoint separator tool. Remove the nut, and lever the end of the lower arm down to release it from the hub carrier.

7 Remove the nut securing the front of the lower arm to the mounting pin, and recover the washer. Discard the nut - a new one must be used on refitting.

8 Slide the lower arm forwards from the front mounting pin, and withdraw the lower arm from under the vehicle. Note that on 1.6 litre engine models, it will be necessary to pivot the lower arm down to release it from the anti-roll bar drop link before the lower arm can be withdrawn from the front mounting pin - recover the remaining bush and washer from the drop link.

Overhaul

9 With the lower arm removed, examine the lower arm itself, and the mounting bushes, for wear, cracks or damage.

10 Check the balljoint for wear, excessive play, or stiffness. Also check the balljoint dust boot for cracks or damage.

11 The mounting bushes and balljoint assembly are integral with the lower arm, and cannot be renewed independently. If either the bushes or the balljoint are worn or damaged, the complete lower arm assembly must be renewed.

Refitting

Note: *Final tightening of all fixings should be carried out with the vehicle resting on its wheels.*

12 Slide the lower arm into position on the front mounting pin. On 1.6 litre engine models, engage the lower arm with the anti-roll bar

drop link (ensure that the upper washer and bush are fitted to the drop link - the concave side of the washer should be against the bush). Refit the washer and the new nut to the front mounting pin. Do not fully tighten the nut at this stage.

13 Engage the lower arm balljoint with the hub carrier, then refit the balljoint nut. Do not fully tighten the nut at this stage.

14 Refit the lower arm rear mounting clamp, and refit the securing bolts. Do not fully tighten the bolts at this stage.

15 On 1.6 litre engine models, refit the lower bush and washer to the anti-roll bar drop link (the concave side of the washer should be against the bush), then fit a new securing nut. Again, do not fully tighten the nut at this stage.

16 Refit the roadwheel, and lower the vehicle to the ground.

17 Make sure that the vehicle is parked on level ground, then release the handbrake. Roll the vehicle backwards and forwards, and bounce the front of the vehicle to settle the suspension components.

18 Chock the wheels, then tighten all relevant nuts and bolts to the specified torque. After tightening, fit a new split pin to the lower arm balljoint nut.

19 On completion the front wheel alignment should be checked, with reference to Chapter 1.

Estate models
Removal

Note: *The lower arm balljoint securing nuts, anti-roll bar drop link nut, and lower arm front mounting nut, should be renewed on refitting.*

20 Chock the rear wheels, apply the handbrake, then jack up the front of the vehicle and support securely on axle stands (see *"Jacking, towing and wheel changing"*). Remove the relevant roadwheel.

21 Unscrew the nuts securing the lower arm balljoint to the lower arm, and remove the mounting plate to free the hub carrier from the lower arm. Discard the nuts - new ones should be used on refitting.

22 If necessary, counterhold the anti-roll bar pin, using a suitable spanner, and unscrew the nut securing the anti-roll bar to the lower arm **(see illustration)**. Recover the washer

10

and bush. Discard the nut - a new one should be used on refitting.

23 Unscrew the two bolts securing the lower arm rear mounting clamp to the vehicle floor, and remove the clamp.

24 Remove the nut securing the front of the lower arm to the mounting pin, and recover the washer. Discard the nut - a new one should be used on refitting.

25 Pivot the lower arm down to release it from the anti-roll bar drop link, then slide the lower arm forwards from the front mounting pin, and withdraw it from under the vehicle. Recover the remaining bush and washer from the anti-roll bar drop link.

Overhaul

26 Examine the lower arm itself, and the mounting bushes, for wear, cracks or damage. The bushes are integral with the lower arm, and if they are worn or damaged, the complete lower arm must be renewed.

Refitting

Note: *Final tightening of all fixings should be carried out with the vehicle resting on its wheels.*

27 Slide the lower arm into position on the front mounting pin, and engage the lower arm with the anti-roll bar pin (ensure that the upper washer and bush are fitted to the anti-roll bar pin - the concave side of the washer should be against the bush), then refit the washer and the new nut to the front mounting pin. Do not fully tighten the nut at this stage.

28 Refit the lower arm rear mounting clamp, and refit the securing bolts. Do not fully tighten the bolts at this stage.

29 Refit the mounting plate (engage the studs with the lower arm balljoint, which is still attached to the hub carrier), then fit the new nuts to secure the balljoint to the lower arm. Do not fully tighten the nuts at this stage.

30 Refit the lower arm bush and washer to the anti-roll bar drop pin (the concave side of the washer should be against the bush), then fit a new securing nut. Again, do not fully tighten the nut at this stage.

31 Refit the roadwheel, and lower the vehicle to the ground.

32 Make sure that the vehicle is parked on level ground, then release the handbrake. Roll

the vehicle backwards and forwards, and bounce the front of the vehicle to settle the suspension components.

33 Chock the wheels, then tighten all relevant nuts and bolts to the specified torque.

34 On completion, the front wheel alignment should be checked with reference to Chapter 1.

---

5 Front suspension lower arm balljoint - renewal

Saloon and Hatchback models

1 On Saloon and Hatchback models, the balljoint is integral with the lower arm. If the balljoint is worn or damaged, the complete lower arm must be renewed as described in Section 4.

Estate models

Note: *A balljoint separator tool may be required for this operation. A new lower arm balljoint split pin will be required on refitting.*

2 Chock the rear wheels, apply the handbrake, then jack up the front of vehicle and support securely on axle stands (see "*Jacking, towing and wheel changing*").

3 Unscrew the nuts securing the lower arm balljoint to the lower arm, and remove the mounting plate to free the hub carrier from the lower arm **(see illustration)**. Discard the nuts - new ones should be used on refitting.

4 Remove the split pin, then unscrew the nut securing the lower end of the hub carrier to the balljoint. Discard the split pin - a new one must be used on refitting.

5 Separate the hub carrier from the balljoint. If necessary, use a balljoint separator tool. Remove the nut, then withdraw the balljoint.

6 Fit the new balljoint using a reversal of the removal procedure, but use a new split pin to secure the balljoint-to-hub carrier nut.

---

6 Front suspension centre link assembly - removal, overhaul and refitting

General

1 The centre link assembly has two bearings fitted to its upper end, which act as "kingpin" bearings. When the steering is turned, the hub carrier pivots in these bearings.

2 Normally, the bearings should not require maintenance, and should last for the lifetime of the vehicle. However, if the vehicle has covered a very high mileage, or has been subjected to frequent hard cornering, bearing wear may be evident.

3 Bearing wear is likely to result in a growling noise when the steering is turned during normal driving, particularly under hard cornering. If the hub carrier is turned by hand with the front of the vehicle jacked up,

dragging or roughness may be noticed if the bearings are worn.

Removal

Note: *A new hub carrier-to-centre link nut, suspension strut-to-centre link nut, centre link-to-upper link nut and, on 2.0 litre engine models, a new anti-roll bar drop link-to-centre link nut, will be required on refitting.*

4 Chock the rear wheels, apply the handbrake, then jack up the front of the vehicle and support on axle stands (see "*Jacking, towing and wheel changing*"). Remove the appropriate front roadwheel.

5 On 2.0 litre engine models, unscrew the nut securing the anti-roll bar drop link to the suspension centre link, and recover the washer and bush. Note that it may be necessary to counterhold the drop link pin as the nut is unscrewed. Discard the nut - a new one must be used on refitting.

6 Prise off the dust cap, then unscrew the nut securing the hub carrier to the centre link assembly **(see illustration)**. Recover the washer. Pull the hub carrier downwards to separate it from the centre link assembly. Discard the nut - a new one must be used on refitting.

7 Remove the nut from the bolt securing the lower end of the suspension strut to the centre link assembly, then withdraw the bolt. Discard the nut - a new one must be used on refitting.

8 Remove the nut from the bolt securing the upper end of the centre link assembly to the suspension upper link, then withdraw the bolt, and manipulate the centre link out from under the vehicle. Discard the nut - a new one must be used on refitting. On 2.0 litre engine models, recover the remaining bush and washer from the anti-roll bar drop link.

Overhaul

9 Check the centre link casting for signs of cracking or damage, and renew the assembly if necessary.

10 If the bearings require renewal, which is unlikely (see paragraphs 1 to 3), consult a Nissan dealer for advice - it may be that the most economical course of action is to renew the complete centre link assembly.

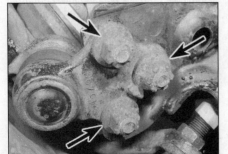

5.3 Lower arm balljoint-to-lower arm nuts (arrowed) - Estate model

6.6 Prise the dust cap from the nut securing the hub carrier to the centre link assembly - Saloon and Hatchback models

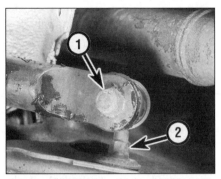

7.2 Front anti-roll bar-to-drop link nut (1) and drop link pin (2) - Estate model

7.4 Front anti-roll bar-to-floor clamp bolts (arrowed) - 2.0 litre Hatchback model

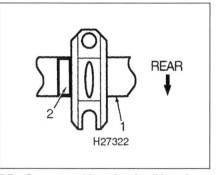

7.7a Correct position of anti-roll bar clamp

1 Anti-roll bar   2 Paint mark

Refitting

Note: *Final tightening of the fixings should be carried out with the vehicle resting on its wheels.*

11 Before refitting the assembly, ensure that the hub carrier pin (kingpin) is clean, and apply a thin layer of grease to the pin.

12 Pack the bearing housing with grease.

13 On 2.0 litre engine models, refit the lower washer and bush to the anti-roll bar drop link (note that the concave side of the washer should fit against the bush).

14 Engage the centre link assembly with the suspension upper link (and the anti-roll bar drop link on 2.0 litre engine models), and refit the bolt and a new nut, noting that the nut should face the rear of the vehicle. Do not fully tighten the nut and bolt at this stage.

15 Engage the lower end of the suspension strut with the centre link assembly, and refit the bolt and a new nut, again noting that the nut should face the rear of the vehicle. Do not fully tighten the nut and bolt at this stage.

16 Engage the hub carrier pin with the centre link assembly, then refit the washer and the new nut. Tighten the nut to the specified torque, then pack the dust cap with grease, and tap the cap into position.

17 On 2.0 litre engine models, refit the anti-roll bar drop link upper bush, washer (the concave side of the washer should fit against the bush), and the new securing nut. Again, do not fully tighten the nut at this stage.

18 Refit the roadwheel, and lower the vehicle to the ground.

19 Make sure that the vehicle is parked on level ground, then release the handbrake. Roll the vehicle backwards and forwards, and bounce the front of the vehicle to settle the suspension components.

20 Chock the wheels, then tighten all relevant nuts and bolts to the specified torque.

21 On completion, the front wheel alignment should be checked with reference to Chapter 1.

---

7 Front suspension anti-roll bar - removal and refitting

Anti-roll bar

Removal

Note: *New anti-roll bar-to-drop link nuts should be used on refitting.*

1 Chock the rear wheels, apply the handbrake, then jack up the front of the vehicle and support on axle stands (see "*Jacking, towing and wheel changing*"). Remove the front roadwheels.

2 Working at one side of the anti-roll bar, where necessary counterhold the drop link pin, then unscrew the nut securing the end of the anti-roll bar to the drop link **(see illustration)**. Recover the washer. Discard the nut - a new one should be used on refitting.

3 Repeat the operation on the remaining side of the anti-roll bar.

4 Unscrew the bolts, and withdraw the clamps securing the anti-roll bar to the vehicle floor **(see illustration)**.

5 Manipulate the anti-roll bar out from under the vehicle.

Refitting

6 Inspect the mounting clamp rubbers for cracks or deterioration. If renewal is necessary, slide the old rubbers from the bar, and fit the new rubbers. Note that the rubbers should be positioned with the paint marks on the bar against their inner edges.

7 Refitting is a reversal of removal, bearing in mind the following points **(see illustrations)**:

a) When refitting the clamps, make sure that the clamps are positioned with the paint marks on the anti-roll bar against the inner edges of the clamps, and that the cut-out bolt holes in the clamps are positioned towards the rear of the vehicle.

b) When reconnecting the drop links to the anti-roll bar, make sure that the drop link balljoint is positioned centrally in its arc of movement, and is not under strain; use new nuts.

c) Do not fully tighten the clamp bolts until the vehicle is resting on its roadwheels, and the suspension has been settled.

Drop link

Removal

Note: *New securing nuts should be used on refitting.*

8 To improve access, chock the rear wheels, apply the handbrake, then jack up the front of the vehicle and support securely on axle stands (see "*Jacking, towing and wheel changing*"). Remove the relevant front roadwheel.

9 Counterhold the drop link pin, then unscrew the nut securing the end of the anti-roll bar to the drop link. Recover the washer. Discard the nut - a new one should be used on refitting.

10 Again, counterhold the drop link pin, then unscrew the nut securing the anti-roll bar drop link to the lower arm, or the suspension centre link, as applicable **(see illustration)**. Recover the washer and bush. Again, discard the nut - a new one should be used on refitting.

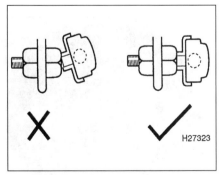

7.7b Correct positioning of anti-roll bar drop link balljoint

7.10 Anti-roll bar drop link-to-suspension centre link securing nut (arrowed) - Hatchback model

10

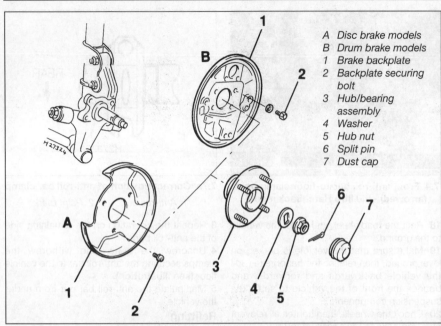

A Disc brake models
B Drum brake models
1 Brake backplate
2 Backplate securing bolt
3 Hub/bearing assembly
4 Washer
5 Hub nut
6 Split pin
7 Dust cap

8.1 Rear hub components - Saloon/Hatchback model shown

11 Lift out the drop link, and recover the remaining bush and washer.

Refitting

12 Check the condition of the drop link bushes, and renew if necessary.
13 Refitting is a reversal of removal, bearing in mind the following points:
a) Note that the concave sides of the washers should be positioned against the bushes.
b) When reconnecting the drop links to the anti-roll bar, make sure that the drop link balljoint is positioned centrally in its arc of movement, and is not under strain.
c) Use new drop link securing nuts, and tighten them to the specified torque.

8 Rear hub bearings - renewal

Note: *The bearing will be destroyed during the removal operation, and a new rear hub/bearing assembly must be used on refitting - the old assembly cannot be re-used. A new rear hub nut and split pin must be used on refitting.*

1 The rear hub bearings are integral with the rear hubs, and cannot be renewed independently **(see illustration)**. If the bearings require renewal, the complete hub assembly must be renewed as follows.
2 Chock the front wheels, then jack up the rear of the vehicle and support securely on axle stands (see *"Jacking, towing and wheel changing"*). Remove the appropriate rear roadwheel.
3 On models with rear disc brakes, remove the brake caliper and the brake disc, as described in Chapter 9. Note that there is no need to disconnect the brake fluid hose from the caliper - suspend the caliper with wire or string, to avoid straining the hose. **Do not** depress the brake pedal whilst the caliper is removed.
4 On models with rear drum brakes, remove the brake drum as described in Chapter 9. **Do not** depress the brake pedal whilst the brake drum is removed.
5 Prise the dust cap from the hub, then remove the split pin from the end of the stub axle **(see illustrations)**. Discard the split pin - a new one should be used on refitting.
6 The rear hub must now be loosened, using a suitable socket and extension bar.

⚠ **Warning: Take care, the nut is very tight! Do not remove the nut at this stage.**

7 Remove the hub nut and washer, then withdraw the hub assembly from the stub axle **(see illustrations)**. Discard the hub nut - a new one should be used on refitting.
8 Thoroughly clean the stub axle, then slide the new hub assembly into position.
9 Fit the washer, then fit a new hub nut - do not fully tighten the nut at this stage.

8.5a Prise the dust cap (arrowed) from the hub . . .

8.5b . . . then remove the split pin

8.7a Remove the hub nut . . .

8.7b . . . and the washer . . .

8.7c . . . then withdraw the hub assembly

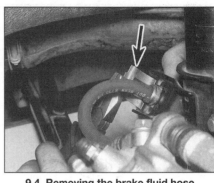

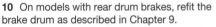

9.2 Unscrewing the anti-roll bar drop link-to-rear suspension strut nut - Hatchback model

9.3 Unbolting the ABS wiring from the rear strut - Hatchback model

9.4 Removing the brake fluid hose securing clip (arrowed) from the rear strut - Hatchback model

10 On models with rear drum brakes, refit the brake drum as described in Chapter 9.

11 On models with rear disc brakes, refit the brake disc and the caliper as described in Chapter 9.

12 Hold the hub stationary as during removal, then tighten the hub nut to the specified torque.

13 Check that the hub spins freely, then fit a new split pin, then tap the dust cap into position.

14 Refit the roadwheel, then lower the vehicle to the ground.

9 Rear suspension components (Saloon and Hatchback models) - removal, overhaul and refitting

Suspension strut

Removal

Note: *New suspension strut upper and lower securing nuts, a new top mounting gasket, and a new anti-roll bar drop link securing nut should be used on refitting.*

1 Chock the front wheels, then jack up the rear of the vehicle and support on axle stands (see *"Jacking, towing and wheel changing"*). Remove the relevant rear roadwheel.

2 Unscrew the nut securing the upper end of the anti-roll bar drop link to the lower end of the suspension strut **(see illustration)**.

Discard the nut - a new one should be used on refitting. Separate the drop link from the strut.

3 Where applicable, unbolt ABS wiring from lower end of strut **(see illustration)**.

4 Pull out the securing clip, and disconnect the brake fluid hose from the bracket at the lower end of the suspension strut **(see illustration)**.

5 Unscrew the nuts from the bolts securing the lower end of the suspension strut to the hub carrier, then withdraw the bolts **(see illustration)**. Discard the nuts - new ones must be used on refitting.

6 Remove the rear seat back side bolster as described in Chapter 11. On Saloon models, remove the rear parcel shelf (see Chapter 11, Section 28). Unclip the carpet trim panel to expose the suspension strut top mounting cover.

7 Prise the plastic cover from the top of the suspension strut top mounting, to expose the three securing nuts **(see illustration)**.

8 Have an assistant support the suspension strut from under the wheel arch, then unscrew the three top securing nuts, and lower the strut assembly from the vehicle **(see illustration)**. Discard the nuts - new ones must be used on refitting.

Overhaul

Note: *Suitable coil spring compressor tools will be required for this operation, and a new*

9.5 Removing a rear suspension strut-to-hub carrier bolt - Hatchback model

damper rod top nut must be used on reassembly.

Note: *On 1.6 litre engine models, there are two types of strut with different diameter damper rods, and therefore different bump rubbers. If the bump rubber is renewed, ensure that the correct replacement part is obtained.*

9 Clamp the lower end of the strut in a vice fitted with jaw protectors.

10 Temporarily refit two of the strut upper securing nuts to their studs then, using a suitable bar inserted between the upper mounting studs, counterhold the upper strut mounting whilst loosening the damper rod top nut. **Do not** remove the nut **(see illustrations)**.

9.7 Rear suspension strut securing nuts (arrowed) - Hatchback model

9.8 Removing a rear strut - Hatchback model

9.10a Loosening the rear strut damper rod top nut - Hatchback model

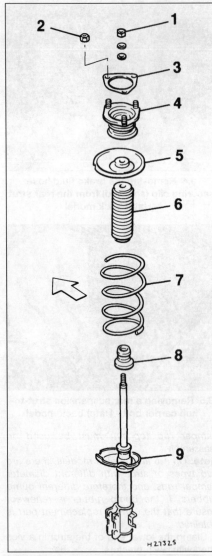

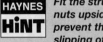

9.10b Rear suspension strut components - Saloon and Hatchback models

1 Damper rod top nut
2 Top mounting nuts
3 Gasket
4 Top mounting
5 Upper spring seat
6 Rubber gaiter
7 Coil spring
8 Bump rubber
9 Damper

> **HAYNES HiNT**
> *Fit the strut upper securing nuts upside-down, to prevent the bar from slipping off the studs.*

11 Fit suitable spring compressors to the spring, and compress the spring sufficiently to enable the upper spring seat to be turned by hand.

⚠️ *Warning: Do not use makeshift or improvised tools to compress the spring, as there is a danger of serious injury if the spring is not retained properly and released slowly.*

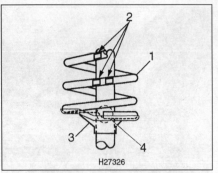

9.19 Rear suspension strut coil spring orientation - Saloon and Hatchback models

1 Coil spring
2 Paint marks
3 Lower spring seat
4 Spring locating shoulder

12 Fully unscrew and remove the damper rod top nut. Note that it will be necessary to counterhold the damper rod, using a suitable spanner, as the nut is unscrewed. Discard the nut - a new one must be used on reassembly.

13 Withdraw the washers, gasket, top mounting, and upper spring seat.

14 Withdraw the spring, complete with compressors, then lift the rubber gaiter and the bump rubber from the damper rod.

15 With the strut assembly now dismantled, examine all the components for wear, damage or deformation. Renew any of the components as necessary.

16 Examine the damper for signs of fluid leakage. Check the damper rod for signs of pitting along its entire length, and check the strut body for signs of damage. While holding it in an upright position, test the operation of the strut by moving the damper rod through a full stroke, and then through short strokes of 50 to 100 mm. In both cases, the resistance felt should be smooth and continuous. If the resistance is jerky, or uneven, or if there is any visible sign of wear or damage to the strut, renewal is necessary. Note that the damper cannot be renewed independently, and if leakage or damage is evident, the complete strut/damper assembly must be renewed (in which case, the spring, upper mounting components, bushes, and associated components can be transferred to the new strut).

17 If any doubt exists about the condition of the coil spring, carefully remove the spring compressors, and check the spring for distortion and signs of cracking. Renew the spring if it is damaged or distorted, or if there is any doubt as to its condition.

18 Clamp the strut body in a vice, as during dismantling, then refit the bump rubber and the rubber gaiter.

19 Ensure that the coil spring is compressed sufficiently to enable the upper mounting components to be fitted, then fit the spring over the damper rod, noting that two paint marks on the spring coils must be positioned towards the bottom of the strut **(see**

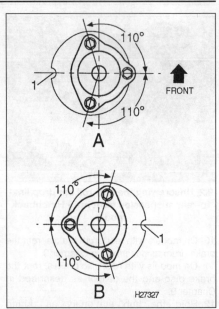

9.20 Rear suspension strut upper spring seat orientation - Saloon and Hatchback models

A Left-hand side
B Right-hand side
1 Cut-out

illustration). Make sure that the lower end of the spring is correctly located on the lower spring seat.

20 Refit the upper spring seat, noting that the seat must be positioned as shown **(see illustration)**. Ensure that the top end of the spring is correctly located on the upper spring seat.

21 Refit the top mounting, then refit the washers and a new top nut to the damper rod. Tighten the top nut to the specified torque, counterholding the damper rod as during removal.

22 Remove the spring compressors.

Refitting

23 Fit a new gasket to the top mounting, then manoeuvre the strut assembly into position under the wheel arch, passing the mounting studs through the holes in the body turret. Note that the cut-out in the upper spring seat must be positioned nearest the outer edge of the suspension turret (ie, the side nearest the roadwheel - see illustration 9.20). Fit the new upper mounting nuts, and tighten them to the specified torque.

24 Engage the lower end of the strut with the hub carrier, then refit the bolts and fit the new nuts, noting that the nuts fit on the forward side of the strut, and tighten to the specified torque.

25 Reconnect the anti-roll bar drop link to the suspension strut, and secure with a new nut. Ensure that the balljoint is positioned in the centre of its arc of movement, and is not under strain, then tighten the nut to the specified torque.

26 Refit the roadwheel, and lower the vehicle to the ground.

9.28a Remove the securing nut . . .

9.28b . . . and recover the washer . . .

9.28c . . . then withdraw the parallel link-to-hub carrier through-bolt - Hatchback model

Parallel links

Removal

Note: *New parallel link mounting nuts should be used on refitting. On completion of refitting, the rear wheel alignment must be checked with reference to Chapter 1.*

27 Chock the front wheels, then jack up the rear of the vehicle and support securely on axle stands (see "*Jacking, towing and wheel changing*"). Remove the relevant rear roadwheel.

28 Unscrew the nut from the through-bolt securing the outboard ends of the two parallel links to the hub carrier. Recover the washer and withdraw the bolt **(see illustrations)**. Discard the nut - a new one must be used on refitting.

29 If the rear parallel link is being removed, make a careful note of the position of the eccentrics on the inboard securing bolt **(see illustration)**. The eccentrics have graduations on the outer edges, and the position of the eccentrics determines the rear wheel toe-setting (see Chapter 1). Note that one eccentric is integral with the bolt head, and the other locates in a groove in the shank of the bolt, under the nut. Make alignment marks between the eccentric and the body bracket.

30 Unscrew the nut from the bolt securing the inboard end of the parallel link to the bracket on the body. Note that it will be necessary to counterhold the bolt. Recover the eccentric, then withdraw the bolt, and

lower the parallel link from under the vehicle. Discard the nut - a new one must be used on refitting **(see illustrations)**.

Overhaul

31 Inspect the parallel link for cracks or other signs of damage, and examine the bushes for wear and deterioration.

32 The bushes are integral with the parallel links, and if worn or damaged, the complete link assembly must be renewed.

Refitting

33 Manoeuvre the link into position beneath the vehicle, then refit the bolt securing the inboard end of the link to the bracket on the body (note that the bolt fits from the front of the vehicle). Where applicable, refit the washer, and fit a new securing nut, but do not tighten it fully at this stage.

34 Refit the through-bolt securing the outboard ends of the parallel links to the hub carrier (note that the bolt fits from the rear of the vehicle), then refit the washer, and a new nut, but do not fully tighten the nut at this stage.

35 Refit the roadwheel, and lower the vehicle to the ground.

36 Make sure that the vehicle is parked on level ground, then release the handbrake. Roll the vehicle backwards and forwards, and bounce the front of the vehicle to settle the suspension components.

37 Chock the wheels, then tighten the outboard parallel link securing nut to the specified torque.

38 Set the eccentric on the inboard parallel link securing bolt to the position noted before removal, then check the rear wheel alignment (see Chapter 1), and tighten the nut to the specified torque. If no suitable equipment is available to check the wheel alignment, tighten the nut with the eccentric positioned as noted before removal, then have the rear wheel alignment checked at the earliest opportunity by a Nissan dealer or a suitably-qualified tyre specialist.

Radius rod

Removal

Note: *A new radius rod front mounting nut should be used on refitting.*

39 Chock the front wheels, then jack up the

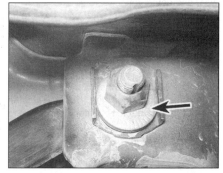

9.29 Note the position of the eccentric (arrowed) on the inboard parallel link securing bolt

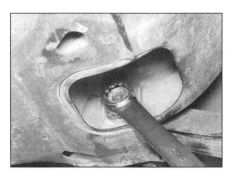

9.30a Unscrew the parallel link inboard securing nut while counterholding the bolt . . .

9.30b . . . then recover the eccentric . . .

9.30c . . . and withdraw the bolt

10

9.40 Radius rod-to-hub carrier nut (arrowed)

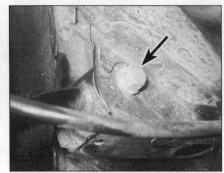

9.41 Radius rod-to-body bolt (arrowed)

9.67 Rear anti-roll bar securing bolt (arrowed) - Hatchback model

rear of the vehicle and support securely on axle stands (see "*Jacking, towing and wheel changing*"). To improve access, remove the relevant rear roadwheel.

40 Where applicable, remove the cover from the nut securing the rear end of the radius rod to the hub carrier, then unscrew the nut and recover the washer **(see illustration)**.

41 Unscrew the nut from the bolt securing the front of the radius rod to the bracket on the vehicle body, then remove the bolt, and withdraw the radius rod from under the vehicle **(see illustration)**. Discard the nut - a new one should be used on refitting.

Overhaul

42 Inspect the radius rod for cracks or other signs of damage, and examine the bushes for wear and deterioration.

43 The bushes are integral with the radius rods, and if worn or damaged, the complete assembly must be renewed.

Refitting

44 Manoeuvre the radius rod into position under the vehicle, and position the rear of the rod on the hub carrier stud. Refit the washer and nut, but do not fully tighten the nut at this stage.

45 Move the front of the rod into position in the front mounting bracket, then refit the front securing bolt, noting that the bolt fits from the inboard edge of the bracket. Fit a new nut, but do not fully tighten the nut at this stage.

46 Refit the roadwheel, and lower the vehicle to the ground.

47 Make sure that the vehicle is parked on level ground, then release the handbrake. Roll the vehicle backwards and forwards, and bounce the front of the vehicle to settle the suspension components.

48 Chock the wheels, then tighten the radius rod securing nuts to the specified torque. On completion, where applicable, refit the cover to the rear radius rod securing nut.

Hub carrier

Removal

Note: *A new parallel link outboard mounting nut, and new suspension strut-to-hub carrier nuts, should be used on refitting.*

49 Chock the front wheels, then jack up the rear of the vehicle and support securely on axle stands (see "*Jacking, towing and wheel changing*"). Remove the relevant rear roadwheel.

50 On models with rear disc brakes, unbolt the brake caliper from the hub carrier as described in Chapter 9. Note that there is no need to disconnect the brake fluid hose - suspend the caliper using wire or string.

51 On models with rear drum brakes, remove the brake shoes, and disconnect the brake fluid pipe from the rear wheel cylinder, as described in Chapter 9 - be prepared for fluid spillage. Plug the open ends of the pipe and wheel cylinder, to reduce fluid spillage and to prevent dirt ingress.

52 Where applicable, remove the cover from the nut securing the rear end of the radius rod to the hub carrier, then unscrew the nut and recover the washer.

53 Unscrew the nut from the through-bolt securing the outboard ends of the two parallel links to the hub carrier. Recover the washer and withdraw the bolt. Discard the nut - a new one must be used on refitting.

54 Unscrew the nuts from the bolts securing the lower end of the suspension strut to the hub carrier, then withdraw the bolts, and remove the hub carrier from under the vehicle. Discard the nuts - new ones must be used on refitting.

Overhaul

55 Examine the hub carrier for signs of cracking or damage. If desired, the hub bearings can be renewed as described in Section 8.

Refitting

56 Move the hub carrier into position, engaging the radius rod with the hub carrier stud, then fit the two bolts securing the hub carrier to the lower end of the suspension strut, noting that the bolts fit from the rear of the hub carrier. Fit new nuts to the bolts, and tighten them to the specified torque.

57 Reconnect the parallel links to the hub carrier, then refit the through-bolt, noting that the bolt fits from the rear of the hub carrier. Refit the washer and a new securing nut, but do not fully tighten the nut at this stage.

58 Refit the radius rod-to-hub carrier securing nut, ensuring that the washer is in place, but do not fully tighten the nut at this stage.

59 On models with rear drum brakes, refit the brake shoes, and reconnect the brake fluid pipe to the wheel cylinder, then bleed the brake hydraulic circuit, as described in Chapter 9.

60 On models with rear disc brakes, refit the brake caliper as described in Chapter 9.

61 Refit the roadwheel, and lower the vehicle to the ground.

62 Make sure that the vehicle is parked on level ground, then release the handbrake. Roll the vehicle backwards and forwards, and bounce the front of the vehicle to settle the suspension components.

63 Chock the wheels, then tighten the radius rod securing nut, and the parallel link outboard securing nut, to the specified torque. On completion, where applicable, refit the cover to the rear radius rod securing nut.

64 Have the rear wheel alignment checked at the earliest opportunity (see Chapter 1).

Anti-roll bar

Removal

Note: *New anti-roll bar clamp nuts, and new anti-roll bar-to-drop link nuts, should be used on refitting.*

65 Chock the front wheels, then jack up the rear of the vehicle and support securely on axle stands (see "*Jacking, towing and wheel changing*"). To improve access, remove the rear roadwheels.

66 Unscrew the nuts securing the lower ends of the drop links to the anti-roll bar. Discard the nuts - new ones should be used on refitting.

67 Unscrew the nuts and bolts securing the anti-roll bar mounting clamps to the brackets on the body **(see illustration)**, then withdraw the clamps, and manipulate the anti-roll bar out from under the vehicle. Discard the clamp nuts - new ones should be used on refitting.

Overhaul

68 Inspect the mounting clamp rubbers for cracks or deterioration. If renewal is necessary, slide the old rubbers from the bar,

9.72 Disconnecting a rear anti-roll bar drop link from the suspension strut - Hatchback model

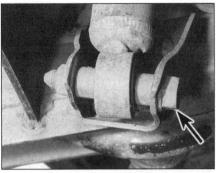

10.2 Rear shock absorber lower securing bolt (arrowed) - Estate model

10.13 Panhard rod upper securing bolt (arrowed) - Estate model

and fit the new rubbers. Note that the rubbers should be positioned with their slits at the top of the bar.

Refitting

69 Refitting is a reversal of removal, bearing in mind the following points:
a) *When refitting the anti-roll bar clamps, note that the elongated bolt holes should be positioned at the bottom.*
b) *When reconnecting the drop links to the anti-roll bar, make sure that the drop link balljoint is positioned centrally in its arc of movement, and is not under strain, and use new nuts.*
c) *Use new clamp nuts, and new anti-roll bar-to-drop link nuts.*

Anti-roll bar drop link

Removal

Note: *New anti-roll bar-to-drop link nuts should be used on refitting.*

70 Chock the front wheels, then jack up the rear of the vehicle and support securely on axle stands (see *"Jacking, towing and wheel changing"*). To improve access, remove the relevant rear roadwheel.

71 If necessary, counterhold the drop link pin, then unscrew the nut securing the end of the anti-roll bar to the drop link. Discard the nut - a new one should be used on refitting.

72 Again, if necessary counterhold the drop link pin, then unscrew the nut securing the drop link to the lower end of the suspension strut, and withdraw the drop link **(see illustration)**. Discard the nut - a new one should be used on refitting.

Overhaul

73 Check the drop link balljoints for wear and damage, and if necessary renew the drop link.

Refitting

74 Refitting is a reversal of removal, bearing in mind the following points:
a) *Make sure that the drop link balljoints are positioned centrally in their arcs of movement, and are not under strain.*
b) *Use new drop link securing nuts, and tighten them to the specified torque.*

10 Rear suspension components (Estate models) - removal, overhaul and refitting

Shock absorber

Removal

Note: *Shock absorbers should always be renewed in pairs - ie, renew BOTH rear shock absorbers, even if only one actually needs to be renewed. New shock absorber mounting nuts should be used on refitting.*

1 Chock the front wheels, then jack up the rear of the vehicle and support securely on axle stands (see *"Jacking, towing and wheel changing"*). Remove the relevant rear roadwheel.

2 Place a trolley jack and interposed block of wood under the centre of the axle tube, then raise the axle slightly to tension the coil springs. Unscrew the nut from the bolt securing the shock absorber to the axle assembly. Discard the nut - a new one must be used on refitting. Withdraw the bolt **(see illustration)**.

3 Unscrew the nut securing the top of the shock absorber to the stud on the underbody, then recover the washer, and withdraw the shock absorber. Discard the nut - a new one should be used on refitting.

Overhaul

4 Examine the shock absorber for signs of fluid leakage. Check the shock absorber rod for signs of pitting, and check the shock absorber body for signs of damage. While holding it in an upright position, test the operation of the shock absorber by moving the rod through a full stroke, and then through short strokes of 50 to 100 mm. In both cases, the resistance felt should be smooth and continuous. If the resistance is jerky, or uneven, or if there is any visible sign of wear or damage to the shock absorber, renewal is necessary.

5 Inspect the mounting bushes for signs of cracking or wear. Note that the bushes are not available separately, and if worn or damaged, the complete shock absorber must be renewed.

Refitting

6 Position the top of the shock absorber over the mounting stud on the underbody, then refit the washer (the larger diameter of the washer fits against the nut), and a new securing nut. Do not fully tighten the nut at this stage.

7 Position the lower end of the shock absorber in the mounting bracket on the axle assembly, then refit the bolt (note that the bolt fits from the inboard side of the trailing arm) and a new securing nut. Do not fully tighten the nut at this stage.

8 Withdraw the trolley jack from under the axle, then refit the roadwheel and lower the vehicle to the ground.

9 Make sure that the vehicle is parked on level ground, then release the handbrake, roll the vehicle backwards and forwards, and bounce the rear of the vehicle to settle the suspension components.

10 Chock the wheels, then tighten the shock absorber securing nuts to the specified torque.

Coil spring
Removal

Note: *Coil springs should always be renewed in pairs - ie, renew BOTH rear springs, even if only one actually needs to be renewed. As it is necessary to lower the complete axle assembly, both coil springs should be removed at the same time. New shock absorber lower mounting nuts, and a new Panhard rod upper mounting nut, should be used on refitting.*

11 Chock the front wheels, then jack up the rear of the vehicle and support securely on axle stands (see *"Jacking, towing and wheel changing"*). Remove the rear roadwheels.

12 Place a trolley jack and interposed block of wood under the centre of the axle tube, then raise the axle slightly to tension the coil springs. Unscrew the nuts from the bolts securing the shock absorbers to the axle assembly, then withdraw the bolts. Discard the nuts - new ones should be used on refitting.

13 Unscrew the nut from the bolt securing the Panhard rod to the bracket on the underbody, then withdraw the bolt **(see illustration)**. Discard the nut - a new one should be used on refitting.

10

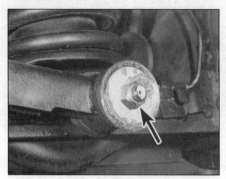

10.24 Panhard rod lower securing nut (arrowed)

10.37 Disconnect the brake fluid hoses from the pipes at the brackets on the rear axle - Estate model

10.39 Disconnect the rear brake pressure-regulating valve spring (arrowed) from the bracket on the axle tube - Estate model

14 Lower the jack sufficiently to relieve the tension in the coil springs, then withdraw the coil springs.

Overhaul

15 If any doubt exists about the condition of the coil spring, check the spring for distortion and signs of cracking. Renew the spring if it is damaged or distorted, or if there is any doubt as to its condition

Refitting

16 Locate the springs in position between the axle and the upper seats, then raise the jack sufficiently to position the upper end of the Panhard rod in its mounting bracket on the underbody.
17 Refit the Panhard rod upper securing bolt, noting that the bolt fits from the rear of the vehicle, then fit a new nut to the bolt. Do not fully tighten the nut at this stage.
18 Position the lower ends of the shock absorbers in the mounting brackets on the axle assembly, then refit the bolts (note that the bolts fit from the inboard sides of the trailing arms). Fit new securing nuts to the bolts, but do not fully tighten them at this stage.
19 Refit the roadwheels, and lower the vehicle to the ground.
20 Make sure that the vehicle is parked on level ground, then release the handbrake, roll the vehicle backwards and forwards, and bounce the rear of the vehicle to settle the suspension components.
21 Chock the wheels, then tighten the shock absorber lower securing nuts and the Panhard rod upper securing nut.

Panhard rod

Removal

Note: *New Panhard rod mounting nuts should be used on refitting.*
22 Chock the front wheels, then jack up the rear of the vehicle and support securely on axle stands (see "*Jacking, towing and wheel changing*").
23 Place a trolley jack and interposed block of wood under the centre of the axle tube, then raise the axle slightly to tension the coil springs.

24 Ensure that the axle assembly is still adequately supported, then unscrew the nut securing the lower end of the Panhard rod to the axle assembly **(see illustration)**. Discard the nut - a new one should be used on refitting. Recover the washer.
25 Unscrew the nut from the bolt securing the top end of the Panhard rod to the body bracket, then withdraw the bolt, and remove the Panhard rod. Discard the nut - a new one should be used on refitting. Recover the remaining washer from the Panhard mounting stud on the axle assembly.

Overhaul

26 Examine the Panhard rod for cracks or signs of damage. Similarly, examine the mounting bushes.
27 The lower mounting bushes (Panhard rod-to-rear axle mounting) can be renewed, but if the top mounting bush is worn or damaged, the complete Panhard rod must be renewed.
28 To renew the lower bushes, simply prise them from the Panhard rod (if they are not already loose), then press the new bushes into position.

Refitting

29 Ensure that the lower mounting bushes are in position, then refit the lower end of the Panhard rod to the stud on the axle assembly. Make sure that the inboard washer is in place (note that the concave side of the washer should be positioned against the stud, ie, away from the Panhard rod).
30 Refit the outboard washer to the Panhard rod stud (the concave side should be against the securing nut), then fit a new securing nut. Do not fully tighten the nut at this stage.
31 Manoeuvre the top end of the Panhard rod into position in the top mounting bracket (if necessary, raise or lower the jack to align the mounting bolt holes in the rod and bracket). Refit the mounting bolt, noting that the bolt fits from the rear of the vehicle. Fit a new nut to the bolt, but do not fully tighten it at this stage.
32 The jack used to support the axle assembly can now be withdrawn.
33 Lower the vehicle to the ground.
34 Make sure that the vehicle is parked on

level ground, then roll the vehicle backwards and forwards, and bounce the rear of the vehicle to settle the suspension components.
35 Chock the wheels, then tighten the Panhard rod securing nuts to the specified torque.

Rear axle assembly

Removal

Note: *New shock absorber mounting nuts, new Panhard rod mounting nuts, and trailing arm securing nuts, should be used on refitting.*
36 Chock the front wheels, then jack up the rear of the vehicle and support securely on axle stands (see "*Jacking, towing and wheel changing*"). Remove the rear roadwheels.
37 Disconnect the brake fluid hoses from the pipes at the brackets on the rear axle tube, with reference to Chapter 9 **(see illustration)**. Be prepared for fluid spillage, and plug the open ends of the pipes and hoses, to reduce fluid spillage and to prevent dirt ingress.
38 Where applicable, remove the ABS wheel sensors, and disconnect the wiring harnesses from any clips or brackets on the rear suspension components, as described in Chapter 9. Note the routing of the cables to ensure correct refitting.
39 Disconnect the rear brake pressure-regulating valve spring from the bracket on the axle tube **(see illustration)**.
40 Disconnect the handbrake cables from the rear brake shoes or calipers, as applicable, as described in Chapter 9, then release the handbrake cables from any clips or brackets on the rear suspension components. Note the routing of the cables to ensure correct refitting.
41 Remove the shock absorbers, the Panhard rod, and the coil springs, as described previously in this Section.
42 Counterhold the nuts, and unscrew the pins securing the fronts of the trailing arms to the body brackets. Note that a suitable long-reach socket will be required to unscrew the pins. Discard the nuts - new ones must be used on refitting.
43 Ensure that the axle assembly is adequately supported, then withdraw the pins

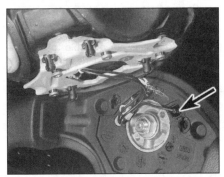

11.3 Pull the horn pad from the centre of the steering wheel, and disconnect the horn wiring (arrowed) . . .

11.4 . . . then remove the screw securing the wiring bracket

11.6 Unscrewing the steering wheel securing nut

securing the trailing arms to the body brackets, and lower the assembly sufficiently to withdraw it from under the vehicle. Take care not to drop the assembly off the jack - the help of an assistant to support the assembly on the jack will ease the operation greatly.

Overhaul

44 Examine the metal components of the assembly for cracks or signs of damage. Similarly, examine the trailing arm front mounting bushes.

45 The trailing arm mounting bushes can be removed/renewed using metal tubes of suitable diameter, as follows. Ideally, a press should be used.

46 Support the trailing arm using a suitable tube positioned around the bush housing, then press or drive the bush from the housing.

47 Lubricate the new bush with a little soapy water (washing-up liquid is ideal) to aid installation. Note that the arrows on the outer face of the bush must point towards the front and rear of the vehicle.

48 Again support the trailing arm, then press or tap the new bush into position, using a tube of suitable diameter, which must bear on the outer metal sleeve of the bush - **do not** tap the end face of the bush directly with a hammer.

Refitting

49 Support the axle assembly on a jack, as during removal, then manoeuvre the assembly into position under the vehicle.

50 Refit the pins securing the fronts of the trailing arms to the body brackets, then fit the new nuts, but do not fully tighten them at this stage.

51 Refit the coil springs, Panhard rod, and shock absorbers as described previously in this Section. Do not fully tighten the mountings until the vehicle is resting on its wheels.

52 The jack used to support the axle assembly can now be withdrawn.

53 Clip the handbrake cables into position in the securing clips and brackets, ensuring that the cables are routed as noted before removal. Reconnect the cables to the rear

brake shoes or calipers, as applicable, as described in Chapter 9.

54 Reconnect the rear brake pressure-regulating valve spring to the bracket on the axle tube.

55 Where applicable, refit the ABS wheel sensors, and clip the wiring harnesses into position, as described in Chapter 9. Ensure that the wiring is routed as noted before removal.

56 Reconnect the brake fluid hoses to the pipes, with reference to Chapter 9.

57 Refit the roadwheels, and lower the vehicle to the ground.

58 Make sure that the vehicle is parked on level ground, then roll the vehicle backwards and forwards, and bounce the rear of the vehicle to settle the suspension components.

59 Chock the wheels, then tighten the trailing arm, Panhard rod, and rear shock absorber fixings to the specified torque.

60 Bleed the brake hydraulic system as described in Chapter 9.

61 Check the handbrake adjustment as described in Chapter 1.

62 Check the adjustment of the rear brake pressure-regulating valve as described in Chapter 9.

11 Steering wheel - removal and refitting

> **Warning: Later models are equipped with an air bag system. The air bag is mounted in the steering wheel centre pad. Make sure that the safety recommendations given in Chapter 12 are followed, to prevent personal injury.**

Models without air bag
Removal

1 Disconnect the battery negative lead.

2 Set the front wheels in the straight-ahead position, then release the steering lock by inserting the ignition key.

3 Pull the horn pad from the centre of the steering wheel, and disconnect the horn wiring from the pad **(see illustration)**.

4 Remove the screw securing the horn wiring bracket to the steering wheel **(see illustration)**.

5 Make alignment marks between the steering wheel and the end of the steering column shaft.

6 Slacken and remove the steering wheel securing nut **(see illustration)**.

7 Lift the steering wheel off the column splines. If it is tight, tap it up near the centre, using the palm of your hand, or twist it from side to side, whilst pulling upwards to release it from the shaft splines. If the wheel is particularly tight, a suitable puller should be used.

Refitting

8 Before commencing refitting, lightly coat the surfaces of the direction indicator cancelling mechanism components and the horn contact slip ring components with grease.

9 Refitting is a reversal of removal, bearing in mind the following points:

a) *Ensure that the direction indicator switch is in the central (cancelled/off) position, otherwise the switch may be damaged as the wheel is refitted.*

b) *Align the marks made on the wheel and the steering column shaft before removal.*

c) *Tighten the securing nut to the specified torque.*

10 Note that if necessary, the position of the steering wheel on the column shaft can be altered in order to centralise the wheel (ensure that the front roadwheels are pointing in the straight-ahead position), by moving the wheel the required number of splines on the shaft.

Models with air bag

> **Warning: Refer to the precautions given in Chapter 12 before proceeding. Take great care not to drop the steering wheel centre pad, or to allow objects to impact the steering wheel centre pad, during this procedure.**

Removal

11 Ensure that the ignition is switched off, then disconnect the battery negative lead. *Wait for at least ten minutes before carrying out any further work.*

10

12.3a Remove the grub screw . . .

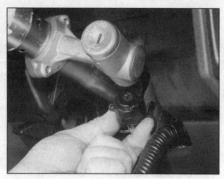

12.3b . . . and withdraw the ignition switch

12 Carefully prise the lower cover from the rear of the air bag unit, and disconnect the now-exposed air bag wiring connector.

13 Prise the side covers from the rear of the air bag unit, to expose the securing bolts.

14 Using a suitable Torx bit, remove the two air bag unit securing bolts (one each side), then carefully lift the unit from the steering wheel. **Take care not to drop the air bag unit, and do not attempt to dismantle it.** Discard the bolts, new ones must be used on refitting. Always store the air bag unit with the pad side (visible side) facing upwards.

15 Set the front wheels in the straight-ahead position, then release the steering lock by inserting the ignition key.

16 Disconnect the horn wiring connector.

17 Proceed as described in paragraphs 5 to 7 inclusive. Unclip the wiring harnesses,

and feed them through the steering wheel as the wheel is withdrawn.

Refitting

18 Refitting is a reversal of removal, bearing in mind the following points:

a) Ensure that the direction indicator switch is in the central (cancelled/off) position, otherwise the switch may be damaged as the wheel is refitted.

b) Feed the wiring harnesses through the steering wheel, and clip the connector into position as the wheel is refitted.

c) Align the marks made on the wheel and the steering column shaft before removal, and align the steering wheel with the guide pins on the air bag contact assembly.

d) Tighten the steering wheel securing nut to the specified torque.

e) Secure the air bag unit to the steering wheel using new Torx bolts, and tighten the bolts to the specified torque.

19 Note that it is not possible to alter the position of the steering wheel on the column shaft in order to centralise the wheel.

12 Ignition switch/steering column lock - removal and refitting

Removal

Note: New shear-screws must be used when refitting the lock assembly.

1 Disconnect the battery negative lead.

2 Remove the steering column shrouds as described in Chapter 11.

3 To remove the ignition switch, disconnect the wiring plug from the switch, then remove the grub screw from the rear of the lock (using a suitable cranked key), and withdraw the switch **(see illustrations)**.

4 To remove the lock assembly, drill out and remove the two shear-screws, then withdraw the two sections of the lock casting from the steering column. Note that the lock assembly cannot be removed from the casting.

Refitting

5 Refitting is a reversal of removal, but when refitting the lock assembly, use new shear-screws, and tighten the screws until the heads break off.

13 Steering column - removal, inspection and refitting

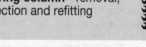

> **Warning: Later models are equipped with an air bag system. The air bag is mounted in the steering wheel centre pad, and the control module is mounted under the steering column. Make sure that the safety recommendations given in Chapter 12 are followed, to prevent personal injury.**

Removal

1 Disconnect the battery negative lead.

2 Remove the steering wheel as described in Section 11.

3 Remove the steering column stalk switches with reference to Chapter 12 **(see illustration)**.

4 Disconnect the wiring plug from the ignition switch.

5 If desired, to improve access, remove the driver's side lower facia panel as described in Chapter 11, Section 30.

6 Working in the driver's footwell, release the steering shaft lower gaiter securing clip, then unclip the gaiter from the metal cover, and

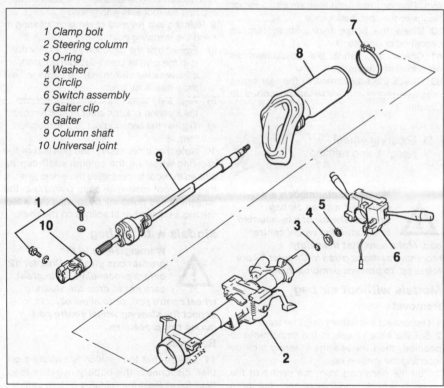

1 Clamp bolt
2 Steering column
3 O-ring
4 Washer
5 Circlip
6 Switch assembly
7 Gaiter clip
8 Gaiter
9 Column shaft
10 Universal joint

13.3 Steering column components - Saloon and Hatchback models

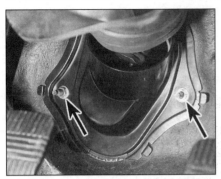

13.6 Slide the gaiter up the steering shaft to expose the metal cover securing nuts (arrowed) . . .

13.7 . . . then remove the metal cover

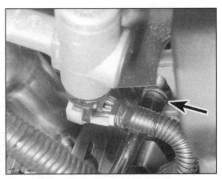

13.10 Unscrewing a steering column upper securing bolt (arrowed)

slide the gaiter up the steering shaft **(see illustration)**. Alternatively, on models with a plastic steering column lower cover, remove the clips and securing screws, and separate the two halves of the cover.

7 Unscrew the three securing nuts, and withdraw the metal cover from the studs in the footwell **(see illustration)**. Slide the cover up the steering column to expose the lower universal joint.

8 Temporarily refit the steering wheel, and turn the steering column as necessary for access to the universal joint clamp bolt.

9 Unscrew and remove the universal joint clamp bolt.

10 Unscrew the two steering column upper securing bolts **(see illustration)**, and the two lower nuts, and withdraw the steering column.

Inspection

11 The steering column incorporates a telescopic safety feature. In the event of a front-end crash, the shaft collapses and prevents the steering wheel injuring the driver. Before refitting the steering column, examine the column and mountings for signs of damage and deformation, and renew as necessary.

12 Check the steering shaft for signs of free play in the column bushes, and check the universal joints for signs of damage or roughness in the joint bearings. If any damage or wear is found in the steering column

universal joints or shaft bushes, the column must be renewed as an assembly.

13 Measure the length of the steering column from the centre of the universal joint pin to the top of the column shaft **(see illustration)**. If the measurement is outside the specified limits, this is probably due to accident damage, and the complete column assembly should be renewed.

Refitting

14 Commence refitting by sliding the rubber gaiter (where applicable), and the metal cover onto the lower end of the shaft. Where applicable, refit and tighten the clip securing the upper end of the gaiter to the steering column **(see illustration)**.

15 Offer the steering column into position, and engage the lower end of the column shaft with the universal joint. Note that there is a master spline, so that the column shaft can only be fitted in one position.

16 Refit the steering column lower securing nuts and the upper bolts, then tighten them to the specified torque.

17 Refit and tighten the universal joint clamp bolt.

18 Position the metal cover over the universal joint, then refit and tighten the securing nuts.

19 Clip the lower end of the rubber gaiter into position in the metal cover, then fit a new lower gaiter securing clip (cable-tie) **(see illustration)**. Alternatively, refit the two halves of the plastic cover.

20 Where applicable, refit the driver's side lower facia panel.

21 Reconnect the ignition switch wiring plug.

22 Refit the steering column stalk switches.

23 Refit the steering wheel, with reference to Section 11.

24 Reconnect the battery negative lead.

---

14 Steering gear assembly - removal, overhaul and refitting

> ⚠ **Warning: Later models are equipped with an air bag system. The air bag is mounted in the steering wheel centre pad, and the control module is mounted under the steering column. Make sure that the safety recommendations given in Chapter 12 are followed, to prevent personal injury.**

Manual steering gear

Removal

Note: *A balljoint separator tool will be required for this operation. A new track-rod end nut split pin should be used on refitting.*

1 Chock the rear wheels, apply the handbrake, then jack up the front of the vehicle and support securely on axle stands (see *"Jacking, towing and wheel changing"*). Remove the roadwheels.

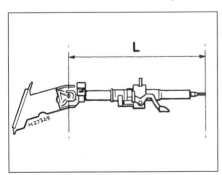

13.13 Steering column length measurement

L = 556.2 to 557.8 mm

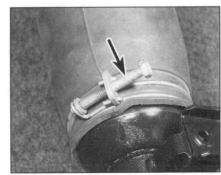

13.14 Refit and tighten the clip (arrowed) securing the upper end of the gaiter to the steering column

13.19 Use a new cable-tie (arrowed) to secure the lower end of the steering column gaiter

10

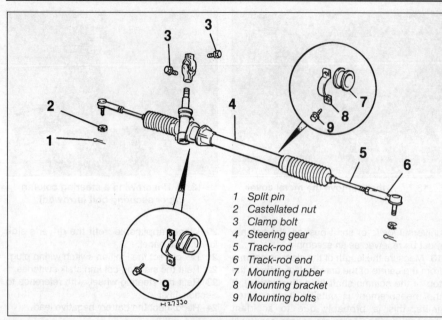

1 Split pin
2 Castellated nut
3 Clamp bolt
4 Steering gear
5 Track-rod
6 Track-rod end
7 Mounting rubber
8 Mounting bracket
9 Mounting bolts

14.3a   Steering gear assembly

2 Move the steering wheel so that the front wheels are pointing in the straight-ahead position.
3 Working on one side of the vehicle, remove the split pin, then partially unscrew the castellated nut securing the track-rod end to the steering arm. Using a balljoint separator tool, separate the track-rod end from the steering arm **(see illustrations)**. Remove the nut. Discard the split pin - a new one must be used on refitting.
4 Repeat the procedure to disconnect the track-rod end on the other side of the vehicle.
5 Working in the driver's footwell, release the steering shaft lower gaiter securing clip, then unclip the gaiter from the metal cover, and slide the gaiter up the steering shaft. Alternatively, on models with a plastic steering column lower cover, remove the clips and securing screws, and separate the two halves of the cover.
6 Unscrew the three securing nuts, and withdraw the metal cover from the studs in the footwell. Slide the cover up the steering column to expose the lower universal joint.
7 Temporarily refit the steering wheel, and turn the steering column as necessary for access to the universal joint clamp bolt.
8 Unscrew and remove the universal joint clamp bolt.
9 Working in the engine compartment, unscrew the bolts securing the steering gear mounting brackets to the bulkhead. Support the steering gear, then withdraw the brackets.
10 Rotate the steering gear, and manipulate it out through the right-hand wheel arch. Note that on left-hand-drive models, it will be necessary to lift the steering gear over the mounting brackets before it can be withdrawn.

Overhaul

11 Examine the assembly for obvious signs of wear or damage.
12 Check the rack for smooth operation through its full stroke of movement, and check that there is no binding or free play.
13 Check the track-rods for deformation and cracks.
14 Check the condition of the steering gear rubber gaiters, and renew if necessary with reference to Section 15.
15 Examine the track-rod ends for wear or damage, and renew if necessary with reference to Section 18.
16 No overhaul of the manual steering gear is possible, and if worn or damaged, the complete assembly (including track-rods) must be renewed.

Refitting

17 Ensure that the steering gear is centralised as follows:
a) *Turn the pinion to rotate the steering from lock-to-lock, and count the number of turns of the pinion.*
b) *With the steering on full lock, turn the pinion back through half the number of turns noted for lock-to-lock, to achieve the centralised position.*
18 Manoeuvre the steering gear into position through the right-hand wheel arch, then refit the mounting brackets, and refit and tighten the securing bolts. **Note:** *On Estate models, lightly tighten the lower clamp bolts (do not fully tighten the bolts at this stage), then tighten all the clamp bolts to the specified torque, starting with the upper bolts, in the order shown* **(see illustration)**.
19 Engage the lower end of the steering column shaft with the universal joint, then refit and tighten the clamp bolt.
20 Position the metal cover over the universal joint, then refit and tighten the securing nuts.
21 Clip the lower end of the rubber gaiter into position in the metal cover, then fit a new lower gaiter securing clip (cable-tie). Alternatively, refit the two halves of the plastic cover.
22 Working on one side of the vehicle, reconnect the track-rod end to the steering arm, then refit the castellated nut, and tighten to the specified torque.
23 If necessary, tighten the nut further (ensure that the maximum torque for the nut is

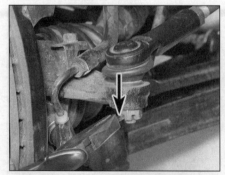

14.3b   Removing the split pin (arrowed) from a track-rod end nut

14.3c   Using a balljoint separator tool to disconnect the track-rod end from a steering arm

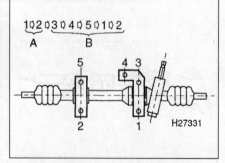

14.18   Steering gear securing bolt tightening sequence - Estate models

A Initial tightening   B Final tightening

not exceeded) until the nearest grooves in the nut are aligned with the split pin hole in the track-rod end, then fit a new split pin.

24 Repeat the procedure to reconnect the track-rod end on the other side of the vehicle.

25 Refit the roadwheels, and lower the vehicle to the ground.

Power steering gear

Removal

26 Chock the rear wheels, apply the handbrake, then jack up the front of the vehicle and support securely on axle stands (see "*Jacking, towing and wheel changing*"). Remove the roadwheels.

27 Position a suitable container beneath the fluid feed pipe unions on the steering gear, then unscrew the union nut, and disconnect the pipe from the steering gear. Similarly, disconnect the fluid return hose from the steering gear. Drain the fluid into the container, then plug or cover the open ends of the pipe/hose and steering gear to reduce further fluid loss, and to prevent dirt ingress.

28 Remove the exhaust front section as described in the relevant Part of Chapter 4.

29 Disconnect the track-rod ends from the steering arms as described previously for the manual steering gear in paragraphs 2 to 4.

30 Where applicable, unclip the wiring harness from the clip on the front subframe mounting bracket.

31 Disconnect the steering column universal joint from the steering gear pinion as described previously for the manual steering gear in paragraphs 5 and 8.

32 Place a trolley jack with an interposed block of wood beneath the transmission, and raise the jack to just take the weight of the engine/transmission assembly.

33 Unscrew the through-bolt securing the rear engine/transmission mounting to the lower crossmember.

34 Unscrew the securing bolts, and withdraw the crossmember from under the vehicle.

35 Unbolt the rear engine/transmission mounting bracket from the engine/transmission assembly.

36 Working in the engine compartment, unscrew the bolts securing the steering gear mounting brackets to the bulkhead. Support the steering gear, then withdraw the brackets.

37 Manipulate the steering gear around the wiring harness (where applicable), then slide the assembly to the right-hand side of the vehicle, and withdraw the assembly from under the left-hand side of the vehicle.

Overhaul

38 Overhaul of the power steering gear should be entrusted to a Nissan dealer.

Refitting

39 Ensure that the steering gear is centralised as follows:

a) *Turn the pinion to rotate the steering from lock-to-lock, and count the number of turns of the pinion.*

b) *With the steering on full lock, turn the pinion back through half the number of turns noted for lock-to-lock, to achieve the centralised position.*

40 Manoeuvre the steering gear into position from under the left-hand side of the vehicle, then refit the mounting brackets, and refit and tighten the securing bolts. **Note:** *On Estate models, lightly tighten the lower clamp bolts (do not fully tighten the bolts at this stage), then tighten all the clamp bolts to the specified torque, starting with the upper bolts, in the order shown (see illustration 14.18).*

41 Refit the rear engine/transmission mounting bracket, and tighten the fixings to the specified torque (see Chapter 2B).

42 Refit the crossmember, and tighten the securing bolts to the specified torque (see Chapter 2B), then refit the through-bolt securing the engine/transmission mounting to the crossmember. Where applicable, clip the wiring harness into position on the crossmember.

43 Withdraw the jack used to support the engine/transmission assembly.

44 Refit the exhaust front section with reference to the relevant Part of Chapter 4.

45 Proceed as described in paragraphs 19 to 24.

46 Reconnect the fluid feed pipe and the return hose to the steering gear.

47 Refit the roadwheels, then bleed the power steering hydraulic system as described in Section 16.

48 On completion, lower the vehicle to the ground.

---

15 Steering gear rubber gaiters - renewal

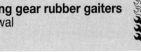

Note: *New gaiter retaining clips should be used on refitting.*

1 Remove the relevant track-rod end as described in Section 18.

2 If not already done, unscrew the track-rod end locknut from the end of the track-rod.

3 Mark the correct fitted position of the gaiter on the track-rod, then release the gaiter securing clips. Slide the gaiter from the steering gear, and off the end of the track-rod.

4 Thoroughly clean the track-rod and the steering gear housing, using fine abrasive paper to polish off any corrosion, burrs or sharp edges, which might damage the new gaiter sealing lips on installation. Scrape off all the grease from the old gaiter, and apply it to the track rod inner balljoint. (This assumes that grease has not been lost or contaminated as a result of damage to the old gaiter. Use fresh grease if in doubt.)

5 Carefully slide the new gaiter onto the track-rod, and locate it on the steering gear housing. Align the outer edge of the gaiter with the mark made on the track-rod prior to removal, then secure it in position with new retaining clips.

6 Screw the track-rod end locknut onto the end of the track-rod.

7 Refit the track rod end as described in Section 18.

---

16 Power steering hydraulic system - bleeding

General

1 The following symptoms indicate that there is air present in the power steering hydraulic system:

a) *Generation of air bubbles in fluid reservoir.*

b) *"Clicking" noises from power steering pump.*

c) *Excessive "buzzing" from power steering pump.*

2 Note that when the vehicle is stationary, or while moving the steering wheel slowly, a "hissing" noise may be produced in the steering gear or the fluid pump. This noise is inherent in the system, and does not indicate any cause for concern.

Bleeding

3 Chock the rear wheels, apply the handbrake, then jack up the front of the vehicle and support securely on axle stands (see "*Jacking, towing and wheel changing*").

4 Check the fluid level in the power steering fluid reservoir (bear in mind that the vehicle will be tilted, so the level cannot be read accurately), and if necessary top-up to just above the relevant level mark.

5 Have an assistant turn the steering quickly from lock to lock, and observe the fluid level. If the fluid level drops, add more fluid, and repeat the operation until the fluid level no longer drops. Failure to achieve this within a reasonable period may indicate a leak in the system.

6 Start the engine and repeat the procedure described in the previous paragraph.

7 Once the fluid level has stabilised, and all air has been bled from the system, lower the vehicle to the ground.

---

17 Power steering pump - removal and refitting

1.6 litre engine models

Removal

Note: *New sealing rings must be used when reconnecting the high-pressure fluid hose to the pump.*

1 For improved access, apply the handbrake, then jack up the front of the vehicle, and support securely on axle stands (see "*Jacking, towing and wheel changing*").

2 Remove the pump drivebelt as described in Chapter 1, Section 21.

10

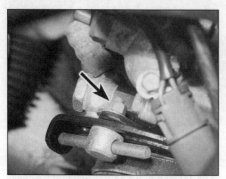

17.5a Unscrew the nut (arrowed) from the power steering pump adjuster stud - 1.6 litre engine models

17.5b Power steering pump adjuster bracket lower securing bolts (arrowed) - 1.6 litre engine

17.6 Turn the pump pulley until one of the holes lines up with the through-bolt (arrowed)

3 Place a suitable container beneath the power steering pump, then unscrew the banjo bolt from the high-pressure fluid hose union, and disconnect the hose from the pump. Recover the sealing rings and discard them - new ones should be used on refitting. Drain the escaping fluid into the container. Plug or cover the open ends of the hose and pump, to reduce further fluid loss, and to prevent dirt ingress.

4 Similarly, disconnect the fluid return hose from the pump, noting that the hose is secured by a hose clip rather than a banjo union.

5 Unscrew the nut from the adjuster stud, then unscrew the two lower bolts securing the adjuster bracket to the engine, and withdraw the adjuster bracket assembly **(see illustrations)**.

6 Turn the pump pulley until one of the holes in the pulley lines up with the through-bolt, then unscrew the nut from the end of the through-bolt, and recover any washers **(see illustration)**.

7 Support the pump, then withdraw the through-bolt, and manipulate the pump out from above the engine. Note that on certain models surrounding components may prevent the pump from being withdrawn from above - in this case, it will be necessary to unbolt the pump mounting bracket from the engine, and withdraw the pump from underneath the vehicle.

Refitting

8 Refitting is a reversal of removal, but use new sealing rings when reconnecting the high-pressure fluid hose, and on completion, refit and tension the drivebelt as described in Chapter 1, Section 21.

2.0 litre engine models

Removal

9 Proceed as described in paragraphs 1 to 4 inclusive.

10 Working at the top of the pump, unscrew the bolt securing the pump to the adjuster bracket.

11 Working underneath the vehicle, unscrew the through-bolt securing the pump to the main mounting bracket.

12 If necessary, to allow additional clearance to remove the pump, unbolt the rear bracket from the pump.

13 Lower the pump, and manipulate it out from underneath the vehicle.

Refitting

14 Refer to paragraph 8.

---

18 Track-rod end -
removal and refitting

Removal

Note: *A balljoint separator tool will be required for this operation. A new track-rod end nut split pin should be used on refitting.*

1 Chock the rear wheels, apply the handbrake, then jack up the front of the vehicle and support on axle stands (see *"Jacking, towing and wheel changing"*). Remove the relevant front roadwheel.

2 Remove the split pin, then partially unscrew the castellated nut securing the track-rod end to the steering arm. Using a balljoint separator tool, separate the track-rod end from the

steering arm. Remove the nut. Discard the split pin - a new one must be used on refitting.

3 Counterhold the track-rod end using the flats provided, then loosen the track-rod end locknut.

4 Counting the exact number of turns required to do so, unscrew the track-rod end from the track-rod.

Refitting

5 Carefully clean the track-rod end and the track-rod threads.

6 Renew the track-rod end if the rubber dust cover is cracked, split or perished, or if the movement of the balljoint is either sloppy or too stiff. Also check for other signs of damage such as worn threads.

7 Screw the track-rod end onto the track-rod by the number of turns noted before removal.

8 Ensure that the balljoint taper is clean, then engage the taper with the steering arm on the hub carrier.

9 Refit the castellated nut, and tighten to the specified torque.

10 If necessary, tighten the nut further (ensure that the maximum torque for the nut is not exceeded) until the nearest grooves in the nut are aligned with the split pin hole in the track-rod end, then fit a new split pin.

11 Refit the roadwheel, and lower the vehicle to the ground.

12 Check the front wheel alignment as described in Chapter 1, and adjust if necessary, then tighten the track-rod end locknut. **Note:** *If the vehicle is to be driven to have the wheel alignment checked, the track-rod end locknut should be tightened before driving the vehicle.*

Chapter 11 Bodywork and fittings

Contents

Degrees of difficulty

Easy, suitable for novice with little experience	**Fairly easy,** suitable for beginner with some experience	**Fairly difficult,** suitable for competent DIY mechanic	**Difficult,** suitable for experienced DIY mechanic	**Very difficult,** suitable for expert DIY or professional

Specifications

Torque wrench settings	Nm	lbf ft
Door hinge bolts	32	24
Door lock striker bolts	15	11
Front seat securing bolts	50	37
Seat belt mounting bolts	50	37

1 General information

The bodyshell is made of pressed-steel sections, and is available in four-door Saloon, five-door Hatchback, and five-door Estate versions. Most components are welded together, but some use is made of structural adhesives; the front wings are bolted on.

The bonnet, door, and some other vulnerable panels, are made of zinc-coated metal, and are further protected by being coated with an anti-chip primer, prior to being sprayed.

Extensive use is made of plastic materials, mainly in the interior, but also in exterior components. The outer sections of the front and rear bumpers are injection-moulded from a synthetic material which is very strong, and yet light. Plastic components such as wheel arch liners are fitted to the underside of the vehicle, to improve the body's resistance to corrosion.

2 Maintenance - bodywork and underframe

The general condition of a vehicle's bodywork is the one thing that significantly affects its value. Maintenance is easy, but needs to be regular. Neglect, particularly after minor damage, can lead quickly to further deterioration and costly repair bills. It is important also to keep watch on those parts of the vehicle not immediately visible, for instance the underside, inside all the wheel arches, and the lower part of the engine compartment.

The basic maintenance routine for the bodywork is washing - preferably with a lot of water, from a hose. This will remove all the loose solids which may have stuck to the vehicle. It is important to flush these off in such a way as to prevent grit from scratching the finish. The wheel arches and underframe need washing in the same way, to remove any

accumulated mud, which will retain moisture and tend to encourage rust. Paradoxically enough, the best time to clean the underframe and wheel arches is in wet weather, when the mud is thoroughly wet and soft. In very wet weather, the underframe is usually cleaned of large accumulations automatically, and this is a good time for inspection.

Periodically, except on vehicles with a wax-based underbody protective coating, it is a good idea to have the whole of the underframe of the vehicle steam-cleaned, engine compartment included, so that a thorough inspection can be carried out to see what minor repairs and renovations are necessary. Steam-cleaning is available at many garages, and is necessary for the removal of the accumulation of oily grime, which sometimes is allowed to become thick in certain areas. If steam-cleaning facilities are not available, there are some excellent grease solvents available which can be brush-applied; the dirt can then be simply hosed off. Note that these methods should not be used on vehicles with wax-based underbody protective coating, or the coating will be removed. Such vehicles should be inspected annually, preferably just prior to Winter, when the underbody should be washed down, and any damage to the wax coating repaired. Ideally, a completely fresh coat should be applied. It would also be worth considering the use of such wax-based protection for injection into door panels, sills, box sections, etc, as an additional safeguard against rust damage, where such protection is not provided by the vehicle manufacturer.

After washing paintwork, wipe off with a chamois leather to give an unspotted clear finish. A coat of clear protective wax polish will give added protection against chemical pollutants in the air. If the paintwork sheen has dulled or oxidised, use a cleaner/polisher combination to restore the brilliance of the shine. This requires a little effort, but such dulling is usually caused because regular washing has been neglected. Care needs to be taken with metallic paintwork, as special non-abrasive cleaner/polisher is required to avoid damage to the finish. Always check that the door and ventilator opening drain holes and pipes are completely clear, so that water can be drained out. Brightwork should be treated in the same way as paintwork. Windscreens and windows can be kept clear of the smeary film which often appears, by the use of proprietary glass cleaner. Never use any form of wax or other body or chromium polish on glass.

3 Maintenance - upholstery and carpets

Mats and carpets should be brushed or vacuum-cleaned regularly, to keep them free of grit. If they are badly stained, remove them from the vehicle for scrubbing or sponging, and make quite sure they are dry before refitting. Seats and interior trim panels can be kept clean by wiping with a damp cloth. If they do become stained (which can be more apparent on light-coloured upholstery), use a little liquid detergent and a soft nail brush to scour the grime out of the grain of the material. Do not forget to keep the headlining clean in the same way as the upholstery. When using liquid cleaners inside the vehicle, do not over-wet the surfaces being cleaned. Excessive damp could get into the seams and padded interior, causing stains, offensive odours or even rot.

> **HAYNES HiNT** *If the inside of the vehicle gets wet accidentally, it is worthwhile taking some trouble to dry it out properly, particularly where carpets are involved. Do not leave oil or electric heaters inside the vehicle for this purpose.*

4 Minor body damage - repair

Note: *For more detailed information about bodywork repair, Haynes Publishing produce a book by Lindsay Porter called "The Car Bodywork Repair Manual". This incorporates information on such aspects as rust treatment, painting and glass-fibre repairs, as well as details on more ambitious repairs involving welding and panel beating.*

Repairs of minor scratches in bodywork

If the scratch is very superficial, and does not penetrate to the metal of the bodywork, repair is very simple. Lightly rub the area of the scratch with a paintwork renovator, or a very fine cutting paste, to remove loose paint from the scratch, and to clear the surrounding bodywork of wax polish. Rinse the area with clean water.

Apply touch-up paint to the scratch using a fine paint brush; continue to apply fine layers of paint until the surface of the paint in the scratch is level with the surrounding paintwork. Allow the new paint at least two weeks to harden, then blend it into the surrounding paintwork by rubbing the scratch area with a paintwork renovator or a very fine cutting paste. Finally, apply wax polish.

Where the scratch has penetrated right through to the metal of the bodywork, causing the metal to rust, a different repair technique is required. Remove any loose rust from the bottom of the scratch with a penknife, then apply rust-inhibiting paint to prevent the formation of rust in the future. Using a rubber or nylon applicator, fill the scratch with bodystopper paste. If required, this paste can be mixed with cellulose thinners to provide a very thin paste which is ideal for filling narrow scratches. Before the stopper-paste in the scratch hardens, wrap a piece of smooth cotton rag around the top of a finger. Dip the finger in cellulose thinners, and quickly sweep it across the surface of the stopper-paste in the scratch; this will ensure that the surface of the stopper-paste is slightly hollowed. The scratch can now be painted over as described earlier in this Section.

Repairs of dents in bodywork

When deep denting of the vehicle's bodywork has taken place, the first task is to pull the dent out, until the affected bodywork almost attains its original shape. There is little point in trying to restore the original shape completely, as the metal in the damaged area will have stretched on impact, and cannot be reshaped fully to its original contour. It is better to bring the level of the dent up to a point which is about 3 mm below the level of the surrounding bodywork. In cases where the dent is very shallow anyway, it is not worth trying to pull it out at all. If the underside of the

dent is accessible, it can be hammered out gently from behind, using a mallet with a wooden or plastic head. Whilst doing this, hold a suitable block of wood firmly against the outside of the panel, to absorb the impact from the hammer blows and thus prevent a large area of the bodywork from being "belled-out".

Should the dent be in a section of the bodywork which has a double skin, or some other factor making it inaccessible from behind, a different technique is called for. Drill several small holes through the metal inside the area - particularly in the deeper section. Then screw long self-tapping screws into the holes, just sufficiently for them to gain a good purchase in the metal. Now the dent can be pulled out by pulling on the protruding heads of the screws with a pair of pliers.

The next stage of the repair is the removal of the paint from the damaged area, and from an inch or so of the surrounding "sound" bodywork. This is accomplished most easily by using a wire brush or abrasive pad on a power drill, although it can be done just as effectively by hand, using sheets of abrasive paper. To complete the preparation for filling, score the surface of the bare metal with a screwdriver or the tang of a file, or alternatively, drill small holes in the affected area. This will provide a really good "key" for the filler paste.

To complete the repair, see the Section on filling and respraying.

Repairs of rust holes or gashes in bodywork

Remove all paint from the affected area, and from an inch or so of the surrounding "sound" bodywork, using an abrasive pad or a wire brush on a power drill. If these are not available, a few sheets of abrasive paper will do the job most effectively. With the paint removed, you will be able to judge the severity of the corrosion, and therefore decide whether to renew the whole panel (if this is possible) or to repair the affected area. New body panels are not as expensive as most people think, and it is often quicker and more satisfactory to fit a new panel than to attempt to repair large areas of corrosion.

Remove all fittings from the affected area, except those which will act as a guide to the original shape of the damaged bodywork (eg headlight shells etc). Then, using tin snips or a hacksaw blade, remove all loose metal and any other metal badly affected by corrosion. Hammer the edges of the hole inwards, in order to create a slight depression for the filler paste.

Wire-brush the affected area to remove the powdery rust from the surface of the remaining metal. Paint the affected area with rust-inhibiting paint, if the back of the rusted area is accessible, treat this also.

Before filling can take place, it will be necessary to block the hole in some way. This can be achieved by the use of aluminium or plastic mesh, or aluminium tape.

Aluminium or plastic mesh, or glass-fibre matting, is probably the best material to use for a large hole. Cut a piece to the approximate size and shape of the hole to be filled, then position it in the hole so that its edges are below the level of the surrounding bodywork. It can be retained in position by several blobs of filler paste around its periphery.

Aluminium tape should be used for small or very narrow holes. Pull a piece off the roll, trim it to the approximate size and shape required, then pull off the backing paper (if used) and stick the tape over the hole; it can be overlapped if the thickness of one piece is insufficient. Burnish down the edges of the tape with the handle of a screwdriver or similar, to ensure that the tape is securely attached to the metal underneath.

Bodywork repairs - filling and respraying

Before using this Section, see the Sections on dent, deep scratch, rust holes and gash repairs.

Many types of bodyfiller are available, but generally speaking, those proprietary kits which contain a tin of filler paste and a tube of resin hardener are best for this type of repair. A wide, flexible plastic or nylon applicator will be found invaluable for imparting a smooth and well-contoured finish to the surface of the filler.

Mix up a little filler on a clean piece of card or board - measure the hardener carefully (follow the maker's instructions on the pack), otherwise the filler will set too rapidly or too slowly. Using the applicator, apply the filler paste to the prepared area; draw the applicator across the surface of the filler to achieve the correct contour and to level the surface. As soon as a contour that approximates to the correct one is achieved, stop working the paste - if you carry on too long, the paste will become sticky and begin to "pick-up" on the applicator. Continue to add thin layers of filler paste at 20-minute intervals, until the level of the filler is just proud of the surrounding bodywork.

Once the filler has hardened, the excess can be removed using a metal plane or file. From then on, progressively-finer grades of abrasive paper should be used, starting with a 40-grade production paper, and finishing with a 400-grade wet-and-dry paper. Always wrap the abrasive paper around a flat rubber, cork, or wooden block - otherwise the surface of the filler will not be completely flat. During the smoothing of the filler surface, the wet-and-dry paper should be periodically rinsed in water. This will ensure that a very smooth finish is imparted to the filler at the final stage.

At this stage, the "dent" should be surrounded by a ring of bare metal, which in turn should be encircled by the finely "feathered" edge of the good paintwork. Rinse the repair area with clean water, until all of the dust produced by the rubbing-down operation has gone.

Spray the whole area with a light coat of primer - this will show up any imperfections in the surface of the filler. Repair these imperfections with fresh filler paste or bodystopper, and once more smooth the surface with abrasive paper. Repeat this spray-and-repair procedure until you are satisfied that the surface of the filler, and the feathered edge of the paintwork, are perfect. Clean the repair area with clean water, and allow to dry fully.

 If bodystopper is used, it can be mixed with cellulose thinners to form a really thin paste which is ideal for filling small holes.

The repair area is now ready for final spraying. Paint spraying must be carried out in a warm, dry, windless and dust-free atmosphere. This condition can be created artificially if you have access to a large indoor working area, but if you are forced to work in the open, you will have to pick your day very carefully. If you are working indoors, dousing the floor in the work area with water will help to settle the dust which would otherwise be in the atmosphere. If the repair area is confined to one body panel, mask off the surrounding panels; this will help to minimise the effects of a slight mis-match in paint colours. Bodywork fittings (eg chrome strips, door handles etc) will also need to be masked off. Use genuine masking tape, and several thicknesses of newspaper, for the masking operations.

Before commencing to spray, agitate the aerosol can thoroughly, then spray a test area (an old tin, or similar) until the technique is mastered. Cover the repair area with a thick coat of primer; the thickness should be built up using several thin layers of paint, rather than one thick one. Using 400-grade wet-and-dry paper, rub down the surface of the primer until it is really smooth. While doing this, the work area should be thoroughly doused with water, and the wet-and-dry paper periodically rinsed in water. Allow to dry before spraying on more paint.

Spray on the top coat, again building up the thickness by using several thin layers of paint. Start spraying at one edge of the repair area, and then, using a side-to-side motion, work until the whole repair area and about 2 inches of the surrounding original paintwork is covered. Remove all masking material 10 to 15 minutes after spraying on the final coat of paint.

Allow the new paint at least two weeks to harden, then, using a paintwork renovator, or a very fine cutting paste, blend the edges of the paint into the existing paintwork. Finally, apply wax polish.

Plastic components

With the use of more and more plastic body components by the vehicle manufacturers (eg bumpers. spoilers, and in some cases major body panels), rectification of more serious damage to such items has become a matter of either entrusting repair work to a specialist in this field, or renewing complete components. Repair of such damage by the DIY owner is not really feasible, owing to the cost of the equipment and materials required for effecting such repairs. The basic technique involves making a groove along the line of the crack in the plastic, using a rotary burr in a power drill. The damaged part is then welded back together, using a hot-air gun to heat up and fuse a plastic filler rod into the groove. Any excess plastic is then removed, and the area rubbed down to a smooth finish. It is important that a filler rod of the correct plastic is used, as body components can be made of a variety of different types (eg polycarbonate, ABS, polypropylene).

Damage of a less serious nature (abrasions, minor cracks etc) can be repaired by the DIY owner using a two-part epoxy filler repair material. Once mixed in equal proportions, this is used in similar fashion to the bodywork filler used on metal panels. The filler is usually cured in twenty to thirty minutes, ready for sanding and painting.

If the owner is renewing a complete component himself, or if he has repaired it with epoxy filler, he will be left with the problem of finding a suitable paint for finishing which is compatible with the type of plastic used. At one time, the use of a universal paint was not possible, owing to the complex range of plastics encountered in body component applications. Standard paints, generally speaking, will not bond to plastic or rubber satisfactorily. However, it is now possible to obtain a plastic body parts finishing kit which consists of a pre-primer treatment, a primer and coloured top coat. Full instructions are normally supplied with a kit, but basically, the method of use is to first apply the pre-primer to the component concerned, and allow it to dry for up to 30 minutes. Then the primer is applied, and left to dry for about an hour before finally applying the special-coloured top coat. The result is a correctly-coloured component, where the paint will flex with the plastic or rubber, a property that standard paint does not normally possess.

5 Major body damage - repair

Where serious damage has occurred, or large areas need renewal due to neglect, it means that complete new panels will need welding-in, and this is best left to professionals. If the damage is due to impact, it will also be necessary to check completely the alignment of the bodyshell, and this can only be carried out accurately by a Nissan dealer using special jigs. If the body is left misaligned, it is primarily dangerous, as the car will not handle properly, and secondly, uneven stresses will be imposed on the steering, suspension and possibly transmission, causing abnormal wear, or complete failure, particularly to such items as the tyres.

11

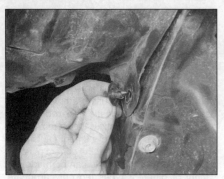

6.2 Remove the screw and release the clips securing the wheel arch liner to the body - Hatchback model

6.3 Unscrew the bumper side securing nuts - Hatchback model

6.4a Unscrew the front . . .

6 Front bumper - removal and refitting

Saloon and Hatchback models

Removal

1 To improve access, chock the rear wheels, apply the handbrake, then jack up the front of the vehicle, and support on axle stands (see "*Jacking, towing and wheel changing*").

2 Working under one of the wheel arches, remove the securing screw and release the two clips securing the lower end of the wheel arch liner to the body and the bumper. Repeat the procedure on the remaining side of the vehicle (**see illustration**).

3 Unscrew the bumper side securing nuts (one on each side) (**see illustration**).

4 Working under the front of the vehicle, unscrew the bumper lower securing bolts (two on each side) (**see illustrations**).

5 Working through the aperture in the front of the bumper, release the two clips securing the plastic section of the bumper to the lower front body panel (**see illustration**).

6 On models with front foglights, disconnect the battery negative lead, then disconnect the foglight wiring connectors.

7 Withdraw the bumper forwards from the vehicle (**see illustration**).

8 If desired, release the securing clips to remove the plastic outer section of the bumper from the metal main section.

Refitting

9 Refitting is a reversal of removal.

Estate models

Removal

10 To improve access, chock the rear wheels, apply the handbrake, then jack up the front of the vehicle, and support on axle stands (see "*Jacking, towing and wheel changing*").

11 Working at the lower corners of the bumper, remove the screws (one on each side), securing the bumper to the lower support brackets (**see illustration**).

12 Working at the upper corners of the bumper, unscrew the upper securing nuts (one on each side, accessible through the apertures in the wheel arch liner) (**see illustration**).

13 Open the bonnet, then carefully pull the front grille panel from the body to release the securing clips.

14 Working though the grille panel aperture, release the four plastic clips securing the plastic outer section of the bumper to the upper body panel (**see illustration**).

15 Working through the aperture in the front of the bumper (behind the number plate),

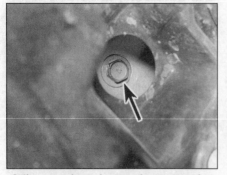

6.4b . . . and rear bumper lower securing bolts (arrowed) - Hatchback model

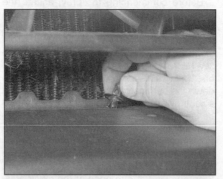

6.5 Release the clips securing the plastic section of the bumper to the lower front body panel - Hatchback model

6.7 Withdrawing the front bumper from the vehicle - Hatchback model

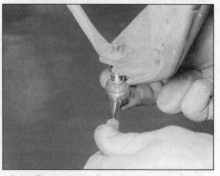

6.11 Removing a front bumper-to-lower support bracket screw - Estate model

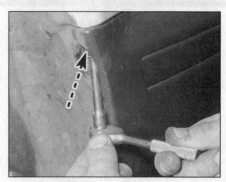

6.12 Unscrewing a front bumper upper securing nut - Estate model

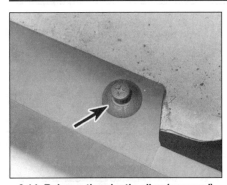

6.14 Release the plastic clips (arrowed) securing the bumper to the upper body panel

6.15 Release the plastic clips (arrowed) securing the bumper to the lower body panel

6.17 Pull the bumper forwards and release the securing clips (arrowed)

release the two plastic clips securing the bumper outer section to the lower body panel **(see illustration)**.

16 Pull the wheel arch liners back towards the rear of the vehicle to release them from the bumper.

17 Carefully pull the bumper plastic outer section forwards, and reach behind the bumper to release the clips securing the plastic outer section to the main metal section **(see illustration)**.

18 Withdraw the plastic outer section of the bumper from the vehicle.

19 If desired, the metal section of the bumper can now be unbolted from the vehicle. The metal section of the bumper is secured by two bolts on each side, accessible from the front of the vehicle **(see illustration)**.

Refitting

20 Refitting is a reversal of removal, but ensure that all the plastic clips are correctly engaged.

7 Rear bumper - removal and refitting

Saloon and Hatchback models

Removal

1 To improve access, chock the front wheels, apply the handbrake, then jack up the rear of the vehicle, and support on axle stands (see *"Jacking, towing and wheel changing"*).

2 On Hatchback models, remove the rear number plate lights from the bumper as described in Chapter 12.

3 Working at the rear of the wheel arches, unscrew the bumper side securing screws (two on each side, which secure the bumper to the body) **(see illustrations)**.

4 Working in the luggage compartment, lift up the carpet panel, then prise out the rubber covers, and unscrew the bolts (two on each side) securing the bumper mounting brackets to the floor **(see illustration)**.

5 Withdraw the bumper assembly **(see illustration)**.

6 If desired, the bumper plastic outer section can be removed from the metal bumper section after releasing the plastic securing clips **(see illustration)**.

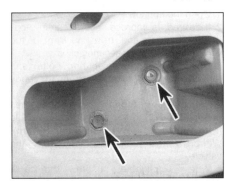

6.19 Front bumper metal section securing bolts (arrowed) - Estate model

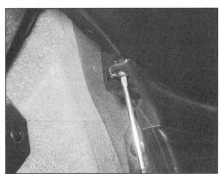

7.3a Unscrew the upper . . .

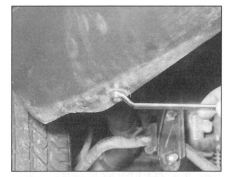

7.3b . . . and lower bumper side securing screws - Hatchback model

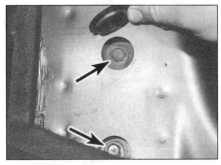

7.4 Prise out the covers to expose the bumper mounting bracket bolts (arrowed) - Hatchback model

7.5 Withdrawing the rear bumper assembly - Hatchback model

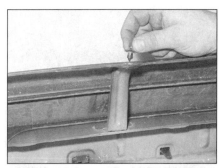

7.6 Release the plastic securing clips to remove the plastic bumper section from the metal section - Hatchback model

11

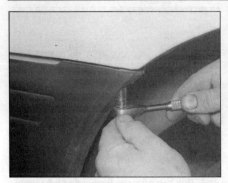

7.9a Unscrew the rear bumper upper . . .

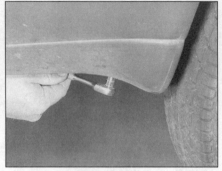

7.9b . . . and lower securing screws - Estate model

7.10 Releasing a rear bumper plastic securing clip - Estate model

Refitting

7 Refitting is a reversal of removal.

Estate models

Removal

8 To improve access, chock the front wheels, apply the handbrake, then jack up the rear of the vehicle, and support on axle stands (see "*Jacking, towing and wheel changing*").

9 Working at the rear of the wheel arches, unscrew the bumper upper and lower securing screws (one upper and one lower screw on each side) **(see illustrations)**.

10 Working under the rear of the bumper, release the two plastic securing clips (one on each side), and unscrew the central securing nut **(see illustration)**.

11 Pull the bumper rearwards from the vehicle.

Refitting

12 Refitting is a reversal of removal.

8 Bonnet - removal, refitting and adjustment

Removal

1 Open the bonnet and have an assistant support it. Using a pencil or felt tip pen, mark the outline of each bonnet hinge relative to the bonnet, to use as a guide on refitting.

2 Disconnect the windscreen washer fluid supply hose from the connector under the bonnet, then release the hose from the clips under the bonnet **(see illustration)**.

3 Unscrew the bolts securing the bonnet to the hinges **(see illustration)** and, with the help of an assistant, carefully lift the bonnet clear. Store the bonnet out of the way in a safe place.

4 Inspect the bonnet hinges for signs of wear and free play at the pivots, and if necessary renew. Each hinge is secured to the body by two bolts.

Refitting

5 With the aid of an assistant, offer up the bonnet, and loosely fit the retaining bolts. Align the hinges with the marks made on removal, then tighten the retaining bolts securely.

6 Reconnect the windscreen washer fluid supply hose, and clip it into position under the bonnet.

7 Adjust the alignment of the bonnet as follows.

Adjustment

8 Close the bonnet, and check for alignment with the adjacent panels. If necessary, slacken the hinge bolts and re-align the bonnet to suit. Once the bonnet is correctly aligned, tighten the relevant hinge bolts securely.

9 Once the bonnet is correctly aligned, check

that the bonnet fastens and releases in a satisfactory manner. If adjustment is necessary, slacken the bonnet lock retaining bolts, and adjust the position of the lock to suit. Once the lock is operating correctly, securely tighten its retaining bolts.

10 If necessary, align the front edge of the bonnet with the wing panels by turning the rubbers screwed into the body front panel, to raise or lower the front edge as required.

9 Bonnet release cable - removal and refitting

Removal

1 Open the bonnet.

2 If desired, to improve access, carefully pull the front grille panel from the front of the vehicle to release the securing clips.

3 Unscrew the three securing bolts, and remove the lock assembly from the body panel.

4 Pull the return spring to one side, then unhook the end of the bonnet release cable from the lock lever **(see illustration)**. Withdraw the lock assembly from the vehicle.

5 Where applicable, unscrew the cable securing clip from the front body panel.

6 Working in the driver's footwell, remove the

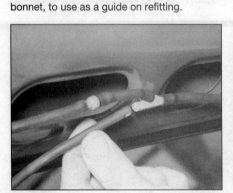

8.2 Disconnect the washer fluid hose from the bonnet connector

8.3 Unscrew the bonnet securing bolts (arrowed) and release the sealant from the edge of the hinges

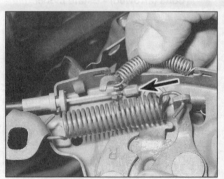

9.4 Pull the return spring to one side, and unhook the end of the release cable (arrowed)

Bodywork and fittings 11•7

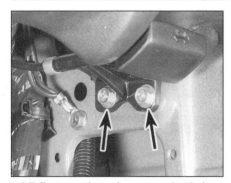

9.7 Bonnet release lever securing bolts (arrowed)

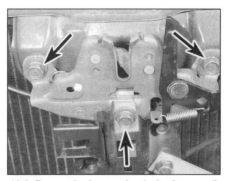

10.3 Bonnet lock securing bolts (arrowed)

securing screw from the footwell side trim panel. Release the plastic securing clip, then pull the weatherstrip from the edge of the panel. Pull the panel from the footwell to release the remaining securing clips.

7 Unscrew the two now-exposed securing bolts, and withdraw the bonnet release lever **(see illustration)**. Unhook the cable end from the lever.

8 Note the routing of the cable, and release it from any clips in the engine compartment, then feed the cable through the bulkhead grommet into the engine compartment. On some models, it may be necessary to move certain components in the engine compartment to one side, to gain access to the cable clips. It is advisable to tie a length of string to the release lever end of the cable before removal, to aid refitting. Pull the cable through into the engine compartment, then untie the string and leave it place until the cable is to be refitted.

Refitting

9 Refitting is a reversal of removal, but use the string to pull the cable into position, and ensure that the bulkhead grommet is securely located. Make sure that the cable is routed as noted before removal, and reposition the cable in its securing clips in the engine compartment. Check the bonnet release mechanism for correct operation on completion.

10 Bonnet lock - removal and refitting

Removal

1 Open the bonnet.

2 If desired, to improve access, carefully pull the front grille panel from the front of the vehicle to release the securing clips.

3 Unscrew the three securing bolts, and remove the lock assembly from the body panel **(see illustration)**.

4 Pull the return spring to one side, then unhook the end of the bonnet release cable from the lock lever, and withdraw the assembly from the vehicle.

Refitting

5 Refitting is a reversal of removal. If necessary, adjust the position of the lock, as described in Section 8.

11 Door - removal, refitting and adjustment

Removal

Note: *A new door check strap roll-pin will be required on refitting.*

1 Disconnect the battery negative lead.

2 Remove the door inner trim panel, as described in Section 12.

3 Disconnect all relevant wiring from the components inside the door, and unclip the wiring harnesses from inside the door. Take careful note of the way the wire is routed, to aid refitting.

4 Carefully feed the wiring through the aperture in the front edge of the door (pull out the grommet if necessary).

5 Using a suitable punch, drive out the roll-pin securing the door check strap to the body bracket **(see illustration)**.

6 Mark the positions of the hinges on the door, to aid alignment of the door on refitting.

7 Have an assistant support the door, then unscrew the bolts securing the door hinges to the door, and lift the door from the vehicle **(see illustration)**.

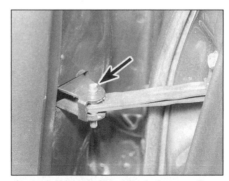

11.5 Remove the roll-pin (arrowed) securing the door check strap to the body bracket

8 Examine the hinges for wear and damage. If necessary, the hinges can be unbolted from the body and renewed.

Refitting

9 Refitting is a reversal of removal, but align the hinges with the marks made on the body before removal, and before finally tightening the hinge securing bolts, check the door adjustment as described in the following paragraphs. Use a new roll-pin to secure the door check strap to the body bracket.

Adjustment

10 Close the door (**carefully**, in case the alignment is incorrect, which may cause scratching on the door or the body as the door is closed), and check the fit of the door with the surrounding panels.

11 If adjustment is required, loosen the hinge securing bolts (the hinge-to-door and the hinge-to-body bolt holes are elongated), and move the hinges as required to achieve satisfactory alignment. Tighten the securing bolts to the specified torque when the alignment is satisfactory.

12 Check the operation of the door lock. If necessary, slacken the securing bolts, and adjust the position of the lock striker on the body pillar to achieve satisfactory alignment. Tighten the bolts to the specified torque on completion.

12 Door inner trim panel - removal and refitting

Front door trim panel

Removal

1 Disconnect the battery negative lead.

2 On models with manual windows, use a length of bent wire to hook out the regulator handle wire clip (pass the wire down behind the handle, and press back the plastic trim plate) until the handle can be withdrawn. Recover the plastic trim plate.

3 Carefully prise the interior door handle

11.7 Unscrew the bolts (arrowed) securing the door hinges to the door

11

12.3 Prise off the interior door handle surround

12.4 Prise out the electric window switch for access to the trim panel securing screw

12.5 Prise off the cover for access to the rear trim panel securing screw

surround from the door panel **(see illustration)**.

4 Prise the electric window switch, or the blanking plate, as applicable from the armrest, to expose the door trim panel securing screw. Remove the securing screw **(see illustration)**.

5 Unscrew the remaining door panel securing screws. One screw is located at the rear edge of the panel, with two screws at the front edge, and three screws at the bottom of the panel **(see illustration)**.

6 Using a suitable forked tool, release the securing clips at the edge of the panel, then lift the trim panel upwards to release the central locating pawl. Pull the panel from the door, and where applicable, separate the two halves of the electric window switch wiring connector **(see illustrations)** Note that the

lower window aperture weatherstrip is integral with the trim panel, and must be released from the door as the panel is withdrawn.

7 If work is to be carried out on the door internal components, it will be necessary to remove the plastic sealing sheet from the inside of the door, as follows.

8 Disconnect the electric window control unit wiring plug, then unscrew the two screws securing the electric window control unit bracket to the door, and remove the control unit/bracket assembly **(see illustration)**.

9 Unscrew the trim clip bracket from the rear of the door, noting its orientation to ensure correct refitting.

10 Remove the two securing screws, and withdraw the armrest bracket from the door **(see illustration)**.

11 Remove the loudspeaker from the door, with reference to Chapter 12 if necessary.

12 Where applicable, pull the electric window switch wiring connector from the door **(see illustration)**.

13 Carefully pull the plastic sealing sheet from the door **(see illustration)**. Try to keep the sealant intact as far as possible, to ease refitting.

Refitting

14 Refitting is a reversal of removal, bearing in mind the following points:

a) *Ensure that the sealing sheet is correctly refitted, and sealed around its edge. It should be possible to use the original mastic sealant, but if necessary, new*

12.6a Using a forked tool to release the door trim panel securing clips

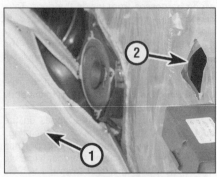

12.6b Release the central pawl (1) from the hole (2) in the door

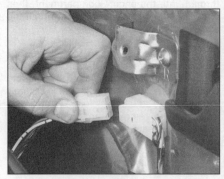

12.6c Separate the two halves of the electric window switch wiring connector

12.8 Remove the two screws securing the electric window control unit to the door

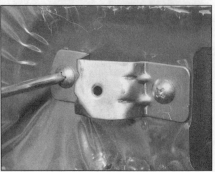

12.10 Remove the armrest bracket

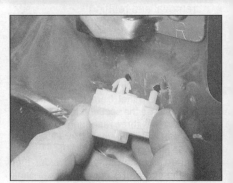

12.12 Pull the electric window switch wiring connector from the door

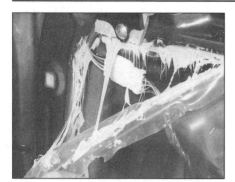

12.13 Pull the plastic sealing sheet from the front door

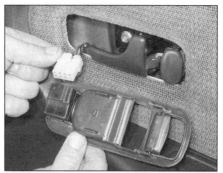

12.16 Pull off the interior handle surround, and disconnect the electric window switch wiring plug

12.18a Remove the securing screw . . .

sealant can be obtained from a Nissan dealer.

b) *Ensure that the plastic bracket at the rear of the door is refitted correctly, as noted before removal.*

c) *Where applicable, before refitting the trim panel, feed the electric window switch wiring through the aperture in the front of the panel.*

d) *Make sure that the trim panel central securing pawl engages correctly with the bracket, and that the weatherstrip engages securely with the edge of the door and the trim panel as the panel is refitted.*

Rear door trim panel - Saloon and Hatchback models

Removal

15 Disconnect the battery negative lead.

16 Pull off the interior handle surround, complete with the electric window switch, where applicable, and disconnect the switch wiring plug **(see illustration)**.

17 On models with manual windows, use a length of bent wire to hook out the regulator handle wire clip (pass the wire down behind the handle and press back the plastic trim plate) until the handle can be withdrawn. Recover the plastic trim plate.

18 Prise the screw cover from the ashtray housing, then remove the securing screw, and

withdraw the ashtray housing **(see illustrations)**.

19 Pull the panel from the door to release the securing clips, then pull the panel up to release the weatherstrip (integral with the trim panel) from the lower edge of the window aperture.

20 If work is to be carried out on the door internal components, it will be necessary to remove the plastic sealing sheet as follows.

21 Remove the two securing screws, then withdraw the metal bracket from the door **(see illustration)**.

22 Carefully pull the plastic sealing sheet from the door. Try to keep the mastic sealant intact as far as possible, to aid refitting.

Refitting

23 Refitting is a reversal of removal, bearing in mind the following points:

a) *Ensure that the sealing sheet is correctly refitted, and sealed around its edge. It should be possible to use the original mastic sealant, but if necessary, new sealant can be obtained from a Nissan dealer.*

b) *Make sure that the weatherstrip engages securely with the edge of the door and the trim panel as the panel is refitted.*

Rear door trim panel - Estate models

24 The procedure is as described previously

in this Section for the rear door on Saloon and Hatchback models, noting that the trim panel is secured by six securing screws - two screws at the rear edge, two at the front edge, and two at the bottom of the panel.

13 Door handle and lock components - removal and refitting

Interior door handle

Removal

1 Remove the door inner trim panel and the plastic sealing sheet, as described in Section 12.

2 Release the plastic clip securing the lock operating rods to the door panel **(see illustration)**.

3 Remove the screw securing the front of the interior handle to the door, then slide the handle towards the front of the door to release the rear securing lug.

4 Withdraw the handle assembly from the door, then release the securing clips, and disconnect the lock operating rods, noting their routing **(see illustrations overleaf)**.

Refitting

5 Refitting is a reversal of removal, bearing in mind the following points:

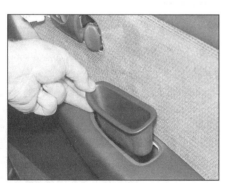

12.18b . . . and withdraw the ashtray housing - Saloon and Hatchback models

12.21 Remove the metal bracket to enable removal of the rear door plastic sealing sheet - Saloon and Hatchback models

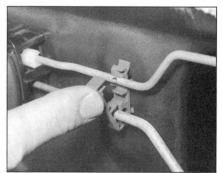

13.2 Release the plastic clips securing the lock operating rods to the door panel

11

13.4a Release the securing clips (arrowed) . . .

13.4b . . . and disconnect the lock operating rods from the interior handle

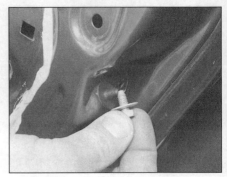

13.7a Remove the securing bolt . . .

a) Ensure that the lock operating rods are routed as noted before removal.
b) Check the operation of the handle/lock mechanism before refitting the door inner trim panel.
c) Refit the door inner trim panel with reference to Section 12.

Front door exterior door handle
Removal

6 With the window fully raised, remove the door inner trim panel and the plastic sealing sheet, as described in Section 12.

7 Remove the bolt securing the window rear guide channel to the rear edge of the door. Lift the guide channel up to improve access to the exterior handle rear securing nut **(see illustrations)**.

8 Unscrew the three bolts securing the metal shield to the inside of the door, and remove the shield for improved access to the handle assembly **(see illustrations)**.

9 Disconnect the lock operating rods from the bellcrank assembly at the rear of the door, then unscrew the securing bolt, and withdraw the bellcrank/mounting plate assembly **(see illustration)**.

10 Disconnect the lock operating rod from the exterior handle, and lift the rod from the door **(see illustrations)**.

11 Working through the door aperture, unscrew the two handle securing nuts **(see illustration)**.

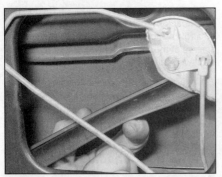

13.7b . . . and lift up the window rear guide channel

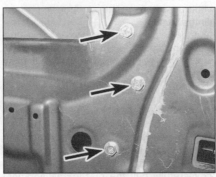

13.8a Unscrew the three bolts (arrowed) . . .

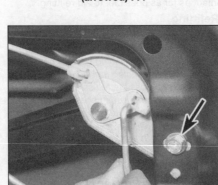

13.9 Disconnect the lock operating rods from the bellcrank. Bellcrank/mounting plate securing bolt arrowed

13.8b . . . and remove the metal shield (arrowed) from the door

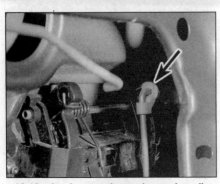

13.10a Lock operating rod securing clip (arrowed)

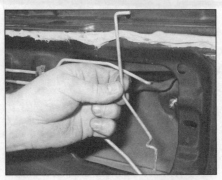

13.10b Lifting out the lock operating rod

13.11 Exterior door handle securing nut (arrowed)

13.12 Recover the metal shield plate from the handle rear stud

12 Recover the metal shield plate from the handle rear stud, then lift handle assembly from the outside of the door **(see illustration)**.

Refitting

13 Refitting is a reversal of removal, bearing in mind the following points:

a) *Ensure that all lock operating rods are correctly reconnected, and that the metal shield and shield plate are correctly refitted.*

b) *Check the operation of the handle/lock mechanism before refitting the door inner trim panel.*

c) *Refit the door inner trim panel with reference to Section 12.*

Rear door exterior handle - Saloon and Hatchback models

Removal

14 With the window fully raised, remove the door inner trim panel and the plastic sealing sheet as described in Section 12.

15 Remove the interior handle and the door lock assembly, as described elsewhere in this Section.

16 Working through the door aperture, remove the two securing nuts, then withdraw the exterior handle assembly from the door **(see illustrations)**.

Refitting

17 Refitting is a reversal of removal, but refit the interior handle and the door lock assembly as described in the relevant paragraphs of this

13.16a Unscrew the two securing nuts (arrowed) . . .

Section, and refit the plastic sealing sheet and the door inner trim panel with reference to Section 12.

Rear door exterior handle - Estate models

Removal

18 Fully raise the window, then remove the door inner trim panel and the plastic sealing sheet as described in Section 12.

19 Working at the lower edge of the door, remove the screw securing the window rear guide channel. Lift the guide channel out through the aperture in the door **(see illustrations)**.

20 Prise the plastic cover plate from the rear of the door for access to the rear exterior handle securing nut **(see illustration)**.

21 Unscrew the two handle securing nuts, and withdraw the handle from outside the door. Disengage the handle operating rod from the lock rod as the handle is withdrawn.

Refitting

22 Refitting is a reversal of removal, bearing in mind the following points:

a) *Ensure that the top of the window rear guide channel engages correctly with the weatherstrip.*

b) *Check the operation of the handle/lock mechanism before refitting the plastic sealing sheet.*

c) *Refit the door inner trim panel with reference to Section 12.*

13.16b . . . and withdraw the rear door exterior handle - Saloon and Hatchback models

Front door lock cylinder

Removal

23 With the window fully raised, remove the door inner trim panel and the plastic sealing sheet, as described in Section 12.

24 Disconnect the lock operating rods from the bellcrank at the rear of the door, then unscrew the securing bolt, and remove the bellcrank/mounting plate assembly **(see illustration)**.

25 Unscrew the three securing bolts, and withdraw the metal shield plate from inside the door.

26 Working through the door aperture, slacken the exterior door handle rear securing nut, and move the metal shield plate to prevent the lever on the lock cylinder from

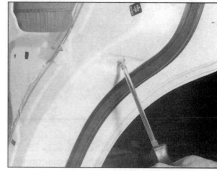

13.19a Remove the securing screw . . .

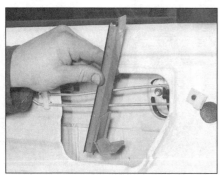

13.19b . . . and lift out the window rear guide channel - Estate model

13.20 Prise out the cover plate for access to the rear exterior handle securing nut - Estate model

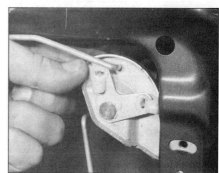

13.24 Removing the bellcrank/mounting plate assembly

11

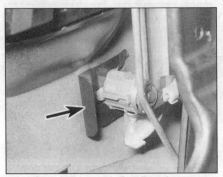

13.27a Prise off the lock cylinder securing plate (arrowed) . . .

13.27b . . . then withdraw the lock cylinder from outside the door

13.33a Unscrew the three lock securing bolts

fouling the plate as the lock cylinder is removed.

27 Using a suitable screwdriver or a pair of pliers, prise off the lock cylinder securing plate, then withdraw the lock cylinder from outside the door. Note that the lock cylinder securing plate has raised tangs which lock against the inner door skin - this means that some force is required to prise the plate free **(see illustrations)**.

Refitting

28 Refitting is a reversal of removal, bearing in mind the following points:
a) *Ensure that the lock operating rods are correctly reconnected.*

13.33b Withdraw the lock, and disconnect the central locking motor/switch wiring plug

b) *Ensure that the exterior handle rear securing nut is re-tightened.*
c) *Check the operation of the handle/lock mechanism before refitting the door inner trim panel.*
d) *Refit the door inner trim panel as described in Section 12.*

Front door lock

Removal

29 With the window fully raised, remove door inner trim panel and the plastic sealing sheet, as described in Section 12.
30 Unscrew the three securing bolts, and withdraw the metal shield plate from inside the door.
31 Remove the bolt securing the window rear guide channel to the rear edge of the door. Lift the guide channel up, clear of the lock.
32 Reach in through the door aperture, and disconnect the four lock operating rods from the lock, noting their locations and routing.
33 Working at the rear edge of the door, unscrew the three securing bolts, then lift the lock out through the door. Disconnect the central locking motor/switch wiring plug from the lock assembly **(see illustrations)**.

Refitting

34 Refitting is a reversal of removal, bearing in mind the following points:
a) *Ensure that the lock operating rods are correctly reconnected and routed, as noted before removal.*

b) *Check the operation of the handle/lock mechanism before refitting the door inner trim panel.*
c) *Refit the door inner trim panel as described in Section 12.*

Rear door lock - Saloon and Hatchback models

Removal

35 With the window fully raised, remove the door inner trim panel and the plastic sealing sheet, as described in Section 12.
36 Remove the two bolts securing the window glass rear guide channel to the door, then pull the guide channel clear of the lock **(see illustration)**.
37 Disconnect the lock operating rods from the door interior handle, then remove the securing screw, and slide the handle forwards to release it from the door.
38 Working inside the door, remove the screw securing the lock motor to the door panel **(see illustration)**.
39 Working at the rear edge of the door, unscrew the three lock securing screws, then manipulate the lock assembly, complete with operating rods, out through the door aperture **(see illustrations)**.
40 Disconnect the wiring plug from the central locking motor, and withdraw the assembly from the door.

Refitting

41 Refitting is a reversal of removal, bearing in mind the following points:

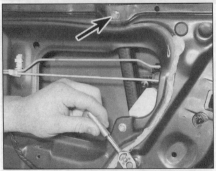

13.36 Remove the two bolts securing the window glass rear guide channel to the door

13.38 Remove the screw securing the lock motor to the door panel

13.39a Unscrew the three lock securing screws . . .

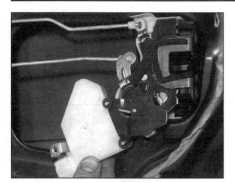

13.39b ... and withdraw the lock assembly

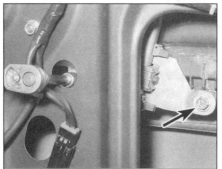

14.4 Remove the two bolts securing the window glass to the regulator mechanism

14.5 Lift the glass out through the window aperture

a) *Ensure that the lock operating rods are correctly reconnected.*
b) *Check the operation of the handle/lock mechanism before refitting the door inner trim panel.*
c) *Refit the door inner trim panel as described in Section 12.*

Rear door lock - Estate models

Removal

42 With the window fully raised, remove the door inner trim panel and the plastic sealing sheet, as described in Section 12.

43 Working at the lower edge of the door, remove the screw securing the window rear guide channel. Lift the guide channel out through the aperture in the door.

44 Disconnect the wiring plug from the door lock motor.

45 Remove the door interior handle as described previously in this Section.

46 Working at the rear edge of the door, remove the three lock securing screws.

47 Manipulate the lock out through the aperture in the door panel, disconnecting the exterior handle operating rod as the lock is withdrawn.

Refitting

48 Refitting is a reversal of removal, bearing in mind the following points:
a) *Ensure that the lock operating rods are correctly reconnected.*

b) *Ensure that the top of the window rear guide channel engages correctly with the weatherstrip.*
c) *Check the operation of the handle/lock mechanism before refitting the door inner trim panel.*
d) *Refit the door inner trim panel as described in Section 12.*

14 Door window glass and regulator - removal and refitting

Front door window glass
Removal

1 Remove the door inner trim panel and the plastic sealing sheet, as described in Section 12.

2 Temporarily reconnect the electric window switch, and the battery negative lead, or refit the window regulator handle, as applicable.

3 Lower the window until the front bolt securing the lower edge of the window glass to the regulator mechanism is accessible through the hole in the inside of the door.

4 Support the glass, then remove the two bolts securing the window glass to the regulator mechanism **(see illustration)**.

5 Lift the glass out through the window aperture in the top of the door, manipulating the glass past the weatherstrips as it is withdrawn **(see illustration)**.

Refitting

6 Refitting is a reversal of removal, bearing in mind the following points:
a) *Take care not to dislodge the weatherstrips when fitting the glass.*
b) *Check the operation of the window mechanism before refitting the door inner trim panel.*
c) *Refit the door inner trim panel with reference to Section 12.*

Front door window regulator

Removal

7 Proceed as described in paragraphs 1 to 4.

8 Fully raise the window glass, and secure the glass in position using suitable tape, or by wedging the glass in position using rags between the glass and the edge of the door - ensure that the glass cannot drop into the door. Alternatively, lift the glass panel out through the window aperture.

9 Where applicable, separate the two halves of the regulator motor wiring connector **(see illustration)**.

10 Unscrew the three bolts securing the motor assembly to the door **(see illustration)**.

11 Unscrew the two upper and the two lower regulator mechanism securing bolts, then manipulate the complete motor/regulator assembly out through the aperture in the door **(see illustrations)**.

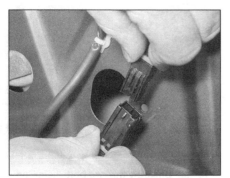

14.9 Separate the two halves of the regulator motor wiring connector

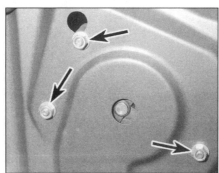

14.10 Unscrew the three bolts (arrowed) securing the motor assembly to the door

14.11a Unscrew the two upper . . .

11

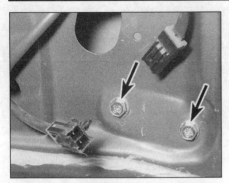

14.11b ... and two lower regulator mechanism securing bolts (arrowed) ...

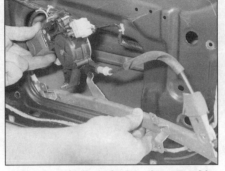

14.11c ... then manipulate the assembly from the door

14.14a Unscrew the lower securing bolt ...

Refitting

12 Refer to paragraph 6.

Rear door sliding window glass - Saloon and Hatchback models

Removal

13 With the window glass fully raised, remove the door inner trim panel and the plastic sealing sheet, as described in Section 12.

14 Unscrew the lower securing bolt, and withdraw the window front guide channel down through the aperture in the front of the door **(see illustrations)**. Note that the upper end of the guide channel engages with the weatherstrip.

15 Temporarily reconnect the electric window switch and the battery negative lead,

or refit the window regulator handle, as applicable, then fully lower the window glass.

16 Prise the inner weatherstrip from the window aperture, and withdraw it from the door. Note how the weatherstrip fits, to aid refitting.

17 Carefully pull the outer weatherstrip from the top rear corner of the window aperture **(see illustration)**.

18 Remove the two bolts securing the lower end of the window rear guide channel to the inside of the door **(see illustration)**.

19 Unscrew the two nuts securing the top of the window rear guide channel to the top of the door, then manipulate the guide channel out through the window aperture **(see illustrations)**.

20 Unscrew the two bolts securing the lower edge of the window glass to the regulator mechanism, then carefully manipulate the glass out through the outside of the window aperture **(see illustrations)**.

Refitting

21 Refitting is a reversal of removal, bearing in mind the following points:
a) Ensure that the weatherstrips are correctly refitted to the window aperture, as noted before removal, and ensure that the upper edge of the window front guide channel engages with the outer weatherstrip (the guide channel should be refitted before the weatherstrip).
b) Check the operation of the window

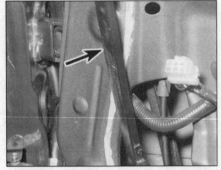

14.14b ... and withdraw the window front guide channel (arrowed) - Saloon and Hatchback models

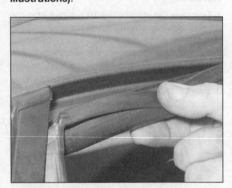

14.17 Pull the outer weatherstrip from the top rear corner of the window - Saloon and Hatchback models

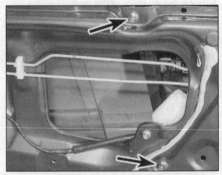

14.18 Remove the two bolts (arrowed) securing the lower end of the rear guide channel - Saloon and Hatchback models

14.19a Unscrew the two nuts securing the top of the window rear guide channel ...

14.19b ... then manipulate the guide channel (arrowed) out through the window aperture - Saloon and Hatchback models

14.20a Unscrew the two bolts securing the glass to the regulator mechanism

14.20b . . . manipulate the glass out through the window aperture - Saloon and Hatchback models

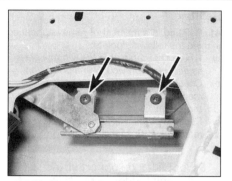

14.29 Unscrew the two bolts (arrowed) securing the glass to the regulator mechanism - Estate model

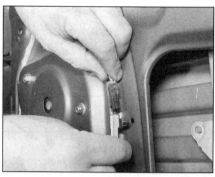

14.33 Separate the two halves of the regulator motor wiring connector - Saloon and Hatchback models

mechanism before refitting the door inner trim panel.
c) Refit the door inner trim panel with reference to Section 12.

Rear door fixed window glass - Saloon and Hatchback models

Removal

22 Remove the sliding window glass, as described previously in this Section.
23 Carefully pull the fixed window glass, complete with its surrounding weatherstrip, from the window aperture.
24 If desired, pull the weatherstrip from the edge of the window.

Refitting

25 Refitting is a reversal of removal, but ensure that the weatherstrip seals securely on both the window aperture and the window glass, and refit the sliding window glass as described previously in this Section.

Rear door window glass - Estate models

Removal

26 With the window glass fully raised, remove the door inner trim panel and the plastic sealing sheet as described in Section 12.
27 Working at the lower edge of the door, remove the screw securing the window rear guide channel. Lift the guide channel out through the aperture in the door.
28 Temporarily reconnect the window

switch, or refit the regulator handle, as applicable, and fully lower the window glass.
29 Unscrew the two bolts securing the lower edge of the window glass to the regulator mechanism, then lift the window glass out through the door window aperture **(see illustration)**. It may be necessary to prise the weatherstrips from the edge of the window aperture to allow the glass to pass through.

Refitting

30 Refitting is a reversal of removal, bearing in mind the following points:
a) Where applicable, ensure that the weatherstrips are correctly engaged with the door.
b) Ensure that the top of the window rear guide channel engages correctly with the weatherstrip.
c) Check the operation of the window mechanism before refitting the door inner trim panel.
d) Refit the door inner trim panel with reference to Section 12.

Rear door window regulator - Saloon and Hatchback models

Removal

31 Remove the door inner trim panel and the plastic sealing sheet, as described in Section 12.
32 Unscrew the two bolts securing the lower edge of the sliding window glass to the regulator mechanism, then fully raise the

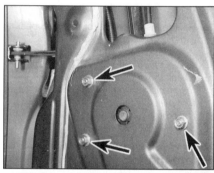

14.34 Unscrew the three bolts (arrowed) securing the motor assembly - Saloon and Hatchback models

window glass, and secure the glass in position using suitable tape, or by wedging the glass in position using rags between the glass and the edge of the door - ensure that the glass cannot drop into the door. Alternatively, remove the sliding window glass, as described previously in this Section.
33 Where applicable, release the regulator motor wiring connector from the door, and separate the two halves of the connector **(see illustration)**.
34 Unscrew the three bolts securing the motor assembly to the door **(see illustration)**.
35 Unscrew the two upper and two lower regulator mechanism securing bolts, then manipulate the complete motor/regulator assembly out through the aperture in the door **(see illustrations)**.

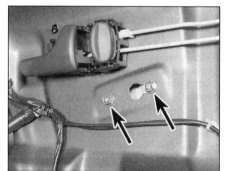

14.35a Unscrew the two upper . . .

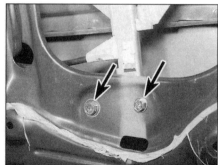

14.35b . . . and the two lower regulator mechanism securing bolts (arrowed) . . .

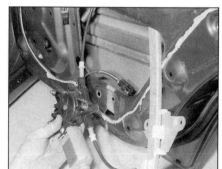

14.35c . . . then withdraw the assembly - Saloon and Hatchback models

11

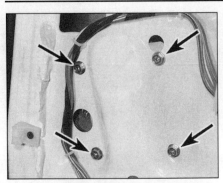

14.40 Unscrew the four bolts (arrowed) securing the regulator mechanism to the door - Estate model

Refitting

36 Refitting is a reversal of removal, bearing in mind the following points:
a) *Where applicable, refit the window glass as described previously in this Section.*
b) *Check the operation of the window mechanism before refitting the door inner trim panel.*
c) *Refit the door inner trim panel with reference to Section 12.*

Rear door window regulator - Estate models

Removal

37 Remove the door inner trim panel and the plastic sealing sheet, as described in Section 12.
38 Unscrew the two bolts securing the lower edge of the sliding window glass to the regulator mechanism, then fully raise the window glass, and secure the glass in position using suitable tape, or by wedging the glass in position using rags between the glass and the edge of the door - ensure that the glass cannot drop into the door. Alternatively, remove the sliding window glass, as described previously in this Section.
39 Where applicable, unclip the regulator motor wiring connector from the door, and separate the two halves of the connector.
40 Unscrew the four bolts securing the regulator mechanism to the door, then manipulate the mechanism out through the aperture in the door **(see illustration)**.

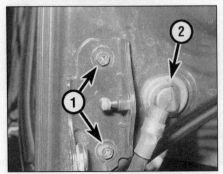

15.7 Boot lid securing bolts (1) and wiring grommet (2)

Refitting

41 Refitting is a reversal of removal, bearing in mind the following points:
a) *Where applicable, refit the window glass as described previously in this Section.*
b) *Check the operation of the window mechanism before refitting the door inner trim panel.*
c) *Refit the door inner trim panel with reference to Section 12.*

15 Boot lid and support struts (Saloon models) - removal, refitting and adjustment

Boot lid
Removal

1 Disconnect the battery negative lead.
2 Open the boot lid, and have an assistant support it in the open position.
3 Release the securing clips, and remove the trim panel from the rear of the boot lid.
4 Working inside the boot lid, disconnect the main wiring harness connector, located on the left-hand side of the boot lid. Tie a length of string to the wiring connector, then prise the wiring harness grommet from the front left-hand corner of the boot lid, and feed the wiring through the aperture in the boot lid. Untie the string from the wiring connector, and leave the string in place in the boot lid, to aid refitting.
5 Prise off the securing spring clip, then pull the boot support strut from the balljoint on the boot lid bracket.
6 Using a pencil or felt tip pen, mark the outline of each boot hinge relative to the boot lid, to use as a guide on refitting.
7 Unscrew the bolts securing the hinges to the boot lid, then lift the boot lid from the vehicle - take care not to scratch the bodywork as the boot lid is removed **(see illustration)**.

Refitting

8 With the aid of an assistant, offer up the boot lid, and loosely fit the retaining bolts. Align the hinges with the marks made on removal, then tighten the retaining bolts securely.

15.15 Releasing a boot lid strut lower spring clip

9 Tie the string to the wiring harness connector, and use the string to pull the wiring harness through the aperture, and into the boot lid.
10 Adjust the alignment of the boot lid as follows.

Adjustment

11 Close the boot lid (**carefully**, in case the alignment is incorrect, which may cause scratching on the lid or the body as the boot lid is closed), and check for alignment with the adjacent panels. If necessary, slacken the hinge bolts and re-align the boot lid to suit. Once the boot lid is correctly aligned, tighten the hinge bolts to the specified torque.
12 Once the boot lid is correctly aligned, check that the boot lid fastens and releases in a satisfactory manner. If adjustment is necessary, slacken the boot lid lock retaining bolts, and adjust the position of the lock to suit. Once the lock is operating correctly, securely tighten its retaining bolts.

Support struts
Removal

13 Ensure that the boot lid is adequately supported.
14 Working at one end of the strut, prise off the securing spring clip, then pull the strut from the balljoint on the hinge assembly.
15 Repeat the procedure at the remaining end of the strut, and withdraw the strut **(see illustration)**.

Refitting

16 Refitting is a reversal of removal, but ensure that the spring clips are securely engaged with the strut.

16 Tailgate and support struts - removal, refitting and adjustment

Tailgate
Removal

1 Disconnect the battery negative lead.
2 Remove the tailgate interior trim panels as described in Section 28.
3 Working inside the tailgate, disconnect the wiring plugs from the luggage compartment light switch (integral with the tailgate lock), the tailgate wiper motor, the heated rear window element, and the rear number plate lights (Estate models). Also unbolt the earth lead(s). Check for any other wiring connectors which must be disconnected to facilitate tailgate removal.
4 Tie a length of string to the wiring harness(es), then prise the wiring harness grommet(s) from the front corner(s) of the tailgate, and feed the wiring through the aperture in the tailgate. Untie the string from the wiring connector, and leave the string in place in the tailgate, to aid refitting.
5 Remove the tailgate washer nozzle, as

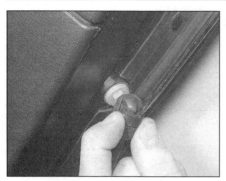

16.8 Releasing a tailgate strut from the tailgate balljoint pin - Hatchback model

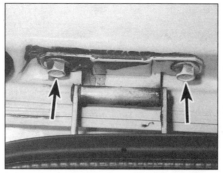

16.10 Tailgate hinge-to-tailgate bolts (arrowed) - Estate model

16.19 Unscrew the lower balljoint pin from the body - Estate model

described in Chapter 12, then tie a length of string to the fluid hose, and repeat the procedure carried out on the wiring harness.

6 Have an assistant support the tailgate in the open position.

7 Using a pencil of felt tip pen, mark the outline of each hinge relative to the tailgate, to use as a guide on refitting.

8 On Hatchback models, prise off the spring clips, and pull the upper ends of the support struts from the balljoints on the tailgate (**see illustration**).

9 On Estate models, unscrew the upper strut balljoint pins from the tailgate - **do not** attempt to separate the struts from the balljoint pins.

10 Unscrew the bolts securing the hinges to the tailgate (**see illustration**), then lift the tailgate from the vehicle.

Refitting

11 Refitting is a reversal of removal, bearing in mind the following points.

12 Tie the string to the wiring harness(es), and use the string to pull the wiring harness(es) through the aperture(s) and into the tailgate.

13 Do not fully tighten the hinge bolts until the tailgate adjustment has been checked, as described in the following paragraphs.

Adjustment

14 Close the tailgate (**carefully**, in case the alignment is incorrect, which may cause scratching on the tailgate or the body as the

tailgate is closed), and check for alignment with the adjacent panels. If necessary, slacken the hinge bolts and re-align the tailgate to suit. Once the tailgate is correctly aligned, tighten the hinge bolts to the specified torque.

15 Once the tailgate is correctly aligned, check that the tailgate fastens and releases in a satisfactory manner. If adjustment is necessary, slacken the tailgate lock retaining bolts, and adjust the position of the lock to suit. Once the lock is operating correctly, securely tighten its retaining bolts.

Support struts - Hatchback models

16 Proceed as described for the boot lid support struts in Section 15.

Support struts - Estate models

Removal

17 The balljoint pins are integral with the struts, and the balljoints cannot be separated.

18 To remove a strut, first ensure that the tailgate is adequately supported.

19 Unscrew the upper balljoint pin from the tailgate, then unscrew the lower balljoint pin from the body, and withdraw the strut (**see illustration**). Note the positions of any washers and/or spacers on the balljoint pins.

Refitting

20 Refitting is a reversal of removal. Ensure that any washers and spacers are positioned on the balljoint pins as noted before removal.

17 Boot lid lock components (Saloon models) - removal and refitting

Boot lid lock

Removal

1 Using a suitable forked tool, prise out the plastic clips securing the trim panel, then unhook the panel from the rear of the boot lid (**see illustrations**).

2 Unclip the plastic cover from the lock (**see illustration**).

3 Push out the plastic clip securing the luggage compartment light switch wiring connector to the inside of the boot lid (**see illustration**).

4 Unscrew the two securing bolts, and

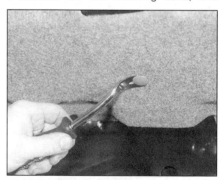

17.1a Release the securing clips . . .

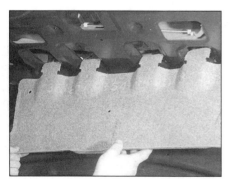

17.1b . . . and withdraw the boot lid trim panel - Saloon model

17.2 Unclip the cover from the lock - Saloon model

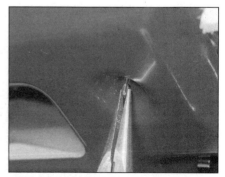

17.3 Push out the wiring connector clip - Saloon model

11

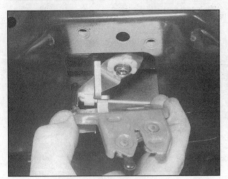

17.4 Withdraw the lock . . .

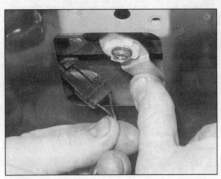

17.5 . . . and the wiring connector - Saloon model

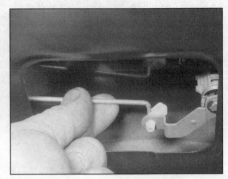

17.9 Disconnect the lock operating rod . . .

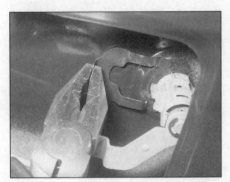

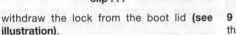

17.10a . . . then pull out the securing clip . . .

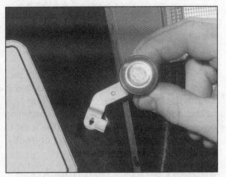

17.10b . . . and withdraw the boot lid lock cylinder - Saloon model

withdraw the lock from the boot lid **(see illustration)**.

5 Using the key, operate the boot lid lock cylinder to allow the lock operating rod to be pushed back - this will provide clearance for the switch wiring connector to pass through **(see illustration)**.

6 Separate the two halves of the wiring connector, and withdraw the lock.

Refitting

7 Refitting is a reversal of removal.

Boot lid lock cylinder

Removal

8 Using a suitable forked tool, prise out the plastic clips securing the trim panel, then unhook the panel from the rear of the boot lid.

9 Release the securing clip, and disconnect the lock operating rod from the lock cylinder **(see illustration)**.

10 Using a suitable pair of pliers, pull out the metal lock cylinder securing clip, then withdraw the lock cylinder from outside the boot lid **(see illustrations)**.

Refitting

11 Refitting is a reversal of removal, but ensure that the lock cylinder securing clip is securely refitted.

Boot lid lock striker

Removal

12 Pull the weatherstrip from the plastic trim panel at the rear of the boot, then pull the trim panel from the body.

13 Using a suitable forked tool, prise out the plastic clips securing the rear carpet trim panel to the body.

14 Unscrew the two securing bolts, then withdraw the lock striker assembly, and disconnect the boot lid release cable from the lever on the striker assembly.

Refitting

15 Refitting is a reversal of removal, but check the operation of the boot lid release mechanism before refitting the luggage compartment trim panels.

18 Tailgate lock and handle components - removal and refitting

Tailgate lock - Hatchback models

Removal

1 Disconnect the battery negative lead.

2 Remove the tailgate inner trim panels as described in Section 28.

3 Unscrew the two lock securing bolts **(see illustration)**.

4 Disconnect the lock operating rod from the lock cylinder **(see illustration)**.

5 Detach the luggage compartment light switch wiring connector from the tailgate, and separate the two halves of the connector (the light switch is integral with the lock assembly) **(see illustrations)**.

18.3 Unscrew the lock securing bolts - Hatchback model

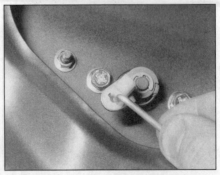

18.4 Disconnect the lock operating rod from the lock cylinder - Hatchback model

18.5a Detach the light switch wiring connector from the tailgate . . .

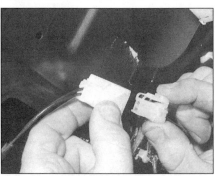

18.5b . . . and separate the two halves of the connector - Hatchback model

18.6 Manipulate the lock out through the tailgate aperture - Hatchback model

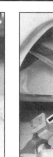

18.10 Disconnect the lock operating rods (arrowed) - Estate model

6 Manipulate the lock out through the right-hand aperture in the tailgate **(see illustration)**.

Refitting

7 Refitting is a reversal of removal.

Tailgate lock - Estate models

Removal

8 Disconnect the battery negative lead.
9 Remove the tailgate inner trim panels as described in Section 28.
10 Disconnect the lock operating rods from the lock, noting their locations **(see illustration)**.
11 Separate the two halves of the door lock wiring connector.
12 Working at the lower edge of the tailgate, unscrew the two lock securing bolts, then

manipulate the lock out through the aperture in the inside of the tailgate **(see illustrations)**.

Refitting

13 Refitting is a reversal of removal, but ensure that the lock operating rods are correctly reconnected, and check the operation of the lock before refitting the trim panel.

Tailgate lock cylinder - Hatchback models

Removal

14 Disconnect the battery negative lead, and remove the tailgate inner trim panels, as described in Section 28.
15 Working inside the tailgate, unscrew the

four nuts securing the tailgate outer trim panel/handle, then withdraw the trim panel/handle **(see illustrations)**.
16 Disconnect the lock operating rod from the lock cylinder.
17 Unscrew the two securing bolts, and withdraw the lock cylinder from outside the tailgate **(see illustrations)**.

Refitting

18 Refitting is a reversal of removal.

Tailgate lock cylinder - Estate models

Note: *A new gasket may be required when refitting the lock cylinder.*

Removal

19 Disconnect the battery negative lead, and

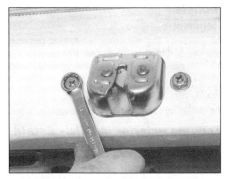

18.12a Unscrew the two lock securing bolts . . .

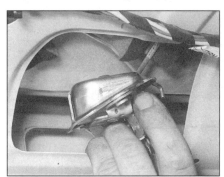

18.12b . . . then manipulate the lock from the tailgate

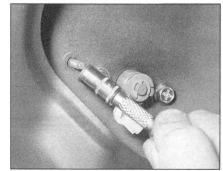

18.15a Unscrew the four nuts . . .

18.15b . . . and withdraw the trim panel/handle - Hatchback model

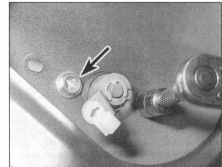

18.17a Unscrew the two securing bolts . . .

18.17b . . . and withdraw the lock cylinder - Hatchback model

11

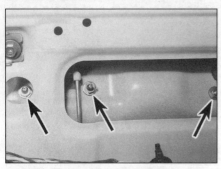

18.20 Three of the four tailgate outer trim/handle panel securing nuts (arrowed) - Estate model

18.21 Tailgate outer trim/handle panel securing clip (arrowed) - Estate model

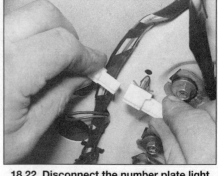

18.22 Disconnect the number plate light wiring connectors - Estate model

remove the tailgate inner trim panel as described in Section 28.

20 Working inside the tailgate, unscrew the four nuts securing the tailgate outer trim/handle panel **(see illustration)**.

21 Release the two outer trim/handle panel securing clips (one at each end of the panel, accessible from the inside of the tailgate) **(see illustration)**.

22 Disconnect the two number plate wiring connectors **(see illustration)**.

23 Disconnect the operating rod from the exterior handle, then pull the panel from the outside of the tailgate, and pull the number plate light wiring grommets from their apertures in the tailgate **(see illustration)**.

24 Disconnect the operating rod from the lock cylinder.

25 Working inside the tailgate, remove the

two securing screws, then withdraw the lock cylinder from outside the tailgate, and recover the rubber gasket **(see illustration)**.

Refitting

26 Refitting is a reversal of removal, bearing in mind the following points:
a) If necessary, use a new rubber gasket when refitting the lock cylinder.
b) Ensure that the lock operating rods are correctly reconnected.
c) Check the operation of the lock components before refitting the tailgate inner trim panel.

Tailgate lock striker - Hatchback models

Removal

27 Prise out the plastic screw covers, and unscrew the four rear luggage compartment

trim panel securing screws. Pull the panel from the body to release the securing clips.

28 Lift up the rear of the luggage compartment carpet panel.

29 Using a suitable forked tool, prise out the plastic clips securing the rear carpet trim panel to the body **(see illustration)**.

30 Unscrew the two securing bolts, then withdraw the lock striker assembly, and disconnect the tailgate release cable from the lever on the striker assembly **(see illustration)**.

Refitting

31 Refitting is a reversal of removal, but check the operation of the tailgate release mechanism before refitting the luggage compartment trim panels.

Tailgate lock striker - Estate models

Removal

32 Release the securing clips, and remove the luggage compartment rear trim panel.

33 Unscrew the two securing bolts, and remove the lock striker.

Refitting

34 Refitting is a reversal of removal.

Tailgate exterior handle - Estate models

Removal

35 Proceed as described in paragraphs 19 to 23 inclusive.

36 Working at the rear of the tailgate outer

18.23 Pull the outer trim/handle panel from the tailgate - Estate model

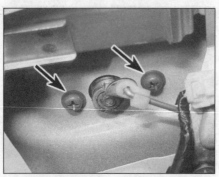

18.25 Tailgate lock cylinder securing screws (arrowed) - Estate model

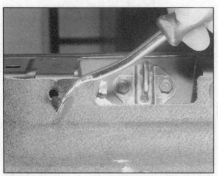

18.29 Prise out the rear carpet trim panel securing clips - Hatchback model

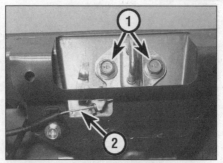

18.30 Unscrew the two lock striker securing bolts (1) and disconnect the release cable (2) - Hatchback model

18.36 Tailgate exterior handle securing screws (arrowed) - Estate model

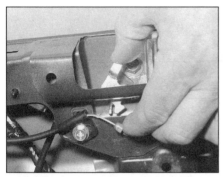

19.1 Disconnecting the release cable from the tailgate lock striker - Hatchback model

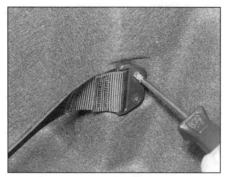

19.3 Remove the luggage strap - Hatchback model

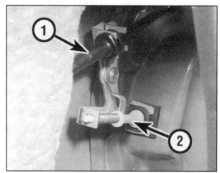

19.6 Fuel filler flap release cable (1), and release rod (2) - Hatchback model

trim/handle panel, remove the two securing screws, and withdraw the handle from the panel **(see illustration)**.

Refitting

37 Refitting is a reversal of removal, bearing in mind the following points:
a) *Ensure that the lock operating rods are correctly reconnected.*
b) *Check the operation of the lock components before refitting the tailgate inner trim panel.*

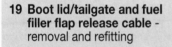

19 Boot lid/tailgate and fuel filler flap release cable - removal and refitting

Saloon and Hatchback models

Note: *If the release cable breaks, or the mechanism is faulty, and the fuel filler flap cannot be released, the flap can be released manually. Proceed as described in paragraphs 2 to 5, then reach in through the body aperture, and pull the release rod to compress the spring and release the filler flap.*

Removal

1 Disconnect the end of the cable from the boot lid/tailgate lock striker, as described during removal of the lock striker in Section 18 **(see illustration)**.
2 Lift out the luggage compartment carpet panel.
3 Unscrew the four bracket securing screws,

and remove the luggage strap from the side of the luggage compartment **(see illustration)**.
4 Where applicable, unscrew the two securing screws, and remove the luggage compartment light.
5 Release the securing clips, and release the side carpet trim panel from the side of the luggage compartment.
6 Disconnect the cable from the fuel filler flap release assembly, then feed the cable through from the boot lid/tailgate lock striker to the fuel filler flap **(see illustration)**.
7 Fold the rear seat cushion forwards for access to the cable.
8 Working on the driver's side of the vehicle, for access to the tailgate/fuel filler flap release lever, pull the sill trim panel from the sill, then pull back the carpet panel to expose the lever securing bolts.
9 Unscrew the two securing bolts, then manipulate the lever assembly out through the aperture in the carpet, and disconnect the cable from the lever **(see illustrations)**.
10 The cable can now be withdrawn from the vehicle, but take careful note of the cable routing, to aid refitting.

Refitting

11 Refitting is a reversal of removal, but ensure that the cable is routed as noted before removal, and check the operation of the release mechanism before refitting the carpet and trim panels.

Estate models

12 The procedure is similar to that described

previously in this Section for Hatchback models, noting the following points:
a) *The cable operates the fuel filler flap only, and is not connected to the tailgate.*
b) *For access to the fuel filler flap mechanism, prise the weatherstrip from the rear edge of the luggage compartment side carpet trim panel, then release the securing clips, and pull the trim panel back to expose the mechanism.*

20 Central locking system components - removal and refitting

Note: *Certain later models are equipped with a remote-control central locking system. At the time of writing, no information was available for the transmitter and receiver units used with this system.*

Electronic control unit

Removal

1 The electronic control unit is located in the driver's footwell.
2 Disconnect the battery negative lead.
3 Remove the driver's side footwell trim panel, with reference to Section 28 if necessary.
4 Remove the securing screw, then withdraw the unit, complete with the mounting bracket, and disconnect the wiring plugs **(see illustration)**.

19.9a Unscrew the two tailgate/boot lid/fuel filler flap release lever securing bolts (arrowed) . . .

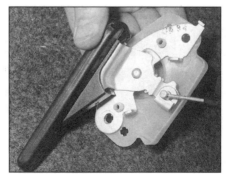

19.9b . . . then withdraw the lever and disconnect the cable

20.4 Removing the central locking system electronic control unit

11

20.7a Remove the two securing screws ...

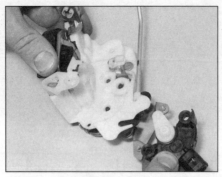

20.7b ... and withdraw the driver's door lock switch

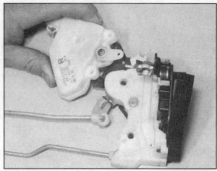

20.10 Removing the central locking motor from the rear door lock - Hatchback model

Refitting

5 Refitting is a reversal of removal.

Driver's door lock switch

Removal

6 Remove the door lock as described in Section 13.

7 The switch is secured to the lock by two screws (see illustrations).

Refitting

8 Refit the door lock as described in Section 13.

Door lock motor

Removal

9 Remove the door lock as described in Section 13.

10 The motor is secured to the lock assembly by two screws (see illustration).

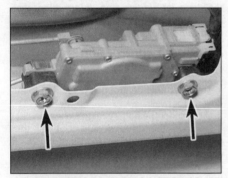

20.16 Tailgate central locking motor securing screws (arrowed) - Estate model

Refitting

11 Refit the door lock as described in Section 13.

Tailgate lock motor - Estate models

Removal

12 Disconnect the battery negative lead.

13 Remove the tailgate inner trim panel, as described in Section 28.

14 Working inside the tailgate, disconnect the wiring plug from the lock motor.

15 Disconnect the two lock operating rods from the motor, noting their locations.

16 Remove the two securing screws, and withdraw the motor from the tailgate (see illustration).

Refitting

17 Refitting is a reversal of removal, but check the operation of the lock mechanism before refitting the tailgate trim panel.

21 Electric window components - removal and refitting

Electronic control unit

Removal

1 The unit is located in the driver's door, behind the door inner trim panel.

2 Disconnect the battery negative lead.

3 Remove the door inner trim panel as described in Section 12.

4 Disconnect the control unit wiring plug, then unscrew the two securing bolts, and withdraw the electronic control unit/bracket assembly from the door (see illustration).

Refitting

5 Refitting is a reversal of removal, but check the operation of the electric window mechanism before refitting the trim panel, and refit the door trim panel as described in Section 12.

Window switches

6 The procedure is described in Chapter 12.

Window regulator motors

7 The regulator motors are integral with the regulators, and cannot be renewed independently of the regulator assemblies. Removal and refitting of the regulator assemblies is described in Section 14.

22 Exterior mirror and associated components - removal and refitting

Mirror assembly

Removal

1 If working on an electric mirror, disconnect the battery negative lead.

2 Remove the door inner trim panel, as described in Section 12.

3 Remove the two securing screws, and remove the mirror trim panel from the inside edge of the door (see illustrations).

21.4 Disconnecting the wiring plug from the electric window electronic control unit

22.3a Remove the two securing screws ...

22.3b ... and remove the mirror trim panel

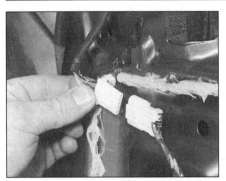

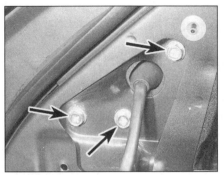

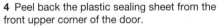

22.5 Disconnecting the door mirror wiring connector

22.6a Remove the three securing screws (arrowed) . . .

22.6b . . . and withdraw the door mirror

4 Peel back the plastic sealing sheet from the front upper corner of the door.

5 Reach through the aperture in the door, and disconnect the mirror wiring connector **(see illustration)**. Unclip the mirror wiring from the door, noting its routing.

6 Remove the three securing screws, and withdraw the mirror from the outside of the door **(see illustrations)**.

Refitting

7 Refitting is a reversal of removal, ensuring that the mirror wiring is routed as noted before removal.

Mirror glass

Removal

8 On models with electrically-heated mirror glass, disconnect the battery negative lead.

9 Insert a suitable thin plastic or wooden tool between the mirror glass and the mirror body, and lever the glass forward to release the securing clips **(see illustrations)**.

10 Where applicable, disconnect the wiring from the rear of the glass, and withdraw the glass from the mirror.

Refitting

HAYNES HiNT	*To aid refitting, lightly grease the securing clips on the rear of the mirror glass.*

11 Where applicable, reconnect the wires to the rear of the mirror glass, then push the glass into position to engage the securing clips.

Mirror adjustment mechanism

Removal

12 On models with electric mirrors, the electric adjuster mechanism can be removed from the mirror as follows.

13 Remove the mirror as described previously in this Section.

14 Remove the mirror glass as described previously in this Section.

15 Remove the securing screws, and separate the two halves of the mirror casing.

16 Similarly, remove the securing screws, and withdraw the adjuster mechanism. Feed the wiring through the mirror casing, noting its routing.

Refitting

17 Refitting is a reversal of removal, ensuring that the wiring is routed as noted before removal.

23 Windscreen, tailgate and fixed windows - general information

These areas of glass are secured by the tight fit of the weatherstrip in the body aperture, and are bonded in position with a special adhesive. Renewal of such fixed glass is a difficult, messy and time-consuming task, which is beyond the scope of the home mechanic. It is difficult, unless one has plenty of practice, to obtain a secure, waterproof fit. Furthermore, the task carries a high risk of

breakage; this applies especially to the laminated glass windscreen. In view of this, owners are strongly advised to have this sort of work carried out by one of the many specialist windscreen fitters.

24 Sunroof - general information

General information

1 Due to the complexity of the sunroof mechanism, considerable expertise is needed to repair, replace or adjust the sunroof components successfully. Removal of the roof first requires the headlining to be removed, which is a complex and tedious operation, and not a task to be undertaken lightly. Therefore, any problems with the sunroof should be referred to a Nissan dealer.

2 On models with an electric sunroof, if the sunroof motor fails to operate, first check the relevant fuse. If the fault cannot be traced and rectified, the sunroof can be opened and closed manually using a screwdriver to turn the motor spindle. To gain access to the motor spindle, ensure that the ignition key is in the "off" position, then prise the spindle cover from the overhead console for access to the spindle. Engage the screwdriver with the spindle, then push the centre of the spindle and turn clockwise to close the sunroof **(see illustration)**.

22.9a Insert a suitable lever behind the mirror glass . . .

22.9b . . . and lever the glass forwards to release the securing clips

24.2 Using a screwdriver to close the electric sunroof

11

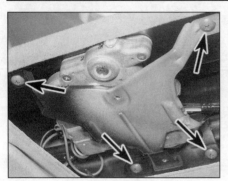

24.8 Sunroof motor bracket securing bolts (arrowed)

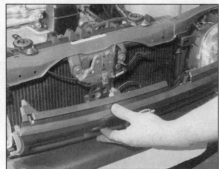

25.1 Removing the front grille panel

25.3 Releasing a front wheel arch liner securing clip

Electric motor - removal and refitting

Removal

3 On models with an electric sunroof, the motor can be removed as follows.

4 Disconnect the battery negative lead.

5 Using a suitable screwdriver, carefully prise the map reading light lens from the roof console.

6 Similarly, prise the spindle cover from the sunroof motor.

7 Remove the two securing screws, then lower the roof console, disconnect the wiring plugs, and withdraw the console.

8 Unscrew the four bolts securing the motor bracket to the roof, noting that one of the bolts also secures an earth lead, then lower the motor assembly from the roof **(see illustration)**.

9 If desired, the motor can be unbolted from the bracket.

Refitting

10 Refitting is a reversal of removal.

25 Body exterior fittings - removal and refitting

Front grille panel

1 Open the bonnet, and pull the grille panel forwards from the body to release the securing clips **(see illustration)**.

2 Refitting is a reversal of removal.

Wheel arch liners

3 The wheel arch liners are secured by a combination of self-tapping screws and plastic clips, and removal is self-evident **(see illustration)**.

Body trim strips and badges

4 The various body trim strips and badges are held in position with a special adhesive tape. Removal requires the trim/badge to be heated, to soften the adhesive, and then cut away from the surface. Due to the high risk of damage to the vehicle paintwork during this operation, it is recommended that this task should be entrusted to a Nissan dealer.

26 Seats - removal and refitting

Front seat

 Warning: Some later models are equipped with automatic seat belt tensioners. The mechanism is designed to instantaneously take up any slack in the seat belt, in the event of a sudden frontal impact, therefore reducing the possibility of injury to the front seat occupants. Take care when

removing the front seats, as the tensioners may cause personal injury if triggered inadvertently - if in doubt, consult a Nissan dealer for advice.

Removal

1 Move the seat fully forwards.

2 Unclip the trim cover from the rear corner of the seat outer rail **(see illustration)**.

3 Remove the securing screw, and remove the trim cover from the rear corner of the seat inner rail **(see illustration)**.

4 Unscrew the seat rail rear securing bolts.

5 Slide the seat fully rearwards, then unscrew the seat rail front securing bolts **(see illustration)**.

6 Lift the seat, complete with the rails, from the vehicle.

Refitting

7 Refitting is a reversal of removal, but tighten the securing bolts to the specified torque.

Rear seat back

Removal

8 Fold the relevant rear seat section forwards, then release the clips, and pull the trim panel from the rear edge of the seat back **(see illustration)**.

9 Remove the four nuts or bolts, as applicable (two on each side) securing the seat back to the hinges, or the hinges to the floor, as desired, then withdraw the seat back from the vehicle **(see illustration)**.

26.2 Removing the trim cover from the rear of the front seat outer rail

26.3 Removing the securing screw from the front seat inner rail rear trim cover

26.5 Unscrewing a seat rail front securing bolt

26.8 Pull the trim panel from the rear seat back . . .

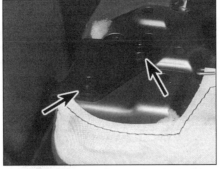

26.9 . . . to expose the seat back securing bolts (arrowed) - Estate model

26.11 Rear seat cushion securing bolts (arrowed)

Refitting

10 Refitting is a reversal of removal.

Rear seat cushion

Removal

11 Fold the seat cushion forwards, then unscrew the four bolts securing the hinges to the floor, and withdraw the seat cushion, complete with the hinges **(see illustration)**.

Refitting

12 Refitting is a reversal of removal.

Rear seat back side bolster - Saloon and Hatchback models

Removal

13 Fold the relevant rear seat cushion forwards, and fold the seat back down.

14 Remove the securing screw from the bottom of the side bolster, then unhook the top of the side bolster and remove it from the vehicle **(see illustration)**.

Refitting

15 Refitting is a reversal of removal.

---

27 Seat belt components - removal and refitting

Front seat belt

Removal

1 Remove the screw from the bottom of the centre pillar lower trim panel, then open the rear door, and remove the two trim panel securing clips. Pull the panel from the pillar **(see illustrations)**.

2 Prise the weatherstrips from the edge of the centre pillar upper trim panel, then pull the panel from the pillar to release the securing clips **(see illustration)**.

3 Prise off the trim cap, and unscrew the seat belt lower anchor bolt, noting that the bolt also secures the inertial reel. Recover the spacer from the bolt **(see illustration)**.

4 Remove the screw securing the upper end of the inertia reel assembly to the body pillar, then lift out the inertia reel **(see illustrations)**.

5 Unscrew the seat belt upper anchor nut, and recover any spacers and washers from the stud, noting their locations.

6 Feed the seat belt through the centre pillar

26.14 Removing a rear seat back side bolster (securing hook arrowed) - Hatchback model

27.1a Remove the securing clips . . .

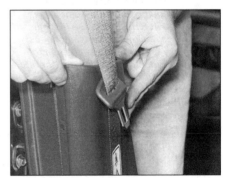

27.1b . . . and remove the centre pillar lower trim panel

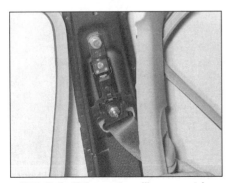

27.2 Pull off the centre pillar upper trim panel

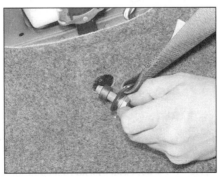

27.3 Unscrew the seat belt lower anchor bolt

27.4a Remove the upper securing screw . . .

11

27.4b . . . then lift out the front seat belt inertia reel

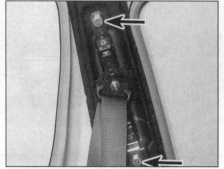

27.7 Front seat belt height adjuster securing bolts (arrowed)

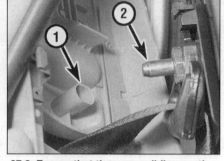

27.8 Ensure that the upper sliding portion of the trim panel (1) engages with the adjuster pin (2)

trim panel, and withdraw the assembly from the vehicle.

7 If desired, the height adjuster can be removed from the centre pillar by unscrewing the two securing bolts **(see illustration)**.

Refitting

8 Refitting is a reversal of removal, bearing in mind the following points:

a) When refitting the upper pillar trim panel, make sure that the sliding portion of the trim panel engages with the pin on the adjuster **(see illustration)**.

b) Tighten the anchor bolts to the specified torque.

Front seat belt stalk

⚠ *Warning: Some later models are equipped with automatic seat belt tensioners. The mechanism is designed to instantaneously take up any slack in the seat belt, in the event of a sudden frontal impact, therefore reducing the possibility of injury to the front seat occupants. Do not attempt to remove the seat belt stalks on models equipped with automatic seat belt tensioners - consult a Nissan dealer for advice.*

Removal

9 Remove the securing screws, and release the clip, then remove the plastic trim panel

from the inner edge of the seat to expose the seat belt stalk securing bolt.

10 Unscrew the bolt and withdraw the stalk assembly.

Refitting

11 Refitting is a reversal of removal, but tighten the stalk anchor bolt to the specified torque.

Rear side seat belt - Saloon models

Removal

12 Fold the rear seat cushion forwards, and unbolt the seat belt lower anchor.

13 Remove the rear parcel shelf, as described in Section 28, and feed the seat belt through the shelf.

14 Remove the seat belt inertia reel lower securing screw, noting that the screw also secures a wiring bracket **(see illustration)**.

15 Unscrew the inertia reel securing bolt, and withdraw the seat belt assembly.

Refitting

16 Refitting is a reversal of removal, but tighten the seat belt anchor bolts to the specified torque.

Rear side seat belt - Hatchback models

Removal

17 Remove the luggage compartment

side/parcel shelf support panel, as described in Section 28.

18 Unscrew the four bracket securing screws, and remove the luggage strap from the side of the luggage compartment.

19 Unscrew the two securing screws, and remove the luggage compartment light.

20 Using a suitable forked tool, release the relevant clips securing the side carpet trim panel to the body, and pull the panel from the side of the luggage compartment to expose the seat belt inertia reel assembly.

21 Unscrew the inertia reel securing bolt **(see illustration)**.

22 Fold the rear seat cushion forwards to expose the seat belt lower anchor bolt, then unscrew the lower anchor bolt.

23 Prise the seat belt surround from the luggage compartment side/parcel shelf support panel, then feed the seat belt through the panel, and withdraw the assembly **(see illustration)**.

Refitting

24 Refitting is a reversal of removal, but tighten the seat belt anchor bolts to the specified torque.

Rear side seat belt - Estate models

Removal

25 Open the relevant rear door, and fold the rear seat back forwards.

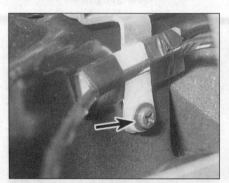

27.14 Rear seat belt inertia reel lower securing screw (arrowed) - Saloon model

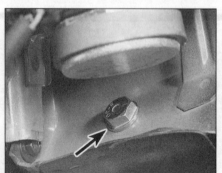

27.21 Rear seat belt inertia reel securing bolt (arrowed) - Hatchback model

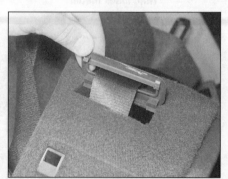

27.23 Prise the seat belt surround from the luggage compartment side/parcel shelf trim panel - Hatchback model

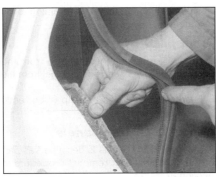

27.26 Prise the weatherstrip from the rear edge of the door aperture - Estate model

27.27 Prise the seat belt surround from the luggage compartment side trim panel - Estate model

27.28 Prise back the side carpet trim panel for access to the inertia reel securing bolt (arrowed)

26 Carefully prise the weatherstrip from the rear edge of the door aperture **(see illustration)**.

27 Prise the seat belt surround from the luggage compartment upper side trim panel, and feed the seat belt through the slot in the surround **(see illustration)**.

28 Peel back the luggage compartment side carpet trim panel to expose the inertia reel unit **(see illustration)**.

29 Unscrew the lower seat belt anchor bolt, noting the positions of any washers and/or spacers.

30 Prise off the trim plate, then unscrew the seat belt upper anchor bolt, again noting the locations of any washers and/or spacers.

31 Unscrew the inertia reel securing bolt, then withdraw the seat belt assembly from the vehicle.

Refitting

32 Refitting is a reversal of removal, but ensure that any washers and/or spacers are positioned on the anchor bolts as noted before removal, and tighten all fixings to the specified torque.

Rear centre seat belt and buckles

Removal

33 Fold the rear seat cushion forwards to

expose the seat belt anchor bolts **(see illustration)**.

34 Unscrew the anchor bolts, and withdraw the seat belt assembly.

Refitting

35 Refitting is a reversal of removal, but tighten the anchor bolts to the specified torque.

28 Interior trim panels - removal and refitting

General

1 The interior trim panels are secured by a combination of metal and plastic clips and

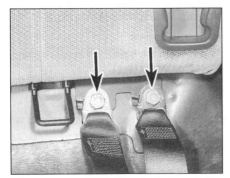

27.33 Rear seat cushion folded forwards to expose rear centre seat belt anchor bolts (arrowed)

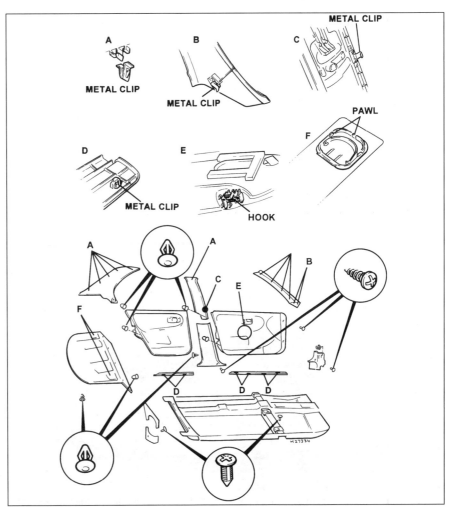

28.1a Passenger compartment trim panels and fixings - Saloon and Hatchback models

11

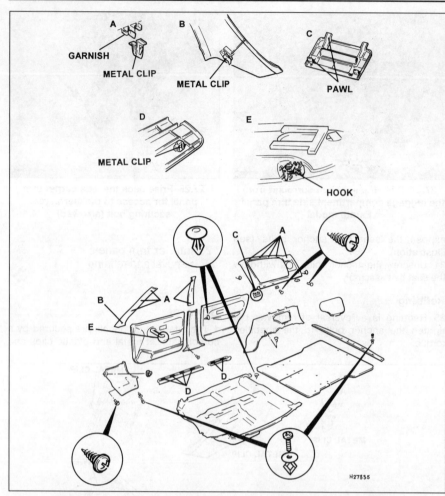

28.1b **Passenger compartment trim panels and fixings - Estate models**

screws. When releasing certain types of securing clips, a suitable forked tool will prove invaluable to avoid damage to the panel and clips. In some cases, it may be necessary to remove surrounding panels before a particular panel can be released (**see illustrations**).

Footwell trim panels

2 Using a screwdriver, carefully prise out the trim plate to reveal the trim panel securing screw. Remove the screw.

3 Twist the rear securing clip to release it, then withdraw the clip, and pull the trim panel from the footwell.
4 Refitting is a reversal of removal.

Sill trim panels

5 Where necessary, pull the weatherstrip from the edge of the panel, then pull the panel from the body to release the securing clips.
6 To refit the panel, simply push it back into

position, ensuring that the retaining clips engage.

Front pillar trim panels

7 Carefully prise the weatherstrip from the edge of the panel, then pull the panel from the pillar.
8 Ensure that the weatherstrip is correctly seated on refitting.

Centre pillar trim panels

9 Removal of the panels is described as part of the front seat belt removal procedure in Section 27.

Door inner trim panels

10 Refer to Section 12.

Rear parcel shelf - Saloon models

11 Remove the rear seat back side bolster, as described in Section 26.
12 Remove the two plastic clips securing the front of the parcel shelf (**see illustration**).
13 Pull up the rear of the parcel shelf to release the rear securing clips, then withdraw the shelf (**see illustration**).
14 If the shelf is to be removed completely, it will be necessary to unbolt the seat belt lower anchor, and pass the belt through the flap in the shelf belt surround plate.
15 Refitting is a reversal of removal, but where applicable, tighten the seat belt anchor bolt to the specified torque.

Luggage compartment trim panels - Saloon models

16 The rear luggage compartment trim panel can be removed by pulling the weatherstrip from the rear of the panel, then pulling the panel upwards to release the securing clips.
17 The luggage compartment carpet trim panels are secured by plastic clips, which are most easily released using a suitable forked tool. Where applicable, remove the luggage strap brackets, and/or the luggage compartment light, to enable the panels to be removed.
18 Refitting is a reversal of removal.

Luggage compartment trim panels - Hatchback models

Rear trim panels

19 Prise out the plastic screw covers, and unscrew the four rear luggage compartment trim panel securing screws. Pull the panel from the body to release the securing clips.
20 If desired, the rear carpet trim panel can be removed as follows.
21 Lift up the rear of the luggage compartment carpet panel.
22 Using a suitable forked tool, prise out the plastic clips securing the rear carpet trim panel to the body.
23 Refitting is a reversal of removal.

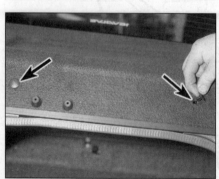

28.12 **Remove the two front securing clips (arrowed) ...**

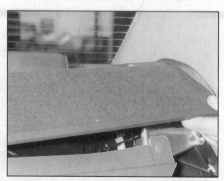

28.13 **... and withdraw the rear parcel shelf - Saloon model**

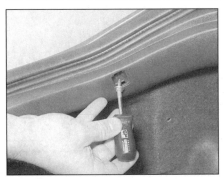

28.25 Prise out the screw cover, and remove the side/parcel shelf support panel securing screw - Hatchback model

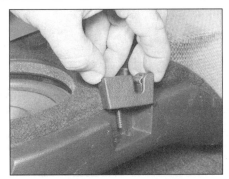

28.27 Withdraw the parcel shelf clip assemblies - Hatchback model

28.28 Pull out the loudspeaker cover panel - Hatchback model

Side/parcel shelf support panels - Hatchback models

24 Remove the luggage compartment rear trim panel as described previously in this Section. Lower the rear seat back.

25 Prise the screw cover from the side/parcel shelf support panel, then remove the securing screw **(see illustration)**.

26 Remove the securing screw from the rear corner of the trim panel.

27 Remove the securing screws, and withdraw the two parcel shelf clip assemblies **(see illustration)**.

28 Lever up the front edge of the loudspeaker cover panel, then pull the cover panel out to reveal the loudspeaker **(see illustration)**.

29 Unscrew the two now-exposed side/parcel shelf trim panel securing screws, then pull the panel from the body to release the securing clips **(see illustrations)**.

30 If the panel is to be removed completely, it will be necessary to feed the seat belt through the aperture in the panel. To do this, prise the seat belt surround from the panel, then unbolt the lower seat belt anchor, and feed the belt buckle and lower anchor plate through the panel.

31 Refitting is a reversal of removal, but where applicable, tighten the seat belt lower anchor bolt to the specified torque.

Luggage compartment trim panels - Estate models

Rear trim panel

32 The luggage compartment rear trim panel can be removed after releasing the plastic securing clips.

Side lower carpet trim panel

33 The luggage compartment side lower carpet trim panels can be pulled back from the body after prising the weatherstrips from their front and/or rear edges, and releasing the plastic securing clips, as applicable.

Side upper trim panel

34 Remove the luggage cover, where applicable.

35 Release the plastic securing clips at the rear edge of the trim panel **(see illustration)**.

36 Remove the securing screws, and withdraw the luggage cover supports from the trim panel **(see illustrations)**.

37 Prise off the trim plate, then unbolt the seat belt upper anchor bolt, noting the locations of any washers and/or spacers on the bolt.

38 Support the tailgate in the open position, then unscrew the tailgate support strut lower balljoint pin from the body.

39 Prise the seat belt surround panel from the trim panel.

40 Pull the panel from the body to release the rest of the retaining clips.

41 Refitting is a reversal of removal, but

28.29a Unscrew the two side/parcel shelf trim panel securing screws . . .

28.29b . . . then pull the panel from the body - Hatchback model

28.35 Release the securing clips at the rear edge of the luggage compartment side upper trim panel - Estate model

28.36a Remove the securing screws . . .

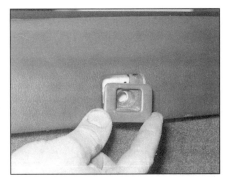

28.36b . . . and withdraw the luggage cover supports

11

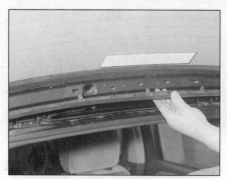

28.45 Removing the tailgate top trim panel - Hatchback model

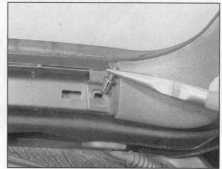

28.46a Pull out the side trim panel clips . . .

28.46b . . . then pull out the parcel shelf support cord anchors . . .

ensure that any washers and/or spacers on the seat belt anchor bolt are positioned as noted before removal, and tighten the anchor bolt to the specified torque.

Boot lid inner trim panel - Saloon models

42 Using a suitable forked tool, remove the plastic securing clips, then unhook the rear of the panel from the boot lid, and withdraw the panel.

43 Refitting is a reversal of removal.

Tailgate inner trim panels - Hatchback models

Removal

44 To remove the side trim panels, the top panel must be removed first. To remove the

lower trim panel, the top and side trim panels must be removed first.

45 To remove the top panel, simply pull the panel from the tailgate to release the securing clips (**see illustration**).

46 The side trim panels can now be removed as follows. Pull out the side trim panel upper plastic clips (one each side, exposed by removal of the top panel), then carefully pull the parcel shelf support cord top anchors from the sides of the tailgate (take care, as the clips are easily broken). The side trim panels can now be pulled from the tailgate (**see illustrations**).

47 To remove the lower trim panel, first remove the two upper securing screws (one each side, exposed by removal of the side trim panels). Prise out the plastic covers, and

remove the remaining trim panel side securing screws (two on each side). Pull the cover plate from the tailgate inner hand grip to expose the remaining securing screw, then remove the screw, and withdraw the hand grip. Carefully pull the trim panel from the tailgate to release the securing clips (**see illustrations**).

Refitting

48 Refitting is a reversal of removal, but ensure that all clips are securely engaged.

Tailgate inner trim panel - Estate models

49 Remove the two securing screws from the panel (one at each upper side of the panel).

50 Release the plastic securing clips from the lower edge of the panel (**see illustration**).

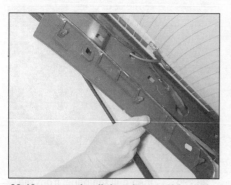

28.46c . . . and pull the trim panel from the tailgate - Hatchback model

28.47a Remove the two upper securing screws . . .

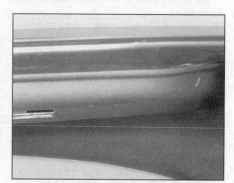

28.47b . . . the remaining side securing screws . . .

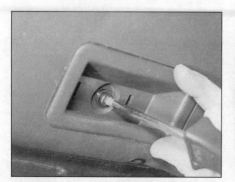

28.47c . . . then remove the remaining screw from the inner hand grip . . .

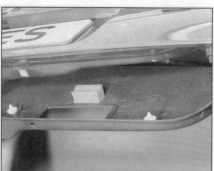

28.47d . . . and pull the trim panel from the tailgate - Hatchback model

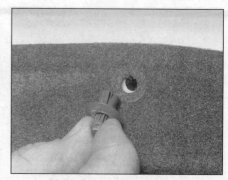

28.50 Release the lower . . .

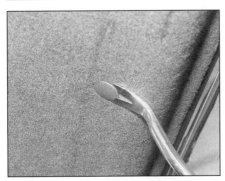

28.51 . . . and upper securing clips from the tailgate inner trim panel - Estate model

51 Using a suitable forked tool, release the upper securing clips **(see illustration)**, then pull the panel from the tailgate.
52 Refitting is a reversal of removal.

29 Centre console - removal and refitting

Warning: Later models are equipped with an air bag system. The air bag sensor is mounted underneath the centre console. Make sure that the safety recommendations given in Chapter 12 are followed, to prevent personal injury.

Removal

1 Disconnect the battery negative lead.
2 Where applicable, prise out the covers, then unscrew the console front securing screws (one screw on each side) **(see illustration)**.
3 Similarly, remove the console rear securing screws **(see illustration)**.
4 Prise the cover plate from the top of the console, and unscrew the two console upper securing screws **(see illustration)**.
5 On models with manual transmission, unclip the gear lever gaiter surround from the top of the centre console **(see illustration)**.
6 On models with automatic transmission, unclip the selector lever cover from the centre console.

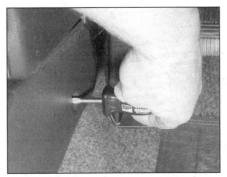

29.2 Unscrew the front . . .

7 Move the console assembly rearwards from the facia, then carefully lift the console up, and disconnect the wiring plugs from the switches mounted in the console. Note the locations of the connectors, to ensure correct refitting.
8 Withdraw the console.

Refitting

9 Refitting is a reversal of removal, but ensure that the wiring plugs are correctly reconnected.

30 Facia panels - removal and refitting

Warning: Later models are equipped with an air bag system. The air bag is mounted in the steering wheel centre pad, and the control module is mounted under the steering column. On some models, a passenger's air bag is fitted in the passenger's side facia. Make sure that the safety recommendations given in Chapter 12 are followed, to prevent personal injury.

Glovebox

Removal

1 Working under the glovebox, remove the two securing screws (one on each side of the

29.3 . . . and rear centre console securing screws

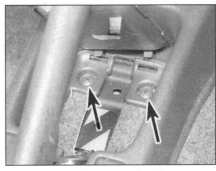

29.4 Prise out the cover plate for access to the two upper securing screws (arrowed)

glovebox), then lower the glovebox from the facia **(see illustrations)**.

Refitting

2 Refitting is a reversal of removal.

Passenger's side lower facia panel

Removal

3 Remove the glovebox, as described previously in this Section.
4 Remove the three securing screws, and withdraw the panel from the facia **(see illustrations)**.

Refitting

5 Refitting is a reversal of removal.

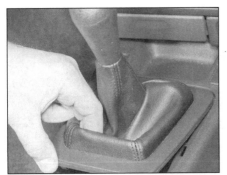

29.5 Unclip the gear lever gaiter from the centre console

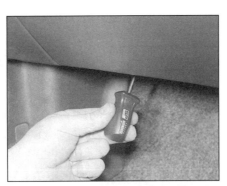

30.1a Remove the two securing screws . . .

30.1b . . . and withdraw the glovebox

11

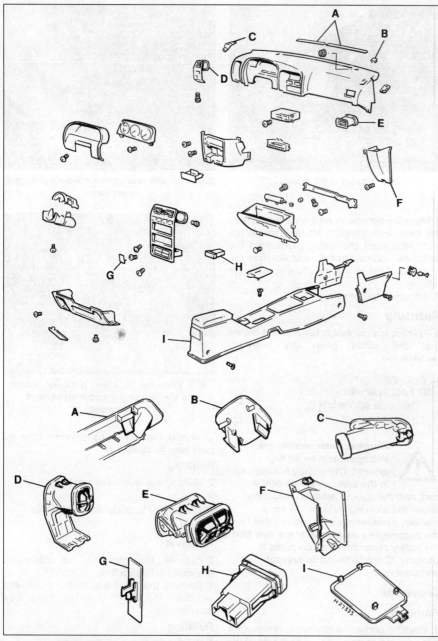

30.1c Facia components and fixings - left-hand-drive model shown

30.4a Remove the three securing screws . . .

30.4b . . . and withdraw the passenger's side lower facia panel

30.6a Remove the screw under the fusebox . . .

30.6b . . . the two screws (arrowed) at the top right-hand side of the panel . . .

30.6c . . . the two top left-hand screws . . .

30.6d . . . and the lower left-hand screw . . .

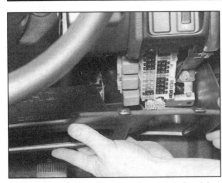

30.6e . . . then withdraw the driver's side
lower facia panel

30.9 Remove the two lower securing
screws . . .

30.10 . . . then prise out the ventilation
nozzle . . .

Driver's side lower facia panel

Removal

6 Remove the six securing screws, and lower
the panel from the facia. One screw is located
under the fusebox, two screws at the top
right-hand side of the panel (the middle of the
three screws in this location does not have to
be removed), two screws at the top left-hand
corner of the panel, and one screw at the
lower left-hand corner of the panel (see
illustrations).

Refitting

7 Refitting is a reversal of removal.

Driver's side switch/ventilation panel

Removal

8 Disconnect the battery negative lead.
9 Remove the two securing screws from the
lower edge of the panel (see illustration).
10 Prise the ventilation nozzle from the panel.
It will be necessary to lever at the sides of the
nozzle to release the swivel pins (see
illustration).
11 Using a suitable screwdriver, release the
two upper securing clips, then pull the panel
forwards from the facia (see illustrations).
12 Disconnect the switch wiring plugs, and
withdraw the panel.

Refitting

13 Refitting is a reversal of removal, but refit
the ventilation nozzle to the panel before
refitting the panel to the facia.

Facia centre switch/ventilation nozzle housing

Removal

14 Disconnect the battery negative lead.
15 Remove the two upper and two lower
securing screws, then pull the panel forwards
from the facia (see illustrations).
16 Disconnect the switch wiring plugs, and
withdraw the panel.
17 If further work is to be carried out, note

the routing of the wiring harnesses, to ensure
correct routing on refitting.

Refitting

18 Refitting is a reversal of removal, but
ensure that the wiring is routed as noted
before removal, and ensure that the air
ducting engages correctly with the rear of the
ventilation nozzles.

Facia lower centre panel

Removal

19 Remove the facia centre switch/
ventilation nozzle housing, the driver's side
lower facia panel, and the glovebox, as
described previously in this Section.

30.11a . . . release the securing clips . . .

30.11b . . . and pull the driver's side
switch/ventilation panel from the facia

30.15a Remove the two upper . . .

30.15b . . . and the two lower securing
screws . . .

30.15c . . . then pull the facia centre
switch/ventilation nozzle housing from the
facia

11

30.21a Remove the top left-hand securing screw . . .

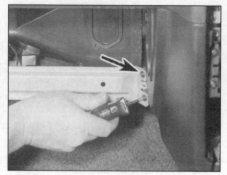

30.21b . . . the two screws securing the panel to the metal bracket . . .

30.21c . . . the top right-hand screw . . .

20 Remove the centre console, as described in Section 29.

21 Unscrew the ten panel securing screws, located as follows:

a) *One screw at the top left-hand corner of panel (see illustration).*

b) *Two screws securing the panel to the metal bracket in the glovebox aperture (see illustration).*

c) *One screw at the top right-hand corner of the panel (see illustration).*

d) *Four screws at the front of the panel, securing the panel to the heater control panel (see illustration).*

e) *Two or four screws (as applicable) at the front of the panel, accessible through the cassette tray aperture (see illustration).*

22 Pull the panel forwards from the facia (see

illustration), then disconnect the wiring plugs from the ashtray illumination bulb and the cigarette lighter. Note the routing of all wiring, to ensure correct routing on refitting.

Refitting

23 Refitting is a reversal of removal, but ensure that all wiring is routed as noted before removal. If the heater control panel has been removed, ensure that it is refitted before refitting the facia panel.

Steering column shrouds

Removal

24 Disconnect the battery negative lead.

25 Working under the steering column lower shroud, remove the six shroud securing screws, then unclip the trim plate from the

ignition switch/steering column lock, and pull the lower shroud down to unclip it from the upper shroud (**see illustrations**).

26 Carefully manipulate the upper shroud from the column (on models with an adjustable steering column, this is aided by fully lowering the column) (**see illustration**).

Refitting

27 Refitting is a reversal of removal, but ensure that the shroud clips engage correctly.

Instrument panel surround

Removal

28 Remove the steering column shrouds, as described previously in this Section.

29 Loosen the two steering column upper

30.21d . . . the four screws securing the heater control panel . . .

30.21e . . . the screws accessible through the cassette tray aperture . . .

30.22 . . . then pull the facia lower centre panel from the facia

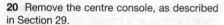

30.25a Remove the steering column shroud securing screws . . .

30.25b . . . then unclip the ignition switch/steering column lock trim plate

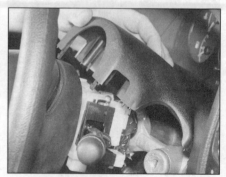

30.26 Removing the upper steering column shroud

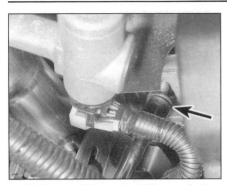

30.29 Loosening one of the steering column upper securing bolts (arrowed)

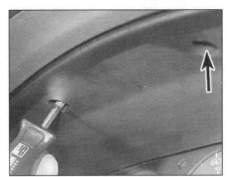

30.30a Unscrew the two top . . .

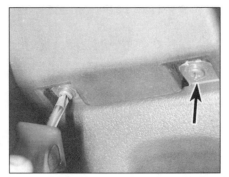

30.30b . . . two left-hand . . .

securing bolts, and lower the steering column slightly **(see illustration)**.

30 Unscrew the five instrument panel shroud securing screws. Two screws are located at the top of the panel, two on the left, and one on the right **(see illustrations)**.

31 Carefully withdraw the shroud from the facia **(see illustration)**. If necessary, lower the steering column further to provide sufficient clearance.

Refitting

32 Refitting is a reversal of removal, but tighten the steering column upper securing bolts to the specified torque.

Upper facia assembly

Note: *This is an involved procedure, and it is suggested that this complete Section is read through thoroughly before beginning the operation. It is advisable to make careful note of all wiring connections, and the routing of all wiring, to aid refitting.*

Removal

33 Remove the following facia panels, as described previously in this Section. Note the routing of all wiring, and keep all securing screws and fixings with the relevant panels to avoid confusion on refitting.

a) *Glovebox.*
b) *Passenger's side lower facia panel.*
c) *Driver's side lower facia panel.*
d) *Driver's side switch/ventilation panel.*

e) *Facia centre switch/ventilation nozzle housing.*
f) *Facia lower centre panel.*
g) *Steering column shrouds.*
h) *Instrument panel surround.*

34 Disconnect the control cable and the wiring plugs from the heater/ventilation control unit, and remove the unit from the facia (refer to Chapter 3 if necessary).

35 Remove the four securing screws, then withdraw the radio/cassette player from the facia, and disconnect the aerial lead and the wiring plugs.

36 Remove the steering column stalk switches, with reference to Chapter 12 if necessary.

37 Unscrew the two upper and two lower instrument panel securing screws.

38 Working in the engine compartment, disconnect the speedometer cable from the gearbox (see Chapter 12), then push the cable through the engine compartment bulkhead sufficiently to enable the instrument panel to be pulled forwards.

39 Pull the instrument panel forwards, and disconnect the wiring plugs and the speedometer cable from the rear of the panel. Withdraw the instrument panel.

40 Working behind the driver's side of the upper facia panel, remove the securing screw, and detach the "lights-on" warning buzzer from the rear of the facia **(see illustration)**.

41 Working at the passenger's side of the

30.30c . . . and single right-hand securing screw . . .

facia, pull the wiring connector from the glovebox light switch.

42 Pull the glovebox light bulbholder from the rear of the facia panel.

43 Reach up behind the passenger's side of the facia, and disconnect the two wiring harness connectors.

44 On models fitted with an anti-theft alarm, reach up behind the passenger's side of the facia, and disconnect the alarm LED wiring connector (the LED is located on top of the passenger's side of the facia).

45 Unscrew the upper facia panel lower securing nuts (one nut located at each bottom corner of the panel) **(see illustration)**.

46 Unscrew the upper facia panel centre securing bolt, which is located in the centre of

30.31 . . . then withdraw the instrument panel shroud

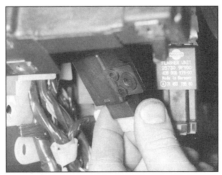

30.40 Detach the "lights-on" warning buzzer from the rear of the facia panel

30.45 Upper facia panel lower right-hand securing nut (arrowed)

11

30.46 Upper facia panel centre securing bolt (arrowed)

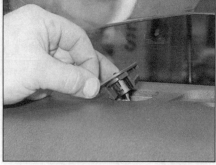

30.47a Prise out the upper securing nut cover plates . . .

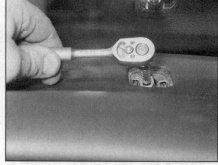

30.47b . . . then unscrew the facia panel upper securing nuts

the instrument panel aperture **(see illustration)**.

47 Working at the top of the upper facia panel, prise out the two upper securing nut cover plates (on models equipped with an anti-theft alarm, the passenger side cover plate houses the alarm LED), then unscrew the upper securing nuts **(see illustrations)**.

48 Make a final check to ensure that all relevant wiring has been disconnected, then pull the upper facia panel towards the rear of the car to disengage it from the scuttle - some manipulation may be required **(see illustration)**.

49 Once the facia panel has been released, withdraw it through the passenger's door aperture.

Refitting

50 Commence refitting by manoeuvring the upper facia panel into position against the scuttle.

51 Ensure that all relevant wiring is fed through the appropriate apertures in the facia,

and is not trapped. Particularly, ensure that the speedometer cable, and the instrument panel wiring is fed through the instrument panel apertures.

52 Ensure that the air ducting engages with the ventilation nozzle housings in the facia panel.

53 Refit the upper facia panel securing nuts, and the central bolts, and tighten them.

54 Refit the upper securing nut cover plates. Where applicable, feed the alarm LED wiring down through the top of the facia panel, and reconnect the two halves of the wiring connector.

55 Further refitting is broadly a reversal of the removal procedure described previously, bearing in mind the following points:

a) *Ensure that all wiring is correctly reconnected, and routed as noted before removal.*

b) *When reconnecting the speedometer cable, reconnect the cable to the speedometer, then pull the cable through the bulkhead, back into the engine*

30.48 Pull the facia panel towards the rear of the car to disengage the panel from the scuttle

compartment, until the instrument panel can be seated securely in the facia. Reconnect the speedometer to the gearbox with reference to Chapter 12.

c) *Refit all surrounding facia panels with reference to the relevant paragraphs of this Section.*

Chapter 12 Body electrical systems

Contents

Degrees of difficulty

Easy, suitable for novice with little experience	**Fairly easy,** suitable for beginner with some experience	**Fairly difficult,** suitable for competent DIY mechanic	**Difficult,** suitable for experienced DIY mechanic	**Very difficult,** suitable for expert DIY or professional

Specifications

Bulb ratings
	Watts
Courtesy light	10
Front direction indicator light	21
Front direction indicator repeater light	5
Front driving light	55
Front foglight	55
Front sidelight	5
Headlights	60/55
High-level stop-light:	
Saloon models	5
Hatchback models	2
Luggage compartment light:	
Saloon and Hatchback models	3.4
Estate models	5
Map reading light	10
Rear direction indicator light	21
Rear foglight	21
Rear number plate light	5
Reversing light	21
Stop/tail light	21/5

1 General information and precautions

General information

The body electrical system consists of all lights, wash/wipe equipment, interior electrical equipment, and associated switches and wiring.

The electrical system is of the 12-volt negative earth type. Power to the system is provided by a 12-volt battery, which is charged by the alternator (see Chapter 5A).

The engine electrical system (battery, alternator, starter motor, ignition system, etc) is covered separately in Chapter 5.

Precautions

 Warning: Before carrying out any work on the electrical system, read through the precautions given in "Safety first!" at the beginning of this manual, and in Chapter 5.

 Warning: Later models are equipped with an air bag system. When working on the electrical system, refer to the precautions given in Section 24, to avoid the possibility of personal injury.

Caution: If the radio/cassette player fitted to the vehicle has an anti-theft security code (as does the unit fitted as standard), refer to the information given in the preliminary Sections of this manual before disconnecting the battery.

12

Prior to wiring on any component in the electrical system, the battery negative lead should first be disconnected, to prevent the possibility of electrical short-circuits and/or fires.

2 Electrical fault-finding - general information

Note: *Refer to the precautions given in "Safety first!" and in Section 1 of this Chapter before starting work. The following tests relate to testing of the main electrical circuits, and should not be used to test delicate electronic circuits (such as anti-lock braking systems), particularly where an electronic control module is used.*

General

1 A typical electrical circuit consists of an electrical component, any switches, relays, motors, fuses, fusible links or circuit breakers related to that component, and the wiring and connectors which link the component to both the battery and the chassis. To help to pinpoint a problem in an electrical circuit, wiring diagrams are included at the end of this manual.

2 Before attempting to diagnose an electrical fault, first study the appropriate wiring diagram, to obtain a more complete understanding of the components included in the particular circuit concerned. The possible sources of a fault can be narrowed down by noting whether other components related to the circuit are operating properly. If several components or circuits fail at one time, the problem is likely to be related to a shared fuse or earth connection.

3 Electrical problems usually stem from simple causes, such as loose or corroded connections, a faulty earth connection, a blown fuse, a melted fusible link, or a faulty relay (refer to Section 3 for details of testing relays). Visually inspect the condition of all fuses, wires and connections in a problem circuit before testing the components. Use the .wiring diagrams to determine which terminal connections will need to be checked, in order to pinpoint the trouble-spot.

4 The basic tools required for electrical fault-finding include a circuit tester or voltmeter (a 12-volt bulb with a set of test leads can also be used for certain tests); a self-powered test light (sometimes known as a continuity tester); an ohmmeter (to measure resistance); a battery and set of test leads; and a jumper wire, preferably with a circuit breaker or fuse incorporated, which can be used to bypass suspect wires or electrical components. Before attempting to locate a problem with test instruments, use the wiring diagram to determine where to make the connections.

5 To find the source of an intermittent wiring fault (usually due to a poor or dirty connection, or damaged wiring insulation), a "wiggle" test can be performed on the wiring. This involves wiggling the wiring by hand, to see if the fault occurs as the wiring is moved. It should be possible to narrow down the source of the fault to a particular section of wiring. This method of testing can be used in conjunction with any of the tests described in the following sub-Sections.

6 Apart from problems due to poor connections, two basic types of fault can occur in an electrical circuit - open-circuit, or short-circuit.

7 Open-circuit faults are caused by a break somewhere in the circuit, which prevents current from flowing. An open-circuit fault will prevent a component from working, but will not cause the relevant circuit fuse to blow.

8 Short-circuit faults are caused by a "short" somewhere in the circuit, which allows the current flowing in the circuit to "escape" along an alternative route, usually to earth. Short-circuit faults are normally caused by a breakdown in wiring insulation, which allows a feed wire to touch either another wire, or an earthed component such as the bodyshell. A short-circuit fault will normally cause the relevant circuit fuse to blow.

Finding an open-circuit

9 To check for an open-circuit, connect one lead of a circuit tester or voltmeter to either the negative battery terminal or a known good earth.

10 Connect the other lead to a connector in the circuit being tested, preferably nearest to the battery or fuse.

11 Switch on the circuit, bearing in mind that some circuits are live only when the ignition switch is moved to a particular position.

12 If voltage is present (indicated either by the tester bulb lighting or a voltmeter reading, as applicable), this means that the section of the circuit between the relevant connector and the battery is problem-free.

13 Continue to check the remainder of the circuit in the same fashion.

14 When a point is reached at which no voltage is present, the problem must lie between that point and the previous test point with voltage. Most problems can be traced to a broken, corroded or loose connection.

Finding a short-circuit

15 To check for a short-circuit, first disconnect the load(s) from the circuit (loads are the components which draw current from a circuit, such as bulbs, motors, heating elements, etc).

16 Remove the relevant fuse from the circuit, and connect a circuit tester or voltmeter to the fuse connections.

17 Switch on the circuit, bearing in mind that some circuits are live only when the ignition switch is moved to a particular position.

18 If voltage is present (indicated either by the tester bulb lighting or a voltmeter reading, as applicable), this means that there is a short-circuit.

19 If no voltage is present, but the fuse still blows with the load(s) connected, this indicates an internal fault in the load(s).

Finding an earth fault

20 The battery negative terminal is connected to "earth" - the metal of the engine/transmission and the car body - and most systems are wired so that they only receive a positive feed, the current returning via the metal of the car body. This means that the component mounting and the body form part of that circuit. Loose or corroded mountings can therefore cause a range of electrical faults, ranging from total failure of a circuit, to a puzzling partial fault. In particular, lights may shine dimly (especially when another circuit sharing the same earth point is in operation), motors (eg wiper motors or the radiator cooling fan motor) may run slowly, and the operation of one circuit may have an apparently-unrelated effect on another. Note that on many vehicles, earth straps are used between certain components, such as the engine/transmission and the body, usually where there is no metal-to-metal contact between components, due to flexible rubber mountings, etc.

21 To check whether a component is properly earthed, disconnect the battery, and connect one lead of an ohmmeter to a known good earth point. Connect the other lead to the wire or earth connection being tested. The resistance reading should be zero; if not, check the connection as follows.

22 If an earth connection is thought to be faulty, dismantle the connection, and clean back to bare metal both the bodyshell and the wire terminal or the component earth connection mating surface. Be careful to remove all traces of dirt and corrosion, then use a knife to trim away any paint, so that a clean metal-to-metal joint is made. On reassembly, tighten the joint fasteners securely; if a wire terminal is being refitted, use serrated washers between the terminal and the bodyshell, to ensure a clean and secure connection. When the connection is remade, prevent the onset of corrosion in the future by applying a coat of petroleum jelly or silicone-based grease, or by spraying on (at regular intervals) a proprietary ignition sealer.

3 Fuses and relays - general information

Fuses

1 Fuses are designed to break a circuit when a predetermined current is reached, in order to protect the components and wiring which could be damaged by excessive current flow. Any excessive current flow will be due to a fault in the circuit, usually a short-circuit (see Section 2).

2 The main fuses are located in the fusebox on the driver's side of the facia.

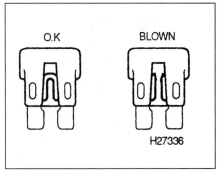

3.3 Fusebox cover removed to expose fuses - spare fuses arrowed

3.4 Auxiliary fusebox in engine compartment (cover removed)

3.5 Checking the condition of a fuse

3 For access to the fuses, pull open the cover flap **(see illustration)**.

4 Additional fuses and circuit-breakers are located in an auxiliary fusebox in the engine compartment, attached to a bracket on the left-hand body panel, next to the battery **(see illustration)**.

5 A blown fuse can be recognised from its melted or broken wire **(see illustration)**.

6 To remove a fuse, first ensure that the relevant circuit is switched off.

7 Using the plastic tool clipped to the main fusebox lid, pull the fuse from its location.

8 Spare fuses are provided in the main fusebox.

9 Before renewing a blown fuse, trace and rectify the cause, and always use a fuse of the

correct rating (fuse ratings are specified on the inside of the fusebox cover flap). Never substitute a fuse of a higher rating, or make temporary repairs using wire or metal foil; more serious damage, or even fire, could result.

10 Note that the fuses are colour-coded as follows. Refer to the wiring diagrams for details of the fuse ratings used and the circuits protected.

Colour	Rating
Orange	5A
Red	10A
Blue	15A
Yellow	20A
Clear or White	25A
Green	30A

11 The radio/cassette player fuse is located in the rear of the unit, and can be accessed after removing the radio/cassette player.

Relays

12 A relay is an electrically-operated switch, which is used for the following reasons:
a) A relay can switch a heavy current remotely from the circuit in which the current is flowing, therefore allowing the use of lighter-gauge wiring and switch contacts.
b) A relay can receive more than one control input, unlike a mechanical switch.
c) A relay can have a timer function - for example, the intermittent wiper relay.

13 Various relays are located behind the

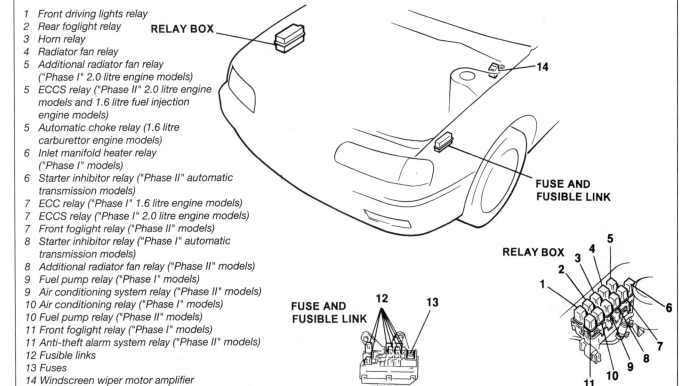

1 Front driving lights relay
2 Rear foglight relay
3 Horn relay
4 Radiator fan relay
5 Additional radiator fan relay ("Phase I" 2.0 litre engine models)
5 ECCS relay ("Phase II" 2.0 litre engine models and 1.6 litre fuel injection engine models)
5 Automatic choke relay (1.6 litre carburettor engine models)
6 Inlet manifold heater relay ("Phase I" models)
6 Starter inhibitor relay ("Phase II" automatic transmission models)
7 ECC relay ("Phase II" 1.6 litre engine models)
7 ECCS relay ("Phase I" 2.0 litre engine models)
7 Front foglight relay ("Phase II" models)
8 Starter inhibitor relay ("Phase I" automatic transmission models)
8 Additional radiator fan relay ("Phase II" models)
9 Fuel pump relay ("Phase I" models)
9 Air conditioning system relay ("Phase II" models)
10 Air conditioning relay ("Phase I" models)
10 Fuel pump relay ("Phase II" models)
11 Front foglight relay ("Phase I" models)
11 Anti-theft alarm system relay ("Phase II" models)
12 Fusible links
13 Fuses
14 Windscreen wiper motor amplifier

3.13a Engine compartment relay locations - Saloon and Hatchback models

12

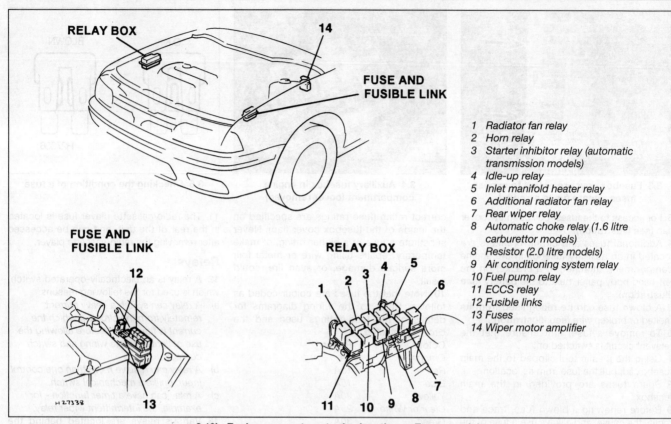

RELAY BOX

14

FUSE AND
FUSIBLE LINK

FUSE AND
FUSIBLE LINK

12

13

RELAY BOX

1 Radiator fan relay
2 Horn relay
3 Starter inhibitor relay (automatic transmission models)
4 Idle-up relay
5 Inlet manifold heater relay
6 Additional radiator fan relay
7 Rear wiper relay
8 Automatic choke relay (1.6 litre carburettor models)
8 Resistor (2.0 litre models)
9 Air conditioning system relay
10 Fuel pump relay
11 ECCS relay
12 Fusible links
13 Fuses
14 Wiper motor amplifier

3.13b Engine compartment relay locations - Estate models

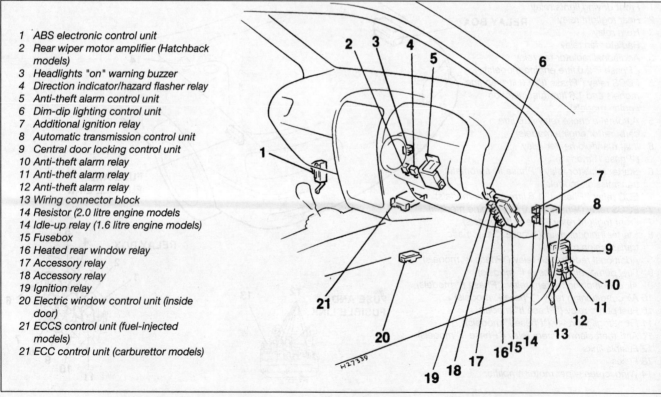

1 ABS electronic control unit
2 Rear wiper motor amplifier (Hatchback models)
3 Headlights "on" warning buzzer
4 Direction indicator/hazard flasher relay
5 Anti-theft alarm control unit
6 Dim-dip lighting control unit
7 Additional ignition relay
8 Automatic transmission control unit
9 Central door locking control unit
10 Anti-theft alarm relay
11 Anti-theft alarm relay
12 Anti-theft alarm relay
13 Wiring connector block
14 Resistor (2.0 litre engine models
14 Idle-up relay (1.6 litre engine models)
15 Fusebox
16 Heated rear window relay
17 Accessory relay
18 Accessory relay
19 Ignition relay
20 Electric window control unit (inside door)
21 ECCS control unit (fuel-injected models)
21 ECC control unit (carburettor models)

3.13c Facia-mounted relay and control unit locations - Saloon and Hatchback models

facia, next to the fusebox, and in various other locations, depending on model. Most of the engine-related relays are located in the relay box on the right-hand side of the engine compartment **(see illustrations)**.

14 On most models, the direction indicator/hazard warning flasher unit is located on a bracket behind the facia, to the left of the steering column, and can be accessed once the driver's side lower facia panel has been removed (see Chapter 11) **(see illustration)**.

15 The "headlights on" warning buzzer is screwed to the rear of the facia, above the direction indicator/hazard warning flasher unit (see paragraph 14).

16 Relays may be located in various other locations, depending on model - for example, on Hatchback models, the tailgate wiper relay is located in the luggage compartment, behind the rear trim panel **(see illustration)**.

17 If a circuit or system controlled by a relay develops a fault, and the relay is suspect, operate the system. If the relay is functioning, it should be possible to hear it "click" as it is energised, If this is the case, the fault lies with the components or wiring of the system. If the relay is not being energised, then either the relay is not receiving a main supply or a switching voltage, or the relay itself is faulty. Testing is by the substitution of a known good unit, but be careful - while some relays are identical in appearance and in operation, others look similar but perform different functions.

18 To remove a relay, first ensure that the relevant circuit is switched off. The relay can then simply be pulled out from the socket, and pushed back into position.

4 Switches - removal and refitting

Note: *Disconnect the battery negative lead before removing any switch, and reconnect the lead after refitting the switch. Refer to the caution in Section 1 if a security-coded radio/cassette player is fitted.*

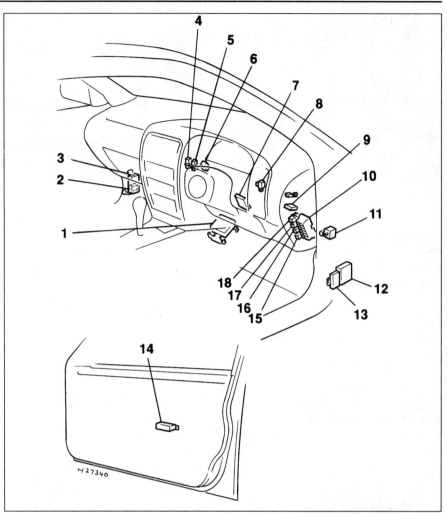

3.13d Facia-mounted relay and control unit locations - Estate models

1 ECCS control unit	10 Fusebox
2 Electric aerial timer	11 Connector block
3 ABS control unit	12 Remote control central door locking control unit
4 Rear foglight relay	
5 Heated rear window relay	13 Central door locking control unit
6 Direction indicator/hazard flasher relay	14 Electric window control unit (inside door)
7 Time control unit (wash/wipe, courtesy light, clock, electric windows delay, etc)	15 Electric windows relay
	16 Accessory relay
8 Headlights "on" warning buzzer	17 Accessory relay
9 Dim-dip lighting control unit	18 Ignition relay

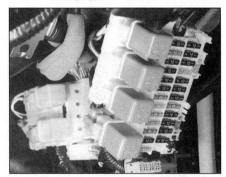

3.13e Driver's side lower facia panel removed to expose relays next to fusebox

3.14 Driver's side lower facia panel removed to expose direction indicator/ hazard warning flasher unit (arrowed)

3.16 Luggage compartment rear trim panel removed to expose tailgate wiper relay (arrowed) - Hatchback model

12

4.3 Sliding the wash/wipe switch from the steering column bracket

Ignition switch/steering column lock

1 Refer to Chapter 10.

Steering column combination switches

2 Remove the steering column shrouds, as described in Chapter 11, Section 30.
3 Where applicable, depress the securing clips, then slide the relevant switch from the bracket on the steering column, and disconnect the wiring plugs **(see illustration)**.
4 Refitting is a reversal of removal.

Centre facia-mounted pushbutton switches

5 Remove the facia centre switch/ventilation nozzle housing as described in Chapter 11.

4.11a Release the securing clips . . .

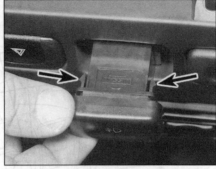

4.7 Removing the rear foglight switch from the facia centre switch/ventilation nozzle housing - securing clips arrowed

6 Working at the rear of the panel, disconnect the wiring plug from the relevant switch.
7 Push the switch forwards from the panel to release the securing clips **(see illustration)**.
8 Refitting is a reversal of removal.

Heater blower motor switch

9 Remove the heater/ventilation control unit as described in Chapter 3.
10 Carefully pull off the blower motor control knob **(see illustration)**. If using pliers, wrap a suitable piece of cloth or card around the knob to protect it.
11 Release the securing clips (two at the bottom and one at the top of the switch), using a screwdriver if necessary, then pull the blower motor switch from the rear of the control panel **(see illustrations)**.

4.11b . . . then pull the switch from the control panel

4.10 Pulling the knob from the heater blower motor switch

12 Refit the switch using a reversal of the removal procedure, then refit the heater/ventilation control unit as described in Chapter 3.

Driver's side switch/ventilation panel-mounted switches

13 These switches include the electric door mirror switch, the instrument panel illumination switch, and the front foglight switch.
14 Remove the driver's side switch/ventilation panel, as described in Chapter 11, Section 30.
15 Working at the rear of the panel, release the securing clips, then push the relevant switch out through the front of the panel **(see illustration)**.
16 Refit the switch by pushing it into position in the panel, then refit the panel with reference to Chapter 11, Section 30.

Centre console-mounted switches

17 Remove the centre console, as described in Chapter 11.
18 To remove the electric window switches, working under centre console, remove the two securing screws and withdraw the switch assembly **(see illustrations)**. Note that the switches are integrated in pairs - ie, front and rear switches cannot be renewed individually.
19 To remove any of the other switches, working at the rear of the centre console,

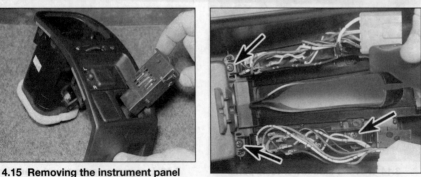

4.15 Removing the instrument panel illumination switch from the driver's side switch/ventilation panel

4.18a Remove the securing screws (two for each switch - arrowed) . . .

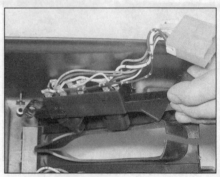

4.18b . . . and withdraw the switch from the rear of the centre console

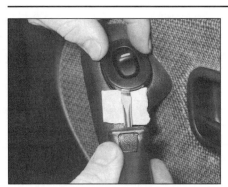

4.21 Prising an electric window switch from the front door. Note card used to protect door trim

4.29a Remove the securing screws . . .

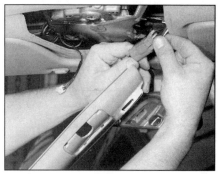

4.29b . . . and lower the roof console . . .

release the securing clips, then push the switch out through the top of the centre console.

20 Refit the relevant switch using a reversal of the removal procedure, then refit the centre console.

Electric window switches

Front door switch

21 To remove a front door switch, simply prise the switch from the door trim panel, and disconnect the wiring connector **(see illustration)**. Note that the wiring connector is clipped to the inside of the door, and it may be necessary to remove the door inner trim panel (see Chapter 11) for access to the connector.

22 Where applicable, refit the door inner trim panel as described in Chapter 11, and refit the switch by pushing it into position.

Rear door switch

23 Pull the interior door handle surround from the door, complete with the switch, then disconnect the switch wiring plug.

24 Push the switch out through the rear of the interior handle surround.

25 Refitting is a reversal of removal.

Centre-console-mounted switches

26 Refer to paragraphs 17 to 20.

Electric sunroof switch

27 Carefully prise the lens from the map reading lights in the overhead console.

28 Prise the cover plate from the rear of the overhead console.

29 Remove the two now-exposed securing screws, and lower the console from the roof **(see illustrations)**.

30 Disconnect the wiring plugs.

31 Working at the rear of the panel, remove the two securing screws, and withdraw the switch from the rear of the panel **(see illustration)**.

32 Refitting is a reversal of removal.

Courtesy light/door ajar warning switches

33 Open the door to expose the switch in the door pillar.

34 Remove the securing screw, then withdraw the switch from the door pillar. Disconnect the wiring connector as it becomes accessible **(see illustration)**.

 HAYNES HiNT *Tape the wiring to the door pillar, or tie a length of string to the wiring, to retrieve it if it falls back into the door pillar.*

35 Refitting is a reversal of removal, but ensure that the rubber gaiter is correctly seated on the switch.

Glovebox light switch

36 Open the glovebox, then prise the switch from the lower edge of the facia, and disconnect the wiring plug **(see illustration)**.

37 Refitting is a reversal of removal.

Luggage compartment light switch

38 The switch is integral with the boot lid/tailgate lock. Removal and refitting details for the boot lid/tailgate lock are provided in Chapter 11.

Map reading light switches

39 The switches are integral with the light assembly, and cannot be renewed independently.

---

5 Bulbs (exterior lights) - renewal

General

1 Whenever a bulb is renewed, note the following points:

a) *Disconnect the battery negative lead before starting work.*

b) *Remember that, if the light has just been in use, the bulb may be extremely hot.*

c) *Always check the bulb contacts and holder, ensuring that there is clean metal-to-metal contact between the bulb and its live contact(s) and earth. Clean off any corrosion or dirt before fitting a new bulb.*

d) *Wherever bayonet-type bulbs are fitted, ensure that the live contact(s) bear firmly against the bulb contact.*

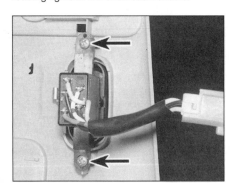

4.31 . . . for access to the sunroof switch securing screws (arrowed)

4.34 Removing a courtesy light switch

4.36 Removing the glovebox light switch

12

5.3 Disconnecting a headlight bulb wiring plug - Saloon and Hatchback models

5.4 Pulling the rubber boot from the headlight - Saloon and Hatchback models

5.6 Removing a headlight bulb - Saloon and Hatchback models

e) Always ensure that the new bulb is of the correct rating (see Specifications), and that it is completely clean before fitting it; this applies particularly to headlight/foglight bulbs (see following paragraphs).

Headlight - Saloon and Hatchback models

2 Open the bonnet.
3 Squeeze the securing lugs, and disconnect the wiring plug from the rear of the bulb (see illustration).
4 Pull the rubber boot from the rear of the headlight (see illustration).
5 Squeeze the retaining spring-clip lugs, and release the clip from the rear of the bulb.
6 Withdraw the bulb (see illustration).

7 When handling the new bulb, use a tissue or clean cloth, to avoid touching the glass with the fingers; moisture and grease from the skin can cause blackening and rapid failure of this type of bulb. If the glass is accidentally touched, wipe it clean using methylated spirit.
8 Install the new bulb, ensuring that its locating tabs are correctly located in the light unit cut-outs. Secure the bulb in position with the retaining clip, then refit the rubber boot and reconnect the wiring plug. Note the "TOP" mark on the rubber boot which should be uppermost.

Headlight - Estate models

9 Open the bonnet.
10 Unclip the plastic cover from the rear of

the headlight, then pull the wiring plug from the bulb contacts (see illustrations).
11 Pull the rubber cover from the rear of the light unit (see illustration).
12 Proceed as described in paragraphs 4 to 7 inclusive.
13 Install the new bulb, ensuring that its locating tabs are correctly located in the light unit cut-outs. Secure the bulb in position with the retaining clip, then refit the rubber cover to the rear of the light unit.
14 Reconnect the wiring plug, then refit the plastic cover to the rear of the light unit.

Front sidelight - Saloon and Hatchback models

15 Open the bonnet.
16 Squeeze the securing lugs, and disconnect the wiring plug from the rear of the headlight bulb.
17 Pull the rubber boot from the rear of the headlight.
18 Pull the bulbholder from the rear of the light unit (see illustration).
19 The bulb is a push fit in the bulbholder.
20 Fit the new bulb using a reversal of the removal procedure.

Front sidelight - Estate models

21 Open the bonnet.
22 Working at the rear of the headlight unit, twist the sidelight bulbholder anti-clockwise, and withdraw it from the light unit (see illustration).
23 The bulb is a push fit in the bulbholder.

5.10a Unclip the plastic cover . . .

5.10b . . . then pull the wiring plug from the bulb contacts - Estate models

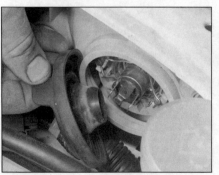

5.11 Pull the rubber cover from the rear of the headlight unit - Estate models

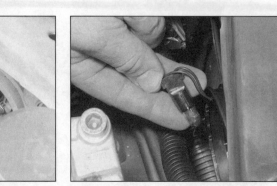

5.18 Removing a sidelight bulbholder - Saloon and Hatchback models

5.22 Removing a sidelight bulbholder - Estate models

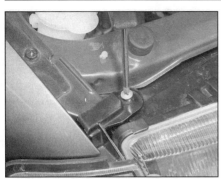

5.25 Removing a direction indicator light securing screw - Saloon and Hatchback models

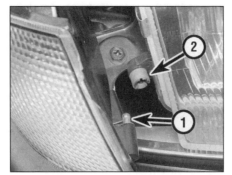

5.26 Release the direction indicator light unit balljoint (1) from the socket (2) - Saloon and Hatchback models

5.27 Withdrawing the bulbholder from the direction indicator light unit - Saloon and Hatchback models

24 Fit the new bulb using a reversal of the removal procedure.

Front direction indicator - Saloon and Hatchback models

25 Remove the direction indicator light unit securing screw (located at the outer top corner of the light unit) **(see illustration)**.
26 Using a suitable screwdriver, carefully release the light unit lower balljoint **(see illustration)**.
27 Withdraw the light unit forwards from the wing panel, then twist the bulbholder anti-clockwise and withdraw it from the light unit **(see illustration)**.
28 The bulb is a bayonet fit in the bulbholder.
29 Fit the new bulb, then refit the light assembly using a reversal of the removal procedure. Ensure that the light unit lower balljoint is securely engaged.

Front direction indicator - Estate models

30 Remove the direction indicator light unit securing screw (located at the outer top corner of the light unit).
31 Remove the light unit lower securing screw **(see illustration)**.
32 Withdraw the light unit forwards from the wing panel, then twist the bulbholder anti-clockwise and withdraw it from the light unit.
33 The bulb is a bayonet fit in the bulbholder.
34 Fit the new bulb, then refit the light

assembly using a reversal of the removal procedure.

Front direction indicator side repeater

35 Push the light unit towards the front of the vehicle, and on Estate models, squeeze the ends of the unit to release it from the wing panel.
36 Withdraw the light unit, then twist the bulbholder anti-clockwise to release it from the light unit **(see illustration)**.
37 The bulb is a push fit in the bulbholder.
38 Fit the new bulb using a reversal of the removal procedure.

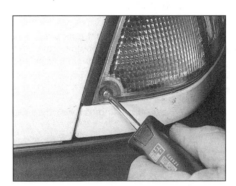

5.31 Unscrewing the front direction indicator light unit lower securing screw - Estate models

5.36 Removing the bulbholder from the direction indicator side repeater light

Front driving light - Saloon and Hatchback models

39 Open the bonnet.
40 Pull up the retaining clip, and remove the plastic cover from the rear of the headlight unit **(see illustration)**.
41 Release the retaining clip from the rear of the bulb, then withdraw the bulb from the rear of the light unit, and disconnect the wiring connector **(see illustrations)**.
42 When handling the new bulb, use a tissue or clean cloth, to avoid touching the glass with the fingers; moisture and grease from the skin can cause blackening and rapid failure of this type of bulb. If the glass is

5.40 Remove the plastic cover from the light unit . . .

5.41a . . . then release the retaining clip . . .

5.41b . . . and remove the bulb from the driving light - Saloon and Hatchback models

12

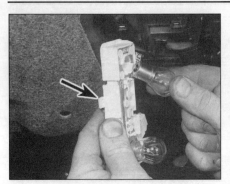

5.51 Removing a bulb from the stop/tail/rear direction indicator light unit - Saloon model

Bulbholder securing clip arrowed

5.56 Removing a bulb from the reversing light/rear foglight bulbholder - Saloon model

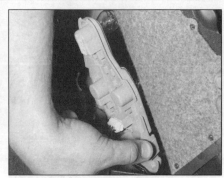

5.60 Removing the rear light cluster bulbholder - Hatchback model

accidentally touched, wipe it clean using methylated spirit.

43 Install the new bulb, ensuring that its locating tabs are correctly located in the light unit cut-outs.

44 Secure the bulb with the retaining clip, then refit the plastic cover, and secure with the clip.

Front driving light - Estate models

45 The procedure is as described previously for Saloon and Hatchback models, noting that the bulb cover is a twist-fit on the rear of the light unit. Twist the cover anti-clockwise to release it from the light unit.

Front foglight

46 Remove the two lens surround securing screws, then withdraw the surround, lens, and reflector.

47 Disconnect the wiring from the bulb, then release the spring clip, and withdraw the bulb from the rear of the light unit.

48 Fit the new bulb using a reversal of the removal procedure.

Stop/tail light and rear direction indicator light - Saloon models

49 Open the boot lid.

50 Working at the side of the luggage compartment, release the securing clip, and lift up the light unit cover flap.

51 Release the bulbholder securing clip, and withdraw the bulbholder from the rear of the light unit **(see illustration)**.

52 The bulbs are a bayonet fit in the bulbholder.

53 Fit the new bulb using a reversal of the removal procedure. Note that the stop/tail light bulb has offset pins, to ensure correct installation.

Reversing light and rear foglight - Saloon models

54 Open the boot lid.

55 Working through the light aperture in the boot lid, squeeze the bulbholder retaining clips, and withdraw the bulbholder from the boot lid.

56 The bulbs are a bayonet fit in the bulbholder **(see illustration)**.

57 Fit the new bulb using a reversal of the removal procedure.

Rear light cluster - Hatchback models

58 Open the tailgate.

59 Working at the side of the luggage compartment, prise open the light unit cover.

60 Squeeze the securing clips to release the

bulbholder from the rear of the light unit **(see illustration)**.

61 The bulbs are a bayonet fit in the bulbholder **(see illustration)**.

62 Fit the new bulb using a reversal of the removal procedure. Note that the stop/tail light bulb has offset pins, to ensure correct installation.

Rear light cluster - Estate models

63 Open the tailgate.

64 Remove the two screws securing the light unit to the rear body panel **(see illustration)**.

65 Lift the light unit slightly to release the lower retaining lug, then withdraw the unit from the body panel, taking care not to strain the wiring.

66 Twist the relevant bulbholder anti-clockwise to release it from the rear of the light unit **(see illustration)**.

67 The bulbs are a bayonet fit in the bulbholders.

68 Fit the new bulb using a reversal of the removal procedure. Note that the stop/tail light bulb has offset pins, to ensure correct installation.

Rear number plate light - Saloon and Estate models

69 Remove the two securing screws, and

5.61 Removing a rear light cluster bulb - Hatchback model

5.64 Remove the two rear light unit securing screws - Estate model

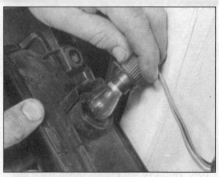

5.66 Removing a bulb from the rear light unit - Estate model

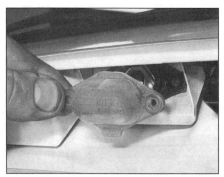

5.69 Removing the rear number plate light unit lens - Estate model

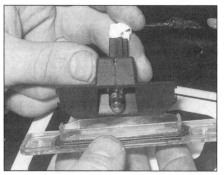

5.70 Unclipping the lens from the rear number plate light - Saloon model

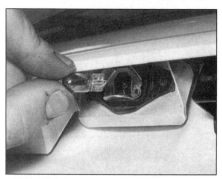

5.71 Withdrawing the rear number plate light bulb - Estate model

withdraw the light unit lens from the boot lid/tailgate **(see illustration)**.

70 On Saloon models, unclip the lens from the light unit for access to the bulb **(see illustration)**.

71 The bulb is a push fit in the light unit **(see illustration)**.

72 Fit the new bulb using a reversal of the removal procedure.

Rear number plate light - Hatchback models

73 Using a small flat-bladed screwdriver, carefully prise the light unit from the rear bumper.

74 Pull the rubber cover from the rear of the light, then pull the bulbholder from the rear of the light unit **(see illustration)**.

75 The bulb is a push fit in the bulbholder **(see illustration)**.

76 Fit the new bulb using a reversal of the removal procedure.

6 Bulbs (interior lights) - renewal

General

1 Refer to Section 5, paragraph 1.

Courtesy light

2 Carefully prise the lens from the light unit (if necessary, carefully use a flat-bladed screwdriver) **(see illustration)**.

3 The bulb is a push fit in the light unit **(see illustration)**.

4 Fit the new bulb using a reversal of the removal procedure.

Map reading light - models with single light

5 Proceed as described previously for the courtesy light.

Map reading lights - models with twin lights

6 Carefully prise the lens from the light unit (if necessary, use a flat-bladed screwdriver) **(see illustration)**.

7 Where applicable, remove the securing screw, and withdraw the light cover plate.

8 The bulbs are a push fit in the light unit **(see illustration)**.

5.74 Pulling the rubber cover from the rear number plate light - Hatchback model

5.75 Removing a rear number plate light bulb - Hatchback model

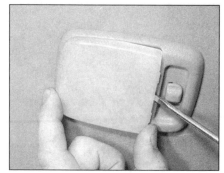

6.2 Prise off the lens . . .

6.3 . . . for access to the courtesy light bulb

6.6 Prise the lens from the light unit . . .

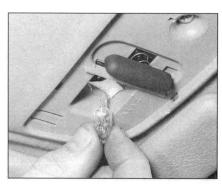

6.8 . . . for access to the twin map reading light bulbs

12

6.13 Removing the luggage compartment light bulb - Hatchback model

9 Fit the new bulb using a reversal of the removal procedure.

Luggage compartment light

10 Open the tailgate or boot lid, as applicable.
11 Where applicable, remove the two securing screws, then prise the light assembly from the body panel.
12 Unclip the lens from the light.
13 The bulb is a push fit in the light assembly **(see illustration)**.
14 Fit the new bulb using a reversal of the removal procedure.

Glovebox light

15 Remove the glovebox, with reference to Chapter 11.

6.25 Pull the top cover from the heater control panel for access to the bulbs

16 Pull the bulbholder from the rear of the facia **(see illustration)**.
17 The bulb is a push fit in the bulbholder.
18 Refitting is a reversal of removal.

Instrument panel lights

19 Remove the instrument panel, as described in Section 9.
20 Twist the relevant bulbholder anti-clockwise to remove it from the rear of the instrument panel **(see illustration)**.
21 The bulbs are integral with the bulbholders.
22 Fit the new bulb, and twist it clockwise to lock it into position.
23 Refit the instrument panel as described in Section 9.

Heater control panel illumination bulbs

24 Remove the heater/ventilation control unit as described in Chapter 3.
25 Pull the top cover from the control unit, to expose the circuit board and the bulbs **(see illustration)**.
26 Twist the relevant bulbholder anti-clockwise, using a screwdriver if necessary, and withdraw the bulbholder from the rear of the control unit. Note that an access hole is provided in the connector board for one of the bulbs **(see illustration)**. The bulbs are integral with the bulbholders.
27 Fit the new bulb using a reversal of the removal procedure, then refit the heater/

6.16 Removing the glovebox light bulb

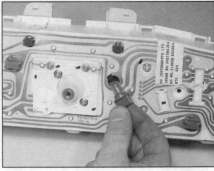

6.20 Removing an instrument panel light bulb

ventilation control unit as described in Chapter 3.

Switch illumination bulbs

28 All of the switches are fitted with illuminating bulbs, and some are also fitted with a bulb to show when the circuit concerned is operating.
29 In most cases, if a bulb blows, the complete switch must be renewed, but on Estate models, certain switch bulbs can be renewed. Check with a Nissan dealer for information on the availability of spare bulbs.
30 On switches where the bulbs can be renewed, remove the relevant switch as described in Section 4, then pull the bulbholder from the top of the switch. The bulbs are integral with the bulbholders.

Cigarette lighter illumination bulb

31 Remove the facia lower centre panel as described in Chapter 11, Section 30.
32 Working at the rear of the panel, pull out the bulbholder.
33 The bulb is a push fit in the bulbholder **(see illustration)**.
34 Refitting is a reversal of removal, but refit the facia lower centre panel with reference to Chapter 11.

Ashtray illumination bulb

35 Proceed as described previously for the cigarette lighter illumination bulb **(see illustration)**.

6.26 Removing a heater control panel bulb via the access hole in the circuit board

6.33 Removing the cigarette lighter illumination bulb

6.35 Removing the ashtray light bulbholder

7.2 Removing the front grille panel

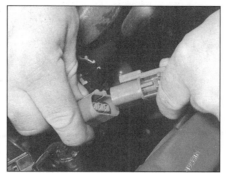

7.3 Disconnect the headlight unit wiring harness connector - Saloon and Hatchback models

7.4 Unscrew the two headlight side securing bolts . . .

7 Exterior light units - removal and refitting

Note: *Disconnect the battery negative lead before removing any light unit, and reconnect the lead after refitting the light. Refer to the caution in Section 1 if a security-coded radio/cassette player is fitted.*

Headlight - Saloon and Hatchback models

Removal

1 Remove the relevant direction indicator light as described later in this Section.

2 Pull the front grille panel forwards from the front of the vehicle to release the securing clips **(see illustration)**.

3 Disconnect the headlight bulb wiring plug, then separate the two halves of the headlight unit wiring harness connector **(see illustration)**.

4 Unscrew the two headlight side securing bolts **(see illustration)**.

5 Similarly, unscrew the two headlight rear securing nuts **(see illustration)**.

6 Unscrew the lower headlight securing bolt, and withdraw the headlight unit from the vehicle **(see illustrations)**.

7 If desired, unbolt the lower trim panel from the headlight unit.

Refitting

8 Refitting is a reversal of removal, but check that the direction indicator light unit lower balljoint is securely engaged. On completion, it is wise to have the headlight beam alignment checked with reference to Section 8.

Headlight - Estate models

Removal

9 Proceed as described in paragraphs 1 and 2.

10 Disconnect the headlight bulb wiring plug.

11 Working in the direction indicator light aperture, unscrew the two headlight outer securing nuts **(see illustration)**.

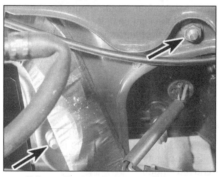

7.5 . . . the two rear securing nuts (arrowed) . . .

12 Working behind the headlight, unscrew the two headlight rear securing nuts **(see illustration)**.

13 Withdraw the headlight from the vehicle, and disconnect the sidelight wiring plug.

14 If desired, unbolt the lower trim panel from the headlight unit.

Refitting

15 Refitting is a reversal of removal, but reconnect the sidelight bulb wiring plug before refitting the light. On completion, it is wise to have the headlight beam alignment checked with reference to Section 8.

Front direction indicator light

16 The procedure is described as part of the bulb renewal procedure in Section 5.

7.6a . . . and the lower securing bolt . . .

7.6b . . . then withdraw the headlight - Saloon and Hatchback models

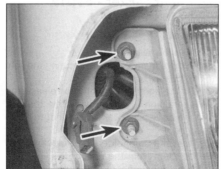

7.11 Unscrew the two headlight outer securing nuts (arrowed) - Estate models

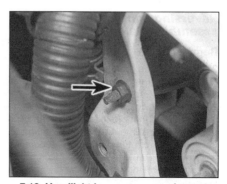

7.12 Headlight lower rear securing nut (arrowed) - Estate models

12

7.20 Rear stop/tail/direction indicator light unit securing nuts - Saloon model

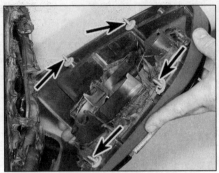

7.30 Removing the rear light cluster - Hatchback model (securing studs arrowed)

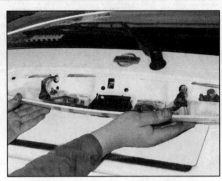

7.48 Removing the tailgate outer trim/handle panel - Estate models

Front direction indicator side repeater light

17 The procedure is described as part of the bulb renewal procedure in Section 5.

Front foglight

18 The procedure is described as part of the bulb renewal procedure in Section 5.

Stop/tail and rear direction indicator light assembly - Saloon models

Removal

19 Remove the bulbholder assembly, as described for the bulb renewal procedure in Section 5.
20 Working inside the luggage compartment, unscrew the three securing nuts (release the wiring clips from the studs, where applicable), then withdraw the light unit from the rear of the vehicle **(see illustration)**. Note that the light unit is held in place with a sealing compound.

Refitting

21 Before refitting the light unit, clean all traces of sealant from the light unit and the rear wing panel.
22 Apply the new sealing strip to the rear of the light unit (the sealing strip is supplied in rolls, and may have to be trimmed to the required length).
23 Refit the light unit using a reversal of the removal procedure.

Reversing light and rear foglight assembly - Saloon models

Removal

24 Remove the bulbholder assembly, as described for the bulb renewal procedure in Section 5.
25 Working inside the boot lid, unscrew the three securing nuts (release the wiring clips from the studs, where applicable), then pull the light unit from the outside of the boot lid. Note that the light unit is held in place with a sealing compound.

Refitting

26 Before refitting the light unit, clean all

traces of sealant from the light unit and the boot lid.
27 Apply the new sealing strip to the rear of the light unit (the sealing strip is supplied in rolls, and may have to be trimmed to the required length).
28 Refit the light unit using a reversal of the removal procedure.

Rear light cluster - Hatchback models

Note: *A new light unit sealing strip will be required on refitting.*

Removal

29 Remove the bulbholder assembly, as described for the bulb renewal procedure in Section 5.
30 Working inside the luggage compartment, unscrew the four securing nuts (one at each corner of the light unit), then pull the light unit from the rear of the vehicle **(see illustration)**. Note that the light unit is held in place with a sealing compound.

Refitting

31 Before refitting the light unit, clean all traces of sealant from the light unit and the wing panel.
32 Apply the new sealing strip to the rear of the light unit (the sealing strip is supplied in rolls, and may have to be trimmed to the required length).
33 Refit the light unit using a reversal of the removal procedure.

Rear light cluster - Estate models

Removal

34 Open the tailgate.
35 Remove the two screws securing the light unit to the rear body panel.
36 Lift the light unit slightly to release the lower retaining lug, then withdraw the unit from the body panel, taking care not to strain the wiring.
37 Twist the bulbholders anti-clockwise to release them from the rear of the light unit (note the locations of the bulbholders to ensure correct refitting), then withdraw the light unit.

Refitting

38 Refitting is a reversal of removal, but ensure that the bulbholders are refitted to their correct locations, as noted before removal.

Rear number plate light - Saloon models

Removal

39 Remove the two securing screws, and withdraw the light unit from the boot lid/tailgate.
40 Trace the wiring back from the light unit, and separate the two halves of the wiring connector.

Refitting

41 Refitting is a reversal of removal.

Rear number plate light - Hatchback models

42 The procedure is described as part of the bulb renewal procedure in Section 5.

Rear number plate light - Estate models

Removal

43 Disconnect the battery negative lead.
44 Remove the tailgate inner trim panels as described in Chapter 11, Section 28.
45 Working inside the tailgate, unscrew the four nuts securing the tailgate outer trim/handle panel.
46 Release the two outer trim/handle panel securing clips (one at each end of the panel, accessible from the inside of the tailgate).
47 Working inside the tailgate, disconnect the two number plate wiring connectors.
48 Disconnect the operating rod from the exterior handle, then pull the panel from the outside of the tailgate, and pull the number plate light wiring grommets from their apertures in the tailgate **(see illustration)**.
49 Remove the two securing screws, and where applicable release the clips, then withdraw the light assembly from the outer trim/handle panel.

Refitting

50 Refitting is a reversal of removal.

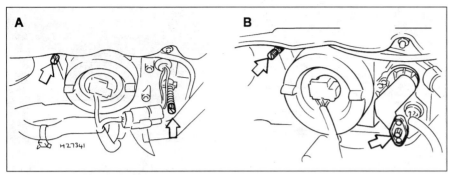

8.2 Headlight beam adjusting screws (arrowed)

A Models without electric headlight adjusters　　*B Models with electric headlight adjusters*

9.3a Remove the two upper . . .

8 Headlight beam alignment - general information

1 Accurate adjustment of the headlight beam is only possible using optical beam-setting equipment, and this work should therefore be carried out by a Nissan dealer or suitably-equipped workshop.

2 For reference, the locations of the beam adjusting screws are as shown **(see illustration)**. The outer screw (nearest the vehicle wing) is used to adjust the horizontal alignment, and the inner screw (located on the rear of the aim adjustment motor on models with electric aim adjustment) is used to adjust the vertical alignment. Note that on models with electric aim adjustment, the adjustment switch must be set to position "0" when carrying out beam alignment.

3 Certain models are equipped with a headlight beam adjustment switch, located on the centre console, which allows the aim of the headlights to be adjusted to compensate for the varying loads carried in the vehicle. The switch should be positioned according to the load being carried in the vehicle - eg; position "0" for driver with no passengers or luggage; up to position "3" for maximum load, or towing.

9 Instrument panel - removal and refitting

Removal

1 Disconnect the battery negative lead.

2 Remove the instrument panel surround as described in Chapter 11, Section 30.

3 Remove the two upper and the two lower instrument panel securing screws **(see illustrations)**.

4 Working in the engine compartment, disconnect the speedometer cable from the gearbox (see Section 14), then push the cable through the engine compartment bulkhead sufficiently to enable the instrument panel to be pulled forwards.

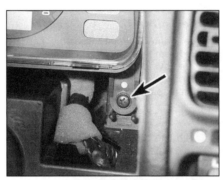

9.3b . . . and two lower instrument panel securing screws (arrowed)

5 Pull the instrument panel forwards, and disconnect the wiring plugs and the speedometer cable from the rear of the panel **(see illustration)**. Withdraw the instrument panel.

Refitting

6 Refitting is a reversal of removal, bearing in mind the following points:

a) When reconnecting the speedometer cable, reconnect the cable to the speedometer, then pull the cable through the bulkhead, back into the engine compartment, until the instrument panel can be seated securely in the facia. Reconnect the speedometer to the gearbox with reference to Chapter 12.

b) After refitting the instrument panel surround, tighten the steering column

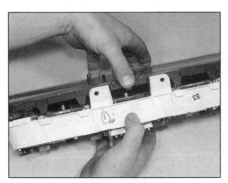

10.2 Unclipping the lens assembly from the instrument panel

9.5 Disconnecting the speedometer cable from the rear of the instrument panel

upper securing bolts to the specified torque.

10 Instrument panel components - removal and refitting

General

1 Remove the instrument panel as described in Section 9, then proceed as described under the relevant sub-heading.

Speedometer

2 Unclip the lens assembly from the front of the instrument panel **(see illustration)**.

3 Remove the four securing screws from the rear of the instrument panel, then withdraw

10.3a Remove the four securing screws (arrowed) . . .

12

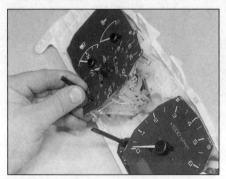

10.3b ... and withdraw the speedometer

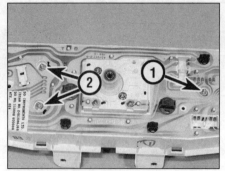

10.5 Tachometer securing nut (1) and gauge securing nuts (2)

11.2 Removing the "lights-on" warning buzzer (driver's side lower facia panel removed)

the speedometer from the front of the panel **(see illustrations)**.

4 Refitting is a reversal of removal, but refit the instrument panel with reference to Section 9.

Tachometer

5 Proceed as described previously for the speedometer, but note that the tachometer is secured by a single nut **(see illustration)**.

Analogue clock

6 Proceed as described previously for the speedometer, but note that the clock is secured by a single nut.

Digital clock

7 The digital clock is an integral part of the tachometer, and cannot be removed independently.

Fuel gauge, temperature gauge and oil pressure gauge

8 Proceed as described previously for the speedometer, but note that the gauges are secured by two nuts.

Illumination and warning light bulbs

9 Twist the relevant bulbholder anticlockwise, and withdraw it from the rear of the instrument panel.
10 The bulbs are integral with the bulbholders.

Printed circuit

11 The printed circuit assembly can be removed from the rear of the instrument panel after removing all the instruments, as described previously in this Section, and the instrument panel illumination and warning light bulbs.

11 "Lights on" warning system - general information

1 On all models, a "lights-on" warning buzzer is fitted. The buzzer will sound if the driver's door is opened when the headlights or sidelights are switched on.
2 The buzzer unit is located behind the facia, to the left of the steering column, and is secured by a single screw. The unit can be accessed once the driver's side lower facia panel has been removed (see Chapter 11, Section 30) **(see illustration)**.

12 Cigarette lighter - removal and refitting

Removal

1 Remove the facia lower centre panel, as described in Chapter 11, Section 30.
2 Pull the cigarette lighter from its socket.

3 To remove the metal housing, depress the retaining lugs, accessible from inside the plastic housing, then push the metal housing out through the front of the panel **(see illustration)**.
4 The plastic housing can be withdrawn from the front of the panel after releasing the retaining lugs.

Refitting

5 Refitting is a reversal of removal, but refit the facia lower centre panel with reference to Chapter 11.

13 Horn - removal and refitting

Removal

1 Disconnect the battery negative lead.
2 Open the bonnet, then pull the front grille panel from the front of the vehicle to release the securing clips.
3 Disconnect the wiring from the horn.
4 Unscrew the securing bolt, and withdraw the horn complete with its mounting bracket **(see illustration)**.

Refitting

5 Refitting is a reversal of removal.

14 Speedometer drive cable - removal and refitting

Removal

1 Remove the instrument panel as described in Section 9.
2 Working in the engine compartment, unscrew the sleeve securing the cable end to gearbox, then pull the cable from gearbox **(see illustration)**.
3 Where applicable, release the cable from the bracket on the engine compartment bulkhead, then pull the cable through into the engine compartment. If necessary, pull the cable grommet from the bulkhead.

12.3 Removing the cigarette lighter metal housing

13.4 Horn bracket securing bolt (arrowed) - viewed with front grille panel removed

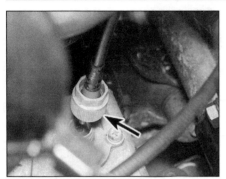

14.2 Unscrew the sleeve (arrowed) securing the speedometer cable end to the gearbox

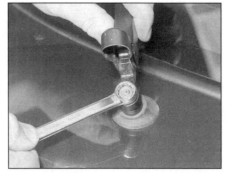

15.3 Unscrewing the tailgate wiper arm spindle nut - Hatchback model

16.3 Pull the weatherstrip (arrowed) from the bulkhead cowl panel

Refitting

4 Refitting is a reversal of removal, bearing in mind the following points:

a) *Ensure that the bulkhead grommet is securely seated.*

b) *Refit the instrument panel with reference to Section 9.*

c) *Note that certain models have alignment marks on the cable outer for use when refitting. The marks should be aligned with the bulkhead bracket when the cable is correctly refitted and routed.*

15 Wiper arm - removal and refitting

Removal

1 Operate the wiper motor, then switch it off so that the wiper arm returns to the at-rest/parked position.

2 If a windscreen or tailgate wiper is being removed, stick a piece of tape along the edge of the wiper blade, to use as an alignment aid on refitting.

3 Where applicable, lift up the wiper arm spindle nut cover, then slacken and remove the spindle nut **(see illustration)**. Lift the blade off the glass, and pull the wiper arm off its spindle. If necessary, the arm can be levered off the spindle using a suitable flat-bladed screwdriver. If both windscreen wiper

arms are removed, note their locations, as different arms are fitted to the driver's and passenger's sides.

Refitting

4 Ensure that the wiper arm and spindle splines are clean and dry.

5 When refitting a windscreen or tailgate wiper arm, refit the arm to the spindle, aligning the wiper blade with the tape fitted before removal. If both windscreen wiper arms have been removed, ensure that the arms are refitted to their correct positions as noted before removal.

6 When refitting a headlight wiper arm, hold the arm below the stops at the bottom of the headlight unit, until the spindle nut has been refitted and tightened.

7 Refit the spindle nut, tighten it securely, and where applicable, clip the nut cover back into position. If refitting a headlight wiper arm, once the spindle nut has been tightened, position the wiper blade against the upper surfaces of the stops on the headlight.

16 Windscreen wiper motor and linkage - removal and refitting

Motor
Removal

1 Disconnect the battery negative lead.
2 Open the bonnet.

3 Pull the weatherstrip from the front edge of the bulkhead cowl panel **(see illustration)**.
4 Remove the securing screw(s) and plastic clip(s), and withdraw the cowl panel **(see illustration)**.
5 Disconnect the motor wiring plug **(see illustration)**.
6 Using a suitable screwdriver, prise the crank arm from the motor drive balljoint **(see illustration)**.
7 Unscrew the four motor securing bolts, and withdraw the motor **(see illustrations)**.

Refitting

8 Refitting is a reversal of removal, but ensure that the motor drive is in the "parked" position before reconnecting the crank arm.

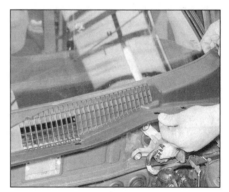

16.4 Withdrawing the bulkhead cowl panel

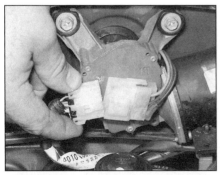

16.5 Disconnect the wiper motor wiring plug.

16.6 Prising the crank arm from the motor drive balljoint

16.7a Unscrew the four securing bolts . . .

12

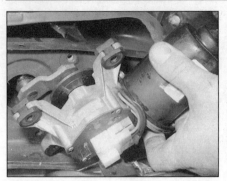

16.7b ... and withdraw the wiper motor

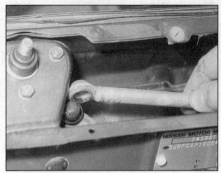

16.12 Prise the crank arm from the spindle unit

16.13 Withdrawing a spindle unit

Linkage

Removal

9 Each spindle unit can be removed individually.

10 Proceed as described in paragraphs 1 to 4 inclusive.

11 Remove the relevant wiper arm.

12 Using a suitable screwdriver, prise the crank arm from the spindle unit balljoint **(see illustration)**.

13 Unscrew the three securing nuts, and withdraw the spindle unit **(see illustration)**.

Refitting

14 Refitting is a reversal of removal, but ensure that motor drive is in the "parked" position before reconnecting the crank arm.

17 Tailgate wiper motor - removal and refitting

Hatchback models

Removal

1 Disconnect the battery negative lead.

2 Remove the tailgate inner trim panels as described in Chapter 11, Section 28.

3 Remove the wiper arm with reference to Section 15.

4 Working inside the tailgate, disconnect the tailgate wiper motor wiring plug.

5 Unscrew the three bolts securing the motor mounting bracket to the tailgate, noting that

one of the bolts also secures an earth lead **(see illustration)**.

6 Withdraw the motor assembly through the aperture in the tailgate **(see illustration)**.

7 The motor is secured to the mounting bracket by three bolts.

8 If desired, the motor spindle grommet can be pulled from the hole in the tailgate.

Refitting

9 Refitting is a reversal of removal, but where applicable, ensure that the grommet is correctly located in the tailgate, and refit the wiper arm with reference to Section 15.

Estate models

Removal

10 Disconnect the battery negative lead.

11 Remove the tailgate inner trim panel, with reference to Chapter 11, Section 28.

12 Remove the wiper arm with reference to Section 15.

13 Disconnect the motor wiring plug **(see illustration)**.

14 Unscrew the two bolts securing the auxiliary motor bracket to the tailgate, and the bolt securing the bracket to the main motor bracket **(see illustration)**.

15 Unscrew the three bolts securing the main motor bracket to the tailgate, then lift out the motor assembly **(see illustration)**.

Refitting

16 Refitting is a reversal of removal, but

17.5 Unscrew the tailgate wiper motor securing bolts (arrowed) ...

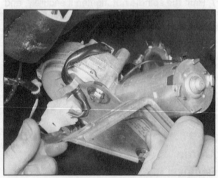

17.6 ... then withdraw the wiper motor - Hatchback model

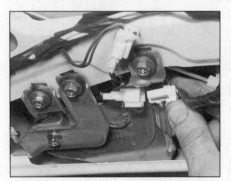

17.13 Disconnecting the tailgate wiper motor wiring plug - Estate model

17.14 Removing the tailgate wiper motor auxiliary bracket - Estate model

17.15 Lifting out the tailgate wiper motor - Estate model

18.4 Remove the wheel arch liner for access to the washer fluid reservoir

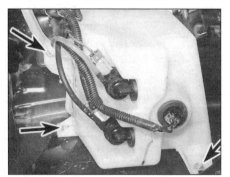

18.8 Washer fluid reservoir securing screws (arrowed)

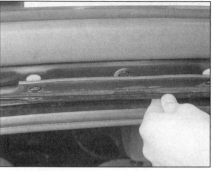

18.18 Remove the weatherstrip securing plate and the weatherstrip . . .

ensure that the grommet is correctly located in the tailgate, and refit the wiper arms with reference to Section 15.

18 Windscreen/tailgate washer system components - removal and refitting

Washer fluid reservoir

Removal

1 Working in the engine compartment, twist the reservoir filler neck clockwise, then pull it from the top of the reservoir.

2 Disconnect the battery negative lead.

3 Chock the rear wheels, apply the handbrake, then jack up the front of the vehicle and support securely on axle stands (see "*Jacking, towing and wheel changing*"). Remove the front right-hand roadwheel.

4 Remove the wheel arch liner **(see illustration)**.

5 Disconnect the wiring plug(s) from the washer pump(s), and from the fluid level sensor, where applicable.

6 Disconnect the fluid hose(s) from the washer pump(s) - if the reservoir still contains fluid, be prepared for fluid spillage.

7 Where applicable, release the wiring harness from its clips, and move the harness to one side to allow sufficient clearance to remove the reservoir.

8 Working under the wheel arch, remove the three reservoir securing screws, then lower the reservoir from under the wheel arch **(see illustration)**.

Refitting

9 Refitting is a reversal of removal.

Washer pump(s)

Removal

10 Proceed as described in paragraphs 2 to 4.

11 Disconnect the wiring plug and the fluid hose from the relevant washer pump.

12 Pull the washer pump from the reservoir, and where applicable, recover the grommet. If the reservoir still contains fluid, be prepared for fluid spillage.

Refitting

13 Refitting is a reversal of removal.

Windscreen washer nozzle

Removal

14 Open the bonnet.

15 Working under the bonnet, release the securing tabs using a suitable screwdriver, then push the nozzle from the bonnet. Disconnect the fluid hose, and withdraw the nozzle.

Refitting

16 Refitting is a reversal of removal.

Tailgate washer nozzle - Hatchback models

Removal

17 Open the tailgate.

18 For access to the washer nozzle, unscrew the two securing bolts, and remove the weatherstrip securing plate and the weatherstrip **(see illustration)**.

19 Prise off the rubber cover, then push out the washer nozzle though the outside of the tailgate, and disconnect the fluid hose **(see illustrations)**.

Refitting

20 Refitting is a reversal of removal, but ensure that the fluid hose is securely reconnected before refitting the rubber cover.

Tailgate washer nozzle - Estate models

Removal

21 Open the tailgate, and working at the inside top edge, pull the cover and the fluid hose from the washer nozzle **(see illustration)**.

22 Unscrew the securing nut, then withdraw the nozzle from outside the tailgate.

Refitting

23 Refitting is a reversal of removal.

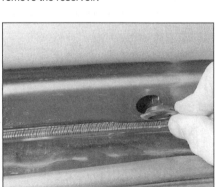

18.19a . . . then prise off the rubber cover . . .

18.19b . . . and push out the washer nozzle - Hatchback model

18.21 Pulling the cover and the fluid hose from the tailgate washer nozzle - Estate model

12

19.3 Remove the radio/cassette player securing screws (arrowed) . . .

19.4 . . . then pull the unit forwards and disconnect the wiring plugs and aerial lead

20.2a Remove the four loudspeaker housing securing screws . . .

19 Radio/cassette player - removal and refitting

Warning: If the radio/cassette player fitted to the vehicle has an anti-theft security code (as does the unit fitted as standard), refer to the information given in the preliminary Sections of this manual before removing the unit.

Removal

1 Disconnect the battery negative lead.
2 Remove the facia centre switch/ventilation nozzle housing as described in Chapter 11, Section 30.
3 Remove the four now-exposed radio/cassette player securing screws **(see illustration)**.
4 Pull the unit forwards from the facia, then disconnect the wiring plugs and the aerial lead from the rear of the unit **(see illustration)**.
5 Note the bayonet fuse, which is a push fit in the rear of the unit.

Refitting

6 Refitting is a reversal of removal, ensuring that the wiring is freely routed behind the unit.

20 Loudspeakers - removal and refitting

Front door-mounted loudspeakers

Removal

1 Remove the door inner trim panel as described in Chapter 11.
2 Remove the four securing screws, and withdraw the loudspeaker housing from the door, then disconnect the wiring plug **(see illustrations)**.
3 If desired, the loudspeaker can be withdrawn from the housing after removing the four securing screws.

Refitting

4 Refitting is a reversal of removal, but refit the inner door trim panel with reference to Chapter 11.

Front body pillar-mounted loudspeakers

Removal

5 Disconnect the battery negative lead.
6 Open the relevant front door, and pull the weatherstrip from the edge of the body pillar trim panel.
7 Carefully pull the trim panel from the pillar to release the securing clips **(see illustration)**.

8 Remove the two screws securing the loudspeaker to the pillar, then lift out the loudspeaker, and separate the two halves of the wiring connector (where necessary, pull the insulating foam from the connector) **(see illustration)**.

Refitting

9 Refitting is a reversal of removal.

Rear parcel shelf-mounted loudspeakers - Saloon models

Removal

10 Disconnect the battery negative lead.
11 Remove the parcel shelf, as described in Chapter 11, Section 28.
12 Remove the four securing screws, then withdraw the loudspeaker from the body panel, and disconnect the wiring plug (where necessary, release the wiring harness from the securing clips).

Refitting

13 Refitting is a reversal of removal.

Rear loudspeakers - Hatchback models

Removal

14 Disconnect the battery negative lead.
15 Remove the relevant luggage compartment side/parcel shelf support panel, as described in Chapter 11, Section 28.
16 Unscrew the four loudspeaker securing screws, then withdraw the loudspeaker from

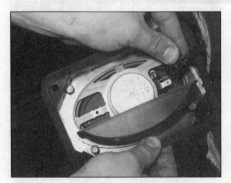

20.2b . . . then withdraw the housing and disconnect the wiring plug

20.7 Pull the trim panel from the front body pillar . . .

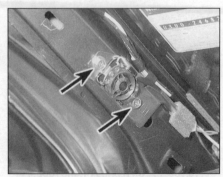

20.8 . . . to expose the loudspeaker - securing screws arrowed

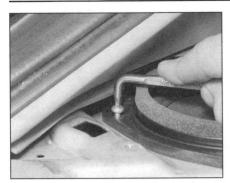

20.16a Unscrew the securing screws . . .

20.16b . . . then lift out the rear loudspeaker and disconnect the wiring plug - Hatchback model

20.23a Remove the securing screws . . .

the mounting bracket, and disconnect the wiring plug **(see illustrations)**.

Refitting

17 Refitting is a reversal of removal.

Rear loudspeakers - Estate models

Removal

18 Disconnect the battery negative lead.
19 Remove the luggage cover, where applicable.
20 Remove the securing screws, and withdraw the luggage cover supports from the trim panel.
21 Support the tailgate in the open position, then unscrew the tailgate support strut lower balljoint pin from the body. Note the positions of any spacers and/or washers on the balljoint pin.
22 Release the plastic securing clips at the rear edge of the trim panel, then pull the panel from the body to release the rest of the retaining clips. Pull back the panel sufficiently to expose the loudspeaker.
23 Remove the four loudspeaker securing screws, then disconnect the wiring plug and withdraw the loudspeaker **(see illustrations)**.

Refitting

24 Refitting is a reversal of removal, but ensure that any spacers and/or washers on the balljoint pin are correctly refitted, as noted before removal.

21 Radio aerial -
removal and refitting

Rear window aerial

1 Certain models may have a radio aerial incorporated in the rear window glass, with the heating element. In the event of a suspected fault, consult a Nissan dealer for advice.

Rear wing-mounted aerial - Saloon and Hatchback models
Removal

2 Disconnect the battery negative lead.

20.23b . . . then withdraw the rear loudspeaker and disconnect the wiring plug - Estate model

3 Remove the carpet panel from the floor of the luggage compartment.
4 Release the securing clips, and pull the carpet trim panel from the side of the luggage compartment.
5 Working through the aperture in the body panel, disconnect the aerial motor wiring connector **(see illustration)**.
6 Remove the screw securing the aerial earth lead to the body **(see illustration)**.
7 Unclip the aerial lead from the body, and disconnect the lead from the aerial **(see illustration)**.
8 Working outside the vehicle, unscrew the securing nut from the top of the aerial. This can be carried out using two short pieces of metal rod and a suitable screwdriver as shown **(see illustrations)**.

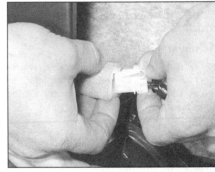

21.5 Disconnect the aerial motor wiring connector

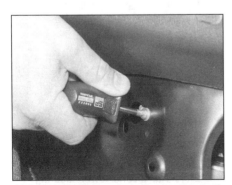

21.6 Remove the screw securing the earth lead to the body

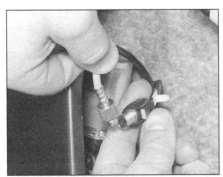

21.7 Disconnect the aerial lead

21.8a Using improvised tools . . .

12

21.8b ... unscrew the top aerial securing nut

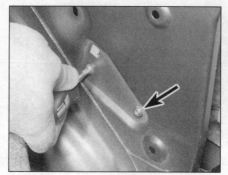

21.9 Unscrew the two screws securing the aerial to the body

21.10a Manipulate the aerial through the body aperture ...

9 Working in the luggage compartment, remove the two screws securing the aerial assembly to the body (see illustration).
10 Manipulate the assembly out through the aperture in the body, and disconnect the water drain tube from the bottom of the assembly (see illustrations).

Refitting

11 Refitting is a reversal of removal, bearing in mind the following points:
a) *Ensure that the drain hose is reconnected to the aerial before manipulating the assembly into position.*
b) *Refit the screws securing the assembly to the body, but do not fully tighten them until the top securing nut has been refitted and tightened.*

Roof-mounted aerial - Estate models

Removal

12 Working on the roof of the vehicle, remove the two securing screws, then carefully pull the aerial from the roof, and disconnect the aerial lead.

Refitting

13 Refitting is a reversal of removal, but ensure that the aerial housing is securely engaged with the roof panel.

Front wing-mounted aerial - Estate models

Removal

14 Disconnect the battery negative lead.
15 Chock the rear wheels, then apply the handbrake, jack up the front of the vehicle, and support securely on axle stands (see "*Jacking, towing and wheel changing*"). Remove the front left-hand roadwheel.
16 Remove the securing screws and release the clips, and withdraw the wheel arch liner (see illustration).
17 Disconnect the aerial lead wiring connector, and the motor wiring connector. On certain models, one or both of the connectors may be located inside the passenger compartment, behind the facia - where necessary, remove the passenger's side footwell trim panel and/or the glovebox (see Chapter 11, Section 30) for access to the connector(s).
18 Working at the top of the aerial, unscrew the securing nut from the top of the aerial. This can be carried out using two short pieces of metal rod and a pair of pliers (see paragraph 8).
19 Remove the two screws securing the aerial lower mounting bracket to the wing panel, then lower the assembly from the wing (see illustration). Where applicable, pull the

wiring grommet from the inner wing panel as the aerial is withdrawn.

Refitting

20 Refitting is a reversal of removal, bearing in mind the following points:
a) *Where applicable, ensure that the wiring grommet is correctly located in the inner wing panel.*
b) *Refit the screws securing the mounting bracket to the wing panel, but do not fully tighten them until the top securing nut has been refitted and tightened.*

22 Anti-theft alarm system - general information

Note: *This information is applicable only to the anti-theft alarm system fitted by Nissan as standard equipment.*

Some models in the range are fitted with an anti-theft alarm/engine immobiliser system as standard equipment. The alarm is automatically armed and disarmed when the driver's door is locked using the key. When the system is first activated, the alarm indicator LED, located on the facia, will glow continuously for 30 seconds. If the LED flashes during this time, this indicates that one of the doors, the bonnet. or the boot lid/tailgate is open. The system will

21.10b ... and disconnect the water drain tube

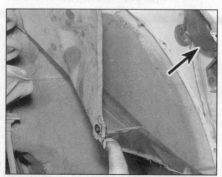

21.16 Withdraw the wheel arch liner for access to the wing-mounted aerial (arrowed) - Estate model

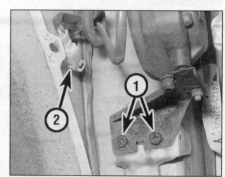

21.19 Radio aerial lower securing screws (1). Note wiring connector (2) - Estate model

not be activated until all the doors, the bonnet, and the boot lid/tailgate are closed. Additionally, if a door is unlocked, or the ignition switch is operated during this 30 seconds, the system will not activate.

After 30 seconds, the indicator LED should flash intermittently, indicating that the system is activated.

If the alarm is set off, the horn will sound for 30 seconds, and the direction indicator lights will flash for 5 minutes. Additionally, the starter motor will not operate.

The alarm can only be stopped by unlocking a door, or the boot lid/tailgate, using the key.

Any suspected faults with the system should be referred to a Nissan dealer.

23 Heated front seat components - general information

Certain models may be with heated front seats. The seats are heated by electrical elements built into the seat cushions.

For access to the heating elements, the seats must be dismantled, and this work should be entrusted to a Nissan dealer.

Removal and refitting details for the heated seat switches are given in Section 4.

24 Air bag system - general information and precautions

General information

On later models, an air bag system is fitted, which is designed to prevent serious chest and head injuries during an accident. A driver's side air bag is fitted in the steering wheel centre pad. Additionally, on certain models, a passenger's side air bag is located in the facia.

The system is armed when the ignition key is in the "ON" or "START" positions (note that the system remains armed for a time after the ignition is switched off), and is activated by a "g" sensor (deceleration sensor) mounted inside the vehicle, under the centre console. The system is controlled by an electronic control unit mounted under the steering column.

The air bag is inflated by a gas generator, which forces the bag out from its location in the steering wheel or facia.

Precautions

Warning: The following precautions must be observed when working on vehicles with an air bag system, to prevent the possibility of personal injury.

a) *Do not attempt to test any of the air bag system circuits using test meters or any other test equipment.*

b) *Before working on any vehicle components located near air bag system components (steering wheel, steering column, facia and centre console), switch the ignition off, and disconnect the battery negative lead, then wait for at least 10 minutes before carrying out any further work.*

c) *Do not attempt to remove the system electronic control unit (located under the steering column), or the sensor (located under the centre console).*

d) *Do not attempt to turn the steering wheel or column with the steering gear removed.*

e) *If the air bag warning light comes on, or any fault in the system is suspected, consult a Nissan dealer without delay.* **Do not** *attempt to carry out fault diagnosis, or any dismantling of the components.*

12

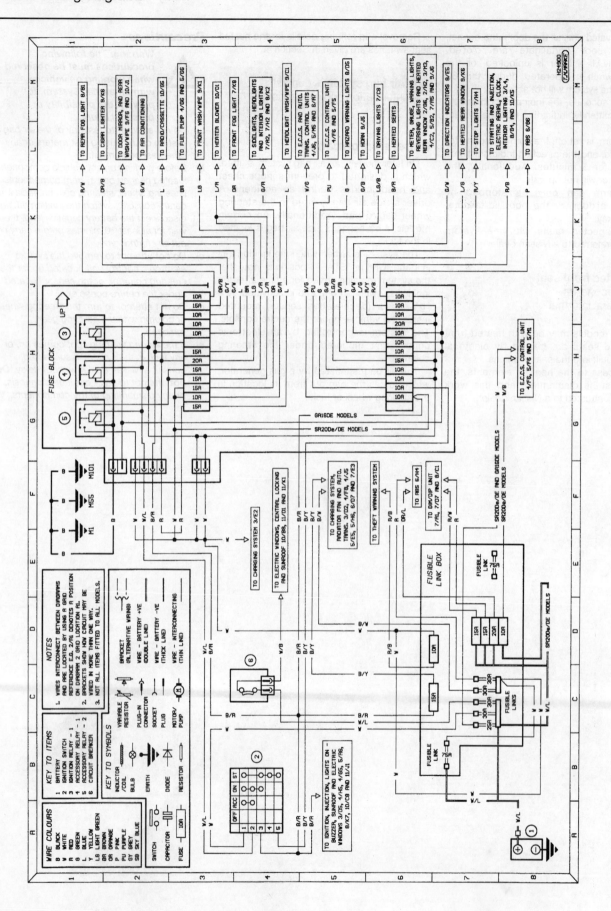

Diagram 1: Notes, key to symbols, and typical power supply routing

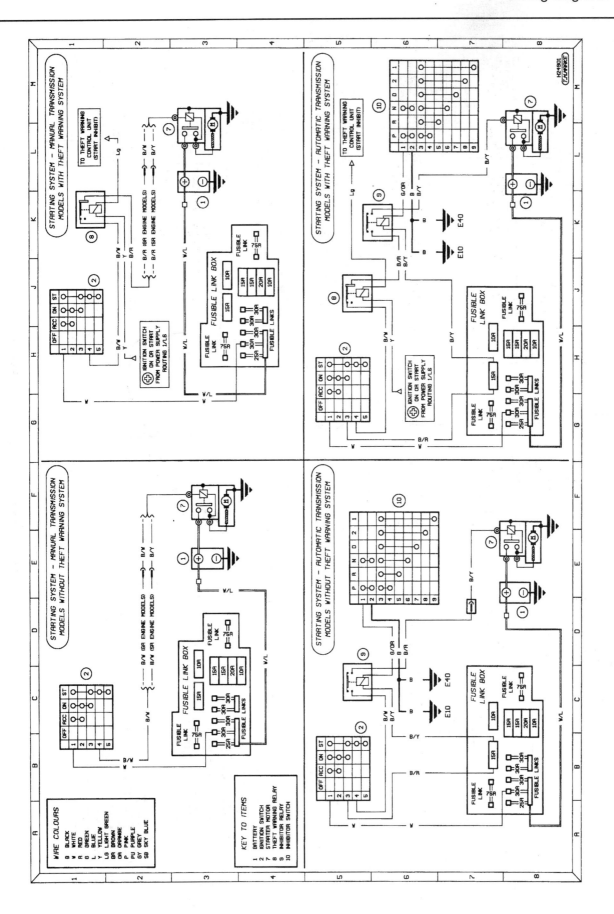

Diagram 2: Typical starting system

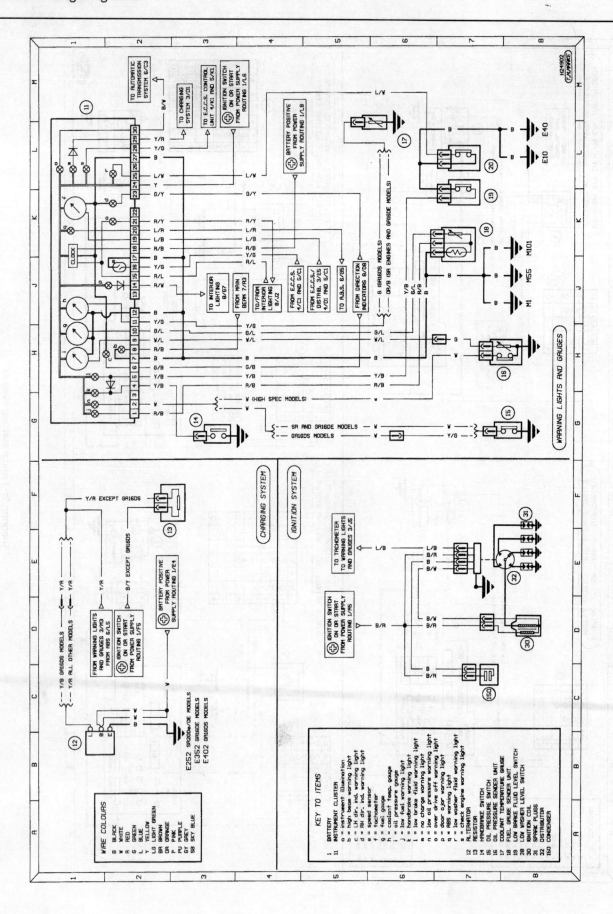

Diagram 3: Typical charging system, ignition system, warning lights and gauges

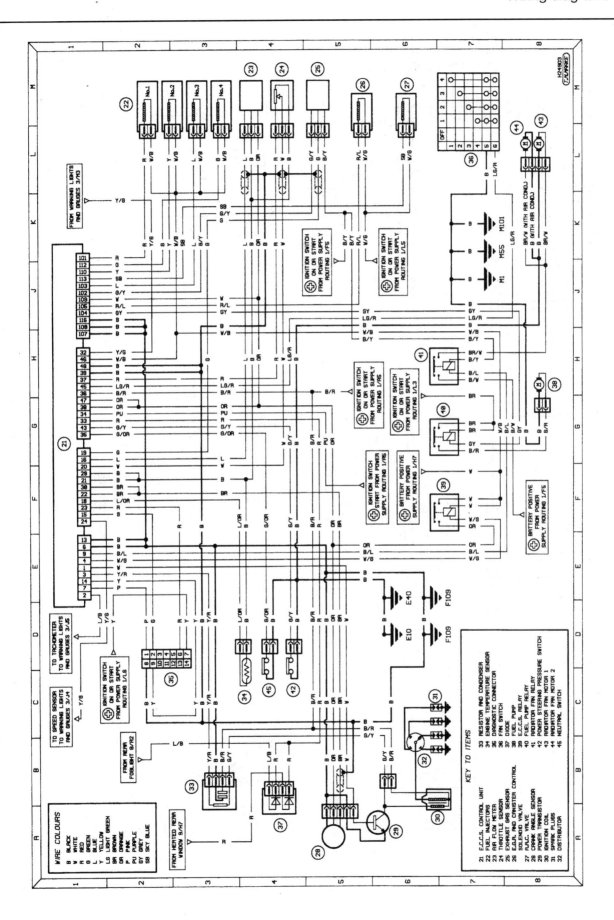

Diagram 4: Typical multi-point fuel injection system - 1.6 litre engine

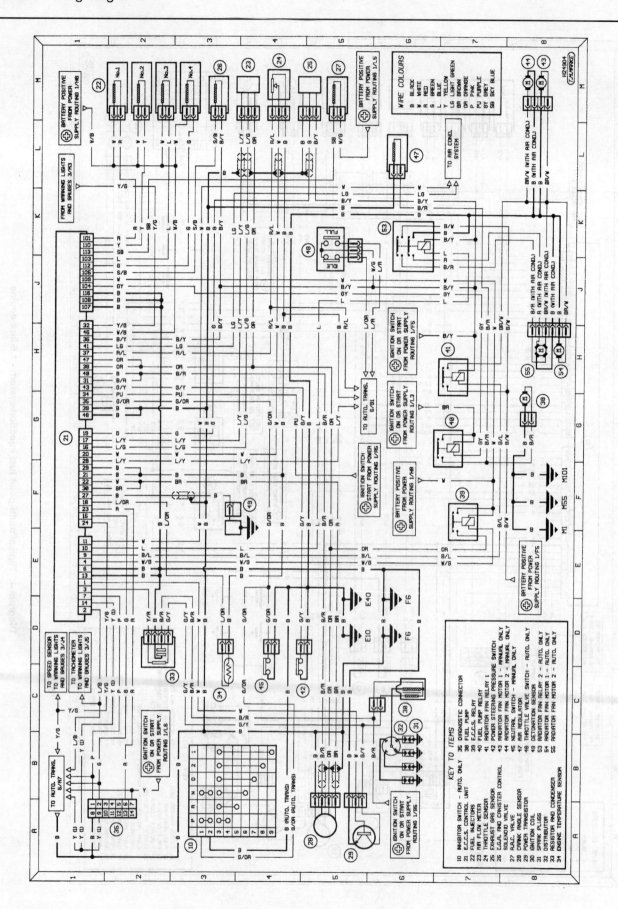

Diagram 5: Typical multi-point fuel injection system - 2.0 litre engine

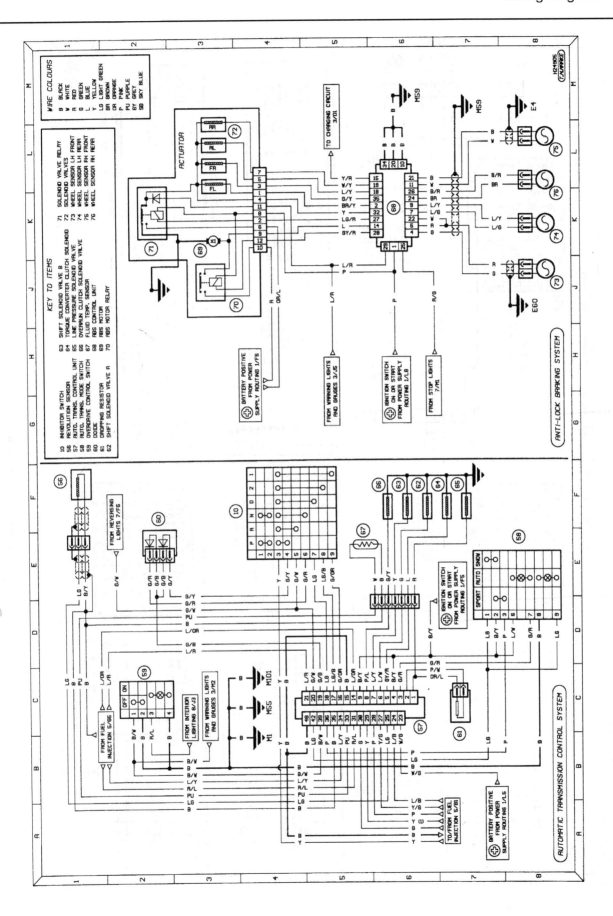

Diagram 6: Typical automatic transmission control system and Anti-lock Braking System (ABS)

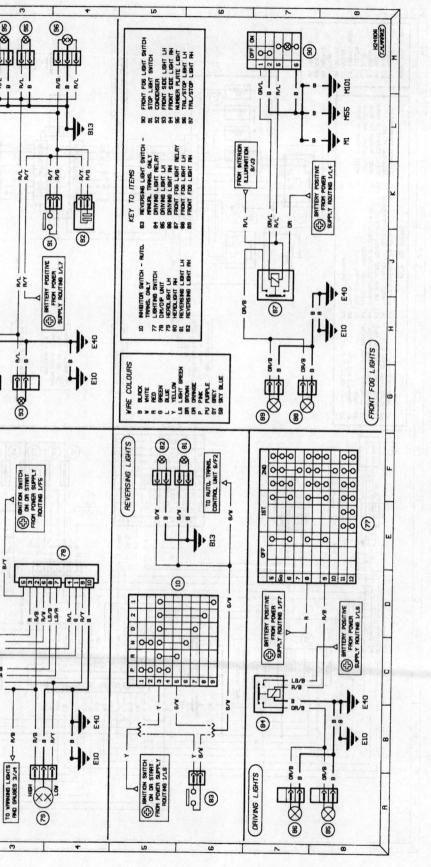

Diagram 7: Typical exterior lighting

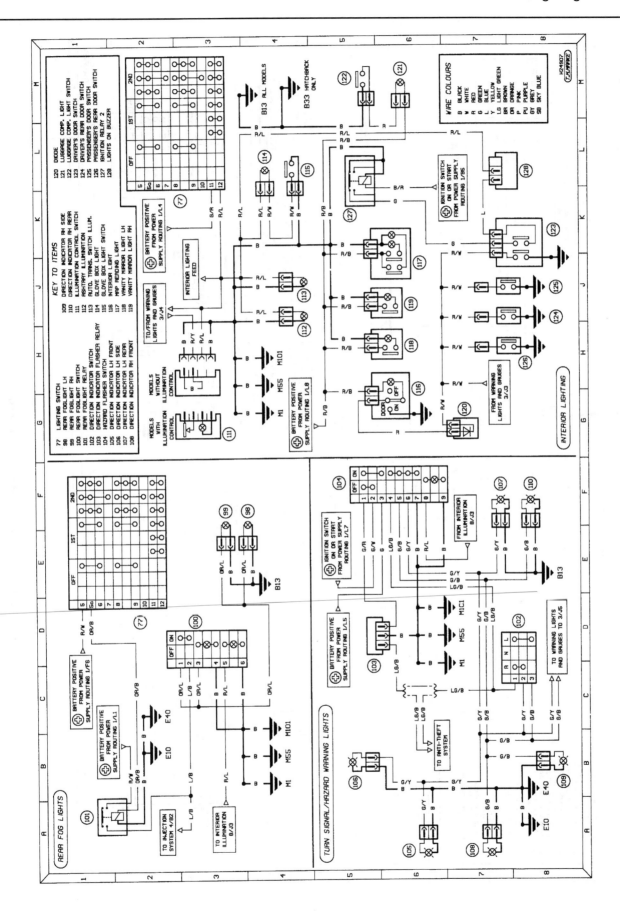

Diagram 8: Typical exterior lighting (continued) and interior lighting

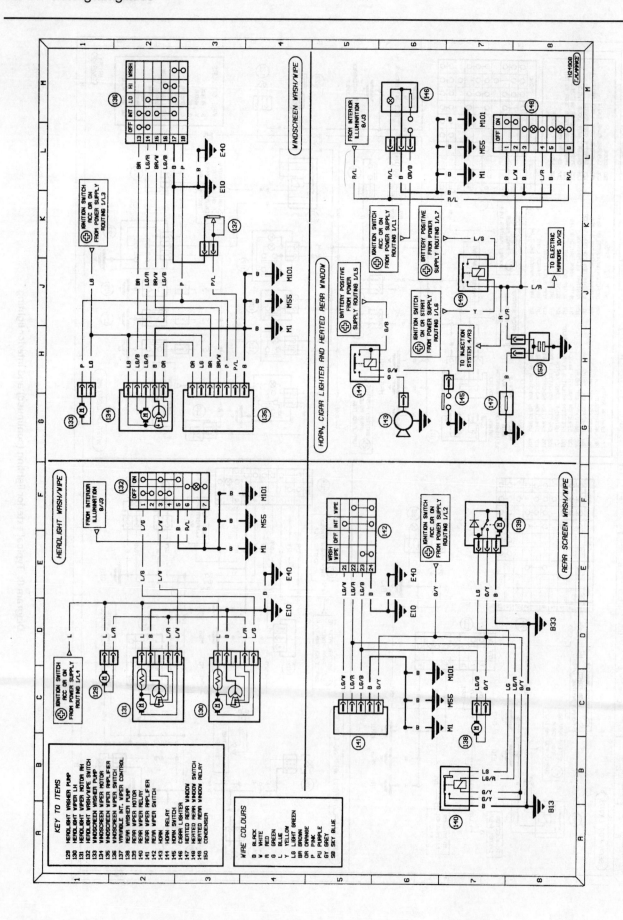

Diagram 9: Typical wash/wipe system, horn, cigar lighter and heated rear window

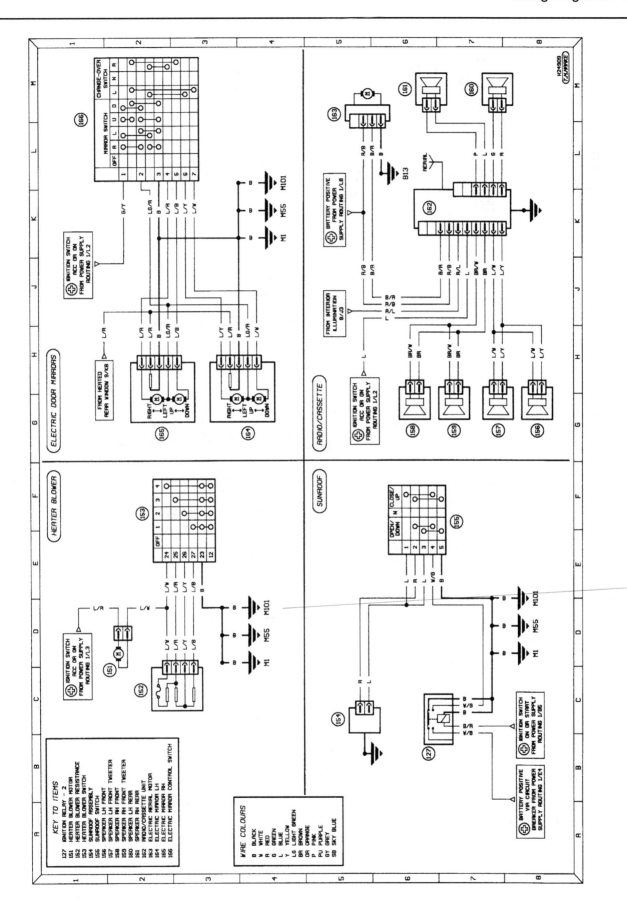

Diagram 10: Typical heater blower, electric mirrors, sunroof and radio/cassette

12

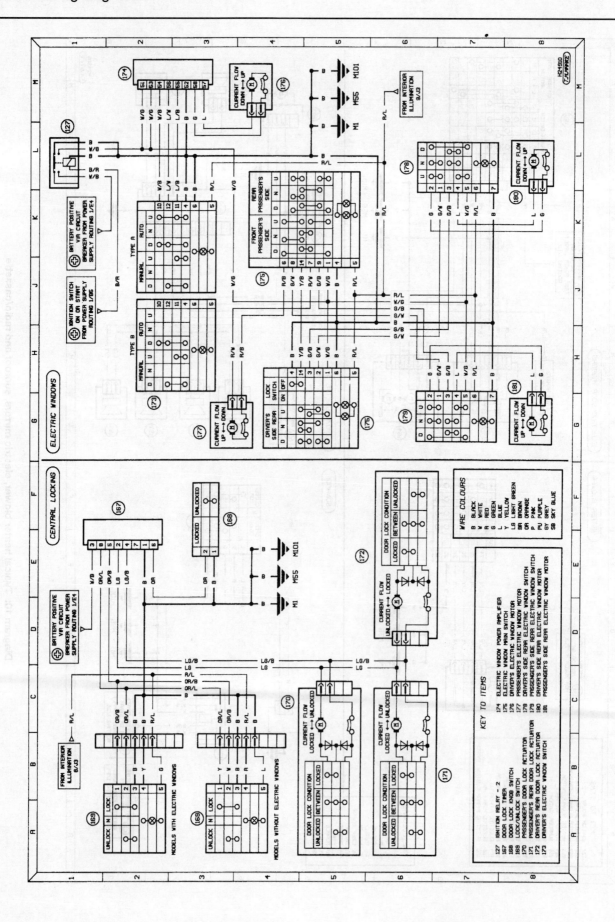

Diagram 11: Typical central locking system and electric windows

This is a guide to getting your vehicle through the MOT test. Obviously it will not be possible to examine the vehicle to the same standard as the professional MOT tester. However, working through the following checks will enable you to identify any problem areas before submitting the vehicle for the test.

Where a testable component is in borderline condition, the tester has discretion in deciding whether to pass or fail it. The basis of such discretion is whether the tester would be happy for a close relative or friend to use the vehicle with the component in that condition. If the vehicle presented is clean and evidently well cared for, the tester may be more inclined to pass a borderline component than if the vehicle is scruffy and apparently neglected.

It has only been possible to summarise the test requirements here, based on the regulations in force at the time of printing. Test standards are becoming increasingly stringent, although there are some exemptions for older vehicles. For full details obtain a copy of the Haynes publication Pass the MOT! (available from stockists of Haynes manuals).

An assistant will be needed to help carry out some of these checks.

The checks have been sub-divided into four categories, as follows:

1 Checks carried out **FROM THE DRIVER'S SEAT**

2 Checks carried out **WITH THE VEHICLE ON THE GROUND**

3 Checks carried out **WITH THE VEHICLE RAISED AND THE WHEELS FREE TO TURN**

4 Checks carried out on **YOUR VEHICLE'S EXHAUST EMISSION SYSTEM**

---

1 Checks carried out **FROM THE DRIVER'S SEAT**

Handbrake

☐ Test the operation of the handbrake. Excessive travel (too many clicks) indicates incorrect brake or cable adjustment.

☐ Check that the handbrake cannot be released by tapping the lever sideways. Check the security of the lever mountings.

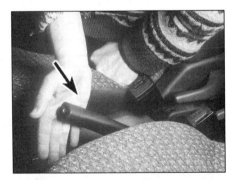

Footbrake

☐ Depress the brake pedal and check that it does not creep down to the floor, indicating a master cylinder fault. Release the pedal, wait a few seconds, then depress it again. If the pedal travels nearly to the floor before firm resistance is felt, brake adjustment or repair is necessary. If the pedal feels spongy, there is air in the hydraulic system which must be removed by bleeding.

☐ Check that the brake pedal is secure and in good condition. Check also for signs of fluid leaks on the pedal, floor or carpets, which would indicate failed seals in the brake master cylinder.

☐ Check the servo unit (when applicable) by operating the brake pedal several times, then keeping the pedal depressed and starting the engine. As the engine starts, the pedal will move down slightly. If not, the vacuum hose or the servo itself may be faulty.

Steering wheel and column

☐ Examine the steering wheel for fractures or looseness of the hub, spokes or rim.

☐ Move the steering wheel from side to side and then up and down. Check that the steering wheel is not loose on the column, indicating wear or a loose retaining nut. Continue moving the steering wheel as before, but also turn it slightly from left to right.

☐ Check that the steering wheel is not loose on the column, and that there is no abnormal

movement of the steering wheel, indicating wear in the column support bearings or couplings.

Windscreen and mirrors

☐ The windscreen must be free of cracks or other significant damage within the driver's field of view. (Small stone chips are acceptable.) Rear view mirrors must be secure, intact, and capable of being adjusted.

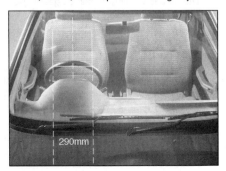

Seat belts and seats

Note: *The following checks are applicable to all seat belts, front and rear.*

☐ Examine the webbing of all the belts (including rear belts if fitted) for cuts, serious fraying or deterioration. Fasten and unfasten each belt to check the buckles. If applicable, check the retracting mechanism. Check the security of all seat belt mountings accessible from inside the vehicle.

☐ The front seats themselves must be securely attached and the backrests must lock in the upright position.

Doors

☐ Both front doors must be able to be opened and closed from outside and inside, and must latch securely when closed.

2 Checks carried out WITH THE VEHICLE ON THE GROUND

Vehicle identification

☐ Number plates must be in good condition, secure and legible, with letters and numbers correctly spaced – spacing at (A) should be twice that at (B).

☐ The VIN plate and/or homologation plate must be legible.

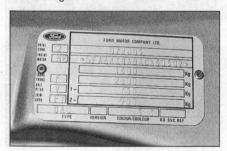

Electrical equipment

☐ Switch on the ignition and check the operation of the horn.

☐ Check the windscreen washers and wipers, examining the wiper blades; renew damaged or perished blades. Also check the operation of the stop-lights.

☐ Check the operation of the sidelights and number plate lights. The lenses and reflectors must be secure, clean and undamaged.

☐ Check the operation and alignment of the headlights. The headlight reflectors must not be tarnished and the lenses must be undamaged.

☐ Switch on the ignition and check the operation of the direction indicators (including the instrument panel tell-tale) and the hazard warning lights. Operation of the sidelights and stop-lights must not affect the indicators - if it does, the cause is usually a bad earth at the rear light cluster.

☐ Check the operation of the rear foglight(s), including the warning light on the instrument panel or in the switch.

Footbrake

☐ Examine the master cylinder, brake pipes and servo unit for leaks, loose mountings, corrosion or other damage.

☐ The fluid reservoir must be secure and the fluid level must be between the upper (**A**) and lower (**B**) markings.

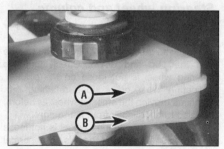

☐ Inspect both front brake flexible hoses for cracks or deterioration of the rubber. Turn the steering from lock to lock, and ensure that the hoses do not contact the wheel, tyre, or any part of the steering or suspension mechanism. With the brake pedal firmly depressed, check the hoses for bulges or leaks under pressure.

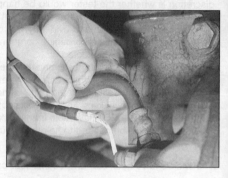

Steering and suspension

☐ Have your assistant turn the steering wheel from side to side slightly, up to the point where the steering gear just begins to transmit this movement to the roadwheels. Check for excessive free play between the steering wheel and the steering gear, indicating wear or insecurity of the steering column joints, the column-to-steering gear coupling, or the steering gear itself.

☐ Have your assistant turn the steering wheel more vigorously in each direction, so that the roadwheels just begin to turn. As this is done, examine all the steering joints, linkages, fittings and attachments. Renew any component that shows signs of wear or damage. On vehicles with power steering, check the security and condition of the steering pump, drivebelt and hoses.

☐ Check that the vehicle is standing level, and at approximately the correct ride height.

Shock absorbers

☐ Depress each corner of the vehicle in turn, then release it. The vehicle should rise and then settle in its normal position. If the vehicle continues to rise and fall, the shock absorber is defective. A shock absorber which has seized will also cause the vehicle to fail.

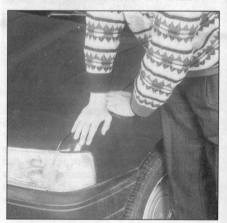

Exhaust system

☐ Start the engine. With your assistant holding a rag over the tailpipe, check the entire system for leaks. Repair or renew leaking sections.

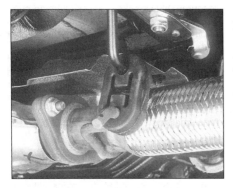

3 Checks carried out
WITH THE VEHICLE RAISED AND THE WHEELS FREE TO TURN

Jack up the front and rear of the vehicle, and securely support it on axle stands. Position the stands clear of the suspension assemblies. Ensure that the wheels are clear of the ground and that the steering can be turned from lock to lock.

Steering mechanism

☐ Have your assistant turn the steering from lock to lock. Check that the steering turns smoothly, and that no part of the steering mechanism, including a wheel or tyre, fouls any brake hose or pipe or any part of the body structure.

☐ Examine the steering rack rubber gaiters for damage or insecurity of the retaining clips. If power steering is fitted, check for signs of damage or leakage of the fluid hoses, pipes or connections. Also check for excessive stiffness or binding of the steering, a missing split pin or locking device, or severe corrosion of the body structure within 30 cm of any steering component attachment point.

Front and rear suspension and wheel bearings

☐ Starting at the front right-hand side, grasp the roadwheel at the 3 o'clock and 9 o'clock positions and shake it vigorously. Check for free play or insecurity at the wheel bearings, suspension balljoints, or suspension mountings, pivots and attachments.

☐ Now grasp the wheel at the 12 o'clock and 6 o'clock positions and repeat the previous inspection. Spin the wheel, and check for roughness or tightness of the front wheel bearing.

☐ If excess free play is suspected at a component pivot point, this can be confirmed by using a large screwdriver or similar tool and levering between the mounting and the component attachment. This will confirm whether the wear is in the pivot bush, its retaining bolt, or in the mounting itself (the bolt holes can often become elongated).

☐ Carry out all the above checks at the other front wheel, and then at both rear wheels.

Springs and shock absorbers

☐ Examine the suspension struts (when applicable) for serious fluid leakage, corrosion, or damage to the casing. Also check the security of the mounting points.

☐ If coil springs are fitted, check that the spring ends locate in their seats, and that the spring is not corroded, cracked or broken.

☐ If leaf springs are fitted, check that all loaves are intact, that the axle is securely attached to each spring, and that there is no deterioration of the spring eye mountings, bushes, and shackles.

☐ The same general checks apply to vehicles fitted with other suspension types, such as torsion bars, hydraulic displacer units, etc. Ensure that all mountings and attachments are secure, that there are no signs of excessive wear, corrosion or damage, and (on hydraulic types) that there are no fluid leaks or damaged pipes.

☐ Inspect the shock absorbers for signs of serious fluid leakage. Check for wear of the mounting bushes or attachments, or damage to the body of the unit.

Driveshafts
(fwd vehicles only)

☐ Rotate each front wheel in turn and inspect the constant velocity joint gaiters for splits or damage. Also check that each driveshaft is straight and undamaged.

Braking system

☐ If possible without dismantling, check brake pad wear and disc condition. Ensure that the friction lining material has not worn excessively, (A) and that the discs are not fractured, pitted, scored or badly worn (B).

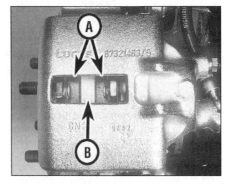

☐ Examine all the rigid brake pipes underneath the vehicle, and the flexible hose(s) at the rear. Look for corrosion, chafing or insecurity of the pipes, and for signs of bulging under pressure, chafing, splits or deterioration of the flexible hoses.

☐ Look for signs of fluid leaks at the brake calipers or on the brake backplates. Repair or renew leaking components.

☐ Slowly spin each wheel, while your assistant depresses and releases the footbrake. Ensure that each brake is operating and does not bind when the pedal is released.

☐ Examine the handbrake mechanism, checking for frayed or broken cables, excessive corrosion, or wear or insecurity of the linkage. Check that the mechanism works on each relevant wheel, and releases fully, without binding.

☐ It is not possible to test brake efficiency without special equipment, but a road test can be carried out later to check that the vehicle pulls up in a straight line.

Fuel and exhaust systems

☐ Inspect the fuel tank (including the filler cap), fuel pipes, hoses and unions. All components must be secure and free from leaks.

☐ Examine the exhaust system over its entire length, checking for any damaged, broken or missing mountings, security of the retaining clamps and rust or corrosion.

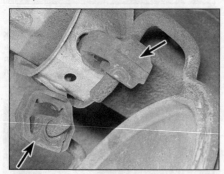

Wheels and tyres

☐ Examine the sidewalls and tread area of each tyre in turn. Check for cuts, tears, lumps, bulges, separation of the tread, and exposure of the ply or cord due to wear or damage. Check that the tyre bead is correctly seated on the wheel rim, that the valve is sound and

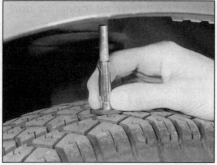

properly seated, and that the wheel is not distorted or damaged.

☐ Check that the tyres are of the correct size for the vehicle, that they are of the same size and type on each axle, and that the pressures are correct.

☐ Check the tyre tread depth. The legal minimum at the time of writing is 1.6 mm over at least three-quarters of the tread width. Abnormal tread wear may indicate incorrect front wheel alignment.

Body corrosion

☐ Check the condition of the entire vehicle structure for signs of corrosion in load-bearing areas. (These include chassis box sections, side sills, cross-members, pillars, and all suspension, steering, braking system and seat belt mountings and anchorages.) Any corrosion which has seriously reduced the thickness of a load-bearing area is likely to cause the vehicle to fail. In this case professional repairs are likely to be needed.

☐ Damage or corrosion which causes sharp or otherwise dangerous edges to be exposed will also cause the vehicle to fail.

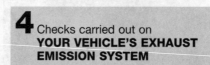

4 Checks carried out on **YOUR VEHICLE'S EXHAUST EMISSION SYSTEM**

Petrol models

☐ Have the engine at normal operating temperature, and make sure that it is in good tune (ignition system in good order, air filter element clean, etc).

☐ Before any measurements are carried out, raise the engine speed to around 2500 rpm, and hold it at this speed for 20 seconds. Allow

the engine speed to return to idle, and watch for smoke emissions from the exhaust tailpipe. If the idle speed is obviously much too high, or if dense blue or clearly-visible black smoke comes from the tailpipe for more than 5 seconds, the vehicle will fail. As a rule of thumb, blue smoke signifies oil being burnt (engine wear) while black smoke signifies unburnt fuel (dirty air cleaner element, or other carburettor or fuel system fault).

☐ An exhaust gas analyser capable of measuring carbon monoxide (CO) and hydrocarbons (HC) is now needed. If such an instrument cannot be hired or borrowed, a local garage may agree to perform the check for a small fee.

CO emissions (mixture)

☐ At the time of writing, the maximum CO level at idle is 3.5% for vehicles first used after August 1986 and 4.5% for older vehicles. From January 1996 a much tighter limit (around 0.5%) applies to catalyst-equipped vehicles first used from August 1992. If the CO level cannot be reduced far enough to pass the test (and the fuel and ignition systems are otherwise in good condition) then the carburettor is badly worn, or there is some problem in the fuel injection system or catalytic converter (as applicable).

HC emissions

☐ With the CO emissions within limits, HC emissions must be no more than 1200 ppm (parts per million). If the vehicle fails this test at idle, it can be re-tested at around 2000 rpm; if the HC level is then 1200 ppm or less, this counts as a pass.

☐ Excessive HC emissions can be caused by oil being burnt, but they are more likely to be due to unburnt fuel.

Diesel models

☐ The only emission test applicable to Diesel engines is the measuring of exhaust smoke density. The test involves accelerating the engine several times to its maximum unloaded speed.

Note: *It is of the utmost importance that the engine timing belt is in good condition before the test is carried out.*

☐ Excessive smoke can be caused by a dirty air cleaner element. Otherwise, professional advice may be needed to find the cause.

Whenever servicing, repair or overhaul work is carried out on the car or its components, observe the following procedures and instructions. This will assist in carrying out the operation efficiently and to a professional standard of workmanship.

Joint mating faces and gaskets

When separating components at their mating faces, never insert screwdrivers or similar implements into the joint between the faces in order to prise them apart. This can cause severe damage which results in oil leaks, coolant leaks, etc upon reassembly. Separation is usually achieved by tapping along the joint with a soft-faced hammer in order to break the seal. However, note that this method may not be suitable where dowels are used for component location.

Where a gasket is used between the mating faces of two components, a new one must be fitted on reassembly; fit it dry unless otherwise stated in the repair procedure. Make sure that the mating faces are clean and dry, with all traces of old gasket removed. When cleaning a joint face, use a tool which is unlikely to score or damage the face, and remove any burrs or nicks with an oilstone or fine file.

Make sure that tapped holes are cleaned with a pipe cleaner, and keep them free of jointing compound, if this is being used, unless specifically instructed otherwise.

Ensure that all orifices, channels or pipes are clear, and blow through them, preferably using compressed air.

Oil seals

Oil seals can be removed by levering them out with a wide flat-bladed screwdriver or similar implement. Alternatively, a number of self-tapping screws may be screwed into the seal, and these used as a purchase for pliers or some similar device in order to pull the seal free.

Whenever an oil seal is removed from its working location, either individually or as part of an assembly, it should be renewed.

The very fine sealing lip of the seal is easily damaged, and will not seal if the surface it contacts is not completely clean and free from scratches, nicks or grooves. If the original sealing surface of the component cannot be restored, and the manufacturer has not made provision for slight relocation of the seal relative to the sealing surface, the component should be renewed.

Protect the lips of the seal from any surface which may damage them in the course of fitting. Use tape or a conical sleeve where possible. Lubricate the seal lips with oil before fitting and, on dual-lipped seals, fill the space between the lips with grease.

Unless otherwise stated, oil seals must be fitted with their sealing lips toward the lubricant to be sealed.

Use a tubular drift or block of wood of the appropriate size to install the seal and, if the seal housing is shouldered, drive the seal down to the shoulder. If the seal housing is unshouldered, the seal should be fitted with its face flush with the housing top face (unless otherwise instructed).

Screw threads and fastenings

Seized nuts, bolts and screws are quite a common occurrence where corrosion has set in, and the use of penetrating oil or releasing fluid will often overcome this problem if the offending item is soaked for a while before attempting to release it. The use of an impact driver may also provide a means of releasing such stubborn fastening devices, when used in conjunction with the appropriate screwdriver bit or socket. If none of these methods works, it may be necessary to resort to the careful application of heat, or the use of a hacksaw or nut splitter device.

Studs are usually removed by locking two nuts together on the threaded part, and then using a spanner on the lower nut to unscrew the stud. Studs or bolts which have broken off below the surface of the component in which they are mounted can sometimes be removed using a stud extractor. Always ensure that a blind tapped hole is completely free from oil, grease, water or other fluid before installing the bolt or stud. Failure to do this could cause the housing to crack due to the hydraulic action of the bolt or stud as it is screwed in.

When tightening a castellated nut to accept a split pin, tighten the nut to the specified torque, where applicable, and then tighten further to the next split pin hole. Never slacken the nut to align the split pin hole, unless stated in the repair procedure.

When checking or retightening a nut or bolt to a specified torque setting, slacken the nut or bolt by a quarter of a turn, and then retighten to the specified setting. However, this should not be attempted where angular tightening has been used.

For some screw fastenings, notably cylinder head bolts or nuts, torque wrench settings are no longer specified for the latter stages of tightening, "angle-tightening" being called up instead. Typically, a fairly low torque wrench setting will be applied to the bolts/nuts in the correct sequence, followed by one or more stages of tightening through specified angles.

Locknuts, locktabs and washers

Any fastening which will rotate against a component or housing during tightening should always have a washer between it and the relevant component or housing.

Spring or split washers should always be renewed when they are used to lock a critical component such as a big-end bearing retaining bolt or nut. Locktabs which are folded over to retain a nut or bolt should always be renewed.

Self-locking nuts can be re-used in non-critical areas, providing resistance can be felt when the locking portion passes over the bolt or stud thread. However, it should be noted that self-locking stiffnuts tend to lose their effectiveness after long periods of use, and should then be renewed as a matter of course.

Split pins must always be replaced with new ones of the correct size for the hole.

When thread-locking compound is found on the threads of a fastener which is to be re-used, it should be cleaned off with a wire brush and solvent, and fresh compound applied on reassembly.

Special tools

Some repair procedures in this manual entail the use of special tools such as a press, two or three-legged pullers, spring compressors, etc. Wherever possible, suitable readily-available alternatives to the manufacturer's special tools are described, and are shown in use. In some instances, where no alternative is possible, it has been necessary to resort to the use of a manufacturer's tool, and this has been done for reasons of safety as well as the efficient completion of the repair operation. Unless you are highly-skilled and have a thorough understanding of the procedures described, never attempt to bypass the use of any special tool when the procedure described specifies its use. Not only is there a very great risk of personal injury, but expensive damage could be caused to the components involved.

Environmental considerations

When disposing of used engine oil, brake fluid, antifreeze, etc, give due consideration to any detrimental environmental effects. Do not, for instance, pour any of the above liquids down drains into the general sewage system, or onto the ground to soak away. Many local council refuse tips provide a facility for waste oil disposal, as do some garages. If none of these facilities are available, consult your local Environmental Health Department, or the National Rivers Authority, for further advice.

With the universal tightening-up of legislation regarding the emission of environmentally-harmful substances from motor vehicles, most vehicles have tamperproof devices fitted to the main adjustment points of the fuel system. These devices are primarily designed to prevent unqualified persons from adjusting the fuel/air mixture, with the chance of a consequent increase in toxic emissions. If such devices are found during servicing or overhaul, they should, wherever possible, be renewed or refitted in accordance with the manufacturer's requirements or current legislation.

Note: It is antisocial and illegal to dump oil down the drain. To find the location of your local oil recycling bank, call this number free.

OIL CARE

FOLLOW THE CODE

O I L   B A N K   L I N E
0800 66 33 66

Introduction

A selection of good tools is a fundamental requirement for anyone contemplating the maintenance and repair of a motor vehicle. For the owner who does not possess any, their purchase will prove a considerable expense, offsetting some of the savings made by doing-it-yourself. However, provided that the tools purchased meet the relevant national safety standards and are of good quality, they will last for many years and prove an extremely worthwhile investment.

To help the average owner to decide which tools are needed to carry out the various tasks detailed in this manual, we have compiled three lists of tools under the following headings: *Maintenance and minor repair, Repair and overhaul*, and *Special*. Newcomers to practical mechanics should start off with the *Maintenance and minor repair* tool kit, and confine themselves to the simpler jobs around the vehicle. Then, as confidence and experience grow, more difficult tasks can be undertaken, with extra tools being purchased as, and when, they are needed. In this way, a *Maintenance and minor repair* tool kit can be built up into a *Repair and overhaul* tool kit over a considerable period of time, without any major cash outlays. The experienced do-it-yourselfer will have a tool kit good enough for most repair and overhaul procedures, and will add tools from the *Special* category when it is felt that the expense is justified by the amount of use to which these tools will be put.

Maintenance and minor repair tool kit

The tools given in this list should be considered as a minimum requirement if routine maintenance, servicing and minor repair operations are to be undertaken. We recommend the purchase of combination spanners (ring one end, open-ended the other); although more expensive than open-ended ones, they do give the advantages of both types of spanner.

- ☐ *Combination spanners: 8, 9, 10, 11, 12, 13, 14, 15, 16, 17, 19, 21, 22, 24 & 26 mm*
- ☐ *Adjustable spanner - 35 mm jaw (approx)*
- ☐ *Set of feeler gauges*
- ☐ *Spark plug spanner (with rubber insert)*
- ☐ *Spark plug gap adjustment tool*
- ☐ *Brake bleed nipple spanner*
- ☐ *Screwdrivers: Flat blade and cross blade – approx 100 mm long x 6 mm dia*
- ☐ *Combination pliers*
- ☐ *Hacksaw (junior)*
- ☐ *Tyre pump*
- ☐ *Tyre pressure gauge*
- ☐ *Grease gun*
- ☐ *Oil can*
- ☐ *Oil filter removal tool*
- ☐ *Fine emery cloth*
- ☐ *Wire brush (small)*
- ☐ *Funnel (medium size)*

Repair and overhaul tool kit

These tools are virtually essential for anyone undertaking any major repairs to a motor vehicle, and are additional to those given in the *Maintenance and minor repair* list. Included in this list is a comprehensive set of sockets. Although these are expensive, they will be found invaluable as they are so versatile - particularly if various drives are included in the set. We recommend the half-inch square-drive type, as this can be used with most proprietary torque wrenches. If you cannot afford a socket set, even bought piecemeal, then inexpensive tubular box spanners are a useful alternative.

The tools in this list will occasionally need to be supplemented by tools from the *Special* list:

- ☐ *Sockets (or box spanners) to cover range in previous list (including Torx sockets)*
- ☐ *Reversible ratchet drive (for use with sockets) (see illustration)*
- ☐ *Extension piece, 250 mm (for use with sockets)*
- ☐ *Universal joint (for use with sockets)*
- ☐ *Torque wrench (for use with sockets)*
- ☐ *Self-locking grips*
- ☐ *Ball pein hammer*
- ☐ *Soft-faced mallet (plastic/aluminium or rubber)*
- ☐ *Screwdrivers:*
  Flat blade - long & sturdy, short (chubby), and narrow (electrician's) types
  Cross blade - Long & sturdy, and short (chubby) types
- ☐ *Pliers:*
  Long-nosed
  Side cutters (electrician's)
  Circlip (internal and external)
- ☐ *Cold chisel - 25 mm*
- ☐ *Scriber*
- ☐ *Scraper*
- ☐ *Centre-punch*
- ☐ *Pin punch*
- ☐ *Hacksaw*
- ☐ *Brake hose clamp*
- ☐ *Brake bleeding kit*
- ☐ *Selection of twist drills*

- ☐ *Steel rule/straight-edge*
- ☐ *Allen keys (inc. splined/Torx type) (see illustrations)*
- ☐ *Selection of files*
- ☐ *Wire brush*
- ☐ *Axle stands*
- ☐ *Jack (strong trolley or hydraulic type)*
- ☐ *Light with extension lead*

Special tools

The tools in this list are those which are not used regularly, are expensive to buy, or which need to be used in accordance with their manufacturers' instructions. Unless relatively difficult mechanical jobs are undertaken frequently, it will not be economic to buy many of these tools. Where this is the case, you could consider clubbing together with friends (or joining a motorists' club) to make a joint purchase, or borrowing the tools against a deposit from a local garage or tool hire specialist. It is worth noting that many of the larger DIY superstores now carry a large range of special tools for hire at modest rates.

The following list contains only those tools and instruments freely available to the public, and not those special tools produced by the vehicle manufacturer specifically for its dealer network. You will find occasional references to these manufacturers' special tools in the text of this manual. Generally, an alternative method of doing the job without the vehicle manufacturers' special tool is given. However, sometimes there is no alternative to using them. Where this is the case and the relevant tool cannot be bought or borrowed, you will have to entrust the work to a franchised garage.

- ☐ *Valve spring compressor (see illustration)*
- ☐ *Valve grinding tool*
- ☐ *Piston ring compressor (see illustration)*
- ☐ *Piston ring removal/installation tool (see illustration)*
- ☐ *Cylinder bore hone (see illustration)*
- ☐ *Balljoint separator*
- ☐ *Coil spring compressors (where applicable)*
- ☐ *Two/three-legged hub and bearing puller (see illustration)*

Sockets and reversible ratchet drive

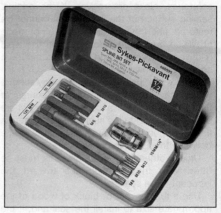

Spline bit set

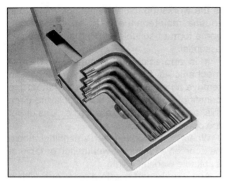

Spline key set

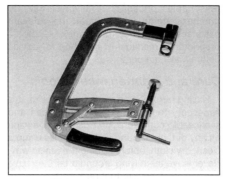

Valve spring compressor

Piston ring compressor

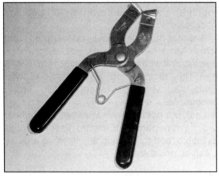

Piston ring removal/installation tool

Cylinder bore hone

Three-legged hub and bearing puller

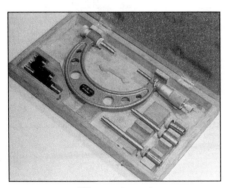

Micrometer set

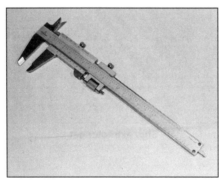

Vernier calipers

Dial test indicator and magnetic stand

Compression testing gauge

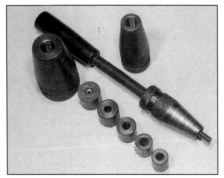

Clutch plate alignment set

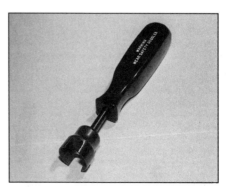

Brake shoe steady spring cup removal tool

- ☐ *Impact screwdriver*
- ☐ *Micrometer and/or vernier calipers* **(see illustrations)**
- ☐ *Dial gauge* **(see illustration)**
- ☐ *Universal electrical multi-meter*
- ☐ *Cylinder compression gauge* **(see illustration)**
- ☐ *Clutch plate alignment set* **(see illustration)**
- ☐ *Brake shoe steady spring cup removal tool* **(see illustration)**
- ☐ *Bush and bearing removal/installation set* **(see illustration)**
- ☐ *Stud extractors* **(see illustration)**
- ☐ *Tap and die set* **(see illustration)**
- ☐ *Lifting tackle*
- ☐ *Trolley jack*

Buying tools

For practically all tools, a tool factor is the best source, since he will have a very comprehensive range compared with the average garage or accessory shop. Having said that, accessory shops often offer excellent quality tools at discount prices, so it pays to shop around.

Remember, you don't have to buy the most expensive items on the shelf, but it is always advisable to steer clear of the very cheap tools. There are plenty of good tools around at reasonable prices, but always aim to purchase items which meet the relevant national safety standards. If in doubt, ask the proprietor or manager of the shop for advice before making a purchase.

Care and maintenance of tools

Having purchased a reasonable tool kit, it is necessary to keep the tools in a clean and serviceable condition. After use, always wipe off any dirt, grease and metal particles using a clean, dry cloth, before putting the tools away. Never leave them lying around after they have been used. A simple tool rack on the garage or workshop wall for items such as screwdrivers and pliers is a good idea. Store all normal spanners and sockets in a metal box. Any measuring instruments, gauges, meters, etc, must be carefully stored where they cannot be damaged or become rusty.

Take a little care when tools are used. Hammer heads inevitably become marked, and screwdrivers lose the keen edge on their blades from time to time. A little timely attention with emery cloth or a file will soon restore items like this to a good serviceable finish.

Working facilities

Not to be forgotten when discussing tools is the workshop itself. If anything more than routine maintenance is to be carried out, some form of suitable working area becomes essential.

It is appreciated that many an owner-mechanic is forced by circumstances to remove an engine or similar item without the benefit of a garage or workshop. Having done this, any repairs should always be done under the cover of a roof.

Wherever possible, any dismantling should be done on a clean, flat workbench or table at a suitable working height.

Any workbench needs a vice; one with a jaw opening of 100 mm is suitable for most jobs. As mentioned previously, some clean dry storage space is also required for tools, as well as for any lubricants, cleaning fluids, touch-up paints and so on, which become necessary.

Another item which may be required, and which has a much more general usage, is an electric drill with a chuck capacity of at least 8 mm. This, together with a good range of twist drills, is virtually essential for fitting accessories.

Last, but not least, always keep a supply of old newspapers and clean, lint-free rags available, and try to keep any working area as clean as possible.

Bush and bearing removal/installation set

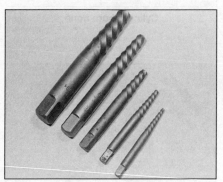

Stud extractor set

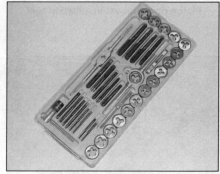

Tap and die set

Buying spare parts

Spare parts are available from many sources; for example, Nissan garages, other garages and accessory shops, and motor factors. Our advice regarding spare part sources is as follows.

Officially-appointed Nissan garages - This is the best source for parts which are peculiar to your car, and are not generally available (eg complete cylinder heads, internal gearbox components, badges, interior trim etc). It is also the only place at which you should buy parts if the vehicle is still under warranty. To be sure of obtaining the correct parts, it will be necessary to give the storeman your car's vehicle identification number, and if possible, take the old parts along for positive identification. Many parts are available under a factory exchange scheme - any parts returned should always be clean. It obviously makes good sense to go straight to the specialists on your car for this type of part, as they are best equipped to supply you.

Other garages and accessory shops - These are often very good places to buy materials and components needed for the maintenance of your car (eg oil filters, spark plugs, bulbs, drivebelts, oils and greases, touch-up paint, filler paste, etc). They also sell general accessories, usually have convenient opening hours, charge lower prices, and can often be found not far from home.

Motor factors - Good factors will stock all the more important components which wear out comparatively quickly (eg exhaust systems, brake pads, seals and hydraulic parts, clutch components, bearing shells, pistons, valves etc). Motor factors will often provide new or reconditioned components on a part-exchange basis - this can save a considerable amount of money.

Vehicle identification numbers

Modifications are a continuing and unpublicised process in vehicle manufacture, quite apart from major model changes. Spare parts manuals and lists are compiled upon a numerical basis, the individual vehicle identification numbers being essential to correct identification of the component concerned.

When ordering spare parts, always give as much information as possible. Quote the car model, year of manufacture, body and engine numbers as appropriate.

The *Vehicle Identification Number (VIN)* plate is riveted to the engine compartment bulkhead, and can be viewed once the bonnet is open. The plate carries the VIN, vehicle weight information, and paint and trim colour codes. The vehicle identification number is also stamped into the bulkhead by the side of the plate **(see illustrations)**.

The *engine number* is stamped on a machined surface on the front side of the cylinder block, at the flywheel end. The first part of the engine number gives the engine code - eg "SR20".

The vehicle identification number (VIN) plate is riveted to the engine compartment bulkhead . . .

. . . and the vehicle identification number is also stamped onto the bulkhead

Buying Spare Parts & Vehicle Identific

Engine

- ☐ Engine fails to rotate when attempting to start
- ☐ Engine rotates, but will not start
- ☐ Engine difficult to start when cold
- ☐ Engine difficult to start when hot
- ☐ Engine starts, but stops immediately
- ☐ Starter motor noisy or excessively-rough in engagement
- ☐ Engine idles erratically
- ☐ Engine misfires at idle speed
- ☐ Engine misfires throughout the driving speed range
- ☐ Engine hesitates on acceleration
- ☐ Engine lacks power
- ☐ Engine backfires
- ☐ Oil pressure warning light illuminated with engine running
- ☐ Engine runs-on after switching off
- ☐ Engine stalls
- ☐ Engine noises

Cooling system

- ☐ Overheating
- ☐ Overcooling
- ☐ External coolant leakage
- ☐ Internal coolant leakage
- ☐ Corrosion

Fuel and exhaust systems

- ☐ Excessive fuel consumption
- ☐ Fuel leakage and/or fuel odour
- ☐ Excessive noise or fumes from exhaust system

Clutch

- ☐ Pedal travels to floor - no pressure or very little resistance
- ☐ Clutch fails to disengage (unable to select gears)
- ☐ Clutch slips (engine speed increases, with no increase in vehicle speed)
- ☐ Judder as clutch is engaged
- ☐ Noise when depressing or releasing clutch pedal

Manual gearbox

- ☐ Noisy in neutral with engine running
- ☐ Noisy in one particular gear
- ☐ Difficulty engaging gears
- ☐ Jumps out of gear
- ☐ Vibration
- ☐ Lubricant leaks

Automatic transmission

- ☐ Fluid leakage
- ☐ Transmission fluid brown, or has burned smell
- ☐ General gear selection problems
- ☐ Transmission will not downshift (kickdown) with accelerator fully depressed
- ☐ Engine will not start in any gear, or starts in gears other than Park or Neutral
- ☐ Transmission slips, shifts roughly, is noisy, or has no drive in forward or reverse gears

Braking system

- ☐ Vehicle pulls to one side under braking
- ☐ Noise (grinding or high-pitched squeal) when brakes applied
- ☐ Excessive brake pedal travel
- ☐ Brake pedal feels spongy when depressed
- ☐ Excessive brake pedal effort required to stop vehicle
- ☐ Judder felt through brake pedal or steering wheel when braking
- ☐ Brakes binding
- ☐ Rear wheels locking under normal braking

Driveshafts

- ☐ Clicking or knocking noise on turns (at slow speed on full-lock)
- ☐ Vibration when accelerating or decelerating

Suspension and steering systems

- ☐ Vehicle pulls to one side
- ☐ Wheel wobble and vibration
- ☐ Excessive pitching and/or rolling around corners, or during braking
- ☐ Wandering or general instability
- ☐ Excessively-stiff steering
- ☐ Excessive play in steering
- ☐ Lack of power assistance
- ☐ Tyre wear excessive

Electrical system

- ☐ Battery will not hold a charge
- ☐ Ignition/no-charge warning light remains illuminated with engine running
- ☐ Ignition/no-charge warning light fails to come on
- ☐ Lights inoperative
- ☐ Instrument readings inaccurate or erratic
- ☐ Horn inoperative, or unsatisfactory in operation
- ☐ Wipers inoperative, or unsatisfactory in operation
- ☐ Washers inoperative, or unsatisfactory in operation
- ☐ Electric windows inoperative, or unsatisfactory in operation
- ☐ Central locking system inoperative, or unsatisfactory in operation

Introduction

The vehicle owner who does his or her own maintenance according to the recommended service schedules should not have to use this section of the manual very often. Modern component reliability is such that, provided those items subject to wear or deterioration are inspected or renewed at the specified intervals, sudden failure is comparatively rare. Faults do not usually just happen as a result of sudden failure, but develop over a period of time. Major mechanical failures in particular are usually preceded by characteristic symptoms over hundreds or even thousands of miles. Those components which do occasionally fail without warning are often small and easily carried in the vehicle.

With any fault-finding, the first step is to decide where to begin investigations. Sometimes this is obvious, but on other occasions, a little detective work will be necessary. The owner who makes half a dozen haphazard adjustments or replacements may be successful in curing a fault (or its symptoms), but will be none the wiser if the fault recurs, and ultimately may have spent more time and money than was necessary. A calm and logical approach will be found to be more satisfactory in the long run. Always take into account any warning signs or abnormalities that may have been noticed in the period preceding the fault - power loss, high or low gauge readings, unusual smells, etc - and remember that failure of components such as fuses or spark plugs may only be pointers to some underlying fault.

The pages which follow provide an easy-reference guide to the more common problems which may occur during the operation of the vehicle. These problems and their possible causes are grouped under headings denoting various components or systems, such as Engine, Cooling system, etc. The Chapter and/or Section which deals with the problem is also shown in brackets. Whatever the fault, certain basic principles apply. These are as follows:

Verify the fault. This is simply a matter of being sure that you know what the symptoms are before starting work. This is particularly important if you are investigating a fault for someone else, who may not have described it very accurately.

Don't overlook the obvious. For example, if the vehicle won't start, is there petrol in the tank? (Don't take anyone else's word on this particular point, and don't trust the fuel gauge either!) If an electrical fault is indicated, look for loose or broken wires before digging out the test gear.

Cure the disease, not the symptom. Substituting a flat battery with a fully-charged one will get you off the hard shoulder, but if the underlying cause is not attended to, the new battery will go the same way. Similarly, changing oil-fouled spark plugs for a new set will get you moving again, but remember that the reason for the fouling (if it wasn't simply an incorrect grade of plug) will have to be established and corrected.

Don't take anything for granted. Particularly, don't forget that a "new" component may itself be defective (especially if it's been rattling around in the boot for months), and don't leave components out of a fault diagnosis sequence just because they are new or recently-fitted. When you do finally diagnose a difficult fault, you'll probably realise that all the evidence was there from the start.

Engine

Engine fails to rotate when attempting to start

- ☐ Battery terminal connections loose or corroded (Chapter 1).
- ☐ Battery discharged or faulty (Chapter 5).
- ☐ Broken or disconnected wiring in the starting circuit (Chapter 5).
- ☐ Defective starter solenoid or switch (Chapter 5).
- ☐ Defective starter motor (Chapter 5).
- ☐ Starter pinion or flywheel ring gear teeth loose or broken (Chapters 5 and 2A or 2B).
- ☐ Engine earth strap broken or disconnected (Chapter 5).
- ☐ Automatic transmission not in Park/Neutral position or starter inhibitor switch faulty (Chapter 7B).

Engine rotates, but will not start

- ☐ Fuel tank empty.
- ☐ Battery discharged (engine rotates slowly) (Chapter 5).
- ☐ Battery terminal connections loose or corroded (Chapter 1).
- ☐ Ignition components damp or damaged (Chapters 1 and 5).
- ☐ Broken, loose or disconnected wiring in the ignition circuit (Chapters 1 and 5).
- ☐ Worn, faulty or incorrectly-gapped spark plugs (Chapter 1).
- ☐ Carburettor/fuel injection system fault (Chapter 4A, 4B or 4C).
- ☐ Major mechanical failure (eg camshaft drive) (Chapters 2A or 2B).

Engine difficult to start when cold

- ☐ Battery discharged (Chapter 5).
- ☐ Battery terminal connections loose or corroded (Chapter 1).
- ☐ Worn, faulty or incorrectly-gapped spark plugs (Chapter 1).
- ☐ Choke mechanism faulty - carburettor models (Chapter 4A).
- ☐ Faulty fuel cut-off solenoid - carburettor models (Chapter 4A).
- ☐ Fuel injection system fault - fuel-injected models (Chapter 4B or 4C).
- ☐ Other ignition system fault (Chapters 1 and 5).
- ☐ Low cylinder compressions (Chapter 2A or 2B).

Engine difficult to start when hot

- ☐ Air filter element dirty or clogged (Chapter 1).
- ☐ Choke mechanism faulty - carburettor models (Chapter 4A).
- ☐ Faulty fuel cut-off solenoid - carburettor models (Chapter 4A).
- ☐ Fuel injection system fault - fuel-injected models (Chapter 4B or 4C).
- ☐ Other ignition system fault (Chapters 1 and 5).
- ☐ Low cylinder compressions (Chapter 2A or 2B).

Engine starts, but stops immediately

- ☐ Loose or faulty electrical connections in the ignition circuit (Chapters 1 and 5).
- ☐ Vacuum leak at the carburettor/throttle body or inlet manifold (Chapter 4A, 4B or 4C).
- ☐ Blocked carburettor jet(s) or internal passages - carburettor models (Chapter 4A).
- ☐ Blocked injector/fuel injection system fault - fuel-injected models (Chapter 4B or 4C).

Starter motor noisy or excessively-rough in engagement

- ☐ Starter pinion or flywheel ring gear teeth loose or broken (Chapters 5 and 2A or 2B).
- ☐ Starter motor mounting bolts loose or missing (Chapter 5).
- ☐ Starter motor internal components worn or damaged (Chapter 5).

Engine idles erratically

- ☐ Air filter element clogged (Chapter 1).
- ☐ Vacuum leak at the carburettor/throttle body or inlet manifold (Chapter 4A, 4B or 4C).
- ☐ Worn, faulty or incorrectly-gapped spark plugs (Chapter 1).
- ☐ Uneven or low cylinder compressions (Chapter 2A or 2B).
- ☐ Camshaft lobes worn (Chapter 2A or 2B).
- ☐ Timing chain(s) incorrectly fitted (Chapter 2A or 2B).
- ☐ Blocked carburettor jet(s) or internal passages - carburettor models (Chapter 4A).
- ☐ Blocked injector/fuel injection system fault - fuel-injected models (Chapter 4B or 4C).

Engine misfires at idle speed

- ☐ Worn, faulty or incorrectly-gapped spark plugs (Chapter 1).
- ☐ Faulty spark plug HT leads (Chapter 1).
- ☐ Vacuum leak at the carburettor/throttle body, inlet manifold or associated hoses (Chapter 4A, 4B or 4C).
- ☐ Blocked carburettor jet(s) or internal passages - carburettor models (Chapter 4A).
- ☐ Blocked injector/fuel injection system fault - fuel-injected models (Chapter 4B or 4C).
- ☐ Distributor cap cracked or tracking internally (Chapter 1).
- ☐ Uneven or low cylinder compressions (Chapter 2A or 2B).
- ☐ Disconnected, leaking, or perished crankcase ventilation hoses (Chapter 4D).

Engine misfires throughout the driving speed range

- ☐ Fuel filter choked (Chapter 1).
- ☐ Fuel pump faulty, or delivery pressure low (Chapter 4A, 4B or 4C).
- ☐ Fuel tank vent blocked, or pipes restricted (Chapter 4A, 4B or 4C).
- ☐ Vacuum leak at the carburettor/throttle body, inlet manifold or associated hoses (Chapter 4A, 4B, 4C or 4D).
- ☐ Worn, faulty or incorrectly-gapped spark plugs (Chapter 1).
- ☐ Faulty spark plug HT leads (Chapter 1).
- ☐ Distributor cap cracked or tracking internally (Chapter 1).
- ☐ Faulty ignition coil (Chapter 5).
- ☐ Uneven or low cylinder compressions (Chapter 2A).
- ☐ Blocked carburettor jet(s) or internal passages - carburettor models (Chapter 4A).
- ☐ Blocked injector/fuel injection system fault - fuel-injected models (Chapter 4B or 4C).

Engine (continued)

Engine hesitates on acceleration

- ☐ Worn, faulty or incorrectly-gapped spark plugs (Chapter 1).
- ☐ Vacuum leak at the carburettor/throttle body, inlet manifold or associated hoses (Chapter 4A, 4B or 4C).
- ☐ Blocked carburettor jet(s) or internal passages - carburettor models (Chapter 4A).
- ☐ Blocked injector/fuel injection system fault - fuel-injected models (Chapter 4B or 4C).

Engine lacks power

- ☐ Timing chain(s) incorrectly fitted (Chapter 2A or 2B).
- ☐ Fuel filter choked (Chapter 1).
- ☐ Fuel pump faulty, or delivery pressure low (Chapter 4A, 4B, or 4C).
- ☐ Uneven or low cylinder compressions (Chapter 2A or 2B).
- ☐ Worn, faulty or incorrectly-gapped spark plugs (Chapter 1).
- ☐ Vacuum leak at the carburettor/throttle body, inlet manifold or associated hoses (Chapter 4A, 4B or 4C).
- ☐ Blocked carburettor jet(s) or internal passages - carburettor models (Chapter 4A).
- ☐ Blocked injector/fuel injection system fault - fuel-injected models (Chapter 4B or 4C).
- ☐ Brakes binding (Chapters 1 and 9).
- ☐ Clutch slipping - manual transmission models (Chapter 6).

Oil pressure warning light illuminated with engine running

- ☐ Low oil level, or incorrect oil grade (Chapter 1).
- ☐ Faulty oil pressure sensor (Chapter 5).
- ☐ Worn engine bearings and/or oil pump (Chapter 2C).
- ☐ High engine operating temperature (Chapter 3).
- ☐ Oil pressure relief valve defective (Chapter 2A or 2B).
- ☐ Oil pick-up strainer clogged (Chapter 2A or 2B).

Engine backfires

- ☐ Timing chain(s) incorrectly fitted (Chapter 2A or 2B).
- ☐ Vacuum leak at the carburettor/throttle body, inlet manifold or associated hoses (Chapter 4A, 4B or 4C).
- ☐ Blocked carburettor jet(s) or internal passages - carburettor models (Chapter 4A).
- ☐ Blocked injector/fuel injection system fault - fuel-injected models (Chapter 4B or 4C).

Engine runs-on after switching off

- ☐ Excessive carbon build-up in engine (Chapter 2C).
- ☐ High engine operating temperature (Chapter 3).
- ☐ Faulty fuel cut-off solenoid - carburettor models (Chapter 4A).
- ☐ Fuel injection system fault - fuel injection models (Chapter 4B or 4C).

Engine stalls

- ☐ Vacuum leak at the carburettor/throttle body, inlet manifold or associated hoses (Chapter 4A, 4B or 4C).
- ☐ Fuel filter choked (Chapter 1).
- ☐ Fuel pump faulty, or delivery pressure low (Chapter 4A, 4B or 4C).
- ☐ Fuel tank vent blocked, or fuel pipes restricted (Chapter 4A, 4B, 4C or 4D).
- ☐ Blocked carburettor jet(s) or internal passages - carburettor models (Chapter 4A).
- ☐ Blocked injector/fuel injection system fault - fuel-injected models (Chapter 4B or 4C).

Engine noises

Pre-ignition (pinking) or knocking during acceleration or under load

- ☐ Ignition timing incorrect/ignition system fault (Chapters 1 and 5).
- ☐ Incorrect grade of spark plug (Chapter 1).
- ☐ Incorrect grade of fuel (Chapter 1).
- ☐ Vacuum leak at the carburettor/throttle body, inlet manifold or associated hoses (Chapter 4A, 4B or 4C).
- ☐ Excessive carbon build-up in engine (Chapter 2C).
- ☐ Blocked carburettor jet(s) or internal passages - carburettor models (Chapter 4A).
- ☐ Blocked injector/fuel injection system fault - fuel-injected models (Chapter 4B or 4C).

Whistling or wheezing noises

- ☐ Leaking inlet manifold or carburettor/throttle body gasket (Chapter 4A, 4B or 4C).
- ☐ Leaking exhaust manifold gasket or pipe-to-manifold joint (Chapter 4A, 4B, 4C or 4D).
- ☐ Leaking vacuum hose (Chapters 4A, 4B, 4C, 4D, 5 and 9).
- ☐ Blowing cylinder head gasket (Chapter 2A or 2B).

Tapping or rattling noises

- ☐ Worn valve gear or camshaft (Chapter 2A or 2B).
- ☐ Ancillary component fault (water pump, alternator, etc) (Chapters 3, 5, etc).

Knocking or thumping noises

- ☐ Worn big-end bearings (regular heavy knocking, perhaps less under load) (Chapter 2C).
- ☐ Worn main bearings (rumbling and knocking, perhaps worsening under load) (Chapter 2C).
- ☐ Piston slap (most noticeable when cold) (Chapter 2C).
- ☐ Ancillary component fault (water pump, alternator, etc) (Chapters 3, 5, etc).

Cooling system

Overheating

- ☐ Insufficient coolant in system (Chapter 1).
- ☐ Thermostat faulty (Chapter 3).
- ☐ Radiator core blocked, or grille restricted (Chapter 3).
- ☐ Electric cooling fan or thermoswitch faulty (Chapter 3).
- ☐ Pressure cap faulty (Chapter 3).
- ☐ Ignition timing incorrect (Chapters 1 and 5).
- ☐ Inaccurate temperature gauge sender unit (Chapter 3).
- ☐ Airlock in cooling system (Chapter 1).

Overcooling

- ☐ Thermostat faulty (Chapter 3).
- ☐ Inaccurate temperature gauge sender unit (Chapter 3).

External coolant leakage

- ☐ Deteriorated or damaged hoses or hose clips (Chapter 1).
- ☐ Radiator core or heater matrix leaking (Chapter 3).
- ☐ Pressure cap faulty (Chapter 3).
- ☐ Water pump seal leaking (Chapter 3).
- ☐ Boiling due to overheating (Chapter 3).
- ☐ Cylinder block core plug leaking (Chapter 2B).

Internal coolant leakage

- ☐ Leaking cylinder head gasket (Chapter 2A or 2B).
- ☐ Cracked cylinder head or cylinder bore (Chapter 2A or 2B).

Corrosion

- ☐ Infrequent draining and flushing (Chapter 1).
- ☐ Incorrect coolant mixture or inappropriate coolant type (Chapter 1).

Fuel and exhaust systems

Excessive fuel consumption

- [ ] Air filter element dirty or clogged (Chapter 1).
- [ ] Choke mechanism faulty - carburettor models (Chapter 4A).
- [ ] Fuel injection system fault - fuel-injected models (Chapter 4B or 4C).
- [ ] Ignition timing incorrect/ignition system fault (Chapters 1 and 5).
- [ ] Tyres under-inflated (Chapter 1).

Fuel leakage and/or fuel odour

- [ ] Damaged or corroded fuel tank, pipes or connections (Chapter 4A, 4B, 4C or 4D).

- [ ] Carburettor float chamber flooding (float height incorrect) - carburettor models (Chapter 4A).

Excessive noise or fumes from exhaust system

- [ ] Leaking exhaust system or manifold joints (Chapters 1 and 4A, 4B, or 4C).
- [ ] Leaking, corroded or damaged silencers or pipe (Chapters 1 and 4A, 4B or 4C).
- [ ] Broken mountings causing body or suspension contact (Chapter 1).

Clutch

Pedal travels to floor - no pressure or very little resistance

- [ ] Broken clutch cable (Chapter 6).
- [ ] Incorrect clutch cable adjustment (Chapter 6).
- [ ] Broken clutch release bearing or fork (Chapter 6).
- [ ] Broken diaphragm spring in clutch pressure plate (Chapter 6).

Clutch fails to disengage (unable to select gears)

- [ ] Incorrect clutch cable adjustment (Chapter 6).
- [ ] Clutch disc sticking on gearbox input shaft splines (Chapter 6).
- [ ] Clutch disc sticking to flywheel or pressure plate (Chapter 6).
- [ ] Faulty pressure plate assembly (Chapter 6).
- [ ] Clutch release mechanism worn or incorrectly assembled (Chapter 6).

Clutch slips (engine speed increases, with no increase in vehicle speed)

- [ ] Incorrect clutch cable adjustment (Chapter 6).
- [ ] Clutch disc linings excessively worn (Chapter 6).
- [ ] Clutch disc linings contaminated with oil or grease (Chapter 6).
- [ ] Faulty pressure plate or weak diaphragm spring (Chapter 6).

Judder as clutch is engaged

- [ ] Clutch disc linings contaminated with oil or grease (Chapter 6).
- [ ] Clutch disc linings excessively worn (Chapter 6).
- [ ] Clutch cable sticking or frayed (Chapter 6).
- [ ] Faulty or distorted pressure plate or diaphragm spring (Chapter 6).
- [ ] Worn or loose engine or gearbox mountings (Chapter 2A or 2B).
- [ ] Clutch disc hub or gearbox input shaft splines worn (Chapter 6).

Noise when depressing or releasing clutch pedal

- [ ] Worn clutch release bearing (Chapter 6).
- [ ] Worn or dry clutch pedal bushes (Chapter 6).
- [ ] Faulty pressure plate assembly (Chapter 6).
- [ ] Pressure plate diaphragm spring broken (Chapter 6).
- [ ] Broken clutch disc cushioning springs (Chapter 6).

Manual gearbox

Noisy in neutral with engine running

- [ ] Input shaft bearings worn (noise apparent with clutch pedal released, but not when depressed) (Chapter 7A).*
- [ ] Clutch release bearing worn (noise apparent with clutch pedal depressed, possibly less when released) (Chapter 6).

Noisy in one particular gear

- [ ] Worn, damaged or chipped gear teeth (Chapter 7A).*

Difficulty engaging gears

- [ ] Clutch fault (Chapter 6).
- [ ] Oil level low (Chapter 1).
- [ ] Worn or damaged gear linkage (Chapter 7A).
- [ ] Incorrectly-adjusted gear linkage (Chapter 7A).
- [ ] Worn synchroniser units (Chapter 7A).*

Jumps out of gear

- [ ] Worn or damaged gear linkage (Chapter 7A).
- [ ] Incorrectly-adjusted gear linkage (Chapter 7A).
- [ ] Worn synchroniser units (Chapter 7A).*
- [ ] Worn selector forks (Chapter 7A).*

Vibration

- [ ] Oil level low (Chapter 1).
- [ ] Worn bearings (Chapter 7A).*

Lubricant leaks

- [ ] Leaking differential output oil seal (Chapter 7A).
- [ ] Leaking housing joint (Chapter 7A).*
- [ ] Leaking input shaft oil seal (Chapter 7A).*

Although the corrective action necessary to remedy the symptoms described is beyond the scope of the home mechanic, the above information should be helpful in isolating the cause of the condition, so that the owner can communicate clearly with a professional mechanic.

Automatic transmission

Note: *Due to the complexity of the automatic transmission, it is difficult for the home mechanic to properly diagnose and service this unit. For problems other than the following, the vehicle should be taken to a dealer service department or automatic transmission specialist.*

Fluid leakage

☐ Automatic transmission fluid is usually deep red in colour. Fluid leaks should not be confused with engine oil, which can easily be blown onto the transmission by airflow.
☐ To determine the source of a leak, first remove all built-up dirt and grime from the transmission housing and surrounding areas, using a degreasing agent, or by steam-cleaning. Drive the vehicle at low speed, so air flow will not blow the leak far from its source. Raise and support the vehicle, and determine where the leak is coming from. The following are common areas of leakage.
  a) Oil pan.
  b) Dipstick tube (Chapter 1).
  c) Transmission-to-fluid cooler fluid pipes/unions (Chapter 7B).

Transmission fluid brown, or has burned smell

☐ Transmission fluid level low, or fluid in need of renewal (Chapter 1).

Transmission will not downshift (kickdown) with accelerator pedal fully depressed

☐ Low transmission fluid level (Chapter 1).
☐ Incorrect selector cable adjustment (Chapter 7B).
☐ Incorrect kickdown cable adjustment (Chapter 7B).

General gear selection problems

☐ Chapter 7B deals with checking and adjusting the selector cable on automatic transmissions. The following are common problems which may be caused by a poorly-adjusted cable.
  a) Engine starting in gears other than Park or Neutral.
  b) Indicator on gear selector lever pointing to a gear other than the one actually being used.
  c) Vehicle moves when in Park or Neutral.
  d) Poor gearshift quality or erratic gearchanges.
☐ Refer to Chapter 7B for the selector cable adjustment procedure.

Engine will not start in any gear, or starts in gears other than Park or Neutral

☐ Incorrect starter inhibitor switch adjustment (Chapter 7B).
☐ Incorrect selector cable adjustment (Chapter 7B).

Transmission slips, shifts roughly, is noisy, or has no drive in forward or reverse gears

☐ There are many probable causes for the above problems, but the home mechanic should be concerned with only one possibility - fluid level. Before taking the vehicle to a dealer or transmission specialist, check the fluid level and condition of the fluid as described in Chapter 1. Correct the fluid level as necessary, or change the fluid and filter if needed. If the problem persists, professional help will be necessary.

Braking system

Note: *Before assuming that a brake problem exists, make sure that the tyres are in good condition and correctly inflated, that the front wheel alignment is correct, and that the vehicle is not loaded with weight in an unequal manner. Apart from checking the condition of all pipe and hose connections, any faults occurring on the anti-lock braking system should be referred to a Nissan dealer for diagnosis.*

Vehicle pulls to one side under braking

☐ Worn, defective, damaged or contaminated front brake pads or rear brake shoes/pads on one side (Chapters 1 and 9).
☐ Seized or partially-seized front brake caliper or rear wheel caliper/cylinder piston (Chapters 1 and 9).
☐ A mixture of brake pad/shoe lining materials fitted between sides (Chapters 1 and 9).
☐ Front brake caliper mounting bolts loose (Chapter 9).
☐ Rear brake caliper/backplate mounting bolts loose (Chapter 9).
☐ Worn or damaged steering or suspension components (Chapters 1 and 10).

Noise (grinding or high-pitched squeal) when brakes applied

☐ Brake pad or shoe friction lining material worn down to metal backing (Chapters 1 and 9).
☐ Excessive corrosion of brake disc or drum. (May be apparent after the vehicle has been standing for some time (Chapters 1 and 9).
☐ Foreign object (stone chipping, etc) trapped between brake disc and shield (Chapters 1 and 9).

Excessive brake pedal travel

☐ Inoperative rear brake self-adjust mechanism - drum brake models (Chapters 1 and 9).
☐ Faulty master cylinder (Chapter 9).
☐ Air in hydraulic system (Chapters 1 and 9).
☐ Faulty vacuum servo unit (Chapter 9).

Brake pedal feels spongy when depressed

☐ Air in hydraulic system (Chapters 1 and 9).
☐ Deteriorated flexible rubber brake hoses (Chapters 1 and 9).
☐ Master cylinder mounting nuts loose (Chapter 9).
☐ Faulty master cylinder (Chapter 9).

Excessive brake pedal effort required to stop vehicle

☐ Faulty vacuum servo unit (Chapter 9).
☐ Disconnected, damaged or insecure brake servo vacuum hose (Chapter 9).
☐ Primary or secondary hydraulic circuit failure (Chapter 9).
☐ Seized brake caliper or wheel cylinder piston(s) (Chapter 9).
☐ Brake pads or brake shoes incorrectly fitted (Chapters 1 and 9).
☐ Incorrect grade of brake pads or brake shoes fitted (Chapters 1 and 9).
☐ Brake pads or brake shoe linings contaminated (Chapters 1 and 9).

Judder felt through brake pedal or steering wheel when braking

☐ Excessive run-out or distortion of front discs or rear discs/drums (Chapters 1 and 9).
☐ Brake pad or brake shoe linings worn (Chapters 1 and 9).
☐ Brake caliper or rear brake backplate mounting bolts loose (Chapter 9).
☐ Wear in suspension or steering components or mountings (Chapters 1 and 10).

Brakes binding

☐ Seized brake caliper or wheel cylinder piston(s) (Chapter 9).
☐ Incorrectly-adjusted handbrake mechanism (Chapter 9).
☐ Faulty master cylinder (Chapter 9).

Rear wheels locking under normal braking

☐ Rear brake shoe linings contaminated (Chapters 1 and 9).
☐ Faulty brake pressure regulator (Chapter 9).

Driveshafts

Clicking or knocking noise on turns (at slow speed on full-lock)

☐ Lack of constant velocity joint lubricant, possibly due to damaged gaiter (Chapter 8).
☐ Worn outer constant velocity joint (Chapter 8).

Vibration when accelerating or decelerating

☐ Worn inner constant velocity joint (Chapter 8).
☐ Bent or distorted driveshaft (Chapter 8).

Suspension and steering

Note: *Before diagnosing suspension or steering faults, be sure that the trouble is not due to incorrect tyre pressures, mixtures of tyre types, or binding brakes.*

Vehicle pulls to one side

☐ Defective tyre (Chapter 1).
☐ Excessive wear in suspension or steering components (Chapters 1 and 10).
☐ Incorrect front wheel alignment (Chapter 10).
☐ Accident damage to steering or suspension components (Chapter 1).

Wheel wobble and vibration

☐ Front roadwheels out of balance (vibration felt mainly through the steering wheel) (Chapters 1 and 10).
☐ Rear roadwheels out of balance (vibration felt throughout the vehicle) (Chapters 1 and 10).
☐ Roadwheels damaged or distorted (Chapters 1 and 10).
☐ Faulty or damaged tyre (Chapter 1).
☐ Worn steering or suspension joints, bushes or components (Chapters 1 and 10).
☐ Wheel bolts loose (Chapters 1 and 10).

Excessive pitching and/or rolling around corners, or during braking

☐ Defective shock absorbers (Chapters 1 and 10).
☐ Broken or weak spring and/or suspension component (Chapters 1 and 10).
☐ Worn or damaged anti-roll bar or mountings (Chapter 10).

Wandering or general instability

☐ Incorrect front wheel alignment (Chapter 10).
☐ Worn steering or suspension joints, bushes or components (Chapters 1 and 10).
☐ Roadwheels out of balance (Chapters 1 and 10).
☐ Faulty or damaged tyre (Chapter 1).
☐ Wheel bolts loose (Chapters 1 and 10).
☐ Defective shock absorbers (Chapters 1 and 10).

Excessive play in steering

☐ Worn steering track rod end balljoints (Chapters 1 and 10).
☐ Worn rack-and-pinion steering gear (Chapter 10).
☐ Worn steering or suspension joints, bushes or components (Chapters 1 and 10).

Excessively-stiff steering

☐ Lack of steering gear lubricant (Chapter 10).
☐ Seized track rod end balljoint or suspension balljoint (Chapters 1 and 10).
☐ Broken or incorrectly-adjusted auxiliary drivebelt (Chapter 1).
☐ Incorrect front wheel alignment (Chapter 10).
☐ Steering rack or column bent or damaged (Chapter 10).

Lack of power assistance

☐ Broken or incorrectly-adjusted auxiliary drivebelt (Chapter 1).
☐ Incorrect power steering fluid level (Chapter 1).
☐ Restriction in power steering fluid hoses (Chapter 1).
☐ Faulty power steering pump (Chapter 10).
☐ Faulty rack-and-pinion steering gear (Chapter 10).

Tyre wear excessive

Tyres worn on inside or outside edges

☐ Tyres under-inflated (wear on both edges) (Chapter 1).
☐ Incorrect camber or castor angles (wear on one edge only) (Chapter 10).
☐ Worn steering or suspension joints, bushes or components (Chapters 1 and 10).
☐ Excessively-hard cornering.
☐ Accident damage.

Tyre treads exhibit feathered edges

☐ Incorrect toe setting (Chapter 10).

Tyres worn in centre of tread

☐ Tyres over-inflated (Chapter 1).

Tyres worn on inside and outside edges

☐ Tyres under-inflated (Chapter 1).

Tyres worn unevenly

☐ Tyres/wheels out of balance (Chapter 1).
☐ Excessive wheel or tyre run-out (Chapter 1).
☐ Worn shock absorbers (Chapters 1 and 10).
☐ Faulty tyre (Chapter 1).

Electrical system

Note: *For problems associated with the starting system, refer to the faults listed under "Engine" earlier in this Section.*

Battery will not hold a charge

☐ Battery defective internally (Chapter 5).
☐ Battery terminal connections loose or corroded (Chapter 1).
☐ Auxiliary drivebelt worn or incorrectly adjusted (Chapter 1).
☐ Alternator not charging at correct output (Chapter 5).
☐ Alternator or voltage regulator faulty (Chapter 5).
☐ Short-circuit causing continual battery drain (Chapters 5 and 12).

Ignition/no-charge warning light remains illuminated with engine running

☐ Auxiliary drivebelt broken, worn, or incorrectly adjusted (Chapter 1).
☐ Alternator brushes worn, sticking, or dirty (Chapter 5).
☐ Alternator brush springs weak or broken (Chapter 5).
☐ Internal fault in alternator or voltage regulator (Chapter 5).
☐ Broken, disconnected, or loose wiring in charging circuit (Chapter 5).

Ignition/no-charge warning light fails to come on

☐ Warning light bulb blown (Chapter 12).
☐ Broken, disconnected, or loose wiring in warning light circuit (Chapter 12).
☐ Alternator faulty (Chapter 5).

Lights inoperative

☐ Bulb blown (Chapter 12).
☐ Corrosion of bulb or bulbholder contacts (Chapter 12).
☐ Blown fuse (Chapter 12).
☐ Faulty relay (Chapter 12).
☐ Broken, loose, or disconnected wiring (Chapter 12).
☐ Faulty switch (Chapter 12).

Instrument readings inaccurate or erratic

Instrument readings increase with engine speed

☐ Faulty voltage regulator (Chapter 12).

Fuel or temperature gauges give no reading

☐ Faulty gauge sender unit (Chapters 3 or 4).
☐ Wiring open-circuit (Chapter 12).
☐ Faulty gauge (Chapter 12).

Fuel or temperature gauges give continuous maximum reading

☐ Faulty gauge sender unit (Chapters 3 or 4).
☐ Wiring short-circuit (Chapter 12).
☐ Faulty gauge (Chapter 12).

Horn inoperative, or unsatisfactory in operation

Horn operates all the time

☐ Horn push either earthed or stuck down (Chapter 12).
☐ Horn cable-to-horn push earthed (Chapter 12).

Horn fails to operate

☐ Blown fuse (Chapter 12).
☐ Cable or cable connections loose, broken or disconnected (Chapter 12).
☐ Faulty horn (Chapter 12).

Horn emits intermittent or unsatisfactory sound

☐ Cable connections loose (Chapter 12).
☐ Horn mountings loose (Chapter 12).
☐ Faulty horn (Chapter 12).

Wipers inoperative, or unsatisfactory in operation

Wipers fail to operate, or operate very slowly

☐ Wiper blades stuck to screen, or seized (Chapters 1 and 12).
☐ Blown fuse (Chapter 12).
☐ Cable or cable connections loose, broken or disconnected (Chapter 12).
☐ Faulty relay (Chapter 12).
☐ Faulty wiper motor (Chapter 12).

Wiper blades sweep over too large or too small an area

☐ Wiper arms incorrectly positioned on spindles (Chapter 1).
☐ Excessive wear of wiper linkage (Chapter 12).
☐ Wiper motor or linkage mountings loose or insecure (Chapter 12).

Wiper blades fail to clean the glass effectively

☐ Wiper blade rubbers worn or perished (Chapter 1).
☐ Wiper arm tension springs broken, or arm pivots seized (Chapter 12).
☐ Insufficient windscreen washer additive to adequately remove road film (Chapter 1).

Washers inoperative, or unsatisfactory in operation

One or more washer jets inoperative

☐ Blocked washer jet (Chapter 1).
☐ Disconnected, kinked or restricted fluid hose (Chapter 12).
☐ Insufficient fluid in washer reservoir (Chapter 1).

Washer pump fails to operate

☐ Broken or disconnected wiring or connections (Chapter 12).
☐ Blown fuse (Chapter 12).
☐ Faulty washer switch (Chapter 12).
☐ Faulty washer pump (Chapter 12).

Washer pump runs for some time before fluid is emitted

☐ Faulty one-way valve in fluid supply hose (Chapter 12).

Electric windows inoperative, or unsatisfactory

Window glass will only move in one direction

☐ Faulty switch (Chapter 12)

Window glass slow to move

☐ Incorrectly-adjusted door glass guide channels (Chapter 11).
☐ Regulator seized or damaged, or in need of lubrication (Chapter 11).
☐ Door internal components or trim fouling regulator (Chapter 11).
☐ Faulty motor (Chapter 11).

Window glass fails to move

☐ Incorrectly-adjusted door glass guide channels (Chapter 11).
☐ Blown fuse (Chapter 12).
☐ Faulty relay (Chapter 12).
☐ Broken or disconnected wiring or connections (Chapter 12).
☐ Faulty motor (Chapter 11).

Central locking system inoperative, or unsatisfactory in operation

Complete system failure

☐ Blown fuse (Chapter 12).
☐ Faulty relay (Chapter 12).
☐ Broken or disconnected wiring or connections (Chapter 12).
☐ Faulty control unit (Chapter 11).

Latch locks but will not unlock, or unlocks but will not lock

☐ Faulty master switch (Chapter 12).
☐ Broken or disconnected latch operating rods or levers (Chapter 11).
☐ Faulty relay (Chapter 12).
☐ Faulty control unit (Chapter 11).

One solenoid/motor fails to operate

☐ Broken or disconnected wiring or connections (Chapter 12).
☐ Faulty solenoid/motor (Chapter 11).
☐ Broken, binding or disconnected latch operating rods or levers (Chapter 11).
☐ Fault in door latch (Chapter 11).

A

ABS (Anti-lock brake system) A system, usually electronically controlled, that senses incipient wheel lockup during braking and relieves hydraulic pressure at wheels that are about to skid.

Air bag An inflatable bag hidden in the steering wheel (driver's side) or the dash or glovebox (passenger side). In a head-on collision, the bags inflate, preventing the driver and front passenger from being thrown forward into the steering wheel or windscreen.

Air cleaner A metal or plastic housing, containing a filter element, which removes dust and dirt from the air being drawn into the engine.

Air filter element The actual filter in an air cleaner system, usually manufactured from pleated paper and requiring renewal at regular intervals.

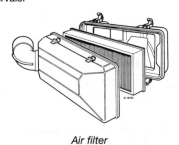

Air filter

Allen key A hexagonal wrench which fits into a recessed hexagonal hole.

Alligator clip A long-nosed spring-loaded metal clip with meshing teeth. Used to make temporary electrical connections.

Alternator A component in the electrical system which converts mechanical energy from a drivebelt into electrical energy to charge the battery and to operate the starting system, ignition system and electrical accessories.

Ampere (amp) A unit of measurement for the flow of electric current. One amp is the amount of current produced by one volt acting through a resistance of one ohm.

Anaerobic sealer A substance used to prevent bolts and screws from loosening. Anaerobic means that it does not require oxygen for activation. The Loctite brand is widely used.

Antifreeze A substance (usually ethylene glycol) mixed with water, and added to a vehicle's cooling system, to prevent freezing of the coolant in winter. Antifreeze also contains chemicals to inhibit corrosion and the formation of rust and other deposits that would tend to clog the radiator and coolant passages and reduce cooling efficiency.

Anti-seize compound A coating that reduces the risk of seizing on fasteners that are subjected to high temperatures, such as exhaust manifold bolts and nuts.

Asbestos A natural fibrous mineral with great heat resistance, commonly used in the composition of brake friction materials.

Asbestos is a health hazard and the dust created by brake systems should never be inhaled or ingested.

Axle A shaft on which a wheel revolves, or which revolves with a wheel. Also, a solid beam that connects the two wheels at one end of the vehicle. An axle which also transmits power to the wheels is known as a live axle.

Axleshaft A single rotating shaft, on either side of the differential, which delivers power from the final drive assembly to the drive wheels. Also called a driveshaft or a halfshaft.

B

Ball bearing An anti-friction bearing consisting of a hardened inner and outer race with hardened steel balls between two races.

Bearing The curved surface on a shaft or in a bore, or the part assembled into either, that permits relative motion between them with minimum wear and friction.

Bearing

Big-end bearing The bearing in the end of the connecting rod that's attached to the crankshaft.

Bleed nipple A valve on a brake wheel cylinder, caliper or other hydraulic component that is opened to purge the hydraulic system of air. Also called a bleed screw.

Brake bleeding Procedure for removing air from lines of a hydraulic brake system.

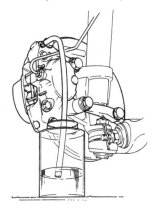

Brake bleeding

Brake disc The component of a disc brake that rotates with the wheels.

Brake drum The component of a drum brake that rotates with the wheels.

Brake linings The friction material which contacts the brake disc or drum to retard the vehicle's speed. The linings are bonded or riveted to the brake pads or shoes.

Brake pads The replaceable friction pads that pinch the brake disc when the brakes are applied. Brake pads consist of a friction material bonded or riveted to a rigid backing plate.

Brake shoe The crescent-shaped carrier to which the brake linings are mounted and which forces the lining against the rotating drum during braking.

Braking systems For more information on braking systems, consult the *Haynes Automotive Brake Manual*.

Breaker bar A long socket wrench handle providing greater leverage.

Bulkhead The insulated partition between the engine and the passenger compartment.

C

Caliper The non-rotating part of a disc-brake assembly that straddles the disc and carries the brake pads. The caliper also contains the hydraulic components that cause the pads to pinch the disc when the brakes are applied. A caliper is also a measuring tool that can be set to measure inside or outside dimensions of an object.

Camshaft A rotating shaft on which a series of cam lobes operate the valve mechanisms. The camshaft may be driven by gears, by sprockets and chain or by sprockets and a belt.

Canister A container in an evaporative emission control system; contains activated charcoal granules to trap vapours from the fuel system.

Canister

Carburettor A device which mixes fuel with air in the proper proportions to provide a desired power output from a spark ignition internal combustion engine.

Castellated Resembling the parapets along the top of a castle wall. For example, a castellated balljoint stud nut.

Castor In wheel alignment, the backward or forward tilt of the steering axis. Castor is positive when the steering axis is inclined rearward at the top.

Catalytic converter A silencer-like device in the exhaust system which converts certain pollutants in the exhaust gases into less harmful substances.

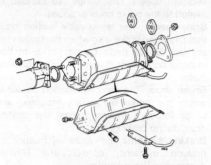

Catalytic converter

Circlip A ring-shaped clip used to prevent endwise movement of cylindrical parts and shafts. An internal circlip is installed in a groove in a housing; an external circlip fits into a groove on the outside of a cylindrical piece such as a shaft.

Clearance The amount of space between two parts. For example, between a piston and a cylinder, between a bearing and a journal, etc.

Coil spring A spiral of elastic steel found in various sizes throughout a vehicle, for example as a springing medium in the suspension and in the valve train.

Compression Reduction in volume, and increase in pressure and temperature, of a gas, caused by squeezing it into a smaller space.

Compression ratio The relationship between cylinder volume when the piston is at top dead centre and cylinder volume when the piston is at bottom dead centre.

Constant velocity (CV) joint A type of universal joint that cancels out vibrations caused by driving power being transmitted through an angle.

Core plug A disc or cup-shaped metal device inserted in a hole in a casting through which core was removed when the casting was formed. Also known as a freeze plug or expansion plug.

Crankcase The lower part of the engine block in which the crankshaft rotates.

Crankshaft The main rotating member, or shaft, running the length of the crankcase, with offset "throws" to which the connecting rods are attached.

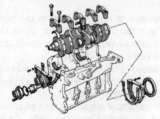

Crankshaft assembly

Crocodile clip See Alligator clip

D

Diagnostic code Code numbers obtained by accessing the diagnostic mode of an engine management computer. This code can be used to determine the area in the system where a malfunction may be located.

Disc brake A brake design incorporating a rotating disc onto which brake pads are squeezed. The resulting friction converts the energy of a moving vehicle into heat.

Double-overhead cam (DOHC) An engine that uses two overhead camshafts, usually one for the intake valves and one for the exhaust valves.

Drivebelt(s) The belt(s) used to drive accessories such as the alternator, water pump, power steering pump, air conditioning compressor, etc. off the crankshaft pulley.

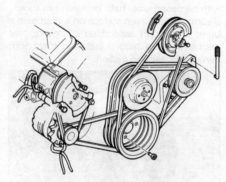

Accessory drivebelts

Driveshaft Any shaft used to transmit motion. Commonly used when referring to the axleshafts on a front wheel drive vehicle.

Drum brake A type of brake using a drum-shaped metal cylinder attached to the inner surface of the wheel. When the brake pedal is pressed, curved brake shoes with friction linings press against the inside of the drum to slow or stop the vehicle.

E

EGR valve A valve used to introduce exhaust gases into the intake air stream.

Electronic control unit (ECU) A computer which controls (for instance) ignition and fuel injection systems, or an anti-lock braking system. For more information refer to the *Haynes Automotive Electrical and Electronic Systems Manual*.

Electronic Fuel Injection (EFI) A computer controlled fuel system that distributes fuel through an injector located in each intake port of the engine.

Emergency brake A braking system, independent of the main hydraulic system, that can be used to slow or stop the vehicle if the primary brakes fail, or to hold the vehicle stationary even though the brake pedal isn't depressed. It usually consists of a hand lever that actuates either front or rear brakes mechanically through a series of cables and linkages. Also known as a handbrake or parking brake.

Endfloat The amount of lengthwise movement between two parts. As applied to a crankshaft, the distance that the crankshaft can move forward and back in the cylinder block.

Engine management system (EMS) A computer controlled system which manages the fuel injection and the ignition systems in an integrated fashion.

Exhaust manifold A part with several passages through which exhaust gases leave the engine combustion chambers and enter the exhaust pipe.

F

Fan clutch A viscous (fluid) drive coupling device which permits variable engine fan speeds in relation to engine speeds.

Feeler blade A thin strip or blade of hardened steel, ground to an exact thickness, used to check or measure clearances between parts.

Feeler blade

Firing order The order in which the engine cylinders fire, or deliver their power strokes, beginning with the number one cylinder.

Flywheel A heavy spinning wheel in which energy is absorbed and stored by means of momentum. On cars, the flywheel is attached to the crankshaft to smooth out firing impulses.

Free play The amount of travel before any action takes place. The "looseness" in a linkage, or an assembly of parts, between the initial application of force and actual movement. For example, the distance the brake pedal moves before the pistons in the master cylinder are actuated.

Fuse An electrical device which protects a circuit against accidental overload. The typical fuse contains a soft piece of metal which is calibrated to melt at a predetermined current flow (expressed as amps) and break the circuit.

Fusible link A circuit protection device consisting of a conductor surrounded by heat-resistant insulation. The conductor is smaller than the wire it protects, so it acts as the weakest link in the circuit. Unlike a blown fuse, a failed fusible link must frequently be cut from the wire for replacement.

G

Gap The distance the spark must travel in jumping from the centre electrode to the side electrode in a spark plug. Also refers to the spacing between the points in a contact breaker assembly in a conventional points-type ignition, or to the distance between the reluctor or rotor and the pickup coil in an electronic ignition.

Adjusting spark plug gap

Gasket Any thin, soft material - usually cork, cardboard, asbestos or soft metal - installed between two metal surfaces to ensure a good seal. For instance, the cylinder head gasket seals the joint between the block and the cylinder head.

Gasket

Gauge An instrument panel display used to monitor engine conditions. A gauge with a movable pointer on a dial or a fixed scale is an analogue gauge. A gauge with a numerical readout is called a digital gauge.

H

Halfshaft A rotating shaft that transmits power from the final drive unit to a drive wheel, usually when referring to a live rear axle.

Harmonic balancer A device designed to reduce torsion or twisting vibration in the crankshaft. May be incorporated in the crankshaft pulley. Also known as a vibration damper.

Hone An abrasive tool for correcting small irregularities or differences in diameter in an engine cylinder, brake cylinder, etc.

Hydraulic tappet A tappet that utilises hydraulic pressure from the engine's lubrication system to maintain zero clearance (constant contact with both camshaft and valve stem). Automatically adjusts to variation in valve stem length. Hydraulic tappets also reduce valve noise.

I

Ignition timing The moment at which the spark plug fires, usually expressed in the number of crankshaft degrees before the piston reaches the top of its stroke.

Inlet manifold A tube or housing with passages through which flows the air-fuel mixture (carburettor vehicles and vehicles with throttle body injection) or air only (port fuel-injected vehicles) to the port openings in the cylinder head.

J

Jump start Starting the engine of a vehicle with a discharged or weak battery by attaching jump leads from the weak battery to a charged or helper battery.

L

Load Sensing Proportioning Valve (LSPV) A brake hydraulic system control valve that works like a proportioning valve, but also takes into consideration the amount of weight carried by the rear axle.

Locknut A nut used to lock an adjustment nut, or other threaded component, in place. For example, a locknut is employed to keep the adjusting nut on the rocker arm in position.

Lockwasher A form of washer designed to prevent an attaching nut from working loose.

M

MacPherson strut A type of front suspension system devised by Earle MacPherson at Ford of England. In its original form, a simple lateral link with the anti-roll bar creates the lower control arm. A long strut - an integral coil spring and shock absorber - is mounted between the body and the steering knuckle. Many modern so-called MacPherson strut systems use a conventional lower A-arm and don't rely on the anti-roll bar for location.

Multimeter An electrical test instrument with the capability to measure voltage, current and resistance.

N

NOx Oxides of Nitrogen. A common toxic pollutant emitted by petrol and diesel engines at higher temperatures.

O

Ohm The unit of electrical resistance. One volt applied to a resistance of one ohm will produce a current of one amp.

Ohmmeter An instrument for measuring electrical resistance.

O-ring A type of sealing ring made of a special rubber-like material; in use, the O-ring is compressed into a groove to provide the sealing action.

Overhead cam (ohc) engine An engine with the camshaft(s) located on top of the cylinder head(s).

Overhead valve (ohv) engine An engine with the valves located in the cylinder head, but with the camshaft located in the engine block.

Oxygen sensor A device installed in the engine exhaust manifold, which senses the oxygen content in the exhaust and converts this information into an electric current. Also called a Lambda sensor.

P

Phillips screw A type of screw head having a cross instead of a slot for a corresponding type of screwdriver.

Plastigage A thin strip of plastic thread, available in different sizes, used for measuring clearances. For example, a strip of Plastigage is laid across a bearing journal. The parts are assembled and dismantled; the width of the crushed strip indicates the clearance between journal and bearing.

Plastigage

Propeller shaft The long hollow tube with universal joints at both ends that carries power from the transmission to the differential on front-engined rear wheel drive vehicles.

Proportioning valve A hydraulic control valve which limits the amount of pressure to the rear brakes during panic stops to prevent wheel lock-up.

R

Rack-and-pinion steering A steering system with a pinion gear on the end of the steering shaft that mates with a rack (think of a geared wheel opened up and laid flat). When the steering wheel is turned, the pinion turns, moving the rack to the left or right. This movement is transmitted through the track rods to the steering arms at the wheels.

Radiator A liquid-to-air heat transfer device designed to reduce the temperature of the coolant in an internal combustion engine cooling system.

Refrigerant Any substance used as a heat transfer agent in an air-conditioning system. R-12 has been the principle refrigerant for many years; recently, however, manufacturers have begun using R-134a, a non-CFC substance that is considered less harmful to the ozone in the upper atmosphere.

Rocker arm A lever arm that rocks on a shaft or pivots on a stud. In an overhead valve engine, the rocker arm converts the upward movement of the pushrod into a downward movement to open a valve.

Rotor In a distributor, the rotating device inside the cap that connects the centre electrode and the outer terminals as it turns, distributing the high voltage from the coil secondary winding to the proper spark plug. Also, that part of an alternator which rotates inside the stator. Also, the rotating assembly of a turbocharger, including the compressor wheel, shaft and turbine wheel.

Runout The amount of wobble (in-and-out movement) of a gear or wheel as it's rotated. The amount a shaft rotates "out-of-true." The out-of-round condition of a rotating part.

S

Sealant A liquid or paste used to prevent leakage at a joint. Sometimes used in conjunction with a gasket.

Sealed beam lamp An older headlight design which integrates the reflector, lens and filaments into a hermetically-sealed one-piece unit. When a filament burns out or the lens cracks, the entire unit is simply replaced.

Serpentine drivebelt A single, long, wide accessory drivebelt that's used on some newer vehicles to drive all the accessories, instead of a series of smaller, shorter belts. Serpentine drivebelts are usually tensioned by an automatic tensioner.

Serpentine drivebelt

Shim Thin spacer, commonly used to adjust the clearance or relative positions between two parts. For example, shims inserted into or under bucket tappets control valve clearances. Clearance is adjusted by changing the thickness of the shim.

Slide hammer A special puller that screws into or hooks onto a component such as a shaft or bearing; a heavy sliding handle on the shaft bottoms against the end of the shaft to knock the component free.

Sprocket A tooth or projection on the periphery of a wheel, shaped to engage with a chain or drivebelt. Commonly used to refer to the sprocket wheel itself.

Starter inhibitor switch On vehicles with an automatic transmission, a switch that prevents starting if the vehicle is not in Neutral or Park.

Strut See MacPherson strut.

T

Tappet A cylindrical component which transmits motion from the cam to the valve stem, either directly or via a pushrod and rocker arm. Also called a cam follower.

Thermostat A heat-controlled valve that regulates the flow of coolant between the cylinder block and the radiator, so maintaining optimum engine operating temperature. A thermostat is also used in some air cleaners in which the temperature is regulated.

Thrust bearing The bearing in the clutch assembly that is moved in to the release levers by clutch pedal action to disengage the clutch. Also referred to as a release bearing.

Timing belt A toothed belt which drives the camshaft. Serious engine damage may result if it breaks in service.

Timing chain A chain which drives the camshaft.

Toe-in The amount the front wheels are closer together at the front than at the rear. On rear wheel drive vehicles, a slight amount of toe-in is usually specified to keep the front wheels running parallel on the road by offsetting other forces that tend to spread the wheels apart.

Toe-out The amount the front wheels are closer together at the rear than at the front. On front wheel drive vehicles, a slight amount of toe-out is usually specified.

Tools For full information on choosing and using tools, refer to the *Haynes Automotive Tools Manual*.

Tracer A stripe of a second colour applied to a wire insulator to distinguish that wire from another one with the same colour insulator.

Tune-up A process of accurate and careful adjustments and parts replacement to obtain the best possible engine performance.

Turbocharger A centrifugal device, driven by exhaust gases, that pressurises the intake air. Normally used to increase the power output from a given engine displacement, but can also be used primarily to reduce exhaust emissions (as on VW's "Umwelt" Diesel engine).

U

Universal joint or U-joint A double-pivoted connection for transmitting power from a driving to a driven shaft through an angle. A U-joint consists of two Y-shaped yokes and a cross-shaped member called the spider.

V

Valve A device through which the flow of liquid, gas, vacuum, or loose material in bulk may be started, stopped, or regulated by a movable part that opens, shuts, or partially obstructs one or more ports or passageways. A valve is also the movable part of such a device.

Valve clearance The clearance between the valve tip (the end of the valve stem) and the rocker arm or tappet. The valve clearance is measured when the valve is closed.

Vernier caliper A precision measuring instrument that measures inside and outside dimensions. Not quite as accurate as a micrometer, but more convenient.

Viscosity The thickness of a liquid or its resistance to flow.

Volt A unit for expressing electrical "pressure" in a circuit. One volt that will produce a current of one ampere through a resistance of one ohm.

W

Welding Various processes used to join metal items by heating the areas to be joined to a molten state and fusing them together. For more information refer to the *Haynes Automotive Welding Manual*.

Wiring diagram A drawing portraying the components and wires in a vehicle's electrical system, using standardised symbols. For more information refer to the *Haynes Automotive Electrical and Electronic Systems Manual*.

Note: *References throughout this index relate to Chapter•page number*

Haynes Manuals – The Complete List

Title	Book No.
ALFA ROMEO	
Alfa Romeo Alfasud/Sprint (74 - 88)	0292
Alfa Romeo Alfetta (73 - 87)	0531
AUDI	
Audi 80 (72 - Feb 79)	0207
Audi 80, 90 (79 - Oct 86) & Coupe (81 - Nov 88)	0605
Audi 80, 90 (Oct 86 - 90) & Coupe (Nov 88 - 90)	1491
Audi 100 (Oct 76 - Oct 82)	0428
Audi 100 (Oct 82 - 90) & 200 (Feb 84 - Oct 89)	0907
AUSTIN	
Austin Ambassador (82 - 84)	0871
Austin/MG Maestro 1.3 & 1.6 (83 - 95)	0922
Austin Maxi (69 - 81)	0052
Austin/MG Metro (80 - May 90)	0718
Austin Montego 1.3 & 1.6 (84 - 94)	1066
Austin/MG Montego 2.0 (84 - 95)	1067
Mini (59 - 69)	0527
Mini (69 - Oct 96)	0646
Austin/Rover 2.0 litre Diesel Engine (86 - 93)	1857
BEDFORD	
Bedford CF (69 - 87)	0163
Bedford Rascal (86 - 93)	3015
BL	
BL Princess & BLMC 18-22 (75 - 82)	0286
BMW	
BMW 316, 320 & 320i (4-cyl) (75 - Feb 83)	0276
BMW 320, 320i, 323i & 325i (6-cyl) (Oct 77 - Sept 87)	0815
BMW 3-Series (Apr 91 - 96)	3210
BMW 3-Series (sohc) (83 - 91)	1948
BMW 520i & 525e (Oct 81 - June 88)	1560
BMW 525, 528 & 528i (73 - Sept 81)	0632
BMW 5-Series (sohc) (81 - 91)	1948
BMW 1500, 1502, 1600, 1602, 2000 & 2002 (59 - 77)	0240
CITROEN	
Citroen 2CV, Ami & Dyane (67 - 90)	0196
Citroen AX Petrol & Diesel (87 - 94)	3014
Citroen BX (83 - 94)	0908
Citroen CX (75 - 88)	0528
Citroen Visa (79 - 88)	0620
Citroen Xantia Petrol & Diesel (93 - Oct 95)	3082
Citroen XM Petrol & Diesel (89 - 97)	3451
Citroen ZX Diesel (91 - 93)	1922
Citroen ZX Petrol (91 - 94)	1881
Citroen 1.7 & 1.9 litre Diesel Engine (84 - 96)	1379
COLT	
Colt 1200, 1250 & 1400 (79 - May 84)	0600
DAIMLER	
Daimler Sovereign (68 - Oct 86)	0242
Daimler Double Six (72 - 88)	0478
DATSUN *(see also **Nissan**)*	
Datsun 120Y (73 - Aug 78)	0228
Datsun 1300, 1400 & 1600 (69 - Aug 72)	0123
Datsun Cherry (71 - 76)	0195
Datsun Pick-up (75 - 78)	0277
Datsun Sunny (Aug 78 - May 82)	0525
Datsun Violet (78 - 82)	0430

Title	Book No.
FIAT	
Fiat 126 (73 - 87)	0305
Fiat 127 (71 - 83)	0193
Fiat 500 (57 - 73)	0090
Fiat 850 (64 - 81)	0038
Fiat Panda (81 - 95)	0793
Fiat Punto (94 - 96)	3251
Fiat Regata (84 - 88)	1167
Fiat Strada (79 - 88)	0479
Fiat Tipo (88 - 91)	1625
Fiat Uno (83 - 95)	0923
Fiat X1/9 (74 - 89)	0273
FORD	
Ford Capri II (& III) 1.6 & 2.0 (74 - 87)	0283
Ford Capri II (& III) 2.8 & 3.0 (74 - 87)	1309
Ford Cortina Mk IV (& V) 1.6 & 2.0 (76 - 83)	0343
Ford Cortina Mk IV (& V) 2.3 V6 (77 - 83)	0426
Ford Escort (75 - Aug 80)	0280
Ford Escort (Sept 80 - Sept 90)	0686
Ford Escort (Sept 90 - 97)	1737
Ford Escort Mk II Mexico, RS 1600 & RS 2000 (75 - 80)	0735
Ford Fiesta (inc. XR2) (76 - Aug 83)	0334
Ford Fiesta (inc. XR2) (Aug 83 - Feb 89)	1030
Ford Fiesta (Feb 89 - Oct 95)	1595
Ford Fiesta Petrol & Diesel (Oct 95 - 97)	3397
Ford Granada (Sept 77 - Feb 85)	0481
Ford Granada (Mar 85 - 94)	1245
Ford Mondeo 4-cyl (93 - 96)	1923
Ford Orion (83 - Sept 90)	1009
Ford Orion (Sept 90 - 93)	1737
Ford Sierra 1.3, 1.6, 1.8 & 2.0 (82 - 93)	0903
Ford Sierra 2.3, 2.8 & 2.9 (82 - 91)	0904
Ford Scorpio (Mar 85 - 94)	1245
Ford Transit Petrol (Mk 1) (65 - Feb 78)	0377
Ford Transit Petrol (Mk 2) (78 - Jan 86)	0719
Ford Transit Petrol (Mk 3) (Feb 86 - 89)	1468
Ford Transit Diesel (Feb 86 - 95)	3019
Ford 1.6 & 1.8 litre Diesel Engine (84 - 96)	1172
Ford 2.1, 2.3 & 2.5 litre Diesel Engine (77 - 90)	1606
FREIGHT ROVER	
Freight Rover Sherpa (74 - 87)	0463
HILLMAN	
Hillman Avenger (70 - 82)	0037
HONDA	
Honda Accord (76 - Feb 84)	0351
Honda Accord (Feb 84 - Oct 85)	1177
Honda Civic (Feb 84 - Oct 87)	1226
Honda Civic (Nov 91 - 96)	3199
HYUNDAI	
Hyundai Pony (85 - 94)	3398
JAGUAR	
Jaguar E Type (61 - 72)	0140
Jaguar MkI & II, 240 & 340 (55 - 69)	0098
Jaguar XJ6, XJ & Sovereign (68 - Oct 86)	0242
Jaguar XJ6 & Sovereign (Oct 86 - Sept 94)	3261
Jaguar XJ12, XJS & Sovereign (72 - 88)	0478

Title	Book No.
JEEP	
Jeep Cherokee Petrol (93 - 96)	1943
LADA	
Lada 1200, 1300, 1500 & 1600 (74 - 91)	0413
Lada Samara (87 - 91)	1610
LAND ROVER	
Land Rover 90, 110 & Defender Diesel (83 - 95)	3017
Land Rover Discovery Diesel (89 - 95)	3016
Land Rover Series IIA & III Diesel (58 - 85)	0529
Land Rover Series II, IIA & III Petrol (58 - 85)	0314
MAZDA	
Mazda 323 fwd (Mar 81 - Oct 89)	1608
Mazda 626 fwd (May 83 - Sept 87)	0929
Mazda B-1600, B-1800 & B-2000 Pick-up (72 - 88)	0267
MERCEDES-BENZ	
Mercedes-Benz 190, 190E & 190D Petrol & Diesel (83 - 93)	3450
Mercedes-Benz 200, 240, 300 Diesel (Oct 76 - 85)	1114
Mercedes-Benz 250 & 280 (68 - 72)	0346
Mercedes-Benz 250 & 280 (123 Series) (Oct 76 - 84)	0677
Mercedes-Benz 124 Series (85 - Aug 93)	3253
MG	
MGB (62 - 80)	0111
MG Maestro 1.3 & 1.6 (83 - 95)	0922
MG Metro (80 - May 90)	0718
MG Midget & AH Sprite (58 - 80)	0265
MG Montego 2.0 (84 - 95)	1067
MITSUBISHI	
Mitsubishi 1200, 1250 & 1400 (79 - May 84)	0600
Mitsubishi Shogun & L200 Pick-Ups (83 - 94)	1944
MORRIS	
Morris Ital 1.3 (80 - 84)	0705
Morris Marina 1700 (78 - 80)	0526
Morris Marina 1.8 (71 - 78)	0974
Morris Minor 1000 (56 - 71)	0024
NISSAN *(See also Datsun)*	
Nissan Bluebird 160B & 180B rwd (May 80 - May 84)	0957
Nissan Bluebird fwd (May 84 - Mar 86)	1223
Nissan Bluebird (T12 & T72) (Mar 86 - 90)	1473
Nissan Cherry (N12) (Sept 82 - 86)	1031
Nissan Micra (K10) (83 - Jan 93)	0931
Nissan Micra (93 - 96)	3254
Nissan Primera (90 - Oct 96)	1851
Nissan Stanza (82 - 86)	0824
Nissan Sunny (B11) (May 82 - Oct 86)	0895
Nissan Sunny (Oct 86 - Mar 91)	1378
Nissan Sunny (Apr 91 - 95)	3219
OPEL	
Opel Ascona & Manta (B Series) (Sept 75 - 88)	0316
Opel Ascona (81 - 88)	3215
Opel Astra (Oct 91 - 96)	3156
Opel Corsa (83 - Mar 93)	3160
Opel Corsa (Mar 93 - 94)	3159
Opel Kadett (Nov 79 - Oct 84)	0634

Title	Book No.
Opel Kadett (Oct 84 - Oct 91)	3196
Opel Omega & Senator (86 - 94)	3157
Opel Rekord (Feb 78 - Oct 86)	0543
Opel Vectra (88 - Oct 95)	3158
PEUGEOT	
Peugeot 106 Petrol & Diesel (91 - June 96)	1882
Peugeot 205 (83 - 95)	0932
Peugeot 305 (78 - 89)	0538
Peugeot 306 Petrol & Diesel (93 - 95)	3073
Peugeot 309 (86 - 93)	1266
Peugeot 405 Petrol (88 - 96)	1559
Peugeot 405 Diesel (88 - 96)	3198
Peugeot 406 Petrol & Diesel (96 - 97)	3394
Peugeot 505 (79 - 89)	0762
Peugeot 1.7 & 1.9 litre Diesel Engines (82 - 96)	0950
Peugeot 2.0, 2.1, 2.3 & 2.5 litre Diesel Engines (74 - 90)	1607
PORSCHE	
Porsche 911 (65 - 85)	0264
Porsche 924 & 924 Turbo (76 - 85)	0397
PROTON	
Proton (89 - 97)	3255
RANGE ROVER	
Range Rover V8 (70 - Oct 92)	0606
RELIANT	
Reliant Robin & Kitten (73 - 83)	0436
RENAULT	
Renault 5 (72 - Feb 85)	0141
Renault 5 (Feb 85 - 96)	1219
Renault 9 & 11 (82 - 89)	0822
Renault 12 (70 - 80)	0097
Renault 15 & 17 (72 - 79)	0763
Renault 18 (79 - 86)	0598
Renault 19 Petrol (89 - 94)	1646
Renault 19 Diesel (89 - 95)	1946
Renault 21 (86 - 94)	1397
Renault 25 (84 - 92)	1228
Renault Clio Petrol (91 - 93)	1853
Renault Clio Diesel (91 - June 96)	3031
Renault Espace (85 - 96)	3197
Renault Fuego (80 - 86)	0764
Renault Laguna (94 - 96)	3252
Renault Mégane Petrol & Diesel (96 - 97)	3395
ROVER	
Rover 111 & 114 (95 - 96)	1711
Rover 213 & 216 (84 - 89)	1116
Rover 214 & 414 (89 - 96)	1689
Rover 216 & 416 (89 - 96)	1830
Rover 618, 620 & 623 (93 - 97)	3257
Rover 820, 825 & 827 (86 - 95)	1380
Rover 2000, 2300 & 2600 (77 - 87)	0468
Rover 3500 (76 - 87)	0365
Rover Metro (May 90 - 94)	1711
SAAB	
Saab 90, 99 & 900 (79 - Oct 93)	0765
Saab 9000 (4-cyl) (85 - 95)	1686

Title	Book No.
SEAT	
Seat Ibiza & Malaga (85 - 92)	1609
SIMCA	
Simca 1100 & 1204 (67 - 79)	0088
Simca 1301 & 1501 (63 - 76)	0199
SKODA	
Skoda Estelle 105, 120, 130 & 136 (77 - 89)	0604
Skoda Favorit (89 - 92)	1801
SUBARU	
Subaru 1600 & 1800 (Nov 79 - 90)	0995
SUZUKI	
Suzuki SJ Series, Samurai & Vitara (82 - 97)	1942
Suzuki Supercarry (86 - Oct 94)	3015
TALBOT	
Talbot Alpine, Solara, Minx & Rapier (75 - 86)	0337
Talbot Horizon (78 - 86)	0473
Talbot Samba (82 - 86)	0823
TOYOTA	
Toyota Carina E (May 92 - 97)	3256
Toyota Celica (Feb 82 - Sept 85)	1135
Toyota Corolla (fwd) (Sept 83 - Sept 87)	1024
Toyota Corolla (rwd) (80 - 85)	0683
Toyota Corolla (Sept 87 - 92)	1683
Toyota Corolla (Aug 92 - 97)	3259
Toyota Hi-Ace & Hi-Lux (69 - Oct 83)	0304
Toyota Starlet (78 - Jan 85)	0462
TRIUMPH	
Triumph Acclaim (81 - 84)	0792
Triumph Herald (59 - 71)	0010
Triumph Spitfire (62 - 81)	0113
Triumph Stag (70 - 78)	0441
Triumph TR7 (75 - 82)	0322
VAUXHALL	
Vauxhall Astra (80 - Oct 84)	0635
Vauxhall Astra & Belmont (Oct 84 - Oct 91)	1136
Vauxhall Astra (Oct 91 - 96)	1832
Vauxhall Carlton (Oct 78 - Oct 86)	0480
Vauxhall Carlton (Nov 86 - 94)	1469
Vauxhall Cavalier 1300 (77 - July 81)	0461
Vauxhall Cavalier 1600, 1900 & 2000 (75 - July 81)	0315
Vauxhall Cavalier (81 - Oct 88)	0812
Vauxhall Cavalier (Oct 88 - Oct 95)	1570
Vauxhall Chevette (75 - 84)	0285
Vauxhall Corsa (93 - 97)	1985
Vauxhall Nova (83 - 93)	0909
Vauxhall Rascal (86 - 93)	3015
Vauxhall Senator (Sept 87 - 94)	1469
Vauxhall Vectra Petrol & Diesel (95 - 98)	3396
Vauxhall Viva HB Series (ohv) (66 - 70)	0026
Vauxhall Viva & Firenza (ohc) (68 - 73)	0093
Vauxhall/Opel 1.5, 1.6 & 1.7 litre Diesel Engines (82 - 96)	1222
VOLKSWAGEN	
VW Beetle 1200 (54 - 77)	0036
VW Beetle 1300 & 1500 (65 - 75)	0039
VW Beetle 1302 & 1302S (70 - 72)	0110

Title	Book No.
VW Beetle 1303, 1303S & GT (72 - 75)	0159
VW Golf Mk 1 1.1 & 1.3 (74 - Feb 84)	0716
VW Golf Mk 1 1.5, 1.6 & 1.8 (74 - 85)	0726
VW Golf Mk 1 Diesel (78 - Feb 84)	0451
VW Golf Mk 2 (Mar 84 - Feb 92)	1081
VW Golf Mk 3 Petrol & Diesel (Feb 92 - 96)	3097
VW Jetta Mk 1 1.1 & 1.3 (80 - June 84)	0716
VW Jetta Mk 1 1.5, 1.6 & 1.8 (80 - June 84)	0726
VW Jetta Mk 1 Diesel (81 - June 84)	0451
VW Jetta Mk 2 (July 84 - 92)	1081
VW LT vans & light trucks (76 - 87)	0637
VW Passat (Sept 81 - May 88)	0814
VW Passat (May 88 - 91)	1647
VW Polo & Derby (76 - Jan 82)	0335
VW Polo (82 - Oct 90)	0813
VW Polo (Nov 90 - Aug 94)	3245
VW Santana (Sept 82 - 85)	0814
VW Scirocco Mk 1 1.5, 1.6 & 1.8 (74 - 82)	0726
VW Scirocco (82 - 90)	1224
VW Transporter 1600 (68 - 79)	0082
VW Transporter 1700, 1800 & 2000 (72 - 79)	0226
VW Transporter with air-cooled engine (79 - 82)	0638
VW Transporter (82 - 90)	3452
VW Vento Petrol & Diesel (Feb 92 - 96)	3097
VOLVO	
Volvo 66 & 343, Daf 55 & 66 (68 - 79)	0293
Volvo 142, 144 & 145 (66 - 74)	0129
Volvo 240 Series (74 - 93)	0270
Volvo 262, 264 & 260/265 (75 - 85)	0400
Volvo 340, 343, 345 & 360 (76 - 91)	0715
Volvo 440, 460 & 480 (87 - 92)	1691
Volvo 740 & 760 (82 - 91)	1258
Volvo 850 (92 - 96)	3260
Volvo 940 (90 - 96)	3249
YUGO/ZASTAVA	
Yugo/Zastava (81 - 90)	1453
TECH BOOKS	
Automotive Brake Manual	3050
Automotive Carburettor Manual	3288
Automotive Diesel Engine Service Guide	3286
Automotive Electrical & Electronic Systems	3049
Automotive Engine Management and Fuel Injection Systems Manual	3344
Automotive Tools Manual	3052
Automotive Welding Manual	3053
In-Car Entertainment Manual (3rd Edition)	3363
CAR BOOKS	
Automotive Fuel Injection Systems	9755
Car Bodywork Repair Manual	9864
Caravan Manual (2nd Edition)	9894
Haynes Technical Data Book (89 - 98)	1998
How to Keep Your Car Alive	9868
Japanese Vehicle Carburettors	1786
Small Engine Repair Manual	1755
SU Carburettors	0299
Weber Carburettors (to 79)	0393

CL05.01/98

Preserving Our Motoring Heritage

< The Model J Duesenberg Derham Tourster. Only eight of these magnificent cars were ever built – this is the only example to be found outside the United States of America

Almost every car you've ever loved, loathed or desired is gathered under one roof at the Haynes Motor Museum. Over 300 immaculately presented cars and motorbikes represent every aspect of our motoring heritage, from elegant reminders of bygone days, such as the superb Model J Duesenberg to curiosities like the bug-eyed BMW Isetta. There are also many old friends and flames. Perhaps you remember the 1959 Ford Popular that you did your courting in? The magnificent 'Red Collection' is a spectacle of classic sports cars including AC, Alfa Romeo, Austin Healey, Ferrari, Lamborghini, Maserati, MG, Riley, Porsche and Triumph.

A Perfect Day Out

Each and every vehicle at the Haynes Motor Museum has played its part in the history and culture of Motoring. Today, they make a wonderful spectacle and a great day out for all the family. Bring the kids, bring Mum and Dad, but above all bring your camera to capture those golden memories for ever. You will also find an impressive array of motoring memorabilia, a comfortable 70 seat video cinema and one of the most extensive transport book shops in Britain. The Pit Stop Cafe serves everything from a cup of tea to wholesome, home-made meals or, if you prefer, you can enjoy the large picnic area nestled in the beautiful rural surroundings of Somerset.

> John Haynes O.B.E., Founder and Chairman of the museum at the wheel of a Haynes Light 12.

< Graham Hill's Lola Cosworth Formula 1 car next to a 1934 Riley Sports.

The Museum is situated on the A359 Yeovil to Frome road at Sparkford, just off the A303 in Somerset. It is about 40 miles south of Bristol, and 25 minutes drive from the M5 intersection at Taunton.
Open 9.30am - 5.30pm (10.00am - 4.00pm Winter) 7 days a week, *except Christmas Day, Boxing Day and New Years Day*
Special rates available for schools, coach parties and outings Charitable Trust No. 292048